Piracy and Privateering in the Golden Age Netherlands

Piracy and Privateering in the Golden Age Netherlands

Virginia West Lunsford

PIRACY AND PRIVATEERING IN THE GOLDEN AGE NETHERLANDS
© Virginia West Lunsford, 2005.

All rights reserved. No part of this book may be used or reproduced in any manner whatsoever without written permission except in the case of brief quotations embodied in critical articles or reviews.

First published in 2005 by
PALGRAVE MACMILLAN™
175 Fifth Avenue, New York, N.Y. 10010 and
Houndmills, Basingstoke, Hampshire, England RG21 6XS
Companies and representatives throughout the world.

PALGRAVE MACMILLAN is the global academic imprint of the Palgrave Macmillan division of St. Martin's Press, LLC and of Palgrave Macmillan Ltd.
Macmillan® is a registered trademark in the United States, United Kingdom and other countries. Palgrave is a registered trademark in the European Union and other countries.

ISBN 1–4039–6692–3

Library of Congress Cataloging-in-Publication Data

Lunsford, Virginia West.
  Piracy and privateering in the golden age Netherlands / Virginia West Lunsford.
    p. cm.
  Includes bibliographical references and index.
  ISBN 1–4039–6692–3
  1. Privateering—Netherlands—History—17th century. 2. Pirates—Netherlands—History—17th century. 3. Netherlands—History, Naval. I. Title.

DJ158.L86 2004
910.4′5—dc22   2004061772

A catalogue record for this book is available from the British Library.

Design by Newgen Imaging Systems (P) Ltd., Chennai, India.

First edition: May 2005

10 9 8 7 6 5 4 3 2 1

Printed in the United States of America.

To Beatrice, Jackson, and Greta

Contents

Acknowledgments ix
List of Abbreviations xi
Glossary xiii
List of Figures xv
Chronology xvii

Introduction 1

Part I The Dutch Sea Robber Defined 7

1. *Kapers* and *Commissievaarders*: The Dutch Privateer 9
2. A "Malicious Business": Piracy in the Dutch Republic 35

Part II Cultural Underpinnings 65

3. Collective Identity, Nationalism, and the Golden Age Netherlands 67
4. Piracy, the Dutch, and the Seventeenth-Century Seas 101

Part III Conclusions 139

5. Prizes and "Excesses": The Golden Age Pirate 141
6. The Dutch Freebooter in the Golden Age 177

Appendices 211
Appendix I   Sample Privateer Instructions 213
Appendix II Income of Amsterdam Privateers and Their *Rederijen* 217
Appendix III Some Dutch Privateer Captures 219

Appendix IV	Privateering Activity Sponsored by the Admiralty of the Maas	227
Appendix V	"Slave Roll" of Dutch Sailors	229
Appendix VI	Origins of the Barbary Corsairs	233
Notes		235
Bibliography		311
Index		349

Acknowledgments

There is not space enough to convey my deep sense of appreciation for the help and encouragement I have received on this project. While all errors and faulty reasoning are my own, any positive qualities this book contains stem directly from the generous assistance I have received from others. I offer my heartfelt thanks to the following individuals and institutions who have made its completion possible.

My research in the Netherlands and Spain was funded by a J. William Fulbright Foreign Scholarship and a Krupp Foundation Fellowship in European Studies. I thank the sponsoring institutions—the Institute of International Education, the Netherlands America Commission for Educational Exchange (NACEE), and the Minda de Gunzburg Center for European Studies at Harvard University—for their incredible generosity. Thank you also to the Department of History at Harvard University for a summer research grant during the early stages of this project, and to the United States Naval Academy Research Council for financial support to enable its completion. I would like to express my special appreciation to NACEE and the Institute of European Expansion at the University of Leiden for their warm hospitality and invaluable help while I was in the Netherlands.

My thanks go out to all of the various librarians, archivists, and curators who so kindly and patiently assisted me in my research in Europe, at the Algemeen Rijksarchief (The Hague, the Netherlands), Koninklijke Bibliotheek (The Hague, the Netherlands), Nederlands Sheepvaart Museum (Amsterdam, the Netherlands), Rijksuniversiteit Leiden Bibliotheek (Leiden, the Netherlands), Zeeuwse Bibliotheek (Middelburg, the Netherlands), Stichting Atlas van Stolk (Rotterdam, the Netherlands), and Archivo General de Indias (Seville, Spain). In this regard, I especially thank J.D. Cramer, M.F.J. Vermetten, A. Poortvliet, G.J.D. Wildeman, G.A.C. van der Lem, Jenny de Roode, and Carl Nix. In the United States, I am grateful for the resources and librarians at Harvard University and the United States Naval Academy. I especially thank Barbara Manvel for all that she has done to assist me. I am also very appreciative of Connie Grigor's administrative help and support.

This project began as a Ph.D. dissertation under the tutelage of Simon Schama. His passion for and knowledge of Golden Age Dutch history, coupled with his insightful methods and interpretations as a cultural historian, are absolutely fundamental to the conception of this project. I am indebted to him for his inspiration, interest, enthusiasm, suggestions, and support.

During the original research phase, I also appreciated the help and comments given by Dr. E.S. van Eyck van Heslinga, Professor Cynthia Lawrence, Professor Pieter Emmer, Professor Stephen Mitchell, Professor Caroline Ford, Professor Charles Maier, Professor David Hancock, and David Marley.

I am most grateful for the encouragement of my civilian and military colleagues in the History Department at the United States Naval Academy. They have shown great interest in my research and ideas, and provided a forum for engaging and thought-provoking intellectual exchange. I consider myself very fortunate to be a member of such a truly collegial academic community. Mary DeCredico, Richard Abels, and Anne Quartararo have been especially generous in giving me their time, helpful suggestions, and general kindness. In particular, I thank William McBride for his clear-eyed advice, spirited conversation, thoughtful support at every turn, and all-around friendship.

I am indebted to my students at the United States Naval Academy who have shown such a keen interest in the subject of piracy, and history in general. I have benefited from their enthusiasm, questions, and knowledge. I am honored and privileged to serve as the teacher of such intelligent and dedicated young men and women.

I am deeply grateful to Brendan O'Malley, the History Editor at Palgrave, for his interest and enthusiasm in this project. Thank you also to his assistants, Heather Van Dusan, Melissa Nosal, and Laura Morrison, who responded to my inquires and patiently helped to shepherd this manuscript into its final incarnation. I appreciated greatly the help of Yasmin Mathew, the services of the copyediting team at Newgen Imaging Systems, as well as those of the peer reviewers who read my original manuscript submission. Thank you for your incisive remarks.

I cannot forget the contributions of friends and family. When I wrote the original dissertation draft, Rennie Mapp, Raf Alvarado, Kevin Cramer, and Robert Fisher were great sources of encouragement, advice, and humor. In Annapolis, I have been blessed by the friendship of Terri Trauth. Wilford and Mollye Poe were very supportive of this project along the way, and I thank them sincerely. Leslie Poe gave much of himself to enable the realization of this book and helped me in innumerable ways; I am deeply appreciative of his generosity. My dear mother, Barbara West Lunsford, has been a source of tremendous support in every sense of the word. And finally, I must extend my most profound appreciation to my children, Beatrice, Jackson, and Greta, all of whom were born during the course of this project. They have kept my spirits up continuously, filling my life with love, laughter, occasional consternation, and much joy.

Note on the Text

Throughout the text, notes, and bibliography, there are several variations in the capitalization and spelling of place names and manuscript titles, which are characteristic of the time and place. These inconsistencies have been left such for authenticity, and are reproduced exactly as listed originally in the sources.

Abbreviations

Archives and Collections

AA	Admiraliteits Archieven (The Hague, the Netherlands)
AGI	Archivo General de Indias (Seville, Spain)
ARA	Algemeen Rijksarchief (The Hague, the Netherlands)
AVS	Stichting Atlas Van Stolk (Rotterdam, the Netherlands)
Dousa Kamer	Dousa Kamer Westerse Gedrukte Werken (Rare Books Division), Rijksuniversiteit Leiden Bibliotheek (Leiden, the Netherlands)
KB	Koninklijke Bibliotheek (The Hague, the Netherlands)
Realia	*Realia. Register op de Generale Resolutien van het Kasteel Batavia, 1632–1805**
RLP	Rijksuniversiteit te Leiden Pamfletten, Rijksuniversiteit Leiden Bibliotheek, (Leiden, the Netherlands)
Thysius	Thysius Collection, Rijksuniversiteit te Leiden Bibliotheek, (Leiden, the Netherlands)
VOC	Vereenigde Oost Indische Compagnie (The Hague, the Netherlands)
WIC	West Indische Companie (The Hague, the Netherlands)
ZB	Zeeuwse Bibliotheek (Middelburg, the Netherlands)
ZBP	Zeeuwse Bibliotheek Pamfletten (Middelburg, the Netherlands)

Terms

Verz.	Verzameling (Collection)
GGR	Gouveneur Generaal en Raden (of the Dutch East India Company)

---

* J.A. van der Chijs, ed. *Realia. Register op de Generale Resolutien van het Kasteel Batavia, 1632–1805* (Batavia and 's-Gravenhage: W. Bruining and Mart. Nijhoff, 1882–1886). This is a published version of the incomplete subject index of the "*kopie-resoluties*" of the VOC Governor-General and Council in the East Indies; the index is in Jakarta, Indonesia. Another unpublished index can be found in the VOC Archive, #835–839 (*Repertorium op de realia (onderwerpen) in de resoluties van gouverneur-general en raden*).

Glossary

article brief, *article brieven*. "Article letters"; shipboard regulations issued by various shipping concerns, as well as the Dutch Navy, which prescribed conduct for the sailors aboard a ship; stipulated which behavior was appropriate and expected.

Batavia. Main colony in the Dutch East Indies; today's Jakarta, Indonesia.

boekhouder. "Ship's husband" or "bookkeeper"; land-based bureaucrat who was responsible for overseeing a privateering venture; member of a privateering firm who was in charge of arranging for a ship's privateering commission, supervising its financial administration, outfitting it for its cruise, and ensuring its proper conduct.

commissie. Commission; specifically, a privateering commission.

commissie van retorsie. Privateering commission; document that sanctioned privateering; a license issued by the state that gave an individual the legal right to attack and capture enemy ships.

commissievaarder. Privateer.

courant. Newspaper.

f. Abbreviation for "guilder," the primary unit of Dutch currency.

guilder. Primary unit of Dutch currency.

Hof van Holland. The High Court of Holland and Zeeland.

kaper. Privateer.

kaperbrief. Privateering commission; document that sanctioned privateering; a license issued by the state that gave an individual the legal right to attack and capture enemy ships.

knevelrijen. Criminal extortion through physical coercion; kidnapping in order to earn money from a ransom.

krant; kranten. Newspaper; newspapers.

lijve gestraft. Corporal punishment.

octrooigebied. Trade company "patent territory," that is, a trade company's monopoly jurisdiction.

piraat; piraten. Pirate; pirates.

placaat. Proclamation.

polder. An area of land that has been reclaimed from the sea or from below sea level by the use of dikes.

praatje. "Little conversation," a genre of pamphlet literature in which characters hold a conversation about topical issues of the day.

reder; reders. Member/members of a firm or partnership.

rederij; rederijen. Partnership/partnerships; investment firm(s).

rijksdaalder. Unit of Dutch currency.

rover. Robber or pirate.

schrijver. Clerk/scrivener; the person aboard a ship charged with keeping the official records.

Stadholder. The quasi-head of state in the Dutch Republic, although most real power was held by the federal assembly of the States-General; a holdover from the time when the Netherlands was part of the greater Spanish Empire, when the office of the "Stadholder" had been the Spanish-appointed governor.

States-General. Highest governing authority in the Netherlands; a sort of national parliamentary assembly.

stroomroverij. River piracy.

United Provinces. United Provinces of the Netherlands, that is, the Dutch Republic.

Vendumeester. "Auctioneer"; an Admiralty bureaucrat charged with supervising the sale of the plunder obtained from a privateering venture.

vrijbuiter. Freebooter.

zeerover. Pirate.

zeeroverij. High seas piracy.

Figures

2.1 "Rock, de Brasiliaen Genaemt . . . ," (Rock, called the Brazilan . . .) engraving, in A.O. Esquemelin, *De Americaensche Zee-Roovers . . .* (Amsterdam: Jan ten Hoorn, 1678), fol. 43. Dousa Kamer. 63

3.1 Title page engraving, Olfert Dapper, *Historische Beschryvinghe van Amsterdam* (Amsterdam: Iacob van Meurs, 1663). Dousa Kamer. 71

3.2 Jan and Caspar Luiken, "Mannier Hoe de Gevange Kristen Slaven tot Algiers Verkoft Worden" (manner in which the captured Christian slaves are sold in Algiers), engraving, in Simon de Vries, *Historie van Barbaryen, En de zelfs Zee-Roovers . . .* , Vol. II (Amsterdam: Jan ten Hoorn, 1684), fol. 384. Dousa Kamer. 81

3.3 Jan and Caspar Luiken, Torments of Christian Slaves, engraving, in Simon de Vries, *Historie van Barbaryen, En de zelfs Zee-Roovers . . .* , Vol. II (Amsterdam: Jan ten Hoorn, 1684), fol. 384. Dousa Kamer. 82

3.4 Title page woodcut, *Belegering ende het Ontset der Stadt Leyden* by Reynerius Bontius (Leyden: Iacob Tinnekens, 1646). Dousa Kamer. 92

4.1 Portrait of François Lolonois, engraving, in A.O. Exquemelin, *De Americaensche Zee-Roovers . . .* (Amsterdam: Jan ten Hoorn, 1678), fol. 47. Dousa Kamer. 102

4.2 Woodcut, *Bekentenisse van Hugo Clerck Capiteyn der ZeeRoovers/die met zyn Complicen ende aenhang gejusticeert zijn tot Amsterdam . . .* (Amsterdam, 1615). Verzameling Thysius. 129

4.3 Buccaneer Cruelty, engraving, in A.O. Exquemelin, *De Americaensche Zee-Roovers . . .* (Amsterdam: Jan ten Hoorn, 1678), fol. 83. Dousa Kamer. 132

4.4 A.O. Exquemelin, title page engraving, *De Americaensche Zee-Roovers . . .* (Amsterdam: Jan ten Hoorn, 1678). Dousa Kamer. 133

4.5 Jan and Caspar Luiken, "Elendige Straffen Die de Turcken de Slaaven doen Leyden" (dreadful punishments which the Turks make the slaves suffer), engraving, in Simon de Vries, *Historie van Barbaryen, En de zelfs Zee-Roovers . . .* , Vol. II (Amsterdam: Jan ten Hoorn, 1684), fol. 407. Dousa Kamer. 135

5.1 Title page engraving, Dionysis van der Sterre, *Zeer Aenmerkelyke Reysen van Jan Erasmus Reyning door Verscheyde Gevesten des Werelds* (Amsterdam: Jan ten Hoorn, 1691). Dousa Kamer.   147

5.2 Title page engraving, *'t Begin, Midden en Eynde Der Zee-Rooveryen van den Alderfamieusten Zee-Roover Claes G. Compaen* . . . (1659). Verzameling Thysius.   162

5.3 *Sententie By mijn Ed: Heeren van den Gerechte der Stadt Dordrecht . . . tegens Laurens Davidsz . . . Ter saecke van . . . Zee-rooveryen ende pirateryen . . .* (Dordrecht: Mattheus van Nispen, 1663). Verzameling ZBP.   173

6.1 Jan Erasmus Reyning and Comrades Adrift, engraving, in Dionysis van der Sterre, *Zeer Aenmerkelyke Reysen van Jan Erasmus Reyning door Verscheyde Gevesten des Werelds* (Amsterdam: Jan ten Hoorn, 1691), fol. 91. Dousa Kamer.   203

6.2 Jan and Caspar Luiken, Drifting Supplicant Sailors, engraving, in Simon de Vries, *Historie van Barbaryen, En de zelfs Zee-Roovers . . .*, Vol. II (Amsterdam: Jan ten Hoorn, 1684), fol. 147. Dousa Kamer.   204

Chronology

1568–1648	Eighty Years War (with Spain); the Dutch Revolt
1579	Union of Utrecht, which establishes the United Provinces of the Netherlands, or what will come to be called the Dutch Republic
1602	Foundation of the Dutch East India Company (VOC)
1609–1621	Twelve Years' Truce with Spain
1621	Foundation of the Dutch West India Company (WIC)
1628	Piet Heyn captures the Silver Fleet in Cuba
1648	Treaty of Münster with Spain, ending the Eighty Years War
1652–1654	First Anglo-Dutch War
1665–1667	Second Anglo-Dutch War
1672–1674	Third Anglo-Dutch War and invasion of the Republic by France
1688–1697	League of Augsburg
1702–1713	War of Spanish Succession
1713	Treaty of Utrecht, ending the War of Spanish Succession

Introduction

During the early years of the seventeenth century, a young man grew up in Oostzaan, a village in the region of Kennemerland in the province of North Holland. This lad, reputedly "fair of form," bourgeois in his origins, and respectable in his personal comportment,[1] maintained "a deep yearning to go to sea."[2] And so to sea he went, during that time immediately after the war with Spain recommenced (1621), working as an "Adventurer"— a privateer—"in the service of his Fatherland."[3] He enjoyed great success, attacking and plundering numerous ships belonging to his homeland's enemies, Spain and Portugal, as well as fighting the privateers of Dunkirk, Oostende, and Cadiz.[4]

Soon, however, he began to grow dissatisfied with his lot. He was not alone in this sentiment—other privateers, too, sought to augment their earnings and expand their horizons. So he and his comrades, ignoring the instructions of the Dutch authorities, began preying upon ships belonging to their nation's allies and friends.[5] Despite such transgressions, they still considered themselves to be patriotic Adventurers, marauders for their homeland, stalwart and stouthearted privateers whose first and foremost goal was disabling the ships of the Dutch Republic's enemies.

Unfortunately, this expansion in the pool of potential victims was not enough to gratify this rebellious seaman. Still disgruntled with his meager cut of the booty, he became increasingly discontented. Finally, he made a fateful decision. He resolved to quit his work as a privateer—even a corrupt privateer—and seek his fortune on his own terms. Thus did Claes Gerritszoon Compaen make a momentous, dramatic, and willful choice. He resolved to leave behind the privateering profession—to shed its rules and regulations, its shipboard hierarchies, and the limited cut of the plunder it delivered—and to become a full-fledged, independent pirate.[6]

This was easy enough to do. Armed with a letter of commission signed by the most powerful Dutch officials, the States-General and the Prince of Orange[7]—in other words, carrying a legal license to privateer—he cajoled his privateer bosses into entrusting him with a ship mounted with seventeen cannons and crewed by eighty men. Appearances notwithstanding, however, he used this vessel to commence his new, nefarious occupation. Accosting a Dutch fishing craft, he deceived the hapless fishermen into believing that he, Compaen, was "a pious Captain from the homeland," and removed a ton of salted herring from its hold. Leaving the plundered men with a fraudulent IOU, which Compaen claimed Dutch authorities would honor (and which, in truth, they did not), he sailed off with his ill-begotten and valuable prize, his inauguration into his new lifestyle complete.[8]

More captures quickly followed, and Compaen soon acquired a reputation among both the authorities and the maritime *grauw* (rabble). In but a short time, so famous and esteemed did he become among the Republic's riffraff, in fact, that when he sought shelter in the Dutch city of Vlissingen during a bad storm, he was able to recruit another fifty sailors right away.[9] By now, he had established himself as such an accomplished and efficient pirate, seventeenth-century Dutch chronicler Nicolaes Wassenaer reports, that "everyone was afraid of him, yes, Spaniards, Portuguese, Frenchmen, Englishmen . . . all seafaring people were terrified . . ." They feared "the violent attacks which he committed with his accomplices . . . [assaults in which] everything which was encountered in the fury was destroyed," incredible damage which was wrought with relish and "in cold blood . . ."[10] Now, the government of the Dutch Republic officially pronounced him a "pirate" (*Zee-Roover*) and "villain" (*Schelm*), an individual who, to the officials' great chagrin, applied his efforts "against the welfare of the Fatherland . . ."[11]

Indeed, before his time on earth had ended, Claes Compaen had become not only a pirate, but rather, according to his biography, the most famous Dutch sea robber of all, a marauder whose equal the maritime world, "in the so many centuries that the Dutch have sailed the seas, had never seen . . ."[12] But what is even more remarkable is that ultimately, after years of unbridled and remunerative success as a pirate, after years of assailing and plundering the ships of myriad states, including his own, Claes Compaen was pardoned by the government he had spurned, returned to the village of his birth, and lived out his days as an eccentric yet celebrated figure in lawful, bourgeois, Golden Age Dutch society.

* * *

I begin with the story of Claes Compaen because it exemplifies perfectly the topic and themes that this book addresses. In one narrative, Compaen's biography embodies the fascinating tension that existed in Golden Age Dutch culture between the "heroic" privateer who fought for his Fatherland and the "monstrous" pirate who sowed violence and fear on the open seas. One might think that Compaen was a unique figure, a wild exception to the upright mores of seventeenth-century Dutch culture. How could a fallen former privateer such as himself—a hugely successful pirate who went so far as to prey upon his own people, who lived among the Barbary corsairs of North Africa, and who with his minions inspired dread on the seas—return to dwell among the upstanding denizens of the village of Oostzaan? How indeed, when Dutch law explicitly affirmed that actions such as Compaen's had been criminal, ungodly, and even evil, and Dutch culture branded pirates as moral reprobates and maritime beasts?

What other seventeenth-century Dutch sources reveal, however, is that Claes Compaen was not alone. The Dutch Republic, it turns out, was a bastion of maritime pillaging in all its forms. And Compaen, while more successful than his Golden Age sea robber colleagues, was not, in essence, so different from a lot of them. For while it is true that some were ultimately branded as outright "criminal pirates" and were sentenced to die, numerous others escaped this fate. Why was this so? This study contends that Dutch pirates and privateers possessed complicated, ambiguous identities in Golden Age culture. Contemporary evidence shows that the line between privateer and pirate—despite all of the Republic's myriad, emphatic statutes and ordinances affirming and reinforcing the distinction—was often murky, gray, permeable, and migratory. The slope from licit privateer to unlawful pirate was, apparently, a slippery one indeed. (The behavior of Compaen's original Adventurer colleagues is evidence enough of that.)

What is especially important to underscore is the cultural understanding of and reaction to these transgressions. Surprisingly, despite the Dutch Republic's own exacting legal codes and its generally principled moral culture, authorities often looked the other way in cases of maritime robbery. Although legally criminals, Dutch "pirates" were often not identified as such, were often not punished very stringently, and at times even ended up serving the state in a lawful capacity. Adding to the confusion, the Dutch often employed the same word—*vrijbuiterij* (freebooting)—to refer to the ostensibly different phenomena of "privateering" and "piracy," especially when these activities were practiced by their own countrymen. And exploiting these inherent ambiguities, those accused of piracy frequently pleaded the profession of privateer, whether they carried the appropriate documents or not. In short, then, despite the strict legal definition of a "piratical" identity and cultural affirmations of pirates' depravity, Golden Age Dutch society could forgive such "lapses," as happened in the case of Claes Compaen. In the culture of the Golden Age Dutch Republic, privateering and piracy were points along a continuum, and men who qualified as pirates could escape the punishments the laws prescribed and rejoin the world of legitimate—even patriotic—maritime enterprise.

How is it that the pirate—an individual whose conduct should have branded him as a feared and despised pariah—still found a place in the Golden Age community? In the face of so many laws explicitly proscribing "piratical" actions and vowing punishment, and in a society whose people claimed to revile piracy as a "godless" and "beastly" enterprise, why were the Dutch authorities and citizenry willing to accept such deviant behavior? The reasons are complex and stem from particular cultural values that both shaped how Dutch society perceived the activities of "piracy" and "privateering" and how the authorities punished those who were eventually found guilty of piratical crimes. Indisputably, certain practical exigencies had something to do with the existence of this magnanimous attitude. Commercial mastery was the saving grace of the new United Provinces of the Netherlands, compensating for the state's small size and ostensible vulnerability. Despite their lack of sheer brute force or copious numbers, the Dutch managed to dominate in global trade.[13] Dutch privateers, and even pirates, it turns out, contributed to this vital economic order. Moreover, privateering itself was a remunerative business, creating opportunities for personal profit and the further extension of capital. Members from all classes of Golden Age society invested in privateering concerns. At the same time, privateers were an important part of the Netherlands' military arsenal during a period of evolving naval warfare. As a veritable branch of the Dutch Navy during times of war, privateers' appointed task of assaulting adversaries' shipping, seizing goods, and inspiring insecurity was a significant one. These reasons help to explain why the strict rules governing privateer conduct at times fell by the wayside in the rush to form privateering companies, recruit sailors, and seek booty. In this respect, the maritime predators of the Dutch Republic were not so different from their socially tolerated and even esteemed brethren in other European societies, most notably, the Sea Dogs of Elizabethan England (the most famous of whom was Sir Francis Drake).

As important as these immediate economic and military exigencies were, however, certain deeply rooted and uniquely *Dutch* cultural predispositions were just as significant. Fundamentally, the Netherlands was a "water culture." In a small, coastal country lying largely below sea level, fashioned out of reclaimed land, subject to floods, and reliant upon the bounty of the ocean, water itself assumed a powerful, dualistic character. Where the Dutch learned to control and work with the sea, the sea responded by offering blessings of food and success in commerce. Conversely, however, water also maintained a malevolent face, which manifested itself in deluges, sea monsters, and other forces of destruction. The success of the state—and indeed people's very survival—depended upon the actions of those who worked on, in, and with the water. Such efforts were necessary but perilous, whether one be a sailor, fisherman, merchant, explorer, or dike keeper.

Within this context, the Dutch Republic's maritime warriors were especially important to its existence as an independent, flourishing state. From the inception of the Dutch Revolt, the Republic's seagoing guerilla fighters, the Sea Beggars, used the water as their arena and a veritable weapon in battling Spanish "enslavement." The Sea Beggars themselves embodied the essential ambiguity—were they pirates or privateers? Already in the seventeenth century, these patriotic *vrijbuiters* (freebooters), as the Dutch typically called them, were subjects of widespread adulation in the Republic. Never mind that in actuality the Sea Beggars were a ragtag assemblage of Dutch aristocrats, ultra-Calvinists, and riffraff who could be quite indiscriminate as to whom they victimized. Early on, they began to maintain an esteemed place in the public imagination and the collective memory[14] of the newly forged "Dutch" people. Ultimately, they became a key touchstone in the symbolic articulation of a Northern Netherlands identity—a *national Dutch* identity. (Indeed, by the late nineteenth century, the "memory" of the "piratical" Beggars had so instilled itself in the Dutch psyche that poet W.J. Hofdijk celebrated his country's sixteenth-century origins by entitling his patriotic panegyric *The Triumph of the Pirates: A Celebratory Offering for the Netherlands' Tercentennial*.[15]) And as the United Provinces continued to develop into a cohesive political and cultural entity, the Sea Beggars' successors—the navy and the privateers—inherited the Beggars' cultural role and also assumed a place of vibrant symbolic importance.

These deeply embedded cultural values had everything to do with why the seventeenth-century Dutch were not more aggressive in labeling, prosecuting, and punishing their errant maritime pillagers. For despite their manifold laws defining and decrying transgressive, piratical acts, the Dutch had a great deal of trouble even recognizing the illegalities the laws forbade. Paradoxical though it may have been, their values blinded them, preventing them from seeing what their own copious laws on the subject shrilly prohibited. The multiplicity of regulations just did not ring true, and ultimately served only as a means for the Dutch to delude themselves—and others—that they were actively delimiting and controlling a dangerously criminal sphere of activity, maintaining an upright, pious demeanor in the midst of so much theoretical "godlessness" and immorality. Golden Age culture may have identified the pirate as a wicked miscreant, but ultimately this was a characterization whose full thrust was applied to non-Dutch seamen. For the Dutch pirate's corrupted identity was leavened with the residue of national self-creation, transforming him from an identifiable criminal into a liminal[16] freebooter whose transgressions were often recast as mere "excesses," and who retained the potential to help the state "heroically."

Fascinating though this might be, until now, such issues have remained completely unexplored. While historians such as Jaap Bruijn and J.Th.H. Verhees-van Meer have produced excellent work on the institution and practices of Dutch privateering during particular Golden Age wars,[17] the subject of Dutch piracy has been almost completely and inexplicably neglected, untouched by scholarly research and analysis. This is surprising, considering the Netherlands' great commercial and maritime prowess during the early modern period. Scholarship about piracy (and privateering) tends to focus again and again on the same British seamen. But Dutch sea robbers represented a sizeable and aggressive contingent of maritime pillagers during piracy's "great age," and it is important that their activities be documented. Moreover, until now, no scholar has investigated the rich and complex cultural identities that the privateer and pirate maintained in the early modern Netherlands, the special place the sea robber held in the Golden Age Republican *mentalité*.

This book endeavors to rectify these omissions from the scholarly record. Certainly, it provides more factual information about Dutch privateering. More important, it introduces some of the first raw data we have on the subject of Dutch piracy during the Republic's Golden Age. But it goes beyond this, devoting itself to what anthropologist Clifford Geertz terms the "thick description"[18] of the Netherlands' maritime predators, delving into the symbolic *meaning* of these men and their occupations within the intricate context of Golden Age Republican culture.

The format of the book is as follows. Part I defines the activities of privateering and piracy in the Dutch Republic and documents its scope and place in Golden Age society. It underscores the distinctions in Dutch law between privateering and piracy and clarifies how those convicted of criminal piracy were viewed and punished. Part II explores aspects of the cultural context that shaped how the Dutch public "processed" and interpreted these acts of maritime predation. Especially significant in this regard were the following: the Dutch relationship with the sea; a burgeoning sense of national identity and how this identity was articulated and experienced; and how piratical activity in general affected the Republic's economy and citizenry. Part III documents the surprising fact that the Golden Age Dutch, for all of their stringent legislation concerning piracy, often refrained from disciplining culprits. It then goes on to analyze and explain why this happened.

It is not entirely surprising that the history of Dutch piracy and privateering remains poorly documented until now. A paucity of remaining evidence makes this enterprise a challenging one. As Dutch historian R.B. Prud'homme van Reine explains, "Pirates and privateers have not made it easy for the historian to describe their history. Written and published sources and objects concerning Dutch privateering and piracy are extremely rare."[19] A calamitous fire in 1844 destroyed much of the relevant material in the Dutch Admiralty archives, many trading company records have disappeared, and pirates, like other criminal sorts, did their best to avoid leaving a paper trail of evidence. Fortunately, however, important and unresearched source material survives in the archives of the Dutch Admiralties and the High Court of Holland, the most revelatory of which are criminal sentencing records from the Admiralty of the Maas (Rotterdam). Moreover, as a study in cultural history, this book draws upon diverse forms of cultural production, including criminal prosecution records, government pronouncements, pamphlet literature, newspapers and almanacs, contemporary books, laws and legal commentary, popular imagery, songs and poetry, and decorative arts.

The Dutch freebooter—that maritime figure who floated between licit and illicit marauding—was an ambiguous character, a stalwart seafarer who occupied some blurred, liminal zone between legitimate, patriotic action and iniquitous, proscribed conduct. Modern historians and the laws of the Dutch Republic might make a sharp distinction between the figure of the privateer and that of the pirate, but careful study reveals that such mutually exclusive, academic, and de jure categories did not correspond to the complex, messy, de facto maritime world of the seventeenth century. Claes Compaen's life, while especially flamboyant, extreme, and infamous, ultimately serves as a telling illustration of other Dutchmen who, while gainfully employed as privateers, navy seamen, or other legitimate mariners for the Fatherland, indulged in the enticing yet forbidden life of piracy, and yet reemerged as full-fledged members of law-abiding Dutch society. He exemplifies the ambiguous and complex identity of the Dutch Republican freebooter and embodies the fundamental tension between the "pious mariner" and the "godless scoundrel" in the Netherlands' Golden Age.

Part I

The Dutch Sea Robber Defined

1

Kapers and *Commissievaarders*: The Dutch Privateer

Claes Compaen's original occupation, privateering—the legal practice of attacking and capturing enemy ships and goods—was widely practiced throughout Europe during the Golden Age.[1] Indeed, it was a feature of Dutch maritime life long before then, arising as a distinct and recognizable activity by the end of the fourteenth century.[2] After the establishment of the first Admiralty in the Netherlands, in the city of Veere in 1488, privateering became somewhat more institutionalized and prevalent.[3] It flourished, especially from 1551 to 1556, when at least 20–30 privateering ships per year set sail to hound and harass the French.[4] During this era, it probably found its most ardent practitioners in Zeeland, but Friesland, too, produced privateers, most notably in the legendary figure of "Grote Piet."[5]

Such patterns carried over to the new Dutch Republic, which was established formally in 1579, after the Netherlands broke away from Spain in 1568. On February 20, 1570, rebellion leader and Stadholder William of Orange (also known as William the Silent) made his first privateering appointments, whose legality his Spanish opponents rejected. The new state's first official privateer was Sea Beggar Diederik van Sonoy. From such modest beginnings, an "industry" quickly developed, and by 1584–1586, privateering had blossomed in the new United Provinces of the Netherlands.[6] Indeed, by 1599, it was evidently so popular that privateers were streaming from the Republic into the West Indies, hunting down the riches transported by Spanish ships.[7]

The seventeenth century only witnessed the further intensification and institutionalization of these activities, as the Republic was almost continuously at war. It expanded considerably during the three Anglo-Dutch Wars,[8] and continued to increase during the War of the Spanish Succession. Entirely legal and potentially lucrative, privateering was a popular target for investment and business enterprise, as well as an effective means to expand and augment the Republic's naval forces. While the denizens of coastal Zeeland were especially devoted to the business of privateering—activities there at mid-century, for example, were at least as great as those taking place at the storied Dunkirk[9]—the endeavor was encouraged and supported throughout the maritime Republic. At the same time, however, from the first days of the Republic's existence, privateering was strictly defined and regulated by the States-General, the Admiralties, and the Prince of Orange, as well as by the Dutch East and West India Companies, which were entitled to license privateers within their Company jurisdictions.[10]

What were the rules governing privateering in the United Provinces? First and most fundamentally, Dutch (and theoretically all) privateering was allowed only in time of war with another country *and at no other time*. (It is important to note, however, that a state did not have to be in a declared state of war per se to permit privateering. Rather, all that mattered was that a state's governing authorities considered their country to be in a hostile relationship vis-à-vis another.) Moreover, once hostilities commenced, the Republic's highest officials had to explicitly declare that privateering was permissible before *kapers* or *commissievaarders* (as privateers were typically called in the Netherlands) could set sail.

Second, per the Republic's laws, it was mandatory that all Dutch privateer captains carry a pre-registered privateering license or commission, the so-called letter of commission or letter of marque (*commissie van retorsie* or *kaperbrief*).[11] These papers were issued and signed by either the Stadholder in his capacity as Admiral General, or during those periods when there was no Stadholder (1650–1672 and 1702–1747), the States-General.[12] Such documents were used from the time of the Republic's inception, when they were signed either by William of Orange or his brother Lodewijk of Nassau. (The Spanish claimed that these letters were illegal, since in their eyes, the Dutch Republic was simply a rebellious region in the Spanish Empire. However, by virtue of William's identity as sovereign of the principality of Orange, in southern France, he was legally entitled to issue such commissions. Still, those signed by his brother—who was not a sovereign authority—were worthless.) Typically, Dutch commissions presented privateering as a justified and legitimate response to egregious transgressions, referring to the injustices committed by the Republic's enemies and the consequent need for redress. The language contained in a 1672 *commissie van retorsie*, presented to a Dordrecht seaman by the States-General, is representative:

> Thus the Kings of France and Great Britain have . . . [shown] hatred to attack and injure these provinces, as well as [its] good inhabitants everywhere. So is it that the . . . States-General of the United Netherlands, with God's blessing, have found it necessary because of this, so as to obtain reparations for the damage suffered by the aforementioned inhabitants, as well as to prevent as much as is feasible the great ruin of the commerce and navigation [of this state], and to this end employ all means of retaliation . . . have conceded that Jan Adriaense Noot, . . . Shipper from Dordrecht . . . may attack and capture . . . all ships, and goods belonging to the subjects of the said Kings, and their . . . allies . . . as well as persons . . . in those territories and allegiances . . . .[13]

Dutch privateering commissions automatically lost their validity when a war ended, but they also could be withdrawn (and quite often were) at any point during the hostilities.[14] *Kapers* who were far out at sea did enjoy a reprieve of sorts from this rule—they were permitted to bring in prizes for months after the Dutch government had rescinded privateering commissions—but ultimately they, too, had to cease and desist. Moreover, depending upon the conflict and the Republic's foreign policy considerations, the pool of potential privateer victims was greater or smaller. Sometimes, Dutch authorities formally stipulated that only enemy ships and their allies were fair game;[15] at other times, however, they permitted the Republic's privateers to prey upon neutral ships trading with the enemy or using the enemy's ports.[16] In 1643, for example, the States of Holland went so far as to permit Dutch privateers to capture *any vessel* using *any* Flemish harbor.[17] Such decisions warranted careful examination by the various authorities, including the Stadholder, the States-General, the Admiralty officials, and the provincial States.[18] Those privateers who transgressed by capturing prizes deemed illegal during a particular conflict were subject to disciplinary measures—at the least, prohibitive fines.[19]

Who applied for these letters of commission? The applicants were private individuals, generally merchants and *boekhouders*, that is, "book-keepers" or "ship's husbands."[20] *Boekhouders* were the men who represented the owners of the actual privateering vessels. While sometimes individuals owned these ships, more often partnerships or firms—*rederijnen*—held title, thereby enabling collective financing and the spreading of the risk among a number of people. Each owner's share in the profits directly corresponded to his or her share of the financing, and generally ranged from $\frac{1}{2}$ to $\frac{1}{128}$.[21] While it is difficult to ascertain how large these partnerships were, they probably ranged anywhere from four to forty investors in number. Also, partners usually owned shares in more than one enterprise, so as to diminish their risk even more.[22] So continuously was the Dutch Republic involved in wars during this era that certain shipowners and firms were able to dedicate themselves exclusively to the practice of privateering.[23] A relatively high number of privateering partnerships were concentrated in the cities of Amsterdam, Middelburg, and Vlissingen, although firms existed in other places in the maritime provinces as well (e.g., Rotterdam, Hoorn, and Dordrecht). As with other business opportunities in the Netherlands, investors were inveigled to participate by means of cajoling posters and subscription lists. Among a vessel's multiple owners, the "ship's husbands" or "book-keepers" were especially important figures, for they were responsible for equipping and outfitting the privateering vessel, overseeing its financial administration, hiring a crew, paying any necessary sureties or bonds, providing the privateering captain with his instructions and rules, and maintaining contact with the authorities and the captain while the ship was at sea.[24] The *boekhouders* tended to be Dutch for it was difficult for nonresidents of the United Provinces to obtain Dutch *commissies van retorsie*, at least before the early eighteenth century.[25]

Although the States-General and the Prince of Orange were formally in charge of the Republic's privateers, the five Admiralties actually oversaw them on a day-to-day basis. Each privateer captain, and thus the men who sailed under him, had to be affiliated with one of the Admiralties. The privateering ship and its *boekhouder* were registered there as well. The Admiralty investigated the captain, who was sometimes called a "captain adventurer," before it would clear him for work.[26] Furthermore, it was incumbent upon the owners of privateering ships, whether an individual or a *rederij* (partnership), to pay a surety to the Admiralty, a security deposit or "caution-money" of approximately ƒ.20,000–30,000 per vessel, which was intended to guarantee a privateering ship's upright conduct. The authorities could confiscate this bond if and when a privateer misbehaved.[27] Sometimes responsibility for paying the surety was divided between the owners and the privateer captain, serving as an immediate check on the commanding officer.[28]

Such rules were only the beginning. Throughout the Golden Age, the Dutch Republic maintained very rigorous and specific regulations regarding privateering, and they differed little through the years.[29] For example, each privateer captain was responsible for keeping a detailed journal of his journey; upon the vessel's return, he submitted this diary to his respective Admiralty and his ship's owners.[30] The States-General mandated that these logs be accurate and up-to-date, and they, too, reserved the right to peruse it.[31] All privateer captains also had to swear an oath before their Admiralty, vowing that they would treat their crews—as well as any seamen from captured prize ships—decently and properly. Should a seized prize still contain a crew, the privateer commander was instructed to arrest the enemy captain and some officers, without harming them, and to bring them back to the appropriate Admiralty authorities. At the same time, the Admiralty affirmed that privateer captains were entitled to support and no obstruction from Dutch naval officers.[32]

Like their colleagues working for the Dutch Navy or the trade companies,[33] Dutch privateer seamen were also obligated to accept the micro-management of their shipboard lives in the form of detailed instructions (e.g., see appendix I), the so-called *Article Brieven* (article letters). In turn, the Admiralties closely regulated and supervised these instructions, ensuring that they corresponded with the wishes of the States-General. Moreover, it was incumbent upon the bookkeeper to swear an oath that he had given no conflicting orders to his captain.[34] An *Article Brief* issued by the Admiralty of Zeeland[35] in 1665 serves as a characteristic example of the very specific directions such documents contained.

Long and very detailed, the "letter" included some thirty-odd rules. A number of the commandments are logical. For instance, the Admiralty naturally proscribed such serious offences as mutiny, assault, and murder.[36] Moreover, they obviously forbade Dutch privateers from attacking vessels belonging to the Dutch Republic and its allies.[37] Likewise, it is understandable that privateers would be expected to follow such sound and safe nautical practices as maintaining respect and order within the chain of command,[38] keeping one's weapons cleaned and ready,[39] staying put throughout one's watch,[40] and properly outfitting and arming the privateer ship.[41]

And instructions detailing the appropriate treatment of a prize[42] and resolutely declaring that the captain, officers, and crewmembers should obtain and carry a suitable commission[43] make sense.

The Admiralty authorities, however, did not stop there. Privateer sailors were ordered to participate in twice-daily public prayers (led by the captain), and to be satisfied with their wages and rations.[44] They were also forbidden to take the Lord's name in vain and charged to stay with their ship at all times.[45] They could not bring a knife aboard or disturb the rations, nor could they ever leave the service of their particular captain, no matter how poor or cruel a commander he might be.[46] Above all else, they had to do everything in their power to maximize the profits of the business concern that was financing their privateering adventure.[47] And they were obliged to declare and abide by the following oath:

> We promise and swear to the High and Powerful Gentlemen of the States-General of the United Netherlands, committed and loyal, in addition to the noble [and] powerful Gentlemen of the Commissioned Council of the Admiralty . . . to be obedient, and that we shall regulate ourselves according to our Commission, Instructions, and Article-Letter, and moreover, to do everything that good, pious Captains, Officers, Warriors, Soldiers, and Sailors are bound to do and ought to do, So help us truly, God Almighty.[48]

Since Dutch laws governing privateering were so detailed and exacting, it is not surprising that the prescribed penalties for breaking them were, in turn, severe and tailored to the particular transgression. The 1665 *Article Brief* relentlessly itemized punishments for each violation, and Dutch privateers were told to expect neither mercy nor clemency.[49] Captains who did not lead public prayers at least twice daily were subject to fines and, after the third offense, eight days in chains and a diet of bread and water (the same reproof given to those sailors who left the ship without a commander's permission).[50] Those taking the Lord's name in vain were to be lashed to the mast and forced to pay money to poor relief.[51] Those striking another seaman with a stick, rope, or their fists were to be thrown three times from the yardarm. (This was a severe disciplinary measure in which the perpetrator, his arms fastened behind his back, was taken to one of the upper booms on a ship. There, a long rope was tied to his wrists and secured to the boom. He was then pushed off. The resulting drop of 40 or 50 feet inevitably dislocated his shoulders and sometimes crushed the bones in his arms and wrists. A sentence of three throws from the yardarm meant going through this grueling process three separate times.) Those caught smuggling aboard a knife were themselves to suffer its blade, which would be used to skewer the violator's hand to the mast.[52] Any sailor who injured another was to be keelhauled three times. (In keelhauling, the arms of the victim were tied above his head and his legs bound. His limbs were then fastened to a long rope that passed beneath the ship, so that he could be "hauled" under the ship, from one side to the other. Death was a distinct possibility, not just from drowning, but also from myriad lacerations caused by the razor-sharp barnacles on the ship's bottom, or decapitation if the victim's head crashed into the hull. During the course of the seventeenth century, the Dutch refined the punishment, developing a harness for the victim, which made the process easier, more efficient, and much safer.[53]) Those who left their watch prematurely were to be thrown from the yardarm and then whipped.[54] A sailor paid a fine each time he did not have his weapon completely clean,[55] and forfeited all his earnings if he expressed dissatisfaction with his wages, did not fulfill the duties of his position, opened a prize's cargo containers or disturbed its official papers, or took more than his fair portion of the plunder.[56] If, God forbid, one seaman killed another, the culprit was to be bound to the corpse, back to back, and thrown overboard.[57] Unspecified "corporal punishment" awaited those who neglected to serve their commanding officers when battling the enemy; showed any violent, inappropriate, or "nuisance" behavior toward their captain; impeded an officer from performing his duty; instigated a mutiny; or took a captured vessel anywhere but to the United Provinces.[58] And those who committed what the *Article Brief* singled out as the worst crimes of all—attacking Dutch or allied ships, or leaving the service of their captain—earned the sentence of execution, as well as confiscation of all of their wages and booty.[59] While such rules were punctilious about prescribed penalties, they permitted no recourse for sailors who might have legitimate grievances, such as a cruel or foolhardy captain. Moreover, they gave broad powers to the officers to interpret their crews' behavior, and provided no formal, institutionalized means for enlisted seamen to voice their side of the story.

As intimidating as such *Article Brieven* were—with their demanding regulations and fear-inducing punishments—they were only the beginning. Privateers were also subject to any new rules disseminated in government proclamations, as well as to revised Admiralty instructions, and relevant clauses in treaties forged between the Republic and other countries.[60] If wayward privateers did not comply, at the very least they were sure to forfeit the bond they and/or their financers had paid to their respective Admiralty. A States-General proclamation, issued on January 8, 1691, and officially terminating privateering at that time, exemplifies such punitive threats. Promising to confiscate the ships, goods, and booty of any Dutch privateer who did not return to the Republic immediately, the government further promised to mete out the vague but ominous punishment of "arbitrary correction" to any transgressors.[61]

It was not as if these seamen had any choice about the matter, however. Those who wished to work as privateers had to abide by the codes, however myriad, picayune, and exacting they might be, for the Dutch authorities absolutely forbade that any of their citizens sail as privateers for another state.[62] Holding a so-called double commission (i.e., letters of marque from both the Netherlands and another country) was also explicitly proscribed, and those caught doing so were subject to the destruction of their ships.[63] Ultimately, Dutch law dictated that a Dutch privateer who broke the rules—for example, by seizing the ships of neutral or allied states—should be classified and treated as a "pirate." Such an ignominious declaration resulted in, at the least, the forfeiture of a privateer's "caution-money," his financial ruin, and corporal punishment.[64]

To ensure that their privateers would follow such regulations, the Admiralties instituted a loose surveillance system to supervise the privateers' conduct when they were away from home. Dutch naval ships that encountered Dutch *kapers* at sea stopped the privateers long enough to ascertain their identity and homeport, check the validity of their letters of commission, perhaps inquire about the duration of their voyage, and receive a report on any captures they had made.[65] Additionally, officials in foreign locales—usually merchants and called, in the parlance of the day, "consuls"—supervised the sale of Dutch privateer prizes abroad and regularly reported the proceeds to the Admiralties at home.[66] A privateer ship's *boekhouder* also monitored the conduct and status of his charge, communicating with the captain via an extensive network of representatives (usually merchants and relatives of the *boekhouder*) in far-flung foreign ports, such as Smyrna, Livorno, Genoa, Venice, Lisbon, London, and Plymouth. These representatives also extended credit to the privateer captain and helped him to further provision his ship during the course of the journey.[67]

So, if the privateering trade involved such ostensible disadvantages, such exacting regulation and micromanagement, why did seamen still choose to go "adventuring"? The answer, in a word, was money. In the greater scheme of things, privateer captains and sailors put up with no more real aggravation and regulation than their merchant shipping and naval service brethren, and they stood to profit handsomely from the capture of valuable plunder. While every privateering venture did not result in winning the proverbial pot of gold—some 91 out of 276 Zeelands privateer captains working during the War of the Spanish Succession enjoyed no success, for instance[68]—the results could be quite alluring.

Dutch privateers seized diverse and valuable goods, ranging from the very pedestrian (e.g., salt)[69] to the exotic (e.g., ginger)[70] to the dazzling (e.g., hard currency and jewels).[71] A report, sent mid-adventure from a privateer ship to officials at the Admiralty of the Maas, provides but one example of the lucrative spoils to be had. So far, the *Saint Benita* already had captured two rich Portuguese prizes, one of which was transporting "600 casks of sugar and around the same amount of leather, tobacco and Brazilwood," and the other carrying "400 casks of sugar, and some leather, tobacco and Brazilwood."[72] Such booty represented typical fare for ships en route from the Caribbean, and sea robbers frequently targeted them.[73] African slaves were especially sought out by privateers cruising that region.

Documents from the Admiralty of Amsterdam provide further details about the variety of merchandise privateers captured. Plunder officially recorded during the 1660s and 1670s included butter, herring and other salted fish, tobacco, lemons, oranges, coal, ordnance, salted meat, grain, wine, almonds, salt, cotton, honey, beer, whale meat, wooden wares, iron, brandy, vinegar, and many instances of unspecified "goods."[74] Likewise, mid-century documents from the Admiralty of the Maas (Rotterdam) list the following types of privateer spoils: oatmeal, fish, coal, apples, vinegar, leather, tobacco, rye, malt, butter, willow, quick-lime, linen, tallow, yarn/thread, beer, salt, herring, wine, brandy, turpentine, animal skins, iron, English soap, sugar, bacon, meat, corn, prunes, tar, flour, pitch, and ballast.[75] During the War of the Spanish Succession (1702–1713), Dutch privateers registered booty including tar, copper, whale and fish oil, salt, brandy, wine, raisins, almonds, wool, coffee, lemons, figs, animal hides, peas, chestnuts, cologne, shark skins, cocoa, herring, dyewood, whale baleen, tin, steel, piece goods, various sorts of lumber, bluing, staves, paper, turpentine, cork, oil, tobacco, indigo, licorice, currants, starch, prunes, vinegar, ordnance, saffron, peat, molasses, rope, firewood, rye, meat, and butter.[76] Such booty was not the end of it, for any prize brought in by a Dutch privateer included the captured ship, which by itself was valuable. (For further examples of privateer booty, see appendices IV and V.)

The Admiralty colleges adjudicated privateer prizes on behalf of the States-General and the Prince of Orange. First, a captured prize underwent intense scrutiny by the Admiralty authorities, so as to ensure that the prize had been a valid target and that it had been legally apprehended and conveyed.[77] If this was the case, the Admiralty officials declared it a "good prize." The Admiralty's auctioneer then set a date for a public auction, which was advertised by means of posters and announcements in the local newspapers. To generate more interest, a day was even put aside for the public to come and look over the goods, to "window shop" so to speak, before the event took place.[78] On the day of the auction itself, the prize ships and their cargoes were sold. Some charges were imposed—storage and auctions costs, for instance. Beyond these fees, however, the cash returned from the sale represented sheer profit, and was divided up according to a government-stipulated formula ensuring the financial enrichment of the relevant parties.[79] While the proceeds of such auctions probably only amounted to half the actual value of the seized vessels' and cargoes,[80] the profits were still handsome (table 1.1).[81]

Table 1.1 Value of privateer booty auctioned in Amsterdam

Year	Booty's value at auction (in guilders)
1665	160,006.91
1666	163,390.05
1667	208,702.54
1668	11,494.4
1672	475,849.55
1673	802,127.76
1674	181,027.88
1675	2,653.11
Total	ƒ.2,005,252.2

Such numbers were not unusual, and if anything, represent smaller takes than were otherwise prevalent. For instance, between 1575 and 1577, Zeelands privateers alone captured booty worth ƒ.432,000.[82] Likewise, between 1654 and 1662, during the First and Second Anglo-Dutch Wars, *kapers* from Zeeland seized some ƒ.3.5 million worth of prizes.[83] Moreover, while the total value of privateer prizes sold outside of the Republic—in France, Spain, and elsewhere—is unknown, incidental data suggests that the profits were very high. And while Admiralty records do not record prizes captured in the West Indies—a region within the jurisdiction of the West India Company (WIC)—such prizes were extremely valuable.[84] Similarly, *kapers* from Zeeland were highly active during the Nine Years War. The proceeds of their auctions—almost ƒ.10 million—reflect only a part of the total value of their hauls because much of the loot was sold in Mediterranean ports.[85] But most impressive was the fact that Zeelands privateers captured some 1,800 prizes worth a staggering ƒ.23.7 million (at least) during the eleven years of the War of the Spanish Succession. These proceeds certainly rival those of the infamous Dunkirk (1,685 prizes) and St. Malo (1,275 prizes).[86]

With all the potential money to be made in privateering, it comes as no surprise that the division of the booty was both subject to specific legal instructions and a source of great dissension between the various parties who stood to benefit. Indeed, the division of prize profits represented a problem from the time of the Republic's inception. Back then, William of Orange endeavored to regulate such profits, ordering that between 10 and 50 percent of the proceeds should revert to him, as Admiral-General. For the most part, however, he was ignored; these privateers operated mostly out of reach of government control, and sold their prizes in various places where William had no representatives. He probably never collected much money at all from these seizures.[87]

Efforts to regulate privateering profits increased as the seventeenth century unfolded and state control became more institutionalized. While government regulations stipulating who would receive which portion of a privateer's plunder changed frequently, several laws were especially important and were oft cited as precedents in legal surveys and disputes. First and foremost was a States-General act dating from 1602. This law—which was reissued in a 1672 proclamation—was viewed as the most generally useful and applicable.[88] It ordered the following allotments in the division of profits raised from privateer booty: 12 percent to the state and the sponsoring Admiralty, 6 percent to the Admiral-General (a.k.a. the Stadholder), and the rest to the individual or business concern that had sponsored the privateering venture. This last party, in turn, would compensate the actual seamen.[89] In cases when Dutch Navy vessels seized enemy ships, the captors' share was much less generous: the sponsoring Admiralty was to retain the "tenth penny," or one-tenth, of the profit; the state would recoup five-sixths; and the surplus, approximately one-sixth, would to go to the seamen who had made the seizure. A 1653 resolution further specified that in these cases the Admiral-General was to receive one-thirtieth of the take retained by the state.[90]

During the course of the seventeenth century, such ostensibly neat and clean conclusions were put to the test again and again, however. The governing authorities certainly complicated the process by periodically issuing new rules on the subject. In 1632, for example, the States-General determined that privateers and their *rederijen* could keep *all* of the profits produced from prizes captured along the coast of Flanders, in the North Sea, and in the English Channel; this law was reaffirmed in 1639.[91] And during the First and Second Anglo-Dutch Wars, the state and officials (whose take was earmarked for poor relief) received 6 percent, while the Admiralty council members retained 1 percent after 1672, and the Admiral-General was entitled to 10 percent.[92] The amount extracted by the state rose to 7 percent during the War of the Spanish Succession.[93] Also clouding the issue were the different guidelines applied to the navy and privateers, as well as simple cupidity on the part of the parties involved, which could impel them to demand a bigger share. Confusing, too, was the issue of who should serve as judge in such matters. Privateering and prize adjudication, as a rule, was officially the domain of the Admiralties. However, as one case from early in the seventeenth century demonstrates, other bodies were only too happy to stick their noses in when it suited them.

In 1605, a merchant ship named *the Lamb*, which was carrying a Dutch privateering commission, captured a Spanish ship in the vicinity of Bermuda. The Spanish vessel was transporting a valuable cargo of ginger, and the crew of *the Lamb* brought their prize back to the Netherlands, to the city of Dordrecht. After the prize had been sold at auction and the profits distributed, two of the men from the partnership that owned *the Lamb* initiated legal action, formally contesting the apportionment of the profits. During the course of the legal proceeding, a number of institutional bodies became involved in the affair, including the Admiralty of the Maas, the States-General, and even the Sheriff of Dordrecht.[94]

Ultimately, then, much confusion existed over privateering profit distribution procedures.[95] Indeed, what was supposed to be a relatively straightforward process was instead often complex and misleading. Consequently, archival documents attest to the bewilderment, rancor, indignation, and avarice that could arise.[96] One mid-century case illustrates this especially well. Although all those involved may have been naval officers (this is unclear—it is entirely possible that one of the men was a privateer), the case still serves as a model of just how bitter the apportionment process could become.

In 1645, a fleet of six Dutch warships recaptured a Dutch vessel, the *Castle of Medemblick*, from the clutches of the Dunkirk corsairs. Almost immediately, a heated debate arose as to which officer—Navy Admiral Maarten Tromp of Holland or (privateer? navy?) Captain Ringelszoon of Zeeland—had boarded the *Castle* first, and thus could claim the ship as his prize. (A States-General resolution from 1631, which decreed that any prize captured by a group of warships working together should be split equally among the entire fleet,[97] was ignored because apparently Tromp and

Ringelszoon belonged to different fleets.) Each man affirmed that the other was lying in claiming the prize as his own. Tromp furthermore maintained that his rival had illegally boarded the captured vessel and removed as much booty as he and his men could carry, an act that represented a flagrant violation of protocol. Ringelszoon responded by professing his innocence and his right to the booty. While Tromp commandeered the actual ship and Ringelszoon allegedly took a handsome share of the plunder, neither one was satisfied with his lot. The situation culminated in Tromp composing an angry correspondence to the States of Zeeland, demanding that the ships of Ringelszoon and his cronies be inspected, and that the Zeelands captain be punished.[98]

Such squabbling was not confined to the Admiralties. Indeed, the trade companies caused problems as well, whether by stubbornly laying claim over any and all prizes captured in their jurisdictions, or by refusing to pay the Admiralty colleges a share of the companies' own prize proceeds, a practice that at least the Dutch East India Company (VOC) was apparently expected to honor.[99] The archives of the Company are replete with resolutions dealing with the thorny issue of prize apportionment.[100] For their part, the States-General did endeavor to prevent non-VOC seamen and privateers from "poaching" in Company waters. A 1606 proclamation, for instance, ordered home any non-VOC privateers cruising Company seas, and insisted, moreover, that no more should set out for the East Indies.[101] Such copious regulations, however, did not prevent controversies from arising.

In June of 1610, for instance, several VOC directors met with officials from the Admiralties of the Maas, Zeeland, Amsterdam, and Hoorn in order to settle the troublesome question as to who maintained jurisdiction over several prize ships captured in East Indian waters by two Dutch admirals. Most valuable among these vessels was a Portuguese carrack, the *St. Anthonio*, whose cargo was so ample that several Dutch ships were required to convey the goods back to the Republic. This prize booty fetched ƒ.200,000 at auction. It was bad enough that four Admiralties all sought a share of the profits, but now the VOC officials demanded a portion as well. Although prior to this date the admirals already had made three payments (amounts undisclosed) to the VOC, recognizing the fact that the captures had been made in VOC waters, the Company authorities still insisted on another ƒ.50,000 (or one-fifth of the proceeds). In the end, the Company's demands—adamant though they were—were ignored, and the prize money was divided among the Admiralties.[102]

If anything, such conflicts with the WIC were only worse, for one of the principle reasons the States-General cited to justify the Company's establishment was, in fact, to attack and seize enemy shipping.[103] The WIC issued its own letters of marque to its captains according to the Company's standards and needs, and in 1653, instituted its own prize court in Recife, Brazil, to adjudicate its captures.[104] All of this was further complicated by the fact that the WIC also allowed some non-Company merchant ships—vessels that had transported Company munitions, soldiers, and supplies from the

Netherlands to the Americas—to engage in a sort of "auxiliary privateering." That is, it permitted them—now empty of their cargoes and en route back to the Netherlands—to capture non-Dutch ships transporting goods within the Company's monopoly jurisdiction. These Company ships thus had the potential to make money on both legs of the journey.

With so many WIC-licensed *kapers* already active within the Company's domain, then, Company personnel certainly did not wish for any "invaders." To this end, the Company's founding charter of 1621 specifically affirmed that the Admiralties reserved no right to prize booty belonging to the Company,[105] and that the Company possessed the privilege of adjudicating prizes found within its delimited waters.[106] Such rules, however, did not prevent the Company and Admiralties from bickering back and forth, asserting that their respective rights were being violated. The vast expanse within the Company's monopoly area—which included the Atlantic, the Caribbean, and the waters off South America, North America, and parts of Africa—were a rich hunting ground indeed; prizes captured there were worth a fight.[107]

In 1650, for example, the WIC became very irritated by the presence of Dutch privateers from Zeeland who, the Company averred, were cruising the Company's waters in South America. Although the Zeelands seamen were carrying appropriate letters of commission from the Republic's authorities, the WIC argued that the Company maintained the right to the valuable prizes that the privateers were capturing. In a letter of complaint to the States-General, the Company's Zeeland Chamber provided specific examples of seizures that had taken place. In 1648, for instance, one privateer had apprehended a Portuguese vessel, and brought 250 casks of sugar, plus the ship, back to Vlissingen for auction. Another had captured a Portuguese caravel full of sugar and tobacco. This same privateer had already seized a load of sugar and syrup, which he conveyed home to Zeeland. And another had snared a Portuguese ship loaded with sugar in the West Indies. Other loads of sugar, the Company's letter protested, had been seized off the coast of Brazil itself. Citing their founding document, and specifically, the clause stipulating that the States-General had given the Company the right to prizes located within their delineated waters, the letter demanded that the interloping privateers' prizes be returned to the WIC.[108] To the Company's chagrin, however, the States-General spurned their claim. Instead, the government authorities took the stance that the WIC and the Admiralty of Zeeland both possessed a right to the prizes, and ordered the disputants to employ a set of strict guidelines to divide the plunder. The States-General even determined that the Admiralty must be the party to declare the prizes when the privateers brought them into port.[109]

Such disputes also went the other way too, of course, a point that is evident in a case which arose in 1676. In July of that year, privateer Ephraim Turner, captain of a ship named the *Eendracht*, captured a French prize transporting salt. According to the WIC, this seizure was made within Company waters, approximately 50 miles off the coast of Newfoundland. Consequently, the Company declared the prize as its own, and scheduled it to go up for auction on the twentieth of that month. Meanwhile, however, Dutch Admiralty officials learned of the capture and went on to contend that Captain Turner had apprehended his prize outside of the Company's domain. Therefore, they concluded, the French ship and its cargo belonged to the Admiralty. The WIC, of course, would have none of this and vehemently expressed this, reiterating the relevant clauses addressing prize jurisdiction and adjudication from the WIC's charter. Ignoring the Admiralty's protestation, the Company auctioned Turner's prize on August 3.[110]

Still another problem with the issue of prize possession and division was the conundrum of who enjoyed the right of legal ownership over captured goods once a war had ended. After the cessation of hostilities, victimized merchants often sought to retrieve their commandeered property. A lengthy and tangled legal proceeding from 1675 exemplifies this issue perfectly. In this case, various parties from different states—the Netherlands, England, and France, to be exact—were all disputants, seeking proprietary claims over a ship and goods legally captured by a Dutch privateer during the Nine Years War.[111] The Dutch themselves were troubled by this same thorny question, and often endeavored to recapture ships and merchandise that enemy privateers had seized from them and resold to new owners. A decision reached by the States of Holland in 1631, for instance, affirmed that any Dutch ships that had been captured by the Dunkirk corsairs and then resold to the French would be reclaimed if these vessels ever entered the Republic's waters.[112] Two years before, seamen from Medemblik had also sought the States of Holland's permission to attack any Dutch vessels that had been seized and subsequently resold by the Dunkirkers, a matter that the States did not dismiss out of hand and passed along to the Admiralty colleges for consideration.[113] Other legislation served to maintain a victim's claim to legal ownership over a captured vessel, even if such seized ships came up on the market. For example, a States-General resolution from 1678 prohibited any Dutch citizens, other than the victims themselves, from purchasing captured Dutch fishing vessels from the enemy.[114]

Even with all of these inherent problems and confusion, seamen working as privateers still stood to profit from their take of the plunder. The portion of the prize profits that went to the successful privateer seamen is unknown. However, it is certain that they did reap some revenue from the plunder, for before they departed from port, they arranged their share of the take with whomever was financing the actual venture.[115] Figures from the Admiralty of Amsterdam during the Second Anglo-Dutch War provide some information about the proportion of profit that went to the privateer captain, and how much his *rederij* earned;[116] this data is summarized in Appendix II. What is interesting here is that the percentage of prize income each privateer captain received was consistent, hovering around 1 percent.[117] This is not a terribly high amount. Of course, one must remember that such prize money represented additional remuneration in addition to the wages the privateer had negotiated with his sponsors, as well as any premiums he had earned (see later).

From time to time, Dutch authorities added further inducements to whet the appetite of prospective *commissievaarders*, extra honey to sweeten the already enticing pot. In 1632, for example, the States-General decreed that privateers (and their backers) were now entitled to keep *all* of the proceeds from the sale of their captured prizes at auction (as opposed to their usual set percentage).[118] Likewise, in October 1673, when the States-General sought to attract more privateers to fight against the French during the Nine Years War, they promised that all privateers could keep in addition to their cut of the booty (which they set at 1.5 percent of whatever a privateer had helped to obtain), the anchors and ropes from the ships they had seized, plus the contents of the enemy sailors' sea chests.[119] So frequently would the States-General offer these last particular incentives that they became the common and expected practice by the time of the War of the Spanish Succession (1702–1713).[120]

Periodically, the States-General also used the lure of special "premiums," bonus awards to encourage Dutch privateers to pursue the ships of certain parties with particular zeal and/or to do their work with exceptional efficiency. In 1632, for instance, the States-General pledged additional cash rewards for the capture or destruction of any enemy vessel, especially those using Flemish ports. The stipulated amounts ranged according to the size and make of the prize vessel and the strength of its weaponry, but all of the sums were alluring.[121] And in 1672, the States-General promised special rewards to those privateers and navy men who could capture any English or French warships. A privateer stood to earn still more if he could target particular naval vessels, for the higher the rank of the enemy officer commanding these warships, the higher the amount of the promised premium. The government also pledged extra compensation to those individuals who could seize the flags of the enemy Admirals' (and lesser officers') ships, supply additional vessels to the Republic's naval fleet, or recapture seized Dutch warships.[122]

Sometimes the premiums involved very specific instructions. In February 1678, for instance, the States-General promised special rewards again, but this time only to those privateers who *recaptured* Dutch ships seized by the enemy. According to the terms of the arrangement, those who retrieved a Dutch ship within 48 hours of its seizure would receive "a lawful fifth of the established value of the freed ship and goods"; those who recaptured one within 96 hours would receive "a legal third of the prescribed value"; and those who reclaimed one after 96 hours would receive "the lawful half of the prescribed value . . ."[123] The Republic's authorities even offered compensation to foreign privateers and naval crews who were able to recapture Dutch ships from the hands of the enemy. In 1627, for instance, the government made a policy of paying fair restitution to English crews who had apprehended Dutch vessels seized by Spain.[124]

Such premiums represented pragmatic and sensible policy, at least according to one mid-century pamphlet,[125] which discussed the remuneration of Zeelands privateers. Published in 1653 during the First Anglo-Dutch War, this *praatje* or "little conversation" criticized the States-General's decision to withhold offering special monetary incentives to privateer seamen; the government had paid inducements such as these to the privateers who had combated the Dunkirk menace earlier in the century. According to the character of the "Burger from Zeeland," Zeelands privateers were a resolute, brave, and hardworking bunch, talented, seafaring soldiers who sought to aid their fatherland. However, the scanty compensation offered by the privateering business at the time represented a real disincentive to such men, he explained, for they needed enough capital to operate their ships and make a profit. Consequently, he said, the number of actual privateers from Zeeland currently serving the Republic was small. Simply offer premiums, the "Burger" contended, and the number of enthusiastic privateers would increase accordingly:

> *Burger*: [The reason why the States-General] sees so few privateers at sea at this time is because the expenses, if premiums are not added, can not be paid . . . but if a premium on the ordnance and ships was promised, then men could equip brave ships to destroy her [England's] fleet . . . and from the ships which were not destroyed, men could obtain good profits . . . and so long as this [i.e., a policy of premiums and bigger profits] is not put into effect, we shall have no good service from the men of Zeeland, because it is certainly true that they are good warriors and indeed would like to take on the enemy, but this is a matter of state which keeps them in check.[126]

The Burger's comments aside, seamen from Zeeland and the other Dutch provinces seem to have responded quite eagerly to the privateering call. Three different pamphlets dating from 1649, all claiming to relay the sentiments of "fireside conversations," "discussions around the table," or "chit-chat in the Central Square" of Amsterdam noted and even fretted about the abundant numbers of privateers cruising the waters of Brazil at that time. Such a plentitude of privateers (many hailing from Zeeland) were disconcerting, the pamphlets recounted, for they threatened the Republic's peace with Portugal.[127] "So many privateers here have set sail and left in a mad dash," one work confided in a worried tone, fearing the international repercussions.[128] Likewise, a "conversation" among a fictional Hollander, Zeelander, Geldersman (i.e., a man hailing from the Dutch province of Gelderland), and Englishman addressed the problems posed by the teeming numbers of avaricious and aggressive privateers on both sides of the contest during the First Anglo-Dutch War. Lamented the Geldersman, ". . . I fear that these Republics will ruin each other. Through [Privateering], the Great Equipage of the water. And for that reason, I truly wish for a good accord between the two of them."[129]

The claims of these pamphlets are probably not too far off the mark. Privateer recruitment was easy, in fact, at least during the First and Second Anglo-Dutch Wars, simply because of the lure of big prize money. Indeed, captains of naval men-of-war were at a distinct disadvantage in trying to muster a crew, and there were cases in which an individual or even large groups of navy seamen deserted their warships in order to join a privateering venture. Several States-General edicts dating from the Second Anglo-Dutch War addressed this issue directly. In 1665, the States-General prohibited all further privateer sailings until the Dutch Navy was completely manned. They restricted privateering again in the spring and summer of 1666 and 1667, for this was the time of year when naval campaigns were fought and seamen were sorely needed for the Republic's military efforts. It was only during the autumn, winter, and early spring that the government dropped these prohibitions and privateering was permitted. The restrictions were even more severe during the Third Anglo-Dutch War. Still, the Dutch authorities sometimes encouraged privateering during the spring and summer months, when Dutch merchant shipping (except for the VOC and the inshore fishery) temporarily ceased, ships sat idle, and more seahands were available.[130]

Although at least 30 Dutch privateering ships went to sea each year,[131] it is difficult to determine how many sailors worked as *kapers* for the Republic during the Golden Age, and who they were. The archival records, unfortunately, are fragmentary and often silent on these points. Typically, a captain was the only person aboard a privateering vessel who carried a letter of commission. Therefore, even if documents reveal that a commission was granted to a particular commander, the number of crewmen who sailed under him is unknown. Some historians have made estimates of the number of commissions that were issued. Still, their numbers pertain only to specific wars or campaigns, and usually to only one Admiralty. And even in these cases, their calculations are not exhaustive. Anecdotal evidence suggests that 31 men per ship serves as a general, if conservative, rule of thumb.[132] These assessments, then, represent a workable if somewhat crude means to extrapolate the size of the Dutch privateering population at certain times during the Golden Age. Table 1.2[133] summarizes these estimates.

The privateering trade, like merchant shipping, used a variety of ship types ranging in size and requiring various numbers of hands. No kind of vessel was particularly favored; the only requirements were that it be quick, maneuverable, well-armed, and versatile. Ultimately, the typical Dutch privateering vessel was nothing more than a heavily armed merchant or fishing ship.[135] Although Dutch privateers frequently used a "frigate" as their ship of choice, what that term meant is hard to grasp.[136] What the Golden Age Dutch termed "frigates" ranged greatly in size, with the largest of them being similar to a small man-of-war. Even so, some of the so-called smaller ships carried crews of 180 hands.[137] For this reason, the projections based upon 31 crewmen per ship are only partly helpful—we have no way of knowing whether privateering ships routinely called for more or fewer crew hands. At the same time, however, these numbers, too, may be exaggerated, for sailors who worked on one privateering venture probably went on to work on another. After all, this is what happened in the case of numerous captains during the War of the Spanish Succession.[138] It is highly likely that certain sailors, too, worked on multiple privateering cruises. This means that these mariners could be represented any number of times in the estimates above.

Table 1.2 Estimated size of the Dutch privateer population

Source	War	Admiralty	Estimated number of commissions issued	Estimated number of privateer seamen (if 31 per ship)[134]
Bruijn	Second Anglo-Dutch	Amsterdam	37	1,147
Bruijn	Second Anglo-Dutch	Zeeland	93	2,883
Bruijn	Second Anglo-Dutch	Maas	5	150
Bruijn	Third Anglo-Dutch	Amsterdam	75	2,325
Bruijn	Third Anglo-Dutch	Zeeland	184	5,704
Bruijn	Third Anglo-Dutch	Maas	15	465
Clark	Nine Years	Amsterdam	95	2,945
Bromley	Spanish Succession	Zeeland	300	9,300
Verhees-van Meer	Spanish Succession	Zeeland	276	8,556
Verhees-van Meer	Spanish Succession	Amsterdam	100	3,100
Verhees-van Meer	Spanish Succession	Maas	38	1,178
Verhees-van Meer	Spanish Succession	VOC	28	868
Verhees-van Meer	Spanish Succession	WIC	26	806

It is also important to note that possession of a valid letter of commission apparently did not mean that one was a dedicated *kaper* per se. For instance, of the 276 commissions issued by the Admiralty of Zeeland during the War of the Spanish Succession, more than 50 were given to merchant vessels that were used primarily for trading journeys, usually to Africa, the West Indies, or the Mediterranean. These captains utilized their privateering commission only when they encountered an enemy along the way. To put it simply, their men did not go out searching for booty as their central goal; they simply acted if a prize crossed their paths.[139] Should, then, such sailors be considered "real" privateers?

Even so, when all is said and done, the population of privateering seamen in the Golden Age Republic was not insignificant. Such estimates indicate that they numbered in the thousands. For instance, the calculations in table 1.2 suggest that perhaps some 14,000 Dutch seamen from Amsterdam, Rotterdam, and Zeeland crewed aboard privateering vessels during the War of the Spanish Succession; the number on Zeelands privateering ships alone probably ranged up to 7,000.[140] This is a formidable number of people, even within the context of the general Dutch seafaring population, estimated at 64,500 in 1670 and 52,500 in 1725.[141]

Alas, little information survives about privateer seamen from Amsterdam, Rotterdam, and Dordrecht, all cities that supported a healthy privateering industry. Illuminating data can be found sometimes by compiling bits and pieces from the remaining archival records. Appendix III lists prize booty that was brought to Amsterdam and Rotterdam (among other ports) in 1652. Likewise, appendix IV lists a number of privateers sponsored by the Admiralty of the Maas, revealing a tantalizing tidbit about the privateering activity in Rotterdam at mid-century. Frustrating, too, is the anonymity that surrounds the individuals who remained at home: the shipowners, *rederijen* partners, investors, and bookkeepers who supplied the money and institutional structure to finance such privateering ventures. Most of them remain enshrouded in the obscuring fog of historical mystery. Moreover, while it is clear that the majority of these men served as the representatives of the shareholders for one or two ships, their other activities are not clear.[142] Were they otherwise employed?

The form and practices of privateering partnerships were well established by the height of the Golden Age. It is true that the Republic's first privateers were not backed by such an institutionalized financing system. They needed ships for their guerilla activities against Spain and therefore tended to retain the vessels they had captured instead of selling them at public auction; their "adventures" thus represented a poor prospect for investors. Any economic help they received tended to be in the form of loans, which, it turns out, usually were not repaid. By the beginning of the seventeenth century, however, standards for financing privateering ventures had solidified and privateering *rederijen* arose, especially in the cities of Amsterdam, Middelburg, and Vlissingen.[143]

The process of privateering was uniform throughout the Republic. Each privateering consortium used the investment capital at its disposal to acquire a vessel (which it purchased or had built to order), equip it properly (ships' supplies were typically procured from merchants who were fellow partners and investors in the venture),[144] and pay the prospective crew's wages. The firm might also purchase insurance. (This was a prudent idea, for probably one of every four privateering ships that set off to seek booty was lost, either through storms or battles at sea.[145]) One especially important task was the outfitting of the ship with weaponry. During the Nine Years War, privateering vessels likely were armed with 2–44 cannons, and during the War of the Spanish Succession, 2–54 (during the latter conflict at least 45 vessels were armed with more than 28 cannons).[146] During the Second and Third Anglo-Dutch Wars, guns probably numbered 4–44.[147] Appendix III provides a few details about the number of cannons carried by privateers in 1652, during the First Anglo-Dutch War. Their numbers range from 4 to 14.[148] In any case, such heavy artillery was supplemented by smaller guns, such as mortars, which were placed on the deck, and hand weapons, such as knives, swords, and pistols, which were given to the men aboard.[149]

Sometimes, it was also incumbent upon the partners to come up with names for their privateering ships. This was always the case with new vessels, of course. However, while many pre-owned ships retained the names that they had borne in commercial shipping, this was not always the case.[150] Naming could be symbolically significant, providing an opportunity to commemorate the privateering vessel's new career, to reflect the character of its new purpose. During the Second and Third Anglo-Dutch Wars, for instance, a number of privateering ships took on new names, titles full of confidence, pluck, and swagger. Examples included *Revenge* and the *Wheel of Adventure*.[151] Similarly, Zeelands privateering ships during the War of the Spanish Succession were emblazoned with daring, forceful, and martial designations alluding to the privateers' cunning, courage, ire, strength, military skill, and inevitable triumph over its adversaries. Such names included the *Tiger's Restitution*, *Mars*, the *Flying Eagle*, *Wheel of Adventure*, *Revenge*, the *Warrior*, *Victory*, the *Black Eagle*, the *Young Warrior*, *Jealousy*, the *Eagle*, the *Great Amazon*, *Justice*, *Adventure*, the *Cunning Fox*, the *Hand Grenadier*, the *Little Amazon*, the *Golden Mortar* (meaning a short cannon), *The Impetuous Ones*, *Fame*, the *Springing Fox*, *Good Adventure*, the *Falcon*, *Tenacity*, *Diligence*, the *Taunted Cat*, *Power*, the *Adventurer*, *Watch Out*, and the *Tiger*.[152] Some of these, such as *Revenge* and *Victory*, were especially popular and were used several times over.

At the same time, the bookkeeper had to hire a captain and crew, as well as request the necessary letter of commission from the authorities. During the early years of the Dutch Republic, when the Dutch were still actively combating the Spanish, William of Orange required that captains be of Dutch descent. They were also often of noble origin, and usually hailed from Holland, Friesland, and to a lesser extent, Zeeland. As the seventeenth century unfolded, however, such citizenship requirements loosened a bit, and some foreigners found employment as privateer captains (this was especially the case in the eighteenth century).[153] Additionally, after the dawn of the 1600s, few came from the nobility, although some were members of the distinguished regent families. At this point, the most important criteria were simply that a captain be trustworthy, reliable, and law-abiding.[154]

Extensive nautical experience was also necessary, of course. During the War of the Spanish Succession, for instance, captains had served in various facets of the maritime trades before accepting privateering commissions. Some 40 Zeelands captains who had served as *kaper* captains during the Nine Years War again received commissions during the War of the Spanish Succession. These individuals, of course, were especially adept at commanding a privateering ship. Others, following family tradition, were the sons and brothers of privateers who had fought in the Nine Years War. Still others had cut their teeth as captains in merchant shipping, the slave trade, the WIC, and even smuggling.[155] And like the ships they commanded, they sometimes assumed a special name for privateering, a sobriquet suggesting mystery and inspiring fear, such as "the Stranger."[156]

While the captain's job was a dangerous one, it offered many advantages. Of course, the wages were good and the plunder and premiums often extremely remunerative. Moreover, if one nursed a sense of adventure and stalwart patriotism, privateering represented exciting and noble work. Also relevant, however, was the industry's capability to elevate the social standing of its commanding officers. It could imbue its more senior workers with the means and "complexion" for social advancement. During the Second and Third Anglo-Dutch Wars, for instance, various privateer captains settled down and became *rederij* partners, and even went on to represent their firms as bookkeepers.[157]

In any event, once the bookkeeper had hired his man, the commission was inscribed with the captain's name, thus further ensuring the captain's accountability and legitimacy. (Only the WIC dispensed commissions with blank spaces for names.) Finally, the newly appointed captain was presented with multiple copies of his commission (upward of 15 or so) for his own needs at sea, and set to work.[158] The captain's first major responsibility was hiring the crew. Of course, men were needed to sail the ship and battle enemy vessels, but additional crew were essential to guard apprehended seamen, and to bring captured prize ships back to port. To actually attack the enemy, especially in a hand-to-hand combat situation, Dutch privateering ships typically carried a complement of soldiers. Moreover, everyone on board was expected to fight, and, to that end, was supplied with personal weapons. Officers included the captain, lieutenants, skipper, the underskipper, the navigator, and the clerk/recorder. The lower officer staff consisted of the surgeon, the sailmaker, the carpenter(s), the cook, the cook's mate, the quartermaster, the boatswain, and the boatswain's mates. The *Gouden Dolfijn*, which went to sea during the War of the Spanish Succession, was typical of Golden Age privateering vessels. Present on that ship were 30 officers, 89 sailors, 11 cabin boys, and 25 extra men.[159]

One position, that of the clerk/recorder, was appointed by the Admiralty, for his job—to keep the mandatory ship's log, supervise the business activities of the captain, maintain the ship's documents and itemize its cargo, and make a careful inventory of the contents of any captured prizes—was essential to preserving the integrity of the government's regulatory measures. The captain secured the rest of the crew. Availability of seamen was usually not a problem. Sailors were recruited primarily from the Republic's maritime provinces, especially Zeeland and Holland. Appendix III reveals that in 1652, for instance, privateer captains came from Zeeland, Amsterdam, Rotterdam, Enkhuizen, and Hoorn.[160] As in merchant shipping, however, foreign sailors—especially those from Scandinavia and Germany—were hired as well. Moreover, privateer captains occasionally went to sea with the intention of augmenting their crews in foreign locales, such as ports in Italy, England, and Ireland.[161] And one privateer captain in 1600 even enlarged his crew by purchasing African slaves.[162]

In theory at least, privateer seahands were supposed to be good, honest men, but crewmembers could come from literally anywhere, even the local prisons. Indeed, during the War of the Spanish Succession, privateer sailors were "recruited" from the Vlissingen jail. For help in the task of mustering a crew, the captains sometimes made use of special brokers. These agents provided food and lodging to homeless and unemployed sailors, as well as clothing and necessary seamen's equipment, in exchange for a portion of the seaman's wages when he eventually located work on a ship. Typically, the broker demanded an advance of two months wages, as well as an IOU for any remainder.[163] Sadly for the sailors, such businesses could be extremely unscrupulous. Although these establishments were scattered throughout the Republic—by the late eighteenth century, even provincial towns boasted 20–40 or even more—the biggest cluster of them was concentrated in Amsterdam, home to some 200. The worst of them—the so-called soul sellers—confined their "clients" in dim, poorly ventilated cellars or garrets, and provided horrible food and filthy sanitary arrangements. The death rate was high.[164]

Privateer seamen received fair compensation according to the standards of the time. For example, they earned $f.10$, $f.12$, or $f.15$ per month during the War of the Spanish Succession, the maximum amount permitted by law. (Officers usually made more.) Furthermore, such wages were supplemented by each seaman's share of any plunder and premiums (which together often resulted in a greater sum than a man's wages). While the seamen's share of the booty was subject to change—it was the result of a private agreement and was worked out between the bookkeeper and the sailors before the privateer ship departed on its cruise—the portion was not negligible. During the War of the Spanish Succession, the sailors received a full 10 percent of the take, which was divided among them according to the amount of effort each had exerted in making the captures. And this was not all that privateer seahands received by way of remuneration—add to this the extra financial rewards they often enjoyed, such as "anchor money," "rope money," and "sail money," as well as compensation for injuries suffered while at sea.[165]

In any event, no matter who made up the crew or where they were from, once the men had been hired and the letter of commission signed and registered, the privateering ship could leave on its voyage—its *kruistocht* (crusade, cruise)—to seek enemy booty. This excursion generally lasted anywhere from two to twenty-four months.[166] Although victims' nationalities changed depending upon the conflict, the privateers' hunting grounds generally did not. Dutch *kapers* monitored those waters through which the established trade routes traversed. Many patrolled the neighboring North Sea, English Channel, and Atlantic Ocean. Others traveled south, preying upon the rich Levant and West Indian trade routes, and using foreign ports (such as La Rochelle, Bilbao, and Cadiz) as bases where they could bring their prizes. Sometimes the *Article Brief* supplied by their Admiralty and bookkeeper stipulated where they were permitted to cruise, but often they were free to go anywhere. At least occasionally, Dutch privateers pooled their resources and formed fleets. For example, in 1674, 14 *kaper* ships, manned by 1,300–1,400 hands, joined forces near Cadiz.[167] Also, Spanish documents make note of "dense" fleets of Dutch privateers in 1571;[168] and a fleet of 42–44 Dutch "rebel" ships in 1600 and 1601.[169] However, it was more typical for Dutch privateers to go to sea alone, or at most in pairs or very small groups of three to five ships.[170] Why? Probably as a pamphlet (a *praatje*) dating from 1649 suggested, because of ambition laced with avarice, an "each to his own" mentality that precluded cooperative action:

> *Little Kees speaks*: But Uncle Jan, the privateers will then . . . flock together and with fleets attack and capture [other ships] . . .
> *Jan Propheet*: Where have you ever experienced that, my friend Kees? . . . The [privateers] have no faith in one another, but rather all run to sea separately, each following his own judgment, where they think that they will get the best booty, as one has always seen.[171]

Conditions on board Dutch privateering vessels were presumably no different from those found aboard merchant and navy ships.[172] An extant log from the privateering ship the *Jonge Krijgsman*, which served the Republic during the War of the Spanish Succession, provides a window into this lost world. For instance, sailors were expected to say the morning and evening prayers (prayer books were supplied for that purpose); more than 20 crewmembers perished during the cruise (due to causes such as falling overboard, dying in battle, and falling ill); and 40–50 men had become so sick from "scurvy and heavy heat and raging fever" that they all lay in their bunks, completely incapacitated. Indeed, like that of other early modern seamen, privateers' state of health was often simply miserable. They suffered from scurvy, fevers, and others sorts of maritime illnesses, and came into contact with deadly diseases such as the plague.[173]

Nor were social relations on board necessarily very healthy. The rapport between the officers and the crew was often poor, characterized by tension and conflict. Reports from consuls in the Mediterranean ports note the lack of respect that Dutch privateer seamen—those from Zeeland in particular—maintained for their superiors. Moreover, crimes ranging from common theft to large-scale mutiny were fairly common. Consequently, captains, per the Admiralties' orders, were ever armed to protect themselves. On the other hand, as in merchant shipping, captains could be cruel taskmasters. New policies formulated by the Admiralties in 1705 recognized this reality and promised to take seriously the complaints that sailors had about their commanders and other officers.[174]

The world of the privateer seafarer did not end with the boundaries of the ship. Life at sea was also punctuated by encounters with other vessels, some sailed by compatriots, others belonging to neutrals or allies, and still others manned by the enemy. Should a vessel belong to fellow Dutchmen, the meeting would typically consist of a friendly check of the ships' papers and convivial greetings and conversation all around.[175] In the case of a neutral or allied vessel, the privateer ship would engage in a procedure called "visit and search" in which the Dutch ship would lie alongside the other vessel and the *kaper* captain and several of his officers would inspect the neutral/allied vessel's documents, paying close attention to the bill of lading, which itemized the contents of the cargo. The Dutch officers might also inspect the actual goods in the hold. Should the captain's suspicions be aroused, and the neutral/allied vessel be caught transporting contraband or using false papers, the vessel likely could be considered a good prize. Otherwise, if after the "visit and search" all appeared in order, the ship would be released. Finally, should the confronted vessel be of the adversarial variety, the Dutch privateer seamen immediately readied their weapons and prepared for attack.

Indisputably, the business of privateering in the Dutch Republic was most entrenched, popular, and supported in Zeeland. The province had long roots in the practice, reaching back at least into the fifteenth century.[176] Such tendencies only intensified over time. During the early phase of the Dutch Revolt, for example, from 1584 to 1586, the city of Vlissingen alone boasted some 50 privateering ships.[177] Zeeland privateers were very active in Spanish America by 1600, with numerous "corsairs" departing from "Mediburg" (Middelburg) in "Zelanda," lured by the great riches of the West Indies.[178] By the mid-seventeenth century, the privateering industry in Vlissingen and Middelburg rivaled those that had taken place at Dunkirk during its heyday between 1621 and 1646.[179] A pamphlet published at mid-century notes that Zeelands *kaper* ships were ever willing, able, and prepared to privateer, outfitted and ready to set sale the minute the government issued letters of commission.[180] Likewise, a Spanish source dating from 1682 complains about the infestation of "Zeelands ships" along the coast of Panama.[181] So numerous did privateering *rederijen* in Vlissingen become during the Second Anglo-Dutch War, in fact, that a number of them formed a sort of confederation, the *Directie van de Nieuwe Equipage* (Directorate of the New Equipage), so as to exert even more influence. Indeed, the Zeelanders dominated the industry by virtue of their sheer numbers. The majority of letters of commission issued by the Dutch government during the Second and Third Anglo-Dutch Wars and the War of the Spanish Succession went to Zeelands captains and *rederijen* (see table 1.2).[182]

This Zeelands presence, however, was not without its problems. Throughout the course of the Golden Age, tensions arose as a consequence of how the Zeelanders conducted business, how they privateered just a bit too aggressively and indiscriminately. They exhibited an insatiable ardor in pursuing booty, a tendency which often resulted in legally dubious captures.[183] Indeed, the Zeelanders were more hawkish than their brethren from Holland, a sentiment that is clearly apparent in a 1653 pamphlet—a *praatje*—about the First Anglo-Dutch War. The characters are presented as a Hollander, a Gelderlander, a Zeelander, and an Englishman, and the topic of their discussion is how to end the war between the Netherlands and England. In opposition to his colleagues' call for a peace treaty achieved through diplomacy and mediation, the Zeelander enthusiastically suggests that the Dutch arm themselves even more heavily. Only through the further amplification of sea power would the Dutch Republic prevail against their English adversaries, the Zeelander argued.[184] And one crucial and effective element of this military effort, he energetically declared, was privateering, a task that the vigorous Zeelanders would be only too happy to fulfill. "And . . . now our Zeelands men again will have the opportunity to privateer, and will work lustily . . .," he proclaims eagerly.[185]

On occasion, Zeeland's stubborn recalcitrance, combined with its mariners' talent and passion for privateering, did engender real tensions. A pamphlet printed during the Second Anglo-Dutch War contains a *praatje* that angrily bemoans the States-Generals' current refusal to issue privateering commissions. The character of the "Sailor"—a Zeelander who has been robbed at sea by the English and thus now seeks a commission so that he can retaliate in kind—caustically complains about the national government, shrilly protesting, ". . . the Gentlemen [of the States-General] are scoundrels/they take our bread out of our mouths." Bridling at the States-General's authority, he insists that the Admiralty of Zeeland should be permitted to do whatever it wants.[186]

A more serious episode with real political repercussions occurred in the late 1640s, when the Republic was endeavoring to forge peace with Portugal. Many unsettled issues were preventing the realization of a treaty, among which, according to one pamphlet from the time, were Portugal's seizure of Angola, as well as Portugal's violence against Dutch colonial interests in Bahia, Brazil.[187] Also a principle obstacle, however, in the opinion of at least three pamphlets printed in 1649, were overly zealous Zeeland privateers.[188]

By this time, the Zeelanders had been practicing unbridled privateering against the Portuguese for years.[189] The privateers' ferocity and plentitude, as well as their sheer success, apparently upset the Portuguese tremendously, and engendered intractable tension between the Dutch Republic and the Iberian kingdom. (For their part, the WIC was none too happy about this situation, and complained bitterly to the States-General about the Zeelanders' encroachment in WIC waters.[190] They also accused the privateers of violent actions toward Company personnel.[191]) According to contemporary pamphlets, *commissievaarders* from Zeeland trolled the waters of coastal Brazil, capturing whatever moved in or out of the ports there. A great number of them did the same in the seas around Lisbon, Pôrto, and Viana, targeting any vessel traveling to or from Brazil. It had been this way for a long, long time, sighed one of the participants in the pamphlet entitled *Conversation in Amsterdam's Dam Square*: "Over the years, already a hundred privateers have left the province and gone there . . .," he grumbled.[192]

The Portuguese king had responded by ordering that all Portuguese merchant ships bound for South America had to be heavily armed, travel in convoys, and be escorted by a fleet of warships. These naval vessels would, of course, protect the merchant ships they chaperoned. At the same time, however, they were commanded to attack and reclaim—to "liberate"—the Brazilian coast.[193] Not surprisingly, this "offensive defensiveness" on the part of the Portuguese, while understandable from their point of view, served only to perpetuate the problem, for as Dutch ships and colonialists in Brazil were assailed, Zeelands privateers responded in kind against their Iberian adversaries. It was difficult to imagine a way to halt the cycle without the Zeelands privateers first ceasing and desisting their activities.

Such was the situation that the three pamphlets described, and their words about the Zeelands *kapers* are often bitter and angry. One declared the

Zeelands privateers to be outright "devils," avaricious opportunists who thought only of their own profits and who resisted a treaty with the Portuguese at every turn, even though such an accord was in the best interest of the Republic and the WIC. So as to continue their "Godless privateering . . . The Zeelands seamen, with force and violence and a hundred thousand practices, have obstructed . . . the ship named the *West India Company* . . ."[194] Another castigated the Zeelands *kapers* even more, deploring their "pernicious, scandalous, ungodly and unchristian practices of thievery and raiding," which showed "great contempt towards the Peace with Portugal," and which was done purely for the sake of augmenting the Zeelanders' own profits.[195] Still another sneered that the Zeelanders cloaked themselves in pious religiosity to justify their behavior, but that they were really just "thieves of heaven, church rogues, disgraces to the religion, all of whom cover up what they do with God's word. . . . What conscientious brothers they are, aren't they?"[196] Provincial enmity inevitably manifested itself in the conversation, as the noble path of Holland was contrasted with the ignominious deeds of its sister province to the south. While the characters spoke highly of the maritime folk of Holland who were endeavoring to make peace with the Portuguese, they rebuked "the Zeelanders and those from Utrecht, who as violent, young devils were against it, and so sought to prevent it . . ."[197] Ultimately, such behavior was to Zeeland's own detriment, one of the characters preached, for the Zeelanders were so accustomed to privateering, so wedded to this type of baneful maritime activity, that their merchant shipping trade was abysmal. They had allowed privateering to become their true industry.[198]

Ultimately, the Republic did not forge peace with Portugal until 1661, and this was only at the strong urging of Holland. Characteristically, the States of Zeeland refused to recognize the treaty, forcefully proclaiming to the States-General that Zeeland had not acceded to the agreement. Consequently, Zeeland did not assent to the accord until 1662, at which point they finally retired their infamously committed and feisty privateers.[199]

The enthusiasm of these privateers must have been frustrating to the Dutch authorities and populous as well. After all, according to contemporary opinion, the corsairs' steadfast independence, unchecked aggressiveness, and unilateral interpretation of the situation did ostensibly forestall peace negotiations with the Portuguese. These privateers skirted illegality while simultaneously jeopardizing their state's relationship with other European powers. Their cavalier disregard for the consequences of their actions must have been vexing. Considering the degree to which the privateering industry was regulated and supervised by the Dutch authorities, it is perhaps surprising that they were permitted to engage in such conduct for so long.

But complaints of disgruntled citizens aside, it appears that the Zeelanders—at least in this instance—had not acted illegally per se. While they may have been guilty of "pushing the envelope," they were privateering with proper letters of commission and against the intended targets. Their actions, while excessive, apparently did not constitute "piracy." For the

Dutch did not suffer acts of piracy lightly and instituted stern laws against it. Moreover, according to criminal sentences enacted by both the High Court of Holland and the Admiralty of the Maas, they were prepared to punish severely those who made the mistake of breaking those laws. This is the focus of Chapter 2.

2

A "Malicious Business": Piracy in the Dutch Republic

From the early years of the Dutch Republic, the laws condemning and proscribing *zeerooverij*—piracy—were serious and manifold. The charter document of the five Admiralty colleges, drafted in 1597, explicitly forbade the crime.[1] In 1611, the States-General promulgated a general proclamation "against the Pirates," the first sweeping regulation treating the misdeed.[2] Denouncing Dutch *zeeroovers* as "scum" and "rabble" who were "Enemies of the human race," and whose "robbery [and] plundering" represented transgressions "against all the Law[s] of Nature and People," the edict declared the authorities' intention to "pursue, quell, punish, and demolish" those who committed such grievous acts. It also stated the government's firm intention to discipline the perpetrators by threatening their lives and possessions, corrective measures that also awaited those who aided and abetted the scoundrels.[3]

Such prohibitions against the crime of piracy also appeared in formal peace agreements between the Republic and other states. In 1648, for instance, the States-General banned piracy and vowed to punish the crime strenuously; this time the law was enshrined in the Treaty of Münster which formally ended the Eighty Years War with Spain.[4] Such firm sentiments were also manifested in mid-century treaties with Portugal (August 6, 1661),[5] France (April 27, 1662),[6] and England (September 14, 1662).[7]

Even at the local level, piracy received serious attention. Provincial laws devoted to the creation and preservation of public order, such as those promulgated in Zeeland in 1596 and 1607, excoriated the crime, grouping it with other offenses that the local authorities believed upset the smooth workings of civil society. Transgressors were threatened with interrogation under torture, branding, banishment, imprisonment, confiscation of possessions, and ultimately, execution.[8] Even in the non-maritime provinces, such as Gelderland, such sentiments were evident; there, in 1621, the fear was of "river pirates" (*stroomrovers*) who would make their way up tributaries and wreak havoc on quiet inland towns.[9]

These measures were not all, of course. The Admiralties, too, formulated their own regulations, which were, in turn, usually supported by the provincial and national governing authorities. These injunctions were especially specific and firm when it came to the regulation of privateering. Generally speaking, Admiralty statutes—which were often mirrored in States-General proclamations—stipulated that privateers who violated their letters of commission were automatically considered *zeeroovers*. As a matter of course, privateers were forbidden to carry double commissions or to accept commissions from a foreign government.[10] The Admiralties and government also warned privateers that if they did not return home to the Republic when summoned, their status as lawful *kapers* could suddenly change, and they would be considered pirates.[11]

In sum, then, at every level—provincial, military, and confederal—the citizenry of the Dutch Republic were enjoined to refrain from that most notorious of maritime misdeeds, piracy. The language was admonishing and serious, and the promised punishments severe. Moreover, these proclamations did not represent mere rhetorical utterances expressed in some removed legislative chamber, but appeared in rather forceful, printed documents, which were disseminated throughout the city and towns of the Republic, posted and announced so that all could see and hear.[12]

But was such a proliferation of laws against the crime really necessary? Indeed, the Dutch authorities had good reason to be concerned and upset. For while the laws discussed above were *preventive* measures aimed at averting the eruption of *zeerooverij* in the first place, other regulations and ordinances represented *reactive* legislation, manifestly acknowledging that throughout the Golden Age, many Dutch seamen fell into a life of piracy. Whether such actions represented something as ostensibly minor as the possession of fraudulent papers, or, on the other hand, the practice of savage maritime banditry, the effect was the same: the government deplored their seafarers' descent into illicit maritime activity and vowed to punish it.

Probably one of the earliest laws of this type was an ordinance promulgated in 1583.[13] This lengthy edict complained bitterly about Dutch "pirates" (*zeeroovers*) who were infesting the seas and preying upon residents of the fledging Republic as well as its friends and allies. These violent seamen—copious in number and armed and dangerous—were truly damaging, the ordinance avowed. They had "committed enormous abuses, excesses, [and] offenses" of an "evil" nature, harming the trade of good, upright commercial people. Consequently, it promised swift and severe retribution to these despicable lawbreakers, and outlined a strict set of measures aimed at creating a controlled privateering trade that could employ such aggressive and rapacious seamen in legitimate enterprise. It also invested particular institutions with the power to prosecute and regulate such predatory maritime activities.

A States-General mandate from 1607 represents another excellent example. The law angrily recognized the manifold "excesses" of Dutch privateers-gone-bad who had taken to preying on neutral states and the Republic's allies. In a strong reproach, the States-General vowed to bring these wayward mariners to heel:

> The complaints which come to us daily about the great excesses and tyrannies which are committed by the freebooters departing out of these provinces, on the neutral friends of these Provinces, are so numerous and frequent, and displease us so much, that we in the service of the country find it necessary that from each College of the Admiralty in Holland and Zeeland, a warship diligently be sent out to sea, to the coasts and harbors of England, and Ireland (where we understand the aforementioned freebooters come to refresh themselves from time to time), with the express . . . order . . . to conquer [these freebooters] and bring [them] to these Provinces, in order that such punishments following the proclamations be done, as the state of their excesses shall demand . . .[14]

While these are tough words directed at men whose original role had been to defend the new and vulnerable independence of their mother country, the Dutch authorities had little choice if they sought to maintain the Republic's relationships with other European states. For other nations—primarily France—had lodged formal complaints against the wayward privateers, demanding punishment, and the Dutch government had to respond in some fashion if it desired to keep such an important neighbor from taking punitive action against Dutch shipping.[15]

What was the substance of the foreign governments' complaints? On September 18, 1605, for instance, the king of France had sent an impassioned letter to the Dutch authorities about the comportment of one J.C. Dreitz (of either Vlissingen or Rotterdam), whom the monarch accused of attacking Frenchmen "tyrannically" at sea and robbing their ships. In response, the Dutch Admiralty officials arrested Dreitz and ordered that all of his sea chests and coffers be seized and searched, in order to ascertain whether any stolen goods or money lay hidden within.[16]

Alas, this was just the beginning. On October 8, 1605, the king of France contacted the Dutch government again, this time demanding the return of more goods that had been captured illegally and taken to Rotterdam. The Admiralty authorities identified two culprits: a mariner named Melknap and a Captain J.C. Rijp. Rijp, they concluded, was certainly guilty of torturing some French sailors, and the two men together, they affirmed, have "greatly violated [others] at sea, and against their [Dutch Admiralty] instructions, have misbehaved against several Frenchmen, from whom they, [using] pain and tyrannical torments, have taken great sums of money and other goods . . ."[17]

At this point, the Dutch authorities made their first official move to curb the behavior of their errant privateers. On July 10, 1606, they drafted a proclamation concerning such freebooter "excesses." These wayward seamen, it acknowledged, whom the Dutch government had sanctioned to attack only those ships and seamen sailing for Spain and the Southern Netherlands, had instead taken to assaulting and "molesting" Dutch allies, and even citizens of the Republic itself. As a result, the proclamation ordered, all Dutch privateers (except those under the command of a trade company) who were presently located on the near side of the Tropic of Cancer should sail home to the Republic by December 31, 1606. Upon arrival, they were to report immediately to the governing council of their respective Admiralty, where they would be interrogated. If any privateer refused to heed this directive, the States-General warned, the Dutch government would automatically assume he was sailing without a proper commission, and, therefore, as a pirate. Such an ignominious distinction would earn the practitioner the promise of corporal punishment and/or removal of his goods and belongings. The *placaat* concluded by forcefully commanding the various local authorities to post the law everywhere, and by admonishing the *reders*, wives, and closest friends of any Dutch privateer to inform their employee/loved one of this latest government decree.[18]

But apparently such efforts were simply not enough. Yet again, on October 8, 1606, authorities in the Republic received notice that the French were up in arms about illegal Dutch depredations. This time, the perpetrators were said to be two privateers, one from Amsterdam and the other from Rotterdam. According to a report sent to Dutch Admiralty officers from French captain Guilleaume Putrel, the two Dutchmen had victimized French seamen, who had been "captured, robbed, and vilely treated . . ." Such acts were, according to Putrel, clearly "against [the men's] Instructions and Commission . . ." Now the French were angry and demanding punishment.[19] By March 1607, things had gotten so bad that the States-General felt the pressure to make a grand, public response to the international community's strident protests.[20] Consequently, they drafted their mandate of March 6, calling for the arrest of any refractory Dutch privateers.

Unfortunately for the Dutch authorities, these incidents were only the beginning of their woes, for other edicts mention the alarming activities of Dutch pirates. For example, a 1611 proclamation bewailed the burgeoning number of Dutch pirates, a multitude of "riffraff" that "grows more and more each day."[21] The immediate cause of this particular situation probably lay in the Twelve Years' Truce with Spain (1609–1621). Once this cease-fire was enacted, many Dutch soldiers and sailors who had been serving in the Republic's military were dismissed or thrown out of work. Consequently, as a result of sheer desperation, lack of other employment opportunities, or merely a desire to maintain their seagoing, martial life, they assumed criminal careers.[22] Similarly, the early-seventeenth-century development of the *fluit*—the flute or flyboat—which made the shipping of cargo so much more efficient and economical, also had the unintended effect of throwing many Dutch seamen out of work. As a result, a number of these now unemployed mariners enlisted with the Barbary corsairss.[23]

But other cases are not so easily explained. Why, for instance, did a plethora of Dutchmen take up piratical life in 1651? The war with Spain had been over for some three years, the First Anglo-Dutch War had not yet commenced, and Dutch shipping was enjoying huge success. And yet a States-General proclamation from August 25 of that year bemoans the large number of Dutch seamen—and those who had served in the Republic's navy, no less—who had taken up piracy:

> Thus it is that some officers, as well as seamen and sailors, [who are] inhabitants of these . . . United Provinces, having been previously in the Country's service, as well as several having remained outside of the Country's service, have bestowed themselves outside of the Land's service, going [instead] to the pirates and thieves, who presently are so strongly rampant at sea, and with their ships help to perpetrate all sorts of violence, to the great detriment and harm—indeed, the total ruin—of the good residents of these provinces, and the destruction of the general commerce and trade . . .[24]

Sheer expediency explains why numerous Dutch privateers carried double commissions during the late 1650s (resulting in "great damage and harm"), a fact that the States-General formally complained about in a statement in 1658.[25] After all, the more commissions one carried, the more outwardly "legal" captures one could make, even if holding a multiplicity of such documents branded one a pirate. But why, in 1665, would the Dutch have so much trouble with their own privateers that the seamen would desert the cause of their country and support that of the enemy? As a March 1665 States-General proclamation makes clear, Dutch sailors (as well as those "of neighboring kingdoms and lands") were earning the title of "pirate" by joining up as privateers for England, a perfidious as well as criminal offense when one considers that the Republic and England were currently at war. Employment as a privateer in King Charles II's navy could only mean that Dutch *kapers*, as a matter of course, were attacking and plundering the ships of their fellow compatriots, truly unthinkable behavior. The *placaat* firmly declared such traitorous men to be "*Zeerovers*" and announced the Dutch authorities' intention to punish them "without mercy." All such "pirates" who were captured, the proclamation promised, would be executed, and their possessions confiscated; those who remained at large would be banished forever.[26]

The 1670s only saw an intensification of such problems. A strongly worded States-General proclamation dating from October 10, 1673, adamantly censured the Republic's privateer seamen for all sorts of "great evil-intentions and debauchery" that qualified as piratical deeds, including the plundering of prizes, disobedience and violence toward their sponsors and captains, "rashly" jumping from one privateering firm to another, and "further misbehavior and disorderliness." The *placaat* also condemned the privateer captains', officers', and sailors' proclivity to "extort excessive sums of money" from their *reders*, which they were able to wrest by using the threat that if they, the privateers, were not paid enough, they would simply desert while underway.[27]

The proclamation then went on to lay out a precise list of punishments for all of the cited infractions. Those privateers who plundered or did the "least violence" to their prizes, or who disobeyed their captain by sailing into a foreign harbor, would pay by forfeiting their lives. And, the States-General added, this sentence would be carried out "without any mercy." Similarly, those officers or sailors who chose to defy their captain and leave his service without permission, or to take a course contrary to the one he dictated, were to be executed without any hope of a pardon or clemency. Additionally, privateers were commanded not to expect or demand any payment for their services until two months after the adjudication and sale of a valid prize. The *placaat* also prescribed set limits on the amount of money that bookkeepers could provide to privateer officers and sailors on any given cruise (which the States-General reckoned should last approximately three months in duration). The stipulated sums ranged from ten rijksdaalders for a captain to three rijksdaalders for a regular sailor. Woe to those who chose to carry more money than this while at sea, for the proclamation promised punishments ranging from a meager diet of bread and water during the extent of the cruise, to keelhauling, to being driven away and labeled as a "rogue," to the death penalty. The proclamation also threatened to prosecute any Dutch citizens who abetted the sale of prizes and cargo illegally plundered by wayward privateers. Such accomplices, the States-General vowed, would be disciplined through the vague yet menacing methods of "arbitrary correction."[28]

Apparently such scare tactics did not nip the problem in the bud. On December 23 of that same year (1673), the States-General felt compelled to issue another proclamation,[29] this one complaining about more instances of privateer misconduct. The proclamation denounced the privateers' habit of staying out at sea and hunting for prizes after the expiration of their commissions, and firmly ordered all Dutch privateers to return to the Republic by February 1674. No excuse would be acceptable, and no pretext justified, it admonished, for an arrival later than the stipulated date. Those choosing not to comply were threatened with the forfeiture of their ships and share of their prizes, as well as the ominous "arbitrary correction." Sponsors, too, were warned that they were liable for fines should any of their privateers not cooperate.[30]

Yet another interesting example of legislative hand-wringing appeared in 1677. Issued by the States of Friesland and the provincial stadholder, Hendrik Casimir, this proclamation—an "Alert Concerning Piracy on the Frisian Coast"[31]—bemoaned the sizable number of fishermen who were leaving their unremunerative careers to work with enemy sea robbers cruising Dutch coastal waters. Whether these fishermen were part of such "injurious piracy" voluntarily or against their wills, the proclamation reproached, the result was the same: "damage, trouble, and thievery." As a precaution, the *placaat* advised, fishermen should simply assume that all privateer vessels—and even all ships in general—that they came across were up to no good and should, accordingly, flee. Those fishermen who were foolish or careless enough to end up as members of these criminal bands, the proclamation threatened, would pay for their perfidy. The Frisian authorities vowed to arrest as many of the transgressors as possible, torch their ships, and bring the culprits back to Friesland, where they would be paraded on a "blockhouse" or tower and "further so punished" so as "to serve as an example" to the rest of the population.

Lawless privateers continued to pose a problem for the Dutch government through the last years of the seventeenth century. In 1690, for example, the States-General was forced to issue a proclamation protesting the "abuses" committed by Dutch privateers. The edict claimed that a number of these seamen were, in truth, "faithless citizens" who were using their *kaperbrieven* as "cloaks" to perpetrate an "injurious trade." In fact, the law railed, these disloyal privateers were actually working in collusion with the Republic's enemy, France. The States-General promised strict punishments against such n'eer-do-wells and their *rederij* sponsors, including stiff fines of ƒ.20,000, confiscation of their ships, and eternal banishment from the land.[32] And not once but twice in 1692,[33] and then again in 1694,[34] the States-General had to issue resolutions specifically forbidding Dutch privateers from attacking, plundering and seizing neutral ships. The privateers had been overly zealous in practicing their trade.

These legislative edicts and laments about unlawful privateering and piracy represented only the beginning. For other archival sources, too, reveal that *zeeroverijen* was a significant and recurrent problem throughout the Golden Age. Such sources include pamphlet literature, newspaper articles, almanacs, and trade company documents, as well as criminal records from local communities, provincial courts, and the Admiralties. From the time of the Republic's inception, its citizens displayed a proclivity for piracy, as Dutch law defined it, whether such behavior took the form of overly zealous or careless privateering, or outright, indiscriminate marauding on the high seas.

The uppermost point on the slippery slope of piratical conduct was occupied by those privateers who engaged in less egregious yet still unequivocally criminal behavior. Extant criminal records reveal numerous instances when the Republic's privateers illegally engaged in the plundering of their prizes or attacked vessels not sanctioned by their commissions. In the eyes of Dutch law, this indisputably represented acts of criminal piracy. What is important to underscore here—and one aspect of these cases that apparently troubled the prosecuting Dutch courts—was these wayward privateers' desire to play both sides of the fence, as it were. In other words, while they wished to maintain the facade of legal, state-sponsored and societally acceptable privateers—to retain their identities as admirable warriors for their country—they engaged in behavior that their chagrined government viewed as loathsome and illegal. They sought to reap simultaneously the rewards of both the criminal and virtuous life.[35]

The archive of the High Court of Holland and Zeeland contains several such cases. Although the files are fragmentary and jumbled and do not, as a rule, relate the outcome of the cases, they still reveal that transgressions by Dutch privateers were investigated and prosecuted at the highest judicial level. For example, in 1610, the court began collecting data on the alleged misdeeds of one Cornelis Dielofs. Dielofs was a privateer sponsored by the Admiralty of Enkhuizen who was active in the waters around the Bay of Cork (Ireland). His file contains a letter from Charles de Montmorourcy, the current admiral of France, who complained about Dielof's unlawful conduct as the "head" and "captain" of a ship named *de Fortuin*. The file also includes correspondence between the High Court, the States-General, and officials at the Admiralty of Enkhuizen, all of which endeavored to ascertain the substance of the French accusations.[36]

Likewise, in 1615, the court officials arrested one Cornelis Claeszoon on the charge of piracy. The suspect mariner was incarcerated in the *Voorpoort* (jail) in the Hague. Claeszoon had procured a commission from the Admiralty of France and used this illegal license to justify his capture of Spanish ships.[37] The case of Jan Lievenszoon Rijckewaert,[38] which the court also investigated in 1615, was similar. A marine who had served the Republic, Rijckewaert captured Spanish and French ships in the Mediterranean. Although he claimed that such actions were justified during time of war (i.e., the Eighty Years War against Spain, although this particular event took place during the Twelve Years' Truce), his lack of any commission prompted the court to prosecute him for piracy.

But Jan Lievenszoon Rijckewaert was hardly the only man who had been audacious enough to set to sea without a proper commission, even as he endeavored to maintain a legal front. Willem Jacobszoon Roose had already attempted this feat in 1613. Indeed, Roose's case represents even more temerity when one considers that he evidently convinced a whole *rederij* to support him in his exploits. A skipper aboard a sizable ship known variously as *de Roose* (*the Rose*) and *de Drie Koningen* (*the Three Kings*), Roose was apprehended by the sheriff of Medemblik in the spring of 1613. After ascertaining that Roose carried no valid commission but had committed various undisclosed acts of aggression, the sheriff charged him with "piracy at sea" (*Roeverie ter Zee*). On June 3, 1613, the sheriff had a poster made that summoned all those individuals—*rederij* partners or otherwise—who had any sort of interest in Roose's ship to come to the city on the next Saturday (July 14) and appear before the court. Another document, a July 14 "Register" from the city of Medemblik, indicates that a number of Amsterdam men did indeed show up, affirming that they had invested money in the ship. Alas, the file contains no further details.[39]

Perhaps the most striking such case from the High Court dates from 1687 and concerns one Hendrick Hoogencamp.[40] Hoogencamp was a canny old merchant and married family man who took perfect advantage of a "privateer identity" in order to cover his admittedly piratical crimes. In 1686, Hoogencamp—a resident of Amsterdam, where he was a member of a trade firm—set to sea in a ship named the *St. Joris*. Supplied with a (fraudulent?) commission from the king of Sweden—as well as carrying seamen who held commissions from the king of Denmark and the Admiralty of Amsterdam— Hoogencamp cast off, claiming that he had to travel to Hamburg to resolve some business matters. (Hoogencamp may have also possessed additional commissions—the court was unclear about this fact.) In reality, however, the wily 50-year old did not journey far at all, choosing instead to prowl the waters of the Republic's northern coast. On November 16, 1686, he and his crew made their first strike, seizing a Dutch ship and stealing ordinance and weaponry. Next, they attacked another vessel, again stealing weaponry, after which Hoogencamp "violently" assaulted a Danish ship, and kidnapped four of the men aboard. A short time later, Hoogencamp and his men struck again, this time against a Dutch ship, *de Jonge Tobias* (*the Young Tobias*). After stealing this ship, Hoogencamp and his 18 "scoundrel" henchmen (an international crew that even included an Englishman whom Hoogencamp had liberated from the Algerian corsairs) headed north and attacked yet another ship. Along the way, they also seized a vessel from Hamburg. Upon their return to Dutch waters, Hoogencamp and his fellow rapscallions brought their assorted booty to land and apportioned it among themselves. Somehow or another, the local sheriff caught wind of these happenings and immediately arrested Hoogencamp; the sheriff also discovered 44 weapons aboard Hoogencamp's vessel (including 20 pistols and 4 blunderbusses), all of which must have only confirmed the lawman's worst suspicions. Upon investigation, the authorities also learned of the pain and distress Hoogencamp had inflicted on his victims, including at least one fatal drowning and acts of torture such as finger breaking. He was, as one court document pronounced, a person of true "disorder" and "maliciousness."

The court sentencing records of the Admiralty of the Maas provide even more examples of privateers—as well as naval seamen—who succumbed to the siren call of piracy. As reflected in the sentencing records' index, the Admiralty sometimes engaged in a sort of "spin control," creating euphemistic labels to characterize the misdeeds of such seamen who walked the crooked line, who behaved piratically even while endeavoring to retain the legitimate veneer of the Republican military man. Examples of labels used to soften the sting of a piracy charge included classifications such as "plundering of prizes," "excesses," "extortion," and the ultra-benign "privateering and prizes."[41] Despite such misleading terminology, however, the documents reveal that these men were tried and sentenced on the more serious charges of piracy and banditry, for the actual Admiralty court's sentences typically did away with such obfuscating qualifiers and found the perpetrators culpable of the ignominious crimes of *berovinge* (robbery, despoliation), *roverij* (brigandage, banditry), or *zeeroverij* (sea banditry, piracy).

Take, for example, the 1695 case of navel officer François Sissingh,[42] which in the sentencing records index is referred to as an instance of "Plundering of Prizes." In Sissingh's actual sentence, however, the Admiralty court cited his "capital disobedience and untrustworthiness," charged him with willfully transgressing against specific Dutch laws,[43] and convicted him on the charge of "criminal robbery and plundering of goods." Indeed, Sissingh's conduct easily fulfills the Dutch legal definition of "piracy."

On May 19, 1694, Sissingh—then a naval officer in command of the frigate *'t Sterrenburgh* (*the Sterrenburg*)—sailed to Yarmouth, England, even though this detour was in clear defiance of his official orders. Although the Admiralty authorities in Rotterdam sent a letter to the wayward commander, ordering him to return home, Sissingh forced his crew to go to Zeeland. By June 19, he had returned once again to the coast of Yarmouth, where he stayed for days, flouting his official orders and responsibilities. On July 4, another naval officer found him and enjoined him once again to return to the Netherlands, but Sissingh refused. Instead, on July 15, he and his men plundered a retaken prize ship, the *Catharina*, stealing various crates full of linens and trade goods. After divvying up the booty with his crew and stowing a good amount of the merchandise on board *'t Sterrenburgh*, he sold the rest in Yarmouth. These proceeds, too, he divided with his crew. Although Admiralty officials had ordered Commander Sissingh to appear in court on three different occasions, he flagrantly ignored their summons. They tried him in absentia, and following guidelines stipulated in Dutch law, sentenced him to eternal banishment from the Republic and the promise of execution by hanging should he ever return.

The index of the Admiralty sentencing records also includes a number of instances of "wayward privateer cases" under the heading of "mobs." These examples demonstrate that the Dutch authorities experienced problems with their *commissievaarders* from the time of the Republic's inception. The case of Adriaan Jansen den Brits, Leendert Joppen, and Jan Jacobsen, who were sentenced on April 11, 1575,[44] is illustrative. On the surface, the three seamen were virtuous Republican lads. Hailing from the province of Holland, they carried commissions from the Stadholder to serve the state as Sea Beggar warriors against the Castilian adversary.

The Sea Beggars were the ad hoc naval force that the rebelling Netherlanders founded in 1568. Composed of men from throughout the Netherlands domains,[45] and led by esteemed nobles such William the Silent and Philip de Marnix, they served as a homegrown, insurgent guerrilla force in opposition to the organized Spanish military. Many late-sixteenth-century Dutch people considered them to be an unruly, immoral group whose "piratical" conduct and carousing with prostitutes voided their membership in proper, civilized society.[46] However, the idea of conquest and domination by the Spanish and their loathed Catholic clergy was even more repellent.[47] Moreover, it was the Sea Beggars who initiated the first great, aggressive strike of the Revolt when they seized the port of Den Briel from the Spanish in 1572. Using the foreign bases of Emden, La Rochelle, and Dover,[48] they went on to capture more important towns (e.g., the strategic Zeeland naval base of Vlissingen, an exploit that assured the rebels control over the Scheldt estuary), relieve embattled rebelling populations, vanquish the Spanish in tough and bloody battles (e.g., the October 11, 1573 battle on the Zuiderzee, by Hoorn), and foment internal unrest.

As Sea Beggars, den Brits, Joppen, and Jacobsen had sailed under the command of Captain Herman Janszoon of Rotterdam. Their first offense was illegally keeping booty and prize money that should have gone to their captain. But while such an action did represent a crime, this was not what really upset the court. Rather, what concerned the Admiralty officials was that the three defendants had made a habit out of violently kidnapping innocent Dutch men and women in order to collect hefty ransoms. Although kidnapping was sometimes used as a martial tactic during this early phase of the Eighty Years War, Dutch soldiers and sailors were certainly not supposed to abduct innocent, pro-independence civilians from the sanctuary of their homes. Rather, the practice was intended as a means to intimidate supporters of Spain. Indeed, in order to prevent the capture of honest Dutch citizens, privateers' letters of commission formally ordered that any abductees be brought to the Admiralty Council and the Prince of Orange. The Council, in turn, would ascertain the circumstances of each kidnapping, determine whether it was legal and warranted, and whether a ransom should be set.

Den Brits, Joppen, and Jacobsen eschewed such regulations, however. Nor were they particularly interested in being discriminating about their victims and seizing only champions of the Spanish cause. Rather, the three wayward Sea Beggars stormed the residences of innocent citizens, tore men, women, and young girls away from their homes, and imprisoned them in the domicile of another crony, a smuggler in Holland. They then ascribed ransom amounts, and released their captives only when these sums were paid. As would be expected, they divided up these ill-begotten proceeds between themselves. That the three men inspired dread in their countrymen is quite probable, for their nicknames suggest their base characters: Den Brits was known as *Duinkuit* or "Dune Spawn," while Joppen went under the alias of *Boerenverdriet* or "Farmers Misery," and Jacobsen, perhaps in an ironic and perverse attempt at sarcasm, called himself *Bestekind*, that is, "Best Child."

But such actions were not the worst of it. Among the men's victims was a petite, young "maiden"—an orphan and virgin. Although they tried to ransom her for *f.*12.5 and (to cover the costs of her meals) a crown, the deliverance money did not arrive fast enough. As they had threatened to do, den Brits and Joppen took her to a haystack and assaulted her; den Brits ultimately raped the girl. Likewise, after kidnapping another young girl, Jacobsen "dishonorably attacked her" against her will.

The Admiralty court was horrified by the actions of den Brit, Joppen, and Jacobsen. Such indiscriminate abduction and ransoming, the judges declared, was a sheer transgression against the men's letters of commission as well as the orders of their captain. It also represented public violence, despoliation, robbery, and oppression, which warranted the harshest of punishments. Accordingly, the court sentenced the three criminals to a multifaceted penalty. First, the men were to be whipped. Then they were to be sent to the gallows outside of the city of Leiden, where they would be hanged. And after their deaths, the corpses of the three men were to be left on the gallows, where they would serve as a "spectacle and example" to others.

Unfortunately, "Dune Spawn," "Farmers' Misery," and "Best Child" were not the only Sea Beggars to terrorize innocent bystanders, including their fellow Dutch citizens. Sea Beggar seamen often violated their letters of commission, illegally assaulting and seizing many a hapless, neutral vessel.[49] Furthermore, the Sea Beggars were the only Dutch privateers, who in addition to their actions at sea, operated on the mainland. There, they were notorious for their acts of "extortion" (*knevelarijen*), whereby small, wandering bands of Sea Beggars would break into peoples' homes and force their victims to pay a set sum as a condition of release (similar to what den Brits, Joppen, and Jacobsen had done). Additionally, they ransacked and plundered various cities, villages, and small islands, and virulently anti-Catholic Beggars made a point of sacking and pillaging convents and abbeys.

While the terrified Dutch populace ostensibly deplored such conduct, *knevelrijen*—when falling within certain parameters—was, as was explained above, lawful and legitimate under the terms of the *commissiebrieven* granted by William of Orange.[50] At the same time, there were limits to such behavior, even if such lines could be difficult to determine. When a Sea Beggar's acts of "extortion" became, in the language of the time, "excessive," even the Stadholder and Admiral-General himself was prone to call them "pirates" (*zeerovers*) and take measures to stop them.[51] Surely, such "excessive" behavior was exemplified by a Sea Beggar named *'t Hoen* (the Chicken). This maverick Beggar, who operated with his band of 18 henchmen during the era of the early Dutch Revolt, made the area between Amsterdam and Haarlem most unsafe for innocent Dutch civilians. He robbed, murdered, and terrorized his unsuspecting victims, using as his hunting grounds the Ij River and the inland canals that interlaced the region. He also practiced "extortion" to collect ransoms from his frightened hostages.[52]

But violent inland *knevelrijen* was not the end of it, for another controversial Sea Beggar practice was the kidnapping of wealthy merchants and fishing boat crews while at sea, and they made no exceptions for Dutch citizens. Like their terrified land-based counterparts, these Dutch seafolk were also held for ransom. Typically, after seizing these defenseless vessels while underway, the Beggars took their hostages to some hidden harbor, often in England or along the Eems River, and determined a ransom. At times, the Beggars also commandeered valuable cargo, charging ransoms that were typically higher than what they could garner for the merchandise at market. (One well-known example of this practice was the Sea Beggar capture of the Dutch grain fleet in September 1569; a number of Amsterdam merchants were forced to pay for its release.) If the ransom was duly and efficiently paid by the victims' *reders* or family members, the individual captive and/or cargo was released, and the vessel was furnished with a *rantsoenbrief* (ransom letter). This document served as a sort of passport, ensuring the vessel's safe passage by guaranteeing that it would not be seized a second time.[53]

Perhaps it is not surprising that such "extortionist" practices took place during the wild and woolly days of the Republic's early existence, when its "navy" was, in reality, composed of a ragtag group of rebelling nobles and maritime ruffians, and the boundaries of the Dutch state, as well as affirmations of Dutch identity, were still nebulous, unsettled, and confused. The Sea Beggars apparently felt no obligation to obey the rules laid down by the fledging Dutch Admiralties. At the same time, however, as the Golden Age unfolded and privateering became a more institutionalized enterprise, privateers were compelled to adhere to the official regulations, which included the prohibition of "extortion."[54]

But even as the institutions and identity of the Dutch Republic became more formalized and organized, authorities at Dutch courts still found themselves charging "valorous" Dutch privateers with the crime of "extortion." In October 1624, for instance, the court at the Admiralty of the Maas found three of the Republic's commissioned *kapers*—Marten Jeliszoon, Jan Jacobszoon, and Bartell Thijs—guilty of this crime. All three were members of a crew sailing under privateer Captain Willem Bouwerszoon, with two of them holding specialized positions aboard: Jeliszoon was a steward and Thijs a cook. In April of that year, their ship had departed the Maas to begin its cruise. When Captain Bouwerszoon and his men reached the English Channel, they decided to attack a French ship. During the course of this assault (the legality of which was dubious to begin with), two prisoners were captured and brought over from the French vessel. These two unfortunate men, both Portuguese, would come to be the focus of the defendants' sadistic attention.

In an effort to follow Captain Bouwerszoon's orders (or so the defendants claimed), the three Dutch privateers tried to force the imprisoned Portuguese seamen to reveal whether the French prize was carrying any unfree goods (i.e., those belonging to states that were not neutral or allied with the Republic), and where the prisoners' own money and possessions were stowed. To that end, Jeliszoon, Jacobszoon, and Thijs used extreme physical coercion, torturing the victims unmercifully. Among other cruelties, the victims experienced the agony of "woolding": the three defendants wound cords with stiff knots around the prisoners' heads, and steadily tightened the cords until the prisoners' eyes bulged. They also bludgeoned the Portuguese men in the jaw, and burned the area between the prisoners' fingers with tapers. As a result of these torments, the prisoners did eventually confess to owning some valuable jewelry: a gold chain bedecked with six strands of pearls. Jeliszoon confiscated the item immediately, and refused to surrender it to his captain.

The Admiralty court found such goings-on to be completely unacceptable. In the first place, they affirmed, the Admiralty's rules dictated that the Portuguese prisoners—as unfree persons—should have been delivered to the Admiralty for verification and questioning. And second, the fierce tortures instigated by the three defendants represented the epitome of "cruel sea extortion" (*wreede Zee knevelerije*), as even defendant Jeliszoon himself admitted. Such crimes, the court determined, were not to be committed without the incurring of grave punishment, which should serve as an example to all. Taking into account the defendants' excuses and submissive pleas for clemency, the court sentenced them to a punishment that gave them a chance to retain their lives: they were to be keelhauled twice from the deck of a warship docked in the Maas. Moreover, all of the defendants' booty was to be confiscated, no matter what anyone else—including the privateers' *reders*—might have promised.[55]

"Extortion," as it turns out, was just the beginning of the transgressions that Dutch privateers perpetrated. Seemingly upright Dutch seamen violated their letters of commission or illegally profited from their ostensibly legitimate status in any number of ways. Typically in these instances, the Admiralty sentencing index refers to such cases as pure *zeeroverij* (literally, sea piracy) or *stroomroverij* (river piracy). And in accordance with the privateer letters of instruction and commission, the court sentenced such defendants to the harshest of penalties: usually execution, but at the least, serious corporal punishment.

The crimes of Steven Janszoon and his 11 unidentified cronies, who were convicted of *zeeroverije* by the Admiralty court in 1624, represent a good case in point. These men served under a privateer captain named Huig Willemszoon, who was based in Zeeland. Embarking with Willemszoon in the spring of 1624, they quickly captured a homeward-bound Hamburg ship. However, instead of bringing the prize ship back to the Admiralty where it could be adjudicated, the disobedient privateers located all the money in the hold and divvied it up among themselves. They then went on to detain the Hamburg ship for another two months, during which time they forced it to remain out at sea. Finally, Captain Willemszoon consented that the captured vessel could be taken to England and sold there, and the defendant and his accomplices did so. Then, having left England, the company set out to capture more ships, proceeding to seize a French fishing boat and a large French merchant ship; they were less successful in taking a small English ship. Their plunder included 400 cases of sugar, a great cache of pieces-of-eight, 7–8 tons of beer, 300–400 fish, and other unspecified goods. In the end, these privateers-gone-bad were apprehended by the Dutch Navy and tried by the court of the Admiralty of the Maas, which used strong language in describing the privateers' misdeeds when it handed down the sentence on September 11, 1624. Noting that unbridled "Freebooters" (*Vrijbuiters*) had become an intractable problem at the present time—that "they swarm the seas in great numbers which increase daily," committed insurmountable damage to the residents of the Dutch Republic, and caused great "enmity" between the United Provinces and its friends, allies, and neighbors—the judges convicted the defendants of "criminal piracy" (*Feiten Zeeroverije*) and condemned them to hang.[56]

The case of one Jan de Haas,[57] a privateer captain who was found guilty of piracy on November 22, 1660, is also illustrative. Haas, who had received a commission from the States-General to patrol the "Great Fishery" near Yarmouth, was expressly warned by the Directors of the Fishery to refrain from harassing or attacking those ships belonging to neutral powers or to states that were allied with the Republic. Despite the solemn oath Haas swore, pledging himself to the service of his country and to the rules stipulated in his *Article Brief*, he quickly transgressed, using subterfuge, duplicity, and violence to attack four ships from Hamburg and two ships from France.

Threatening his victims with gunfire, the privateer forcibly detained the foreign vessels and requested to see their passports and other documents. He then announced that their paperwork was improper, at which point he took the opportunity to plunder their cargoes. For his pains, he was able to pillage over a ton of dried and salted fish, wool, linens, textiles, nets, bleach, flour, grain, sugar, 80 rings of copper wire, beer, salt, fish oil, fishing line, smoked meat, olives, cheese, hams, tobacco, and lemons. Add to this the fact that

Haas had coerced the victimized captains into signing fraudulent notes which stated that their vessels had been left unmolested and undamaged. Haas also concealed his identity, using a false name and home harbor, and declined to record his captures in his privateering log, as was required by law. Although he ultimately released all the captive seamen, he kept the cargoes, storing the goods in the hold of his own ship, in his home in Rotterdam, and in other undisclosed locations.

The Admiralty court decried such dastardly actions, dubbing them to be "piracy and extortion," behavior that was "very evil and [which produced] injurious consequences," and which could not be tolerated in a "land of justice." Haas was sentenced to be brought to a special scaffold, which was to be erected in front of the court, where he was to be beheaded (executed "with the sword"). The Admiralty also confiscated his goods.

Or one might consider the example of the 42-year-old mariner Reinier Claaszoon Vonk. On October 16, 1673, the Admiralty of the Maas convicted and sentenced him for his piratical actions at sea, deeds that, in the words of the court, constituted "affairs of very evil consequences." Vonk was the commander of a sloop that had been outfitted with muskets, hand weapons, and ordnance. His sponsoring firm had instructed him to travel to the Maas River, where he should capture all unfree ships and goods, and bring them to the Admiralty, in Rotterdam, for adjudication. To this end, he was furnished with a Dutch privateering commission, but one that was actually intended for another person, one Jan de Vries. The document was, therefore, invalid in Vonk's hands.

Such legal technicalities mattered naught to Vonk, however, for he disobeyed the commission's instructions anyway. Rather than cruise the mouth of the Maas, he headed for the high seas without delay. Right away, he found success, for in the waters beyond the coast of Zeeland, he captured a craft laden with wine, which he brought into the Maas. He and his crew then captured another vessel, this time anchored near Schiedam, and also loaded with wine. Vonk then went on to seize a Flemish ship carrying tobacco, fish, and other goods.

The Admiralty court was angered by Vonk's illegal depredations and made no secret of their feelings when they sentenced the seaman. Citing his transgression of Dutch laws, his guilt in engaging in behavior that contributed to the "destruction" of Dutch maritime trade, and the necessity to ensure the security of Dutch roadsteads and ports, the judges condemned Vonk to be thrown three times from the great yardarm of a warship. Should Vonk survive this punishment, he was then to be tied to the ship's main mast and lashed by the sailors who were currently on watch. Last, Vonk was enjoined to pay the court costs, as well as those of his imprisonment.[58]

It is clear that the court at the Admiralty of the Maas viewed such crimes as reprehensible acts that went against the laws of the Dutch Republic and were inimical to Dutch trade. The offenders who committed such deeds— ostensibly upright privateers who had pledged to honor certain rules and regulations—were condemned by the judges, and duly sentenced to harsh and unforgiving punishments. However, bad as these cases may have been, what most offended the Dutch authorities and populous were the cases in which Dutch privateers (or former privateers) hired themselves out to the Republic's enemies and actively campaigned against their Dutch countrymen. For instance, various instances of such Dutch privateer perfidy occurred during the course of the War of the Spanish Succession (1702–1713). It was not unheard of for large numbers of Dutch privateer seahands to desert in a foreign harbor, and the temptation to join up with the enemy was great. For example, two-third of the crew of the privateer ship the *Walcheren* abandoned their Dutch posts in order to serve on French privateer ships and warships.[59]

Dutch law—which, of course, prohibited such actions—did sometimes catch up with these disloyal individuals. One privateer, Frans Pietersen, deserted his Dutch ship and fled to Oostende, Flanders. There, he took up service as a privateer for the French. Eventually, he was brought back to Zeeland, where he stood trial for his misdeeds and was sentenced to death.[60] Similarly, Albert Rijke, a privateer seaman from Amsterdam, ran away from his Dutch ship, and eventually joined up with the Dunkirkers, serving them as a privateer captain. His job was to prowl the inland rivers and waters of Zeeland. Captured by the Dutch authorities, he too was sentenced to death, a fate he ultimately escaped only because the Dutch government feared reprisals against Dutch prisoners in France.[61]

Turncoat Dutch privateers were a problem from the earliest years of the Republic. On September 22, 1576, for example, in a classic case of what the Admiralty sentencing index referred to as "river piracy" (*stroomroverijen*), the Admiralty court gathered to decide the fate of Hendrik Franszoon Cruidaan and Cornellis Gysbregtszoon. Cruidaan was a former Sea Beggar captain who had served under William of Orange, and Gysbregtszoon—also known as the *Zwaartgen* ("Little Hefty Man" or perhaps "Little Dark Man")—was his partner in crime. After receiving funds from the Admiralty of Amsterdam to recruit sailors for the Dutch war effort, Cruidaan instead absconded with the money and assembled a gang of eight men (including Gysbregtszoon). Together, the band acquired a boat in Dordrecht and journeyed to Antwerp, where they made overtures to the pro-Spanish forces. En route, they also kidnapped a merchant from Utrecht, from whom they stole six pieces of gold, and whom they presented to the enemy as an extra inducement. After promising to serve one Jan Turk, a commander in Antwerp, they accepted an advance of three months salary, for a total of 90 pounds per man (Turk contracted each individual for 30 pounds per month). Cruidaan and his accomplices then returned to Dutch waters with the intention of causing real mayhem.

Before too much time had elapsed, Cruidaan, Gysbregtszoon, and the others had kidnapped a young lad from Zeeland, forcing him to serve as a cabin boy. Now part of a fleet that included some 32–33 Antwerp corsairs spread out between four different vessels, they made their way to the region called the Biesbosch, a murky network of interlacing marshes, shallows, and estuaries where the Waal and Maas Rivers meet. For three days they waited there stealthily with hopes of attacking and raiding the Prince of Orange's ships and galleys. When that goal eluded them, they instead kidnapped a carpenter from a local village, took him to Antwerp, imprisoned him, and ransomed him for some ƒ.400. Returning to the Republic, the men laid low. But in a final dastardly turn, Cruidaan poisoned and killed one of his cronies with whom he had been lodging in a Zeeland village.

The Admiralty court judges wasted no time in calling such crimes "wicked" acts that would not go unpunished. They sentenced the two defendants—at the time imprisoned in the Rotterdam *Vangenhuis* (jail)—to be executed by decapitation. Cruidaan, the former Sea Beggar captain, and his accomplice, Gysbregtszoon, were to be led from the prison to the city gallows. There, the executioner would behead them with a sword. The court did grant that the men were to be given a decent burial, for the sentence stipulated that their bodies were to be retrieved and interred in Rotterdam's *Kerkhove* (church cemetery). But in one final twist, the wily *Zwaartgen*—Cornelis Gysbregtszoon—escaped on the very day that the judges announced his fate.[62]

The preceding examples probably represent only a fraction of the number of Dutch privateers who went astray. After all, precious few archival documents—such as Admiralty of the Maas prosecution records (or any criminal records from the other four Admiralties)—survive. Still, when one is aware of just these misdeeds that Dutch privateers and their sponsors (the *rederijen* and trade companies) perpetrated, it is not surprising that the trade did not always enjoy the highest esteem, either at home or abroad. Some historians claim that Dutch privateers in general, and Zeelands ones in particular, had a bad reputation.[63] Indeed, beyond its shores, the Republic's *kapers*—sometimes referred to as "Pechelingues" or "Pixaringos," a south-European bastardization of the word "Vlissingers"—were often greatly feared.[64] And while criticism at home seems to have been more muted, Dutch *commissievaarders* still had their detractors.

For instance, a 1649 pamphlet, *Amsterdams Vuur-Praetje* (*Fireside Chat in Amsterdam*), was not at all shy about expressing its displeasure with Dutch privateers and their tendency to skirt the law. Framed as a discussion about whether the States-General should issue letters of commission (this time, against the Portuguese), the pamphlet's author accused the Republic's *kapers* of various types of misconduct, including the use of illegal bribes to circumvent the laws and the improper application of violence and aggression against those who stood in their way.[65] Dutch privateers were nothing but "thieves," it affirmed, who tended to rob and plunder their own countrymen if no "legal" victims were immediately available.[66] They were "devils" who sought only to further their own cause and enrich themselves.[67] It also claimed that regulations were useless in controlling these maritime predators—Dutch privateers did what they wanted to anyway.[68] In general, the pamphlet asserted, "godless privateering"[69] was an ignominious industry, a "Devil's trade" that contaminated all of Dutch seafaring and was anathema to Christian mores.[70] And it was foolish—even delusional—to believe that any difference existed between the Netherlands' privateers and the much-despised corsairs of that "illustrious pirate nest," Dunkirk.[71] In sum, the pamphlet argued, Dutch privateers were just pirates by another name.

The authorities of the Golden Age Netherlands were aghast at the misdeeds committed by those Dutch privateers—and their sponsors—who went astray. Such men had taken advantage of the slippery slope that existed between lawful privateering and illicit piracy, to retain the veneer of Republican probity even as they behaved wantonly in the pursuit of ill-gotten plunder. Sometimes, however, reprobate Dutch seamen took no pains to cloak their crimes in legality. They neither justified their actions as deeds that were valid during time of war, nor carried fraudulent privateering commissions. They did not endeavor to create or preserve a "privateer" facade while acting in a "piratical" fashion. Some Dutchmen just resolved to take up the pirate's life, to profit illicitly, sometimes violently, and often at the expense of their fellow countrymen. Working as both ocean-going rogues (*zeeroovers*) and inland river bandits (*stroomroovers*), they made no pretense of their intentions. They simply sought to ambush unsuspecting victims to feather their own iniquitous nests, to aid and abet the enemy, or other such schemes that were anathema to Dutch law, commerce, and mores.

Dutch court records contain convictions of numerous Dutch mariners who succumbed to the siren call of the piratical life. Sadly and not surprisingly, many of these instances concern perfidious Dutchmen who hired themselves out to the Republic's enemies, especially during the its early years. Such men received the full odium of the Dutch authorities. To take but one example, a States-General resolution of April 16, 1627, notes that three Dutch "turn-coats" who had willingly served the Dunkirkers and were subsequently captured by Dutch navel authorities would be prosecuted to the full extent of the law.[72] Likewise, on October 31, 1628, the judges at the High Court of Holland sentenced Dutch sailor Ysbrand Willemzoon Nobel to be hanged to death for the crime of serving "the enemy" (one assumes the Spanish or the Dunkirkers), for whom he had captured numerous Dutch vessels; he had also committed various violent acts ashore.[73]

Admiralty records are still more revealing. For example, on November 24, 1605, Admiralty judges sentenced a Dutch seaman and his 48 unidentified accomplices (some of whom were also citizens of the Republic) to hang for the crime of serving the Dunkirk corsairs. Mariner Jacob Janssen of Enkhuizen had received a commission from the Dunkirkers to privateer against the Republic. Under the command of a Dunkirk vice-admiral, Janssen and his cronies crewed aboard the ship the *Albertius*, patrolling Dutch waters with the intention of capturing, plundering, robbing, and imprisoning Dutch fishermen, merchants, and "other good sea people of the United Netherlands." The *Albertius* had been effective in its efforts, destroying numerous Dutch vessels and imprisoning countless Dutch seafarers in the dismal dungeons of Dunkirk. Finally captured by the Dutch Navy, Janssen and his 48 colleagues were brought back to Rotterdam to face trial.

The court did not hide its feelings of contempt for the defendant and his accomplices. Calling them "villains" who had sold their souls to the enemy, it accused them of practicing a "malicious business" of "hostile intentions" against the upright people of the Dutch Republic. In sum, the judges declared, the actions of these turncoats had led to the "insecurity, disadvantage, and destruction of the Dutch maritime trade," as well as "the utter ruin and decay of many poor fishermen, merchants, and other good residents" of the United Provinces. Such misdeeds, the judges proclaimed, would not be tolerated. Consequently, Janssen and the others were sentenced to be executed at the gallows outside of Rotterdam.[74]

While the Admiralty's criminal sentencing index primly referred to this case as one concerning "Prisoners," the vast majority of the time the court did away with euphemisms and such traitorous Dutchmen were typically labeled pirates, pure and simple. For example, those men who served under the infamous, late-sixteenth-century Dutch pirate the "Devil of Dordrecht"— branded by the Dutch authorities as a "rogue and traitor" to his country— were found guilty of intentionally "destroying, capturing, plundering, and robbing the good merchants, shippers, and householders" of the Republic.[75] The only qualifiers the judges sometimes utilized were those that provided information about which bodies of water these renegade Dutchmen roamed, that is, whether they were *stroomroovers* (river pirates) or *zeeroovers* (sea pirates). Either way, however, the court viewed them with condemnation, repugnance, and anger.

Take the case of Dutchmen Jan Spienink and Egbert Gerrits, both of whom were convicted of piracy by the Admiralty court and sentenced on May 5, 1589.[76] These two men chose to serve the Dunkirkers rather than their own state. Both worked as captains aboard Dunkirk corsair vessels; when a Dutch warship apprehended them, they were jointly commanding a flyboat manned by 37 crewmen. Scouring the North Sea waters surrounding the Republic, they had already captured four Dutch ships loaded with various types of merchandise and fish in only three weeks time. The court considered Spienink and Gerrits to be veteran pirates who went to sea with the sole goal of plundering, robbing, and kidnapping the upright merchants, fishermen, and other sea people of the Republic. Such actions, the judges proclaimed, resulted in damage and destruction to the Dutch maritime trade. The two traitors were duly convicted of "piracy and river hooliganism" and sentenced to be hanged at the Rotterdam city gallows.

Then there was the case of Dutchmen Adriaan Corneliszoon and Lenart Joriszoon, both of whom were sentenced on March 22, 1586. The Admiralty authorities viewed their perfidious behavior as nothing but pure *stroomroverij*. Corneliszoon and Joriszoon had joined other Dutch traitors in robbing and plundering Republican vessels to provision Spanish soldiers. Moreover, they crewed aboard naval ships based in Antwerp. Joriszoon was merely the owner of a barge and had not been involved in the criminal life. But he quickly acceded to Corneliszoon's enticing entreaties to join his piratical gang. Other members included two more turncoat Dutchmen—known only as the *Roosken* (Little Rose) and *Debracte* (the Hound, the Rogue)—who had already given themselves over to the enemy, and who worked as *Stroomschenders* (river violators/desecrators), disturbing the Republic's trade.

Corneliszoon and Joriszoon wasted no time commencing their new career. After sailing to Zandvliet, where they provided the Spanish soldiers garrisoned there with 14 tons of butter, they traveled to Dordrecht, and stole a barge loaded with cheese and bacon. This vessel, too, they brought to Zandvliet. Along the way, Joriszoon consented to travel to Delft, where he retrieved a large load of butter, ham, and cheese. With the help of Corneliszoon, he transported this food again to Zandvliet and into the appreciative arms of the Spanish.

They now took a different tack. Formally entering into an agreement with the Spanish soldiers in Zandvliet, they participated in chasing a warship commanded by the Prince of Orange. When that pursuit proved unsuccessful, they based themselves in Antwerp, and worked as sailors on a pro-Spanish warship. At a later point, when Corneliszoon's and Joriszoon's work brought them back to Dordrecht, the Dutch authorities finally arrested them and imprisoned them in the Hague. As one would expect, the Dutch judges found the defendants' river piracy to constitute acts of "hostility and enmity" against the state, "evil examples" of behavior dedicated to the "total ruin of these provinces." Accordingly, they sentenced them to be hanged in the Hague. Furthermore, following the executions, their corpses were to be brought to "the usual place" outside of the city, where they would be displayed so as to serve as a "terrifying and deterrent Spectacle" for all to see. And last but not least, their goods were to be confiscated for the common good.[77]

Like these defendants, who had worked for the established river pirates *Roosken* and *Debracte*, there were other turncoat Dutchmen who joined organized gangs of *stroomroovers* serving the enemy. One of those apprehended by the Admiralty of the Maas was Adriaan Janssen, who with his six unidentified crewmen was found guilty by the court in 1590. Known by the alias of "*Naartgen*" (tentative trans. "the Horrid/Grim One"), Janssen worked under the command of a pirate captain known as the "*Lange Bagger*" (the "Long Mud Dredging" or alternatively, "the Long Jewel"). As in other exploits Janssen had committed—and as in the types of crimes that the *Lange Bagger* and his followers perpetrated regularly—*Naartgen* and his cronies departed from Geertruidenbergh, a city under control of the enemy, and went ashore in the Zwaluwe region of South Holland, where they had concealed a fully outfitted boat. They then sailed to Willemstad in order to plunder and rob the merchant ships plying the river, and waited stealthily in the harbor. There, they seized two vessels, taking the commander prisoner in the one, and plundering ƒ.400–500, and capturing five soldiers, a merchant, and a woman from the other. With these prisoners and booty, they had set out for Geertruidenberge, where they planned to divvy up their spoils, when the Dutch authorities apprehended them. Taking little time for fuss or ceremony, the justices found Janssen and his crewmen guilty of "enormous" crimes and "river piracy" and sentenced them on December 12, condemning them to be hanged at the gallows outside of Willemstad.[78]

The court was similarly horrified by a group of traitorous men whom they brought to justice on July 11, 1592. Willem Hendrikszoon van Dongen,

Laurens Adriaan Janszoon, and their three unnamed colleagues were found guilty of "heinously enormous" misdeeds and river piracy, which were contrary to the ordinances and proclamations of the Dutch Republic. Van Dongen and his cronies were some of the very many Dutchmen who sailed under the command of the notorious river pirate the *Lagge Bagge* ("the Vile Jewel," or perhaps "the Vile Mud Dredging"), himself a Dutchman who now worked as a "Captain of River Pirates" in Antwerp.[79] Like the *Lagge Bagge*'s other followers, the defendants prowled the rivers of the Republic, attacked and fought Dutch naval vessels, and captured and plundered other Dutch ships they encountered there. They also systematically kidnapped the Dutch people aboard these craft, as well as residents of several Dutch villages, and imprisoned them in Geertruidenberge, a Spanish stronghold. Sometimes Janszoon, Van Dongen, and their fellow crewmen murdered their victims, including one entire family, whose house they burned. For these crimes, as well as because of the fact that they did not hold a legitimate commission from the Dutch admiral-general, the Admiralty authorities sentenced them to be hanged at the Rotterdam gallows.[80]

Unfortunately, these defendants were not the only traitorous Dutchmen to serve that reprehensible traitor from Leiden, the *Lagge Bagge*. The Admiralty of the Maas apprehended other *Baggelingen*—as his followers were apparently known—and likewise found them guilty of the crime of river piracy. For instance, Geraart Janszoon (a.k.a. the *Jonge Bagge* or "Young Jewel") and Willem Janszoon (nicknamed *Vosken* or "the Little Fox"), both served the pirate commander, and were sentenced by the court on April 26, 1594.[81] So, too, did Geert Aartszoon (alias Geert Laps or "Geert the Despicable"), who was convicted and sentenced on August 22 of that same year. Shockingly, all three men had formerly served in Dutch Navy or Sea Beggar fleets, and Aartszoon had even held the distinction of working aboard the ship of General Philips van Nassau. Now, like the other loathed *Baggelingen*, all three prowled the rivers and streams of the Republic, searching for Dutch ships that they could "plunder and rob" and "good people" whom they could kidnap and ransom. Between them, they had succeeded in capturing at least seven different vessels of varying sizes and held several victims hostage, including a village pastor. The Admiralty court, not surprisingly, denounced these attacks as base acts of "piracy" and "river hooliganism," and sentenced all three defendants to hang at the Rotterdam gallows.[82]

Even those men who did not actually *succeed* in abetting the enemy through piratical means could be convicted of piracy, for the mere intention to do so could be enough to determine culpability. This is what happened in the case of Laurens de Rundere, whom the Admiralty court found guilty of "extortion and river piracy" on October 1, 1588. Using a fraudulent Dutch privateering commission, de Rundere and his crew of 16 men set sail with the plan to cruise the Republic's rivers in search of booty. After joining with one Gullis Janszoon of Zierikzee, who, in turn, had other sailors working with him, the whole company gave themselves over to the Spanish forces. At this point, however, any illusions of grandeur De Rundere and his cronies maintained unraveled in spectacular fashion. Indeed, these men were singularly unsuccessful in everything they tried to do. First, their ship was completely unequipped for warfare. Second, their one attempt at following some Dutch warships ended when the buffoonish river pirates became frightened and went ashore. And third, the counterfeit commission they were carrying was so poorly forged that it was easily detected by the local authorities. Of course, such a pathetic comedy of errors earned these defendants no reprieve for the Admiralty judges sentenced De Rundere (as well as his Spanish sidekick Domingo Esteban and 14 of their unidentified accomplices) to death by hanging.[83]

Then there were the faithless Dutchmen, often termed renegades, who joined up with the Barbary corsairs. From the sixteenth through nineteenth centuries, these infamous North African marauders regularly attacked and plundered European vessels trading in the Mediterranean Sea. Early modern Europeans feared them as violent infidel despoilers, as the corsairs—based in various city states (including Algiers, Salé, Tunis, Tripoli, and Mamora) and except for Salé, nominally controlled by the Ottoman Empire—zealously pursued and looted any and all sorts of cargoes, whatever the (Christian) ship's nationality. Dutch seamen were well represented among their ilk from the beginning years of the seventeenth century. For example, a States of Holland resolution from April 1611 addressed the alarming fact that a Dutchmen, one Simon Maartsszoon Stuijt, was currently serving as the captain of "several pirate ships" in the Bay of Mamora.[84] And a criminal investigation conducted by the High Court of Holland in 1615 focused on the behavior of one Grote Piet ("Big Pete," "Great Pete")—as well as a whole gang of Dutch "pirates"—who had rioted and committed acts of violence in the Dutch town of Oudkarspel, plundered ships in the English Channel, and who had connections with the North African rovers.[85] Dutch participation in Barbary corsair activities did not cease as the century unfolded. Indeed, as late as 1686, an edition of the newspaper the *Ordinaire Leydse Courant* contains a reference to a "Renegade from Holland" who was serving as the "lieutenant" aboard a North African corsair vessel armed with 20 cannons and crewed by 200 sailors.[86]

Such anecdotal references represent only the tip of the proverbial iceberg. Dutch participation in Barbary corsair activities was real and significant. Dutchmen working as Barbary corsairs and immersing themselves in North African mores included, for example, Hassan Reis (a.k.a. Meinart Dircxssen or de Jonge Veenboer); Murad Flamenco (Vlaming) van Antwerpen; Saffar Reis (alias Thomas den Gauwdief, from Harlingen); Assam Reis (a.k.a. Jan Marinus from Sommelsdijk); Redgeb Reis (a native of the Hague); Haaggi Mamy Reis (from Akersloot); and Seliman Buffoen (orginally from the Rotterdam suburb of Schoonderloo).[87] Indeed, several were so successful in their pursuits as North African pirates that they became the objects of keen interest in the popular Dutch press.

One of these notorious corsairs was the Dutch seaman who became known by the nickname of the *Veenboer* ("Peat Bog Farmer"). According to seventeenth-century chronicler Nicolaes Wassenaer, this "illustrious pirate" began his career lawfully, as a commissioned Dutch privateer, but hungered for more money than that trade could afford him. Thus, "he fell into committing excesses, and poached on everyone whom he met," Wassenaer disclosed. He became quite rich using such methods,[88] and ended up working with the North Africans. There, according to fellow seventeenth-century historian Simon de Vries, he inveigled more Dutchmen to join the Barbary fold, making them members of his crew and training them in the ways of Barbary corsair seafaring.[89]

Infamous, too, was Simon de Danser the Younger, the progeny of another famous pirate, Simon de Danser the Elder. (The elder de Danser had been a prolific sea robber from Vlissingen. In his early years, he worked as a legitimate privateer for the Dutch, but his real success occurred after he became a free-agent pirate. He also nominally served the French. In the end, he was killed by the North Africans.)[90] Danser the Younger makes an appearance in Claes Compaen's biography, which assumes such universal awareness of Danser's identity and deeds (as well as those of his father) that it goes to no pains to explain more about him. It simply mentions that this young Dutch rogue, "a very renowned pirate," made the conscious decision to join the Barbary corsairs of Salé.[91] Nicolaes Wassenaer also makes note of Danser the Younger, mentioning that he eventually settled down and went into business in Salé, specializing in selling the booty plundered by his corsair colleagues; Claes Compaen himself was a client.[92]

Also among this ilk was the celebrated Ali Pegelin or Pisselingh, the Dutchman who, according to Simon de Vries's *Historie van Barbaryen*, "was for approximately forty years one of the most eminent pirates of Algiers." He amassed "great riches" and became an admiral in command of many ships. Born in Vlissingen—hence the name Pisselingh, a mispronunciation of his place of origin—he inherited a tidy sum from his parents, which he used to procure and outfit eight ships and five galleys. Setting to sea with this personal fleet, de Vries recounts, "Fortune was so kind to him, that he increased his wealth unbelievably much," and eventually settled in Algiers in 1645. There, he continued to grow in affluence and influence, rubbing elbows with the most powerful governing authorities and amassing a family of several wives and children.

It is clear, then, that many of the Republic's *zeerovers* and *stroomrovers* were perfidious characters who offered their services to their country's enemies, most notably Spain, the Southern Netherlands, and the Barbary states. Such traitors, it turns out, made up a good number of those defendants convicted of "piracy" by the court at the Admiralty of the Maas. They also appear in other types of sources from the Golden Age era, including government edicts, books, and High Court of Holland investigatory documents. Beyond this population, however, were those men who felt the tie of no master or leader, those who sought to prowl the seas completely on their own terms. These were the independent souls who, at best, constantly shifted their allegiances, opportunistically serving this state or another when it suited them;

or, at worst, attacked whomever they wanted whenever they wanted, robbing and plundering indiscriminately and without the modicum of "legitimacy" a commissioned appointment purported to impose. The autonomous nature of these seamen—their unaffiliated status and maverick bent—left little recourse to aggrieved merchants and authorities of the Dutch Republic, for there was no foreign government to complain to, no other party from whom one could seek compensation or redress. The Republic's only hope in these cases was to apprehend the reprobates and punish them severely.

The High Court of Holland investigated numerous Dutch individuals on charges of "freelance" piracy. These include the cases of Jacob Billeker and his "consorts" in 1571;[93] Gysbrecht Moos (alias "Smit") in 1572;[94] Jan Quirynk in 1572;[95] Willem Jacobsz Roose in 1613;[96] Jan/Cornelis Janszoon (?) a.k.a. "Grote Piet" in 1614–1615;[97] Jan Theuniszoon Knollendam in 1615;[98] Johan Ruth in 1615;[99] Cornelis and Pieter Pack in 1615;[100] Jan Thoeniss in 1630;[101] Laurens Davids in 1663;[102] Barint vander Linden in 1687;[103] and Gerrits Gyssen Bloek in 1697.[104] Additionally, records show that the court convicted a man—Volchert Janszoon Cattendyk—of piracy (*zeeroverij*) in 1571, and sentenced him to be decapitated. The judges also ordered that Cattendyk's corpse be displayed prominently and publicly, and that all of his possessions be confiscated by the state.[105] Jacob Billeker and Ysbrand Willemszoon Nobel were hanged.

More interesting and detailed, however, are those cases found in the Admiralty of the Maas sentencing records. Take the example of Claas Janszoon van der Pot. Van der Pot united with several other experienced Dutch "freebooters" with the express purpose of attacking local Dutch shipping during the long and arduous Siege of Leiden in 1574. These autonomous miscreants were not in the service of the enemy; rather, they discerned a good opportunity to rob and plunder during a time of great internal strife and institutional dislocation. They succeeded in capturing various ships belonging to people residing in the region, as well as ships traveling the Maas River. Moreover, they seized vessels from the enemy forces as well. Booty included herring, herring nets, rye, malt, grain, 700 pounds of cheese, and money. Not content to simply rob and plunder ships, they also shot a man on a local beach and stole several horses from a residence. While most of the pirates apparently escaped arrest, van der Pot was caught and convicted by the court. Horrified by his actions, on May 22, 1575, the judges sentenced him to be hanged in Delft's central square. Furthermore, his corpse was to be brought outside of the city and displayed there, with the purpose of serving as an "abhorrent and terrifying spectacle." All of his possessions were ordered to be seized by the state as well.[106]

While the misdeeds of van der Pot and his cronies were dastardly, the late-sixteenth-century career of Goris Pieterszoon (also called Goris Prins) was much longer and more nefarious. His first exploits took place when he served as the helmsman aboard a pirate ship commanded by one Jan Merida Mulato. Mulato's vessel was a sizable warship manned by some 90 crewmembers. After taking it out past Scotland, to the "Great Fishery," Mulato and his gang began to attack, rob, and plunder various fishing vessels and merchant ships. Their tactics were forceful, as they opened fire on their numerous victims. And indeed, they were strong, skilled, and tough enough to capture powerful adversaries, including a Dutch warship. Part and parcel of these pirates' *modus operandi* was to remove the cabin boys from the ships they apprehended and send these poor youths off to Spain. Mulato, Pieterszoon, and company continued these escapades for some five years, after which time they sailed to Dunkirk and served with the Dunkirk corsairs for awhile, and then continued on to Scotland, and then to Spain. Ultimately, Pieterszoon traveled back to Vlissingen and commenced a plan to capture small ships from the Republic's inland waterways. After he had seized his first victim and was en route with it to Dunkirk—where he planned to sell both it and its cargo—he and 39 of his cronies were finally apprehended by Dutch forces. Of course, the Republic's authorities were aghast at Pieterszoon's actions. On August 23, 1591, the Admiralty court in Rotterdam convicted him and his 39 unidentified crewmen of the crimes of "enormous river hooliganism" and "piracy." Vowing that no quarter would be given to such miscreants, the judges condemned the defendants to be hanged at the city's gallows.[107]

Another case of piracy involving independent pirates occurred in 1612. In this instance, the court convicted seven seamen—six Dutchmen and one Englishman—who had banded together with the express purpose of victimizing and marauding innocent Dutch seafarers. Dutchman Jacob Gabrielszoon and Englishman Claaszoon Thomaszoon were the ringleaders of this particular gang. From the beginning, Gabrielszoon and Thomaszoon conceived a plan to commit piratical acts, and, to that end, assembled a group of nine to accompany them on their ignoble jaunt. After commandeering a small ship from a naive Dutch mariner, they sailed out past the island of Ameland and seized an anchored, unmanned fishing boat. Heading now for the open seas and in need of weaponry, they proceeded to capture a Dutch cargo ship laden with herring and a crew of four, and removed booty consisting of some thousand rijksdaalders as well as gold, silver, and provisions. (They released the boat and the crew.) Thereafter, they continued on to Yarmouth, where they took a "great boat," and journeyed back to the Republic, to Vlissingen, where they met up with Joris Uitsingam, Pieter d'Oudenaarde, and Jan Joriszoon.

The band, now bigger and stronger, made an agreement "to go adventuring at sea"—that is, to set out in search of ill-begotten booty. Requiring another vessel for this course of action, they traveled to Amsterdam, where they purchased a craft from a Captain Heindrik Wittebak of Dunkirk. They also recruited two more members, for two of Wittebak's crewmen—Jan Simonszoon and Daniel Adriaanszoon—were eager to join the pirates' "evil plan." One of the stipulations of this transaction was that the pirates were to transport Captain Wittebak—very ill and a patient at the Amsterdam *Gasthuis* (hospital)—back to his wife in Dunkirk. This promise was not to be honored, however, for 4–5 hours after the pirates had set sail, Wittebak died, and the "Adventurers" callously threw his body overboard. Thenceforth, they entered the Maas River, where Uitsingam and another man, Jacob de Stierman, disembarked and went to Rotterdam in order to enlist more recruits for their gang.

In their effort to find more members, Uitsingam and de Stierman endeavored to inveigle men off the street in Rotterdam. When that proved unsuccessful, they retired to "the inn in this city where the Black Eagle hangs out." Apparently, this symbol of the "Black Eagle" denoted a rough-and-tumble place where new members likely could be found. There, they met up with Claas Thomaszoon and Jan Claaszoon, as well as four other unnamed seamen, all of whom were willing and able to "assist them in their . . . sea scummery" (*ZeeSchuimerije*). The band now numbered 12. Departing Rotterdam, they set off again, but stopped en route, where they drank and caroused. The four newest recruits—the unnamed mariners from the Black Eagle Inn—reconsidered what they were doing and defected. When the gang, now restored to their original number of eight, arrived in the vicinity of den Briel, they captured a large fishing boat and sailed for Yarmouth, where they provisioned their new vessel. Next, they traveled the Thames, where they overwhelmed a six-man craft from Vlissingen and plundered everything of value, including some money, trade goods, and victuals. Sometime after this, they were apprehended by the Dutch authorities and their six-month "adventure" of robbery and plunder finally ceased.

As one would expect, the court at the Admiralty of the Maas was repulsed by the actions of these six wayward citizens of the Republic. The judges railed that such behavior represented an "evil plan" and "malicious trade," which completely contradicted the edicts of both natural and civil law. Moreover, the court said, their crimes directly transgressed against States-General proclamations from 1606 and 1611, which emphatically declared that anyone found at sea without a proper and legitimate privateering commission would be considered as "pirates and Sea Robbers." Such misdeeds only led to the "insecurity, damage, and destruction of merchant shipping, as well as to the total ruin of the merchants, and fishermen trafficking the sea . . ." The Dutch Republic would not tolerate it, the judges thundered, and would seek immediate and severe punishment. Consequently, the court sentenced the seven men to be brought to the vessel they had purchased from the deceased Dunkirk man, Captain Wittebak, which was now anchored outside of Rotterdam. Once there, they would all be hanged from a crossbeam or transom erected on the ship, "so that death followed," and the state would confiscate all of their possessions.[108]

Admiralty of the Maas criminal records certainly indicate that the Dutch Republic faced a problem with citizens who had metamorphosed into maverick, independent pirates. Other Golden Age sources corroborate this point, revealing that the challenge the Dutch confronted was a large, even global, one. Especially vulnerable to enemy depredations—including those of their own turncoat pirates—were the Republic's trade companies, for both the VOC and WIC were extremely alluring targets. According to Dutch law (if not that of other states), the East and West India Companies held total monopolies over their respective *octrooigebieden* ("patent areas"), lucrative regions that enticed the world with their tantalizing wealth. In many respects, these companies acted as quasi-independent political entities, and guarded their jurisdictions jealously, viewing trespassers in search of goods as illegal invaders with piratical intent. Of course, VOC and WIC authorities had to confront the assaults of other states' seamen. But they contended with the troublesome presence of fellow Dutchmen as well, interloping homegrown predators.

For example, in November 1663 the VOC collaborated with the High Court of Holland in the successful prosecution of Cornelis Claaszoon Wegh for the crime of piracy, which Wegh allegedly had committed in the Red Sea.[109] This case was not dissimilar from that of Hans (Jan?) Dekker, a Dutchmen who served as an "Admiral" in command of two French "pirate ships," the *St. Michiel* and the *St. Malo*, which cruised VOC waters in 1618. Much to the VOC's chagrin, Dekker and his men were noticeably successful. Flying Dutch flags to camouflage their vessels' true identities, they surreptitiously plied the waters of the Red Sea and coastal Mozambique, capturing and plundering the ships of native peoples.[110] According to VOC records, their depredations disturbed East Indies trade and even resulted in loss of life. But eventually, Company personnel apprehended these "*zeerovers*," and placed Dekker under arrest in accordance with States-General laws and VOC policies that mandated the seizure of all Dutchmen sailing on foreign ships. Even so, the slippery Dutch pirate escaped and was sheltered by the English in their outpost in Pangerang.[111]

The WIC had its own woes, of course. The Caribbean was rife with pirates, and the Company frequently found itself to be a target of their assaults. Sometimes these attacks were carried out by fellow Dutchmen. Take the 1683–1684 cases of the *Elisabeth* and the *Stadt Rotterdam*, two extremely valuable WIC ships that were stolen by so-called "French" pirates while en route from Cartagena.[112] As it turns out, the commanders of this band of robbers were really two Dutchmen, Nicolaes van Hoorn and Laurens de Graaf. Purporting to carry a French commission, which was, in fact, invalid, de Graaf served as the captain aboard a ship named the *Neptunus*. He had a long and notorious history as a pirate in the region—where he sometimes was known as Lorencillo—and had gone so far in 1672 as to attack the Spanish treasure port of Campeche, steal 120,000 pieces-of-eight in silver from a rich prize ship, and burn the village of Champotón to the ground.[113] Van Hoorn, for his part, based himself on the island of Hispaniola, a notorious buccaneer haunt. By 1682, his deeds had marked him, according to the WIC, as "famous." In May 1683, for instance, he—along with another Dutchmen, Michiel Andrieszoon, and the French buccaneer the "Chevalier de Grammont"—led the spectacular sack of the city of Vera Cruz. During this astonishing event, van Hoorn and his co-commanders used 13 ships manned by 800 buccaneers to attack the city, ransacking every house and taking some 4,000 residents captive.[114]

In any event, during the early 1680s, both de Graaf and van Hoorn were cruising the Caribbean in search of booty, and at some point, joined forces.

The two may have been working together already during the May 1683 sack of Veracruz, since Spanish sources do claim that "Lorencillo" participated in the event.[115] Accosting the *Elisabeth* and the *Stadt Rotterdam* in the vicinity of Cuba, the traitorous Dutchmen and their minions plundered the ships thoroughly, removing the 100,000 rijksdaalders worth of gold and silver in their holds. The WIC authorities, understandably and predictably, were appalled at this loss, and did everything they could to apprehend the *zeerovers*, exchanging futile correspondences with the French and Spanish governments and proposing strategies to pluck van Hoorn from the refuge of Santo Domingo. Nothing really came of their upset, for de Graaf and van Hoorn continued to assault and plunder Caribbean shipping, with van Hoorn further vexing WIC authorities with his attacks on Company slave ships. Both would go on to have sustained careers as very successful pirates.[116]

The Caribbean was also the setting for another illustrious Dutch sea robber, Rock de Bresiliaan (or as the English called him, Rock Brasiliano). Although not known for his aggressions against the Republic per se, de Bresiliaan (figure 2.1) was famous by dint of his inclusion in Alexander Exquemelin's bestselling 1678 memoir, *The Buccaneers of America*. A native son of Groningen whose given name had long been forgotten, the Dutchman was dubbed "Rock de Bresiliaan" by his buccaneer companions because of his long residence in Dutch Brazil. Forced to leave that colony when the Portuguese retook it in 1652–1654, Rock fled to Jamaica, where his seamanship and natural leadership qualities so impressed the buccaneers there that they elected him to be a captain. Right away, he captured a valuable Spanish ship loaded with great quantities of money, an act that brought him widespread renown and sealed his position as a buccaneer commander. He followed up this deed with at least one other lucrative capture, this time of a Spanish vessel laden with various trade goods and a large haul of pieces-of-eight.

But if Rock de Bresiliaan was an effective and successful leader of his men, some of his other personal qualities left much to be desired. According to Exquemelin, Bresiliaan was hot-tempered and unpredictable, and prone to bullying and fisticuffs. Moreover, he spent lavishly, drinking to great excess and engaging in every manner of debauchery:

> . . . he made all Jamaica tremble. He had no self-control at all, but behaved as if possessed by a sullen fury. When he was drunk, he would roam the town like a madman. The first person he came across, he would chop off his arm or leg, without anyone daring to intervene, for he was like a maniac.[117]

When attacking, he was also a grisly, bloodthirsty predator, treating the Spanish with great cruelty and sadism because of his profound, entrenched odium for them: "He perpetrated the greatest atrocities possible against the Spaniards. Some of them he tied or spitted on wooden stakes and roasted them alive between two fires, like killing a pig . . ."[118]

Rock de Bresiliaan is fortunate that he escaped the exacting arm of Dutch law, for according to the Republic's edicts, he indisputably was a "pirate" and

Figure 2.1 "Rock, de Brasiliaen Genaemt . . .," (Rock, called the Brazilan . . .) engraving, in A.O. Esquemelin, *De Americaensche Zee-Roovers* . . . (Amsterdam: Jan ten Hoorn, 1678), fol. 43. Dousa Kamer.

pirates were a despicable bunch—ungodly, licentious criminals deserving of severe punishment and public censure. Golden Age proclamations by the States-General, as well as laws enacted on a local level, manifest this point plainly. Moreover, criminal records from the High Court of Holland and the Admiralty of the Maas reveal that such decrees were not just hollow criticisms or empty threats. Rather, the Dutch authorities followed through with their promises to prosecute and discipline their wayward seamen, whether such defendants were errant privateers found guilty of a relatively minor infraction or full-fledged, independent, seagoing marauders. Dutchmen convicted of *zeeroverij* and *stroomroverij* in the Republic's courts were typically executed, usually by hanging.[119] At the least, they were condemned to endure severe corporal punishment, such as multiple keelhaulings, whippings, and/or being thrown from the yardarm. Indeed, the authorities of the Dutch Republic were deadly serious in their resolve to eradicate piracy among their citizenry.

Part II
Cultural Underpinnings

3

Collective Identity, Nationalism, and the Golden Age Netherlands

The figures of the Dutch privateer and pirate maintained complicated roles in Golden Age Dutch culture. Integral to the cultural construction of their identities were deep-rooted, fundamental Dutch values. Foremost among these values were both the unique perspective the Dutch maintained about their relationship with the sea, and their blossoming sense of national cohesion.

* * *

In 1686, the *Ordinaire Leydse Courant*, a Leiden-based newspaper, ran a series of dramatic articles about storms and flooding afflicting the Netherlands. Narrated with horror and despair, the paper catalogued the devastation the calamitous deluge had wrought throughout the land. On November 24, initial reports from Amsterdam indicated that the "harsh weather of the last Friday" had brought about "significant destruction," resulting in four shipwrecks. All had sunk along Holland's coast; another ship had made it safely to Enkhuizen, but not before the angry wind and waves had stripped it of its anchors and rigging.[1]

By November 26, the ruination had increased. North of Tilburg, the swollen waters rushed in, reaching the height of "one and a half men" in only eight hour's time. Although the great dike at Waalwijk held, the flood engulfed the land and "many animals, cows as well as horses, were drowned."[2] On November 28, "immediate, direct word" from Amsterdam revealed that the land around Groningen was under water, and that "many hundreds of men and beasts were drowned." The "wretched tidings" from Groningen on November 29 were no better: in some places, the water surged four feet above the dikes, "by which unbelievably many people and animals were drowned. In some villages, no more than two or three persons have survived, narrowly salvaging themselves with planks or small boats." People were killed in the dead of night, "so that today no one knows where they are," and out at sea, numerous ships and their cargoes had been destroyed. Moreover, the paper confessed, "One still fears to hear of further hardships . . . ."[3]

But word of further hardships there would be. A plaintive November 26 correspondence from Noorden, south of Amsterdam, related still more horrors:

> We all live here in a still very desolate state, and not only us, but also our neighboring cities, hoping the Lord will deliver us. We have been abandoned the last few days, without hearing anything of our neighbors, but now we are beginning to hear again tidings of one another, and to learn more daily of the great destruction that the Water has brought to all. There is still a full sea here: the newly-diked polders have all been broken down and . . . submerged, all the houses are ruined and many washed away, [and] many men and animals have drowned.[4]

And a letter to the paper from Emmen, in the province of Overijssel, relayed additional tragedies. "The miserable condition in which we find ourselves," the victim wrote, "cannot be described." Numerous area polders were submerged, and bridges, dikes, and canals were demolished. "One sees here," the letter cried, "dead men and beasts by the hundreds, drifting." Groningen was "half gone," and the towns of Termunterzijl and de Knock "entirely gone." The force of the inundation was such that one man's home, complete with house, barn, horse, cow, and cabbage garden, had been swept away, only to end up in an entirely different area, "where it still sits." "In sum," the letter concluded, "the misery and damage which has occurred cannot be expressed."[5]

Other Dutch newspapers carried accounts of the devastating 1686 floods, detailing lives lost and property destroyed.[6] And sadly, while the damage was drastic, it was no different from the destruction caused by many such natural disasters that took place during the Netherlands' early modern era. For centuries, the people inhabiting the flat, low-lying region of the Netherlands had battled such inundations, and in this respect, the deluge of 1686 represented just another wrenching yet repetitive chapter in an age-old story. Nor were the journalistic reports inspired by this 1686 flood unique, for papers and chronicles in general detailed the various water disasters that periodically beset the country.[7] Beyond flooding, the tempestuous and aggressive power of the water was relayed via other media, too. Marine paintings, a standard genre of the sixteenth- and seventeenth-century Dutch artistic repertoire, depicted numerous scenes of shipwrecks[8] and "sea monsters."[9] And pamphlets circulated the news of Dutch tempests—as well as those affecting other parts of the world[10]—to the Dutch public.

For part and parcel of Dutch existence was the extreme awareness of the awesome and annihilative power of the surrounding waters. Lying almost entirely below sea level, fashioned from hard-won, reclaimed land, and adjacent to the turbulent North Sea, the Netherlands' existence itself was, in the words of one seventeenth-century spokesman, something of a miracle.[11] Violent weather, deluges, shipwrecks, and drownings were perilous features of everyday life in the Dutch Republic. Whether they were viewed as manifestations of divine retribution visited upon a sinful population,[12] or merely wrathful forces of Mother Nature, storms and floods were a fundamental, unifying threat that all Dutch people faced. Indeed, an emblematic report from the 1666 almanac, the *Hollandtze Mercurius*, listing winter storm damages, reads almost like a geographical survey of the Dutch maritime provinces:

> In Zeeland, 3 polders in Cadzand caved in . . . ; In Holland the Klundert dike by Willemstad broke . . . . The dikes on the Maas flowed over . . . . In Scheveningen and Katwijk, many houses washed away . . . and the region around Haarlem also flooded. In Amsterdam, cellars and warehouses filled up. The dike by Durgerdam broke through, [and] all of Waterland was under water, with many lakes spilling out. The island of Marken was overrun by the sea. The dike by Vollenhove and the dike by Groningen broke . . .[13]

The irony of these continual natural threats was, of course, that the Netherlands benefited greatly from the sea. As one 1645 pamphlet affirmed, the Dutch Republic was the "Indies of Europe," the most blessed of lands because of its tremendous merchant shipping, its fortunate location on the sea, its commodious and secure harbors, and its knowledgeable and experienced sailors.[14] Dutch waters teemed with fish, the shipbuilding industry flourished, and domestic communications—which centered upon the networks of canals interlacing the country—were efficient and comprehensive.

In short, then, the great seventeenth-century Dutch "economic miracle" could never have happened without the sea. Dutch success depended fundamentally upon the state's merchant shipping, and additionally rested upon its formidable shipbuilding and fishing industries. As the population of the city of Amsterdam swelled from approximately 30,000 in 1585 to about 105,000 in 1622, immigrants invested their capital in commercial ventures, shipping, and manufacturing. The citizens of the new United Provinces enjoyed special resources and advantages that enabled them to become prodigious maritime traders. Consequently, for more than a half century, the northern Netherlands' rate of economic growth outstripped that of all other states, establishing a true Dutch primacy in many areas of commerce and finance.[15] As C.R. Boxer affirms, "By 1648 the Dutch were indisputably the greatest trading nation in the world, with commercial outposts and fortified 'factories' scattered from Archangel to Recife and from New Amsterdam to Nagasaki."[16]

This great efflorescence in commerce was greatly linked to Dutch success in shipbuilding. "By seventeenth century standards," Richard W. Unger affirms, Dutch shipbuilding "was a massive industry and larger than any shipbuilding industry which had preceded it."[17] During the seventeenth century, the Dutch built some 500 seagoing ships per year, not including those constructed for foreign buyers or the small craft used on the inland waterways.[18] At the same time, the Dutch dominated the European fishing industry. Herring, "the Dutch Gold Mine,"[19] was the crux of this prosperous trade. During an era in Europe when only the rich ate meat often, and Catholic fast days mandated the frequent consumption of fish, Dutch prowess in catching herring became an incredibly lucrative enterprise. As contemporary observer Meynert Semeyns commented in 1639,

> The Dutch catch more herrings and prepare them better than any other nation ever will; and the Lord has, through the instrument of the herring, made Holland an exchange and staple-market for the whole of Europe. The herring keeps Dutch trade going, and the Dutch trade sets the world afloat.[20]

So the water possessed a strange dual role for the Dutch. While on the one hand, it wrought fear and horrific destruction, on the other, it delivered bountiful prosperity that enriched the Netherlands with food, wealth, and resources. Even as the enraged sea shattered dikes and obliterated villages and farms, the nurturing, benevolent sea provided the opportunities for the staggeringly successful industries of merchant shipping, shipbuilding, and fishing. These industries, in turn, catapulted the Dutch into the role of economic leaders of the seventeenth-century world. For as Immanuel Wallerstein has proclaimed, "this 'sand and mud dump left over from the ice age' with a jerry-built and seemingly ineffectual state machinery was the hegemonic power of the capitalist world-economy . . .," a feat equaled in history only by Great Britain and the United States.[21]

The sea's desolation and deliverance, then, was the essential duality with which Dutch people lived daily, and they were not unaware of this peculiar irony. This was a culture, after all, in which depictions of maritime tragedy were very popular, a genre of painting that art historians have variously interpreted as symbolizing both the ironic mutability of fortune (i.e., while disaster is visited upon some, prosperity is delivered to others),[22] and the pitting of "destruction and defeat against survival and victory."[23] This was also the society that, even as it was acutely aware of the devastation caused by inundations and storms, celebrated the 1648 peace with Spain with a spectacular, pageant-like exhibition in which the Netherlands sat upon a throne, supported by the tools of maritime industry, including anchors, sails, flags, rigging, oars, the spirit of commerce, and ships' coats of arms.[24] Or which depicted its capital city of Amsterdam as an enthroned queen receiving homage and the gifts of commerce from the world's continents, all the while attended by the Sea, personified as a muscular Neptune (figure 3.1). Even the Republic's fishermen sang of the sea's ironic presence in their lives, of how the ocean's volatile, mercurial temperament was precisely what brought them happiness, and in fact, made them who they were:

> The sea has created us
> We also find joy there
> Even though it always lurches
> And seldom remains quiet . . .[25]

As a people, the Dutch had succeeded in harnessing the power of the sea and wind to their own advantage, and they were ever mindful of what they had achieved in yoking these particular forces of Mother Nature. Indeed, the

Figure 3.1 Title page engraving, Olfert Dapper, *Historische Beschryvinghe van Amsterdam* (Amsterdam: Iacob van Meurs, 1663). Dousa Kamer.

proverb "God made the Dutch, but the Dutch made Holland" illustrates this Dutch pride in their native resourcefulness and inventiveness. Golden Age sources celebrated the Dutch "miracles" of land reclamation, which had wondrously transformed a "sandy patch of land" into something bigger and better, through dikes, mills, canals, and polders, and extolled the glories of Dutch merchant shipping, claiming that with this vital trade, the Netherlands had escaped being poor and miserable.[26]

This central role of the sea cannot be underestimated and deeply affected the construction of privateer and pirate identity in Golden Age Dutch culture. Whether the water and climate brought devastation or affluence, it maintained a fundamental presence in the Dutch psyche. As Simon Schama asserts, "it is not too much to describe Dutch society as having a diluvian personality . . ." For, as Schama explains, in the mind of the Dutch, they had forged a covenant with God, an agreement in which the "Almighty had endowed them with the wit and the will to conquer the waters, and even to turn the waters against their enemies; and He had raised them to great riches and power, the better to proclaim His omnipotence . . ."[27]

This peculiar relationship with the sea affected Republican society's ideals about social standing and merit. Andries Vierlingh, a humanist and the veteran dike master to the princes of Orange, depicted the Dutch community as the opposite of a delicate court of mannered leisure. Those brave souls who combated the waters, he said, "must be accustomed to hard work from childhood; men who have greased leather boots on their feet and who can stand a rough and harsh climate. In times of storms, wind and hail they must be able to persevere."[28] In keeping with Vierlingh's sentiments, those who received great public esteem were generally the industrious, diligent, and robust burgers and merchants, not elitist, aloof, and splendid courtiers.[29]

This, then, was the foundation of the cultural milieu in which the Dutch freebooter dwelled. In turn, it was this mentality that helped to shape the perceptions the Dutch populous maintained about their ocean-going rogues. Simultaneously cursed and blessed by the mighty force of the sea, the people of the Dutch Republic developed an awareness of themselves as a people who were communitarian, resourceful, brave, pious, plebeian, and blessed by God. All of these qualities colored their understanding of their pirates and privateers.

* * *

At the same time, the Dutch freebooter's role and identity were profoundly affected by a more specific phenomenon that took place during the Golden Age: the Dutch citizenry's developing sense of a national consciousness. The Netherlands' particular history—most significantly, its revolt against Spain—occasioned the creation of a national spirit that unified and motivated Dutch men and women throughout the seven member provinces.

Benedict Anderson's work on the "nation" is useful in illuminating the development of early modern nationalism in the Dutch Republic.[30]

Anderson's definition is an anthropological one, which treats the "nation" as a "cultural artifact" that commands profound emotional allegiance.[31] Rather than emphasizing formal and specific changes in state structure, he defines the nation as "an imagined political community—and imagined as both inherently limited and sovereign." It is "*imagined*," he explains, "because the members of even the smallest nation will never know most of their fellow members, meet them, or even hear of them, yet in the minds of each lives the image of their communion." At the same time, it is imagined "as *a community*, because, regardless of the actual inequality and exploitation that may prevail, the nation is always conceived as a deep, horizontal comradeship." It is this profound fraternal sentiment that "makes it possible . . . for so many . . . people, not so much to kill, as willingly to die for such limited imaginings."[32]

In seeking to understand how the "nation" arose historically, Anderson identifies various economic, social, and scientific changes that precipitated this transformation. Vital among these was the development of capitalism, and most especially, what Anderson terms "print capitalism." During the Reformation, print capitalism both increased the use of the vernacular language and disseminated new ideas on a mass level, efficiently and comprehensively. The newly created "reading publics" were composed of large numbers of people, and printed texts lent a "fixity" or "permanence" to dialects that, in turn, became powerful, unifying languages. These changes made possible a novel form of association: the "imagined community" of the nation.[33]

Also essential to Anderson's assessment is the role of shared history in cementing "national" bonds of attachment. In formulating his position, he draws upon the ostensibly ironic definition of a "nation" put forth by Ernest Renan:

> Now, the essence of a nation is that all the individuals have many things in common but that also they have forgotten many things . . . . Each French citizen *is obliged to have forgotten* the Saint Bartholomew's Day Massacre, [and] the massacres of the Midi in the thirteenth century.[34]

In other words, members of a national community are bound together by the awareness—the memory—of certain fundamental, transformative events whose very divisive details the community has decided to transcend and "forget." In Renan's examples, a French citizen would recognize ("remember") the historical significance of the bloody St. Bartholomew's Day in 1572 Paris and the Albigensian massacres in the thirteenth-century Midi while, at the same time, choose to "forget" that in each event, there were aggressors and victims, winners and losers. Thanks to the national community's "systematic historiographical campaign," these originally violent conflicts and ruptures become resonant, unifying events. As Anderson puts it, "antique slaughters . . . are now inscribed as 'family' history."[35]

Echoing this emphasis on the importance of history in forging communal bonds, the work of Maurice Halbwachs, and most importantly, his theory of "collective memory" is also helpful in understanding the nature of Republican nationalism. A student of sociologist Emile Durkheim and his idea of the "collective conscience," Halbwachs focused on *history* as a vital source of solidarity, contending that memories serve to bind people together, whether the group be as small as the family or as large as the nation. All communities possess distinctive recollections that their members have carefully crafted and maintained, often over long periods of time.[36] Essential to this idea of "collective memory" is its socially constructed and "presentist" character. People consciously and unconsciously forge the history they need so as to reinforce the bonds of the living, current community. Moreover, collective memory is sustained through artificial means so that group members who have not directly experienced historical moments integral to that group can nonetheless enjoy the bonds such events have forged. In other words, individual members who do not recall the events directly can be stimulated to "remember" them by indirect means, such as readings, commemorations, monuments, or communal festive occasions that celebrate the deeds and accomplishments of departed group members.[37]

Anderson's and Halbwachs' models fit the situation in the Golden Age Netherlands, where the individual provinces first united to defeat a common foe—Spain—during the Dutch Revolt. Out of the fire of these events—out of the acrimony, violence, social upheaval, and religious and political dissension—citizens of the Republic weathered specific experiences that formed the foundation of an incipient, shared identity. Later wars and other developments continued to reinforce this new "Dutchness." Scholars might contend that the "nation" and "nationalism" are modern, primarily nineteenth-century phenomena,[38] but the case of the Dutch Republic suggests otherwise.[39] For the seventeenth-century Dutch were members of a "nation."[40] They shared, as a group, collective memories that bound them together in an "imagined community," a community born of a new state structure which became a novel focus of allegiance for its citizens.

* * *

A Golden Age "national" Dutch identity—that is, an identity that transcended mere municipal or provincial ties—was only possible because of the remarkable print culture and mass literacy of the seventeenth-century Netherlands. Print capitalism provided a new means for the dissemination of ideas and for extensive numbers of people to communicate with one another.[41] There was very little censorship in the Republic, and freedom of expression was a typical part of life there.[42] Printing presses were in constant use, producing pamphlets, broadsheets, chapbooks, newspapers, songbooks, and almanacs for popular audiences, in addition to the more highbrow and expensive books for the elite and literati. Between 1565 and 1648, the number of booksellers and printers probably increased eightfold, and during this period, Holland (especially Amsterdam) surpassed Antwerp as the printing center of Europe.[43]

What were the various popular genres? Pamphlets—a medium whose purpose was to inform and persuade readers about current events[44]—were copious and ubiquitous. By 1648, 200–300 were being published each year, typically with 1,000 to 1,240 copies per run. Moreover, many enjoyed multiple reprintings, meaning that 10,000 to 50,000 copies of a pamphlet might be in circulation at any given time.[45] Evidence of this frenetic publishing activity survives in the multitude of pamphlets extant in Dutch archives today.[46]

Similar to pamphlets were works known as "blue books" or "chapbooks" (*volksboeken*), inexpensively produced works intended for a popular audience. Their readers came primarily from the poorer parts of town. Typical subjects included the Bible, mythology, history, Dutch maritime journeys and adventures, old fairy tales, and burlesques.[47] Such chapbooks were last reprinted in 1819,[48] and as Dutch literary scholar, J.M. Buisman avows, "represent a mirror . . . of the wishes and dreams of the common folk."[49] *Volksboeken* contrast noticeably with the works produced for the more privileged reader, which consisted of exquisite tomes bound in leather and illustrated with detailed and nuanced copper-plate engravings.[50] These publications generally devoted themselves to more "elevated" topics, such as politics, history, and world leaders.[51]

Rank-and-file Dutch people also kept up-to-date on current affairs with weekly (sometimes bi- or tri-weekly) newspapers, which began to appear regularly during the 1620s.[52] These *courants* and *kranten* played a key role in disseminating information, bringing the latest news to their readers as quickly as possible by using reports sent from correspondents in far-flung locations.[53] One paper even had war correspondents (the first ever), who followed the Republic's army on its various campaigns.[54] Newspapers, like many pamphlets and almanacs, often pointed out the accuracy and truthfulness of their accounts, stressing that their information came from "reliable sources" with firsthand knowledge.[55]

Still other genres of popular print media existed. Almanacs were published annually, summarizing events and important stories from the past year, and included excerpts from political documents, treaties, and diplomatic correspondences.[56] Additionally, compilations that catalogued "world-wide" political news stories (including those that occurred in the Netherlands), treaties, and important government resolutions appeared periodically.[57] Finally, songbooks containing popular ballads were available from the end of the sixteenth century.

Who read all of these various forms of mass media? After 1600, many—if not the majority—of Dutch people could read.[58] The soundest indicator of this is the Amsterdam Marriage Register, which reflected both urban and rural literacy patterns, as couples from throughout the Republic celebrated their nuptials in Holland's capital city. By 1680, 70 percent of grooms and 44 percent of brides could sign their own names in the Register.[59] Furthermore, anecdotal evidence supplied by contemporary foreign visitors (such as Lodovico Guicciardini and the scribes of Philip II) supports the notion that the Dutch were unusually literate. Calvinist Church records also suggest that literacy was widespread among the Dutch population (pastors felt moved to comment on this issue because they were concerned about congregants reading impious or "heretical" texts). And investigations into the records of seventeenth-century booksellers have revealed that purchasers of books and pamphlets included such middle-class types as goldsmiths, cloth-shearers, oarsmen, cobblers, and brewers, in addition to City Council members.[60] The cost of printed works, and specifically pamphlets, were certainly within the means of the average Dutch citizen. Even among the illiterate, lending and reading aloud frequently took place, and expanded the pamphlet audience a great deal.[61]

Anecdotal archival evidence also confirms the significance of print culture in daily life. The Admiralty of the Maas regularly subscribed to various newspapers.[62] Moreover, municipal leaders used newspapers as a means to learn what was happening in other parts of the Republic. In 1696, for example, Enkhuizen city fathers discovered that a criminal was in their midst when they read about a case in "last Thursday's paper."[63] Businesses utilized newspapers to advertise their enterprises to a wide audience.[64] And a 1653 pamphlet reveals how important print culture was when it used the *omission* of a significant news story from the papers as a means to justify the pamphlet's existence. The actual work, one of the *praatje* ("little conversation") genre, opens with a discussion between characters considering the political situation in England:

> Zeelander: Well, what is the news here in Amsterdam?
> Hollander: I don't know what the big news is, because I have few contacts, and it isn't in print, which you yourself know well . . .
> Geldersman: Well, then, let us discuss what isn't in print . . .[65]

This pervasive Dutch print culture enabled the formation of communal bonds that transcended one's city or province, a fundamental development in making the "imagined community" of the nation possible.[66] Moreover, the character of Dutch nationalism becomes visible in the vestiges of seventeenth-century quotidian media. Golden Age books, pamphlets, newspapers, chapbooks, almanacs, and songbooks all manifest qualities of this new "Dutchness" in which the public participated.

A feeling of Dutch nationhood was rooted, first and foremost, in the Republic's commercial character. To trade was patriotic, and Dutch commercial success was viewed as a special gift from God. "Oh Trade, this land will build its glory fast upon you!"[67] exclaimed a pamphlet, dating from 1630, extolling the praises of the VOC and WIC. This and myriad other such pamphlets lauded the "divine" power of Dutch seaborne commerce, the Republic's trade companies, and the Netherlands' "commercial heroes" who, with ardor and purpose, brought fame and riches to their "Fatherland."[68]

Such publications inevitably emphasized the Dutch ability to triumph over its enemy and oppressor, Spain. "The great maritime commerce . . . is the mother of all," proclaimed an anonymous author, crediting God's help in bestowing this special blesssing that enabled the Netherlands to combat and overwhelm the Spain.[69] Seventeenth-century historian Simon de Vries also gave voice to this sentiment in his narrative of the Republic's past. From the beginning, he claimed, it was the commercial talents of the Dutch people that enabled the Netherlands to triumph and flourish. This was in contrast to the once-wealthy Southern Netherlands, which was now controlled by the detested Spanish, and had consequently withered away into a somnolent and indigent state:

> It is remarkable, that within six years after the ... oath [establishing] the United Netherlands, trade began to bloom ... despite the incessant turmoil and dangers of these times; ... in April ... 1587 alone, 590 ships left from the Vlie for the Baltic, [and] more than 200 departed the [port of] den Briel and Zeeland, together [making] 800 ships ... This prosperity and commercial wealth drew such a great many people here, that in the majority of the cities of our Fatherland, there were no homes available; consequently, men had to extend and enlarge a sizable number of the ... cities. Many villages also were ... developed and enlarged, or [completely] refurbished. Compared to this, the Spanish Netherlands had it very bad. The land remained undeveloped; and no one from the outside could come in.... There ... arose a horrible scarcity [of food], starvation, plague, and consequent poverty; so that many cities became desolate; and in many villages of two or three thousand houses, no inhabitants were found; wolves and wild beasts [laid claim to] the best domiciles, [and] birthed their young in the very beds in which human beings had once lain.[70]

Dutch "trade patriotism" vis-à-vis Spain was especially evident in the early 1620s, when the WIC was being formed. One pamphlet after another—inevitably written by anonymous patriots who claimed to be "lovers of Netherlands freedom" (*Lief-hebber der Nederlantsche vryheyt*) and the like—trumpeted the WIC as the means to slay the Castilian dragon in Spain's prodigiously lucrative yet vulnerable American colonies.[71] One pamphlet claimed that the WIC would transform South America from *Nova Hispania* into *Novum Hollandium*, wiping out Spanish mores and religion through the Company's superior trading tactics.[72] Another declared that God sought to punish the Spanish for their brutal, bloody deeds by using the WIC as his chosen instrument of vengeance against "this murderous Nation."[73] And according to another, the Republic's possession of valiant commercial explorers would enable the Dutch to overcome Spanish tyranny and "slavery."[74]

General hatred of Spain was pervasive and is evident in publications popular among all echelons of the Dutch public. Enmity toward Castile ran so deep, in fact, that a printer of a popular work of translated fiction had to beg his readers not to discriminate against the piece just because of its Spanish origins.[75] It was Las Casas's notorious treatise reporting Spanish abuses perpetuated among the Indians of America that played a large part in generating Spain's

"Black Legend" in the Netherlands. First printed in 1578 as *A Very Short Tale of the Destruction of the Indies* and reissued in 1596 under the title *The Mirror of Spanish Tyranny in West India* with horrifyingly vivid engravings by Jan and Theodor de Bry, Las Casas's inflammatory work was published repeatedly in the Republic during the seventeenth century and enjoyed enormous popularity.[76]

But Las Casas's chronicle of Spanish abuse in the Americas was only the beginning, for the Dutch had their own homegrown horrors to condemn. Indeed, the Netherlands' revolt against Spain provided the Dutch with many purported examples of Spanish brutality and injustice. Numerous pamphlets devoted themselves to disseminating information about the alleged atrocities committed by the Spanish, forming veritable catalogues of Castilian "cruelty, murder, arson, plunder, wildness, excessive burdens, and other violence against body and conscience . . ."[77] during the Revolt and Eighty Years War. Contemporary histories and chronicles, whether written for an elite or popular audience, narrated the ordeal of the Revolt in lurid, macabre fashion, detailing Spanish brutality and barbarity.[78] Testimonies did not stop at the Republic's borders: supposed eyewitness accounts reported Spanish savagery committed against the Dutch far afield, in Germany and in South America, for instance. One such pamphlet related the woeful tale of a luckless Dutchman whom the Spanish had captured in Peru and condemned to be drawn and quartered and then torn apart with burning tongs.[79]

Such reading was not limited to an adult audience. Indeed, one famous and extremely popular work that originally appeared in 1614—*The Youth's Mirror, or A Short History of Netherlands History*—listing the "foremost acts of [Spanish] tyranny and barbaric and inhumane cruelties," purposely served as both a self-proclaimed "eternal memorial," and an illustrated children's schoolbook[80] (which, incidentally, was heavily used until the late eighteenth century).[81] The text's publisher, Herman Coster, who had reworked a famous anti-Spanish pamphlet written by Willem Baudaert,[82] affirmed in his introduction that it was essential for the children of "free Netherlanders" to read his book—to "imprint" upon their hearts and minds the history of the Republic's recent war with Spain—in order to protect "our hard-bought freedom and privileges." The Republic's children, he proclaimed, must "nevermore forget [Spain's] bloody persecutions, tyrannical savagery, murders, extermination of the provinces and cities, rapes, [and] abolishment of the land's dearly-bought rights and privileges."[83]

Texts of all sorts, whether concerning commerce or not, often articulated the Dutch posture toward Spain as that of slaves seeking liberation from their despotic masters. Time after time, this trope was utilized to frame the Dutch relationship vis-à-vis Spain, and was an important element in how the Dutch viewed themselves as a united national group. Repeatedly, contemporary media characterized the Netherlands as "free" and "united" in opposition to the "godless and tyrannical" Spanish, who had "no other goal than to bring the United Provinces under cruel bondage and slavery."[84] Through the shared ordeal of Spanish torments—and later generations' collective memories of these tribulations—the people of the Republic began to view themselves as members of a real "Fatherland"[85] who had, through God's assistance, thrown off the chains of an inhumane servitude.

Pamphlet literature from throughout the seventeenth century manifests this adulation of the free Fatherland vis-à-vis Spanish despotism. For example, a 1599 account of Spanish violence was dedicated to "all Netherlands Fatherland-loving persons."[86] The author of a 1608 publication called himself "an enthusiast of the Fatherland's freedom."[87] The printer of a 1618 pamphlet that professed to expose a nefarious plot to return the Dutch to Spanish subjugation entitled himself "a devotee of the Fatherland," as did numerous pamphlets composed during the 1620s.[88] In 1636, the author of an anti-Spanish pamphlet described himself as an "upright and Fatherland-loving patriot."[89] And by mid-century, a pamphlet characterized the Dutch people as the "good residents and patriots of our beloved and expensively won Fatherland."[90]

This Dutch self-image as a people triumphant over Spanish "bondage" became a way of envisaging themselves among the world at large. In other words, the "slave" in general became an important and resonant concept with the Dutch, and they formed an identity of themselves in opposition to it. Simon Schama considers this phenomenon at length in his discussion of the Dutch admiration for—and conscious association with—the ancient Israelites of the Old Testament. Of all the Biblical analogies available, none was more compelling to the Dutch than Exodus. Indeed, references to the Exodus story abound in early modern Dutch culture, whether in the form of popular songs, paintings, engravings, or theater.[91] All emphasized the deliverance of the enslaved Dutch people from the bondage of the "Pharaonic" Spanish King to the Promised Land of the free Dutch Republic. This self-image as a "delivered people" became a fundamental aspect of Dutch national identity appearing in diverse sources, ranging from the laudatory tombstone eulogy for Admiral Jan Van Galen, which cries "In this cathedral, goes the Batavian / to his grave / Galen, who would choose death rather than to be a slave . . .,"[92] to an emblematic pamphlet from 1653, a bellicose work on the First Anglo-Dutch War, which enthused "Tis better for all of us to die for the Fatherland / Than to rot as slaves . . ."[93]

It is important to remember that slavery was not just a conceptual model for seventeenth-century Dutch people, but an actual, practiced institution that posed a real threat. So the idea of slavery represented not just a collective historical "memory" that formed an intrinsic element of Dutch national identity, but also an immediate and present danger that continued to unite Netherlanders of all stripes. The much-loathed Spanish trafficked in and owned slaves, whom, contemporary Dutch sources reported, they routinely used as labor to row their galleys.[94] Probably even more frightening, however, was the specter of the sailor-kidnapping and Christian-enslaving pirates of North Africa—the Barbary corsairs.

It is true that the Barbary corsairs have become something of a historical myth, greatly renowned for their reputed violence. Whether all the reprehensible deeds attributed to them are actually true or not (and there are certainly scholars who contend that they are not),[95] it is indisputable that the North Africans traded in human flesh. They routinely seized hapless European sailors and enslaved them, using them as forced labor or selling them in the markets of North Africa and Turkey.[96] (Of course, the Barbary Muslims were not alone in this odious practice—Christians too, such as the Knights of St. John in Malta, also worked as corsairs and captured unlucky individuals whom they peddled as slaves. And slave markets could be found in Christian ports such as Livorno, Italy, as well.[97]) Regardless of how bad the Barbary corsairs really were, however, the *perception* among seventeenth-century Europeans was that the North Africans were inhumane, untrustworthy, uncivilized, and savage. The Dutch were no exception in sharing this viewpoint. Too many of their sailors had been captured and enslaved for the Dutch not to react negatively. Moreover, the corsairs' attacks served to cripple Dutch trade, resulting in a hampering of the financial bottom-line.

Dutch interest in the Barbary pirates was quite intense and widespread. Popular works such as Simon de Vries's second volume of the *History of the Barbarians and Their Pirates*[98] recounted the turbulent history of the relationship between the Dutch and the North African marauders. De Vries's allegedly firsthand account relates dreadful places where thousands of Christian slaves (in 1621, supposedly over 32,000 in Algiers alone)[99] were, among other things, barbarously tortured; worked ceaselessly; housed in dark, hot, vermin-infested prisons, where their skin was eaten by lice and fleas; jeered at by Muslim youths, who threw stones, urine, and feces at them; and burned alive.[100] Graphic (and incendiary) engravings by the famous Luyken brothers illustrated the text, depicting anguished Christians being sold in slave markets (figure 3.2) and suffering the torments meted out by their North African captors. Methods of torture included bludgeoning, having feet and hair set afire, public whippings, being impaled on pikes and hooks, genital mutilation, live burial, and even crucifixion (figure 3.3).

Numerous other works concerning the Barbary pirates circulated throughout the Netherlands. Pamphlets reported harrowing news (such as how in 1617, 36 Barbary corsairs kidnapped and enslaved 1,000 Christian men, women, and children from the Canary Islands)[101] and articulated woeful tales, such as that of the Dutch slaves forced to fight in a bitter Moroccan war.[102] Pamphlets and books, reputed to be nonfictional memoirs written by Europeans who had been captured, enslaved, and subsequently liberated or escaped, were published.[103] These books emphasized the North Africans' "ghastly" jurisprudence, sensationalistic details about slavery, tips for survival, and data on the "curious" habits of the enslavers, and enjoyed a healthy readership. For instance, *The Plundered Helen of Amsterdam*,[104] an account of a young Amsterdam woman who was held in "Turkish slavery," was reprinted seven times between 1693 and 1780. Likewise, the title pages of two other pieces—*The Jewish Vagabond, or the History of a Certain Not Unknown Slave* and *The Strange Record of One Unlucky Traveler*[105]—indicate

Figure 3.2 Jan and Caspar Luiken, "Mannier Hoe de Gevange Kristen Slaven tot Algiers Verkoft Worden" (manner in which the captured Christian slaves are sold in Algiers), engraving, in Simon de Vries, *Historie van Barbaryen, En de zelfs Zee-Roovers...*, Vol. II (Amsterdam: Jan ten Hoorn, 1684), fol. 384. Dousa Kamer.

Figure 3.3 Jan and Caspar Luiken, Torments of Christian Slaves, engraving, in Simon de Vries, *Historie van Barbaryen, En de zelfs Zee-Roovers...*, Vol. II (Amsterdam: Jan ten Hoorn, 1684), fol. 384. Dousa Kamer.

the many bookstores where the texts were available. Readers could sate their interest at shops all over the Republic, in large and small cities alike.[106]

News about the Barbary pirates and their treatment of slaves also appeared in Dutch almanacs and newspapers. For example, the almanac *De Snelle Mercurius*, published in Amsterdam in 1686, published dates when North Africans had apprehended ships and kidnapped Christian sailors, and the means taken to liberate the captives.[107] Troubling acts of retaliatory vengeance were also duly noted.[108] Likewise, newspapers such as the *Amsterdamse Dingsdaegse Courant* and the *Ordinaire Leydse Courant* kept their readers fully informed on the latest news from "Barbaria," whether it was the negotiating of a truce between the corsairs and a European state, the impressive strength of a fleet sent to confront the corsairs, or reprisals, battles, or prisoner exchanges between Europeans and the North Africans.[109] Especially upsetting were reports of Europeans who, attracted by the lure of money, would aid and abet the corsairs. One such account related the story of a villainous French captain who promised 500–600 French Huguenot refugees that he would deliver them safely to secure sanctuary in America. Instead, he brought them to Algiers where he sold them to the Turks as slaves.[110]

Such public awareness of alleged Barbary cruelty transformed the corsair into a sort of "bogeyman" within the Dutch cultural psyche. For instance, it was rumored that Dutch children were being kidnapped and transported to the North African slave markets.[111] Whether such legends were true or not, plenty of Dutch men and women did meet the grim fate of becoming slaves after seizure on the high seas. For example, Simon de Vries, to cite but one contemporary observer, contended that as of 1660, 1,000 Dutchmen were enslaved in Algiers alone.[112] Extant "slave rolls" from the seventeenth century list the names of Dutch individuals who were ambushed by corsairs from the various North African cities. Appendix V, detailing the data from one such roll, reveals the information that such documents typically contained.[113] Slaves included citizens from throughout the Republic, individuals of all ages, men and women, and sometimes even entire families.[114] A list of 178 slaves liberated from Algiers and included in Simon de Vries's *The History of the Barbarians and Their Pirates* substantiates this impression, showing that the Dutch men and women delivered from "Barbary bondage" in this case hailed from throughout the country.[115] The overriding, unifying quality shared by these diverse groups of people, as one roll's title attested, was their shared identity as members of the "Netherlands nation."[116]

Enormous effort went into the endeavor to liberate these lost fellow citizens of the Fatherland.[117] The exact process might differ from year to year, depending upon the status of the relationship between the Republic and the various North African cities,[118] but the method was more or less the same. Simply put, slave rescue entailed money, for the slaves' freedom had to be purchased from their North African owners. To this end, the government actively encouraged the formation of liberation societies whose sole purpose was to collect capital for the emancipation of Dutch slaves.[119] Such societies did arise in the maritime cities and towns.[120] Additionally, although the States-General itself took little direct action to free imprisoned and enslaved Dutchmen,[121] they did ply the North Africans with gifts in order to grease the political wheels.[122] Not surprisingly, family members of the enslaved Netherlanders were extremely instrumental in organizing collection activities, but friends maintained a significant presence as well. Moreover, such liberation societies appear to have been a charitable activity held in high esteem and thus received the interest and sponsorship of the general public as well.[123]

The monetary amounts necessary for liberation were highly variable. One sample list from Algiers in 1683 indicates that prices generally ranged from 130 to 600 pieces-of-eight, with most manumissions averaging between 200 and 300. There were, however, a few exceptionally expensive individuals, including an Amsterdam ship captain (2,000 pieces-of-eight), one Cornelis Sievertze van Tessel from Enkhuizen (1,100 pieces-of-eight), a skipper from Alkmaar (900 pieces-of-eight), and a woman from Rotterdam, Elisabet van Meurlijn (900 pieces-of-eight).[124] Likewise, Simon de Vries's liberated slave list from 1682 shows that though the prices ranged from 150 to 2,000 pieces-of-eight, most manumissions cost between 200 and 300.[125] Another list reveals that Dutch sailors captured by the Algerians between 1690 and 1726 cost between 135 and 700 pieces-of-eight to liberate, with the average price being 336 pieces-of-eight.[126] Occasionally, the North Africans would even hold their version of a "fire sale" in which they would offer the slaves for a much lower figure.[127]

In the end, no matter how much liberation cost or how deliverance was obtained, captives' homecomings were treated with jubilation. Word circulated throughout the Netherlands: pamphlets were published, and accounts detailing the particulars appeared in the newspapers. And such happy reports often emphasized the bonds of nationhood in articulating their joyful news, stressing that Dutch slaves had returned to "our Fatherland."[128] (Of course, the Dutch themselves practiced slavery in their American and Asian colonies, a fact that it is important to note; slaves were typically Africans or native peoples. This seems ironic, given the Dutch devotion to freedom and liberty and their loathing of the idea of slavery. This is a very complicated and important topic that necessitates exploring the issues of seventeenth-century racism and warrants further research. Still, that the Dutch themselves held slaves does not invalidate the observation that the Dutch used "slavery" as a model for their own self-identity. If anything, it means that the concept resonated even more, that it held even more immediate and comprehensible meaning for Dutch people.)

According to popular belief, then, the "Moors" were the Republic's maritime nemesis, interfering with the free trade of goods, attacking and destroying valuable ships, and most importantly, seizing pious, God-fearing Dutch men and women and thrusting them into an appalling state of bondage. It is no wonder that when a plague engulfed Salé in 1679, the Dutch interpreted the epidemic as divine justice against the Barbary corsairs, a proper punishment for the North Africans' terrible sins.[129] For the most part, however, the Dutch did not wait for God to reprove the "Barbarians." Rather, they looked to the fortitude and valor of the Dutch Navy, viewing them as agents of vengeance and just retribution.

Naval missions to "purify the coast of [Barbary] pirates," as contemporary documents expressed it,[130] departed regularly and enjoyed some success. Such Admiralty fleets typically cruised the Spanish and Portuguese coasts and the Mediterranean Sea, ever on the lookout for predatory North Africans. When they encountered a corsair vessel, they endeavored to apprehend it, liberate any captive Christians, confiscate the weapons, and auction the goods at the nearest friendly port. Ostensibly inspired by a fight-fire-with-fire mentality, these Dutch Navy crews sometimes also seized the corsairs themselves, selling them as slaves in ports such as Spain's Puerta de Santa Maria.[131] Dutch privateers were also permitted to haul in their Barbary counterparts as legitimate "prizes" whom they could sell to the highest bidder at public auction.[132] Selling these North African prisoners was a lucrative enterprise. Sample records from a 1661–1662 mission led by Admiral Michiel de Ruyter (who led fleets against the corsairs between 1654 and 1657, and 1661 and 1664) indicate that 84 "Moors and Turks" fetched $f.5,224$, with other such sales that year resulting in $f.14,256$, and $f.10,142$ respectively.[133] And going full circle, the prisoners—and the capital generated by their sale—were typically used as instruments of exchange in liberating Dutch men and women held in Barbary servitude.[134]

In general, the Dutch Navy served to protect the interests of the Republic all over the globe, whether this meant convoying with commercial vessels through treacherous waters or engaging in one of the many military conflicts the Netherlands found itself involved in during the Golden Age. The Admiralties and their sailors were the focus of fervid interest and the source of much national pride. Newspapers reported regularly on the navy, listing the dates and reasons for Admiralty meetings and the status of battles,[135] the movements of the fleet while at sea,[136] and the triumphant return of "brave sea heroes" such as the most prominent admirals.[137] Moreover, annual almanacs contained a multitude of details about Dutch war squadrons, such as the names of the relevant ships, the identity of their commanders, the flag each flew, and the varieties and amount of weaponry they carried.[138] Many a pamphlet was also devoted to the navy's valiant deeds,[139] recounting in great specificity the narrative of campaigns between the Dutch and their enemies,[140] and engaging in laudatory commentary on the noble endeavors of the admirals.[141] And all forms of the popular press periodically contained first-hand accounts, written by the foremost admirals themselves, of battles and their experiences at sea.[142]

That the navy was greatly admired and their officers highly esteemed is evident from the language used to discuss them. Successful admirals were held up as models of virtue whom rank-and-file Dutch people should imitate. The richly illustrated 1676 book, *Lives and Deeds of the Illustrious Sea Heroes* by Lambert Van Den Bos, contains flattering biographies and handsome portraits and engravings of Dutch admirals such as Cornelis

Tromp, Michiel de Ruyter, and Opdam van Wassenaer, all presented for the Dutch public's enthusiastic consumption.[143] Likewise, the dedication of Simon de Vries's work, *The Great Arena of Woeful, Bloody, and Murderous Happenings*—a book of didactic moral edification whose self-proclaimed purpose was to provide readers with examples of "the punishment of the godless and the reward of the good"—extolled Tromp, characterizing him as the "Very Noble, Widely-famous and Manly Sea Hero."[144] De Vries singled out Tromp as the epitome of bravery and probity—a patriot who had manifested tremendous courage in facing danger and confronting the enemy in order to secure the freedom of his "*Vaderlandt*."[145] Similarly, a 1653 pamphlet written by an anonymous "heartfelt sailor from Holland" lauded Cornelis's father, Admiral Maarten Tromp, as both "the superlative sea-hero" and "our never-frightened sea-hero," "a good Christian" who died "as a stouthearted hero at arms."[146] Another pamphlet celebrated Admiral de Ruyter (as well as Maarten Tromp, once again) as a "sea lion" who bravely faced the English in the Battle of Lowestoft, a contest of terrible ferocity.[147] And a 1607 pamphlet, articulated as a "Victory Song" to the valor of Admiral Jacob van Heemskerk, declared him the "noble and brave gentleman."[148] The "Victory Song" itself—a patriotic narrative written in verse about the fierce battle between the Dutch and the Spanish at Gibraltar in 1607—described Heemskerk's behavior in combat in the most complimentary of terms, citing his bravery, piety, prowess as a warrior, and patriotism. Popular poems and songs, too, glorified the noble merits of Dutch naval figures,[149] and the epitaphs on navy men's tombstones and monuments reveal the Dutch public's great admiration for their fallen heroes.

The Dutch public avidly read works about the navy's highest-ranking officers. In justifying its own raison d'être, for instance, a 1645 pamphlet about Admiral Maarten Tromp noted that a previously printed pamphlet about the intrepid admiral had been very popular among the reading public, and that people craved even more "blue books" about him.[150] Another pamphlet devoted to Admirals Tromp and de Ruyter cited the popularity of a preceding publication as the justification for its existence. "All good patriots" had read the earlier piece, the pamphlet explained, and "have been well pleased" to learn details about the battle and the "just praise" it offered to "Admiral Tromp and other sea heroes."[151] A 1687 biography of Admiral de Ruyter was so popular that by 1732, it had already been reissued three times.[152] Indeed, the voracious public appetite for such publications is also revealed by the fact that the States-General sometimes attempted to suppress the printing of inflammatory materials about famous admirals in an effort to quell public upset.[153]

Cynthia Lawrence argues that there existed in the seventeenth-century Dutch Republic a "cult of the naval hero" and that, further, naval heroes transcended their identities as mere brave officers to became " 'secular saints' who symbolized national virtue."[154] Naval officers assumed this special role for several reasons. First, unlike the army, which was dominated by foreign mercenaries, the navy's officers and sailors were typically from the Republic (usually the maritime provinces). Thus, the public viewed the navy as a more homegrown, "national" institution with direct, vibrant ties to the Dutch populace.[155] Second, the origins of the navy in the Sea Beggar fleets gave the navy the stamp of historic, patriotic purpose.[156] And finally, the intense adulation that the Dutch maintained for their sea heroes was, Lawrence says, "a consequence of the lack of contemporary flesh-and-blood idols with whom the Dutch could identify." From Admiral Jacob van Heemskerk on, Lawrence asserts, naval heroes "were presented, and widely perceived, as accessible salt-of-the-earth types who remained within the realm of the common man, despite their wealth and fame."[157] Their image reflected the ideal that dikemaster Andries Vierlingh had envisioned: robust, hardworking, upstanding, and courageous "everyday" men who bravely faced the perils of the water. Consequently, these dauntless "sea lions" become official heroes presented by the government for public consumption, and filled a cultural void to become genuine folk heroes as well.

This cult of the naval hero flourished throughout the 1600s, becoming even more pronounced during the third quarter of the century.[158] Its first intense expression appeared in the public mourning and memorials dedicated to Admiral Jacob van Heemskerk. When Heemskerk's inspired and brave leadership brought about a spectacular Dutch victory against the Spanish in the Battle of Gibraltar (1607), public celebrations erupted throughout the Republic. Likewise, when Heemskerk perished soon after due to wounds he suffered in the campaign, the States-General ordered a state funeral and, setting a new precedent in government artistic patronage, mandated a monument in his honor.[159] The memorial's Latin inscription testifies to Heemskerk's sterling character, from his inspirational leadership and navigational skills, to his unassailable courage and compassion. In turn, pamphlets, poems, and songs printed and circulated at this time echoed such sentiments, and brought the tragedy of Heemskerk's "martyrdom" to a wide and intensely interested audience. His dramatic death prompted expressions emphasizing his piety, boldness, sense of sacrifice, and national dedication. At the call of the "cry of war," one such pamphlet recounted, the Admiral "boldly ran out," motivated by "God's word and the country's freedom . . . to die honestly upon the sea."[160] Eulogizing publications assumed the form of hagiographies, comparing Heemskerk's "sacrifice" of his life to the crucifixion of Christ. Hundreds of mourners attended his funerals (the first state funeral in the United Provinces since the assassination of William of Orange in 1584),[161] his armor and the cannonball that killed him became revered relics, and his monument in Amsterdam's Oude Kerk (Old Church) became a shrine.[162] Both the official monument (whose elaborate iconography glorified his heroic virtue)[163] and popular printed materials emphasized that Heemskerk's noble life was one that others—and especially future generations—should emulate.

Many sources manifest such sentiments about other admirals, revealing a fierce passion for these figures. Certainly, the pamphlet literature reveals an intense identification with them as symbols of national rectitude and strength.

For instance, a pamphlet that was published in 1653—a *praatje* between two figurative sailors on the death of Admiral Maarten Tromp—has one seaman exclaiming that he wishes that he could have died in Tromp's place, and that he does not know how to contain himself. Nor, he confesses, can he figure how the Fatherland will survive without "our . . . never frightened sea hero, Admiral Tromp." In the course of this dialogue, he depicts Tromp as a true father of the nation:

> Joris: It saddens me so much that I wish that that cursed bullet had hit me in place of our Faithful Father. Ach! when I think about it, what pain our Fatherland suffers because of his death, I don't know how I shall hold myself together.[164]

In the seventeenth-century idiom, *Trouwen Vader* ("Faithful Father"), the term "Joris" used to describe Tromp, could also mean "uniting/connecting/binding Father," signifying Tromp's capability to unite the seven provinces through the symbolic force of his heroic image. "Joris" also later comments that Tromp has been "our hero who has served as a Father to us."[165]

And "Joris" was not alone in maintaining such sentiments. The Admiral inspired numerous songs and poems, all of which singled him out for his "heroic" piety and stalwart defense of Dutch "freedom." Pieces also employed the familiar trope of slavery to lionize Tromp, crediting him with "delivering" the Netherlands from the bondage of servitude (e.g., "O Hero, Deliverer of our beloved Fatherland . . .").[166] And in keeping with Tromp's patriotic popularity, the Admiral's victories at sea prompted many patriotic engravings.[167] Depictions of him as a god-like, maritime champion circulated among the public. For instance, numerous large and iconographically rich images of "Tromp as Sea Hero" appeared (along with similar representations of Admirals Van Galen and Opdam van Wassenaer) in a triumphal celebration in Amsterdam marking the 1654 peace with England.[168] He was not the only one, of course. During this era when the production of such "heroic" sea imagery was bountiful, prints of renowned sea officers and their naval exploits must have hung in many Dutch homes.[169] Admiral de Ruyter himself inspired fervent devotion. Copious adulatory and eulogizing pamphlet literature—bearing titles such as *The Plaintive Fatherland*—was published upon his death,[170] as well as a plethora of memorializing poems and songs.[171]

Certainly, by using patriotic and nationalistic symbols, the navy intentionally forged a clear identification between itself and the Republic that it served. Naval ships, for example, typically were either named after noble qualities or geographical locations throughout the Netherlands. Examples from a fleet that fought in 1665, in the Second Anglo-Dutch War, included: *Freedom, Gouda, Zeeland, Large Holland, Little Holland, Power, The Provinces, Vlissingen, Rotterdam, Leiden,* and *Zutphen*.[172] One could argue that this naming was a culturally unifying act, since all of these Dutch "places," scattered as they might be in real geographical terms, were out at sea together, battling as one unit. Likewise, the coat of arms for the

Admiralty of the Maas (Rotterdam) showcased the initials "PPP," meaning *Pugno Pro Patria*, or "I fight for the Fatherland," and the stern of the glorious flagship *The Seven Provinces*, commanded by Admiral Michiel de Ruyter in 1665, displayed the carved coat of arms of each province grouped around a large crest containing the lion emblem of the Dutch Republic.[173] Furthermore, naval ships, no matter which Admiralty they belonged to, flew the flag of the Republic, not that of their individual province or region. As one 1666 almanac proudly noted, when the Dutch Navy (under the command of Admiral de Ruyter) captured an English castle in Sierra Leone, the Dutch flag of the "Orange, White, and Blue came to wave in place of the English standard, surely a great sadness for the Englishmen's arrogant hearts."[174]

When one considers the degree to which the navy symbolically identified itself with the fledging Republic that it represented—and how government bodies and the popular press further encouraged and engendered these bonds—one can understand how the public developed and participated in a "cult of the naval hero." Naval champions were depicted and viewed as courageous and unflinching, even as they were pious, moderate, prudent, humble, and modest—all qualities that seventeenth-century Dutch society held especially dear.[175] And while this phenomenon likely had complicated roots, one should underscore that the origin of the navy in the Sea Beggar fleets of the early Dutch Revolt "contributed to a continuing sense of a historic, patriotic mission which played an important role in the cult's ethos and in its long-term popular appeal."[176]

The Sea Beggars had had a checkered past, attacking friend and foe alike. At the same time, their efforts had been absolutely vital to the preservation of the Republic against Spain. As a consequence of their naval achievements, as well as the enhancement (and eventually rehabilitation) of their reputation brought about by the passing of years and the instilling of collective historical memory,[177] the Sea Beggars later inspired widespread praise, enthusiasm, and even exaltation. Quite forgotten was their notoriety as violent carousers, indiscriminate plunderers, and coarse riffraff. Instead, these zealous marauders of the late sixteenth century transformed into "Founding Fathers" and excited nationalistic feelings in the populace of the newly born United Provinces.

One indicator of these sentiments was the popularity of Sea Beggar "songbooks," collections of anti-Spanish and anti-Catholic hymns that the maritime insurgents allegedly sang while battling the Castilians.[178] The compilation and printing of these songs began well before the seventeenth century. By 1581, *Een nieu Geusen Lieden Boecxxken* (*A New Little Book of Sea Beggar Songs*) had appeared, but it was only the most recent publication of its sort, an "expanded and improved" example of earlier editions, as the volume itself proclaimed.[179] During the course of the seventeenth century, and on into the eighteenth, the compilations continued to be very popular, with numerous variations proliferating throughout the Republic. Such works were often illustrated with woodcuts or even engravings, depicting William the Silent, or later Stadholders who were meant to share the founding father's glory by association with these songs of rebellion.[180] They might also include patriotic slogans (e.g., *Vive le Geus*, or "Long live the Sea Beggars"), patriotic emblems, and brief examinations of the history of the Dutch Revolt.[181] Endeavoring to capitalize on the insatiable public demand for such collections, they also often advertised that they had been "improved" and "expanded" over earlier editions.[182]

That the Golden Age Dutch public knew and sang such songs is indisputable. The most popular was the *Wilhelmus*, the patriotic tune attributed to William the Silent himself but probably actually written between 1568 and 1572 by fellow rebel and nobleman Philip de Marnix van Sint Aldegonde. This Sea Beggar hymn became the official anthem of the Netherlands in 1932, but had represented its unofficial patriotic favorite from the late sixteenth century.[183] With lyrics pledging fidelity until death to "the fatherland," service to God, dedication to the values of freedom and piety, and courage to expel "tyranny," the *Wilhelmus* manifests the essence of the "pious patriotism" that underlay seventeenth-century Republican culture. Indeed, contemporary sources, such as this pamphlet dating from 1626, reveal that long after the era of the Sea Beggars, the song continued to sound its stirring patriotic message as naval ships (allied, in this instance, with the English) prepared to go into battle:

> . . . the English and the Dutch swore an oath and promised to send help to one another as long as a drop of blood remained in their bodies. This alliance brought about . . . great courage among the fleet . . . [and] trumpeters blew . . . the old song Wilhelmus van Nassau.[184]

Certain celebratory moments from Sea Beggar history also became the subject of seventeenth-century marine art. In 1621, for instance, artist A. de Verwer painted a battle that took place on the Zuiderzee in October 1574 (which, of course, the Beggars had won). More impressive are Hendrik Vroom's detailed and beautifully crafted "Zeeland Tapestries"—textile masterpieces depicting five decisive Sea Beggar battles from the early years of the Revolt—which were commissioned by the Admiralty of Zeeland for the decoration of their council chamber. Moreover, in some places (such as the town of Oudewater), paintings of significant moments in Sea Beggar history served a didactic function. Placed in prominent locations, so that the townspeople could behold them, they instructed the public about the Republic's hard-won independence and the key role that the Sea Beggars had played.[185]

One event in Sea Beggar history that particularly resonated with the citizens of the seventeenth-century Dutch Republic was the Relief of Leiden in 1574. In October 1574, the city had been under siege by the Spanish for nearly six arduous months. Within its walls, the beleaguered inhabitants were starving to death and plagued by disease. Still, they stalwartly refused to surrender to the Spanish army encircling them. Ultimately, after much suffering and deprivation, the Sea Beggars rescued the people in dramatic fashion, cutting the dikes surrounding the region and flooding the poldered land, thus enabling the Beggar ships to sail five miles inland to Leiden's doorstep. The terrified Spaniards, caught unawares, stampeded to escape the seagoing guerrillas and the waters engulfing the plain. In a final act of salvation, the rebels delivered sustenance—in the form of herring and bread—to the famished yet steadfast citizens of Leiden, thereby ending the siege and staving off disaster.

Leiden's *Ontzet*, or "Relief," was commemorated in manifold ways. Immediately after the event took place, pamphlets appeared recounting the city's terrible experience.[186] Later, printed images sought to render the suffering of the wretched Leideners. For example, the city chronicle written by local historian J.J. Orlers was illustrated with explicit engravings of the besieged and malnourished citizens, graphically depicting their (alleged) miserable diet of cats, dogs, grass, and roots, and showcasing pitiful, starving infants.[187] Beginning in the late sixteenth century, plays—passionate in their patriotism and popular with the public—retold and reenacted the event to later generations. These dramas, written by authors such as Jacob Duym[188] and Reynier Bont,[189] were not only performed, but were printed as pamphlets and circulated to a wide and engaged audience. Bont's rendition, illustrated with a woodcut portraying two Sea Beggars and the emblematic food of salvation, white bread and herring (figure 3.4), was especially well-received and went through numerous editions, all of which claimed to relate Leiden's ordeal in "lively" fashion.

As the years passed, the exciting and stirring story of the Sea Beggar's Relief of Leiden did not diminish in appeal. Theatrical retellings of the *Ontzet*—ever more ornate—continued to be a focus of popular enthusiasm and interest. Over 100 years after the siege itself had taken place, an Amsterdam newspaper from 1686 advertised that the Amsterdam Theatre would present *The Siege and Relief of the City of Leiden*, with "various magnificent and extraordinarily splendid displays."[190] And in the same year, a Leiden newspaper noted that the date of the relief—October 3—had long been considered a holiday by a number of governmental institutions in the province of Holland:

> The Hague, October 3. The members of the States of Holland were initially very busy today from 8 to 10 in the morning, and thereafter were in session until about 1pm. However, the assembly was not complete, for several esteemed members were absent, especially those from Leiden, for the reason that, in that city today, on account of its Relief which happened in the year 1574, a day of atonement, fasting and thanksgiving was held; which day is always a holiday here for the High Court of Holland as well as the Governing Council, the Council of Justice and other colleges. It was 112 years ago today that the forenamed city, through God's almighty rule, was miraculously delivered and liberated from a siege of 23 weeks, out of the hands of the Spanish.[191]

October 3 is still celebrated as a special holiday in Leiden, marked by a ceremony in which town citizens gather together at the symbolically charged Van Der Werff Park,[192] sing Sea Beggar anthems and other patriotic tunes, and then proceed to the city's historic Weigh House, where the municipal

Figure 3.4 Title page woodcut, *Belegering ende het Ontset der Stadt Leyden* by Reynerius Bontius (Leyden: Iacob Tinnekens, 1646). Dousa Kamer.

government dispenses their forebears' food of deliverance: white bread and herring.

There is no doubt that the seventeenth-century citizens of the Dutch Republic considered the Sea Beggars to be historic figures of decisive importance. More than that, however, as the Golden Age unfolded, the Sea Beggars became pervasive symbols of Dutch *national* strength and unity. Dutch people sang Sea Beggar anthems during moments of patriotic enthusiasm, they observed images of Sea Beggar bravado, and read and watched dramas depicting their ancestors' suffering relieved by Sea Beggar bravery. They proudly included Sea Beggar documents in city chronicles.[193] They participated in festivities marking the Sea Beggars' courage and acts of deliverance, from the "day of atonement and thanksgiving" in Leiden, to mock naval battles between the Dutch and Spanish fleets at Enkhuizen, Monnikendam, and Hoorn.[194] Sometimes, they even served patriotic meals featuring the "foods of affliction"—rapeseed cakes, rodent meat, boiled hide, and gruel made from mashed bark—which the besieged Leideners claimed they had ingested to survive.[195] The navy, as the current maritime protectors of the Republic, quite naturally benefited from all of this positive attention directed toward their historical predecessors. They were, of course, happy to encourage such an association—the Admiralty of Zeeland's commissioning of Hendrick Vroom's masterful Sea Beggar tapestries is evidence enough of that. And sources indicate that the Dutch public indeed accepted the navy as honored heirs of the Sea Beggar mantle. Poems and songs commemorating the great Dutch victory over the Spanish at the 1639 Battle at the Downs, for instance, make pointed references to the Republic's maritime fighting men as heroic *Geuzen* ("Beggars," i.e., "Sea Beggars").[196]

Transcendent "national" symbols such as the Sea Beggars, wielding their cultural power through the mechanism of collective historical memory, unified the disparate member provinces of the Dutch Republic. Claims of nationalist sentiment aside, however, tensions did exist between the provinces. Each province had its own sense of identity and history, of course, and in turn, championed its respective interests within the Republic's decentralized, confederated political framework. The 1579 Union of Utrecht—conventionally viewed as the Republic's "founding document"—was really just a treaty of common defense among the provinces, each of which continued to be sovereign. The States-General, in fact, could enact only what the member provinces' assemblies had independently and previously agreed to do. Neither taxes, nor coinage, nor weights, nor measures were uniform throughout the Republic, and each province retained the right to appoint its own Stadholder (who might not necessarily derive from the Orange dynasty). And while the province of Holland unequivocally dominated the political, cultural, and economic arenas of the new state, other provinces—particularly Zeeland—sometimes balked at Holland's supremacy.

Contemporary sources reveal that Zeelanders possessed a keen sense of provincial identity and saw themselves as quite distinct from the denizens of Holland. This was not idle hair-splitting, for sometimes foreigners also distinguished the Zeelanders and Hollanders as separate peoples. For example, a 1625 letter among Spanish government officials (which was intercepted by the Dutch) advocated the establishment of an Admiralty in Seville for the purpose of pursuing "Turks, Hollanders and men from Vlissingen..."[197] Back home, writers published self-proclaimed works of "Zeelands poetry"[198] and indigenous chronicles emphasized Zeeland's clear-cut identity, declaring that the province's fame was ubiquitous, that its people were naturally a courageous seafaring folk renowned for their fighting spirit, and that they had battled boldly and unflinchingly against the Spanish. Both Christianity and the Fatherland, one chronicle expounded, had benefited from Zeeland's bravery and steeliness.[199]

Part and parcel with this strong sense of self, the Zeeland provincial government sometimes resisted the fact that Holland's voice was the prevailing one in the States-General, and in Dutch affairs generally. In 1662, for instance, when the States-General had stopped issuing letters of marque, the States of Zeeland argued forcefully that an exception should be made for them, for in the past, Zeeland had gone above and beyond the call of duty in protecting the Republic. At this moment, Zeeland complained, Portuguese privateers were plaguing the Zeeland coast, "daily robbing the good inhabitants [there]," and the States-General should permit the Zeelanders to fight back. More pointedly, adopting a legalistic tone and quoting particular statutes, the provincial authorities protested that they reserved the right to appoint privateers, both for reasons of self-defense and because the Union of Utrecht granted Zeeland that specific privilege.[200] Such rancorous tensions around the subject of privateering had long existed between Zeeland and the rest of the Republic, and would continue to be a divisive issue through the War of Spanish Succession (1702–1713).[201]

Sometimes such provincial strains were evident in the relations between the various Admiralty colleges—again, especially between those of Zeeland and Holland—and particularly when money or honor was at stake. For example, the Admiralties of Zeeland and Amsterdam occasionally bickered over spoils plucked from enemy ships.[202] On a larger cultural level, these tensions sometimes came to be personified in the famous admirals, as Hollanders and Zeelanders squabbled back and forth, criticizing each other's sea heroes, even as they lionized their own. One infamous and widely circulated pamphlet (ostensibly from Holland) entitled *Rotterdams Zee-Praatjen* (*Rotterdammers' Conversations about Maritime Matters*) condemned popular Zeelands admiral Jan Evertszoon for supposedly displaying cowardice and ignoble behavior in the 1653 Battle of Lowestoft against the English:

> Mate: I believe that he . . . did not behave as an honest man . . . this day, he showed himself to be the greatest scoundrel in the world . . . I certainly believe that Jan Evertsz. [was] the cause of all this hardship and the loss of so many ships . . .[203]

Quite different, the pamphlet proclaimed, was the valorous and courageous comportment of Admirals Maarten Tromp and Michiel de Ruyter, both of Holland.

Evidently, *Rotterdams Zee-Praatjen* caused quite a storm. In an effort to assuage upset Zeelands feelings, the States-General banned the pamphlet and imposed fines on its author and printer.[204] Further, some anonymous Zeelander decided to fight fire with fire. When a second pamphlet appeared—this one a putative sequel entitled *Vervolg van Het Rotterdams Zee-Praatje . . . Noodig, In der haast gelesen te werden* (*The Continuation of the Rotterdammers Conversation about Maritime Matters . . . which Should be Read in Haste*), it bore the imprimatur of a Middelburg publisher, thus revealing its ostensible Zeelands origins. In this version, the character of the Mate now blames Evertszoon's sailors, as well as the English navy's advantages over the Dutch, for Evertszoon's troubles. The admiral, the Mate declares, was not at fault. In fact, the character of the Helmsman confesses that in the first pamphlet, he was simply speaking too freely, without careful thought. Indeed, another character, a merchant, agrees and proclaims that Admiral Evertszoon is, after all, "a good sailor and soldier."[205]

Likewise, the 1645 dispute over captured spoils between Admiral Maarten Tromp of Holland and Zeelands captain Ringelszoon caused enough widespread consternation to generate at least one pamphlet.[206] Composed in the form of a reputed letter from one "friend" in Middelburg (Zeeland) to another in Rotterdam (Holland), the publication was an exercise in public relations designed to support Zeeland's position in the controversy. The pamphlet indicates that other Zeelands captains professed to have witnessed the event, and that they, of course, sided with Captain Ringelszoon. The population of Zeeland frowned deeply upon Tromp's arrogance, the pamphlet concluded, and could only hope that their provincial governors would not believe the admiral's story.[207]

The other Admiral Tromp from Holland—Cornelis—did not fare well in a 1666 pamphlet either. This *praatje* between three characters (a merchant from Amsterdam, a man from Delft, and a sailor from Zeeland) discussed an important sea battle between the Dutch and the English, a campaign in which the Dutch faced great peril and that they ultimately lost. In fulfilling its self-proclaimed mission of "instructing pious and well-intentioned patriots,"[208] the pamphlet lambasted Tromp for his "irresponsible and destructive" behavior in the heat of combat. The Zeelands sailor—here labeled "sincere and honest"—declares that it was largely Tromp's fault that the Dutch fleet faced such danger and eventually succumbed.[209] For 30-odd pages, the Zeelander denounces Tromp, detailing the admiral's many faults, alleging that he conciliated the English, and proclaiming that other admirals were much more talented. In spite of all of this, the sailor complains, Amsterdammers refuse to hear any criticism of their precious admiral.[210]

Such anecdotes illustrate the fact that provincial identities were important in the seventeenth-century Netherlands. Some historians have contended that local identity was everything in the Dutch Republic, that seventeenth-century Netherlanders perceived their town, neighborhood, or province as their home community.[211] According to this point of view, provincial tensions could not truly be overcome, for the vibrancy of such local identities would preclude the development of an allegiance to a higher cultural and political authority. It is absolutely true that provincial ties inspired powerful feelings among Dutch people, whether they be, for example, Hollanders, Zeelanders, Gelderlanders, or Frisians. Certainly, the Republic was not a state where one might suppose, at first glance, that *national* bonds would be strong. Its political structure was loose and decentralized, and truthfully, its birth had been accidental and haphazard. Moreover, as Simon Schama points out, "The straggling shape of the new country was . . . determined more by fortunes of war and pragmatic considerations of policy, than either natural geography or a self-evidently tribal feeling for blood and soil."[212]

However, contemporary evidence reveals that the citizens of the Dutch Republic did transcend such local ties to form an attachment to a higher, *national* community. Yes, inhabitants did ascertain provincial differences and identities, and yes, regional bonds were heartfelt and real. When push came to shove, however, when the hostility of an enemy faced the young Republic, Dutch people discerned that they were members of a larger body, and banded together and fought as one, as one of the characters in this pamphlet "conversation" among a Hollander, a Zeelander, a Gelderlander, and an Englishman explained:

> Hollander: These lands are . . . very divided up—the provinces are seven, each of which has various privileges and customs, and at the same time, each town has its own particular manners. [These lands] are also divided up by different religions. . . . Because of this, they are brought to concord and contentment with difficulty; however, against a common enemy, [union] is much easier . . . [213]

One song, popular during the 1672 war with France, echoed these sentiments, albeit with more passion and lyricism: "Hollanders and Zeelanders / Prove yourselves to be as courageous and valiant as Lions / With the Frisian quarter / . . . Utrecht . . . / Groningen and Ommeland / Overijsel . . . [and] / Gelderland [too] . . . Prove yourselves in battle . . . Long live, long live the Orange . . ."[214]

Ultimately, then, in spite of enduring local identities, citizens of the unified seven provinces, which made up the Dutch Republic, perceived that they were part of something greater. Certainly, they recognized that they belonged to a larger institutional framework. Grand Pensionary Johan de Witt expressed this sentiment unambiguously in remarks he made in the mid-seventeenth century:

> Do not the present seven United Provinces have the same single interest in their own preservation? A same single fear of all foreign powers? Are they not bound to each other by mutual alliances and marriages among both regents and inhabitants, by common bodies, companies and partnerships in trade and other interests, by intercourse, possession of property in each other's lands, common customs and otherwise, are they not indeed so bound and interwoven together that it is almost impossible to split them from each other without extraordinary violence?[215]

Just as important, however, is the fact that citizens of the Republic now shared a keen *emotional* bond because of their newly fashioned national identity. They maintained the profound *feeling* that they were members of a new, inclusive, Northern Netherlands community, a community whose bonds had been forged through the ordeal of a protracted, bloody revolt against Spain, and whose ties were renewed and strengthened through each progressive step of united action. One pamphlet—a mid-seventeenth-century work whose stated purpose was "the instruction of devout and well-intentioned Patriots"—illustrates this point beautifully.

This publication, a *praatje* entitled *The Sincere Sailor from Holland*, was written in 1666 during the Second Anglo-Dutch War by an author who "following the feelings of the best patriots, has done great service for our Fatherland . . ."[216] It was advantageous for "our beloved Fatherland," he affirmed, to print this "conversation," which would serve as instruction for its "good inhabitants." "Read this with an impartial heart and judgment and a healthy and Fatherland-loving mind," the pamphlet directed, "and always remain obedient to your Mighty and lawful government."[217] The pamphlet's action takes place on a canal boat traveling from Dordrecht to Rotterdam. Among the cast of characters the work introduces is a young, fervently patriotic sailor from Zeeland who has worked as a mate on a naval ship in the latest battle against the English. Although wounded, the seaman longs to return to Rotterdam as soon as possible, for he wants to sail again with the fleet, so as to avenge his fatherland against the "murderous English king" and to protect the Republic's liberty.[218] The sailor's Zeeland identity is less important to him; at this moment of military crisis, it is the united *patria* that is the focus of his allegiance. He expresses his undying love for his fatherland, a passionate devotion that has physically manifested itself in his injuries: "The longing and love for my Fatherland, which is the cause of my wounds, is also the cause of my yearning . . ."[219] Those sailors who have not performed valiantly in the face of battle he excoriates as untrue Dutchmen, as individuals who act as if they "were born in Flanders or ran away from Brabant."[220]

In the eyes of the seventeenth-century citizens of the Dutch Republic, then, sentiments of nationalistic oneness were real and vigorous. Although nationalism was a result, and not a cause, of the revolt against Spain,[221] the concept of a common patria quickly became a powerful focus of allegiance to people. Provincial identities resonated deeply, but as the sixteenth century waned and the seventeenth century unfolded, and they fought together as comrades-in-arms, citizens of the Dutch Republic were willing to come together as one "Dutch" people.

This ability to transcend provincial differences is illustrated once again in a pamphlet published in 1653. During this *praatje* among a Hollander, Gelderlander, Zeelander, and Englishman, the Gelderlander proclaims that not just his people, but the Hollanders too, have earned the valorous appellation of "Batavian":

> Geldersman: You, Hollanders, should know yourselves as Batavians. Even though Batavia is actually the Betuwe region, and lies in the heart of our province, and as such, the name of "Batavians" actually belongs to us, because of your courage, and power at sea, so will we let you, in addition to ourselves, use this name . . .[222]

Who were the Batavians? As described by Tacitus, they were the ancient Germanic people who inhabited the Netherlands during classical times. Moreover, they were a hardy folk who had resisted the Roman yoke and practiced a form a self-government. As such, these forebears—the subjects of much Golden Age interest—became a significant symbol for early modern Netherlanders rebelling against Spain. A myriad of chronicles, histories, plays, and the like, all devoted to the brave Batavians, appeared during the seventeenth century,[223] affirming the idea that certain idealized Dutch traits were age-old and had been preserved in the face of tyranny and domination.[224] In dubbing his colleague from Holland a "Batavian," the Gelderlander—who after all, considered his provincial peers as the true Batavians—was invoking a symbol that had historic connotations of bravery and freedom, as well as contemporary implications of cultural solidarity and political unity.

So, by the mid-seventeenth century, the "good patriots" of the Dutch Republic viewed themselves as members of a "nation," a nation that inspired their sacrifice and dedication. Certainly, by this time, contemporary evidence abounds which indicates that the citizens of the United Provinces were conscious of themselves as "Northern Netherlanders" who belonged to one united state. Earlier tendencies to say "these provinces" or "Nether Lands" when referring to the confederation of the United Provinces had by now given way to the more cohesive "this land" or "Netherland";[225] national histories appeared, presenting the Northern Netherlands as a unified political and cultural entity;[226] and by the late seventeenth century, Dutchmen employed the term *natie* (nation) to refer to their homeland.[227] Patriotic displays celebrating the union of the seven provinces, such as a figural representation of the state in Stadholder Maurice's 1618 triumphal entry into Amsterdam,[228] great depictions of the "heroes of Dutch history" (such as the Batavians and the princes of Orange) in a celebration marking the "eternal peace" forged with Spain in 1648,[229] and a "unity pyramid" commemorating the ascension of Stadholder William III as king of England,[230] occurred throughout the century as well.

Such evidence indicates that citizens of the seventeenth-century Dutch Republic participated in the "imagined community" of a nation. The newly born United Provinces inspired its peoples' profound emotional allegiance, resulting in expressions of patriotism, sacrifice, and devotion. Indeed, Dutch people, while still closely identified with their own particular town and province, maintained in their minds an image of their fellow citizens' united, *national* communion. By the early years of the 1600s, the wayward renegades of the breakaway Northern Netherlands had developed a special bond of fraternity, a new identity as citizens of the united Dutch Republic.

Certainly, the actual ordeal of the revolt against Spain, as well as the continuing threats of the seventeenth-century world (such as other wars, commercial competition, and the Barbary corsairs) and Dutch prowess in so many areas (such as world trade, colonial expansion, artistic production) brought together the disparate peoples of the provinces of the Northern Netherlands. Also significant was the new political structure, which, although loose and decentralized, certainly served as a means to unite citizens institutionally. As important, however, was the power of "collective memory," that is, of carefully preserved and reenacted history, which served as a source of solidarity. Through the medium of a pervasive and vibrant print culture, Dutch people established collective memories that enabled them to form an image of themselves as a distinct, united, and potent *nation*. In their minds, they were pious, anti-Spanish, commercially blessed former slaves who had been delivered through God's benediction and Sea Beggar courage. They were the "modern Israelites," the defenders of liberty who possessed a navy replete with upright sea heroes. They were the modern Batavians who, while dedicated to their respective provinces, were unstintingly and selflessly devoted to the perpetuation of their new "Fatherland." All of these qualities would play a significant role in determining how the Dutch defined and viewed their marauding freebooters, whether of the piratical or privateering stripe. For these sentiments created a filter through which the Dutch public conceived of the notions of maritime heroism and roguery.

It is fitting to close this chapter, then, with words from a 1629 pamphlet that trumpets Dutch liberation from Spain and which highlights the essential place of collective memory and history in the formation of Dutch national consciousness. Written in a highly didactic and colloquial style, and thus ostensibly intended for the average reader, this poem of praise to the united "Fatherland" is articulated as a dialogue between two characters, "Freedom" and "Memory." Presenting itself as the guardian of the Fatherland, "Memory" forcefully reminds "Freedom" what has happened to permit "Freedom" to exist and flourish in the Dutch Republic. To this end, "Memory" reviews the Republic's bloody and sacrificial history, highlighting crucial historic events and emphasizing the fundamental role played by maritime commerce, the trade companies, the States-General, the prince of Orange, and most importantly, "our parents" and the "courageous mariners of Holland and Zeeland." History should not be forgotten, and Dutch liberty must not be taken for granted, "Memory" admonishes "Freedom" and the pamphlet's readers; ancestors' sacrifices must be recalled and commemorated. And now that "Freedom" is alive and vigorous, "Memory" also cautions, it must be defended for the sake of the nation:

> Freedom . . .
> With your most powerful, vigorous hand
> Go forth, for our Fatherland.[231]

4

Piracy, the Dutch, and the Seventeenth-Century Seas

> It was *long*, and it was *cruell*, it was *forcible*, and therefore fearefull . . .[1]
> Seventeenth-century chronicler Andrew Barker,
> commenting on a pirate capture

About a third of the way through Alexander Exquemelin's *The Buccaneers of America*,[2] a surgeon's famous account of his life among the seventeenth-century Caribbean buccaneers, the reader encounters a chilling and violent anecdote about one of the author's more nasty brethren, the sadistic and inhumane French captain, François L'Olonnais (figure 4.1):

> The buccaneers . . . took a number of prisoners, whom they treated most cruelly, inflicting on these poor folk every torment imaginable. When l'Olonnais had a victim on the rack, if the wretch did not instantly answer his questions he would hack the man to pieces with his cutlass and lick the blood from the blade with his tongue . . . And if one of the poor Spaniards, driven by fear and the cruel tortures he suffered, promised to lead the buccaneers to the citizens in hiding, and then through bewilderment could not find the way, he would be inflicted with a thousand torments—and then put to death at the end of it all. After most of their prisoners had been done to death by the cruelest atrocities, the buccaneers at last found two who would lead them . . . [L'Olonnais] . . . again asked about the way. The men answered that they knew of no other road. Then l'Olonnais being possessed of a devils' fury, ripped open one of the prisoners with his cutlass, tore the living heart out of his body, gnawed at it, and then hurled it in the face of one of the others, saying, "Show me another way, or I will do the same to you."[3]

Such hair-raising stories have longed served to produce the myths and lore that surround the intriguing character of the early modern pirate. Exquemelin's work, first published in Amsterdam in 1678 as *De Americaensche Zee-Roovers* and thereafter translated into any number of foreign languages and reprinted myriad times, represents an unparalleled primary source for the history of piracy. This colorful and rich text offers a very rare glimpse into an elusive, premodern, maritime, criminal world, a subculture that still piques deep interest and captivates the modern imagination.

Figure 4.1 Portrait of François Lolonois, engraving, in A.O. Exquemelin, *De Americaensche Zee-Roovers* ... (Amsterdam: Jan ten Hoorn, 1678), fol. 47. Dousa Kamer.

At the same time, however, early modern pirates—thanks to their stereotypical image in modern popular culture—have become quite misunderstood. Their actual identities and character—always somewhat veiled because of their outlaw status—have been eroded by the passage of time and popular culture's misrepresentation of them. Who were the pirates, and when and where did they flourish? How much mayhem did they actually sow, and were they all typically as violent as François L'Olonnais? More to the point of this book, did piracy affect the citizens of the Dutch Republic and if so, how much and in which ways? The responses to these questions are important to consider, for not only do they provide information about the particular conditions in which Dutch privateers and pirates operated, they also reveal more about the cultural lens through which Dutch people "processed" and comprehended the activities of piracy and privateering generally.

* * *

Most of the information modern historians have gathered about early modern piracy derives from English sources. Consequently, the lion's share of secondary literature on the subject treats pirates who were Anglo-American in origin and/or those who plagued Britain's colonial possessions.[4] Amidst all of this Anglo-centric source material, a number of important French texts also represent rich sources of evidence about early modern piracy.[5] Interestingly enough, though, in spite of the enduring popular interest in piracy and the vast literature that this fascination has spawned, there is a dearth of sound scholarly treatments of the subject. One significant reason for this paucity of critical historical work is that archival documentation about pirates and privateers remains scanty. As a result, any number of purported "studies" of piracy only reflect and perpetuate the same fictional exaggerations and fallacies that abound in modern films and novels.

The period from approximately 1570 to around 1730 represent the great age of piracy,[6] or, in other words, the era when sea robbery as an "economic" enterprise was most remunerative and from the governing authorities' point of view, threatening. Marcus Rediker isolates the ten years between 1716 and 1726 as especially frenetic, affirming that during this decade Anglo-American pirates, in particular, "created an imperial crisis [in England] with their relentless and successful attacks upon merchants' property and international commerce." Their numbers, he claims, "were extraordinary, and their plunderings were exceptional in both volume and value."[7] Certainly, piracy existed before 1570 and after 1730, but it dwindled to a great extent after the British government's "War Against Piracy"—a campaign in which naval patrols flushed pirates from their maritime hideouts and mass hangings depleted their numbers—concluded in 1725. Complicating things for both people at the time and modern historians endeavoring to decipher piracy's past is the fact that what many imprecisely call "piracy" represented, in actuality, several different forms of predatory maritime activity, some criminal and some not.

The fact that maritime bandits often blurred the lines by becoming involved in several of the various forms of "piratical activity" during the course of their lives, and that one state's pirate might be another's "legitimate" privateer (e.g., the Barbary corsairs), make the study of piracy more challenging. How, for instance, is one to begin to estimate their numbers? Does one include privateers and the Barbary corsairs in the sum total? Or does one simply attempt to tally the number of stateless "deep-sea marauders" who plied the early modern waters? Such ambiguities in pirate identity only further complicate the already bedeviling task of counting people who were often doing their best to hide from the public view. Outlaw pirates, like all other brands of criminals, lived along the obfuscating fringes of society; they did not avail themselves willingly to the governing authorities, they did not fill out censuses, and they did their utmost to remain apart from the legitimate world whose official records historians use to reconstruct the past. In any event, they numbered in the thousands.[8]

While calculating the true size of the early modern pirate population may be impossible, there is more agreement about which parts of the world were especially prone to their depredations. Of course, from the early sixteenth to nineteenth centuries, the Mediterranean was a perilous place for mariners due to the assaults of the Barbary and Maltese corsairs.[9] Likewise, Europeans had, since time immemorial, experienced piratical attacks along the continent's western, southern, and northern coasts; this was no different during the early modern era. An important example of marauders who fit this category were the Dunkirk privateers or corsairs, maritime bandits from the Southern Netherlands who attacked and plundered vessels belonging to or trading with the Dutch Republic.

What was new during the early modern period, however, with the expansion of the known world and the related increase in trade and shipping, was the development of European piratical activity along the "Spanish Main" of South America, in the Caribbean, along coastal North America, and within the waters of the East Indies, the Indian Ocean, and coastal Africa. Piracy was a problem that initially appeared in the Caribbean and along coastal South America in the early sixteenth century (specifically, in the form of French Huguenot privateers).[10] Of course, any merchant ship traveling in the Caribbean could be considered fair game—and quite often was—but the most obvious and tantalizing targets were the Spanish galleons, heavily laden with gold, silver, and other riches, and the Spanish colonial settlements these ships frequented while en route from Mexico to Seville. These so-called treasure ports, which included the cities of Cartagena, Nombre de Dios, Portobello, Maracaibo, and Havana, were vulnerable to the attacks of various European privateers and the buccaneers. Englishmen Sir Francis Drake and Sir Henry Morgan were only two of the more famous sea robbers who ravaged and plundered these outposts. Although the Spaniards—and later, other European powers who maintained colonies there—tried to combat the pirates' assaults by sending more soldiers, amassing greater numbers of arms, and building stronger fortifications,[11] colonial settlements were often quite defenseless.[12] One cautious estimate avers that just between 1655 and 1671, the buccaneers alone sacked 18 cities, 4 towns, and 35 villages, and wrought enormous damage on South American and Caribbean maritime trade.[13]

As settlement in England's North American colonies became denser and circumstances made the Caribbean less hospitable, pirates moved up the coast, attacking merchant vessels transporting slaves and various sorts of staples, which were en route to Boston, New York, Charleston, and Virginia. The attacks of these pirates reached a crescendo in the early eighteenth century and caused enormous damage. Probably most renowned among this group was the infamous Blackbeard (Edward Teach), but he represented only one among many.

Pirates did not just infest the Americas, however. On the other side of the world, they were very active in the East Indies and the Indian Ocean, and along the coast of Africa. In these waters, the primary lures were the merchant ships working the spice trade, ferrying luxury goods such as spices and textiles back to European consumers, and slave ships conveying captured Africans to the plantations of the New World. However, native peoples, such as those inhabiting southern India and the Hadramat (South Arabian coast), were preyed upon as well. Certainly, pirates of European descent—beginning with the Portuguese in the year 1500—were a grave problem. They were not alone in their predatory activities, however, for the Barbary corsairs also carried out assaults there, as did indigenous peoples, such as the Moplahs of Malabar and the Omanis, who took to the seas seeking booty and vengeance against the colonial invaders.[14] Of all the pirates who stalked this region, Englishman Captain Kidd (William Kidd) is probably the most familiar to modern Westerners; however, the predations of other less famous sea robbers, such as those of the Portuguese pirate brotherhood the *Feringhis*, who were active for over a century, were far more dangerous and destructive.[15]

The pirates themselves appear to have been a mixed bunch. According to Marcus Rediker, nearly all early-eighteenth-century Anglo-American pirates had worked as merchant seamen, Royal Navy sailors, or privateersmen and became pirates when their own vessels were captured.[16] This is a description that probably fits many pirates in general, not just those who originally owed their allegiance to Great Britain. However, at the same time, pirate crews were also populated by the occasional escaped African slave,[17] frustrated colonists, and fugitive indentured servants (as often happened with the buccaneers, who originally had been just an assemblage of hunters living in the wild),[18] the very rare woman (as in the cases of the notorious Anne Bonny and Mary Read),[19] and the odd aristocrat (such as Englishman Sir Thomas Cavendish, who sailed in the Pacific). Crews were typically quite international, boasting men from all over the globe, or at least from among the various European colonial powers. In terms of their personal characteristics, Rediker's study of 117 pirates active between 1716 and 1726 indicates that their median age was 27 years, and that they did not have family ties or obligations; they were also, almost without exception, from the lowest social classes.[20]

In terms of violence, plenty of graphic episodes appear in primary sources. Exquemelin's *Buccaneers of America*, praised by modern historians as a vivid and generally accurate description,[21] acknowledges that graphically violent behavior was common among the Caribbean sea robbers. Factually and rather dispassionately, Exquemelin reports some of the typical and brutal means of violence the buccaneers used to achieve their goal of successful plundering. In order to obtain information concerning the whereabouts of desired goods, Exquemelin's pirates put their prisoners on the rack, disjointing their arms; they twisted cords around their victims' foreheads and wrung so hard that their "eyes appeared as big as eggs and were ready to fall out" of the skulls; they hanged prisoners, whipping and bludgeoning them, cutting off noses and ears, singeing faces with burning straws, and finally stabbing them to death. Women were kidnapped, abused, and held for ransom.[22] Men were hung by their genitals, "till the weight of their bodies tore them loose. Then they would give the wretches three or four stabs through the body with a cutlass . . . Others they crucified . . ."[23] The barbarous François L'Olonais stands out for his sheer inventiveness in inflicting sadistic cruelty, such as when he gnawed on the heart of his prisoner.[24]

David Cordingly's study of pirate life and lore, *Under the Black Flag*, includes anecdotes chronicling brutal pirate atrocities, including savage murder, rape, and torture. Cordingly's account tells of pirates who starved, beat, molested, and maimed their victims, sometimes in perversely creative ways. One of his most visceral examples relates the gruesome tale of a woman captive who, according to Spanish reports, was "set bare upon a baking stove and roasted, because she did not confess of money which she had only in their conceit." Equally grisly was the sadistic practice of the buccaneer Montbars of Languedoc, who sliced open the stomach of his victim, removing one end of the intestines, which he nailed to a post, and then forced the prisoner to dance to his death by beating him in the buttocks with an burning log. Cordingly explains that certain acts, such as "woolding"—that is, wrapping a slender cord about a victim's head and twisting it hard, causing intense pressure—were standard practice. Indeed, he affirms that extreme violence was part-and-parcel of pirate life, and represented one of its signature characteristics.[25]

It is no wonder that citizens of the Dutch Republic, from the Admiralties to the trade companies to simple fishing fleets, greatly feared pirate and privateer attacks. VOC records, for instance, complain about both European pirates and privateers who preyed on VOC vessels,[26] and native pirates from Papua New Guinea who posed a threat to trade within the East Indies.[27] VOC ships were also disturbed by Arabian pirates based on the coast of Oran,[28] pirates who targeted the China trade,[29] and pirates who cruised the Red Sea and the Indian Ocean in the vicinity of Mauritius.[30] Company officials noted pirate haunts, such as that of the island of Sainte Marie (off the east coast of modern Madagascar). Here, by 1700, a population of some 500 pirates, presided over by a British "king," Eduart Welsch, came to spend the winter, repair their ships, and participate in a lively trade with vessels arriving from New York, New England, and Bermuda.[31] This same island also served as a site where pirates engaged in slave trading.[32] Figuratively wringing their hands, VOC authorities endeavored to come up with policies to fight all of these maritime bandits.[33]

Likewise, the WIC experienced its own frustrations with pirate and privateer attacks. Newspapers reported the problems the Company faced in the

Caribbean and South America in particular. In 1686, the *Ordinaire Leydse Courant* declared that assaults against the Company by the buccaneers had resulted in "great harm to our Peruvian trade."[34] Other reports indicated that pirates, based in the Cape Verde Islands, had captured passenger vessels en route from Amsterdam to Surinam and plundered ships carrying commodities such as gum and rubber resin.[35] One especially troubling story from November 12, 1686, noted that 150 pirates using three ships were plaguing the coast of Surinam, and already had sacked two luckless Dutch vessels.[36] Indeed, piracy was an ever-present challenge for the WIC,[37] a problem that the Company tried to address by arming Caribbean-bound WIC captains with "letters of reprisal,"[38] and augmenting the amount of weaponry and ammunition on Company ships and in Curaçao (where the Company's Caribbean headquarters was located).[39] Fear of pirate infiltration and attacks also stopped the Company from contracting private parties to transport WIC ammunition and materiel.[40]

The trade companies, of course, were not the only ones to suffer. Pirates and privateers did not discriminate and throughout the course of the Golden Age, Dutch skippers in general became victims of sea robber depredations. Attacks causing serious concern and harm began at least by the late sixteenth century. Such assaults were quite commonplace during the early years of the Revolt, when "pirates" (probably privateers working for the Spanish cause) hid within the rivers, deltas, and inlets between Holland and Zeeland, preying on Dutch shipping and fishing. By 1589, the States-General felt angry enough to issue a government proclamation mandating certain security measures, such as the necessity for ships to convoy and carry soldiers among their crews.[41]

By the later years of the seventeenth century, however, the vexations caused by pirate and privateer predations had only intensified. Nowhere was it truly safe to travel, from the home waters of the North Sea, to the Americas, to the Indies, to the coast of Africa.[42] So commonplace were such attacks—or at least the fear of such attacks—that everyday sea chanteys and poems gave voice to the trepidation Dutch seamen felt about the prospect of encountering hostile marauders on the open seas.[43] Certainly, the Dutch authorities were aware of the problem. The States-General issued various proclamations, especially during the 1670s, complaining about foreign privateers' attacks on Dutch shipping.[44] In an effort to discourage such damaging activities, they periodically swore to combat and suppress foreign privateering,[45] and forbade all such mariners from entering Dutch harbors; those ignoring this mandate would be forced to sell their goods and their vessels.[46] They also prohibited Dutch citizens from paying any ransom for captured ships.[47] Likewise, a 1686 edition of a Leiden newspaper includes a report about a group of merchants and businessmen, all from Rotterdam, Schiedam, and Sluys, who brought their entreaties and complaints to the States of Holland on October 6, seeking help in combating the "great damage which is caused by pirates everyday" who lay in wait along the coast of Ireland. The provincial government responded immediately, promising to send six ships, including two heavily armed warships, to eradicate the predators.[48]

Such reports represent only the tip of the iceberg. Piracy (including enemy privateering) was a nasty thorn in the side of Dutch trade, causing untold damage to ships, the upsetting divestiture of goods, and where sailors were concerned, tragic loss of life. While many such attacks were committed by anonymous sea marauders, whom the sources record only as *zeeroverijen* ("sea robbers," "pirates"), *roovers* ("robbers," "thieves"), and *vrijbuiters* ("freebooters," "pirates"),[49] in other cases, the Dutch were well aware of the identities of the aggressors. Whether in the form of privateering or piracy, sources reveal that the citizens of certain states preyed on Dutch vessels again and again.

Given the history of the Dutch Revolt and the Eighty Years War with Spain, it is not surprising that the Republic had to contend with Spanish marauders. For instance, in 1622, after the Twelve Years' Truce (1608–1621) had ended, the king of Spain, Philip IV, issued a formal proclamation encouraging Spanish privateers to capture and plunder all Dutch ships frequenting Spanish harbors.[50] This call was but one facet of an overall Spanish strategy to use privateers to crush the Dutch at sea, in the words of R.A. Stradling, "to carry the war to the enemy at the sole source of his existence—the areas of sea borne commerce and (more especially) of fishing."[51]

Dutch authorities, both in the Admiralties and the States-General, were incensed by this Spanish call to action, and outlined a series of protective and retaliatory steps to take against such depredations.[52] Measures that the States-General enacted included the offer of premiums for the capture of Spanish warships and privateer vessels; a promise to all Dutch sailors and privateers that they could keep any booty that they might plunder from outgoing Spanish vessels; a vow to punish any Spanish privateers by "binding them back to back" and "throwing them over the side" of the ship; free rein to plunder from Spanish citizens; the creation of a "powerful" squadron for the purposes of attacking Spanish ships "with violence" during that summer season; and finally, during the next year's winter season, a strategy to outfit a powerful "Royal Fleet," a naval detachment dedicated solely to the destruction of all Spanish sea power. By 1625, the States-General was offering premiums for the capture and/or destruction of *all* Spanish ships, no matter whether they be merchant or military vessels,[53] and providing explicit and extensive instructions as to how merchant and fishing vessels should arm and protect themselves.[54]

Even after the cessation of the Eighty Years War, however, the Dutch found themselves to be the victims of marauders from the Spanish Empire. To take one example, in 1649 when the ink on the Treaty of Münster (1648) was barely dry, Spanish privateers were assaulting Dutch ships traveling to and from the Dutch colony of Bahia, Brazil. These "Castilian" privateers accosted and plundered WIC ships carrying sugar and other tropical commodities.[55] A newspaper story from 1686 reports that Spanish attacks still continued decades later. In this particular case, a Dutch vessel, traveling from St. Eustacius and carrying sugar, cotton, and indigo, was captured by a Spanish "pirate" (*zeeroover*) on the coast of West Africa.[56]

Yet another Spanish threat were the "Biscayer Pirates," that is, Spanish Basques. These pirates lay in wait in the Caribbean between Puerto Rico and Hispaniola, preying upon French and English vessels, as well as WIC ships transporting hard currency. The records note that these "Biscayers" massacred at least one of the crews of an unfortunate English vessel they captured.[57] Alas, this seems to have been only the latest incident in a long string of "Biscayer" assaults, for Nicolaes Wassenaer mentioned these same pirates in his chronicle, *Historical Narration of All Memorable Happenings*,[58] published in 1627 and 1628. Wassenaer reported that "At this time two warships were sent from these Netherlands . . . to stop the continual piracy of the Biscayers . . ." Among the Dutch casualties had been eight merchant ships en route to Bordeaux, which were captured as they left Nantes and taken to Bilbao and San Sebastián, ports in Basque Spain. Although the "Biscayers" had in the past sailed for the king of France, Wassenaer explains, they now paid tribute to the king of Spain, for he had driven the Arabs out of their lands. And while Wassenaer was alarmed by their habitual piracy, he could not help but express admiration for their talents as mariners.[59]

The Spanish denizens of the Iberian Peninsula, however, were not the only ones to prey upon Dutch shipping. Indeed, the Dutch also experienced trouble from the Portuguese. Of course, during the early decades of the Golden Age, Dutch and Portuguese ships often engaged in skirmishes and plundering as they fought one another for commercial supremacy in the East Indies. However, Portuguese attacks were confined neither to Asian waters nor to the early years of the century. In 1662, for instance, Portuguese privateers were patrolling the coast of Zeeland, committing "hostilities" and "predations," sources affirm, "in an unbearable manner." The problem was serious enough that the members of the States of Zeeland made a formal plea for help to the States-General, requesting that a fleet of Dutch warships be outfitted to combat the marauders "who everyday rob the good citizens" of the province.[60] Portuguese pirates also used the Cape Verde Islands as a refuge and preyed upon ships that entered the surrounding waters. Dutch ships were warned to avoid stopping there.[61]

As threatening as these Iberian pirates and privateers were, however, they paled in comparison to their comrades-in-arms, the Dunkirk privateers. In 1621, once the Spanish had decided to make large-scale privateering a serious weapon against the Dutch in the Eighty Years War, Dunkirk began its evolution into a maritime den of thieves, a place that the Dutch called the "Algiers of the north." Although the Spanish had maintained privateering fleets in Flemish ports since early on in the Revolt, it was only after the collapse of the Twelve Years' Truce in 1621 that Dunkirk became the headquarters of an official squadron that was devoted specifically to economic warfare. Along with the other Flemish cities of Oostende and Nieuwpoort, Dunkirk emerged as the center of a new privateering industry, one that attracted formidable amounts of private capital.[62] It would remain an important facet of the Spanish military effort until 1646, when it fell to the French (who would also go on to use the city as a privateering base).

There has been considerable debate over how many ships—and therefore how much capital—the Dunkirkers were able to wrest from the Dutch.[63] Still, based upon strong (if varied) scholarly assessments, the numbers were very high. Between the years 1629 and 1638 alone, the Dunkirkers (both the privateers and the official Spanish armada) were able to seize and plunder some 1,880 ships totaling 209,448 tons.[64] The vast majority of these victims were Dutch.[65] Moreover, between 1625 and 1637, the Dunkirkers destroyed as many as 533 Dutch fishing vessels.[66] Other tallies show that the Dunkirkers captured 1499 Dutch ships during the years 1627–1634, and another 495 from 1642 to 1645.[67] And the value of those vessels taken between 1642 and 1645 was nearly five million guilders.[68] The upshot is that the Dunkirkers did the Republic great damage. And yet, as striking and dramatic as these figures are, they represent only the beginning, for the Dunkirkers preyed upon the Dutch for many, many years—under the Spanish from 1583 to 1609 and 1621 to 1646; and under the French from 1672 to 1678 and 1688 to 1697 (the era of the infamous corsair, Jean Bart).[69] In R. Stradling's opinion at least, by 1638, the Dunkirkers' "depredations had become the most serious political issue confronting the States-General."[70]

It is true that Spanish war policy emphasized commerce raiding only after 1621. However, the Dunkirk corsairs represented a serious menace far before this date. The years from 1583 until 1609 was a period of heavy Dunkirk aggression, resulting in substantial damage to Dutch trade.[71] A chronicle of the city of Enkhuizen reveals that from 1589 through 1605, residents of Holland faced steady harassment and violence from Dunkirk *rovers* ("pirates," "robbers"). These marauders plied the seas surrounding the new Dutch Republic, searching for merchant ships and fishing boats. Although the Dutch authorities were quick to retaliate by capturing any enemy vessels they could and imprisoning and hanging the privateers aboard, the Dunkirkers continued to wreak havoc, seizing and burning ships and fishing boats, and kidnapping and killing the crews.[72] Other chronicles relate that the Dunkirkers were such a problem that naval captain Moy Lambert of Rotterdam was explicitly ordered to hunt them down; he captured some 60 of them in 1605, and they were hanged in Rotterdam and Enkhuizen.[73]

As early as 1576, the Dutch were trying and convicting privateers working out of Dunkirk for the crimes of "sea piracy," "river piracy," and "river hooliganism."[74] Although the "Dunkirkers" were actually of diverse national origin (e.g., Flemish, Spanish, and German), used various types of vessels (from small boats crewed by only six men to heavily armed warships), and targeted assorted waterways (from the North Sea to the estuaries of the Biesbosch and Zwaluwe regions), all were united in their goal to rob, plunder, kidnap, and destroy the ships and sailors of the fledging Dutch Republic.[75]

A case from 1589 is typical. On May 5 of that year, the Admiralty of the Maas convicted Captain Jan Spienink and 33 of his crewmen for piracy and river hooliganism, sentencing them to be hanged at the gallows outside of Rotterdam. The court determined that Spienink and his men had captured four of the Republic's vessels, plundering fish and various unspecified trade goods. Such actions, the Admiralty proclaimed, were intended to lead to "the destruction of sea-trade,"[76] a goal that they naturally deplored. Likewise, on August 10, 1594, the Admiralty convicted one Claas van Gan and his crew of 46 for the same crimes. A veteran Dunkirk privateer, he had kidnapped 20 Dutch sailors, for whom he was demanding ransoms of ƒ.43 per man. Seized by a Dutch Navy warship before he and his men could further rob, plunder, and kidnap other "good Dutch sea traders and fishermen," they were hanged at the gallows just outside of Rotterdam.[77] Again, in November of 1599, the Admiralty convicted another 15 Dunkirk privateers for kidnapping Dutch sailors and fishermen from the Flemish and Zeeland coasts and Maas River. These sea robbers were hanged at the same gallows.[78]

A case settled on November 28, 1601, is especially telling. Veteran Dunkirk privateers Laurens Courtszoon and Jan de Segelare, along with 29 of their fellow crewmen, were found guilty of the crime of piracy. Using a small ship aptly named *The Terror*, they had violently attacked and plundered various boats and ships along the coast of England and ransomed a kidnapped victim for 200 guilders. The States-General felt this group to be especially dangerous, given the marauders' stated intention to plunder and imprison any fishing and trading vessels belonging to the Republic or its neighboring lands. When navy captain Moy Lambert apprehended them, they were very quickly questioned and summarily hanged for their especially "wicked and evil" deeds and their "maliciously-intentioned, ungodly enterprise."[79]

After the Spanish instituted their official commerce raiding policy in 1621, conditions only worsened. The Dunkirkers were more formally organized, using larger vessels and sailing in fleets. For example, in 1622, Stein Peterszoon and 23 of his fellow crewmembers departed with two other enemy vessels to plunder and imprison "merchants, fisherman and other good sea people of the United Netherlands." Their "evil intentions" were foiled by Dutch naval warships, but only after violent combat. Like many of their compatriots who had preceded them, they were hanged at the Rotterdam gallows.[80]

By the mid-1620s, the States-General felt the need to formally and regularly issue instructions declaring how Dutch ships should protect themselves from the Dunkirkers' predations. They also resolved to periodically equip and launch special naval detachments expressly dedicated to the eradication of the Dunkirk menace. In February 1626, for example, the States-General pledged to fortify and outfit 30 men-of-war, each formidable in size and carrying 20–22 "good pieces of weaponry" (cannons), and another 6 or 7 "metal pieces" (guns). Every ship was to be manned by at least 75 crewmembers and 20 soldiers. Moreover, another 5 "yachts" were to accompany the fleet; each of these smaller vessels was to carry another 50 men, and more weapons (such as light guns) and ammunition. The States-General mandated that only the best and most courageous sailors were to be hired for this expedition, and that all of the Admiralties should work together on this project, sharing the costs and responsibilities. The fleet was to go to sea in April of that year.[81]

This offensive fleet proved to be the first of many, for the Dutch would continue to launch protective squadrons until 1646. One of their primary goals was to realize an effective blockade of the Dunkirk harbor, as well as to assault and capture or destroy the corsairs' ships. The work was highly dangerous and frightening, but the security and prosperity of the Republic depended upon it. Over the years, many navy men cut their teeth on this hazardous "Dunkirk tour," and, consequently, became heroes in the eyes of their compatriots. Among this group were the highly celebrated admirals Piet Hein and Maarten Tromp.

Especially impressive and effective in this regard were the actions of Zeelands commander Johan Evertsen. On February 18, 1636, while commanding a small squadron of three naval vessels, he was confronted by a group of four Dunkirk ships, led by the notorious captain Jacques Colaert. Colaert was a highly successful veteran corsair who had sailed the seas for Dunkirk for 36 years, and during that time, captured some 100 merchant ships and 27 warships from the Republic. After a pitched battle in which Evertsen and his crews sank 2 of the Dunkirk ships, 48 Dutchmen perished and another 50 were wounded, the Dutch triumphed. Carrying home more than 200 Dunkirk sailors as prisoners, Evertsen and his bedraggled-yet-victorious squadron arrived in Vlissingen 9 days later. The nation cheered, and the grateful Admiralty of Zeeland commissioned a gold coin in commemoration of and gratitude for Evertsen's patriotic service.[82]

In addition to these dedicated naval detachments, the Admiralties enacted other policies to combat the Dunkirk threat. Even in the midst of expeditions devoted to other purposes, the Admiralties made it their responsibility to arrest summarily any Flemish privateer they encountered. Such was the case in October 1657 when a naval ship charged with the suppression of Barbary and French pirates in the Mediterranean captured a Flemish privateer (and its three English prizes, loaded with grain) along the Dutch coast. The Admiralties, along with the States-General, also encouraged Dutch privateers to pursue and attack the Dunkirkers, and to that end, offered special bonus premiums as well as a bigger-than-ordinary cut of the booty for every Dunkirk ship a Dutch privateer seized or destroyed. Despite such inducements, however, the Dutchmen paid more attention to Spanish and Portuguese merchantmen because they represented more valuable prizes and were less dangerous to apprehend.[83]

More than the loss of goods, most upsetting to the Dutch was the Dunkirkers' practice of killing or kidnapping the crew aboard captured vessels. These ill-fated Dutch sailors were drowned at sea or taken back to the Flemish city, where they were hanged, or imprisoned in terrible conditions. Their freedom was sometimes possible, but only for a price. Consequently, Dutch families and communities were ever scrambling to collect the ransom money requisite for the release of their loved ones. In one fell swoop, the Dunkirkers could do grave damage to a Dutch shipping company or fishing outfit, seizing valuable vessels and kidnapping irreplaceable men. Take, for example, a case from 1678. On just one day (January 1), the Dunkirk privateers were able to capture 25 ships and 20 fishermen from the fishery of Maasluis alone. After imprisoning the unlucky sailors in Dunkirk dungeons, the Flemish sea robbers demanded a fantastical ransom of ƒ.48,000–50,000,[84] a catastrophically high sum for families of sea folk who were described at the time as being "miserably poor and wretched . . ."[85]

One pamphlet, published around 1645 and addressing the Dutch public, angrily recounted the various way that the Dunkirkers had harmed the Republic's seamen:

> I beg of you, consider . . . how many of your folk, in all manner of condition, [the Dunkirkers] have thrown off into the deep of the sea, from aboard your ships. Aye, how often have they cut off the [Dutch sailors'] noses and ears? How many more honest and fair people must pay with their lives for this unreasonable cruelty? How many women [will the Dunkirkers] make widows? How many children must be left behind as orphans? How many families have been devastated by their piracy? How many bankruptcies have they brought about, in Amsterdam, as well as in your other best cities?[86]

Another pamphlet, published in 1629, similarly decried the indiscriminate cruelty of the Dunkirkers, citing their cavalier indifference about kidnapping and killing indigent, unarmed civilians,

> [The Dunkirkers] have captured people who go out not with Cannons to fight, but with Nets to fish, to earn their frugal bread-money with difficult Work. And not only do they burn [the fishermen's] Boats and Busses and drive them aground, with fish and all. But they also bind the simple Fishermen back to back against one another, and in this fashion fling them overboard and drown them. It was yet a great mercy, when someone was imprisoned in Dunkirk or transported elsewhere, and put there in a dark and stinking jail.[87]

Yet another, published in 1639, in Holland, was equally repulsed by the aggressive practices of the Dunkirk privateers against defenseless Dutch citizens:

> It is obvious to all people here in the Province that for many years the moaning and complaining of the miserable, wretched Prisoners within Dunkirk has continued. How many times have I seen the Tyranny and oppression of the poor fisherman, shippers, helmsmen, and sailors who must go out to Sea in order to feed and support their poor families? How many pitiful, bitter lamentations must the good Inhabitants of this Land hear all day, when the poor . . . fishermen, shippers, helmsmen and sailors are captured? How often are collections made in the Maritime-cities, such as Rotterdam, Dordrecht, Gouda, Amsterdam, Enkhuizen, Hoorn and in still other places in order to help these poor, oppressed, imprisoned people with, on the one hand, their ransom, [and] on the other, their maintenance, and as they are released again out of the prisons, [they] are already ruined men . . . How many of the Merchants are ruined as their ships and goods are made prizes or booty? Ah! how are the industries of shipping, herring fishing, and fishing ruined here in this province! How many goods and how much blood does each day cost? How unfree is the North Sea made![88]

The Dutch authorities tried to assist in the return of these lost Dutch sailors, both by providing the funds for naval squadrons dedicated to the suppression of the Dunkirkers, and by arranging periodic prisoner exchanges between the Dutch and Dunkirk authorities.[89] Furthermore, endeavoring to eradicate the economic incentive for the Dunkirkers' predatory practices, the States-General periodically issued proclamations forbidding Dutch citizens from purchasing stolen goods and ships from Dunkirk sources.[90] Such efforts were not enough to assuage angry public feelings, however, as the author of one mid-seventeenth-century pamphlet attested when he bewailed the treatment of Dutch seamen rotting away in Dunkirk captivity:

> What treatment do [our Dutch sailors] suffer [at the hands of the Dunkirkers]? They are plundered, stripped, all taken away from here, they are put in prison, and they are all put on the most severe and merciless rations that one can invent. Indeed, so many are given rations [of this sort] . . . that once they come home, a short time afterwards they languish away and die.[91]

For this author and others like him, the Dutch government had to do more to combat this "Algiers and Tunis of the West" whose denizens infested Dutch seas and rivers. The port through which all Spanish sea power had to pass, the pamphlet proclaimed to the government and people, and thus the "mouth that feeds the enemy," Dunkirk "is the firmly-attached splinter in your flesh, which constantly torments you . . . so [that] it will not let you rest." The Dutch government and people had to fight this evil with vigor and persistence, the pamphlet warned, for "This stabbing and painful thorn will never fail to torture the Dutch lion, until the time when it is violently . . . jerked out of your paw . . ."[92]

Although a special menace, the Dunkirkers were not the only Europeans to prey upon Dutch shipping and sailors, of course. Besides the Spanish, the Portuguese, and the privateers of Dunkirk, the Republic was assaulted by the French and the English, both "legally" during official wars between the Republic and the other states, and "illegally" during times of ostensible peace.

French privateers especially targeted the WIC. Company archives from the late seventeenth century record numerous Gallic attacks. Sometimes, documents describe these assaults merely as acts of "French piracy and violence."[93] In other instances, however, Company scribes included details such as the names of victimized Company ships, the cargo, and the dates they were captured by "French privateers." Examples include the *St. Pieter*, transporting a load worth ƒ.6250, and captured on November 13, 1676; the *Pellicaan*, seized on April 1, 1677, and brought to Dunkirk; the *Reus*, taken on September 10, 1677, while en route to Curaçao by a French privateer ship called *de Oranje Boom*, which was fitted with 16 cannons; the *Croon Vogel*, commandeered at the island of "Cajuna" (Cayo, Cuba?); several attacks on unnamed vessels that took place on July 15, 1680;[94] the much-lamented ships the *Elisabeth* and *Stadt Rotterdam*, accosted on August 16, 1684, along the northern coast of

Cuba after leaving Cartagena, and plundered of their loads of gold and silver by "two great French privateer ships";[95] and unnamed ships taken by French "privateers" on November 22, 1696; November 4 and 18, 1704; April 13 and 21, 1706; and October 8, 9, and 10, 1706.[96] At other times, WIC records note the monetary value of French captures. In early 1675, for instance, Company documents note that French "pirate ships" captured the prodigious prize of 100,000 pieces-of-eight.[97]

Of course, the WIC was not the only enterprise to suffer at French hands—the VOC was also victimized. French privateers were especially adept at hunting down VOC ships within the myriad, intricate waterways of the East Indies themselves. Even worse, the French marauders sometimes disguised their vessels by flying Dutch flags, thereby fooling indigenous ships into believing that the French vessels were actually VOC merchantmen.[98] By the late seventeenth and early eighteenth centuries, Company directives ordered VOC officials to apprehend French privateers in places such as the Sunda Strait, the Strait of Malacca,[99] and the Bay of Canton.[100]

French privateer and pirate assaults against Dutch merchant shipping also took place in the Mediterranean. In 1657, the Admiralty of Amsterdam sent a well-armed warship there with the express purpose of reining in "all pirates, Turks, and French pirates from Marseille and Toulon."[101] The log of that ship's journey indicates that the Dutch pursued two French "pirate" ships by the island of Pantalleria (located between Sicily and Tunisia); chased another nine while en route to Livorno, Italy; and captured one in the "Baeij van Porte Spetio" (probably the Gulf of Genoa, near the port city of La Spezia).[102] Moreover, a reference from the 1651 edition of the almanac the *Hollantse Mercurius* contains one case that illustrates perfectly the mercenary and highly mobile tendencies of the privateering business. In January 1650, two Dutch merchant vessels were captured in the Mediterranean by French privateers carrying letters of marque, issued not by their king, but by the Knights of St. John, based in Malta (a fact that technically made them pirates).[103] Indeed, so intensely did French "pirates" attack Dutch shipping in the Mediterranean during the mid-seventeenth century that the Dutch began arresting all French merchant vessels for the sake of security and in retaliation.[104]

As frustrating and painful as French attacks were, English depredations against the Dutch inflicted far more damage. Englishmen were convicted of piracy against the Republic at least as early as 1572,[105] a trend that continued into the early decades of the seventeenth century.[106] It was during the three Anglo-Dutch Wars, however, that the Dutch truly felt the sting of English marauders, for privateering became an important aspect of the naval effort on both sides. The English profited handsomely from their privateer attacks against the Dutch. By the close of the Third Anglo-Dutch War, for instance, a large number of Dutch flyboats had turned up in English hands. Ultimately, during the course of the three conflicts, the Dutch lost to the English at least 1,000–1,700, 522, and 500 ships respectively.[107] English privateers also played an integral military role in the Caribbean. This was especially the case during the Second Anglo-Dutch War, in 1666, when they were able to seize the Dutch-held islands of Saba, St. Eustatius, and Tobago. Although the Dutch retook these colonies a year later, it was not without a good fight and assistance from both the French and the buccaneers.[108]

Popular publications reported on and complained bitterly about English assaults. The 1666 edition of the *Hollandze Mercurius*, published during the course of the Second Anglo-Dutch War, related how English privateers had commandeered Dutch vessels. By January 1665, for instance, English "pirates" (*rovers*, but probably privateers in actuality) had raised the ire of the VOC by capturing three Company ships in the English Channel, and killing some of the men aboard.[109] By February of that year, the almanac reported, the English "who love stealing as much as anyone, and love booty as much as anyone else does," had struck again on numerous occasions, absconding with more than 18 Dutch ships.[110] Perhaps most maddening was that the English—former supporters of the fledging Republic—were not content to encourage just their own countrymen to serve as privateers. Rather, in 1665–1666, they also provided English letters of marque to at least seven Flemish captains from Oostende,[111] employed Flemish seamen in general,[112] and even seriously considered supplying letters of commission to the Maltese corsairs (an option they later declined to exercise).[113] To combat these English and Flemish marauders, the States-General resolved to outfit 72 warships, ordered that any English ship—whether naval or merchant—had to be captured;[114] and issued a warning to neighboring states (as well as to their own subjects) that any person found sailing with the English privateers would be considered a "pirate," and would be either executed, or eternally banished.[115]

Popular songs and poems, typically patriotic in nature, also expressed ardent antipathy toward the English and their nefarious privateers, terming them "pirates" and much worse, sometimes going so far as to equate them with the much-loathed Barbary corsairs. Such pieces also lambasted the English not merely as adversaries but as "betrayers" who ignored the Calvinist sensibilities that had previously united the two states.[116] Moreover, numerous pamphlets bewailing English depredations circulated among the public. Such publications were frequently angry and indignant about what they considered to be acts of violent piracy. One pamphlet, published in 1653 during the First Anglo-Dutch War, accused the "perfidious English government" of employing all sorts of "falsehoods and pretexts" to capture Dutch vessels, all to the Netherlands' great loss.[117] Another one, appearing in 1672, bemoaned the English government's loosely regulated and alluring "piracy procedures," government policies that allowed and encouraged injurious privateering to flourish.[118] Yet another pamphlet—this one in the form of a *praatje* ("conversation") and ostensibly published just before the outbreak of the Second Anglo-Dutch War—found English assaults to be so acute, it argued, that the English could pay their own war costs with captured Dutch booty. Moreover, it accused the English of attacking even while peace still existed between the two states, rendering such acts completely piratical:

> *Burger*: Good day sailor; from where art thou voyaging? It seems to me that thee appears so poor, so shabby.
> *Sailor*: Good day sir. My journey was from Bordeaux, where we were still the master[s] of our ship; but just now, I have come from England, so that it is no wonder that I seem so poor; because I have been completely plundered.
> *Burger*: How was it that your ship was plundered?! . . . After all, ships sail out freely and return home.
> *Sailor*: [The English], They are allowed to act like the Devil—the Englishman takes everything that he can, and . . . [what] good prize[s]—he has well over a hundred of our ships in his harbors.
> *Burger*: What! Does he [i.e., King Charles II] order so many ships captured, [that] verily he shows that he is not a Christian king[?]; people here say that there is still a treaty . . .
> *Sailor*: . . . indeed, he will capture so many ships, that with our own [Dutch]money he can pay for the war.[119]

Yet another pamphlet, written in 1653 during the First Anglo-Dutch War, made more serious allegations against the English privateers. According to this publication, English "pirates" had kidnapped Scottish men and women who (like the majority of the Dutch) were Calvinists. The Englishmen then sold these luckless souls into slavery, both to the Spanish, who took the victims to work in the "tobacco lands"; and to slave dealers in "Guinea" (West Africa), who either sold them, in turn, to others, or had them work in the mines as laborers who, according to the pamphlet, never saw the light of day.[120] (According to the 1651 edition of the *Hollantse Mercurius*, the Scots encouraged privateering against the English as well, although no reference is made to enslaving captives.[121]) Still another pamphlet, this one published in 1672 during the Third Anglo-Dutch War and written by an individual who allegedly had survived capture and persecution by English "pirates" (*zeeroovers*), manifested profound anger at the "godless" English. Written in poetic form, the pamphlet depicts the "enemy" English and their "pirates" as lacking any semblance of law and morality, expresses indignation at their policy of capturing the ships of Christian nations, and judges their privateering practices to be worse than those of the Turks.[122]

Naturally, with the English competing with the Dutch for dominance in the East Indies, the VOC faced its share of troubles from English sea robbers, especially during the late seventeenth century and early eighteenth century. English "pirates" were something of a constant nuisance,[123] pillaging valuable booty from Dutch ships and storehouses.[124] Despite anger and frustration at these predatory English intruders, VOC authorities were often unsure about how to treat the ones they apprehended. This indecisiveness resulted in diverse and erratic judgments, all punitive but varied, ranging from death sentences,[125] to transfer to other VOC jurisdictions[126] and homeland Admiralty courts,[127] to confiscations of goods and vessels,[128] to forced labor as VOC soldiers in the Far East.[129]

Part of this confusion apparently derived from the perennial conundrum surrounding the identities of these marauders—that is, were they "pirates" or "privateers"? While Company records generally reflect language confirming the former characterization, they also show that VOC officials did go out of their way to search for letters of commission that would establish an alleged pirate's lawful privateer identity. A valid letter of commission gave Company authorities pause, as their own documents—which question how intensely the VOC should pursue and assail "Pirates in the Indies with or without Commissions"—patently reveal.[130] For theoretically, according to Western understanding, a proper letter of commission (or "letter of marque") was supposed to serve as some sort of protection, as well as permit its holder to bring any of his prizes into a neutral port and sell them.[131] Even if VOC personnel located such letters of commission, however, they still maintained lingering suspicions, for why was an English privateer cruising the Dutch waters of the East Indies, a place, they felt, he had no right to be? This question seemed especially relevant after 1688, when the Netherlands' Stadholder William of Orange also assumed the English throne as King William III. (The WIC harbored similar reservations about the status of "pirates" and "privateers" in their jurisdiction, even when such sea robbers preyed upon the Company itself. In 1675, for instance, WIC authorities felt obliged to obtain and review the commissions of the French "pirate ships" that had plundered 100,000 pieces-of-eight from the Company.[132])

Take the case of Daniel Kennedy. According to VOC records, Kennedy was a "famous pirate" from England. The Company apprehended him in Batavia in December 1702. Kennedy contended that he carried a letter of marque from King William III of England (who was, of course, also William III, Stadholder of the Dutch Republic). Company officials, however, arrested him, confiscated his ship, and proceeded to inspect carefully his documents, his vessel, and his claims. Even if his papers were legal—even if he were a lawful privateer according to the definition understood by the Dutch—VOC authorities still sought to know why Kennedy was in the Indies.[133] His ultimate fate is unknown, but certainly the records show that despite the language the Company personnel used to describe him (*zeeroover*), international legal norms dictated that they could not immediately dismiss him as a mere criminal "pirate."

Another case dating from the early eighteenth century is equally illustrative. In late 1704 and early 1705, Company officials received word that the renowned English privateer, buccaneer, and explorer William Dampier had arrived in the Indies.[134] Dampier's identity apparently required no explanation—his exploits made his name familiar to the Company's Governing Council. By July 1706, Dampier's ship had fallen into disrepair, and Company officials were able to bring him to Batavia.[135] On August 2, VOC authorities proceeded to question him and examine his vessel, his crew, his intentions, and his belongings; two Spanish prisoners were also taken into custody.[136] By the next day, after their preliminary investigation was complete, Company officials were demanding that Dampier hand over a chest filled with silver, but he resisted.[137] Meanwhile, Company officials grew angry with Dampier's crew, who declined to cooperate further and refused to leave until the VOC had given them fair restitution for the goods that the Company had confiscated. This state of affairs continued until August 12, when the crew finally consented to reboard their vessel (without restitution, it seems).[138] Dampier and the Company persisted in their tussle over the silver-filled chest until October 5, when the Company's governing authorities abruptly decided to close the case, and Dampier was apparently released.[139] He returned safely to England, and later made several more famous voyages, including an ill-fated trip to northwest Australia in 1709, and a very remunerative, around-the-world privateering expedition in 1708–1711.

One of the accusations that the Dutch made against the English privateers was that the English targeted and plundered Christians. This was a practice that, according to the Dutch, made the English no better than the Barbary corsairs, and therefore rendered them despicable and morally degenerate.[140] Such a charge was a very serious and critical one indeed, for along with the Dunkirkers, no privateering group seems to have caused the Dutch more distress and consternation than the Barbary corsairs. These sea robbers from North Africa did worrisome damage to Dutch shipping and were involved in the enslavement and killing of many Dutch seamen. Whether the Dutch called them pirates, privateers, or corsairs, the Barbary marauders represented a real and serious threat to Dutch trade.

It is useful for a moment to consider the confusion over the status of the Barbary corsairs, that is, were they pirates or privateers? In most of their diplomatic communications with the North African authorities, the Dutch politely employed the terms "warships" and "corsairs" to identify the Barbary sea robbers. Within their own domestic media, however, they generally referred to these marauders as "pirates" and "robbers."[141] How did it happen, then, that in the eyes of the Dutch, these North Africans were more often than not viewed as criminal "pirates" (*zeerovers*, *roovers*),[142] while according to North African standards, they were lawful and successful privateers (*kapers*)? Of course, this thorny puzzle of proper identity and nomenclature was a general problem in the early modern maritime world, for the licensed, letter of marque–carrying privateers of one state often were criminal pirates in the eyes of another. Still, the case of the Barbary corsairs was more complicated.

There were two important reasons why the Dutch did not regard the Barbary corsairs as legitimate privateers. The first was because of an international agreement made between the Republic and the Ottoman Empire at the beginning of the seventeenth century: the so-called Capitulation of the Sultan of Turkey, formalized in 1612 (and renewed in 1681).[143] According to this accord, the Ottoman sultan agreed that the Turks would not disturb Dutch shipping, specifically that they would not confiscate goods which were transported in Dutch merchant ships, even if these goods belonged to the sultan's adversaries. Additionally, the sultan promised that any passengers on these Dutch ships—whether they be enemies of the Ottomans or not—would be released immediately.[144] Seventeenth-century historian Simon de

Vries contended that the sultan had struck such a deal because the Dutch had manumitted Muslims enslaved by the Spanish, which had happened when the Dutch captured the city of Sluis during the Dutch Revolt. So appreciative was the sultan, de Vries says, that he invited the Dutch to trade as merchants in his lands.[145] Because the Barbary corsair states were officially under the suzerainty of the Ottoman sultan, the Dutch argued that the 1612 Capitulation should apply to these North African polities. In turn, the Dutch contended that any Barbary molestation of Dutch shipping was illegal and criminal, or, in other words, piratical. For the most part, however, the Barbary states' leaders ignored the Capitulation and did not feel that they were bound to honor it.[146]

The second reason why the Dutch usually considered the Barbary corsairs to be pirates and not privateers was that the letters of marque the North Africans carried did not conform to European standards. According to Western rules, only a sovereign prince or government could issue privateering commissions or letters of marque, and only during time of war. Because the Barbary sea robbers' commissions bore only the mark of their own city's local governing authority and were not signed by their technical overlord, the Ottoman sultan, and, moreover, were not necessarily produced during formal hostilities, the Dutch did not recognize them as legal privateering documents.[147] To the Dutch, the term "privateer" had a strict legal meaning, and to grant a looser definition was to vitiate the spirit of the Dutch mantra of international trade: "free ship, free goods, free people."

Contemporary sources are replete with references to the violence of the Barbary corsairs and the damage they wrought on the Dutch. As early as 1609, a firsthand account written by Andrew Barker, a former English captive in Tunis, reported that the corsairs of that city were greatly "strengthened forces, which continually encreaseth by the Ships of England and Holland, which they daily surprise . . ."[148] By way of example, Barker related that in just one day, the Tunisians had captured "Foure great ships of Holland, of three hundred and foure hundred Tunnes apeece . . ." Other victimized Dutch ships included the *Bull* of Amsterdam (weighing 500 tons), and "two more [in] her company," as well as the *Tobias* of Amsterdam, and an unidentified Dutch vessel of 500 tons, worth 24,000 pounds.[149]

According to Simon de Vries, such attacks had begun only after the commencement of the Netherlands' Twelve Years' Truce with Spain (1609–1621). Before this time, the Barbary peoples—who felt an intense antipathy toward Spain—considered themselves kindred spirits with the citizens of the Dutch Republic, fellow warriors against the despised government of Castile. As soon as the Truce was initiated, however, the Algerians did not lose much time in attacking Dutch ships, and the rest of the North African corsairs quickly followed suit.[150] From this point on, the Dutch were almost relentlessly harassed by the Barbary corsairs. Klaas Heeringa, who drew his material from archives throughout Europe, cites multiple references to Barbary attacks against the Dutch.[151] Dutch trade company logs, too, include notice of seamen who lost their lives while battling the North African marauders.[152]

Simon De Vries also pointed out that from 1609 on, the number of active corsairs increased each year. For example, in 1617, the corsairs of Tunis and Algiers alone comprised more than 60 ships; by 1620, their number had swelled to 80–90 ships.[153] And he cites further evidence of the hardship these corsairs caused when he notes that the States-General received frequent and vociferous complaints from Dutch merchants, particularly in 1614, 1617, 1650–1656, and 1660.[154]

Admiralty of the Maas criminal records provide more specific information about the harm Barbary corsairs inflicted upon the Dutch. A case from December 1614 reveals that a group of Barbary marauders in custody had, during the previous nine months, used not a conventional North African galley, but, instead, a large sailing ship armed with 18 cannons to capture numerous Dutch, English, and French vessels.[155] Another pamphlet further relates that these same corsairs had captured 35–36 ships during their career, and despite a recent truce, had plundered more than 30 tons of merchandise from Amsterdam merchants alone. Booty included lots of money (e.g., from just one heist, they had plundered ƒ.12,000 worth of pieces-of-eight), gold, precious gems, jewelry, tallow, wheat, iron, weapons, herring, and sardines. The pamphlet also complained that these corsairs were but one contingent of Barbary pirates who had "infested" the seas for "innumerable years."[156]

These same sources reveal that the so-called North African pirates involved in this case, were, in actuality, of diverse ethnic and national backgrounds (see Appendix VI). So, while the governments of North African cities such as Mamora, Salé, Algiers, Tripoli, and Tunis actively encouraged and sponsored the Barbary corsairs' activities, it is not at all true that the pirates themselves were always of North African descent. In this particular example, the corsairs included men from England, France, Scotland, Ireland, Norway, the Southern Netherlands, Germany, North Africa, and even the Republic itself.[157] Simon de Vries also affirms that the Barbary corsairs included many lapsed European Christians among their number.[158] He cites by way of example the composition of a "pirate fleet" that set out from Algiers in 1660. Among the 18 ships that departed from that city, 13 of the captains were Christian apostates of European descent: 6 Greeks, 1 Dane, 1 Italian (from Genoa), 1 Welshman, 1 Englishman, 1 Swede, and 2 Frenchmen. Furthermore, of the four corsair vessels that remained in port, three were commanded by "renegade" Christian captains from England and Portugal.[159]

This case provides additional details about the practices of the Barbary corsairs. A number of the men—all Europeans—were seasoned pirates who had worked the Mediterranean for months. Pardoned by the duke of Florence for these first offenses, they sailed to Mamora for the express purpose of joining a corsair crew based there—a crew whose captain and officers, again, were Europeans, with some even being of aristocratic descent (including a general named "Mandarin" and their captain, Hugo Clerck). Once at sea, they augmented their number by impressing sailors whose ships they captured.[160] The Spanish seizure of Mamora in 1614 hindered them not a bit; they simply moved their base of operations to Salé and resumed their predatory patrols. They were a violent gang who used tortures such as "woolding" to obtain what they wanted. By the time the Dutch naval Captains Moy Lambert and Ellert Thomasszoon—both of whom had been dispatched by the States-General per the bitter complaints of Dutch merchants, and who had slyly disguised their warships as French merchant vessels—encountered their quarry, the corsairs numbered approximately 65 men. In the end, Lambert and Thomasszoon vanquished them on November 2, 1614, and while many perished in the battle, the Dutchmen still brought back 52 to face trial in the Netherlands. When the Admiralty officials interrogated and ultimately tortured some of the pirates, the corsairs revealed the hiding places of some of their treasure, including a gold chain set with precious stones (whose worth, a pamphlet breathlessly exclaimed, was "well over 100 pounds"), and two gold plates worth approximately $f.600$.[161] In the end, most of the corsairs were hanged.[162]

It is important to note that while the Barbary corsairs represented a grave threat to Mediterranean shipping, their attacks against the Dutch were by no means confined to that body of water.[163] They also prowled the African coast, and even ventured as far as the Red Sea region,[164] searching for Dutch (and other Christian) prey. North African pirates attacked a WIC ship, the *St. Pieter*, in the vicinity of the Canary Islands in 1687, confiscating a large number of goods, capturing ten seamen, and burning the vessel after a grueling battle.[165] Barbary raiders also assaulted VOC ships in the same location.[166] In general, late-seventeenth-century WIC authorities expressed concern about the trade route between Angola and Curaçao, which they felt was vulnerable to North African depredations. As a result, they vowed to augment their ships' weaponry and crews.[167] These leaders had good cause for concern, for according to Simon de Vries, after 1652, the Barbary corsairs increasingly took to the seas in large, powerful fleets, that typically included at least 20 vessels.[168]

The Barbary corsairs also ventured into Western European waters. Dutch officials worried constantly about attacks by the North Africans along the coasts of Portugal and Spain, and launched naval expeditions to "purify" (as they put it) the seas of their menacing presence there.[169] In 1650–1651, a strongly armed "Turkish pirate ship" (a commonly used seventeenth-century synonym) had been spotted in the English Channel, where already it had captured two ships from Holland, and three from Zeeland.[170] The situation had not changed 30 years later, when a 1686 edition of the *Ordinaire Leydse Courant* reported a similar event.[171] Nor were the North Africans shy about patrolling the French coast; the corsairs from the 1614 Admiralty of the Maas criminal sentencing records, for instance, generally targeted the Spanish and French coasts,[172] although the Dutch apprehended them off the coast of England.[173] Likewise, a 1686 edition of the *Ordinaire Leydse Courant* included a report about two groups of passengers who, while sailing along the western coast of France, had become so frightened of Barbary marauders in the vicinity, that they had abandoned their ships and sought refuge in Brest.[174]

Surely nothing rankled the Dutch more than the fact that the North Africans dared to penetrate actual Dutch waters. As early as 1623, Barbary corsairs cruising the English Channel stopped in Veere, Zeeland, where they were successful in acquiring food and supplies.[175] A late-seventeenth-century edition of the *Ordinaire Leydse Courant* further declared that three vessels belonging to people whom the paper termed Barbary "scoundrels" had been spotted off the coast of Zeeland, anchored only three or four miles from Vlissingen.[176] Such "visits" were not only unwelcome, but in many cases illegal, since the Dutch had a long-term understanding with the North Africans—especially the Algerians—that the Barbary corsairs were not permitted to frequent the Republic's coasts, either to buy war materials or to sell their captured prizes.[177]

Sometimes, the corsairs employed elaborate subterfuges to lend their activities a veneer of legality. In 1686, for instance, the Admiralty of Zeeland complained to the States-General that the "Admiralty of Algiers" (as they politely put it) had captured a number of "richly laden" ships from Zeeland. The Algerians contended that they were perfectly entitled to do this, claiming that the Zeeland ships were carrying improper passports. The States-General strenuously protested these captures in a diplomatic correspondence to the Dey (governor) of Algiers, affirming that the format of Dutch passports was recognized as valid by both the British and the French, and in keeping with the criteria stipulated in the April 30, 1679, peace treaty between Algiers and the Dutch Republic. Nevertheless, in the interest of stopping such seizures, the Dutch authorities decided to print and promptly distribute new passports that the Algerians could not find objectionable.[178]

Such incidents were not unusual. Although the Dutch periodically forged peace agreements with the various Barbary regencies,[179] relations between the North African city states and the Republic were often stormy and hostile. To that end, the States-General issued explicit instructions as to how Dutch ships should protect themselves, and how Dutch seamen should behave in the event that any Dutch vessels—whether naval or merchant—should encounter the Barbary rovers.

A States-General proclamation issued in 1655, which concerned ships traveling to the Mediterranean Sea and the Levant,[180] is representative. In an effort to forestall Barbary depredations against Dutch seamen—depredations that, as the *Placaat* read, involved "evil-doing, captures, loss of life, and shedding of blood"[181]—the States-General instituted a series of protective measures including instructions to shipowners regarding the minimum size ship they could use, the types and quantity of weapons with which they should outfit their craft, and the number of sailors who had to be on board. Ships were also required to convoy with at least one other similar vessel from their company, and were forbidden to transport any ordnance or naval stores (such as masts and rigging) to the cities of Salé, Algiers, or Tunis without the express permission of the States-General. If a shipowner chose to ignore these mandates, the government threatened to declare his vessel uninsurable. Moreover, the States-General vowed to impose a hefty fine of *f.*1000, as well as seize the contents of the offending party's freight. (Should one go so far as to transport contraband materiel and supplies, the punishment was execution.) To detect any recalcitrant shipowners, the government developed an inspection system using the local magistrates of the relevant Dutch ports; they also created incentives for these local authorities (as well as fellow mariners) to report those not in compliance with the rules.[182]

The States-General drafted specific directives for the Dutch Navy as well, usually in the context of special missions to the North African coast. The instructions given to Captain Moy Lambert in 1618 are emblematic.[183] The States-General enjoined the well-equipped fleet of 14 ships to travel to the region around Algiers, Tunis, and "other pirates nests along the coast there"; they were also to patrol the waters around the Spanish islands of Mallorca, Minorca, Ibiza, and any other islands between there and Sicily. The goal of this expedition was clear: the navy was to seek out and destroy the Barbary corsairs—to induce so much fear in them by shooting, burning, and pillaging their ships that the North Africans would flee the seas. The government also pledged to reward handsomely any Dutch ship that apprehended a Barbary vessel. Special incentives included bonus wages (specifically, one month's additional salary for each pirate captured), equal access to profits earned from the sale of the ship's goods, and for the captain of each conquering naval ship, the right to take the prize's provisions and small weaponry. These periodic naval jaunts to hunt down the North African corsairs were successful both in frightening off at least some Barbary ships[184] and in raising money for the Republic's Admiralties.[185]

The protective actions that the Dutch took against the Barbary corsairs[186] were representative of the defensive actions they employed against pirates (and enemy powers) generally. From the time of the Republic's birth, the authorities mandated such measures as a precaution against the myriad of dangers that lurked on the high seas. A proclamation issued by the States of Holland in 1596, concerning merchant vessels traveling to and from Norway and the Baltic, is typical in this regard. The rules were detailed and serious. Ships were not to leave the Republic's shores unless sailing with a proper convoy. Specifically, ships had to travel in a fleet of at least 30 vessels, and were to be accompanied by two warships, each heavily armed and outfitted for combat (the costs of the weaponry and ammunition were to be shared among the convoying ships).[187] Moreover, all ships were to use the Norwegian port of Vleckero as their point of departure before returning to the Netherlands; the ships were to wait there until 30 accumulated and they could begin the trip home. As a disincentive to flout the rules, the government fined ships whose captains or owners refused to travel in convoys, directing the money to one of the Admiralty colleges. Moreover, the authorities warned, vessels that chose to go it alone could not appeal to the government or navy for help—any ship acting so cavalierly and recklessly would bear all costs and damages incurred by an enemy attack.[188]

By the same token, courageous behavior was generously rewarded with special premiums. The authorities promised to compensate any Dutch vessel that suffered damage because its captain and crew were bold enough to attack an enemy ship while underway. Should the brave crew succeed in sinking the hostile ship, the government vowed double compensation; and should they drive the enemy ship aground, the lucky Dutch crew was to enjoy a reward equal to the value of the enemy ship and the goods it was carrying. Likewise, any Dutch crew that was able to seize an enemy vessel was to receive that prize and all of the goods it was transporting.[189] The ordinance also included firm reminders to convoying naval ships to always show their lights when traveling at night; prescriptions for the strength, weight, and number of weapons to be used; and formulas for calculating fines, premiums, and payments to the Admiralties.[190]

Such measures did help to protect vulnerable Dutch merchant vessels during the course of the seventeenth century. Still, of course, by no means did they stem the problem of piracy and privateering altogether. Such maritime predation posed a continual threat to Dutch shipping, and therefore, to the Republic's general welfare. It is not surprising to learn, then, that the Golden Age public was gripped and fascinated by tales of piracy and privateering on the high seas.

Such accounts appeared throughout the Golden Age in all forms of printed media, including newspapers, almanacs, pamphlets and "blue books," engravings and prints, and books. This "pirate literature" was widespread also because it represented a blending of two of the more popular foci of public interest: maritime adventure stories and tales of crime. Indeed, it seems that the appetite for things maritime and criminal was almost insatiable, as particularly well-liked titles often went through any number of reprints. Willem Ysbrantszoon Bontekoe's extremely popular *Memorable Account of the Eight-Years Long and Very Adventurous Voyage*,[191] for example—a narrative of an ill-starred trip to the East Indies—appeared in a plethora of editions throughout the seventeenth and eighteenth centuries. Such reprintings included 32 different editions in the seventeenth century alone, with another 21 during the eighteenth century.[192]

Which types of maritime lore interested the Dutch public? First and foremost, accounts of travels abroad, especially those composed by intrepid Dutchmen.[193] Numerous publications devoted to Dutch sea journeys to far-off lands appeared in both pamphlet and book form. Usually purporting to be nonfictional texts—which, in actuality, represented blendings of fact and fantasy, of realistic reportage and fanciful hyperbole—these accounts detailed the frightening trials and tribulations of the voyage, the exoticism of foreign seas and lands, and the "peculiar" habits and customs of diverse foreign cultures. While some tales used realistic details but ultimately leaned more toward the imaginary (such as the 1624 *Strange Adventure of Two Beautiful Lovers*, the rollicking story of a dauntless couple who discover treasure in the West Indies after overcoming formidable adversities),[194] others endeavored to portray a vivid, informative, and accurate picture of life abroad in Asia, Africa, the Middle East, and the Americas.[195]

Particularly popular were chronicles and descriptions of the East Indies, that dazzling, wondrous, and faraway place in which the Dutch would enjoy a centuries-long colonial presence. Favorite texts related everything from the story of the first Dutch expedition to the Indies, to particular travelers' memoirs, to "shoot-em-up" accounts of battles between the Dutch and other colonial powers.[196] Naturally, works about the West Indies attracted readers too.[197]

At the same time, the Dutch public was not just interested in spectacular stories about distant, exotic places. Pieces devoted to the more pedestrian aspects of the maritime industry were appealing. In almost every edition, Dutch newspapers included updates on the status of the Republic's fleets, whether belonging to the trade companies, the Admiralties, or individual merchants. (The ships of foreign powers often were assessed as well.) For instance, the newspaper *Ordinaire Leydse Courant*, which was published three times per week, always noted all incoming and outgoing Dutch vessels, and provided the ships' names, their captains, their destinations, and their cargoes. Likewise, should there be no maritime activity that day, the paper indicated that "there is no news from the sea [today]."[198] Papers also reported regularly on such subjects as communications from traveling ships and updates on their progress,[199] dramatic weather conditions at sea,[200] government appropriations to the navy,[201] and privateer activity.[202] Affairs within the trade companies and Admiralties were also scrutinized and discussed; one series of articles that ran in the *Ordinaire Leydse Courant* in 1686, for example, divulged a pattern of corruption, fraud, and embezzlement at the Admiralties of the Maas and Amsterdam.[203]

Naturally, newspapers were not the only sources of information about nautical concerns. Notable maritime stories, sometimes accompanied by illustrations, were always featured in the various almanacs, which were published annually. The 1666 edition of the *Hollandtze Mercurius*, for example, included long stories about Dutch naval battles, expeditions, and triumphs that had taken place that year, as well as a description of the devastating English capture of 11 treasure-filled VOC ships returning to the Republic from Batavia.[204] Such almanacs also noted the dates during the year when important trade company fleets, such as the VOC convoy from Batavia, arrived.[205] Additionally, pamphlets devoted to seafaring news and commentary were plentiful, and discussed any and all nautical subjects, such as critiques of the trade companies,[206] firsthand accounts of interesting or harrowing travels,[207] descriptions of naval campaigns (both Dutch and foreign),[208] Dutch captures of enemy vessels,[209] new nautical technology,[210] or anything else pertaining to the maritime industry. And, of course, maritime images produced by Dutch artists—depicting everything from Dutch naval fleets in battle, to tempests at sea, to quiet harbor scenes, to shipwrecks—were widespread and popular.

One subject that especially intrigued the Dutch reading public was that of criminality at sea. Pamphlets and newspapers breathlessly discussed tales of maritime murder,[211] mutiny,[212] and mayhem.[213] Such fervid interest in the sordid underbelly of the shipping trades only reflected the public's broader appetite for anything pertaining to crime and criminals in general.[214]

Countless books, pamphlets, and newspapers disseminated new criminal laws,[215] carried news of efforts to fight crime,[216] and chattered about criminality at home[217] and abroad.[218] "Crime and disaster compendia"—indices of all sorts of horrific happenings that had taken place both within the Republic and beyond its borders—often assumed a moral tone as they reported on sensationalized mayhem.[219] Within this general interest in crime, thieves and robbers attracted so much attention that an entire genre of literature—both fiction and nonfiction—arose to fulfill the public's keen interest.[220]

It is not surprising, then, that given this particular literary context, publications about pirates and enemy privateers were both popular and widespread among Golden Age Dutch readers. For what were pirates other than maritime thieves, wild marauding criminals who used hidden harbors and the indefensible, open seas to practice their own particular and frightening brand of banditry? In one fell swoop, pirate stories combined the excitement and intrigue of maritime adventure with the horror and spine-tingling dread of crime tales. One finds that works such as *The Beginning, Middle, and End of the Pirate Career of the Most Famous Pirate Around, Claes G. Compaen*, Exquemelin's *Buccaneers of America*, William Lithgow's *Rare Adventures and Painful Peregrinations of William Lithgow*, and Captain Charles Johnson's *The General History of the Robberies and Murders of the Most Notorious Pyrates* were wildly popular in the Netherlands during the seventeenth and eighteenth centuries and were reprinted manifold times.[221]

This public fascination with pirates (and, by extension, privateers) pervaded all popular media, from newspapers, pamphlets, and almanacs, to fine books illustrated with carefully crafted engravings. It also manifested itself as an appetite for both nonfictional and fictional descriptions of pirate life. Newspapers and almanacs claimed to recount unvarnished, factual accounts of pirate and privateer attacks, captures, and battles with the Dutch authorities. A 1639 report about the Dunkirk privateers from an Amsterdam paper, the *Courante uyt Italien ende Duytschlandt*,[222] represents a typical example. The article, whose title made a point of its supposed veracity,[223] relates the action of an intense and violent contest between the Dutch and their Dunkirk adversaries. The account was extremely lengthy and detailed by the journalistic standards of the day. But then again, this was a battle that merited public attention, for it had featured a famous Dutch admiral, and resulted in grave casualties on the Dunkirk side (320 dead and wounded), a definitive Dutch victory, and the Dutch capture of three Dunkirk ships and numerous sailors. Other examples of newsworthy subjects were Dutch sailors who survived pirate imprisonment and returned to the homeland,[224] the pirate capture of foreign vessels,[225] the Dutch capture of pirates or enemy privateers, and information about pirates in vital mercantile areas.[226]

The fare of almanacs was somewhat similar, offering, for example, "authentic" accounts of menacing pirates in the various parts of the world, tales of privateer capture of Dutch trade vessels, and efforts by the Dutch government to combat such assaults. A 1686 edition of the *Snelle Mercurius*, for instance, noted that on September 8 of that year, "came news from Jamaica that pirates with seven ships were [now] cruising the South Sea" (i.e., the Pacific Ocean below Central America), having withdrawn from Panama.[227] And a 1666 edition of the *Hollandtze Mercurius* listed the ships captured and the seamen killed or wounded that year in the ongoing battle between the Dutch Navy and English privateers; it also discussed the measures Dutch authorities were taking to deal with these English aggressions.[228]

In the realm of pamphlets and books, however, the character of the pirate—whether fictional or not—usually fulfilled a didactic function, representing evil incarnate or serving as the depraved counterpoint to the noble, "civilized," and pious persons or individual being praised, thereby inculcating in the reader the virtues of ethical and sacrificial moral conduct. Seagoing marauders easily performed this role in texts from such explicitly sermonizing genres as hagiographies[229] and works of moral edification.[230] However, even in such purportedly "authentic" works as the biography of Claas Compaen, Exquemelin's *Buccaneers of America*, and Dionisus van der Sterre's memoir of Dutch privateer, Jan Erasmus Reyning,[231] pirates emerge as resolutely villainous creatures whose whole way of life contrasts with that of the upright culture of the seventeenth-century Dutch Republic.

The Dutch reading public eagerly consumed pamphlets detailing the harrowing experiences of Dutch ships that encountered pirates and enemy privateers,[232] as well as those that recounted Dutch victories over the marauders,[233] translated foreign reports about the capture of pirates and privateers,[234] and related the crimes, confessions, and/or sentences of individual sea robbers.[235] And while such texts claimed to be "truthful" renditions of what had actually taken place, these purportedly factual publications almost always manifested a clear moral voice, with the pirate assuming the role of fallen citizen or evil rogue—characters whose contemptible career choice (and the consequences resulting) were due purely and simply to their own poor judgment and foolish use of free will.

A perfect example is a pamphlet dating from 1615 that relates the events surrounding the mass execution of 24 pirates in Rotterdam and Amsterdam (figure 4.2).[236] This international gang of sea robbers—the band of Barbary corsairs led by Captain Hugo Clerk, a former English gentleman from Southhampton—were sentenced to be hanged after Dutch naval captains Moy Lambert and Ellert Thomasszoon captured them at sea. While the pamphlet articulates in a factual, straightforward, and "journalistic" manner the details of the pirates' crimes and the tale of their arrest, it ostensibly takes some poetic license when it claims to record the call-and-response "Hymn of Lamentation" allegedly sung between the pirates and Captain Clerk. Sung "to the tune of the 'English Fortune' " (or so the pamphlet says), the lamentation runs an extensive 16 verses in length, with Captain Clerck crying out 8 verses, and his corsair crewmen responding in kind. The tone and words are nothing if not morally instructive, containing admissions of guilt, supplications to God, expressions of regret, entreaties for forgiveness, and acknowledgment of the correct moral authority of God and the Dutch judicial

Figure 4.2 Woodcut, *Bekentenisse van Hugo Clerck Capiteyn der ZeeRoovers/die met zyn Complicen ende aenhang gejusticeert zijn tot Amsterdam* . . . (Amsterdam, 1615). Verzameling Thysius.

system. Captain Clerk and his men, so the pamphlet declares, ultimately realized that their behavior had gone beyond the pale.

A second pamphlet dating from around the same time is equally representative. This publication, *On the Glorious Victory Obtained Against the Pirates*,[237] relates the Dutch Navy's triumphant conquest of two bands of Anglo-Irish pirates. While the pamphlet certainly supplies many standard factual details about the conquest—such as that four Dutch men-of-war were used to capture and burn the ships of the pirates lurking near the Irish coast, that the pirates' ships were well-armed and extremely dangerous, and that the gang of sea robbers defeated near Norway included more than 60 men—also patently evident is a clear, morally didactic voice.

This voice certainly manifests itself in the descriptive passages of the text, eliciting sympathy for the Dutch merchants who were the pirates' victims, inspiring admiration for the brave Dutch naval captains who reined in the marauders, and condemning the villainous sea robbers. Of course, the Dutch captains—including, once again, the intrepid Moy Lambert, this time joined by Jacob Janssen, and Captains Cleuter and Pellecoren (whose first names are not recorded)—are all portrayed as exemplars of supreme moral integrity and valor. At the same time, the pirates are denounced "because they have perpetrated much evil," "created many widows and orphans...," and "polluted" the seas.[238] Where this moralistic sermonizing becomes most apparent, however, is in the "Triumphal Hymn on the Victory Secured Against the Pirates," a song of nine verses that immediately follows the more cut-and-dry reportage of the events.

Certainly, the hymn teaches moral lessons about "good" versus "evil" conduct by contrasting the characters of the Dutch Navy men with that of the pirates. The naval captains and their stalwart sailors are "clever," "intrepid," "valorous," "devout," "brave," "contemplative," and "bold"; while the pirates are likened to beastly "tigers and bears" who are "wicked," "merciless," "cruel," "disgraceful," and "godless." The anthem makes this lesson all the more inspiring and heartfelt by directly associating the Dutch seamen's ethical virtue with Republican nationalism, first, by enjoining would-be singers to perform the hymn to the tune of "Wilhelmus van Nassouwen" ("William of Nassau" or "the Wilhelmus," the ever-popular and rousing Sea Beggar song that served as the Republic's unofficial national anthem). Moreover, like so many other Golden Age texts, in describing the deeds of the valiant Dutch captains (and thereby framing the moral action that takes place), the pamphlet invokes the notion of deliverance from slavery. Responding to the mournful entreaties of so many beleaguered and impoverished Dutch merchants whose welfare depends upon the fruits of the lucrative Baltic trade,

> Stout-hearted Captain Cleuter
> and pious Pellecoren
> have during this season
> sought to liberate [*bevrijden*]
> the Norwegian waters
> with outfitted ships . . .[239]

In the end, this Dutch goal of "liberation" succeeds: after two furious battles in which the navy men's "bullets fly lustily," the heroic Dutch captains and their men capture the pirates and bring them in chains to Amsterdam. There, the marauders are imprisoned and ultimately receive their "reward" of "climbing to their grave with a high ladder" (i.e., being hanged). And Dutch trade—now emancipated from the enslaving snares of predatory sea robbers—resumes once again.

This depiction of the pirate as a debauched and debased being is also evident in Dutch books published during this era. In the *Very Considerable Journeys of Jan Erasmus Reyning* (1691),[240] for example, Dionisius van der Sterre claimed that the general reputation of the privateer was that of a drunken and incompetent person who was prone to wickedness and anger; pirates, he implied, were that much worse.[241] Exquemelin's buccaneers, moreover, are wild men who give "themselves freely to all manner of vices and debauchery . . ."; they "are hugely cruel and tyrannical . . . barbarous. . . ."[242] The engravings that accompany Exquemelin's text make this characterization all too clear. Presenting scenes of violence, terror, and mayhem, they depict pirates as brutal sadists inflicting manifold unspeakable tortures on their helpless victims (figure 4.3). The title page only heightens the intensity of this presentation by contrasting the "dandified" appearance of the buccaneers with the pitiful entreaties of their beseeching victims and cartouches showing episodes of horrific buccaneer cruelty, including roasting victims alive on a spit (figure 4.4).

A popular poem dating from the mid-seventeenth century made the additional point that such crimes do not pay. Using famous Dutch pirate Claes Compaen as the moral exemplar one should condemn, the rhyme acknowledges that the *zeerover* indeed acquired riches during his ignoble career, but that such ill-begotten wealth is ephemeral and provides little comfort when one is old and frail. Moreover, the verse affirms, one should not envy the lot of a man such as Compaen, but rather should keep one's heart pure and clean, free from the moral taint of cupidity, robbery, and malice:

> The Pirate Klaas Kompaan,
> Robbed profusely
> on the Ocean,
> But in his old age
> Destitute, meek and bent,
> He had to wander in search of his bread.
> Stolen goods do not prosper.
> A good heart does not envy.[243]

But it is in the preface of Compaen's biography, *The Beginning, Middle, and End of the Pirate Career of the Most Famous Pirate Around, Claes G. Compaen*,[244] that the morally edifying purpose of the seventeenth-century pirate becomes especially apparent. The anonymous author, who went only by the *nom-de-plume* "an enthusiast of novelties," admitted that he was quite aware that he had written a book about a corrupted individual, a man whose infamy was known the world over.[245] To treat such a ignominious person, the author confessed, might seem to some readers a peculiar and even dangerous act, for like a physical illness, Compaen's moral wickedness could

Figure 4.3 Buccaneer Cruelty, engraving, in A.O. Exquemelin, *De Americaensche Zee-Roovers* . . . (Amsterdam: Jan ten Hoorn, 1678), fol. 83. Dousa Kamer.

be "contagious":

> Everyone will probably think it strange that I have taken the trouble to describe the . . . deeds, and injurious journeys of the ultra-famous pirate, Claes Compaen, for indeed, all of his actions . . . have served to bring ruin to various peoples, and in particular, to the inhabitants of our Fatherland, to noble and free maritime commerce, to business conducted in foreign lands, [and] to the

Figure 4.4 A.O. Exquemelin, title page engraving, *De Americaensche Zee-Roovers*... (Amsterdam: Jan ten Hoorn, 1678). Dousa Kamer.

friendship of allies, and what is more, [his deeds] have violated [these people and affairs] in such a manner that many have become poor [as a result] . . . [And many would believe that] such things being written, [are] very dangerous . . . [that] through them [one might] become infected, so that one's heart [also] makes such a journey, [and will] want to put similar actions into effect . . . [246]

But, as the author explained, it is through such perverse accounts that decent people—especially children—learn proper morality, for it is only by studying examples of the "good" and the "bad" that one is able to acquire a real and lasting ethical code. One should use the behavior of "godless, wanton, and resolutely evil men" such as Claes Compaen, he affirmed, as a "mirror" to compare and improve one's own moral character.[247]

Not surprisingly, this particular moral voice was especially evident in works that treated the Barbary corsairs. While it is true that newspapers and almanacs often just employed a "journalistic" voice when discussing the North Africans (e.g., from the 1686 edition of the *Snelle Mercurius* almanac: "Spanish galleys captured a Turkish ship with 200 crewmen aboard, among whom were forty-five Christian slaves who were immediately released"),[248] also typical were tones of sensationalism and horror. Songs and poems addressed the corsairs' alleged perverse lasciviousness, calling them, for example, "scum from Gomorrah."[249] Books such as Simon de Vries's richly illustrated *History of the Barbarians and Their Pirates*,[250] Emanuel de Airanda's *Turkish Slavery*,[251] Albrecht Schiel's *Description of His Life in Barbaria*,[252] and Gallonye's *Disastrous and Very Memorable Trials and Tribulations of a Slave Who Passed Four Years in Salé, Enslaved by the Infidels*[253] illustrated what they described as the wrenchingly barbarous conditions under which Christian slaves lived at the hands of their reputedly depraved North African captors. Books such as *The Beyond-Peculiar History of the Marquess of Frene*, which claimed to tell the "astonishing-yet-true" tale of a French noblewoman whose husband had sold her to a "Turkish pirate," depicted the Barbary corsairs as a European woman's worst nightmare.[254] All together, these texts provide any number of vivid anecdotes testifying to the corsairs' cruelty and rapaciousness. Particularly graphic among de Vries's reminiscences are examples of the various fashions by which the North Africans tortured and killed their recalcitrant captives. Jan Luyken's engravings of these alleged brutalities, moreover, gave graphic and startling visual expression to these passages (figures 4.1 and 4.5). The following two cases are illustrative:

> But the most dreadful thing which one saw here [in Algiers] was that some men at the gate [of the city] heaved a [prisoner] onto hooks, from which they let him hang, until he had given up his spirit [i.e., died]. The [captive] men are thrown onto these iron hooks from above; and the [Algerians] let them hang there until they die. This is one of the most gruesome ways they kill people; [a means] by which the condemned one, slowly and very severely, suffers [and] experiences pain.
>
> Shortly before this there was another even more ghastly punishment given to a Spanish [man] . . . His body was put in iron pins, with outstretched arms; his hands were nailed to a cross; his feet, or heels, were nailed to the block. For 72 hours this [poor] wretch remained in [this] dreadful situation . . . [before he died].[255]

Among these texts, special horror was reserved for the "renegades," those Europeans who had deserted their mother countries and joined up with the

Figure 4.5 Jan and Caspar Luiken, "Elendige Straffen Die de Turcken de Slaaven doen Leyden" (dreadful punishments which the Turks make the slaves suffer), engraving, in Simon de Vries, *Historie van Barbaryen, En de zelfs Zee-Roovers...*, Vol. II (Amsterdam: Jan ten Hoorn, 1684), fol. 407. Dousa Kamer.

detestable Mediterranean predators. While these traitors reportedly lived in indulgent comfort and luxury—one is described as dwelling in Tunis "in a most princely and *magnificent* state"[256]—the price they paid, the sources affirm, was the complete and total contamination of their souls. The North Africans were so corrupt—so base and low—these texts imply, that their culture entirely obliterated any semblance of "civilized Christian behavior" in the Europeans who voluntarily served with them. Consequently, these texts suggest, such Westerners had embraced a depraved and totally degenerate existence. For instance, Andrew Barker's "*True and Certaine Report*" about "*Ward and Danseker, the Two Late Famous Pirates*" claimed to describe the wanton, licentious, and thoroughly immoral lives of these perfidious Western renegades. In detailing the history of the English pirate Ward and his European cronies, Barker painted a picture of lasciviousness and perversity in addition to the expected banditry and violence:

> [These European renegades] accustome their lives to all *disorder*, making their habit and carriage a shore, farre more detestable, and uncomely to be talked of, or by *Christianity* to be condemned and abhorred, then their theeving at Sea, *swearing*, *drinking*, *dicing*, and the utmost enormities that are attended on by consuming *riot* are the least of their *vices*, that can be recited. Unlawfully are their goods got, and more ungodly are they consumed, in that they mix themselves like brute beasts with the enemies of the Savior . . . Nay sinne is grown to that *ranknesse* amongst them, through the fatnesse of *Concupiscence* and *Covetousnesse* . . . I will leave their *Sodomie*, and the rest of their *crying sinnes* . . . to the *Judgement* of the *Just Revenger*, and not give them to be talked of further by my pen.[257]

This was not all, of course. Various forms of media—pamphlets and newspapers, in particular—detailed the difficulties of dealing with the North African rogues, including the various steps the Dutch Navy and other authorities had taken to stop Barbary depredations.[258] Such texts often took a moral tone. Compendia and almanacs listed and elaborated Barbary crimes,[259] and pamphlets related incendiary stories about abused Dutch sailors existing in Barbary captivity.[260] Songs and poems celebrated Dutch—and indeed all Christian—triumphs over the corsairs and depicted the encounters as great moral contests.[261] *Kranten* and *couranten* and pamphlets—such as one 1618 example starring the "valiant" veteran pirate-hunter Moy Lambert, who in this instance, liberated hundreds of slaves from Barbary bondage[262]—presented blow-by-blow accounts of tension-filled battles between the Dutch ships and the North African corsairs, and trumpeted Dutch triumphs as victories of "good" over "evil." (One should note that in 1620, a medallion was struck in honor of Moy Lambert and depicted the stalwart pirate-hunter hanging and throwing overboard 125 Algerian corsairs.)[263] And while the examples cited above were all published during the seventeenth century, such portrayals—especially those that emphasized stories of Europeans helplessly trapped in Barbary bondage—continued to appear through the eighteenth century.[264]

When we see the early modern pirate in a twenty-first-century light—as a quaint rapscallion with a peg leg and parrot perched on his shoulder, a dandy rascal who serves only to entertain and amuse us—we forget the definite and true terror he once inspired centuries ago. While the history of the pirate will always be shrouded in some degree of elusive mystery, modern scholars—even with their dearth of reliable sources—understand that he justifiably intimidated the early modern, maritime world. The pirate was a frightening creature whose very acts of aggression rent at the fabric of the prevailing economic and political order; moreover, their radically communitarian culture represented a revolutionary threat to the early modern status quo.[265] In the eyes of sailors—and, by extension, all those who cared about and relied upon them—the violence that seventeenth-century pirates such as François L'Olonais once sowed was not fictitious, but a real and horrifying threat that might lurk anywhere on the open seas. The fear that the Dunkirk privateers and Barbary corsairs inspired—the dread of mistreatment, imprisonment, bondage, and death—was not make-believe, but based upon actual and immediate happenings, troubling contemporary incidents that could potentially affect any member of the Dutch maritime community, and at any time. Likewise, merchants and governments whose goods were plundered and whose ships were commandeered suffered true pecuniary damage that affected the fortunes of actual families, towns, companies, and nations.

The people of the seventeenth-century Dutch Republic were no exception to this general apprehension that the early modern world maintained vis-à-vis seagoing marauders. In all quarters of the maritime world, Dutch goods became pirate booty, Dutch sailors were maimed, kidnapped, and killed, and the Dutch public was aware of it all. That pirates were feared, loathed, and morally condemned by the citizens of the United Provinces is indisputably true—vanquishing them was a laudatory and even patriotic achievement. This fact becomes apparent when one reads, for example, the mid-seventeenth-century tombstone of Admiral Jan van Galen, who among "his manly and happily-performed deeds," "captured six Dunkirk pirate ships and a very great [amount] of booty from the Barbary peoples . . ."[266] Indeed, many naval tombstones cite the vanquishing of Dunkirk and Barbary marauders as a noble and patriotic accomplishment.[267] To the Golden Age Dutch, the pirate—or at least the foreign pirate or the *zeerover* who attacked Dutch ships—was a moral reprobate and monster, a degenerate who had turned his back on God, endeavored to sack the fine and remunerative workings of "free ship, free goods, free people," and ravaged the lives of innocent seafarers forced to endure his depraved molestations. Thus were pirates condemned in the mass media, hunted by the Admiralties, and hanged in the city gallows. They were creatures indelibly tainted by the stain of their misdeeds, fallen men whose moral compass had gone awry.

Part III

Conclusions

5

Prizes and "Excesses": The Golden Age Pirate

Modern people are quite entertained by the idea of pirates. But in the Golden Age Dutch Republic, piracy—*roverij*—was a base, evil crime, a despicable misdeed that wrought destruction on the Republic's prodigious but vulnerable commerce, terrified mariners, wasted precious naval and judicial resources, alienated allies and neighbors, and even caused occasional domestic tensions. Its practitioners, according to popular sentiment and legal pronouncements, were nothing but depraved, ignoble miscreants, and Dutchmen who fell into this career were profligate, corrupt seamen who opportunistically sought to enhance their own prospects at the expense of their fledging state. Such men were prosecuted and punished to the full extent of Dutch law.

Or were they? As it turns out, when it came to the crime of piracy, the Dutch actually were quite erratic in the dispensation of justice. Dutch authorities often made surprising exceptions to the rules that they themselves had instituted. Within the context of the strict legislative and penal patterns that existed in the Golden Age Netherlands, numerous seamen charged with piracy were punished lightly, pardoned, or even rehabilitated to serve the state. Indeed, some predatory Dutch mariners were never prosecuted at all. In other words, although thieves of other stripes were regularly prosecuted and punished,[1] Dutch pirates often escaped the harsh sanctions that the law claimed they were due. For all of the authorities' pious hand-wringing, protestations of disgust, and dedication to the gallows, they—and the Dutch public in general—sometimes deviated wildly from the professed legal and societal standard when confronted with piracy of a homegrown variety, forgiving convicted criminals or punishing them only with the proverbial slap on the wrist. Even more surprising, they often seem to have looked the other way in these cases, or even to have acted according to the belief that the transgression was minor or inconsequential.

Evidence of this tendency is quite extensive and compelling, and is manifested in numerous types of Golden Age sources, from criminal sentencing records, to contemporary books and pamphlets, to government proclamations. Sometimes, it just took the form of an attitude—a "soft pedaling" sentiment that is reflected in the Dutch authorities' designation of the crime.

For example, the Admiralty of the Maas' criminal sentencing index renamed piratical offenses, thereby eliminating the sting of the label "piracy." Actions that by law constituted *zeeroverij* (piracy on the high seas) and *stroomroverij* (riverine piracy) were given obfuscating or more benign titles such as "plundering of prizes" or "extortion." This propensity also surfaced in laws and proclamations, such as a 1606 States-General *placaat* issued in response to a report that numerous Dutch privateers in search of Spanish victims had instead been attacking the ships of the Republic's allies and even the Dutch themselves. The statesmen admitted that they were aware that these unruly mariners were going beyond the bounds of their privateering commissions—that the "persons and goods" of the Republic's "good citizens" and friends were being "damaged and molested." At the same time, however, they refused to label these alleged actions too harshly, euphemistically calling them "excesses" rather than the more criminal-sounding "piracies" or "robberies."[2] Indeed, the Dutch employed the term "excesses" frequently when referring to Dutch piratical activity.[3]

But the Dutch authorities did more than express this inclination in words and turns of phrase. Sometimes, they went so far as to allow an alleged pirate to slip through their fingers, to run afoul of the law and get away with it. In other words, they chose not to prosecute—or even investigate—the suspect individual. This is what happened, for instance, in an Amsterdam case in which several shipowners were accused of abetting piracy, for the magistrate refused to consider even prosecuting the men.[4] And there is another interesting aspect to this phenomenon as well. Curiously enough, one finds that these supposed reprobates—these reputedly loathsome, fear-inducing pirates—could generate favorable cultural interest. Instead of being vilified, some *zeerovers* were accorded social respect or received approving mention in popular publications. In the just-cited case concerning the Amsterdam shipowners, for example, the suspects' high societal standing made them ineligible for prosecution, or so the magistrate contended.[5]

One discerns this tendency at work in the case of three Dutch "thieves" (*dieven*) who stole "a chest with costly jewels" from the viceroy of Sardinia in December 1650. Absconding with this treasure from the island, the robbers fled on a Dutch ship to convey their booty back to the Netherlands. Upon realizing his loss, the aggrieved viceroy dispatched an armed galley to battle the Dutchmen and retrieve his property. The Sardinians, however, were terrified by the sight of the Dutch thieves "lustily displaying their teeth." So intimidated were the pursuers that "the Galley did not dare to approach / [and] turned back again for Sardinia . . ." The Dutch marauders "came into Texel after several weeks" and landed at Den Helder. They were not prosecuted by the Dutch authorities for their misdeeds. Rather, their exploits were thought exciting and daring enough to warrant mention in the 1651 edition of the annual almanac, *Hollantse Mercurius*, which supplied the details of their adventure without resorting to critical or condemnatory language.[6]

But a much more interesting case in this regard is that of Jan Janszoon, a Dutchman who sailed with the Barbary corsairs during the early decades of the seventeenth century. As Simon de Vries detailed in his second volume of the *Historie van Barbaryen, En de zelfs Zee-Roovers . . . (History of the Barbarians, and Their Pirates)*, Janszoon originally worked as a privateer for his country. Eventually, however, he left the Republic to join the Barbary corsairs of Algiers, where he rose to the rank of admiral. At the height of his power there, he commanded a fleet of some 16 ships and became very rich from the booty he plundered.[7] Later, he relocated to Salé, where he took on the moniker of "Murad Reys" and, once again, assumed the powerful rank of Admiral.[8] He continued to enjoy a successful and lucrative career there, becoming a merchant of sorts (specializing in stolen goods) and even served as a liaison between the North Africans and Dutch merchants and government representatives.[9]

Such are the general biographical details of Janszoon's life. But there are two aspects of his case that are particularly intriguing. First, even though Dutch authorities had the opportunity to arrest or prosecute him for his crimes, they neglected to do so. And second, Janszoon's reputation at home was not necessarily as poor as one might expect. In fact, this Dutchmen-turned-Barbary sea robber found some degree of sympathy in the Republic, despite the fact that he had abandoned his Dutch wife and children when he defected to Algiers (and remarried there),[10] and that he had joined a population of high-seas marauders whose image in the Republic was abominable. Evidently the Dutch could overlook the fact that Janszoon had repudiated his own people, wed himself to a society that enslaved innocent Dutch men and women in allegedly abhorrent conditions, and in the words of Simon de Vries, "had renounced the Lord Christ, destroyed his own soul, condemned his salvation, [and] also prodded other Christians" to do the same.[11]

Let's consider the first point, that is, the fact that the Dutch declined to apprehend Jan Janszoon. In 1622, Janszoon, then a captain aboard a Barbary corsair ship, sought refuge in the city of Veere (in Zeeland) during an intense storm. One might expect that the authorities there would have taken this golden opportunity to capture a renowned Dutch *zeerover*—a lapsed privateer who had renounced his mother country to serve the ignominious North Africans—but they did not. Indeed, rather than arrest Janszoon, they granted his ship shelter, and the renegade captain was received by the city's residents. As it turns out, many of Janszoon's crewmen were Dutch as well, and when the news spread about the arrival of his ship, their Dutch families (including Janszoon's Dutch wife and children) came to Veere and beseeched the renegades to remain in the Netherlands. But Janszoon and his crewmembers staunchly refused, explaining that while it was true that their work as Barbary corsairs enabled them to seek booty, it also gave them the opportunity to attack the Spanish. In 1622, now that war had resumed with Spain, such reasoning fell on sympathetic and receptive ears. A number of Zeelanders were so impressed with this rationale that they helped the stranded corsairs to outfit a ship (an act that Dutch law forbade) and joined up with Janszoon themselves.[12]

Surprisingly enough, the Dutch authorities—this time in Holland—had yet another chance to arrest Jan Janszoon and still they did not act. At some point in the 1620s, the erstwhile Dutchman set sail for Holland with the express purpose of selling booty that he and his fleet had plundered from ships plying the waters of coastal Spain. En route, Janszoon's ship, as well as the two others with him, were attacked and damaged by a Dunkirk corsair ship; both sides experienced casualties. The three Barbary corsair vessels limped into the Rotterdam, Amsterdam, and Texel harbors respectively and sold their goods to make some money. Janszoon himself auctioned off his damaged ship in Amsterdam for some f.1,400. Accompanied by his crewmembers, he then journeyed to Rotterdam and met with upper-level authorities from the Admiralty of the Maas, who although aware of what they termed Janszoon's "dirty business," simply had a discussion with the pirate and then sent him and his cronies on his way. In short, they did nothing to prevent the renowned Dutch *zeerover* from returning to North Africa.[13]

The Dutch authorities' kindly stance toward Jan Janszoon was manifested in the popular media as well, for the pirate made a fairly good name for himself in several Dutch publications. Chronicler Nicolaes Wassenaer, for example, wrote about Janszoon in the 1627–1628 edition of his *Historisch Verhael aller Gedenkwaerdiger Geschiedenissen* (*Historical Tale of All Memorable Happenings*). The chronicler employed no negative or critical language in describing the Haarlem native or recounting his trespasses, and, indeed, complimented Janszoon as a "celebrated" pirate who once had been a "valiant" privateer for the Republic.[14] The hugely popular biography of Claes Compaen, too, includes mention of Janszoon, affirming that Janszoon had once served the Republic as a privateer who had committed acts that went beyond the limits of his commission. He had gone on to become an esteemed member of Salé society, the biography remarked laudatorily, and was certainly "shrewder than any Turk."[15]

Another illustration of this phenomenon—this Dutch refusal to prosecute a known pirate who, at the same time, received cultural approbation—was represented by Jan Erasmus Reyning, the seaman from Vlissingen who enjoyed such a successful career as a buccaneer in the West Indies.[16] The son of a mariner, he commenced work as a privateer crewhand while still a child. From the beginning, Reyning saw how remunerative sea robbery could be, for during his first privateering voyage, on a 21-gun ship, he and his fellow crewmen captured 18 prizes laden with valuable trade goods, all of which they dutifully brought back to Vlissingen.[17] Encouraged by this success, he continued to pursue a maritime life, working aboard merchant trade and privateering vessels. Soon, however, he longed for greener pastures and set off for Surinam, which served as the starting point for his illustrious career in the Caribbean.

It was not long before Jan Erasmus Reyning officially broke Dutch law, for immediately upon his arrival in the Americas, he traveled to Martinique and took up service with the French. Such an act was flagrantly illegal—Dutch seamen were not permitted to work for foreign powers unless granted a special dispensation from the States-General. In fact, a States-General proclamation from 1629 emphasized that this law precluding foreign service should be strictly enforced so as to safeguard the welfare of the country. Moreover, a 1640 reiteration of this same edict went further, ordering the prosecution and punishment of all those persons who had aided and abetted— or even had knowledge of—transgressing seamen.[18] To make matters worse, Reyning quickly voyaged to Hispaniola, a refuge for that notorious pirate brotherhood, the buccaneers, and hired himself out to one of the so-called "*kapers*" there.[19] Almost certainly, this "*kaper*," a Dutchman named Casten, was, in actuality, a pirate. Whatever his status, Casten generally based himself in Jamaica, and sought Reyning's help in attacking and capturing ships belonging to the Spanish.[20]

Supposedly, Reyning received a formal (albeit illegal, under Dutch law) commission to privateer from the governor of Jamaica.[21] By agreement, the Governor received a share of all booty Reyning and his fellow "privateers" captured, but this small requirement served as no impediment to a healthy sea robbing career. Immediately, Reyning found himself enjoying notable success, and the circles in which he now traveled enabled him to meet other thriving Caribbean "privateers," men who had made infamous raids on Spanish colonial ports and towns, as well as seized prodigious numbers of traveling ships.[22] These newfound contacts, in turn, led to work with "celebrity" buccaneers, for soon enough Reyning was hired as the lieutenant for one Captain Rokje—apparently Exquemelin's Rock de Bresiliaan (a.k.a. Rock Brasiliano; q.v., Chapter 2).[23] He then took up service as a captain in a regiment of the renowned Sir Henry Morgan.[24] Indeed, Reyning was one of the men involved in Morgan's famous raid on Panama, sharing in a glittering treasure trove of plunder. Among other things, their booty included:

> . . . money and gold . . . Chinese purslane [an herb] and rare things . . . entire warehouses with precious trade goods / and well-upholstered shops . . . The apothecaries alone were as big as some in Amsterdam. All of their implements and other appurtenances, such as the lids for pots, even the pots themselves, mugs, vessels [were] (. . . of pure silver), so that they found in this city a priceless treasure.[25]

Securing this booty was not without its pressures, however. In order to locate all of the treasure, the buccaneers had to coerce Panama's residents quite forcefully. Exquemelin's description of one particular victim is representative of a general campaign of terror:

> When it became plain that was all he was going to tell them, they strappado'd him until both his arms were entirely dislocated, then knotted a cord so tight round the forehead that his eyes bulged out, big as eggs. Since he still would not admit where the coffer was, they hung him up by his male parts, while one struck him, another sliced off his nose, yet another an ear, and another scorched him with fire . . . At last, . . . they let a Negro stab him to death with a lance.[26]

Such violence and mayhem apparently did not bother Reyning. Enriched and triumphant, he sought out his next opportunity. Cavalierly switching sides, he now received a commission from the Spanish to hunt the English; in just one year, he captured some 32 prizes.²⁷ Next journeying to Curaçao—and for the first time in a long while, seeking legal work—he inquired about a Dutch commission. Far from being arrested or even shunned for his past misdeeds, he was welcomed with open arms. Indeed, the Curaçao authorities immediately granted him permission to use the port of Fort Amsterdam and the governor issued him a *kaperbrief* (privateering commission) allowing him "to capture French and English [ships], to rob and pillage as much as it was in his power . . ." With this official license to plunder, he seized a myriad of prize ships containing cargo such as wine, bread, sugar and other victuals, indigo, and African slaves, indeed "a great plenitude." He also burned ships that had had the misfortune to cross his path. His booty provisioned the colonists in Curaçao with a plethora of supplies; the grateful people there, in turn, heaped appreciation and praise upon him. Within a short time, so prominent had he become that he had an entire fleet under his authority.²⁸ Although offered the command of a ship under the king of Spain, he declined, seeing more remunerative opportunities working for the Dutch. Besides, this lucrative post apparently had transformed him into quite the patriot, "for . . . he had no desire to serve potentates other than his own nation."²⁹ Concluding his West Indian career of "peril and danger" by working for the *Assiento der Negers*, a slave-trading company, he transported African bondsmen by the hundreds.³⁰ Wealthy and accomplished, he returned to the Netherlands and to the wife who had not seen him for nine years.³¹

Jan Erasmus Reyning's career as a Caribbean buccaneer and *commissievaarder* apparently became known to the Dutch reading public, for a full-fledged biography of the erstwhile sea robber appeared in 1691 (figure 5.1). Even more than Barbary corsair Jan Janszoon, Reyning was depicted in complimentary—indeed celebratory—terms. By all accounts, his biographer, Dionysis Van der Sterre, found his subject to be a dashing and admirable figure. Seeking to profile the "wondrous voyages and exciting circumstances" of the successful maritime bandit whom van der Sterre fondly called "our Adventurer," the author painstakingly chronicled Reyning's many pitched battles on sea and land, his dramatic shipwrecks, and terrifying encounters with starvation in his *Very Remarkable Journeys of Jan Erasmus Reyning*. Time and again, he also lauded Reyning's "faithful valor,"³² his kindness and nobility of character,³³ and loyal dedication to those whom he served, including his fellow buccaneer seamen.³⁴

Jan Janszoon and Jan Erasmus Reyning—pirates who were, at the same time, objects of cultural fascination and respect—represent two intriguing cases in which the Dutch authorities neglected to enforce the stringent laws they had made concerning *zeerooverij*. While Golden Age Dutch criminal records reveal that the authorities in the Republic repeatedly prosecuted seamen for the crime of piracy, neither Janszoon or Reyning was arrested or even investigated—never mind disciplined—despite their transgressions against emphatic Dutch legislation. This is curious indeed. But, one might

Figure 5.1 Title page engraving, Dionysis van der Sterre, *Zeer Aenmerkelyke Reysen van Jan Erasmus Reyning door Verscheyde Gevesten des Werelds* (Amsterdam: Jan ten Hoorn, 1691). Dousa Kamer.

ask, do these men represent odd exceptions to the rule, mere anomalies in an otherwise typical pattern of pervasive prosecution and punishment? The surprising answer is "no." Dutch criminal records reveal that even when the Dutch authorities did choose to prosecute wayward seamen, they often put this gentler disposition into effect. Consequently, one finds criminal sentences that were unexpectedly mild and in complete defiance to the officially prescribed punishments in the *Article Brieven* and laws.

The first manifestation one can discern of this tendency is the authorities' inclination to prescribe lighter sentences than the laws stipulated. Sometimes such cases simply involved privateers whose behavior had gone awry. For instance, *Article Brieven*, such as the 1665 example discussed in Chapter 1, mandated severe punishments for those privateers who disobeyed or left the service of their captains. By law, such intransigence was supposed to earn a sentence of corporal punishment or execution, plus the confiscation of all wages and booty.[35] During the Second and Third Anglo-Dutch Wars, however, the Admiralties typically imposed much lighter penalties on those privateer seamen who opposed their commanders, choosing instead to levy fines or mandate assignments on Dutch warships.[36]

Such judicial mildness concerning insubordination appears to have extended into the early eighteenth century. When in 1703–1704 privateer seamen aboard the Dutch vessel the *De Getergde Kat* (*Provoked Cat*) revolted against their captain, mutinied, and took the vessel to England to be readied for an independent cruise,[37] one would expect that the Admiralty officials would have responded harshly. The *Getergde Kat* was a commissioned ship that went to sea during the early years of the War of Spanish Succession. Although the crew had signed contracts in November and December 1703, agreeing to follow faithfully the orders of their captain, some of the seamen quickly began to yearn for their independence. After the ship set sail on December 20, 1703, a number of the men conspired to form a plot against their captain. These crewmembers—including one Heijndrik Florisse, a 36-year-old boatswain's mate from Rotterdam and 21 other seamen—forced him to take the vessel out to the open sea.

The mutineers set forth for England, to Falmouth, where they readied the *Getergde Kat* for future travels. Among other preparations, they added ballast for further unlawful cruises, and sealed her hull to guard against leaks. On January 15, 1704, when the vessel was equipped and fit, they set out to sea. The court record makes no mention of what they did during this time, but does note that they later made a second trip to Falmouth. Eventually, however, those sailors loyal to the captain were able to overcome the mutineers and forced the ship to return to the Netherlands.

The Admiralty court found no justification for the mutineers' actions and termed their uprising as "matters of very damaging and ruinous consequences." Although the insurgents had used the pretext that the *Getergde Kat* was not seaworthy and they had thus been forced to take matters into their own hands, later official inspections conducted by seasoned VOC and privateer carpenters would not corroborate this defense. Court documents also state that the men had no real complaints against their captain. Indeed, according to the Admiralty records, the commander was an able man, the *Getergde Kat* was in seaworthy shape, and the rebellious sailors aboard had no excuse for their conduct. Rather, they had fomented a mutiny simply because of their own insatiable desire to commit criminal acts, to privateer on their own terms—in other words, to act piratically.

The judges convicted Heijndrik Florisse and his 21 collaborators, citing the mutineers' criminal disregard for their privateering *Articlebrief*, their private contract with their sponsor, and their formal privateering *commissies van retorsie*. In taking up their service as privateers for the Dutch Republic, the sentence affirmed, the men had sworn a solemn oath to abide by the rules, strictures, and regulations contained in these official documents. Moreover, the judges pointed out, by the time the mutiny occurred, the sailors had already received *maand geld*, that is, wages, which further cemented their employment and the terms under which they had agreed to work.

But in the end, the court's bark was, in most respects, worse than its bite. Most of the convicted seamen got off lightly, even though their sentences, delivered on April 2, 1704, cited no reason for such clemency. Certainly, Heijndrik Florisse, the boatswain's mate, endured a heavier punishment, for the judges ordered that he be taken to a warship anchored in the Maas and thrown from the yardarm and then lashed 100 times. Additionally, his wages and share of the prize booty were to be confiscated and he was ordered to pay the court costs. The rest of the defendants, however, fared much better. Sixteen unidentified sailors paid the ostensibly stiff price of eternal banishment from the Republic. But banishment was certainly preferable to execution or the maiming caused by corporal punishment. As painful and depriving as it was to be evicted from one's homeland, one still retained one's life, limbs, and faculties. Moreover, banishment was a penalty that one could flout, for it was difficult to regulate and convicts were known to return before their time of exile had expired.[38] Five others—all Dutch and comprising a mix of officers and regular seamen—were sentenced only to the confiscation of their wages and booty, plus the costs of justice. And one other individual had to pay these fines and endure a public whipping.[39]

Other offenses qualified for this more temperate sentencing as well. Lieutenant Adriaan Bank—an officer on a privateer ship under the command of one Captain Halfkraagh—and seven of his fellow seamen who were found guilty of "plundering prizes," were the recipients of lenient sentencing in March 1675. Bank and his accomplices had flagrantly disregarded the orders of their commander in order to enrich themselves. When Captain Halfkraagh and his men captured a ship (called the *Witte Duif*—i.e. the *White Dove*) from two Dunkirk privateers, he ordered Lieutenant Bank and seven other crewmembers to retrieve the cargo—which consisted of pitch and various trade goods—and bring it back to the Admiralty of the Maas, where it would be registered and auctioned. Bank and his unidentified colleagues did otherwise, however. After plundering the *Witte Duif*, they surreptitiously sold the stolen goods and proceeded to divvy up the ill-begotten profits among themselves. According to precedents in Dutch law, such acts constituted criminal piracy and should have earned a heavy punishment, up to and including execution. The court at the Admiralty of the Maas, in fact, specifically cited a States-General *Placaat* of December 1, 1640, which stipulated that at the very least, a privateer convicted of this crime would have to forfeit all earned and unearned salary and premiums as well as surrender any plundered goods to the original owners. In opposition to this legislation, however, the court ordered only that Bank and his cronies forfeit a bit of their salaries (two months' worth for Bank and one month's compensation for the sailors) and turn over the stolen goods to their *reders*; they were even given the option of simply paying the equivalent sum of money if they preferred.[40]

Another interesting example involved a 1697 case concerning the privateer ship *de Faam* (*the Fame*).[41] While the sentencing index of the Admiralty of the Maas tried to downplay the harsh stain of a piracy charge in this instance—categorizing it as simply another occurrence of "Privateering and Prizes"—a careful perusal of the actual sentencing documents reveals that the Admiralty court found the crimes to be much more serious. Indeed, many of the *Faam*'s personnel were involved in criminal misdeeds, and the court ultimately tried and convicted (many in absentia) 5 officers and 14 sailors on charges ranging from "utter faithlessness and profligacy" to "criminal robbery of goods," to "manifest piracy."

What actually happened in this particular case? Captain Floris Maartenszoon was the commander aboard the frigate ship *de Faam* during the spring of 1695. Maartenszoon and his men captured a valuable prize, *de Wijnstok*, on May 6. As was the customary practice, Maartenszoon ordered several of his crewmembers—including first mate Jan Sluis, mate Willem Teunisse Verbrugge, and several sailors—to go aboard the *Wijnstok*, now docked at Leith, the port suburb of Edinburgh, Scotland, to take the vessel home. Against Maartenszoon's orders, however, Sluis and his cronies removed cargo from the prize ship—including copious amounts of wine, brandy, and paper—sold the merchandise, and divided up the proceeds. Sluis had ordered the further removal of even more wine before he was stopped.

But this was not all. Also on May 6, Captain Maartenszoon had installed another chief mate, Engel Samuelszoon, as well as several other men—including quartermaster Claas Abrahamszoon and a number of sailors—aboard the captured prize ship *de Fortuin*. As in the case with the *Wijnstok*, Samuelszoon and his fellow seamen unloaded brandy from its hold, and sold the cargo in Leith. While the errant seamen initially claimed that they had given the proceeds to Captain Maartenszoon, the court later determined that they had actually arranged for it to be sent surreptitiously to land. The privateers now further plundered the *Fortuin*, removing more booty and hiding it aboard *de Faam*. Additional witnesses testified that Samuelszoon had secretly unloaded more brandy from the captured vessel, selling the spirits for more illicit cash. Although he retained a double portion of all of the profits for himself, he divided up the rest of the ill-begotten gains with his helpers before his misconduct was discovered.

Alas, there was still another chapter to the tale. Yet again, on May 6, 1695, members of Maartenszoon's crew had been put aboard a captured prize ship—*de Prins Karel*—in order to guard the booty. These men included an officer—a quartermaster named Groenevelt—and several sailors. When the helmsman was away, Groenevelt and his fellow mariners attacked the cargo, plundering some sugar and selling it, and then pilfering some wine.

The Admiralty court judges heaped scornful condemnation upon *de Faam*'s disgraced privateers. Citing Jan Sluis, Engel Samuelszoon, and quartermaster Groenevelt as the ringleaders, they convicted the errant seamen of very serious charges. Sluis and Samuelszoon were found guilty of "manifest piracy," which, the judges said, went against the laws of the Republic and warranted the harshest of punishments. Their accomplices—Willem Teunisse Verbrugge and quartermaster Claas Abrahamszoon—were convicted of "manifest robbery and banditry" and "notorious banditry" respectively; at least in Verbrugge's case, such crimes were deemed worthy of the "the stiffest punishment." While the modern reader might feel some sympathy for Groenevelt—witness testimony claimed that as quartermaster, he had often complained to his captain about the scarcity of the crew's rations, and had therefore resolved to purchase fresh provisions with the illegally begotten proceeds—the court's response was not so compassionate. Over Groenevelt's protestations, the judges found his actions to be the height of "inexcusable debauchery," which went against the laws of the Republic. They also judged the complicity of his fellow conspirators to be acts of "utter faithlessness and profligacy."[42]

But such roar and thunder would prove to be mere bombast, for the court's sentences belied their words of righteous indignation. The judges meted out the most onerous penalties to a number of rank-and-file sailors who had been involved in the affair but who declined to show themselves in court. Tried in absentia, nine seamen from the *Wijnstok* and *Fortuin* were banished for life from the Republic and ordered to pay a fine. Similarly, another sailor, this time from the *Prins Karel*—who was also tried in absentia and convicted of "criminal robbery of goods," an offense that merited "heavy consequences in a land of justice"—was eternally banished and ordered to pay a fine. But those defendants who were present fared much better. Chief instigators Jan Sluis, Engel Samuelszoon, and quartermaster Gronevelt received sentences of banishment for six years, six years, and four years respectively; the salary and booty they had earned from their last cruise was also confiscated. And although four other sailors were censured for their "utter faithlessness and profligacy," the judges did nothing more than slap them with a fine.[43]

Then there were those cases in which Dutch sailors took up service under foreign governments, and, most perfidiously, with the Republic's enemies. Penalties for this crime could be very severe. Indeed, if the case of mariner Pieter Steenwers is at all indicative, this was certainly so, for on June 24, 1677, the Admiralty of the Maas sentenced the seaman to be thrown from the yardarm three times, after which he was to be lashed.[44] It is hard to imagine that Steenwers survived the ordeal. Why, then, was the Admiralty so mild in its judgment of mariner Jan Janssen, whom the court convicted of having "hired himself in service to the enemy . . . on a Dunkirk privateer vessel . . . ?" For rather than imposing a punishment such as that suffered by the unfortunate Mr. Steenwers, Janssen only had to submit to a whipping. Similarly, shipper Arij Philepszoon—whom the Admiralty of the Maas court found guilty in 1689 of abetting the enemy when he outfitted a ship and sent it to support the hostile forces in Oostende—received only the indignity and inconvenience of a *f.*600 fine, plus the confiscation of his ship.[45] This despite a 1672 law by the States-General, which mandated the penalty of death for anyone, no matter what his rank, who presented a Dutch warship to the enemy. While this particular law was specifically directed at naval personnel and Philepszoon was not a member of the Dutch armed forces, the decree still manifests how critically the Dutch authorities viewed the issue of helping enemy forces with the donation of outfitted ships.[46] Fortunate, too, was privateer Hendrik Jacobsen of Roosendaal, whose service aboard an enemy vessel out of Dunkirk earned him only a term aboard the Dutch warship the *Oranje Galei* (*Orange Galley*).[47] While this is not to say that such penalties were negligible—Janssen, Philepszoon, and Jacobson all felt the sting of the Admiralty court's judgment, whether in the form of the whip, confiscation of expensive property, or forced labor—such discipline was much easier to bear than execution or the severe corporal punishment endured by Pieter Steenwers.

Even in cases that involved true, unadulterated sea marauding, the courts could be curiously lenient. On June 23, 1693, when the court at the Admiralty of the Maas tried and convicted Dutch privateer Dirk de Gelder of piracy in absentia, they declined to sentence him. Although in other similar cases this same court had vowed to punish defendants who chose to flee— and, indeed, had prescribed harsh penalties—in this instance, they did nothing but issue another citation for de Gelder to appear in court (this after he had already defaulted on two summons). The judges admitted that they found the former helmsman to be guilty of "the plundering and robbing of . . . [a] Bus-ship" and the violent assault of a sailor aboard that vessel. In this case, however, they chose to be curiously indifferent about de Gelder's crime rather than thunderously pledge vengeance and punishment, an altogether different response from that which they had displayed on other occasions.[48]

To take an example when the defendant was actually present in court, one could consider the case of Jan Corneliszoon Knole of Amsterdam,[49] whom the Admiralty court convicted of the dual crimes of serving a foreign government and carrying double privateering commissions. Sentenced on June 29, 1651, Knole—a privateer captain aboard the ship the *'t Helsvier*—was sharply criticized for transgressing the instructions of his Dutch commission, forswearing the formal oath he had made when he accepted his Dutch commission, and disregarding the explicit directives of States-General proclamations dating from July 27, 1627, March 23, 1628, and March 29, 1640.

What exactly did Knole do? After receiving a commission from the WIC and Stadholder William II on February 14, 1649, he departed on a WIC ship. Against the regulations of his Dutch *commissiebrief*, Knole then received a commission from a foreign noble, the Grave of Ormond. This document—illegal though it was—purported to give Knole the right to attack and plunder ships along the coast of Zeeland. Utilizing this illicit commission, Knole assailed and captured a ship belonging to Robbert Custus of Rotterdam, seizing the cargo of English grain that Custus was transporting from Yarmouth to Zeeland. The privateer then brought Custus, the prize ship, and booty to Dunkirk, where he forced Custus to abandon his ship, and arranged to sell the captured vessel.

Knole's criminal actions caught up with him, however. Custus made his way back to Rotterdam, where he lodged a formal complaint with the Admiralty concerning Knole's perfidious conduct, and requested compensation for his stolen ship. As a result, the Admiralty authorities arranged for the wayward Dutch privateer to be brought to Rotterdam from Dunkirk, and investigated the charges. After a careful analysis of the evidence, the Admiralty court found him guilty, citing Dutch laws stipulating that under no pretext was a resident of the Republic to serve a foreign government in any capacity. They also denounced him for carrying a double privateering commission. Consequently, he was duly convicted of piracy (*zeeroverij*). However, instead of sentencing Knole to be executed, as Dutch law dictated, the Court instead decreed that his crimes called for corporal punishment and monetary fines. The judges thus condemned Knole to be tied to a scaffold on July 4, flogged, and then incarcerated in the Amsterdam *Tuchthuis* (prison) for 28 years, where he was to work off the court costs of his prosecution; he was also ordered to pay for the costs of his imprisonment. Not an easy sentence, to be sure, but one preferable to execution.

Then there was the case of Cornelis Claaszoon, whom the Admiralty of the Maas tried and convicted of piracy in August 1601.[50] Claaszoon was but one member of a gang of *zeerovers* who sailed under the command of Captain Quinijn den Waterman, a veteran pirate who worked for the Spanish in the Southern Netherlands. From the outset, Claaszoon's intention was to attack and plunder Dutch merchants and fisherman traveling along the coast, and he met this goal, assaulting and stealing with his cronies at least four vessels—two merchantmen and two fishing boats—containing unspecified cargo. And yet when the time came for the court to sentence Claaszoon, the pirate was spared the strict penalty the laws dictated, for he was not executed. Rather, because the States-General sent a letter requesting that Claaszoon not be hanged with his accomplices, and because the court and Prince Maurice, the current Stadholder, claimed to prefer "mercy in preference to the rigor of Justice," Claaszoon was consigned to row for 12 years on a Dutch penal galley; he was also ordered to pay the court costs. While such a sentence was an arduous one, it still compared favorably to the cold finality of the Rotterdam city gallows.

The case of privateer Captain Jop Ariense Stogwoning, whom the Admiralty of the Maas court convicted of "extortion" in September 11, 1692, represents another intriguing example of somewhat atypical sentencing.[51] Commander of the ship *de Vliegende Draak* (*the Flying Drake*) and in possession of a valid Dutch privateering commission dated March 17 of that year, Stogwoning used violence and duplicity to capture a ship belonging to a fellow Dutchman. When Stogwoning attacked and apprehended the ship on June 24, he displayed a fraudulent passport, claiming to be the notorious

Dunkirk corsair Jan Bart, and demanded a ransom of ƒ.1,500 from the captive captain; he also forced the unfortunate man to give him any money that was on his person. And these dictates were not issued gently; Stogwoning employed vicious and menacing means to attain his goal, such as using "a naked saber and other weaponry" to assail the captain and the cabin boy (both of whom were injured in the struggle) and threatening "to drive the ship . . . into the ground."

The Admiralty court, naturally, took issue with Stogwoning's conduct, and implied that this was not the privateer's first offense, for they affirmed that he had committed "still other evil . . . very enormous encounters." They also reminded him that he had sworn an oath to obey his *articulbrief* and instructions, both of which pointedly decreed that he was not to attack merchants or residents of the Dutch Republic. As a consequence of disregarding such blatant instructions, they proclaimed, Stogwoning's punishment should serve as a deterrent to others so that such behavior would not recur. But in the end, for all of the court's moral sermonizing, the judges did not sentence him to die. Rather they ordered that he "be condemned to be publicly and severely punished," although they did not go into what form this "public punishment" should take. They also enjoined the defendant to pay a fine of ƒ.2,000 plus the court costs.

While this sentence is grave, Stogwoning fared better than had he been condemned to the hangman's noose. And for all of Stogwoning's transgressions, *de Vliegende Draak* and its crew continued to serve as privateers—albeit shady ones who got themselves in repeated trouble—for at least another three years. Indeed, the infamous ship crops up on several occasions in later Admiralty records, and these references indicate that the Admiralty authorities, despite their prosecution of the errant Stogwoning, had permitted the ship and its men to privateer again. First, on December 23, 1692, an Admiralty of the Maas resolution affirms the Admiralty's intention to recall the wayward privateers of the *Vliegende Draak*, for the privateers had stayed out at sea beyond the legal deadline stipulated by their commission.[52] Second, on June 2, 1695, the officers and sailors of the privateering "frigate" *de Vliegende Draak* were suspected of plundering their prizes and were ordered to be "taken into detention" in order to ascertain the validity of this allegation.[53] While these documents confirm that the privateers aboard *de Vliegende Draak* were certainly prone to misconduct, they also reveal that such misdeeds did not stop the Admiralty from employing them; they were still deemed acceptable enough to serve the state.

The 1690 case of Cornelis van der Hoeven is particularly surprising.[54] When the Admiralty court found him guilty of acts that constituted "piracy" (*Roverijen*) as well as "excesses, violence, and despoliation," one would expect that the sentence would be harsh and unyielding. After all, according to court testimony, van der Hoeven's conduct had been nothing short of piratical and as an esteemed navy officer—a captain in command of the warship *het Wapen van Rotterdam* (*the Arms of Rotterdam*)—his fall from grace was particularly noteworthy and egregious.

On September 16, 1689, while out on a routine cruise of the Dutch coast, van der Hoeven encountered a Swedish ship, *de Vergulde Vlugt* (*Gilded Flight*), which was en route from Bordeaux and carrying wine. Homeward bound, *de Vergulde Vlugt* was near the mouth of the Maas River when it confronted van der Hoeven and his crew. Perhaps flushed with success from his recent seizure of the French privateer ship *Huisduinen*, van der Hoeven ordered the capture of the neutral Swedish ship as well. Using the *Huisduinen* as their vessel of attack, van der Hoeven's men accosted *de Vergulde Vlugt* and boarded it. Going against the Admiralty's orders to bring any prizes to Rotterdam for adjudication, van der Hoeven instructed his officers instead to forge the Swedish ship's papers and remove the French wine from its hold; according to his plan, they would sell the booty elsewhere and pocket the money. After stealing the wine, the corrupt navy seamen abandoned the Swedish ship. As if this escapade were not enough, the court testimony elaborated, van der Hoeven had been involved in additional assaults against neutral ships, including a raid of the Norwegian vessel the *Hope*; and the plundering of the *St. Anna* of Hamburg. In both of these instances, van der Hoeven and his men had hurled terms of abuse as well as violent blows against the crewmembers of the victimized ships, and had gone on to rob their provisions. Moreover, the captain had embezzled casks of olive oil, which he then concealed illegally in his own warehouse in Delft.

While the court records note that the complaints against van der Hoeven had been many—both from within and without the Republic—the Admiralty had never seen fit to discipline the man. True to form, this episode would prove to be no exception. For although the judges took van der Hoeven to task verbally for his lack of commitment to his commission (which ordered him to serve the Admiralty with trust and honor; to refrain from attacking Dutch allies and neutral parties; to bring all prizes to the Admiralty College; and not to "minimize" the booty in any way) yet again they refrained from punishing him seriously. Yes, they chided him for his "disobedience" and "very evil" behavior, which constituted "piracy" (*Roverijen*). But ultimately, the court sentenced the navy captain only to pay a fine of 1,000 silver ducats plus the court costs; they also suspended him from naval service for a period of 12 months. In contradistinction, van der Hoeven's *articulbrief* called for a much stiffer penalty: confiscation of all the defendant's money within the Republic, loss of rank as captain, declaration of being *inhabil* ("unsuitable, unfit") for any other state service, payment of a *f.*10,000 fine, and banishment from the Republic for a period of six years. (One wonders why the *articulbrief* did not mandate death, in keeping with standard Dutch law.)

Yet another instance of light sentencing occurred in the case of a group of seafarers who were tried by the Admiralty of the Maas in 1589. Although found guilty of intentionally targeting innocent Dutch sea folk and attacking and plundering three vessels in the North Sea, the admiral-general, Prince Maurice, prescribed quite gentle penalties for many of them. While several of their ilk were condemned to the hangman's noose, six others—whose crimes were noted as no less serious—were sentenced only to stand beneath the gallows during their comrades' executions, as well as confinement in a "pit" for eight days, during which they would be given a diet of only bread and water. They were also told to beg forgiveness from God, and proscribed from ever serving the Dutch Republic in any other official capacity.[55]

More mild sentencing—vis-à-vis the penalties mandated by Dutch law and Admiralty contracts—is but one manifestation of a curious Golden Age Dutch tendency to treat some of these piratical crimes with kid gloves. What is perhaps more remarkable is that various individuals—seamen who were indeed found guilty of the crime of *zeeroverij*—were pardoned completely, and never endured any punishment for their misconduct. In other words, despite the Republic's strenuous prohibitions against the crime of piracy, and the severe punishments these laws called for, the governing authorities permitted many a convicted mariner to go scot-free.

Consider the case of Wouter Gijsbregtiszoon, whom the Admiralty of the Maas tried in the fall of 1576. Convicted of piracy along with accomplices Maximus Brant, Hendrikk Cruidman, and his brother Cornelis Gijsbregtszoon (q.v., Chapter 2), he was sentenced to be decapitated at the "place of Justice" in Rotterdam. All of his possessions were to be confiscated as well. However, on September 22, 1576, the young Maritge Cornelisdogter intervened. Humbly appearing at the town hall, with "folded hands," "weeping eyes," and "on bended knees," she begged the Admiralty officials to forgive Gijsbregtszoon, her young love, of his misdeeds, and to pardon him. She swore that he was a good man and that she would marry him and bring him to a better Christian life. When the officials, in turn, questioned Gijsbregtszoon about her entreaty, he promised to marry her and to live "honestly and peacefully," and "with God's help," to earn a decent livelihood for her. Consequently, the Admiralty of the Maas court duly pardoned Gijsbregtszoon on October 23, qualifying their change of heart with the comment that the convicted pirate—despite his depredations, kidnappings, and abetting of the Spanish—had been a pious young man who supported his parents and who had been misled by the evil deceptions of the other defendants.[56]

Perhaps the supplications of the weeping Maritge Cornelisdogter were difficult to resist. But what about situations in which no devout young fiancée tearfully implored the Court for the release of her convicted betrothed? Do examples exist in which a convicted pirate was granted clemency without the intervention of an interested outside party? The answer is an unequivocal "yes." Consider, for instance, the case of 29 unidentified sailors who worked under Captain Hendrik Willemszoon and who were convicted of piracy by the Admiralty of the Maas court on November 10, 1610.[57]

Willemszoon—a denizen of Amsterdam who had originally come from Hamburg—served as the commander aboard the ship *'t Kraantgen* (*the Little Crane*). Although posing as legal privateers and outfitted by an Amsterdam *rederij*, the Admiralty court established that, in fact, the seamen had sailed without any sort of proper commission. Indeed, the *Kraantgen* was made to appear as a legal privateering vessel in order to deceive the Admiralty officials, but the venture was intentionally a piratical one from beginning to end. Embarking upon a cruise to the Cape Verde Islands and the West Indies, the captain and his *reders* pretended that they were sending the ship to these destinations in order to transport lumber. Their real intention, however, was to hunt for booty. Using a load of wood as mock cargo to deceive the Admiralty and fellow convoy members, the ship set out, carrying a fraudulent, illegitimate privateering commission as its ostensible license to act.

Illegal though it was, the *Kraantgen*'s mission was successful. Prowling the waters of, among other places, the Cape Verde Islands, the coast of Brazil, and the island of Madeira,[58] Willemszoon and his men captured five ships of Spanish, French, and Portuguese origin. Their booty included several tons of fish, flour, rice, oil, 50 vats of Canary Island wine, further unspecified amounts of wine, victuals, and a number of unnamed goods. Also, when Willemszoon and his men captured a Portuguese bark, they actively collaborated with a "certain English freebooter's ship." Moreover, because the *Kraantgen*'s sponsors purposely had sent the ship to sea without adequate provisions, Willemszoon and his crew were forced to seize what they needed from other ships, as was the sponsors' intention. One can imagine that this fact alone—this deliberate lack of food and water—was a strong incentive for the seamen aboard the *Little Crane* to attack and capture as many ships as possible.

Ultimately, the Admiralty authorities learned the truth about the *Kraantgen*'s illicit mission and arrested Willemszoon. Citing a 1606 States-General *placaat* that stipulated that any persons found at sea without a proper commission would be considered as "pirates and sea robbers" (*pijratten en . . . Zeerovers*), as well as Articles 1 and 35 of the 1609 Treaty with Spain (cementing the Twelve Years' Truce), the court vociferously condemned the behavior of the captain, his crewmembers, and his financial backers. Sparing no one their censure, the judges declared that Captain Hendrik Willemszoon's "intended piracy" constituted a "wanton business" of "so much . . . evil"; they likewise proclaimed the *rederij*'s behavior in the affair as "intentional villainy." But, in the end, while Willemszoon, the foreign native of Hamburg, was sentenced to hang, his 29 Dutch cronies were pardoned and released by "his Excellency the prince because of Special mercy . . ."[59] This despite the fact that the sentence claims that the 29 crewmembers bore complete responsibility for their actions. Moreover, the judges made no move to punish the *reders* themselves, even though the court had found the privateering firm to be fully complicit in the evil scheme.

Then there was the notorious 1614 case concerning pirate Captain Hugo Clerck and his Barbary corsair minions (q.v., Chapter 4). Jointly tried by the Admiralties of Amsterdam and Rotterdam, this gang of 60–70 sea robbers, a thorn in the Republic's side for years, was found guilty of violently marauding at least 35 ships and reaping plunder such as gold, gems, precious stones, tallow, herring, sardines, wheat, weaponry, trade goods, and copious amounts of money. One pamphlet claims that the merchants of Amsterdam alone had lost over 30 tons of merchandise. Finally apprehended by a Dutch navel detachment specifically assigned to arrest them, the band was brought to trial in very public fashion and duly convicted of piracy. Accordingly, as one would expect, many of the crewmembers—whose number included men from various European and North African states (see Appendix V)—were hanged at the Rotterdam and Amsterdam gallows. Additionally, seven were sentenced to stand beneath the gallows during the execution of their colleagues, and some were still imprisoned pending their trials. Strikingly enough, however, the three Dutch members of the band—Sander Arianszoon of Vlissingen, Joris Janszoon of Enkhuizen, and Hendrik Janszoon of Enkhuizen—were all granted pardons, three of only five defendants who received such merciful sentences.[60]

Perhaps the Admiralty authorities felt that these three Dutchmen had been reluctant participants in the pirates' exploits. After all, a pamphlet printed at the time does note that several of Captain Clerk's *zeerovers* claimed to have been sailors who were taken against their wills from captured ships (this was a very common defense in early modern piracy trials, however). The publication goes on to say that the Admiralties released these persons. Unfortunately, there is no way of establishing whether this is the reason why Arianszoon, Janszoon, and Janszoon were pardoned. (Recall, moreover, that according to the Admiralty records, a number of defendants were still awaiting their trials and their ultimate fate was not recorded.) Furthermore, even if the Admiralty did deem the three Dutchmen to be among this select group of innocent bystanders, why were they singled out as particularly believable or sympathetic? Many a pirate crew was composed of captured merchant seamen who took up life under the "black flag," either voluntarily or against their wills.

All that aside, however, what about a case in which there seems to have been no doubt about the intentionality of the defendants' crimes? The 1696 case of navy officer Hendrick van der Crap, first lieutenant under Captain Barent van der Pot aboard the warship *Rotterdam*, fits this description. The court at the Admiralty of the Maas convicted van der Crap of piracy, along with his comrade Jan Zuijlen, the second lieutenant on the *Rotterdam*. On August 24, 1695, van der Crap and Zuijlen were aboard the *Rotterdam*, which was anchored in a Dutch roadstead. Nearby lay the VOC ship the *Vosmaer*, just back in home waters after the arduous trek from Batavia. After concealing navy pistols on their persons, van der Crap and Zuijlen took a small sloop and made their way over to the *Vosmaer* and to a smaller craft that was accompanying it. Brandishing the guns—which they intended to use against any resistors—they approached the smaller ship and Zuijlen leapt out. The two errant naval officers now forced crewmembers aboard the smaller VOC craft to unload precious cargo from its hold, including bails of tea, rattan, and chests full of other assorted Asian trade goods.

Van der Crap and Zuijlen did not escape with this plunder, however, for they were apprehended by their commander, Captain van der Pot, a man of "distinction" in the employ of the Admiralty of the Maas. Once detained,

Zuijlen tried to pretend that he did not have any of the stolen booty, but was proved a liar. When bluntly confronted with his misconduct, he claimed that van der Crap had ordered him to remove cargo from the vessel, because van der Crap's mother in Batavia had sent goods home to her son in the Netherlands. The Admiralty court, not surprisingly, found these prevarications to be "frivolous pretexts," and denounced Zuijlen and van der Crap's misdeeds. They condemned Zuijlen for trespassing against his *article brief* and other orders, for forsaking military discipline, and for following the "personal" orders of a commanding officer, rather than remembering that his true obligation was to his country. Consequently, the judges convicted him on the charge of public violence and harassment, which they said was made worse by the fact that such actions had been committed by one in the service of the state. For his part, van der Crap was found guilty of "criminal violations, abuse," and "criminal piracy." He was also censured for his "extreme faithlessness" in forgetting his oath and his duty, particularly criticized for trespassing against Article 34 of his *article brief*, and upbraided for abusing the authority granted to him by the Dutch Republic. Additionally, the court convicted him of "willful disobedience" and affirmed that such behavior warranted the forfeiture of his "body and life."

Initially, the court did not refrain from imposing harsh sentences. After ordering Zuijlen to appear in court on three separate occasions—orders that went unheeded—the court tried and convicted the second lieutenant in absentia, and rendered a sentence of eternal banishment from the Dutch Republic. They also promised a stricter penalty should Zuijlen ever return to the country. Van der Crap shared in this ignominy. He, too, was enjoined to appear before the court on three different dates (February 29, 1696, April 4, 1696, and May 15, 1696), but he ignored these commands completely. Assuming that the first lieutenant had flown the country, the judges banished van der Crap for life on June 26, 1698 and also confiscated his goods. Should he ever return, the judges warned, he would pay with his life, for the authorities would execute him "with the sword" (i.e., behead him).

Considering the harshness of these words and the severity of the punishments, it comes as a surprise that in the end, the court changed Hendrick van der Crap's sentence. Per his request, the court reopened the case for examination on September 3, 1700. Curiously enough, after this reappraisal, the court pardoned him, explaining that the Admiralty preferred "mercy before the rigor of Justice." They then went on to say that they had forgiven him and that they would reinstate his good name. Now, the court gently reproached, he need only pay the court costs. Jan Zuijlen's fate remained unchanged (one assumes that he never chose to appear before the court), but Hendrick van der Crap—the erstwhile naval officer and convicted pirate—was now once again a free and honorable man within the realm of the Dutch Republic.[61]

Such acts of clemency were not just a local Rotterdam affair—the Admiralty of the Maas was not the only institution to extend merciful olive branches to convicted Dutch *zeerovers*. Indeed, political bodies such as the States of Holland sometimes became involved in the granting of reprieves. This is what happened, for instance, in the case of Captain Simon Maartszoon Stuijt, who worked as a Barbary corsair during the early years of the seventeenth century. Commander "over several pirate ships, lying in the Bay or Harbor of Mamora in Barbaria," Stuijt requested a pardon for himself and *all* of his crewmembers. An experienced *zeerover*, he had attacked and pillaged many a ship (although nowhere does it state that he targeted Dutch ships in particular). Now, however, he sought to return home, and petitioned his government from abroad. A States of Holland resolution notes that Stuijt made this solicitation several times. With the agreement and support of the States-General, the States of Holland finally consented to his wish on April 28, 1611. The government's rationale for this gesture was that "by that means [it will be possible] to get these people out of the sea and liberate commercial traffic."[62]

Pardons were also granted from the highest level of the Dutch government, the States-General. This is what took place in the case of brothers Pieter and Cornelis Pack, for example, whom the High Court of Holland convicted of piracy in 1615. The two sea robbers had captured a Dutch ship from Hoorn, but, despite this misdeed, were granted pardons by the States-General.[63] Convicted *zeerover* Johan Ruth—perhaps a crony of the Pack brothers—was also tried by the High Court of Holland in 1615 for seizing a Hoorn vessel, and was similarly pardoned.[64] Likewise, convicted pirate Jan Lievenszoon Rijckewaert—who had been a soldier for the Republic but had then taken up piratical attacks against Spanish and French ships in the Mediterranean Sea— was granted a pardon by the States-General (which was also signed by the States of Holland) in 1615.[65]

These pardons all coincidentally date from 1615, but the States-General issued reprieves to pirates before and after that year too. In 1609, for instance, they proclaimed that they had examined the "bandits" aboard two frigates and made the decision to dismiss a great number of them. While approximately 75 individuals were sent to prison to await justice, another 146 were "released and . . . freed." Among these 146 liberated souls were 110 citizens of the Dutch Republic (or 75 percent of the total); the remaining men came from various European states.[66] As part and parcel of this arrangement, the Dutch government also presented the liberated "bandits" with passports.[67]

More startling is a proclamation that the States-General issued on August 25, 1651. This document pardoned *all* Dutchmen who had joined the "pirates and robbers who now are so rampant in the sea" despite the great "violence," "damage and harm," and "indeed total ruin" these marauders had been unleashing upon the "many good inhabitants" of their home country. According to this *placaat*, the pirates now felt "troubled" about the crimes they had perpetuated, "would prefer to return to these provinces, to their friends and relatives . . . ," and were seeking pardons from the Netherlands' highest authority. After "ripe deliberation," the States-General decided to grant this request:

> So is it, that We ... out of unusual mercy, have forgiven, acquitted and pardoned ... the Officers, sailors, and seamen who have deserted [the United Provinces], serving the aforementioned robbers and pirates, or have served them [in the past], [and] all of those persons ... who have sailed with them, breaking the law in the sea and elsewhere ...

The *placaat* also stipulated that those pardoned would not have to suffer any fines, penalties, or punishments for their crimes, and that the grant of clemency was effective immediately. The one stipulation the States-General imposed was that the *rovers* and *piraten* who sought to take advantage of this remarkable reprieve were to return to the Republic within three months.[68]

But probably the most famous pardon the States-General ever issued was to the irascible and renowned *zeerover* Claas Compaen. Perhaps more than anyone else, Compaen incarnates the dual identity of the pirate in the Golden Age Netherlands. For while on the one hand, he had passed most of his life as a highly effective maritime criminal in an ignoble line-of-work, on the other hand, he was ultimately forgiven by his country's authorities and celebrated by his home-culture's popular press. Indeed, Compaen became so renowned for his misdeeds that his actions literally became "proverbial," for Dutch mothers would scold their children "Be nice right now, or I'll call Claes Compaen!"—much as modern American parents have threatened to summon the "bogeyman."[69] He was also the subject of striking fascination. In sum, Compaen the miscreant was, at the same time, Compaen the quasi-folk hero.

Claes Compaen's acts as a maritime predator were indisputably immoral according to the standards of the time. But the story of this erstwhile privateer for the homeland, this maverick mariner who had gone his own way and experienced a dazzling career as a pirate, was apparently too compelling and exciting for the Dutch public to ignore. When Compaen's ghostwriter (evidently a village schoolteacher[70] who interviewed acquaintances of Compaen[71]) recorded the pirate's exploits in a rollicking and detailed biography of his maritime adventures, *'t Begin, Midden en Eynde Der Zee-Rooveryen van den Alderfamieusten Zee-Roover/Claes G. Compaen, Van Oostzanen in Kennermer-landt ...* (*The Beginning, Middle and End of the Pirate Career of the Most Famous Pirate Around, Claes G. Compaen, of Oostzanen in Kennermerland*),[72] the result was a sensation and one of the most consistently popular books in the history of Dutch publishing (figure 5.2). (In addition to two separate printings in 1659, editions of the text appeared in 1662, 1668, 1675, 1682, 1685, 1688, 1726, 1733, 1756, 1762, 1778, 1781, ca. 1790, 1803, and 1910.)[73] Compaen was also included in a number of other important and popular publications, such as the widely read and influential history of the VOC, *Begin ende Voortgangh Van de Vereenighde Nederlantsche Geoctroyeerde Oost-Indische Compagnie* (*The Beginning and Continuing Progress of the United Dutch Patented East India Company*),[74] Nicolaes Wassenaer's chronicle *Historisch Verhael aller Gedenkwaerdiger*

Figure 5.2 Title page engraving, *'t Begin, Midden en Eynde Der Zee-Rooveryen van den Alderfamieusten Zee-Roover Claes G. Compaen* ... (1659). Verzameling Thysius.

Geschiedenissen ... (*Historical Tale of All Memorable Happenings*),[75] Lambert van den Bosch's paean *Leven en Daden der Doorluchtigste Zeehelden* (*Lives and Deeds of the Most Illustrious Sea Heroes*),[76] Johan van Twist's *General Beschrijvinghe van Indien* (*General Description of the Indies*),[77] and the personal reflection of a Dutch VOC vice-admiral who faced Compaen in battle, Wybrant Schram's *Journael ende Verhael Vande Oost-Indische Reyse, gedaen by den Heer Admiral Wybrant Schram* (*Journal and Tale of the East Indies Voyage of Admiral Wybrant Schram*).[78] Compaen's anonymous biographer contended that Compaen's fame as a *zeerover* was global—that he was known not just in Europe but in other far-flung locations too, such as Libya, Mauritania, Morocco, and the other Barbary states, and even the coast of India.[79]

Of course, this widespread interest in Compaen is not evidence that the Dutch public was ignorant of the pirate's culturally condemned lifestyle and misdeeds. Indeed, the decision of the biography's publisher to retain his anonymity—referring to himself only as "a Devotee of all Novelties"—is probably an indication of this realization and representative of a desire to escape guilt by association. After all, this is the same text that began, in the preface, by proclaiming to deplore Compaen's conduct and expressed fear of corrupting readers' souls with descriptions of the pirate's criminal behavior. And yes, Dutch Republican culture did profess to find piratical conduct to be deeply disturbing and problematic. But such cultural disgust was evidently superficial or conditional, for the moral sermonizing and concern was consigned only to the biography's introductory remarks. Once the narrative was underway, the critique ended. The story of Claes G. Compaen was apparently too gripping—and his character too charismatic—for people to ignore. The Golden Age populous was fascinated and enthralled.

The reading public's interest in Dutch pirates—even pirates who should have aroused moral condemnation—was not limited to the flamboyant Compaen. For example, chronicler Simon de Vries found former Zeelander-turned-Barbary corsair Ali Pegelin/Pisselingh so compelling that he felt inspired to describe Pisselingh's "Barbarian" life in somewhat close detail, without moral censure. De Vries's *Historie van Barbaryen* contains quite a bit of complimentary information about the renegade Dutchman, despite the fact that Pisselingh had joined the much-loathed North African corsairs and profited greatly from that association. (And as a further service to his readers, de Vries also made reference to the fact that he had included more about Pisselingh's illustrious career in other texts, the *Historische, Philosophische en Politike Rust-uyren* [he refers readers to page 94], the *Grooote Historische Rariteit-Kamer* [page 297], and Volume IV of the *Curieuse Aenmerckingen der bysonderste Oost en West-Indische verwonderenswaerdige dingen* [page 1360].)[80] It is also interesting that the infamous Dutch buccaneer, Rock de Bresiliaan—a man so brutally violent that he was said to roast Spaniards alive on spits[81]—appeared under the diminutive Rokje ("Little Rok") in Dionysis van der Sterre's biography of Jan Erasmus Reyning.[82] Such a nickname bestows an almost "cute" and certainly affectionate connotation, despite the man's alleged savagery.

In any event, what do various seventeenth-century sources tell us about Claes Compaen's ignominious history as a maritime predator? After making his fateful decision to quit his official post as a privateer for the Republic, Claes Compaen enjoyed terrific success as a pirate, capturing a great number of ships from countries the world over.[83] True to his original affirmation when he entered the pirate life, many of his victims were fellow Dutchmen.[84] He even attacked and absconded with ships under the command of other pirates.[85] Although it is impossible to know exactly how many ships he seized (before he returned home to the Netherlands, Compaen burned the journal that he had used to keep track of his accounts),[86] he estimated that, even at an early point in his career, he had taken at least 350.[87] Such a number of captures would make him among the most successful pirates in history.[88] To market his ill-begotten wares, he struck up relationships with local authorities, corrupt men who gave him refuge in exchange for part of the plunder.[89] For most of his time as a pirate, in fact, Compaen used the Moroccan port of Salé—the notorious "pirates' nest" on the Atlantic coast—as his home base, a place where he could sell goods he had plundered, restock his ships, and rest between voyages.[90] At the pinnacle of his career, he lorded over a fleet of seven ships[91] and up to 400 pirate crew hands.[92] And his craft were typically large and strong—prodigious "Guinea-travelers," for example (i.e., ships used in the West Africa trade). He particularly favored one called *de Omval* (*The Ruin*).[93]

Fulfilling the dark reputation of his fellow maritime marauders, Claes Compaen, too, used violence and fear during his sea robber career. He kidnapped, blackmailed, and threatened his victims as means to his desired end.[94] At times, he could be purposely cruel: once, he went so far as to turn over to the Dunkirkers 70 Dutch sailors he had captured, an inhumane act against his fellow compatriots which resulted in the imprisonment of the poor seamen.[95] And as both Wassenaer and Compaen's biography make clear, he certainly inspired dread on the high seas. Still, relative to the company he was keeping, Compaen was generally not a sadistic man. Instead of threats or violence, he often employed simple duplicity, such as false papers, to outwit his victims. Moreover, he could be downright convivial to those whom he encountered at sea. When he kidnapped and ransomed the *Alcaide* (mayor) of Salé for ƒ.50,000, for instance, he treated the man very well.[96] Likewise, when he captured the ship of fellow Dutchman Evert Corneliszoon, it was only after amiably visiting with Corneliszoon for a spell. Then he released all of Corneliszoon's crew and offered the unlucky captain 50 ducats of traveling money so that Corneliszoon could return home to Holland.[97] When the pirate seized a valuable Dutch ship, coincidentally commanded by his former neighbor Jacob Quick, Compaen proclaimed with hearty good cheer, "Welcome, my good neighbor!" and invited the man to come aboard.[98] And after commandeering the vessel of a Dutchman named Boefje (Little Scoundrel, Little Rascal) and warmly welcoming him aboard his own ship, Compaen affably teased the man, jokingly querying, "How is this so, Boefje? Have you still not had enough bad luck? Must you, also, become my booty?"[99] After further jesting and kidding, Compaen stole only a token amount of plunder from Boefje's ship, requested that the man deliver some money to Compaen's wife back home in the Netherlands, visited and chatted for a spell, and sent the "victim" on his way. A few days later, Compaen caught up with Boefje again; they shared a meal, drank, visited together, and parted once more, wishing one another a pleasant journey.[100]

Both of these aspects of Claes Compaen's character—his threatening mien and affability—came into sharp relief during the most famous moment of his long career as a pirate: his encounter and battle with the VOC ship, the *Hollandia*, in June 1626. Even if all other details about Claes Compaen are apocryphal or enhanced, this chapter of the story really did take place—at least as generally related—for Vice-Admiral Wybrant Schram's original report about the event still survives in the VOC Archive.[101] Espying the Batavia-bound vessel by Sierra Leone (West Africa) where its crew had sought shelter to repair a leak,[102] and ascertaining its Dutch identity, Compaen determined to strike up an acquaintance with the *Hollandia*'s commander, the "brave Wybrant Schram of Enkhuysen."[103] For rather than further riches or treasure, rather than glittering plunder and booty, the pirate had decided that he desired one thing above all else—he wanted to end his career as a pirate and return home to the Netherlands. He composed a note to the VOC ship's captain, requesting that the commander help him to obtain a pardon from the States-General. In exchange, the pirate promised, he would leave the *Hollandia* and her crew unmolested.[104]

Schram, however, refused and ultimately, hostilities ensued. Compaen raised the "Blood-flag,"[105] the respective crews prepared, and the ships opened fire.[106] The pirate's martial prowess quickly became apparent. In the words of his one of his adversaries, he showed himself to be "a seaman whom his enemy can rely on, [a man] with cunning and also with composure."[107] Things continued on this course for hours, with the two crews engaged in hard fighting from 12 noon until 4 o'clock in the afternoon. The result was destruction and a number of casualties. Both ships sustained damage in the form of broken rigging and masts and limped back to the Sierra Leone harbor. And among the crew of the *Hollandia*, four people perished, including the minister, whose leg was shot off; the minister's wife, who lost both of her feet; the ship's carpenter; and an able seaman. Other crewmembers were seriously wounded.[108]

Despite all of his efforts, though, Compaen had not vanquished the stalwart crew of the *Hollandia*. So, jocular character that he was, he switched tacks and sent an amiable letter to Vice-Admiral Schram, expressing his greetings and seeking the friendship of the beleaguered VOC commander. He also wanted assurances that Schram would assist him with his pardon back in the Netherlands.[109] By the time Schram's and Compaen's ships parted a few days later, they had struck up a relationship of sorts, after having shared food and conversation. In the meantime, despite Compaen's hopes for a pardon from the Dutch authorities, he apparently saw no reason to alter his behavior. When Schram spotted the pirate out at sea just a few days later, he could see that Compaen was already back to his old, duplicitous tricks, flying two flags from the mast—"below a French one, and above a Prince Flag (i.e., Dutch flag)"—in an effort to conceal his identity to potential victims.[110] And, indeed, right away, Compaen returned to his usual habits, capturing a richly laden Dutch ship en route from Africa.

Back in the Netherlands, the States-General had come to the conclusion that they would extend amnesty to Claas Compaen. Using the argument that a pardon would serve to remove the dangerous and destructive *zeerover* from the sea, they signed the document and presented it to Heyn Aertszoon, Compaen's half-brother,[111] who later rendezvoused with Compaen in Salé.[112] Landing in the Republic, Compaen docked at Sparendam, and traveled to the Hague, ". . . where he fell on his knees before the Prince of Orange, and his Excellency then went on to confer the permitted Pardon to the Rebel . . ."[113]

The story of Claas Compaen does not end quite yet. Both his biography and Wassenaer's chronicle supply a few details about Compaen's life after he settled into a tranquil and domestic existence in smalltown Holland. As pleasantly placid as life in Oostzaan must have been, where Compaen lived "behind the church, [on] an avenue or boulevard surrounded by trees and water," he retained his colorful demeanor, wearing expensive, foreign clothing such as "scarlet red garments with silver trimmings,"[114] ever arming himself with "pistols and other weapons,"[115] employing servants,[116] and always keeping two loaded guns behind his front door.[117] Around age 40 when he reentered bourgeois Dutch society, he still cut a fine figure, being "long of build and of manly appearance, very well spoken, with great prudence concealing his financial affairs, soberly sharing this [information only] with his friends." And friends he had, for many sought out his company, desiring a relationship with the eccentric, notorious, and now-retired pirate.[118] Marauding adventurer though he had been, he now enjoyed the simple pleasures, for "Up until this point, fishing has been his greatest amusement . . ."[119] He lived to see the spectacular success of his published biography.

As extraordinary as Claes Compaen's pardon was—as amazing as it is to learn that the Dutch authorities let such an accomplished pirate off the hook and that, in turn, Compaen was able to insert himself easily into the simple tranquility of Dutch bourgeois life—this Dutch "spirit of clemency" took yet an even more surprising form. Indeed, some pirates—whether they assumed this identity by dint of mere reputation or by the stamp of a court's conviction—were deemed fit to serve the Republic in an official capacity. In other words, the Dutch Republic overlooked these individuals' notorious pasts, and judged them "clean" and fit enough to work as naval and trade company officers.

Accomplished Caribbean buccaneer Jan Erasmus Reyning represents one example of this phenomenon. Reyning's favorable work experience with the WIC provided the means for the erstwhile buccaneer to obtain legitimate and esteemed employment back home in Netherlands. Gone was any taint of his former misdeeds, such as his collaboration with other pirates, his service under foreign governments, his violent despoliation of innocent ships, his participation in barbarous treatment of captives, and his possession of dubious commissions. What remained, apparently—what the Dutch authorities saw—was simply a gifted, skilled, and effective maritime warrior, a seafaring leader whose talents could be well utilized by his country. Reyning's first stroke of good luck occurred when the governor of Curaçao, Jan Donker, wrote a letter to the chairmen of the WIC on Reyning's behalf, urging them to give the former buccaneer his own ship to command.[120] Reyning had now joined the ranks of official WIC captains. Later, after he had returned home to Zeeland for a visit, he received an invitation from the Admiralty of Amsterdam, a request to take him into official naval service. Offered the command of a small frigate named *de Fortuyn* (*the Fortune*), which was equipped with eight guns and thirteen sails, Reyning set off yet again. Naturally, he enjoyed spectacular success, attacking, plundering, and burning ships, especially those belonging to the French.[121] The Admiralty of Amsterdam must have been pleased with their decision to take him on.

But admittedly, the place where Reyning established his "pirate credentials"—the Caribbean—was a liminal space: an area characterized by murky, vacillating identities, a place where yesterday's criminal pirate could become today's licit and upstanding seaman. This much becomes evident when one looks at archival documents of the time. For such cagey and corrupt double-dealing—of engaging in criminal conduct while seeming to embody legality and virtue—was not just the practice of refractory individuals such as Jan Erasmus Reyning. Indeed, surviving documents from the WIC demonstrate that such criminality-in-disguise took place often and at a high institutional level in that little-policed and unfixed space. Many parties resident in the Caribbean were involved in shady dealings,[122] and the Dutch were no exception. The WIC itself both participated in and permitted crooked schemes with piratical sorts, and directly profited from them. And needless to say, despite emphatic laws prohibiting such contacts, neither Company officials nor Dutch government authorities seemed too quick to prosecute or even stop the individuals involved.

Documents from the later years of the seventeenth century reveal just how corrupt WIC business practices could be. While there had long existed a close connection between merchant shipping and privateering in the Caribbean region (e.g., the WIC itself had a lengthy history of capturing prize ships in its region, and between 1659 and 1661 alone issued some 40 *commissies van retorsie*),[123] the Company did much more than simply sponsor and support licit privateering. Apparently, Company personnel routinely fraternized with both pirates and "privateers" of dubious legality, entering into trade arrangements with them and offering them capital, refuge, and arms. For example, the Dutch were key trading partners with the buccaneers of Hispaniola, giving the pirates there—who tended to be anti-Spanish and fiercely pro-Protestant—gunpowder, cloth, and brandy in exchange for meat.[124] The existence of WIC records about these dubious practices indicates that Company authorities back home were keenly interested in such activities. One senses that the acts treated in these extant papers (which, in the following examples, cover only a short time frame) represented only a fraction of what really went on.

Official statements from Company personnel stationed in Curaçao reveal numerous instances of WIC ties to Caribbean pirates. A 1683 interrogation of one Pieter Doncker, for example, pointedly raised the issue of the Company's relationship with "the pirate" (*piraat*) Willem Riet, whose ship, the *Tyger* (*Tiger*), had been warmly received in Curaçao.[125] Another 1683 interrogation, this time of one Juan Barofso y Pozzo, revealed that the island had been visited by a Dutch "privateer or pirate" (*Caaper off piraat*) who arrived in his ship, *den Propheet Elias* (*the Prophet Elias*), in April 1682. Far from closing the island's harbor to the roguish seaman, Barofso y Pozzo reported, Company authorities welcomed him and supplied him with ammunition; they also sheltered him in Bonaire. This pirate then went on to plunder the Dutch merchant ship *de Somebeeck* near Bonaire in July 1682. The same witness also alleged that WIC official, Willem de Penijn, knowingly supported the "pirate" (*Roover*) Jantjen, turning a blind eye to the sea robber's lack of a valid commission, and taking a direct role in purchasing his stolen goods.[126] Other witnesses revealed that the "privateers and pirates" (*de caepers ende piratten*) Willem Riet and Jantie captured a Spanish ship carrying 116 casks of sugar, which they later traded in Curaçao with the blessings of the WIC authorities there.[127] Another document clarified that a Dutch seaman, Jacob Rijkertzoon, who was sailing illegally under the English flag, had served as the middleman in this transaction.[128] Witness Gisberto Hippesack corroborated this account,[129] and further commented that Riet had plundered Spanish cocoa as well.[130] Hippesack also averred that it was standard if illegal practice in the Caribbean for so-called privateers to carry the commission of one state while working for another,[131] a claim that was buttressed by high-level official Jan Doncker.[132] Hippesack went on to name WIC privateer Antheunis Klincke as a suspect in this regard.[133] (This assertion was verified by other WIC officials, who stated that Klincke was guilty of "perfidy" and "piracy" for serving the French even as he carried a WIC commission.[134]) Meanwhile, witness David Abendana reported that "privateers" (*capers*) from the vicinity of Caracas routinely came to Curaçao to trade; among other goods, high-level WIC authorities purchased pitch, paper, sulfur and rope from them. (It is amusing to note that according to Abendana, these same WIC officials, showing some small sense of moral compunction, did not permit these illicit commercial activities to take place on the Sabbath.[135])

Documents generated by upper-level WIC authorities back in the Republic are just as revealing. Investigatory materials concerning the actions of Curaçao employees Balthazar Beck and Willem de Penijn, for example, indicate that the two WIC officials supplied another pirate, buccaneer "Monsieur de Grammont" (a.k.a. Chevalier de Grammont), with provisions and ammunition. Beck and de Penijn went so far as to dispatch a Company ship to the island where Grammont and his squadron were hiding, to bear the offering.[136] Witnesses further claimed that de Penijn, Beck, and Curaçao director Nicolaas van Liebergen also traded with Grammont, paying cash for goods such as brandy, bacon, tobacco, ammunition, and the like.[137] Other documents claim that de Penijn also took a WIC ship to an island where he purchased sugar from privateer (*Kaper*) Willem Riedt, and brought it back to Curaçao. De Penijn committed the further sin of using Company funds for this illegal transaction.[138] Still other records affirm that Director Nicolaas van Liebergen had supplied this same "privateer or pirate" (*kaper ofte piraat*), Willem Riet, with water and wood when Riet lay hidden in the harbor of Santa Barbara. The document also termed Riet and his cronies "godless men."[139] And in 1688, then director of Curaçao, Willem Kerckrink, committed the trespass of admitting the pirate ship *Anna Elisabeth* to the island's harbor. This last offense apparently went beyond the pale, for in an effort to install some proper order, WIC authorities back in the Republic commanded Kerckrink to punish these criminals as an example to all, and ordered that the papers of all other ships arriving in Curaçao be thoroughly inspected, so as to avoid further accommodation of such maritime riffraff. They also demanded that they be apprised of the names and identities of all incoming ships.[140]

But the WIC was not alone, for the VOC certainly perpetrated misdeeds as well. Evidently, preserving the flow of trade was important enough to warrant illicit acts and grave abuses,[141] and some were of a piratical nature. A States-General proclamation from 1610, for example, acknowledged the "excesses" committed by Company privateers.[142] And in 1714, the High Court of Holland slapped a steep fine of *f.*40,000 against the Company in the matter of the VOC privateer who went by the provocative title of "the Stranger."[143] Indeed, C.G. Roelofson affirms that in matters concerning hegemony over the East Indies trade, the VOC "showed an aggressiveness, which quickly earned the Dutch a reputation as 'pirates.' "[144] The Company also deliberately aided and abetted piracy within the waters of its own jurisdiction. For instance, at the end of the seventeenth century, the VOC provided Company flags and passes to English "pirates" (*Zeerovers*) cruising the Malabar Coast so that that the marauders could more easily catch "Moorish" ships there; Company ships, meanwhile, were spared.[145]

So the WIC's and VOC's *octrooigebieden*—monopoly jurisdictions—were special cultural spaces where identities were fluid and legitimate businesses engaged in illegitimate practices. An "anything goes" attitude prevailed in these far-off colonial outposts, these frontiers where the licit and the illicit not only rubbed shoulders, but enjoyed a symbiotic relationship and intermingled almost seamlessly. To be a pirate in these regions meant that one could evidently wear several different hats simultaneously, acting as either a *kaper* or a *zeerover* in the same instance, depending upon the perceptions of the audience and the exigencies of the moment. Evidence of this is the WIC's seemingly-interchangeable use of terminology for the sea robbers they observed and worked with in the Caribbean; such men were alternatively called *kapers, rovers,* and *piratten* in the Company's own archival records. Jan Erasmus Reyning, a clever fellow apparently, took astute advantage of the special opportunity the cultural space of the Caribbean presented to him. That is, he seized the chance to enjoy the fruits of a piratical career and then recast himself as a fully legitimate servant of the state.

But what about those Dutch pirates whose reputation was not made in the East or West Indies, who earned the moniker of *zeerover* far away from those rough-and-tumble geographical outposts which allowed for such extreme blurring of cultural boundaries? Did the Dutch ever allow men whose identity as pirates was never debated—whose criminal misdeeds were never euphemistically redefined—to return to the good graces of Golden Age society and serve the Republic? The answer is yes. In at least two notable instances, Republican authorities deemed convicted pirates suitable enough not only to serve the state, but to work as leaders—powerful officers—in positions of great prestige and responsibility.

The case of Laurens Davidszoon and Hubert Hugo is probably the most surprising and dramatic of all. By reconstructing their tale through sources in the archives of the VOC and the High Court of Holland, as well as by consulting Davidszoon's actual court sentence delivered in Dordrecht in 1663 and several foreign sources, one can encounter a remarkable instance of how Golden Age Dutch culture could turn the other cheek when it came to the issue of piracy. Hugo, a native of Delftshaven, and Davidszoon (also known as Laurens van Convent), born in Dordrecht, were both respectable family men with legitimate seafaring careers when they decided to embark upon a piratical adventure in the mid-seventeenth century.[146] Hugo had served as an honorable employee of the VOC for 14 years, quickly working his way up the Company's white-collar administrative ladder to the prestigious position of *koopman* (merchant), before returning home to the Netherlands in 1654.[147] Davidszoon, for his part, had worked as a proper merchant seaman and privateer for the Admiralty of the Maas.[148]

At some point in 1660 or 1661, the two men struck up an acquaintance, and, with six other individuals, created a *rederij* to finance a privateering adventure. While the professed intent was to "exchange food with the Moors" (i.e., Arabs), the *rederij*'s actual goal was "to go capture the Moors . . ., to harm Moors in the Red Sea . . ."[149] Each participant invested ƒ.8,000 in the undertaking. Using the ƒ.64,000 collective capital at their disposal, the partnership had a ship built and designated Davidszoon as the captain and Hugo as the "commander." The vessel—a "frigate" of 400 tons—was constructed in Sardam and mounted with 30–36 guns.[150] Outfitting the new ship in Amsterdam with the requisite provisions, rigging, ammunition, and hand weapons, the *reders* gave it the patriotic appellation of the *de Seven Provintien* (*the Seven Provinces*, an obvious reference to the seven-member provinces of the Dutch Republic) and proceeded to hire a crew.[151]

As soon as the ship departed the Netherlands' shores, Davidszoon's and Hugo's seemingly upright demeanor evaporated. Formerly marking the *Zeven Provintien*'s transformation from a stalwart, respectable Republican vessel into a dangerous craft bent on nefarious deeds, the two men renamed their ship *den Swarten Arent* (*the Black Eagle*).[152] Docking in the French port of Havre de Grâce, they received a French commission dated May 24, 1661 from the Duc de Vendôme, uncle of King Louis XIV and "Chief and General Superintendent of the Navigation and Commerce of France." This French letter of marque, while illegal under Dutch law, purported to give Davidszoon and Hugo the right to seize the goods of and take as prisoners "pirates, corsairs and infidel Mahometan people . . . and other savages and enemies of this state . . ."[153] Their only obligation was to bring all booty back to Havre de Grâce for adjudication. So after hiring some additional crew, which now numbered 72 men, and further provisioning their vessel, Davidszoon and Hugo set sail from Havre de Grâce on August 31, 1661 for the Red Sea.[154]

By all accounts, Davidszoon and Hugo were ferocious and effective *zeerovers*. While the official testimonies—found in Dutch, English, Indian, and Arab documents—differ a bit in the details, the consensus is that the two men and their crew violently attacked, plundered, and burned a number of ships in the Indian Ocean and Red Sea. Their crimes commenced on the coast of Madagascar, where they thoroughly pillaged at least one ship.[155] Proceeding thenceforth to the Red Sea, they sailed toward the city of Mocha, assaulting, burning, and sinking "Moorish" vessels along the way. Booty included rice, money, provisions, cowries, cloth, spices, livestock, gold, jewels, and other unspecified goods. They also kidnapped several indigenous mariners and held them for ransom, and stole passports from the VOC and English East India Company.[156] Moreover, when challenged militarily by the local leaders in Mocha, Hugo, and Davidszoon seized and burned more ships, captured ammunition, took prisoners, and killed local soldiers.[157] Reputedly, the pirates also tortured captive sailors and raped women aboard ships they had apprehended.[158] Their most spectacular seizure was probably that of the royal ship of the dowager queen of Bijapur, which was carrying a precious load of tributary treasures to Mecca and Medina. According to one Arabic chronicle, Hugo's and Davidszoon's booty from this capture included 65,000 gold pieces, 150 bales of muslin, carpets, a great horde of money, rosewater aloes, and two beds, one of gold and the other of silver.[159] Another English source reports that the pirates made off with "great riches, amounting to about 5 or 6 Tuns of Gold, in Jewels & other rich Comodities."[160] By any account, that haul alone was staggeringly valuable.

Despite local military opposition, Hugo and Davidszoon pillaged and burned ceaselessly before departing the Red Sea waters. The pirates then made their way to the Caribbean (after stopping at the island of St. Helena), where they attacked ships and seized booty (including 2,500–2,600 leather hides) in the vicinity of the islands of Martinique and St. Kitts.[161] Although Davidszoon himself claimed to have brought booty and prize ships back to Havre de Grâce for adjudication,[162] another source asserts that he returned directly to Amsterdam, where he was eager to divvy up his and Hugo's illbegotten spoils with their fellow *reders*.[163] Hugo himself temporarily disappears from the narrative at this point, apparently having gone to France, where one document relates that he was imprisoned in Havre de Grâce.[164] Whatever the actual sequence of events, the Dutch authorities somehow now caught wind of the scheme, and Davidszoon was apprehended and imprisoned in Dordrecht while awaiting trial; the remaining plunder was confiscated.[165]

Even though Laurens Davidszoon was being held in Dordrecht, the existence of investigatory documents in the archive of the High Court of Holland reveals that this court played a part in indicting and prosecuting the *zeerover*.[166] Although Davidszoon professed his innocence—he claimed that his actions were permissible under the terms of his commission—the High

Court of Holland would have none of his excuses. Indeed, it upbraided Davidszoon for transgressing against the 1606 States-General *placaat*, which proscribed Dutch seamen from working for foreign governments. The court also found Davidszoon to be guilty of trespassing in VOC waters where, the judges proclaimed, Davidszoon and Hugo indisputably acted as *piraten en zeeroovers* (pirates and sea robbers). All of this misconduct, the court determined, constituted egregious criminal behavior for which Davidszoon should be punished with the loss of both his life and possessions. And prior to his execution, the judges declared, Davidszoon should be incarcerated in the *Voorpoorte* (jail facility) of the Court.[167]

Before this judgment could be carried out, however, Davidszoon was removed from the High Court of Holland's custody and tried by the municipal court in his home city of Dordrecht.[168] Although the venue was different, the Dordrecht sentence reiterated the conclusions of the higher court, deeming the erstwhile family man guilty of *Zee-rooveryen ende piraterijen* (Sea-robbery and piracy) in the Red Sea. The judges cited Davidszoon's and Hugo's assaults on innocent ships; their burning, pillaging, and plundering; and their theft of VOC and English passports. They also censured Davidszoon and Hugo for their impiety, specifically, "that . . . during the time that they were in the Red Sea, they never said the ordinary Ship's prayers . . ." All of this, the court declared, constituted "matters of very pernicious consequences, which cannot be tolerated in a land of Justice" and merited "very severe punishment."[169]

While these words sound grave and ominous, it is at this juncture that Davidszoon's spate of bad luck began to turn, for the Dordrecht court's idea of "severe punishment" was milder than that of the High Court of Holland. To be sure, the penalty was still an onerous one, but Davidszoon was to retain his life. Rather than execution, the Dordrecht judges sentenced the convicted pirate "to be brought in chains to such a secure place as shall be decreed by their Honors [the judges] in order to be sequestered there for the time of thirty years, and upon the expiration of the same thirty years, for him to be banned for [his] lifelong days from the city of Dordrecht, and the province of Holland and West Friesland . . ." They also called for the confiscation of his possessions.[170] Since Dordrecht lacked a facility for actually carrying out this sentence—the city did not possess an appropriate prison—a request was made to move Davidszoon to the Amsterdam *Tuchthuis* (house of correction). This solicitation was granted by the Amsterdam authorities, and Laurens Davidszoon was duly transferred to the Amsterdam facility in October 1663 to begin his 30-year term of incarceration.[171]

By itself, the gentler penalty dictated by the Dordrecht court is again evidence of a cultural tendency to treat convicted Dutch pirates more lightly than the law prescribed. The Dordrecht judges did not order Davidszoon to die as the High Court of Holland had dictated and as countless Dutch legal codes enjoined. Likewise, the fact that Davidszoon's sentence was printed in pamphlet form (figure 5.3) reveals that that the Dutch public—or at least the citizens of Dordrecht—was quite interested in the case. But while the Dordrecht sentence is intriguing and compelling in and of itself, it represents

SENTENTIE

By mijn Ed: Heeren van den Gerechte der Stadt Dordrecht, op den xxvj. September, 1663. gepronuncieert tegens Laurens Davidsz., gewesene Capiteyn op het Schip eerst genoemt de seven Provincien, ende daer naer den Swarten Arent, in den Jare 1661. van Amsterdam naer Havre de Grace, ende van daer naer 't Roode Meer uyt-gevaren,

Ter saecke van de Zee-rooverpen ende piraterpen mettet voors: Schip/ in't gesepde Roode Meer gepleeght.

TOT DORDRECHT,

Voor MATTHEUS VAN NISPEN, Boeck-verkooper by de Nieuw-brugh in de Sonne-wijser. 1663.

Figure 5.3 *Sententie By mijn Ed: Heeren van den Gerechte der Stadt Dordrecht . . . tegens Laurens Davidsz . . . Ter saecke van . . . Zee-rooveryen ende pirateryen . . .* (Dordrecht: Mattheus van Nispen, 1663). Verzameling ZBP.

only the mere beginning of the clemency Laurens Davidszoon enjoyed. Indeed, it is really after Davidszoon was transferred to Amsterdam and began his term of imprisonment there that his—as well as Herbert Hugo's–fortunes improved considerably.

Laurens Davidszoon stayed but a short time in the Amsterdam *Tuchthuis*, for two months after his arrival, on November 27, 1663, he managed to escape through a chimney during the still of night. In all probability, he fled now to Havre de Grâce, where his crony Herbert Hugo apparently resided (Hugo's wife moved there in April 1664).[172] While much controversy and international dissension surrounded the distribution of the booty the two Dutch *zeerovers* had violently wrested from their Arab and Indian victims— both the French government and the VOC laid vigorous claim to it, with the French ultimately prevailing[173]—Hugo and Davidszoon were apparently able to live in France without a problem. In any event, the French ostensibly considered both Hugo and Davidszoon to be free men, for surprisingly enough, a letter extant in the French *Archives Nationales* dated November 4, 1664 affirms that the States of Holland had granted pardons to *Laurens David et consors* ("Laurens Davidszoon and consorts") in October 1664.[174] Laurens Davidszoon, the man whom the Dutch authorities had convicted of piracy only a year before, the condemned criminal whom the High Court of Holland had sought to execute and the court of Dordrecht had sentenced to 30 years incarceration and eternal exile, was now, incredibly enough, a free man.

The story actually continues to grow even more surprising. For on July 15, 1665, less than two years after Laurens Davidszoon had been convicted of criminal piracy in a Dutch municipal court, his name appeared in the commissions book of the Admiralty of the Maas. In other words, he had now been accepted into the respectable ranks of the Dutch Navy, and not as any mere sea hand either. Rather, Davidszoon was installed as the captain aboard the state warship the *Gornichem* and actively served in the Second Anglo-Dutch War. He continued in this capacity, commanding several naval warships, including the *Swol*, through 1666. In 1671, records show that the Admiralty made him the captain of the man-of-war *Groot-Hollandia*, and in 1672, he was promoted to serve as the commander of one of the largest warships in the fleet, the *Gelderland*. This prodigious vessel was manned by some 280 crewmembers and carried 36 cannons. This advancement in his occupational fortunes seems to have improved his family's social standing as well, for notarial documents reveal that Davidszoon's wife, the former "Stijntje Pieters" now went by the more refined and formal "Juffrouw Christina Pieters." Davidszoon apparently served the Admiralty of the Maas with courage, fortitude, and distinction until his death from illness in 1672.[175]

For his part, Herbert Hugo fared extremely well too. Far from being prosecuted for piracy in his native country, the former pirate instead resumed his career with the VOC and went on to hold appointments of great power and prestige. He was also compensated most handsomely for these honors. This is somewhat remarkable, considering that just a short time before, Hugo had trespassed in VOC waters, attacked VOC trading partners, forcibly stolen VOC passports, and caused enormous diplomatic damage between the VOC and indigenous political powers in the Red Sea and Malabar Coast regions. How, then, did Hugo's extraordinary rehabilitation come about?

In 1671, the *zeerover* had the audacity to contact the VOC, offering his services to the Company in return for a generous salary. After meeting to discuss the matter, the VOC authorities accepted Hugo's overture and reinstated him as a Company employee. Once again, Hugo found himself on the Company's fast-track, for immediately, in May 1671, he was appointed as the *opperhoofd* (chief) of the island of Mauritius, earning a salary of *f.*100 per month (in comparison, the post of *koopman* [merchant] paid only *f.*65). By the time of Hugo's and his family's arrival at his new assignment, he bore the title of "Commander" of the colony. Although he did have to abide by some special Company demands—for instance, under no circumstances was he to visit the coast of India, where memory of his depredations was still vivid—the VOC leadership entrusted him with great responsibility, such as overseeing the agricultural development of his new island home. By the time of his death in Batavia in 1678, the governing officials in the Indies had named him one of the Company's notable dignitaries, a man worthy of solemn and ceremonious respect.[176] Somehow or another, Hubert Hugo, the former pirate who had flagrantly flouted Dutch law and violently trespassed in Company waters, had transformed into Hubert Hugo, the noble, esteemed, and highly decorated servant of the VOC.

It is undeniably true that the Dutch Republic maintained strict, emphatic laws defining "piracy" and calling for its severe punishment. It is also true that many convicted *zeerovers* and *stroomrovers* did pay a heavy price for their transgressions, earning sentences of extreme corporal punishment and execution by decree of the Dutch courts. What is also indisputable, however, is that many of those seamen who were suspected, accused, or even convicted of piracy walked away with a much more mild reproach, or no reproach at all. Curiously enough, these individuals received much gentler penalties than Dutch law stipulated, or they were pardoned and permitted to rejoin the ranks of respectable seventeenth-century Dutch society. Sometimes, the authorities neglected even to charge these marauders at all, with the result that behavior which was officially "piratical" according to the letter of the law was allowed to continue unabated and uncondemned.

How can it be that the same society which crafted such exacting and specific legislation concerning piracy and its punishment could, at the same time, turn a blind eye to egregious examples of the very conduct it denounced? And why was it that a culture that professed such revulsion for piracy still openly craved to read benign or even complimentary accounts of Dutch practitioners of the crime? The answer lies partly in the allure of monetary enrichment and the exigencies of national defense. But just as important was the fundamental tension in Golden Age Dutch culture between the prescribed word of law and the power of patriotic nationalism and historical memory. Although Dutch culture professed to condemn the figure of the "pirate," the weight of the Republic's own personal history and identity, combined with its economic and military needs, engendered cultural attitudes and values that nullified this claim, with the result that blatant acts of *zeeroverij* by Dutchmen sometimes went "unnoticed" or unpunished. Chapter 6 explores these complicated mores and values that affected the Republic's cultural understanding of criminal piracy.

6

THE DUTCH FREEBOOTER IN THE GOLDEN AGE

It is difficult to reconcile the Golden Age Dutch Republic's stringent legislation regarding privateering and piracy—as well as the Dutch population's loathing for piracy in general—with its courts' erratic dispensation of justice. Numerous Dutch laws meticulously delimited conduct that constituted "piracy" and emphatically forbade Dutch seamen from engaging in it. Yet, surprisingly, the Dutch authorities often neglected to act on these edicts. While judges sometimes did deliver the prescribed harsh penalties, consisting of brutal corporal punishment and execution, many convicted *zeerovers* and *stroomrovers* escaped such severe sanctions, instead receiving lighter sentences, pardons, and even public approval. Occasionally, archival sources disclose reasons why the authorities chose to be merciful.[1] In general, however, one can find no outward, discernable rationale for the Dutch authorities' reasoning. Why were there so many exceptions to explicit Dutch rules about piracy? Why did the Dutch public's proclaimed repugnance for piracy not manifest itself as a zealous commitment to prosecute and punish their own errant seamen? Why did popular Dutch literature claim to demonize pirates but then sometimes instead lionize them? How can one explain the Dutch authorities' peculiar hesitancy to penalize convicted maritime criminals, and, indeed, the Dutch population's apparent support of this position?

These are not simple questions to answer, for the reasons are manifold and complex. By closely analyzing the various forces at work during the Netherlands' Golden Age, however, one discovers the explanation for this seemingly random behavior. In sum, political and economic imperatives—namely, the struggle for independence, the exigencies of military defense, and the importance of trade—as well as special predispositions arising from the Netherlands' maritime traditions, its citizens' growing sense of national consciousness, their interpretations of international legal custom, and their adherence to a particular set of collective memories, forged cultural values that both deviated from the official word of law and mitigated the Dutch public's general disdain for piracy. These cultural values shaped Golden Age society's perceptions, allowing for a softening and blurring of the formal standard and the toleration of a slippery slope between the lawful "privateer" and the illegal "pirate." Ultimately, these countervailing beliefs conditioned the symbolic meaning[2] attached to the figures of the Dutch privateer and pirate, with the result that the marauders' ostensibly distinct identities represented, in actuality, hazy points along a continuum. Consequently, the Dutch public and authorities often failed to recognize the "piratical" behavior that their own laws proscribed. And even if they did discern piracy in their midst, they were prone to relabeling it euphemistically or looking askance. Manifold regulations designed to keep piracy in check fell by the wayside in the face of these inexorably influential cultural predispositions. Fussy edicts and proclamations became mere window dressing, serving to delude the Dutch—and especially foreign governments—that the Republic took piracy seriously and prosecuted its practitioners ruthlessly.

Such cultural values made it difficult indeed to draw a firm line between the two activities of "privateering" and "piracy." This becomes patently clear in a pamphlet published in 1649, which alternates between calling Dutch privateers "*Kapers*" ("privateers"), "*Vrijbuiters*" ("Freebooters"), and "*Rovers*" ("Pirates").[3] It is also revealed in the Index of the Admiralty of the Maas' sentencing records, which instead of merely grouping together all piratical transgressions in one category called "*zeeroverij*" contains a myriad of categories for maritime robbery, ostensibly mitigating and obfuscating the fundamental character of the crime. Moreover, it is further manifested in the research of J.Th.H. Verhees-Van Meer, who acknowledges some difficulty in defining exactly who qualified as a privateer and as a pirate during the War of Spanish Succession. Possession of a valid letter of marque was not the sole criterion, she admits, for sometimes those who held such documents were prosecuted as *zeerovers*, while in other instances, mariners who held no *commissiebrief* were celebrated and rewarded for their capture of enemy ships and booty. And what can one make of Dutch seamen who carried commissions issued by neutral foreign powers, she asks?[4] In short, then, the Dutch privateer/pirate was a liminal sort of person, a "sometimes good," "sometimes bad" maritime predator with an indistinct and elusive identity.

* * *

So how did such blurring of the boundaries come about? How did this permissiveness vis-à-vis piracy evolve? In seeking to understand the unique cultural values that defined and shaped Dutch perceptions of piracy and privateering and engendered such tensions between the rule of law and everyday, lived experience, it is mandatory to consider the very real and integral role that privateers—whether upright and moral or wayward and corrupt—played in the struggle to preserve the independence, prosperity, and vigor of the young Dutch Republic. Since the Dutch were at war during so much of the Golden Age, and since the Republic was, after all, a somewhat small state struggling to combat larger, more populous adversaries, the almost-continuous contributions of the privateers were, through the years, important. At a fundamental level, privateers were a genuine part of the Dutch naval effort, a force of brave and battle-ready men who played their own important role in intimidating, frustrating, and inflicting damage upon the enemy.

Privateering's indisputable military utility in an era of evolving naval warfare was evident to the seventeenth-century Dutch. A 1662 "proposition" drafted by the States of Zeeland, for example, beseeched the States-General to issue letters of commission against the Portuguese. It declared that not only "experience but also most advice from the . . . [Admiralty] College" recommended such an action, for the privateers had delivered "very notable service" in the "suppression" of the Republic's enemies at other times, "and especially in the War against Spain . . . " The Zeelanders further implored the government to provide funding for bountiful premiums to attract stalwart and brave *commissievaarders*.[5] That the States-General itself was already aware of privateering's advantageousness and effectiveness is clear. It issued proclamations that advertised the availability of privateering commissions and urged Dutch seamen to apply to their respective Admiralties.[6] Moreover, during the course of the seventeenth century, the States-General deliberately instituted two privateering concerns dedicated to the repression of the Republic's enemies: the "Duinkerkse Directie" ("Dunkirk Directory"), created in 1642 for the purpose of eradicating the Flemish menace, and the 1646 "Brasilse Directie" ("Brazil Directory"), the goal of which was the removal of the Portuguese from WIC waters.[7] In 1665, during the Second Anglo-Dutch War, several privateering *rederijen* emulated this model and joined forces in the "Directie van de Nieuwe Equipage" ("Directory of the New Equipage"). This conglomerate enjoyed immediate governmental support, with the States-General quickly issuing commissions to their seamen, and the Admiralty of Zeeland loaning them 27 guns.[8] Such concerns were effective in combating the Republic's adversaries and, in turn, in furthering its political goals. Indeed, as one 1649 pamphlet that discussed Portuguese–Dutch relations proclaimed, ferocious Dutch privateering had served as a very effective "means to force Portugal to dance to our pipes . . . " Specifically, the pamphlet proclaimed, zealous Dutch *kapers* would not only aid in keeping the Portuguese out of Brazil, but would "force the Portuguese to return Angola / and . . . let us keep the Island of Sint Thomé and the whole South-Coast of Africa . . . "[9]

Of course, parallel with the necessity to maintain a strong and able national defense was the need to safeguard and defend Dutch maritime commerce. This made especially good sense during a mercantilist age characterized by a Western belief in finite global wealth. After all, only with the lucrative goods and investment opportunities delivered by the "God-given" carrying trade could the small Republic continue to stand tall as a vigorous, affluent, and independent state in the European community of nations. As a States-General *placaat* of 1645 put it, the "entire existence and welfare, as well as the fame of the United Provinces, depends upon its shipping, and foreign trade, and commerce."[10] And a 1687 pamphlet echoed these sentiments, affirming that

> The whole prosperity of the provinces of Holland and Zeeland, and the foundation of its exchequer consists (so everyone is aware) in the free sea trade

and commerce of all kinds of wares and commodities, to which end God the Lord Almighty has bestowed especially upon the aforementioned provinces—above all other lands—good facilities, suitable roadsteads, harbors, rivers, and waters.[11]

Elements of the Dutch population viewed commerce as so integral to the survival of the state that moral niceties were seen as dispensable. For example, despite the various prohibitions the Dutch government had proclaimed against trafficking with the Barbary corsair states, Dutch ships continued to bring merchandise—and even contraband materials—to the North African ports, especially Algiers.[12] Certainly such illegal trading was motivated by opinions such as that manifested in a 1687 pamphlet, which urgently persuaded its readers of the absolute necessity of the Mediterranean trade. Almost hysterical in its voice, the pamphlet vehemently argued that if the Netherlands lost control of the Mediterranean trade, all other Dutch commerce would fall by the wayside. To protect this vital route, he advocated that the Dutch sail everywhere throughout the region and frequent every port there, not just neutral havens such as Marseille, Genoa, and Venice.[13] Such a point of view probably also accounts for the Dutch willingness, both on the part of the government and private parties, to deal with renegade Dutchmen (e.g., Jan Janszoon) who had joined up with the North African corsairs, rather than just hunt them down and prosecute them as pirates. For such men, straddling two cultures as it were, were an advantageous asset in both commercial and slave manumission negotiations.

In any event, Dutch privateers naturally assisted in the endeavor of protecting and furthering Dutch trade by assailing merchant trade vessels that belonged to, worked for, or sustained hostile competitor powers. Especially important in this regard were the VOC and WIC. Without a doubt, the VOC and the WIC were understood as integral to maintaining Dutch predominance in maritime commerce. Popular opinion tended to hold these two institutions as sacred, as divinely bestowed blessings, and most certainly linked to the affluence, security, and indeed *freedom* of the fledgling Dutch Republic. As one 1629 pamphlet put it, in an open prayer to God, "Bless these [Companies] with such Success and Progress that through [them] the Enemy's power is broken, [and] the Trade and Prosperity of these provinces are increased."[14] No matter that VOC and WIC seamen were sometimes involved in questionable conduct or that the commercial mission of the companies was often furthered through pugilistic means. The men who accomplished such deeds were perceived as brave patriots who put their lives on the line to safeguard and enrich their homeland. As one 1630 pamphlet—glowingly entitled *In Homage to the . . . East and West-India Company and Heralded Seagoing Trade of these Free United Netherlands Provinces*—exclaimed,

> Thus people from the *East* to the *West*, and from the *South* to the *North*, are aware of . . . the powerful materiel, and notable exploits of the widely-renowned

East and *West-India* Company ... to [the] great and considerable harm of our ... general enemies; ... [T]hese provinces, by virtue of these companies, are not only enriched, with gold, silver and expensive wares, and commodities, but are also extended, to the laurelled praise of the same ... and ... with manly courage ... .[15]

The author then went on to invoke several of the Republic's most hallowed national symbols—the Sea Beggars and the Batavians—in its litany of praise for the companies.[16]

Public sentiment assigned explicit privateering aims to the trade companies. When the pamphlet *In Homage to the ... East and West-India Companies* poetically extolled the WIC's and VOC's prowess in garnering precious goods, for instance, it used the language of privateering—that is, the search for "prizes"—to express such achievements. Indeed, in the words of this text, the Companies consisted of those brave souls

Who do not spare the Sea / or the mountains or reefs / or the harbors wide and narrow / or terrifying shoals / But seek, in exotic lands / up to the highest summits valiantly to [win] prize[s] for these provinces.[17]

Of course, VOC and WIC seamen actually did capture prizes within their waters, and naturally such deeds were interpreted as victories for the Republic. One pamphlet from 1649, for example, termed the actions of the VOC's privateers "valiant" even as it criticized the extreme behavior of other Dutch *kapers*.[18] And it is important to note that the Companies often presented at least a portion of these prize profits to the Republic's government, for the sake of the common good, or as one mid-century VOC resolution patriotically put it, for the sake of the "nation" (*"natie"*).[19]

Certainly, privateering in the name of commerce was most visibly incarnated by the WIC. It is true that the WIC was first and foremost a monopolistic commercial enterprise dedicated to the exploitation and extraction of commodities from Africa and the Americas. However, the Company's charter cited another equally important reason for the WIC's existence. According to the States-General, who drafted the Company's founding document in 1623, a "general company" dedicated to trade and shipping in Africa and the New World could also enjoy and be enriched by "the great adventure of piracy, extortion, and the like which takes place on such faraway voyages ... " This is a very telling and revealing statement, for not only was the States-General acknowledging that aggressive marauding was one of the fundamental raisons d'être of the new WIC, it explicitly labeled such actions as *"Zee-roverijen,"* that is, piracy. In this case, there was no pretence or euphemistic masking of the intent. Purely and simply, the States-General unequivocally resolved that the WIC should make *zeeroverij*—criminal piracy—one of its essential goals. And apparently, such conduct was deemed completely legal, appropriate, and acceptable. Indeed, so supportive was the States-General of the WIC's mission that the government delegates promised to protect and defend the Company, and to expend considerable sums of money to do so.[20]

The Company certainly followed through with its instructions to target other European powers. Not only did the WIC issue its own letters of marque, which were valid within the Company's jurisdiction, but WIC personnel in general acted ruthlessly to assault and capture the ships and goods of others within "Company" waters. In so doing, the Company became a hybrid commercial/military operation, simultaneously dedicated to the expansion of profits and the destruction and exploitation of the Dutch Republic's enemies. In this regard, Spain enjoyed special pride of place, for since the Company's inception, WIC personnel had endeavored to harass the Spanish. (For that matter, the Dutch had made a practice of zealously pursuing Spain's ships and goods in American waters since the first days of the Republic.)[21] This was clearly evident to everyone; a French document from 1634, for instance, affirmed that in spite of Spain's attempts to be "amiable" in the New World, the WIC persisted in hunting the Castilians ruthlessly.[22] So in addition to the WIC cargo vessels that regularly plied the Atlantic Ocean carrying valuable trade goods, the Company also dispatched fleets of heavily armed "naval" ships to prowl the waters of the Americas, seeking interloping adversaries. Even the designations borne by Company officers reflected this martial spirit, for as in the navy and army, top commanders were called vice admirals, admirals, and generals.

Certainly, WIC tactics could be very aggressive and violent. Take, for example, the tale recounted by one Dutch pamphlet. The source, allegedly an intercepted Spanish letter that described the attempt of WIC admiral Jacques Hermite to capture ships belonging to the Spanish Silver Fleet of 1624, recites a series of bloody Dutch assaults against both Spanish ships and hapless Peruvian colonists. In this case, the WIC fleet was formidable and well-armed. Composed of some 12 ships and a number of attendant sloops, it easily dwarfed the plainly inadequate Spanish detachment of two ships charged with collecting and conveying the massive, dazzling cargo of silver along the coast of Peru. Admiral Hermite's official instructions were to burn Callao, capture Lima if possible, apprehend and burn any Spanish ships he encountered, and seize the Silver Fleet. While he and his men did not achieve these particular goals, they still managed to sow much destruction. By virtue of WIC intelligence (the Company had two spies in Peru whom the Spanish authorities later discovered and tortured), Hermite was aware of crucial information, such as which Peruvian ports were most vulnerable and the proposed itinerary for the Silver Fleet. Acting on this advice, the WIC men captured two Spanish vessels, killing several sailors while they slept and laying claim to gold and silver; burned some three-fourths of the colony of Pesco; captured another 5 ships in the Pesco harbor; slayed some 150 Spanish sailors from another captured vessel; and besieged the colony of Guayaquil, binding prisoners and throwing them overboard alive. In this last incident, their victims numbered at least 15 men, including a monk and teacher. The Spanish letter writer, while acknowledging the fortitude and courage of the man who had led the attack against Guayaquil—WIC Vice-Admiral Jan Huygen—was also quick to cite Huygen's brutality.[23]

News of such "piratical" WIC attacks met with public applause and excitement back home in the Republic. A 1624 pamphlet, for example, which details a successful conquest in Brazil by WIC forces, uses glowing language to describe the assault. The text emphasizes the courage and boldness of the "brave and celebrated Sea-Hero" General Jacob Wilckens, and lauds the "manliness and stout resolution" of his soldiers and sailors. Painting a picture of patriotic valor, the pamphlet presents a blow-by-blow narrative of the pitched battle, complete with the sound of blaring Dutch trumpets and pounding drums and the WIC sailors' vows to fight courageously in the name of the States-General.[24] Likewise, a pamphlet published in 1630 extolled the WIC capture of Olinda, Brazil, with adulatory language and warm appreciation. The text proclaimed that the site, located in Pernambuco, had been "taken with virile daring and great courage . . . Under the command of the very brave and valiant Sea-hero, Lord Henrick Lonck, General . . . over a powerful fleet of ships . . . " Further accentuating Lonck's achievement, the pamphlet also included a list of all captured vessels, the names of enemy prisoners, and an inventory of their ammunition.[25]

Dutch citizens were apparently only too happy to support an official "piratical" venture if it led to the destruction of the Republic's adversaries. That such ventures could be remunerative only made them more attractive. As a result of the WIC's patriotic mission—as well as because of its stated goal to generate tremendous profits and please its shareholders[26]—the Company enjoyed public investment as well as acclaim. Similarly, financial investment in general privateering was widespread. Of course, like any other business venture, privateering carried risks, and some were unique to the profession. Investors feared that a war might end quickly, before they could recoup their money. They also balked at the high security deposit that the Admiralties demanded, and were afraid that privateer seamen might misbehave, thereby ensuring the forfeiture of the bond. And of course, even if the Dutch privateer ship survived tempests at sea or attacks from enemy vessels and triumphantly returned home with booty, there was no guarantee that such spoils would bring a good return at auction. Despite such potential problems, however, the mesmerizing lure of possible profits proved to be a hypnotic aphrodisiac, and good Dutch citizens happily invested funds in numerous privateering ventures. Indeed, the trade served as an esteemed nexus for weaving together the various strata of Golden Age society, for all classes of the Republic were involved in and supported the perpetuation of the industry.

From the very beginning, the partners in Golden Age privateering firms were respectable, stalwart members of bourgeois Republican society. People familiar with the sea were the most frequent participants,[27] and relatives of the bookkeeper were common shareholders as well.[28] Merchants, of course, were well represented—their knowledge of maritime trade and commodities enabled them to be informed and savvy investors. Also heavily involved were local government officials—town council members, sheriffs, bailiffs, and aldermen—as well as directors of the Levant trade companies, and administrators from the VOC and WIC.[29] During the three Anglo-Dutch Wars, prominent men who were leading merchants and regents served as privateering bookkeepers.[30] Indeed, privateering bookkeepers included among their number some of the most influential men in local and provincial circles. Wealthy and prominent, they served on the city councils of Middelburg and Vlissingen (sometimes as mayor), as shareholders or directors of the WIC, and were typically involved in lucrative merchant trades (such as gunpowder), in addition to their work as powerful and successful privateering *reders*.[31]

It must be underscored, however, that involvement in such privateering *rederijen* was not reserved for the mighty and influential alone. Seasoned mariners who worked in the business themselves often invested. Even as captains continued to enjoy careers as active seamen, they might purchase some shares in the ships they commanded.[32] Moreover, among the shareholder participants were tradesmen, individuals who worked as brewers, ship carpenters, ship chandlers, doctors, and rope makers.[33] A pamphlet dating from 1649 indicates that this had been the case for some time, affirming that all echelons of Dutch society (in this instance, in Zeeland)—including the city government and other public agencies—partook in privateering partnerships. Indeed, so popular was the trade that this pamphlet—a *praatje*—likened it to the great Tulip Mania of 1636–1637:[34]

> *Mr. Blue*: . . . is it true what they say, that the *Middelburg* city government itself outfitted several ships to go privateering? or that [the magistrates] are partners or participants with others in [such a venture]?
> *Mr. Yellow*: Oh yes, that's certain / and you must surely believe it, that the Principal partners or participants involved are from all over Zeeland.
> *Mr. Blue*: . . . But just tell me why the city government of *Middelburg* does [this] . . .?
> *Mr. Yellow*: I'll tell you exactly: The Orphanage Department there thought it proper to invest some five tons of gold from its Orphaned Children's Fund in the West-India Company / which was lost . . . because of the run-down state of the [Company]; and they necessarily must come up with . . . this money with the Interest . . . so they have ordered the best means [to do] that . . . People have seen that last year the privateers have done extraordinarily well: and how they now will be successful [again] . . .
> *Mr. Blue*: . . . I hear that this privateering has taken hold so hard / that one hears about almost nothing else in all of *Zeeland*: just as people once behaved about the Tulips / and that Young and Old / Maidens and Youths / Rich and Poor . . . / even Beggars / converse [about it] / [and] that people in the church read aloud about it [to] Women and Men and Youths . . .[35]

In sum, anyone who possessed the requisite cash to invest in privateering firms likely participated; only naval officers and certain Admiralty officials were forbidden by law to do so.[36]

Privateering, then, served as an important focus for investment in the Golden Age Republic. But this was not the trade's only financial role.

Privateering also made a significant contribution to the Dutch economy in general. First, the sale of prize ships and plunder garnered money for the Admiralties and *rederijen*.[37] Second, auctions of seized vessels and booty injected more goods and ships into the market, stimulating the wartime economy of various Dutch cities.[38] (In this regard, one must point out that the Dutch permitted not just their privateers but sometimes those of other states as well to sell their plunder in the Republic.[39]) Third, privateering provided well-paying, sought-after maritime employment, which ostensibly compensated seamen better and offered more freedom than jobs in the navy and merchant shipping. And last, the industry served as an economic catalyst for a whole host of associated activities, presenting opportunities not only to investors, but also to shipbuilders, rope makers, sail makers, chandlers, carpenters, and anyone else whose labor supported and fueled the maritime economy. In this respect, privateering's economic impact extended far beyond the bounds of its intended mission, rippling out to stimulate myriad trades in Golden Age society.

So privateering was an entrenched, significant business in the Dutch Republic, an industry that promised potentially lucrative returns and which, over time, blossomed into a set of institutionalized arrangements, practices, and expectations that served to connect various and disparate facets of Golden Age society. Moreover, it provided an important means to protect and further the Republic's naval and commercial needs. Consequently, the Dutch public could not help but view the trade as generally advantageous and beneficial.

* * *

As important as these military and economic benefits were to privateering's acceptance, however, were fundamental preconditions, traditions, and beliefs that affected how the Dutch perceived the practice of maritime pillaging. A series of events in Zeeland during the War of Spanish Succession illustrates this point. In this example, while military and economic imperatives were extremely influential in how the Dutch understood and defined "privateering" and "piracy," long-standing cultural attitudes were even more so.

What happened in this particular case? Although forbidden by the States-General's letters of instruction to do so, Zeeland privateers began to seize the ships of allied and neutral states as early as the summer of 1702. Technically, such acts constituted criminal piracy. The Admiralty of Zeeland's response only added fuel to the fire. Commanded by the States-General to suspend adjudication of these ill-begotten captures and release the victims, the Admiralty staunchly refused, declaring them "good prizes" and selling several of the vessels and their cargo. The States-General retaliated by ceasing to issue letters of commission.

Although the States of Zeeland and States-General initially settled their differences,[40] unlawful captures by the Zeelanders began again in 1703. So aggressive and indiscriminate were the privateers, in fact, that they inspired one English diplomat to comment that the Zeelanders made "no difference between friends, Neutrals and Enemies, but take all they meet, and immediately declare good prize all they take."[41] The States-General predictably objected to these infractions, but to no avail, for the Zeelanders ignored their demands. Accordingly, the States-General stopped issuing commissions in September 1703. Moreover, in a further attempt at arm-twisting, in June 1704, they ceased to pay premiums for enemy warships and privateer vessels. The Danes—the chief victims of these unlawful seizures and understandably incensed—also brought pressure to bear. They castigated the Zeelanders as "pirates" and threatened reprisals, among which was the withdrawal of Danish troops who were supporting the Dutch in the war against France. In July 1705, some of these threats were borne out when in retaliation, the Danes detained a VOC ship in a Danish-controlled harbor in Norway.[42]

By July 1705, the Zeelanders finally abandoned their illicit practices. They were rewarded for their change of heart—the States-General once again issued commissions and even doubled the stipulated premium payments. This recess, however, was short-lived, and by 1706, Zeeland's privateers were once again actively capturing neutral and allied ships. This time, their unlawful depredations went one step further for they seized a number of vessels belonging to their sister province, Holland. The same set of by now habitual responses recurred: the States-General ordered the vessels' release, the States of Zeeland obstinately refused, and the States-General ceased granting of letters of commission. The all-too-familiar impasse was only resolved after the authorities in Holland conceded to pay considerable sums to Zeeland for the release of the detained ships from Holland.[43]

What possibly could have motivated not only Zeeland's privateers, but also the officials of the States of Zeeland and the Admiralty of Zeeland, to repeatedly engage in such illicit "piratical" behavior, conduct that made victims of such neutral and allied powers as Denmark, Sweden, and the Hansa cities of Hamburg, Lübeck, and Bremen, as well as their fellow Dutchmen?[44] Of course, the Zeelanders had long been known for their overly "enthusiastic" pursuit of privateering (see Chapter 1). But this case was especially serious. As Verhees-Van Meer affirms, "The conflict took such grave form that the international relationships and unity of the Republic of the Seven United Provinces . . . threatened to be upset by it."[45]

The causes were several. First, there were socioeconomic reasons why the Zeelanders perpetrated these dubious captures. Privateering represented a significant economic stimulus to the region—certain members of the city councils went so far as to deem it the most important business in Zeeland. Moreover, many inhabitants of the province had invested in privateering *rederijen*. Obviously, these people sought to realize profits on their shares and were loath to release valuable prizes and booty, whether they came from belligerent or neutral/allied ships. Second, the institutional arrangements of the provincial political bodies, as well as the close relations between the members of these bodies, meant that no government mechanism existed to stop the captures from taking place. The Admiralty's prize court was completely dominated by Zeelanders, with no dissenting voices from outside the province. Even worse, these men were the same people who comprised the board of governors of the States of Zeeland.[46]

Most important, however, was the Zeelanders' adherence to a long-standing cultural idea, a particular political and legal ideal. Simply put, the Zeelanders believed that when the Dutch Republic was in a state of war with another country, all trade to that country—whether carried by ships belonging to the adversary, allied states, or neutral powers—was forbidden. There were *no* exceptions. So the Zeelanders felt no moral compunction about capturing neutral or allied vessels that were traveling to or from the enemy's ports.[47] They viewed such ships as enemies of their beloved fatherland.

This stance was nothing new—the Zeelanders had long nursed such sentiments. In 1627, for instance, after war had resumed with Spain, the States-General, States of Holland, and States of Zeeland met to discuss whether vessels captured by Dutch privateers along the Spanish coast but actually destined for Venice should be considered "good prizes." The Zeeland authorities took a hard line, contending that *all* ships seized in this vicinity were eligible for legal confiscation. Holland disagreed, arguing that all goods that came from Spain were indeed fair game, but not those belonging to neutral parties. Over Zeeland's protestations, the delegates of the States-General concurred with Holland's position, and the policy was established in accordance with Holland's less hawkish viewpoint.[48]

Furthermore, however exasperating and obstructionist they might have been, the Zeelanders' beliefs did not arise out of thin air. Indeed, the Republic as a whole had once supported and enacted the same policy. Before approximately 1650 and the elaboration of new norms in international law, states were entitled to prohibit all trade with their declared enemy's ports, since any commercial activity would only serve to strengthen their adversary. This was the established practice and had developed during the medieval era.[49] In keeping with this custom, and incensed by King Philip III's 1599 mandate forbidding all Spanish (including Southern Netherlands and Portuguese) communications with the "rebel" Dutch provinces, the States-General had angrily decreed on April 2, 1599, that *any* ship headed for the king of Spain's domains would be confiscated, its cargo included.[50] Why such upset on the States-General's part? Philip III's dicta put an end to the Republic's system of controlled Dutch and allied trade with the Southern Netherlands, as well as to its free trade with Spain and Portugal (tacitly permitted by the Spanish and Portuguese authorities despite the state of war between the Republic and Spain). The States-General not only considered Philip's decree as perfidious, but saw it also as a clear attempt to weaken the Dutch economy.

While the States-General could not, in the end, enforce their April 2 legislation, and trade by neutrals (such as Denmark, Scotland, France, the Hansa Towns, and indeed the Dutch themselves) continued unabated, they did not forget it. In 1605–1606, and then again in 1625, they reenacted the policy, albeit in a more gentle form. This time, neutral powers were warned that their ships destined for Spain and Portugal were subject to "visit and search" by Dutch vessels, and that all enemy goods, as well as contraband (rather liberally interpreted), were to be confiscated. And this time, unlike 1599, the Dutch actively implemented their threats. Consequently, the States-General received a spate of complaints from neutral powers about the overly aggressive behavior of Dutch privateers, objections that they cavalierly ignored. While the Dutch authorities did, on occasion, make slight conciliatory gestures, when they feared that the privateers' alleged depredations might truly threaten the Republic's international relationships, they generally allowed the marauding to continue.[51]

So the Zeelanders' perspective was not a new or original one—it was, in fact, a holdover of medieval ideas, coupled with a patriotic tenacity, still alive amidst the new, post-Grotius international legal order. And the Zeelanders "crimes" were not original either. After all, the complaints that the States-General had received in the early seventeenth century concerned privateers from Holland, not their brethren from the province to the south. It is, however, true that the Zeelanders maintained a harder line, a more rigid interpretation of this age-old legal right than their compatriots had had a century before. And they still subscribed to this theory long after the rest of the European world had professed its support for a new set of international norms. Moreover, the Zeelanders' particularly zealous adherence to this outdated legal interpretation had the unintended consequence of engendering very serious domestic and international political tensions, a fact that made their transgressive posture especially dramatic. But what this episode proves is that underlying, traditional beliefs are enormously powerful, and are extremely influential in shaping the very way that a group perceives a given situation. The combined motivations of economic self-interest and fervent political—indeed, patriotic—belief in the preservation of the state by means of the exercise of old legal rights prevented these "intransigents" from grasping the situation any differently. The Zeelanders cultural/legal conservatism colored their interpretation of privateering mores and allowed them to excuse "piratical" conduct as justifiable and right.

But, the questions remains, was the Zeelanders' patriotism directed toward their province or the Dutch Republic as a whole? In acting from this heartfelt cultural belief, this old legal tradition, were their efforts directed at merely protecting the interests of their province or were the Zeelanders patriots for the *nation*? After all, one could argue that their refractory stance vis-à-vis the Republic's central power—the States-General—represented the height of provincial resistance to federal authority, an act of local rebellion against national cohesion. It is undeniably true that provincial patriotism in Zeeland was strong and abiding. For instance, the stirring names borne by some of the province's privateering vessels betrayed Zeelanders' fierce pride in their mother province. Ships used during the War of Spanish Succession present clear evidence of this, for inspiring designations alluding to a deeply felt Zeelands identity were very popular. These names, sometimes used by more than one vessel, referred primarily to the province's appellation and institutions: *Zeeland's Restitution, Little Zeeland, Zeelandia, Zeeland's Prosperity,* the *States of Zeeland,* and the *Court of Zeeland.* Zeeland's towns, regions, and geographical markers were also honored again and again: *Middelburg's Prosperity, Kleverskerke, Cortgene, Walcheren, Oost Beveland, Oostkapelle, Domburg, Hope of Veere, Noordgouwe,* and *Strijenham.*[52]

But simply because Zeelanders boasted a healthy sense of vibrant provincial patriotism does not mean that their ties to the nation were not vital and real, and conversely, that other Dutch citizens' bond to Zeeland and its inhabitants was not fraternal and inclusive. For this is indisputably not the case. Zeelanders were Zeelanders, but they were also *Dutch* men and women, citizens of a united Republic. And this is how other Dutch people saw them.[53] The same applies to Zeeland's privateers. Their profound sense of Zeelands identity might have created periodic tensions, but it did not prevent them from being dedicated citizens of the Dutch Republic, and, in turn, from being viewed by other Dutch people as devoted servants of the state. Even in the midst of his condemnation of overly aggressive Zeelands privateering, a fictional "Hollander" in the 1649 pamphlet *Amsterdams Vuur-Praetje* (*Amsterdam's Fireside Conversation*) affectionately calls these belligerent and roguish Zeelands seamen "*onse Kapers*," "our privateers."[54]

It is true, too, that being a "Zeelands" privateer did not mean that one necessarily hailed from the province, or alternatively, that one even used Middelburg or Vlissingen as a home base. Indeed, such labels could be very misleading. Evidence from the Nine Years' War and the War of Spanish Succession reveals numerous instances of Dutchmen who were not Zeeland natives working as seamen aboard Zeelands privateering vessels. Likewise, "Hollanders" participated as shareholder partners and even bookkeepers in Zeelands privateering concerns.[55] Such patterns were also evident in Zeelands commercial shipping.[56] Moreover, privateers were not exclusive about bringing booty to their province alone, but sold prizes in Amsterdam as well.[57] Even the Admiralty of Zeeland's governing body—the board of governors, which consisted of nine members, and could defend Zeeland's interests quite assertively—included two representatives from the province of Holland: one from Amsterdam, and the other from either Dordrecht, Delft, or Rotterdam.[58]

So heartfelt Zeelands localism—even in the realm of privateering, a vital trade in the province—did not preclude the development of allegiance to the new national state. Quite the contrary, in fact. One must not, therefore, simply attribute Zeeland's privateering intransigence—and indeed illegal behavior—during the War of Spanish Succession as evidence of that. Even if the citizens of Zeeland and Holland were periodically at odds with one another, plenty of evidence (see Chapter 3) indicates that both Zeelanders and Hollanders were committed to the idea of the unified nation of the Dutch Republic. The Zeelanders may have been mavericks, but their recalcitrance was directed toward strengthening and protecting the Republic, not weakening its central authority. And conflicting interpretations of traditional legal custom aside, other cultural beliefs that conditioned the

Golden Age definition of "piracy" and "privateering" served to bind together the disparate residents of the United Provinces into a national collective of likeminded citizens.

Primary among these conditioning cultural forces was the vital symbolic role of the Sea Beggars as the patriotic fathers of the Dutch Republic's freedom and independence. This motley crew of warrior seamen was seized upon by an eager Dutch public in need of an overarching means to bind them together as members of a new "imagined community," as a vehicle to unite them as citizens of the newborn United Provinces of the Netherlands. Through the course of the Golden Age, the Beggars came to incarnate the Dutch people's fervent longings for a collective identity as a *nation*, a nation created via haphazard historical accident, a sense of divine mission, economic puissance, and military success. As Chapter 3 detailed, songs, plays, patriotic imagery, observed ritual holidays, and the like all worked to cement the role of the Sea Beggars as the Dutch Republic's avenging angels, protectors of liberty, and midwives of independence against the "evil empire" of Spain. That these men were considered privateers fighting for a just cause (even if they lacked the proper documentation) could only reflect well on the Republic's later *commissievaarders*, mariners who inherited the mantle of and veneration for an earlier generation of maritime heroism and bravery. In short, the entrenched and pervasive notion that the Sea Beggars were the fathers of Dutch liberty created the cultural conditions in which post–Sea Beggar privateers could be viewed as the progeny and torchbearers for their illustrious forebears.

This "inherited identity" is evident in a 1672 pamphlet, published during the Republic's war with France, which describes events in the beleaguered city of Kampen. Entitled *True Good News of How the BLOCKZYL Fortress was taken by Storm by Holland Privateers*, the text reads like a reprise of Sea Beggar derring-do, with the French now standing in as the requisite villains. Stealthily approaching the besieged city in the early dawn hours, the undermanned yet valiant force of Dutch privateers—just like their celebrated sixteenth-century brethren—assaulted Kampen in a sudden, unexpected rush. As the pamphlet breathlessly recounts, ". . . with the break of day / the Fortress and Fortifications of BLOCKZYL / were taken by Storm / by the Hollanders / who, with [their] small ship, had smashed the [enemy] forces on Land . . ." In a final act of patriotic display, the triumphant privateers "planted the Prince [of Orange]'s Flag on the [Fortress] Tower . . .," the surrounding grounds of which were now littered with the corpses of slain French soldiers.[59]

At the same time, because of the Sea Beggars' actual checkered past, their public image maintained some space to allow for dubious behavior. This, too, became part of the cultural backdrop of Dutch privateer identity. Plenty of Dutch citizens—at least those who lived during the late sixteenth and early seventeenth century—were perfectly aware of instances when Sea Beggar seamen had committed grievous crimes against the very population they were supposed to protect. And yet, in another example manifesting that unique Dutch cultural characteristic of "diluvian duality"—that is, that the sea itself simultaneously brought forth both disaster and deliverance to the Dutch people (see Chapter 3)—such behavior was apparently absorbed, digested, and accepted. Just as the waters visited upon the Republic both savage, devastating tempests and the beneficent blessings of trade, so the virile warrior of the sea, the Republican Sea Beggar—and, by extension, the Golden Age privateer—could contain, in one person, both a villain and a hero. Moreover, it was the Sea Beggars themselves, in perhaps the most celebrated episode of their patriotic careers, who had used the Netherlands' traditional watery nemesis—the flood—to relieve the besieged and starving citizens of Leiden in 1576. In other words, despite their occasional degeneration into "sea monsters," as it were, it was the Sea Beggars who had succeeded in harnessing the very natural force that ever-threatened the Dutch people—the sea—and used it to repel the loathsome invaders who threatened Dutch freedom.

Cultural awareness of this ambiguity in Sea Beggar identity—that is, of the coexistence of the monster and the hero—is evident in the language Dutch people used to describe these seagoing rebels and their actions. Contemporary chroniclers apparently had difficulty defining the Sea Beggars' status—they wrestled with the proper nomenclature to pinpoint what the Beggars were. A letter dating from 1572, which was later included in a chronicle of the city of Goes, for example, calls the Beggars "pirates" ("*Piraaten*") even as it describes their praiseworthy deeds in fighting for the city of den Briel.[60] And the words chosen by the author of a 1666 history of the city of Enkhuizen are even more interesting. Recording a 1572 incident that qualifies as true criminal *piracy*—a case in which the Beggars sailed into the Vlie River and seized an innocent Enkhuizen ship—the text's author groped for the appropriate label, finally calling the marauders "several freebooters or Sea Beggars" ("*eenige vrybuiters of Water-geusen*").[61] Tellingly enough, this is the exact same terminology he employed in a section detailing a 1572 episode of Sea Beggar *heroism*, in which 500 of their number defended Enkhuizen against the Spanish: "After which [the Spanish forces] were turned away by the arrival of the Freebooters or Sea Beggars of Emden . . ." ("*Daerna sijn se afgedankt door de komste der Vrijbuiters of Water-geusen van Emden . . .*").[62] In other words, whether these early Revolt-era fighting men acted as "pirates" or "privateers"—as criminals or brave heroes—the historian utilized the exact same label to identify them: "Freebooters or Sea Beggars." His choice was a revealing one, for *vrijbuiter* (Freebooter)—defined variously as a "buccaneer, pirate, pillager, adventurer, libertine, and free spirit"[63]—represented an imprecise identifier that contained in one convenient Dutch word the notions of both legal marauding (adventuring) and criminal robbery (piracy). In short, it allowed the author to equivocate linguistically, to affirm the existence of a slippery slope of maritime conduct even as he endeavored to record an accurate description of historical events.

Evidence that this chronicler was not the only one to take advantage of the elasticity this ambiguous term *vrijbuiter* offered turns up in other sources as well. For example, a 1577 proclamation issued by the king of Spain notes that the Sea Beggars declared themselves to be Freebooters (*Vrybuiters*), a title that the monarch forbade them to use.[64] Likewise, following in the footsteps of their celebrated Sea Beggar forebears, later Dutch privateers were also referred to as "freebooters." An early-seventeenth-century States-General *placaat* that addressed the allegedly criminal behavior of some of the Republic's licensed privateers, dubbed the misdeeds "excesses committed by Freebooters of these Provinces" (*"Excessen door Vrijbuijters ... dezer Landen ... gepleeft"*).[65] The sentencing records of three separate court cases from the Admiralty of the Maas employed the term *vrijbuiters* (freebooters) or *vrijbuit varen* (to go freebooting) to indicate licensed privateers who were convicted of the crime of piracy in 1574 and 1624.[66] The Admiralty Court also called a Dunkirk privateer who was convicted of piracy in 1594 a freebooter.[67] A 1629 poem lauding privateering repeatedly uses the term Freeboot (*Vrybuyt*) and Freeboot-trade (*Vrybuyt-vaert*) to designate its subject.[68] Another poem, published in 1665 and praising stalwart Dutch privateers, was entitled *To the Freebooters of Holland and Zeeland* (*Aan de Hollantse, en Zeeuwse Vrybuyters*).[69] Perhaps most interesting of all was the 1629 panegyric whose title and text openly referred to the disconcerting liminality incarnated in the identity of the Dutch privateer: *In Praise of the Freeboot Trade, and a Rebuke Against the Abuse of the Same* (*Lof des Vrye Vaearts, ende Berisp Tegen het Misbrvck der Selver*).[70]

And as it turns out, *vrijbuiter* was not the only word in Dutch elastic enough to designate the activities of both privateering and piracy. The terms "Adventurer" and "to go Adventuring" could also function in this way. For example, on the one hand, when Claes Compaen worked as a patriotic *kaper*, he was called an "Adventurer";[71] indeed, this was a typical designation for privateering generally (e.g., see Appendix III).[72] On the other hand, however, when the convicted pirates Jacob Gabrielszoon, Pieter d'Oudenaarde, Joris Uitsingam, Daniel Andriessen, Jan Simonszoon, Jan Claaszoon, and Claas Thomaszoon made a conscious plot to maraud as pirates, the Admiralty Court called their malicious intentions a plan "to go adventuring in the sea" (*"een Avontuur in Zee to maken"*).[73]

So the Golden Age Dutch privateer, as the heir to the Sea Beggar identity, conveniently inherited the Sea Beggar's culturally sanctioned liminal status. As the Sea Beggars had been permitted to be men "betwixt and between" codes of conduct, so were the later privateers. Dutch "pirates," too, obviously benefited from this tacit acceptance of a seamless slippery slope between licit and illicit maritime robbery, for rather than being automatically consigned to a "polluted" realm defined and delineated by despicable criminal conduct,[74] their activities could be viewed as just another point—albeit the terminus—along a continuum of culturally permissible marauding. While it is true that popular Dutch literature often designated "pirates" as moral reprobates, these texts usually pinpointed foreigners as practitioners of that particular sin. The perception of "Dutch" pirates was certainly more complex and nuanced. That the seventeenth-century Dutch themselves were aware of their privateer's "inherited liminality" is apparent in one 1649 pamphlet, a *praatje* in which a character complaining about the illicit behavior of Zeeland privateers still admits, "The Zeelanders are nevertheless... Sea Beggars...."[75] Alternatively labeling these irascible seamen *Kapers* (privateers) and *Rovers* (Pirates), the pamphlet also employs that classic identifier for the Sea Beggars—*vrijbuiter* (freebooter)—when discussing the Zeelanders' predatory activities.[76]

Ambiguous language is not the only evidence of cultural equivocality in regards to Dutch maritime pillaging. This same obfuscating lens was used to interpret the patently problematic actions of Dutch seamen. A 1624 pamphlet that recounted the conquest of a Brazilian settlement by WIC forces, for example, reveals cultural permissiveness and ambiguity regarding pirate-like actions when it simultaneously extolled both the "piratical" behavior and noble restraint of the WIC seamen. Upon the Company warriors' capture of the helpless colony, the text exclaims, they "were very desirous for booty / and . . . fell to plundering / . . . so that all together received good and considerable booty . . . ." Such plunder included ships loaded with African slaves; 30,000 ducats of Jesuit cash; 4,000 chests of sugar; and "a plenitude of money." They also kidnapped the Spanish Viceroy and his son. Still, the pamphlet points out, the WIC men behaved with decorum, refraining from drunkenness despite the presence of "a thousand bottles of Spanish wine," and permitting the settlement's residents to return in peace.[77]

This culturally accorded liminality also ensured that men of dubious character could be accepted—and even invited—into the ranks of the Republic's privateers. With such men sailing as Dutch *kapers*, it is no wonder that maritime crime in the form of piracy took place. A pamphlet from 1629, for example, called for any ablebodied man—no matter what his tarnished personal history—to serve the state, just so long as he was willing to fight for the Netherlands. Even those perfidious mariners who had sailed with the despised Dunkirk corsairs were encouraged to join the corps of Republican privateers:

> Oh!
> in order to fight . . .
> let Dunkirkers, marauders,
> farm-plaguers, traitors
> remain on board, and within the ramparts,
> if they keep hitting until [the enemy] falls . . .[78]

And a 1672 States-General proclamation that sought to discipline transgressive Dutch privateers (who apparently were committing misdeeds such as plundering their prizes, defying their captains, and joining rival companies), simultaneously tried to appease the very seamen it threatened to punish. Even as the edict condemned such privateer infractions and vowed serious penalties, it also enticed these refractory seamen to support the Dutch effort. However unsavory these men might have been, the States-General did not want to lose their support:

> And so that . . . no one may be discouraged as regards these matters, but may be encouraged to serve the country and harm the enemy, we have firmly dictated . . . that all the sailors of a privateer ship, together will enjoy as their share of the plunder one and one percent of the value of all the prizes which the same will have come to capture / in addition to an anchor and a rope from every captured ship / and over and above that all the chests of the enemy sailors. . . .[79]

Ultimately, then, Dutch Republican culture's perception of the Sea Beggars helped Golden Age privateers to emerge as cultural heroes, despite their lapses into "piratical" behavior. Of course, public veneration for their maritime champions certainly found its most elaborate and widespread expression in the idolatry of renowned Dutch naval officers. But seventeenth-century evidence indicates that privateers, too, were the subjects of public approbation, reverence, and accolades of appreciation. After all, in addition to being the heirs to the historic Sea Beggar tradition, the Republic's corps of privateers was also associated with the forces of the revered Dutch Navy. Indeed, given the fact that the Dutch Admiralties both licensed and supervised the privateers' activities, Dutch *kapers* were, in effect, their own quasi-branch of the navy. Evidence of the institutionalization of this consanguineous relationship appeared in government edicts that were intended to apply collectively to both naval and privateer personnel. For instance, a 1672 States-General document outlining the specific protocol for the seizure of enemy ships was addressed to both navy seamen and their privateer colleagues.[80] And there was a constant exchange of personnel between the two enterprises, with privateers becoming navy seamen and vice-versa. No less a figure than the celebrated Admiral Michiel de Ruyter, in fact, had worked as the captain of a *kaper* ship before he commenced his illustrious naval career.[81] By virtue of both his Sea Beggar roots and his institutional association with the current maritime military, then, the Golden Age privateer was apparently deemed worthy of inclusion in the Republic's "cult of the naval hero."

Proof of the privateer's heroic status is contained in sources that run the gamut from official government proclamations, to quotidian publications, to praise poems, to tomb inscriptions, to contemporary books. The 1672 States-General *publikatie* cited above, for instance, uses "heroic" language to describe both privateer and naval seamen. Amidst dry clauses elaborating upon the various premiums to be awarded for prize captures, the document employs effusive, complimentary terminology to typify the deeds of the Republic's maritime fighting men. Privateers and navy men who captured enemy vessels were hailed as "Patriots" of great martial skill, soldiers who exemplified bravery, gallantry, valor, nobility, courage, and manliness.[82] Likewise, when privateers Pieter Hamers and Cornelis Gerrits captured the French warship *The Bourbon* in 1707, the Admiralty of Zeeland termed their accomplishment—a perilous episode that resulted in over 80 causalities—"a heroic deed."[83] The popular media also paid attention. Books recounted episodes of brave privateer feats (see, e.g, Simon de Vries's history of the Barbary corsairs, which relates the tale of how a "valiant" privateer from Zeeland escaped from the clutches of the North African pirates).[84] Newspapers, too, reported on the triumphant exploits of the Republic's *commissievaarders*.[85] And almanacs included entries about exciting privateer captures in their annual list of newsworthy topics, ensuring that the Dutch reading public learned of the *kapers'* thrilling exploits. Such accounts typically included the home city of the privateer ship, the origin and ship type of the prizes they had seized, the location of the capture, and the contents of the booty. Sometimes the names and sizes of the various ships, as well as the name of the privateer captain and the number of guns the ships carried were listed as well.[86]

Pamphlets also circulated news about the Republic's privateers and sang the praises of their prowess and exploits. Printers circulated news of exciting privateer captures.[87] And sources, such as a 1653 *praatje* printed during the First Anglo-Dutch War, singled out the Netherlands' privateers as one of the state's most formidable military assets:

> *Hollander*: . . . And in addition to our War Ships, which demonstrate Maritime Might, so one hears that our Privateers capture everything, [just] like a Swarm of Bees along . . . [England's] Coast, [they seize] whatever they . . . come across, as much as is possible.[88]

Such texts could employ extremely patriotic language in extolling the virtues of the Republic's privateer seamen, patently referring to the *kapers* as "heroes" worthy of public adulation. One pamphlet printed in 1653 and running some 100 pages in length, was a rhapsodic account of Dutch victories against the "murderous" English enemy.[89] Filled with patriotic poems, mini-narratives about the Republic's foremost Admirals, criticism of the English (who are called "thieves," "pirates," and "devils") and reports on actual military achievements, the pamphlet represents one vast celebration of the Dutch Navy and "other Sea–Heroes of this State . . .," that is, the Republic's privateers. While navy and privateer seamen alike are generally referred to as "pious Batavians" and "Lions of the Sea" whose "gallant deeds" help to protect "our Beloved and Dearly-Bought Fatherland,"[90] the work goes on to recount and enumerate in chronological order the specific accomplishments of various privateers (see Appendix III). This list is expressed in extremely vivid and fulsome language, referring to privateers as "brave Batavians," "valiant Netherlands Batavians," "our renowned Lions of the Sea," "upright Batavian[s] for the Fatherland," "Sea Roosters," "Zeelands Adventurer[s]," "Netherlands Adventurers," and the like. Their accomplishments are called "Heroic deeds," which are "Furiously" and "manfully" fought for, "Heroically" and "Victoriously" achieved, and "triumphantly, with the firing of the Canon, brought in on the crest of the tumbling waves..." Likewise, privateer booty is typically "costly" and "rich."[91] One anecdote even invoked the familiar trope of slavery, tapping into that fundamental, resonating quality of Dutch identity and thereby making its privateer protagonists great champions of national virtue as they used their fortitude, cunning, dexterity, and courage to deliver themselves from bondage:

> A *Zeelands Adventurer* from *Vlissingen*, outfitted with 14 pieces [i.e., guns] and 50 Eaters [i.e., crewmembers] was—by misfortune—captured at sea by 4 Pirates ["*Zee-Roovers*"] and the crew fettered in iron chains on their own ship... [A]fter 17 Turks had been installed on their ship, in order to transport them to *Turkey* as *Slaves*, a Sailor—whom I myself have toasted in *Zeeland* with a cool goblet of wine—with the Key from his chest, which he had correctly [stowed] in his Sack, and fit into the shackles, skillfully opened them, so that all 50 were released by this means, and furthermore, threw all of the Turks overboard. Several days later, a new Rich English Street-Conveyer [i.e., a merchant ship which conveyed goods to and from the Mediterranean], mounted with 18 pieces, containing 250 Pipes of Oil, 80 Vats of Spanish Wine, Grain, Hides, Wool, and other commodities, as well as *Eleven Sacks of Pieces of Eight*, came into sight, which [the Dutch privateers] gallantly boarded right away, and after a long and hard battle (resulting in many dead and wounded on both sides), heroically vanquished, and brought into *Veere*.[92]

Even episodes of unrestrained Dutch privateer aggression were worthy of celebration: "... another *Zeelands Adventurer* captured an English coal-ship, and an English frigate, mounted with 36 pieces [i.e., guns], which he [the Dutch privateer] intending to rob as the Prize, furiously hurled into the ground."[93]

Public accolades of admiration and appreciation also took the form of poems or songs. For instance, one seventeenth-century song celebrated the eager Dutch privateer who, braving the bracing sea and elements, left the comforts of home with expectations of winning "rich booty."[94] The 1665 poem *Aan de Hollantse, en Zeeuwse Vrybuyters* (*To the Hollands, and Zeelands Freebooters*) lauded the swagger and daring of Dutch privateers in colorful language, noting the flying bullets and the urge to "Seize, plunder, whatever you can... it is booty..."[95] The epic 1629 poem (spanning 10 pages in length) *In Praise of the Freeboot Trade, and a Rebuke Against the Abuse of the Same* (*Lof Der Vrye Vaerts, Ende Berisp Tegen Het Misbrvvyck Der Selver*), while more cautious, lauded the virtues of *kaapvaart* and the search for booty in glowing, ceremonial language, depicting the trade as an important element in the preservation of the "Fatherland."[96] Likewise, the 1629 *Ode, in Honor of the Freeboot-Trade* (*Lof-Dicht, Ter Eeren Des Vrye Vaerts*), mannered and replete with classical references, presented privateering as a gift from the Olympian gods.[97]

With such widespread awareness of and respect for privateer exploits, it is not surprising that the Dutch sometimes directed special adulation toward particular individuals. Thus, for example, when Zeelands privateer Captain

Pieter Borrens perished "gallantly for the Fatherland" in a battle against the Dunkirkers in 1711, he was memorialized in the following tune, among other tributes:

> Our Captain [is] a Hero of Heroes
> Pieter Borrens triumphant:
> Who put forward his Body and Life
> For his beloved Fatherland . . .[98]

Likewise, Captain Mathys Jacobszoon Pruis—who died in 1665 after capturing four English ships carrying tobacco—also received the grateful appreciation of his people, who saluted him as a "hero" in several eulogistic poems of praise.[99] Also famous and esteemed was the privateer Cornelis Jol, more popularly and affectionately known as "Houtebeen" ("Wooden Leg"), who was involved in many an exploit in Caribbean and South American waters for the WIC. A native of Scheveningen, where a street still bears his name, Jol caused so much damage to the Spanish and Portuguese that they knew him by name.[100] When he assisted Admiral Maarten Tromp in vanquishing the Spanish at the 1639 Battle of the Downs, he became especially well known, inspiring at least one poet to compose an ode in his honor.[101] And years later, in 1653, he was still being recognized as a "valiant Sea-Hero," a "Sea Lion" of "widely-renowned Courage" whose peers, one pamphlet related, included such revered figures as Admiral Jacob van Heemskerk, Piet Heyn, and Moy Lambert.[102]

One finds an especially potent expression of the "cult of the heroic privateer" dedicated, in the words of Golden Age chronicler Olfert Dapper, "to the eternal memory of the valiant and manly Sea hero KORNELIS JANSZ. of Amsterdam, nicknamed HAENTJE."[103] This privateer, whom the Dutch public affectionately called "the Little Rooster" and who perished while fighting the Dunkirk corsairs, was depicted in images[104] and honored in praise-poems and songs that described his noble and selfless martyrdom at the hands of the despicable "pirates" of Dunkirk. Eulogistic odes commended him as a "Hero" and "Sea Rooster" who "sparkled so valiantly" and who was inspired by the Roman God of war, Mars.[105] Songs written in his honor (and sung to the melodies of popular patriotic and religious hymns) acclaimed him as a "pious hero" and "Batavian" full of bravery and fortitude, "his voice thundering" as he stood amidst the flying bullets. They extolled his self-sacrifice "for the Orange" and "for the free Netherlands," called upon God to grant him "eternal life," and "bequeath his soul to the Angels."[106] His grave—an impressive memorial befitting a patriotic martyr—was crowned by a Latin inscription that effusively commended the courageous deeds of this celebrated "martial hero."[107] Entombed in Amsterdam's Oude Kerk in 1633, and in close proximity to the hallowed resting place of the legendary Admiral Heemskerk, Haentje's epitaph—composed by Amsterdam Professor Kasper van Baerle and engraved in gilt letters upon a black marble tablet—cemented the privateer's status as one of the Republic's sanctified national heroes:

> Take heed, beholder, of the miraculous deeds of our people, and the astonishing, honorable Sea Battles so triumphantly [and] fiercely conducted. Here lies one interred, who cruised through the Spanish waters with his [ships'] keels, and dyed the Mediterranean Sea with the blood of the Spanish. Who recently, with the capture of Spanish ships, made Dunkirk tremble. So many times did he victoriously and ferociously attack the enemy, and at the same time plunder the ships of the enemy's merchants and traders, that the Batavian need not come on the sea with the entire fleet in order to seize the Spaniard; but rather one ship, and only one commander, is enough. But while this sea-hero sacrificed his body and life for the Fatherland in the middle of the waves and gave his best, he was furiously and radiantly cut down in battle. Oh Romans! boast no more now about your Decien. Under this marble tombstone also lies buried the body of a Decien.[108]

However much praise "the Little Rooster" received, however, it surely paled in comparison to the public adulation directed toward the great WIC commander Admiral Piet Heyn. Although Heyn was a lieutenant-admiral in the Dutch Navy at the time of his death (he, too, was slain during a battle with the Dunkirk corsairs), he achieved his greatest accomplishments—the deeds that brought him the most renown—while he was serving the WIC. Certainly, Piet Heyn represents the apex of public adulation for Dutch privateers. (So significant and lasting has his place in Dutch history been, in fact, that a ditty about him is still sung today, the "Triumphal Song of the Silver Fleet," which C.R. Boxer has gone so far as to call "the unofficial Dutch national anthem."[109]) Heyn's career was generally brilliant. It is indisputable, however, that the act which brought him such tremendous fame and veneration was his 1628 capture of the Spanish Silver Fleet in the Bay of Matanzas, Cuba. Although the French, English, and Dutch had repeatedly endeavored to seize Spain's entire fleet of treasure ships en route from the Americas, Heyn's conquest was the *only* case in which such an attempt was successful. His achievement was never repeated by any other mariner from any other country.

Aside from his dashing triumphs, Piet Heyn also embodied personal characteristics that endeared him to the Dutch populous. Indeed, he exemplified the Dutch ideal. Born in humble circumstances to a seafaring family in Delfshaven, Holland, he represented the prototypical "pick oneself up by one's bootstraps" type of lad; he was a decent, hardworking, and upright Calvinist whom life rewarded because of his discipline, talents, piety, and dedication. Perhaps even more striking, in terms of Heyn's "symbolic" appeal, was the fact that he had been captured by the detested Spaniards not once, but twice. Each time he was incarcerated for several years and forced to live in very dire conditions: first, as a rower on Spanish penal galleys (1598–1602), and second, as a prisoner in Havana, Cuba (1604–1606). After his release and several years of service with the VOC, he married a well-off Rotterdam widow. By 1618, he had become an affluent burger and by 1622, he had been elected as a Rotterdam city alderman. When joining the WIC in 1623, he was immediately installed as second-in-command of a 26-ship fleet, which eventually captured Bahia, Brazil, in 1624. This victory was followed by other impressive achievements, namely raids of the Portuguese, which resulted in the devastation of their ships and fantastic seizures of booty. In 1627 alone, for instance, he captured 38 vessels. So it was fitting that the Company made him "General" over the fleet of 31 ships (outfitted with some 4,000 men and 689 guns) instructed to intercept the Spanish treasure ships in 1628.

Heyn's spectacular capture of the Silver Fleet was a result of both happy coincidence (e.g., poor communication and sloppy seamanship on the Spanish side) and the Dutch commander's able, decisive, and courageous leadership. In the end, his conquest was bloodless and quite peaceful, with little illegal plundering or abuse of the Spanish sailors and passengers. Spanish eyewitness accounts, in fact, testified to Heyn's gracious treatment of his prisoners, as well as his ability to maintain order and discipline among his own personnel.[110] Such descriptions only enhanced Heyn's reputation at home even more, for in the public's eyes, not only was the commander a dazzlingly effective WIC warrior who had inflicted a terrible wound on the Republic's great nemesis, but at the same time, he was a virtuous, modest, and restrained man of faith as well. He was, in short, a Dutchman of whom all could be unequivocally proud—the ideal made flesh.

When Heyn, his fleet, and their vast treasure arrived home in the Republic, they were greeted with celebratory zeal. En route to Amsterdam, he was received with the firing of salutes, the pealing of church bells, ceremonial addresses in Latin, and choirs singing his praises.[111] The unprecedented capture of the *flota*—the great Spanish Silver Fleet—aroused tremendous public excitement, and with good reason. For this was the prize to end all prizes, a glittering and prodigious haul of masses of silver and gold from Peru and Mexico. The rest of the cargo was not insignificant either, containing as it did precious goods such as cochineal, indigo, sugar, hides, cacao, silks, musk, amber, and pearls. All told, Heyn's heist was valued at the time at 11.5–12 million guilders, a sum equal to more than $25 million in modern terms.[112]

But this initial reception, however enthusiastic, was far from the end of the Dutch citizenry's embrace of Piet Heyn. Public idolatry toward the WIC commander continued unabated, and even intensified after his felling at the hands of the Dunkirkers. His "heroic cult" took many forms, ranging from pamphlets recounting his illustrious deeds (including narratives written by his officers and even Heyn himself),[113] to songs and poems lamenting his martyrdom, to engravings depicting his stalwart visage and heady adventures, to various types of decorative art objects commemorating his name (e.g., medallions and saltcellars),[114] to an elaborate tomb in Delft (adjacent to that of the great naval hero Admiral Maarten Tromp) marking his "sanctified" resting place and memorializing his brilliant career. Artists confessed to a great swelling of patriotic ardor for the "Fatherland" as a direct result of

Heyn's magnificent accomplishment and a yearning to pay tribute to the man—to enable the "collective remembering" of his grand exploits, as it were.[115] In the preface of I. Liefs ceremonial ode, for instance, the poet declared:

> So it is with great passion and joy that I had learned of the widely-renowned, never-before-heard-of, blissfully-rich Victory, of the capture of the King of Spain's SILVER FLEET; and accordingly, greatly rejoicing as a devotee of the Fatherland, I have composed this LAUDATORY POEM with extreme ardor, and . . . because of suggestions from other devotees, have let it be published in print to [bring about] a permanent Memory and the arousal of all good Patriots . . .[116]

Fellow poet Dionysius Spranckhuysen also proclaimed, "Oh you VIII Day of *September*, what a great and joyful memory you shall leave for us and our descendants!" Spranckhuysen went so far as to urge that such remembrance be a communal and multigenerational responsibility, affirming that, "it is not enough that we have given thanks . . . once to the Lord God in the public churches. Rather, each one [of us] should do his utmost, that the memory . . . by us and our descendants might continue always."[117]

Consequently, piece after countless piece[118] extolled Heyn's pluck and courage, his probity, his defense of Dutch freedom against the tyranny of Spain, and his ability to inspire a fierce love for the Fatherland. They also made associations between Heyn and his Sea Beggar predecessors,[119] and in describing his heist of the Silver Fleet employed pirate/privateer terminology—such as *buit* ("booty"), *veroven* ("to capture"), *roven/roof/geroofd* ("to plunder"/"plundering"/"plundered"), *beroven* ("to plunder, despoil"), and *vrije-vaert* ("freeboot trade").[120] Moreover, these works often contrast Heyn's "plundering" very positively to Spain's contemptible "plundering" of the New World. The capture itself was referred to as, "A Glorious Thing, a Heroic deed, a *Batavian* exploit."[121] Poems bombastically termed Heyn a "Neptune [who] brings Gold and Silver to our land, to the honor of the Orange . . . and to the horror of the Castilian . . ."[122] They referred to him as a "Champion" and "Victorious Hero," a "Batavian" who had triumphed for "our Fatherland,"[123] and whose renown would be eternal:

> Who is [this], about whose fame and everlasting Memory
> the world writes, and [who] achieved the greatest glory,
> That every a Hero deserved . . .[?]
> 'Tis *Heyn* the *Batavian* . . .[124]

He was, moreover, depicted as an "instrument of God," a means by which divine grace had been bestowed upon the deserving people of the United Netherlands.[125] Songs were composed to fit the melodies of rousing, patriotic anthems, such as the *Wilhelmus*, thereby transforming Heyn—by means of ritual music—into a revered father of Dutch liberty and nationhood.[126] He was showered with complimentary praise, becoming in the hearts and minds of the Dutch people "the laudable, clever, virile-hearted Gentleman" whose incredible theft of booty served to unite all strata of his fatherland, surmounting all demographic divisions and filling the whole of Golden Age society with jubilation:

> Let abundance be revealed again;
> Children, maidens, men, women . . .
> aristocrat, burger, mariner, farmer,
> . . . all in a joyous stirring!
> All mouths sing the praises
> There is [the] Prize . . .[127]

Rhapsodic verses also encouraged the public to celebrate the patriotic ardor arising from Heyn's illustrious deeds by embracing collectively understood symbols of Dutch nationhood: "Rejoice . . . people! with white-blue-[and] orange flags . . ."[128] And elegiac lamentations marking Heyn's demise expressed the heartfelt grief of a national community united in mourning.[129]

But a privateer did not have to perish at sea in order to receive the adulation of the grateful Dutch public. Take the cases of Cornelis Gerrits and Pieter Hamers. Gerrits and Hamers belonged to that special and unofficial fraternity of privateer captains (consisting of 12 members) who captured more than 40 prizes during the War of Spanish Succession. Their accomplishments were unequivocally impressive, for they had seized some 70 and 131 ships respectively.[130] Their sponsoring Admiralty, Zeeland, was duly appreciative, and honored the pair, lauding them as official "heroes" for their valiant efforts. Upon the event of their capture of a great French warship that brought ƒ.96,900 at auction, the two *kapers* received special rewards—gilded and engraved silver chalices of great monetary value—from the Admiralty in gratitude "for the immortal recognition of this heroic deed."[131]

Willem Credo's stature as a "heroic *commissievaarder*" was even more impressive. Credo served as a Middelburg-based privateering captain from 1689 to 1713. During his career, he singlehandedly captured almost 200 vessels, with a value of some three million guilders. In the words of his son-in-law, minister Gerard Bacot (who published a complimentary biography about him in 1734), he was "one of the most celebrated sea heroes in Zeeland."[132] Credo must have been well-known to the public, for between 1702 and 1713, his name showed up almost continually in newspapers such as the *Amsterdamsche Courant*, with reports on the latest capture he had made (an almost monthly occurrence). Stories about Credo and his ship the *Peerl* (*Pearl*) also appeared regularly in the pages of the almanac, the *Amsterdamsche Mercuuren*. Especially riveting for readers was the tale of his confrontation with the 60-gun French warship commanded by one Captain L'Aigle, a vessel that French king Louis XIV had dispatched specifically to deliver the intrepid Dutch privateer to Paris, dead or alive. (L'Aigle, moreover, was given the tantalizing incentive of a promised ƒ.20,000 reward.) But the Frenchman proved to be no match for the irrepressible Credo. When at last the two captains did meet, L'Aigle was overawed by Credo's reputation and failed to act. As Bacot's 1734 work proclaimed, "Credo (instead of [wreaking] vengeance) took a glass of wine in his hand, in order to drink to [his enemy's] prosperity and called out . . .'*Monsieur L'Aigle, A vostre santé!*' " ("Mr. L'Aigle, to your health!").[133]

Even admittedly dubious characters were depicted as patriotic heroes. Dionysius van der Sterre, for example, expressed glowing praise for the nationalistic zeal evinced by "our fearless Hercules Captain Jan Erasmus," the Dutch sea robber and privateer Jan Erasmus Reyning.[134] Brushing aside the not-so-insignificant facts that Reyning had accepted privateering commissions from other European states, joined up with the buccaneers, and gone so far as to participate in Morgan's infamous and violent raid on Panama, van der Sterre's *Very Remarkable Journeys of Jan Erasmus Reyning* instead depicted his subject as a resolute patriot who had served his nation with filial devotion and brave fortitude. Indeed, van der Sterre took heated issue with Exquemelin's *Buccaneers of America* for suggesting that Reyning had sailed the Caribbean as a "pirate" (*Roover*), an independent marauder who sought only to line his own pockets. Nothing could be further from the truth, van der Sterre angrily clarified, for Reyning's sea robbery "was carried out under a good commission: and it is certain that Jan Erasmus never did anything without a commission . . ."[135] (Never mind that such commissions were invalid and illegal under Dutch law, and that on this point alone, Reyning *did* act as a pirate.) When his country needed him, van der Sterre affirmed, Reyning was there:

> . . . he learned that war was declared between Holland, England and France; whereupon Captain Jan Erasmus came to a decision by himself, to go to Curaçao as quickly as possible, and there to serve his own Nation, and to injure the English and French as much as it was in his power to do so.[136]

According to van der Sterre, Reyning attacked countless ships and seized booty for his country, comporting himself "like an angry lion" amid blaring trumpets and waving banners.[137] At one point, after capturing the French fortress on Granada, so moved was he by patriotic ardor that he fashioned a Dutch flag out of random pieces of fabric he found aboard his ship. Using white linen and blue linen, and white cloth dipped in turkey's blood, he cobbled together an orange, white, and blue ensign—emblem of the prince of Orange—to plant upon the wall of his conquest.[138] And by dint of his seafaring skills and martial prowess, he contributed over 50,000 pieces-of-eight to the coffers of the WIC.[139] Consciously or subconsciously, van der Sterre—and/or his publisher—also chose to depict Reyning according to a visually symbolic idiom of "Dutchness," which would have resonated deeply with his compatriots. To illustrate an episode in which Reyning had survived the loss of his ship and was drifting at sea (figure 6.1), the text pilfered and reworked an image from Simon de Vries's *History of the Barbarians and Their Pirates*—an engraving of luckless, supplicant sailors who have barely escaped enslavement at the hands of

Figure 6.1 Jan Erasmus Reyning and Comrades Adrift, engraving, in Dionysis van der Sterre, *Zeer Aenmerkelyke Reysen van Jan Erasmus Reyning door Verscheyde Gevesten des Werelds* (Amsterdam: Jan ten Hoorn, 1691), fol. 91. Dousa Kamer.

the Barbary corsairs (figure 6.2). Subtly inscribed into this visual presentation of Reyning, then, is the suggestion of his escape from slavery and victimization at the hands of the hated corsairs of North Africa, both of which were notions that carried profound weight within the Dutch psyche. Ultimately, van der Sterre proclaims, Jan Erasmus Reyning was a hero, a privateer champion who "did everything out of a noble affection for his nation, and to serve the West India Company . . ."[140] and later, of course, the Dutch Navy.

Figure 6.2 Jan and Caspar Luiken, Drifting Supplicant Sailors, engraving, in Simon de Vries, *Historie van Barbaryen, En de zelfs Zee-Roovers* . . ., Vol. II (Amsterdam: Jan ten Hoorn, 1684), fol. 147. Dousa Kamer.

Not surprisingly, those *kapers* whose deeds qualified them for inclusion in the culture's esteemed circle of "sea heroes" were also rewarded with enhanced social standing. Certainly, by the late seventeenth and early eighteenth centuries, privateers could be men of real social eminence.[141] For example, of the 12 captains who achieved especially notable success during the War of Spanish Succession by capturing more than 40 prizes each, evidence shows that Salomon Reynders and Willem Credo—who seized some 50 and 97 and ships respectively—received special distinction.[142] As a consequence of their daring martial exploits, they and their families reaped the reward of societal admiration and advancement. The son of Salomon Reynders directly profited from his father's success as a privateer by becoming the vice-admiral of the Admiralty of Zeeland and serving as the director of the *Commercie Compagnie*, a commercial shipping venture in Middelburg.[143] By virtue of his illustrious deeds, Willem Credo was compensated handsomely, receiving a special pension of ƒ.12,000 from his *reders*.[144] By the end of the war, Credo had the means to obtain a country estate in Alphen aan de Rijn, in Holland, in a quarter replete with summerhouses belonging to the ruling elite. According to his will, by the end of his life, the former *kaper* captain owned two houses (the other was in Vlissingen), much gold and silver, and valuable artwork.[145]

This tendency of privateering to elevate its captains socially had existed long before the War of Spanish Succession. Perhaps the most striking example occurred in the case of privateer captain Isaac Rochussen. On July 7, 1672, during the Third Anglo-Dutch War, Rochussen and his ship the *Eendracht* (*Concord*) fought a pitched battle against and ultimately seized the richly laden and heavily armed English East Indiaman, *The Falcon*. This magnificent prize garnered ƒ.350,000 at auction in Amsterdam, the highest price ever paid for a captured vessel at the time. (And this despite the fact that a fair quantity of the diamonds and other jewels that the *Falcon* had been carrying never made it to auction in the first place, because they were illegally embezzled before the sale.) By way of comparison, most prizes during this period yielded only a few thousand guilders profit—perhaps ƒ.10,000 or so at most. While the ƒ.812,000 produced from the sale of 29 other prizes that Zeelands privateers captured at that time (an average of ƒ.28,000 per vessel) was impressive, it still pales in comparison. The sum realized by the sale of Rochussen's prize was, in this context, simply staggering. With his share of the take, Rochussen retired from privateering (after accepting an inscribed gold medal from his grateful *reder*, Abraham van Peere; the medal still survives in the Rijksmuseum in Amsterdam), settled in Vlissingen, and commenced a career as a merchant. During the Nine Years' War, his name again became affiliated with privateering, but this time as a shareholder in a firm. His son followed suit, making a career as a privateering *reder* as well. The reputation of the Rochussen family continued to grow, and soon enough they joined the ranks of the elite. During the eighteenth and nineteenth centuries, the privateer's descendants served the Netherlands in the capacity of diplomat, banker, governor-general of the Dutch Indies, and member of the Council of State. By his one illustrious deed as a Dutch *kaper* captain, Isaac Rochussen had indelibly elevated his family's name, fortune, and prospects forever.[146]

That the Netherlands' privateers understood and appreciated their status as Republican heroes—as exemplars and protectors of the new Dutch *nation*—becomes clear when one notes the names borne by privateering vessels.

Numerous privateering ships during the Second and Third Anglo-Dutch Wars displayed patriotic designations that referred to rousing symbols of Dutch national identity or character, such as *Orangist at Heart*, the *Disturbed Lion* (the "Dutch Lion" being an intensely popular emblem representing the Republic), and the *Provoked Cheese-Maker*, the last of which was used some three times.[147] Even in independently minded Zeeland, home of so many privateering aficionados and zealous defenders of provincial interests, national sentiments ran deep. Privateering vessels during the War of Spanish Succession bore such patriotic appellations as *The Seven Provinces, The Red Lion, Provoked Lion of the Sea, Golden Freedom, House of Nassau, Faithful to the Fatherland, The Lion's Redress, The Country's Prosperity, King William, The Golden Lion, The Black Lion, The Provoked Hollander, Orange Tribe, The Provoked Lion, The Prince of Friesland, The Vigilant Lion, Great King William*, and *Most Loyal*. Some stirring identifiers referred to towns or cities—sometimes quite small and unheralded—located throughout the Republic. Examples included *Swanenburg, Marienburg, Westerbeek, Rozenburg, Zonnebeke, Amsterdam's Pilot Galleon, City of Rotterdam*, and the *Arms of Rotterdam*. Significant, too, were the large number of vessels that contained the word *galei* in their name, a term that designated a "small warship" in the parlance of the day, but one that also connoted a "slave galley." One could argue that this mode of naming represents a manifestation of the fundamental place the issue of bondage and liberation played in the Dutch cultural psyche and sense of national identity. In any case, *galei* was a loaded term, patently invoking either a martial vessel and/or a craft intended for slaves. Such meanings became even more pointed and inspiring in cases where a Dutch city or region, either in the province, the homeland, or the colonies, was honored: *Zeelands Galley, Maas Galley, Middelburg Galley, Galley of the Indies, Zierikze Galley, Curaçao Galley*, and *Vlissingen Galley*.[148]

Feelings of patriotic nationalism, then, appear to have penetrated into the hearts and minds of many Dutch privateers and their sponsors. What is even more interesting is that renegade Dutch pirates could be affected by such sentiments as well. Take the case reported in the 1651 edition of the *Hollantse Mercurius* almanac. In August 1650, English "pirates" (*Roovers*) captured the ship in which a plucky, young, Dutch merchant was traveling to London. Among the crew of this marauding band was another Dutchman who hailed from the same town as the merchant. Despite the pirate gang's intention to plunder the victimized ship ruthlessly, the captive merchant was able to establish a bond with the turncoat Dutchman based upon their shared municipal and national identity:

> ... a certain Soldier serving under these Pirates, saw our Hollands merchant, whom he ... knew / because they were both born in the same City / they spoke and immediately recognizing one another / [the soldier] also asked the aforementioned merchant about his Highness [the Prince of Orange] ... .[149]

As it turns out, this was no idle conversation, for the acknowledgment of these bonds paid off for the merchant in important ways. Bribing the soldier, as well as one of the soldier's shipmates, and bravely professing his dedication to the prince of Orange ("... he ... spoke with courage / and shouting / that he was a Servant of his Highness Prince William ...") the merchant rebelled against the English *zeeroovers*. Finally, in the fracas that ensued, he was able to enlist the help of the two soldiers, attack the other pirates, rescue two female passengers, and escape with his life intact.[150]

So the Dutch pirate, as well as privateer, was embedded in a complicated and multilayered context that defined the de facto (as opposed to de jure) scope of his activities and determined how his home society perceived his identity. Rather than inhabiting two distinct spheres, as Dutch law insisted, the cultural categories of *kaper* (privateer) and *zeerover* (pirate) in fact mingled, fluidly assuming one another's behavior and characteristics as the need or opportunity arose. That Golden Age Dutch society accepted, at least to some degree, this "privateer/pirate continuum"—this "slippery slope" of maritime predation—despite their declared abhorrence for piracy, is clear when one considers the evidence presented in criminal sentencing records and popular media. In the face of this, one might wonder why convicted pirates were ever punished harshly at all. Indeed, sometimes the motivation had nothing to do with internal reasons, but was simply a response to relentless foreign pressure or threats (e.g., persistent French entreaties to the States-General in the early seventeenth century;[151] the 1660 case of Jan de Haas;[152] and the early-eighteenth-century case of Albert Rijke[153]). Complaints expressed by a victimized Dutch citizen also appear to have carried considerable weight (e.g., the case of Jan Corneliszoon Knole of Amsterdam[154]). Moreover, stricter sentences likely reflected the individual sentiments of particular judges who were more stringent in their application of the law, even as they existed within a culture that permitted them to be much more lenient. It also appears that despite the latitude Golden Age Dutch culture provided, certain convicted defendants had crossed some kind of line, that their behavior went beyond the pale, as it were. Working for the Republic's enemies—especially the Dunkirkers—qualified in this regard. The judges also appear to have looked less kindly on those defendants who were convicted in absentia; showing up in court and admitting one's sins, it seems, often paid a tangible reward. And there is the probability that the Republic's authorities felt the need periodically to crack down when they could, or when things appeared to be getting out of hand—to establish control when Dutch privateers were becoming simply too aggressive and insubordinate.

The point is, however, that these tough penalties were not necessarily the norm—punishments were changeable and inconsistent. The category and title of "pirate" was negotiable. It may be, too, that Dutch permissiveness toward piracy was another emanation of a broader cultural tendency to allow great personal autonomy until clearly defined limits were exceeded (consider, e.g., Golden Age approaches to childrearing).[155] In any case, while one finds plenty of examples of men who were convicted of piracy and punished severely, according to the law's prescriptions, it is also indisputable that the crime was also quite tolerated, both by the judicial system and the public at large. Indeed, public acceptance often went beyond mere toleration. In fact, the pursuit of individual profit or national self-interest led many members of the Golden Age Netherlands to actively *embrace* and *encourage* the fluid boundaries defining privateer and pirate traits, to capitalize on the shifting, blurry border supposedly separating the two practices. This is what happened, for example, in the 1610 case of Captain Hendrik Willemszoon and his crew of 29 whose piratical venture aboard the *'t Kraantgen* (*the Little Crane*) was sponsored by an Amsterdam *rederij* (see Chapter 5).[156] It also took place in the case of Herbert Hugo and Laurens Davidszoon (see Chapter 5). For Hugo and Davidszoon did not set sail from Amsterdam as identifiable, visible "pirates." Rather, even as they had maintained piratical aims, they adopted the veneer of "privateers" by establishing a *rederij* to sponsor and support their venture and by obtaining an illegitimate commission from the king of France. Likewise, fellow participants in this sham partnership were not dubious characters from the Netherlands' seamy underbelly, but instead represented upstanding and respectable members of Golden Age society, men who appeared to be "good bourgeois" in every way. Shareholders included Dordrecht merchant Isaac van den Biesheuvel, who would later serve as a member of that city's municipal government; Amsterdam merchant Hendrick Christiaanszoon Brouwer; and Hubrecht de Lairesse, a VOC bureaucrat.[157] Each contributed *f*.8,000 to the *rederij*, a firm that resembled any of the other myriad such enterprises in the Netherlands, but one whose motives were, from the beginning, impure and criminal in intent. These fine men knowingly sought to profit from an intentionally *piratical* venture.

This anecdote aside, such profiteering on the Dutch citizenry's part took place at a much greater level when one considers the actions of the two largest and most esteemed Dutch trade enterprises, the VOC and WIC. Both firms enjoyed societal approval and widespread public interest and investment. And yet the Companies engaged in "piratical" actions in order to further their commercial ambitions. Indeed, the WIC's charter was nakedly explicit about the Company's "piratical" propensities and goals. But the VOC, too, attacked and plundered, captured and pillaged,[158] even as its leaders declined or were unable to brand their policies as such, and all for the sake of increasing the bottom line and augmenting its and the Republic's power and glory.

Sample seventeenth-century pamphlets reveal that the public knew about the Companies' ignoble transgressions. Although representing voices of dissent and reproach, these works bear witness to the fact that Golden Age society was aware that "piratical" conduct had, in many respects, become standard practice for legitimate, even venerated, Dutch institutions. One pamphlet published in 1626, for example, lambasted the VOC's "godless" conduct in the Indies, behavior which it said had resulted in the immoral exploitation of native peoples, extortion of the region's capital and resources, and outright "thievery" of goods. In blistering language, the text condemned the Company's personnel for engaging in the "most godless robbery" and maritime violence that had resulted in the plundering of vessels, the sinking of ships, and the murder of innocent seamen. All of this, the pamphlet declared, constituted "piracy," which besmirched the Netherlands' good name the whole world over. While assuming the disguise of good, bourgeois investors, the pamphlet proclaimed, Dutchmen who had profited from this illicit and corrupt trade actually trafficked in banditry, mayhem, and murder.[159]

Two other pamphlets, published in 1635 and 1638 respectively, similarly attacked the company. The 1635 publication—a long diatribe against current Dutch political and trade policy—claimed that the newfound "freedom" achieved by the Dutch Republic in its break from Spain had actually resulted only in immorality and degradation. Part and parcel of this so-called freedom—which the author viewed only as licentiousness—was the development of Dutch pirates (*zeeroovers*) infesting the seas. Pride of place in this regard had to go to the VOC, the writer declared, for the company engaged in barbarous, villainous conduct in the East Indies, robbing and pillaging rapaciously in order to maximize its profits.[160] While not against the East Indies trade per se, the author railed against the VOC's particular policies and practices and judged them to be the Devil's handiwork. The Company's directors, the author claimed, were "villainous" and had wrought much more destruction on the land and peoples of the East Indies than had the Republic's enemies, Spain and Portugal.[161] "Who can recount," he asked rhetorically, "all of the deceit, miserliness, faithlessness, and barbarous savagery which this Company and [its] godly participants have pursued . . . and still do?"[162] Excoriating the VOC's authorities and personnel as "pirates" and even cannibals who "ate the flesh of men and supped on human blood," the pamphlet pleaded for the public's outrage against the Company's "unchristian" conduct.[163]

But these pamphlets' caustic complaints appear to have fallen on deaf ears, for little outrage arose. The Companies continued to do business as usual and were well supported by the general public. Indeed, in the eyes of the typical Dutchman, the trade companies represented vehicles for personal enrichment and state expansion and glory. Their conduct was perceived as completely appropriate. And why should it have been otherwise, when maritime robbery was so "acceptable" that even rank-and-file seamen, as well as the officers and personnel of the glorified Dutch Navy, engaged in it?[164] The scattered voices of dissent in these pamphlets notwithstanding, there appears to have been little criticism of the VOC's and WIC's tactics. The Companies' "piratical" demeanor mattered naught.

This should not be surprising, considering the particular cultural conditions that shaped how the Golden Age Dutch perceived and "processed" the notion of piracy. The Dutch deplored "piracy" when their people suffered as a result of maritime marauding—when valuable trade goods and fellow Dutchmen were seized by the Dunkirkers, the Barbary corsairs, and other foreigners. Such miscreants were easy to hold up as examples of "godless" moral degeneration. At the same time, however, the Dutch could not always recognize "piracy," or did not always chose to name it as such, when members of their own society committed the crime. Copious and shrill Dutch laws tried to insist that "privateering" and "piracy" were altogether different practices and accorded the two trades separate spheres of action and identity. But while such pronouncements may have been *legally* valid, they were *culturally* untrue, thus accounting for inconsistencies in the prosecution of justice and ostensible lapses in societal judgment. Pervasive cultural values born of special economic, military, and political exigencies and fired in the kiln of deeply embedded maritime traditions engendered a context in which the differences between *kaapvaart* and *zeeroverij* were actually just the differences inherent in a Janus-like opposition, superficial dissimilarities that, at a deeper level, dissolved into a seamless continuum of maritime predation.

At a fundamental cultural level, then, the Golden Age privateer and pirate was one person, an ambiguous, symbolically charged figure who simultaneously incarnated both the glorified hero and the reviled criminal in the eyes of his home culture. And like so many other ironic dualities born of the Netherlands' relationship with the sea, this figure—this liminal freebooter—was simultaneously both a blessing and a curse, two facets of one force. His identity was ambiguous and complex, allowing him to be simultaneously the patriotic Sea Beggar champion, the untamed reprobate of the high seas, and everything in between. The Spanish may have thought that they were insulting the Dutch when they tarred them as rebel pirates,[165] but their description was more accurate than they could have realized. For in very important ways, the maritime predator was profoundly important to the Dutch cultural psyche. Whether he be the pious mariner or the godless scoundrel, the Dutch freebooter was a character whose identity and activities were fundamentally entwined with the national spirit—indeed, with the very conception of the "imagined community"—of the Golden Age Dutch Republic.

Appendices

Appendix I

Sample Privateer Instructions (April 1599)

Data from ARA, AA, Verzameling Bisdom #123: "Uit het Memoriael Admt. de Maze," April 13, 1599, Extract-Resolutien van de Staten Generaal, de Staten van Holland en de Admiraliteit op de Maze, plakaten, reglementen, instructien, enz. betreffende de commissievaart . . .

These are instructions for those privateers who received *Brieven van Marcque* (*Letters of Marque*) from the Admiralty of the Maas in the spring of 1599. The Admiralty warned that recipients who did not abide by the instructions were to be punished as *Piraten en Zeerovers* ("Pirates and Sea Robbers").

Instructie voor de genen brieven van Marcque verkregent hebbende:

1. Eerst en alvoren zullen geen Scheepen mogen uitreden ten Oorloge, ten waere hun reeders ofte Capiteinen verkregen hadden van de Heeren Staten Generl. behoorl. brieven van Marcque, waer naer de Reyse. Capiteinen zullen hebben te lichten van den Admirael Generl. Commissie, ende doende in de Collegien van d'Admt. Staende onder 't restort [ressort?] daer zij uitvaren zullen den nabetij. Eed, ende van denzelven te zullen voldoen, stellen goede en Suffisante vautie voor de voorsz. Raden voor hunne handeling tot alzulke Somme toe als de raden ter Admt. zullen arbitreren, op poene van gehouden en gestraft te worden als Piraten en Zeerovers, indien zij anders uitgevaren, zullen zijn, ende te betalen alle Schaaden en Interessen de reijse. koopl. aentedoen, stellende de voorsz. cautionarissen ter cause van dezen hun Subject de Judicature van 't voorsz. Collegie, Waer naer Zij zullen lichten van de Vice-admiraels inde respe. Quartieren behoorl. brieven van Attache;

2. Sullen overzulks de voorsz. Captnen. mogen aentasten alle Schepen ende goederen aenkomende ende toebehoorende den ondersaten van den Koning van Spagne, in welke zijne rijken ofte Landen die eenig Sints gezeten ofte toebehoorende mogen zijn, van gelijken alle de personen Scheepen en goederen, die zij in Zee zullen vinden, van den geenen, die in die in de gedesunieerde Nederlanden zijn gezeten.

3. Voorts word verstaen, dat zijl. zullen mogen ophalen ende ten goede prinsen hebben alle de goederen Scheepen en persoonen uit de Nederlanden op de Landen en rijken bij den Koning van Spagne +++ [op?] Europa bezeten reisende ofte eenigSints gemunt hebbende.

4. Zonder dat zij zullen mogen ophalen ofte beschadigen eenige Scheepen in deze Vereenigde Nederlanden, andere Konikrijken Landen of republijcquen (uitgenomen d'ondersaten van den Koning van Spagne ende Ingezetenen van de

gedesunieerde Provintien) toekomende, gaende oft komende van de Kusten van Barbarien, Brasil, Guinea, Oost en West Indien, alwaer men verstaet voor hen luiden libere trafficque en negotiatie te verblijven ende toe te laten.

5. Vermogen de Voortz. Captnen. aen allen den Landen den Koning van Spagne Subject zijnde invallen te doen, aldaer hostiliteit te toonen, zoo jegens personen, als dezelve gevangen nemende rantçoenerende, de goederen binnen Scheepsboord brengende, ende alles te doen jegens de voorsz. Vijandl. plaetsen, wes de rechten van Oorloge eenig Sints zijn toelatende, altijds goede respecten ende inzichten nemende op de personen van andere koning rijken ende Landen in die Quartieren te vinden.

6. Ende zullen mede bekomen hebbende eenige Scheepen, dezelve niet vermogen te plunderen, in de grond te booren, goederen versteken ofte persoonen bij maniere van torture aentasten en qualyk te tracteren, maer die brengen in de havenen dae zij Eed gedaen en cautie gestelt hebben, omme de goederen behoorl. geinventariseert bij eenige Special. daer toe te committeren ende getrouwel. bewaert te zullen worden ten proffijte van den geenen, die daer toe bevonden zullen zijn geregtig te wezen, op de poenen van mede als piraten en Zeerovers gestraft te zullen worden. Waer naer de voortz. Captnen. en officieren zullen geven behoorl. Instructien aen de Fiscalen van den Districte, omme hunne zaken voor de Collegien geinstitueert, partije (indien daer eenige is) gehoort, recht daer op gedaen te worden als naer behooren.

7. Sententie tot voordeel van den voortz. Volke van Oorloge gekregen en de goederen bij den Vendumeester verkocht zijnde, zullen van de pennen. geprocedeert van verkochte goederen voorden Captnen. Scheepsvolk ende Rheeders de voortz Schip ofte Schepen tot hunnen Koste uitgerust hebben, de moeten aftrekken voorde geregtigheit van den Lande ofte gemeene zaake (alvoren afgetrokken zijnde de Kosten, zoo ter cause van de lossinge, Inventarisatie, verkopen als in de procederen gevallen) den 5 penn. ende daer naer van de reste den 10en. penn. voor den Admirael Gene. en het Surplus zal blijven ten proffijte van de voortz. reders, Captnen. Officieren en bootsgezellen, onder hun te verdeelen naer costume of zoo anders naer de respe. contracten behooren zal.

8. Des word verstaen dat bij gevallen de voortz. Captnen. rencontreren eenige Vlooten indienst van den Lande zijnde ende bij den Command. versocht worden op een exploict ten dienste van den Lande rakende, gehouden zullen zijn voor den tijd van 8 of 10 dagen hun te laten emploijeren en den dienst doen op zulke recompence van den Lande, als naer gelegentheit van den exploicte ende meriten van de zaake bevonden zal worden te behooren.

9. De Commissien van den voortz. Captnen. zullen hun krachten effect hebben den tijd van een Jaer voor den genen niet varende buiten Europa, ende van twee Jaaren voor die geenen, die naer Oost en West Indien zullen vaaren, naerr de expiratie van welken tijd dezelve Captnen. gehouden zullen zijn wederom te keeren ter plaetsen daer zij uitgevaren zijn.

10. Voor welk wederkeeren de borgen mede zullen geobligeert zijn, ten waere bij de voorn. E Heeren Staten Generl. raedsaem bevonden word, de Commissien binnen dezelve tijd te wederroepen.

11. Ende zullen de Captnen. hun bootsvolk binnen Scheepsboord in goede ordre houden, ende hun voorts in alles reguleren ende naerkomen de Krijgsdiscipline in den Artijkelbrief gementioneert.

12. Ende reserveren de Heeren Staten Generl. aen henl. deze Instr. te mogen veranderen, daer af en toe te doen naerr geleegentheit van zaaken, midsgrs. de Interpretatie van de duisternissen dewelke in dezelve zouden mogen worden bevonden.

Eedt:
Dat Sweeren wij Mijne E. Mo Heeren Staten Generael der Vereenigde Nederlandse Provintien gehouden getrouwd zijne Exce. als Admirael gehoorsaem te zijn en ons te reguleren naer den Artikelbrief midsgrs. alles te doen, dat goede Vroome Officieren, Krijgsluiden en Soldaten en bootsgezellen Schuldig zijn en behooren te doen. Zoo waerlyk helpe ons god Almachtig.

Gearresteert den April 13, 1599

Appendix II

Sample Income Earned by Amsterdam Privateers and Their *Rederijen*

The data in this table was derived from the following sources: ARA, AA #1844, 1845, 1846, and 1847: *Rekeningen van den vendumeester wegens zijn uitgaaf van de prinsen, mulcten en confiscatien*, 1665–1667; and ARA, AA #1806, 1807, and 1808: *Rekeningen van den vendumeester wegens zijn ontvang van de prinsen, mulcten en confiscatien*, 1665–1667.

Year	Total amount	Privateer	Payment to privateer	Payment to *Rederij*
1665	4,763.2	Pieter van den Bergh	48 (1%)	1,918.80 (40.3%)
	5325	Zeeland privateer	53 (.99%)	4,871.40 (91.5%)
	19,203.8	Capt. Jan Oiemers	192 (.99%)	17,857.17 (93%)
	1,014	Cornelis Oromtas [?]	10 (.99%)	752.19 (74%)
	756	Jacob Jacobsz.	8 (1.05%)	587.12 (77.6%)
	172	Oultman Eijldon & Pieter Jansz. de Vries	6 (3.5%)	89.90 (52.3%)
	560	Adriaen Virth	6 (1.07%)	425.19 (76%)
	5,543.19	Oltman Eijldor	55 (.99%)	5,257.16 (95%)
	628.6	Sijmon Cloopersz	6 (.95%)	364.14 (58%)
	6,294	Sijmmon Cloopersz	63 (1%)	5,597.10 (89%)
	1,740	Philip Ras	17 (.98%)	1,497.40 (86%)
	2,250	Pieter Constant	22 (.97%)	1,836.60 (81.6%)
	3,018	Pieter Jansz de Vries	30 (.99%)	2,766.15 (92%)
	19,001	Jan Jacobsz Taul	190 (1%)	18,703.00 (98.4%)
	27,313.18	Jan de Bock	273 (1%)	25,598.50 (94%)
	4,803	Abraham Dominicas	48 (1%)	4,755.00 (99%)
	22,987.6	Mattijs Jacobsz Pruijsl	2298 (1%)	22,707.60 (99%)
1666	5,153.11	Jan Pietersz. Bocq van Zeelant	52 (1%)	4,782.20 (93%)
	1,305	Pieter Jansz de Vries	13 (99.6%)	1,055.16 (81%)
	5,650.5	Hendrick Bruijn Haen	56 (.99%)	5,086.80 (90%)
	3,600	Pieter Willemsz.	36 (1%)	3,405.10 (95%)
	910.10	Hendrick Bruijn Haen	9 (.99%)	664.19 (73%)
	4,483.6	Hendrick Bruijn Haen	45 (1%)	4,078.10 (91%)

Continued

Appendix II

Continued

Year	Total amount	Privateer	Payment to privateer	Payment to *Rederij*
	7,071.2	Jan Wagenaer	71 (1%)	7,000.20 (.99%)
	11,732	Adriaen Bontsz. Vos	117 (.99%)	10,918.00 (93%)
	11,098.16	Adriaen Bonts Vos	111 (1%)	9,150.15 (82.4%)
	4,074.2	Hendrick Bruijn Haen	40 (.98%)	3,727.11 (91.5%)
	17,288.5	Pieter Willemsz & Pieter Goetsem	173 (1%)	17,115.50 (99%)
	4,963.18	Jan Wagenaer	50 (1%)	4,913.18 (99%)
	3,529.2	Lijn Brandt van Zeelant	36 (1.02%)	2,764.11 (78.3%)
	42,292.2	Jan Jansz Lauw van Zeelant	423 (1%)	40,963.20 (97%)
	8,605.9	Zeelant privateer	86 (.99%)	8,519.90 (99%)
1667	18,056.5	Cornelis Poules	180 (.99%)	17,876.50 (99%)
	2,550	Houdrick Bruijn Haen	25 (.98%)	2,525.00 (99%)
	18,478.8	Cornelis Pouldsz.	184 (1%)	18,294.80 (99%)
	259.15	Symon Cloopras	8 (3.1%)	185.15 (71.4%)
	1,314.7	Steven Tomasz.	13 (.99%)	941.10 (72%)
	12,631.4	Adriaen Quast	126 (.99%)	11,450.60 (91%)
	4,900	Steven Tomasz.	49 (1%)	4,851.00 (99%)
	9,219.4	Houdrick Bruijn	92 (1%)	9,127.40 (99%)
	1,520	Adrian Quast	15 (.98%)	1,505.00 (99%)

Appendix III

Some Dutch Privateer Captures (1652)

Elaborated here are details about privateer captures during the first year of the First Anglo-Dutch War (1652) according to the pamphlet, Verz. RLP: *Naerder Openbaringe, van Nederlants Engelschen Oorloge, Oorsake, Ende Tegenweer*. . . . (Leyden: Wilhelm Christiaans vander Boxc, 1653), 40, 54–57, 69–70, 77–87. "Guns" indicates the number of cannons aboard the privateering vessel. I use the term "Dutch Privateers" when the document specified only "our privateers" (*onse kapers*).

Privateer name(s)	Quantity & origin	Guns	Prizes	Victims' nationality	Prize details (i.e., cargo, en route from, guns, etc.)	Where brought
	2 brothers from Zeeland	6 & 10	13	England		Zeeland
Wilh. Bosch & Gillis Boone			7	England	5 from Terre Neuf (fish, etc.); 1 from Carribean ; 1 from London (goods)	Zeeland
	1 from Vlissingen	6	6	England	En route from Iceland	
	2 Dutch privateers		20	England	All were "great coal ships", one ship armed with 14 cannons	
	1 Zeelander		3	England		Vlissingen
	"Batavians"		many	England	Captured along Biscay and other coasts	France (where sold also)
	1 Zeelander			Biscayer		
Capt. Kleyn-Pieck & Capt. Brand	Zeeland		1	England	East Indiaman	Zeeland
	5 Zeelanders		7	England	Very richly laden vessels; 6 en route from Lisbon (sugar, oil, salt); 1 en route from St. Lucas (wool, etc.)	Zeeland
	"Batavians"		15	England	En route from Barbados (sugar, cochineal, tobacco, other wares)	Havre de Grace
	"Batavians"		13	Hamburg & Lübeck	Ships carrying pitch, tar, hemp, flax, and other wares	Amsterdam
	Zeelanders		6	England	6 richly-laden vessels en route from Portugual; 1 sank there	
	Dutch "Sea Lions"		2		1 en route from Bilbao (iron, etc.); and a *Mallegoms-Vaerder*	

Capt. Jan van Rotterdam	Rotterdam?		England	East Indiaman (?)	Rotterdam & Vlissingen
Capt. Koets-Wagen; another unnamed man	Rotterdam; Zeeland; 170 crewhands	4 & 10	England	12	Captured these vessels near Yarmouth; 12 prizes from a fleet of 22 merchant ships; carrying money, *Bukingh* (?), and other wares; one convoy with an 8 cannon ship accompanied the fleet
	1 "Adventurer"	many	England		Plundered many English *kitsen* along the coast of "Rie"	Vlissingen
	Dutch privateers	1			Great coal ship	Vlissingen
	Zeelanders	3	England & Scotland		2 ships from England, 1 from Scotland	Middelburg
	1 Dutch privateer	1	England		Ship carrying 30 *lasten* of wine	Vlissingen
	Dutch privateers	2	England		Ships captured near Jersey; carrying corn, etc	Kauw (where sold also)
Capt. Brand			England?	2	Both ships richly-laden (with sugar, tobacco, etc.); seized on Dover coast	Texel
	"Sea Lions"	1	England		Ship was richly-laden with many fine wares; from London	Rotterdam
	Batavians	1	England		Richly-laden sips en route from Smyrna	
	2 Zeelanders	3	England		Richly-laden merchant ships; stranded another 9 vessels on the English coast	Vlissingen
	Nederlandish "Sea Cocks"	1	England		A great merchant ship (belonging to d'Heer Longhlant) carrying tin	
Ship: *Spaensche Barcke*	Amsterdam	5	England		Merchant ships armed with 14, 14, 12, 8, and 8 cannons respectively; 9 enemy men killed and many injured	Amsterdam
	Zeelanders	5	England		"Costly" prizes carrying "Bayen," "Carsayen" and other wares	Vlissingen
	1 Amsterdammer	3	England		"Beautiful" prizes en route to the Canaries; carrying English textiles, piece-goods, fish, and wheat; worth ƒ.200,000	Nantes

Continued

Continued

Privateer name(s)	Quantity & origin	Guns	Prizes	Victims' nationality	Prize details (i.e., cargo, en route from, guns, etc.)	Where brought
	1 Rotterdammer		1	England		Amsterdam
	1 Amsterdammer		1	England	Merchant ship carrying copper, raisins, sugar, & wine; worth fl. 30,000	Amsterdam?
Capt. Keelman			1	England	Prize was "costly"	Rotterdam
	1 Amsterdammer		3	England	Merchant ships carrying wine, oil, spices, and textiles	Amsterdam
	"Batavians" from Holland		5	Danzig & Lübeck	Ships were en route from Dunkirk; carrying pitch, tar, and naval stores	't Vlie
	Zeelanders		3		Prizes loaded with lead, tin, pitch, and tar	Zeeland
	1 Zeelander		2	England	Merchant ship and frigate (armed with 36 cannons); sank both	
	1 from Enkhuizen		1	England	Merchant ship loaded with butter, cheese, and other food	Texel
	2 from Amsterdam		4	England; Hamburg; & Oostende	English vessels were "great" coal ships; other 2 vessels were flutes	
	"Sea Lions"		1	England	Carrying textiles	't Vlie
	1 from Enkhuizen		3	England	One ship was loaded with lumber and "vijvres"(?); 2 vessels were recaptured Dutch ships (carrying "puyen" [?])	Texel
Kapt. Verstegen & Kapt. Rietbeeck			1	Hamburg	Ship had 65 Englishmen aboard	Amsterdam
	1 Rotterdammer		1		A rich prize with costly wares	Rotterdam
	2 Zeelanders		2	England	Loaded with corn and English textiles	Zeeland

223

Kapt. Vijgh		1	Hamburg	Ship en route to England, carrying pitch and tar	Rotterdam
Kapt. Vijgh		several		Prizes loaded with wares and contraband	Zeeland
Kapt. Vijgh		several		Prizes loaded with wares and contraband	Texel
	1 from Hoorn & 60 "lost" [verloore] children Dutch privateers	12	England	Textile ship with convoy ship, captured while en route Hamburg	Rotterdam
		2			
		1		The *Avonturier de Fortuyn*, a flute-ship carrying coal	Texel
	"Adventurers"	4	England	Ships en route from Gottenberg [Sweden?], loaded with pitch, tar, and pylons/ships masts	't Vlie
Hans Warregaren & comrades		1	Emden	Ship en route from Newcastle, loaded with coal & grindstones (to be used for sharpening "murderous" knives and axes for "chopping off heads")	Amsterdam
	1 from Hoorn, with 50 "daredevils"	4	Sweden; England?	Swedish ship was carrying ammunition; other 3 were loaded with pitch, tar, hemp, and other contraband articles	
	Zeelands "daredevils"	3	England	Loaded with sugar and tobacco; worth ƒ.50,000	Veere
	Lost children [Verlore Kinderen]	2	England		Vlissingen
	1 Zeelander & 1 Amsterdammer	4	England	Rich prizes armed with 16 and 22 cannons; en route to the Virgin Islands; loaded with brandy and other commodities	

Continued

Continued

Privateer name(s)	Quantity & origin	Guns	Prizes	Victims' nationality	Prize details (i.e., cargo, en route from, guns, etc.)	Where brought
Ship: *Spaensche Bercke*			3		Rich prizes; captured while the Dutch ship was en route from La Rochelle	France (where sold also)
	1 Hollander		1	England	prize carrying butter and coins	Maas (Rotterdam?)
	Dutch privateers		1	England	Prize (barque) captured on French coast while en route to Terre-Neuf	
	1 from Vlissingen & 50 crewmen	14	1	England	Rich Mediterranean ship armed with 18 cannons; loaded with oil, Spanish wine, corn, wool, hides, and other commodities, as well as 11 sacks of pieces-of-eight; many dead and wounded on each side	Veere
	1 from Amsterdam		2	England	Ships were en route from the Elbe, loaded with ammunition	Texel
	Netherlands "Batavians" and "Sea Heroes"		4	England	These costly prizes were en route to and from the West Indies; loaded with textiles, tin, clothing, lead, and other commodities	
	1 Dutch "Adventurer"		1		A rich prize loaded with Canary wine and other wares; worth fl. 72,000	Havre de Grace & La Rochelle
	privateers from Holland		2		Good prizes	Enkhuizen

2 Dutch privateers	4	England	Armed with 8, 12, 14, and 16 cannons; loaded with brandy, piece-goods, coal, tine, lead, hats/caps, and "lijwaet"	Vlissingen
"Batavians"	2	England	Great merchant ships, seized en route to Brazil to Portugal; loaded with 1200 chests of sugar	
Dutch privateers	3	England	Loaded with wool, pitch, and tar	Texel
Post-Peert 1 from Enkhuizen	2	England	Carrying coal	Texel
Kapt. Boon 1 from Enkhuizen	2	England	Rich prizes with pitch and tar	Hoorn
	1	England	Large ship of 80 "lasten;" loaded with 700 sacks of bread, 200 tons of butter, 200 tons of beer, several hundred cheeses, many vats of wine, and other provisions, all of which were intended for the fleet of Admiral Black, located by Texel	Amsterdam
Hans Warre-garen	3	England	Rich ships loaded with sugar, indigo, and tobacco; 1 sank	't Vlie
2 from Enkhuizen	4	England	All were coal ships	Enkhuizen
"Adventurers" from Holland	3	England	Costly and richly-laden ships, en route from Canary Islands; carrying 3 half-tons of gold	Zeeland
1 Zeelander	1	England	Richly-laden merchant ship; en route to Rouen	
Ship: *De Avonturier den Diamant*	2	England	Both were costly "Mallegoms-Vaerders" loaded with 140 pipes of wine, 70 pipes of oil, 400 vats of "vijgen" and 400 Korven of raisins	

Continued

Continued

Privateer name(s)	Quantity & origin	Guns	Prizes	Victims' nationality	Prize details (i.e., cargo, en route from, guns, etc.)	Where brought
	1 Zeelander		2	England	Loaded with wool and coal	Vlissingen
	1 from Enkhuizen		2	England	Prizes were en route from London to Hamburg; loaded with many costly manufactured goods	Enkhuizen
	Various privateers from Holland & Zeeland		7	England	Rich prizes armed with 8 and 14 cannons; loaded with English textiles, salt, coal, pitch, tar, and 300 vats of Virginia tobacco	Vlissingen & Texel

Appendix IV

Privateering Activity Sponsored by the Admiralty of the Maas

All data comes from ARA, AA, Verz. Van Der Heim #155: *Extracten uit de rol van Proceduren voor den Raad ter Admiralteit op de Maze over Prinsen der Commissievaarders verovert* ... entries for 1652–53; 1665–67; 1672–73; 1690.

Date	Privateer	# of prizes	Victims origin	Booty
Oct. 1652	Cornelis Kelemans & Jan de Raed	4	England	Oatmeal, Norwegian freight, fish
Nov. 1652	Willem Lenders	1	England	Coal
Nov. 1652	Abraham Heindriks Capellenaar	2	England	Coal, Icelandic fish
Jan. 1653	Wouter Fredriks	2	England	Iron, English soap, Spanish wine, vinegar, cheese, tobacco, corn
Jan. 1653	Cornelis Kelemans	3	England	Apples, vinegar, leather, fish, tobacco, coal
Feb. 1653	Albert Gerritsen	4	England	Rye, malt
Feb. 1653	Jacob Plat & Adriaan Albertsen	1	England	Fish
April 1653	Cornelis Kellemen	1	England	No cargo—privateering ship
July 1653	Ewout Koecketer	1	England	Butter, willow
July 1653	Robbert Gerards Appelburg	2	England	Quicklime, Norwegian freight
Aug. 1653	Dirks Jacobse de Veer	1	England	Fish
July 1665	Lauren Karsseboom	1	?	?
July 1664	Claes Pietersz. de Boer	1	?	?
Oct. 1665	Jacob Sijmons	1	?	?
Jan. 1666	Jan Laurens Koestaert	1	?	?
Sept. 1667	Steeven Pieterse	1	?	Contraband: naval stores
Sept. 1667	Steeven Pieterse	1	Sweden	Contraband: naval stores

Continued

Continued

Date	Privateer	# of prizes	Victims origin	Booty
Sept. 1672	Jan van Vlissingen	2	1 from England; other ?	Coal, linen, tallow, yarn/thread
Sept. 1672	Otto van Aken	3	?	Beer, ballast, empty privateer ship
Nov. 1672	Jan van Vlissingen	1	England	Salt, herring
Jan. 1673	Guirijn (Guinign?) Drooghart	1	France	Wine, brandy, turpentine, oil of turpentine, rye, goat skins
Jan. 1673	Cornelis Boxeel	1	England	?
Feb. 1673	Willem Bloks & Jan Jacobs Springer	?	?	?
Feb. 1673	Quirijn Drooghart	?	?	?
1690	6 privateers	?	2 from France; rest?	Meat, bacon, flour, tar, pitch

Appendix V

"Slave Roll" of Dutch Sailors Captured by the Algerian Corsairs (1690–1712 and 1715–1726)

Lyste of Rolle van alle de Slaaven, so van de Neederlandsche Natie, of die met Scheepen in den Staat der vereenigde Nederlanden t'huis hoorende t'seedert het jaar 1690 tot 1712, en van het jaar 1715 tot 1726 inclius, door de Algiersche Kaapers genoomen, en tot Algiers opgebragt zyn. ARA, AA: Verz. Schrijver #8.

This document is a chronological list enumerating Dutch citizens captured by the Algerian corsairs between 1690 and 1712 and 1715 and 1726. I have included the examples through 1710. Typical details include the names of the ship taken; the name of the shipper and the ship's home port; any enslaved Dutchmen from that vessel who were still alive; their Dutch occupation; their marital status; their age; where they were born; and finally, what type of slave they were in Algiers. Marginalia indicated if the men in question later died; were liberated, and if so, when and how many pieces-of-eight were paid. I have included these remarks in italics at the end of each entry.

1690: Het Schip de Geertrui, waar van Schipper was Laurens N.; zynde de volgende alhier alleen in het leeven,
  1. Thomas Werkholm, voor Jongen uitgevaaren, gebooren tot Labek in het Keiserrijk, oud vyftig jaaren, ongetrouwt, particuliere Slaave.

1691: Het Schip de St. Jan van Rotterdam, Schipper Pieter Jansse, genoomen primo January; waar van de volgende alhier alleen in leeven is,
  2. Leur Gallas, Matroos, een Hamburger, oud vyf en vyftig jaaren, ongetrouwt, te Rotterdam t'huis hoorende, particlier Slaaf. *1730 gelost voor 250.*

1692: Het Schip de Kat van Hoorn, Schipper Pieter Reinier; waar van de volgende Persoon in het leeven is,
  3. Andries Christysse, Matroos, een Deen, oud vyf en sestig jaaren, ongetrouwt, Deyliks Slaave. *als presem [?] Van den Dey Vrye geg. 1730.*

1694: Het Schip de Surgo Clara, Schipper Mecher Bras, genomen den 7 January; waar van de volgende alleen alhier in leeven is,
  4. Johan Christoffel Beryk, Timmerman, een Courlander, oud een en sestig jaaren, ongetrouwt, te Amsterdam t'huis hoorende, particulier. *1730 voor 135.*

1696: Het Schip de Juffrouw Rachel van Amsterdam, Schipper Jan Brouwer, genoomen primo January; waar van de volgende alhier alleen in het leeven is,
  5. Teunis Cornelisse, Matroos, een Noorman, oud vyf en tagtig jaaren, ongetrouwt, te Amsterdam t'huis hoorende, particulier. *Doodt.*

1699: Het Schip de St. Maria van Amsterdam, Schipper Jan Serjan, genoomen den 15 October; waar van de volgende alhier alleen in het leeven is,

  6. Jan Tonnisse, Matroos, nu Timmerman, een Deen, oud vier en vyftig jaaren, ongetrouwt, t'Amsterdam t'huis horrende, particulier. *400—1730*.

1700: Het Schip de goude Druif van Amsterdam, Schipper Pieter Muller; waar van de volgende alhier alleen in het leeven is,
  7. Pieter Hansse, Matroos, een Holsteiner, oud neegen en vyftig jaaren, ongetrouwt, te Amsterdam t'huis hoorende, particulier. *gelost*.

1704: Het Schip Walgert, Schipper Jacob Huigen, ter kaap van Zeeland uitgevaaren; hebbende in hunne kruistogt een Fransche Setia genoomen, die door gemelde Schipper Jacob Huigen van sijn Scheepsvolk wierd beset, ten einde om deese Fransche Setia na Livorno op te brengen, dog op hunne reise door vier Algerynen verovert; van welk Scheepsvolk de volgende alhier nog in het leeven is,
  8. Pieter Walrand, Matroos, gebooren tot Middelburg, oud seeven en veertig jaaren, ongetrouwt, te Middelburg t'huis hoorende, particulier. *1730—700*.

1707: Het Schip de Livornsche Galley van Amsterdam, Schipper Jan Klinkert, genomen 16 Juny; waar van de volgende alleen alhier in het leeven is,
  9. Hans Adolph Douco, Chirurgyn, een Holsteiner, oud vyf en vyftig jaaren, zynde Weduwenaar son-Kinderen, te Amsterdam t'huis hoorende, Deylik. *1730 voor 900*.

1707: Het Schip de Mercurius van Amsterdam, Schipper Pieter coulenburg; waar van de volgende alleen alhier in het leeven is,
  10. Paulus Steynman, Matroos, een Dantzikker, oud een en sestig jaaren, ongetrouwt, te Amsterdam t'huis hoorende, particulier. *Vrye gegaan met gaselle, genomen door de Malteren [?]*.

1707: Het Schip de Triumphant, Schipper Jan de Boot, genomen den 13 July; waar van de volgende alhier nog in het leeven zyn,
  11. Gilliam Bont, Matroos, mu Zeilmaaker, gebooren tot Brugge in Vlaanderen, oud vier en vyftig jaaren ongetrouwt, te Middelburg t'huis hoorende, Deylik. *gelost vande frans Aalmoete*.
  12. Cornelis Jansse, Zeilmaaker, een Deen, oud twee en veertig jaaren, ongetrouwt, te Amsterdam t'huis hoorende, particulier. *300 in 1730*.
  13. Gerrit Somer, Matroos, een Courlander, oud vyftig jaaren, Weduwenaar sonder Kinderen, t'Amsterdam t'huis hoorende, particulier. *240 in 1730*.

1707: Het Schip de Overwinaar, Schipper Jacob Elers, gevaaren van Middelburg naar Oostindien, welk voorschreeve Schip door twee Fransche Kaaper op de hoogte van Ambrosius is genomen en de Equipagie naar Macao in Oost-indiën gevoert, op de te rugreise tot Cadez aan de Wal geset, als wanneer de volgende Matroos sig heeft begeeven aan boord van een Deensch Schip als Passagier, omme wederomme naar het Patria te keeren, dog op de t'huisreise door twee Algerynen genomen; zynde de gemelde Matroos genaamt,
  14. Jurriaan Everse, nu een Syweever, gebooren tot Amsterdam, oud vier en veertig jaaren, ongetwouwt, particulier. *175 in 1730*.

1708: Het Schip de graauwe Haas, Schipper Jan Feyt van Amsterdam, genomen den 9 February; waar van de volgende alleen alhier in het leeven is,
  15. Daniel Adriaanse Kok, gebooren tot Vlissingen, oud vyftig jaaren, ongetouwt, tot Vlissingen, t'huis hoorende, particulier. *400 in 1730*.

1709: Het Schip de St. Jan van Amsterdam, Schipper Jan Reimerse Vos, genomen den 12 April; waar vande volgende in het leeven zyn,
  16. Alexander Dondre, Watermatroos, een Venetiaan, oud sestig jaaren, ongetrouwt, t'Amsterdam t'huis hoorende, particulier. *vrije gegaan met de spaans aalmoese [aalmoete?]*.

17. Andries Oosterman, een Sweed, Bootsman, oud agt en veertig jaaren, ongetrouwt, te Amsterdam t'huis gehoort, particulier. *466 in 1730.*
18. Arent Eertman, Matroos, gebooren tot Straalsond, oud veertig jaaren, ongetrouwt, te Amsterdam t'huis gehoort, particulier. *gelost.*
19. Casper Morit, Matroos, een Venetiaan, oud ses en vyftig jaaren, ongetrouwt, te Amsterdam t'huis gehoort, particulier.
20. Merewys Micherse, Matroos, nu Timmerman, een Brandenborger, oud vier en vyftig jaaren, ongetrouwt, te Amsterdam t'huis gehoort, particulier.

1710: Het Schip de Hollandsche Galley, Schipper Willem Ney, welk Schip door drie Fransche Oorlogscheepen is genomen en den 10 December 1710 tot Malaga opgebragt, als wanneer de Equipagie aan land wierd geset, van welke Equipagie twwe Matroosen sig aan het boord van een Deensch Schip als Passagiers, hebben begeeven, om alsoo te repatrieeren, dog het selve Deensche Schip wierd in hunne voyage door drie Algerynen verover en tot Algiers opgebratt; zynde gemelde twee Matroosen alhier nog in het leeven, als.

21. Pieter Cornelise Matroos, een Sweed, oud vyftig jaaren, getrouwt tot Vlissingen, sonder Kinderen, Deylik.
22. Pieter Gol, Matroos, een Holsteiner, oud twee en veertig jaaren, ongetrouwt, t'Amsterdam t'huis hooren, Deylik. *300–1731.*

The document also includes a list indicating the nationalities of the men:

Nationality	Quantity
Nederlanders	45
Engelsche	6
Fransche	7
Keiserlijke	3
Spanjaards	1
Moscoviters	1
Deenemarken	45
Sweeden	45
Poolsche	1
Brandenburgers	5
Venetianen	4
Holsteinders	30
Lubekkers	4
Hamburgers	33
Breemers	6
Curlanders	3
Straalsunders	2
Dantzigers	9
Rostokkers	1
Koningsbergers	1
Hanoversche	2
Brunswijk	1
Stettynders	2
Vlamingers	4
Griek	1
TOTAL	251

Waar onder 105 Deylik of Deys Slaaven. 146 particuliere.

Appendix VI

Origins of the Barbary Corsairs Captured in November 1614

This data is derived from the following sources: ARA, AA, Verz. Bisdom #167: *Copie-Crimineele vonnissen van de Admiraliteit op de Maas, 1575–1710*; Verz. Thysius: *Belijdenisse, Sententie, ende namen der Zee-roovers, die soo tot Rotterdam als 't Amsterdam met der koorde gheexecuteert zijn enz... den 24 Jan.* (Amsterdam: Broer Jansz., 1615); and Verz. Thysius: *Bekentenisse van Hugo Clerck Capiteyn der Zee Roovers, die met zijn Complicen ende aenhang gejusticeert zijn tot Amsterdam, den 24 Jan. 1615...* (Amsterdam, 1615).

First name	Last name	Hometown	Origin nation	Position
Jan	Archer	Lincoln	England	
Sander	Ariansz	Vlissingen	United Provinces	
Haly	Benaman	Salé	Morocco	
Borca	Benmissou	Salé	Morocco	
Denis	Belere		France	
François	Claving			Midshipman
Hugo	Clerck	Southhampton	England	Gentleman; Captain
Thomas	Clerck	King's Lynn, Norfolk	England	Cabin boy
Thomas	Corel	Sandwich	England	
Steven	Davids	Wilshire	England	
Nicolas	Dru	Barnstable	England	Corporal
David	Fery		Scotland	
Laurens	Fijn	Basthabel [Barnstable?]	England?	
Williem	Fransz			
Willem	Frens	Westport	Ireland	
David	Gibben			
Mathien	Halele	Northampton	England	Quartermaster
Joris	Heinssen	Flanders	Southern Netherlands	Master Gunner's mate
Hendrick	Jansz.	Enkhuizen	United Provinces	
Joris	Jansz.	Enkhuizen	United Provinces	
Willem	Ketly	Dortmuyen [Dartmouth?]	England?	
Richard	Kinge [Ringa?]	London	England	Boatswain
Niclaes	Lijm	Wilshire	England	
Jan	Martin	London	England	Boatswain

Continued

Continued

First name	Last name	Hometown	Origin nation	Position
Thomas	Martin	Schakum [?]		Cabin boy
Joris	Martin	het Conquest [?]	France	Skipper's mate
Pieter	Martsen		Norway	
Abdela	Mehemet	Salé	Morocco	
Francois	Melligen	het Conquest [?]	France	
Michiel	Moer			
Jems	Numan	Wilshire	England	
Samuel	Odler			
Jan/Willem	Ogliby	Angus	Scotland	Lieutenant
Occo	Olof	Vleckero	Norway	
Missach	Oya		North Africa	
David	Pauli	Helisortsz? Helifouts		Steward
Raaf or Gaaf	Peper	Somerset [?]	England?	Cook
Willem	Peyn			
Samuel	Pleyn	King's Lynn, Norfolk	England	
Christoffel	Portleyn			
Thomas	Pottel	Plymouth	England	
Andries	Pouwelsz.	Tonsberghe	Norway	Master Gunner
Jan	Price	Ratley by London	England	Skipper, master
Richard	Rider	Plymouth	England	Trumpeter, Bugler
Edmont	Schors		Scotland	
Seltjman	Sellijman	Ornao [Oran, Algeria?]	Spanish Morisco	
Jan	Sno	London	England	Quartermaster
Nicolaes	Somer	Dorchester?	England?	Skipper's mate
Richard	Stein			Scribe
Willem	Wijtz		Scotland?	Quartermaster
Halijn	Wilsen			Skipper's servant
Joris	Wit [Witsen?]	Brusto [Bristol?]	England	Ship's carpenter

Notes

Introduction

1. *'t Begin, Midden en Eynde der Zee-rooveryen* . . . (1659), 1.
2. Nicolaes Wassenaer, *Historisch Verhael Aller Gedenkwaerdiger Geschiedenissen* . . ., Vol. 13 (Amsterdam: Jan Jansz., 1627–1628), 31.
3. Wassenaer explained that the Adventurers went to sea as a result of a government decree encouraging the capture and plundering of any Spanish vessel (Wassenaer, *Historisch*, 30vs). For more on this Dutch proclamation—which itself was a response to a Spanish pronouncement saying more or less the same thing against the Dutch—see chapter 6 in this book.
4. *'t Begin, Midden en Eynde der Zee-rooveryen* . . ., 1; and Wassenaer, *Historisch*, 31. Cadix here is referred to by a seventeenth-century nickname and spelling: St. Lucaren Calis.
5. Wassenaer, *Historisch*, Vol. 13, 30b. This was taking place in the summer of 1627.
6. *'t Begin, Midden en Eynde der Zee-rooveryen* . . ., 1.
7. *'t Begin, Midden en Eynde der Zee-rooveryen* . . ., 1–2; and Wassenaer, *Historisch*, 31.
8. *'t Begin, Midden en Eynde der Zee-rooveryen* . . ., 2.
9. *'t Begin, Midden en Eynde der Zee-rooveryen* . . ., 3; and Wassenaer, *Historisch*, 31.
10. Wassenear, *Historisch*, 31; and *'t Begin, Midden en Eynde der Zee-rooveryen* . . ., 14.
11. *'t Begin, Midden en Eynde der Zee-rooveryen* . . ., 2.
12. *'t Begin, Midden en Eynde Der Zee-Rooveryen* . . ., 1.
13. Economic historian Immanuel Wallerstein affirms that the Dutch triumphed because they possessed the strongest industrial base in textiles and shipbuilding, encouraged new types of capital organization, and created an efficient commercial network. As a result, Dutch shipping dominated the world carrying trade during the whole of the seventeenth century. See his *The Modern World System II: Mercantilism and the Consolidation of the European World Economy, 1600–1750* (New York: Academic Press, 1980), 46 and 56.
14. Maurice Halbwachs, *The Collective Memory* (New York: Harper-Colophon Books, 1950); and *On Collective Memory*, ed. and trans. Lewis A. Coser (Chicago: University of Chicago Press, 1992).
15. W.J. Hofdijk, *De Triomf der Piraten: Eene Feestgave bij Neerlands derde Jubil'e* (Amsterdam: Funke, 1872).
16. Cultural anthropologist Victor Turner characterized liminality as "that time and space betwixt and between one context of meaning and action and another. It is when . . . [one] is neither what he/she has been nor what he/she will be." Liminal persons are "threshold people," and exist in a state of "social limbo."

Turner, who applied his understanding of the concept of liminality to the study of ritual, also affirmed that the liminal "zone" or "stage" is a place for potential cultural innovation and social structural transformation. See his *The Ritual Process: Structure and Anti-Structure* (Chicago: Aldine, 1969).

17. Jaap R. Bruijn, "Dutch Privateering during the Second and Third Anglo-Dutch "Wars", ed. Commission Internationale d'Histoire Maritime, *Course et Piraterie...*, Vol. I (Paris: Institut de Recherche et d'Histoire des Textes/Editions du Centre National de la Recherche Scientifique, 1975), 397–415; and J.Th.H. Verhees-van Meer, *De Zeeuwse Kaapvaart Tijdens de Spaanse Successieoorlog 1702–1713* (Middelburg: Werken Uitgegeven door het Koninklijk Zeeuwsch Genootschap der Wetenschappen, 1986).

18. For an explication of this term and type of analysis, see Clifford Geertz, "Thick Description: Toward an Interpretive Theory of Culture," *The Interpretation of Cultures* (New York: Basic Books, 1973), 3–32. For a discussion of how a historian influenced by Geertz has applied symbolic anthropological theory to produce "thickly described" analyses, see Robert Darnton, "History and Anthropology," *The Kiss of Lamourette: Reflections in Cultural History* (New York: W.W. Norton, 1990), 329–353.

19. R.B. Prud'homme van Reine and E.W. van der Oest, eds., *Kapers op de Kust: Nederlandse Kaapvaart en Piraterij 1500–1800* (Vlissingen: Uitgeverij ADZ, 1991), 9.

1 *KAPERS* AND *COMMISSIEVAARDERS*: THE DUTCH PRIVATEER

1. For a history of the general practice of Western privateering, see Michel Mollat, "De la Piraterie Sauvage à la Course Réglementée (XIVe–XVe Siècle)," ed. Commission Internationale d'Histoire Maritime, *Course et Piraterie...*, Vol. I (Paris: Institut de Recherche et d'Histoire des Textes/Editions du Centre National de la Recherche Scientifique), 162–184.

2. The oldest extant Dutch letter-of-marque dates from this time. Although little is known about the history of privateering in the Netherlands during this early period, scholars have learned that its influence was felt at both a local level (e.g., fifteenth-century privateers from cities such as Zierikzee and Brouwershaven attacked ships in nearby Flemish waters) and in international relations (e.g., from 1438 to 1441, Holland and Zeeland waged a "privateering war" against the northern cities of the Hanseatic League; and from 1477 to 1482, their privateers fought against the forces of King Louis XI of France). For more on this topic, see J.C.A. de Meij, "Oorlogsvaart, Kaapvaart en Zeeroof," ed. G. Asaert, Ph.M. Bosscher, J.R. Bruijn, and W.J. van Hoboken, *Maritieme Geschiedenis der Nederlanden*, Vol. I (Bussum, 1976–1978), 308. See also H.A.H. Boelmans Kranenburg, "Zierikzee als visscherijplaats," *Zeeuws Tijdschrift*, 20 (1970), 78, cited in J.Th.H Verhees-van Meer, *De Zeeuwse Kaapvaart Tijdens de Spaarse Successieoorlog 1702–1713*, Werken Vitgegeven door het Koninklijk Zeeusch Genootschap der Wetenschappen, Vol. 3 (Middleburg: Koninklijk Zeeusch Genootschap der Wetenschappen, 1986), 7; and de Meij, "Oorlogsvaart," 310–311 and 315.

3. For two examples of sixteenth-century privateering prize cases adjudicated at the Admiralty of Veere, see C.G. Roelofsen, Appendix to the Introduction, *Practice*

and Doctrine in Particular Regard to the Law of Naval Warfare in the Low Countries from Circa 1450 Until the Early 17th Century (Utrecht: Proefschrift, 1991; published under "Studies in the History of International Law"), XIX–XXIII. Before 1488, cases concerning privateering had been overseen, albeit haphazardly, by the judicial institutions of the *Hof van Holland* and the *Raad van Mechelen*. See E.W. van der Oest, "De Praktijk van de Nederlandse Kaapvaart en Piraterij 1500–1800," ed. R.B. Prud'homme van Reine and E.W. van der Oest, *Kapers op de Kust: Nederlandse Kaapvaart en Piraterij 1500–1800* (Vlissingen: Uitgeverij ADZ, 1991), 24.

4. Research suggests that these early privateers were successful. From September 1553 to July 1555, some 60 captured ships supposedly were brought to the Admiralty at Veere. Moreover, the fishermen's guild in Vlissingen claims that 600–700 prizes were captured each year. See de Meij, "Oorlogsvaart," 326.
5. R.B. Prud'homme van Reine, "Nederlandse Kaapvaart en Piraterij in Beeld," in Prud'homme van Reine and van der Oest, *Kapers op de Kust*, 33–35.
6. Verhees-van Meer, *De Zeeuwse Kaapvaart*, 8. See also de Meij, "Oorlogsvaart," 334.
7. AGI, Patronata 268, N. 2, R. 3: *Declaracion de Rodrigo Girardo, Capitan de Filibote Flamenco*, 1600. "Girardo" reported that the privateering industry was very popular in his home country, with many starstruck by the dazzling riches the Spanish had discovered in the New World.
8. Prud'homme van Reine, "Nederlandse Kaapvaart en Piraterij," 51.
9. Jaap R. Bruijn, "Dutch Privateering during the Second and Third Anglo-Dutch Wars," ed. Commission Internationale d'Histoire Maritime, *Course et Piraterie . . .*, Vol. I (Paris: Institut de Recherche et d'Histoire des Textes/Editions du Centre National de la Recherche Scientifique, 1975), 411. See also R. Baetens, "Organisatie en resultaten van de Vlaamse Kaapvaart in de 17e eeuw," *Mededelingen van de Belgische Marine Academie*, 21 (1969/1970), 98–99 and 106–109.
10. For examples of Dutch proclamations and ordinances about privateering, see the following sources, which span the seventeenth century: "Instructie voor de Reeders en Capnen. met Consent van H.H.M. Verkrijgende brieven van Commissie ter Zee . . .," March 16, 1604, in ARA, AA, Verz. Bisdom #34: *Alphabetische index op de extract-resolutien . . .*, Rec. IV, fol. 7, see "Zeevaart" heading; C. Cau, ed., *Groot Placaet-Boeck van de Staten-Generaal en van Holland en Zeeland*, Vol. II (The Hague/Amsterdam: 1658–1796), 1531–1536; *Groot Placaet-Boeck*, Vol. V, 319 sqq.; and from *Recueil van alle de Placaaten, Ordonnaties, Resolutien, Instructies, Lijsten en Waarschuwingen Betreffende de admiraliteiten . . .* ('s-Gravenhage: Isaac Scheltus, 1730–1780): "Instructie voor de Commissievaarders," June 6, 1702, Vol. III, 184; "Instructie voor de Commissievaarders deezer Landen," July 28, 1705, Vol. III, 306; and "Placaat . . . op de . . . Commissievaart deezer Landen," July 28, 1705, Vol. III, 345.
11. This mandate was decreed in the foundation document of the five Admiralty colleges, which were established on August 13, 1597. See J.J. Baud, *Proeve eener Geschiedenis der Strafwetgeving tegen de Zeerooverij* (Utrecht: D. Post Uiterweer, 1854), 80.
12. For examples of Dutch privateering commissions, see "*Commissieboeken*" of the Admiralities, ARA, AA #1328 and #2429–2430, passim; as well as Verhees-van Meer, *De Zeeuwse Kaapvaart*, Appendices I–IV, 174–179. For more on the

particular features of Dutch privateering commissions, especially during the War of the Spanish Succession, see Verhees-van Meer, *De Zeeuwse Kaapvaart*, 20–21 and 23–25.

13. ARA, AA, Verz. Bisdom #107: *Commissie van retorsie voor een Deulsche Schiper*, September 2, 1672.

14. See, e.g., the following proclamations issued by the States-General, all of which revoked the commissions of Dutch privateers and can be found in *Recueil van Alle de Placaten . . . Betreffende de Admiraliteiten . . .*: "Placaat, verbod van alle Vaart uit deeze Landen van Kapers . . .," January 8, 1691, Vol. II, 189; "Placaat tot revocatie van alle Commissievaarders," November 25, 1692, Vol. II, 230 vs.; "Placaat tot revocatie van de Commissievaarders," November 13, 1693, Vol. II, 249 vs; "Placaat verbiedende de Commissievaart . . .," March 28, 1695, Vol. II, 265; and "Placaat, verbod Commissievaarders . . .," October 19, 1695, Vol. II, 270. For an additional proclamation addressing the same issue, see ARA, AA, Verz. Bisdom #123: Placaat, December 23, 1673, "Lyste op de Placaten en Orders Rakende Commissievaarders en Vreemde Kapers," 1627–1673, *Extract-Resolutien van de Staten Generaal, de Staten van Holland en de Admiraliteit op de Maze, plakaten, reglementen, instructien, enz. betreffende de commissievaart, het beheer van de buitgemaakte en gestande vijandelijke schepen en goederen, de vaart der neutralen, enz.*, 1590–1784.

15. For example, see the following ordinances from the States-General in *Recueil van Alle de Placaten . . . Betreffende de Admiraliteiten*: "Resolutie tot nakomminge der Tractaaten met Neutraalen ten reguarde van het opbrengen van Scheepen door Commissievaarders," January 4, 1692, Vol. II, 218 vs; and "Resolutie, ordre omtrent de Commissievaarders en precautie tegens het opbrengen van Neutraale Scheepen," July 10, 1692, Vol. II, 224 vs.

16. See, e.g., a proclamation issued by the States-General in ARA, AA, Verz. Bisdom #123: Placaat, December 15, 1672, "Lyste op de Placaten en Orders Rakende Commissievaarders en Vreemde Kapers," 1627–1673, *Extract-Resolutien van de Staten Generaal, de Staten van Holland en de Admiraliteit op de Maze, plakaten, reglementen, instructien, enz. betreffende de commissievaart . . .*, 1590–1784.

17. This was a practice that, according to legal historian C.G. Roelofsen, had long been Dutch tradition. AA, ARA, Verz. van der Hoop #1: *Aanteekeningen uit de resolutien de Staten van Holland betreffende de Admiraliteiten . . .*, 1575–1716, Section II: Particulariteijten Ontrent Goede of Quade Prises, "Resolution #162," May 8, 1643; and C.G. Roelofsen, "Grotius and State Practice of His Day: Some Remarks on the Place of *De Jure Belli ac Pacis* within the Context of Seventeenth-Century 'Christendom' and the Role of Contemporary Precedents in Grotius' Works," *Grotiana*, 10 (1989), 20–28.

18. See, e.g., a discussion of whether booty removed from ships captured along the Spanish coast but destined for Venice should be considered "good prizes." Participants included the States of Holland, the States of Zeeland, and the States-General. Although Zeeland was resistant, it was decided that all goods from Spain could be confiscated, but not those belonging to neutral parties; the matter was deemed negotiable for those who came from no fixed address. Zeeland sought to confiscate all goods, but lost. AA, ARA, Verz. van der Hoop #1: *Aanteekeningen uit de resolutien de Staten van Holland betreffende de Admiraliteiten . . .*, 1575–1716, "Particulariteijten Ontrent Goede of Quade Prises," September 30, 1627, Section II, fol. 36.

19. Verhees-van Meer, *De Zeeuwse Kaapvaart*, 2. When a privateer seized a ship that the Admiralty did not consider a "good prize," the captured vessel was released and the privateer's sponsors were responsible for paying for the court costs.
20. Bruijn, "Dutch Privateering," 402. This data is based upon Bruijn's investigation of Dutch privateering during the Second and Third Anglo-Dutch Wars (1665–1668 and 1672–1674), and has been corroborated by J.Th.H. Verhees-van Meer's analysis of Zeeland privateering during the War of the Spanish Succession.
21. Verhees-van Meer, *De Zeeuwse Kaapvaart*, 32 and 163.
22. van der Oest, "De Praktijk van de Nederlandse Kaapvaart," 14.
23. Bruijn, "Dutch Privateering," 400.
24. Verhees-van Meer, *De Zeeuwse Kaapvaart*, 34–37 and 163; and Prud'homme van Reine and van der Oest, *Kapers op de Kust*, 14.
25. Verhess-van Meer, *De Zeeuwse Kaapvaart*, 16.
26. See, e.g., these instructions for those who would receive letters of marque ("*Brieven van Marcque*") in the spring of 1599: ARA, AA, Verz. Bisdom # 123: "Uit het Memoriael Admt. de Maze," *Extract-Resolutien van de Staten Generaal, de Staten van Holland en de Admiraliteit op de Maze, plakaten, reglementen, instructien, enz. betreffende de commissievaart* . . ., 1590–1784, April 13, 1599, entry #1.
27. J.K. Oudendijk, "The Dutch Republic and Algiers, 1662–1664," *Course et Piraterie: Etudes présentees à la Commission Internationale d'Histoire Maritime*, Vol. I, ed. Commission Internationale d'Histoire Maritime (Paris: Institut de Recherche et d'Histoire des Textes/Editions du Centre National de la Recherche Scientifique, 1975), 156.
28. This was the case, e.g., in 1665, when the Admiralty of Zeeland ordered privateer shipowners to pay a security deposit of $f.12,000$ per vessel so as to ensure that their privateers would not seize Dutch, allied, or neutral ships; and forced each prospective privateer captain to pay $f.10,000$ in "caution money" per adventure so that he would bring his prizes to the Admiralty for adjudication and not sell them elsewhere, nor remain out at sea for longer than one year. Verz. Thysius: Collegien ter Admiraliteyt, Zeeland Kamer, *Instructie ende Articulen, Waer naer de Capiteynen, Officieren ende Bootsgesellen ter vryer Neeringhe uytvarende, op behoorlicke Commissie hun sullen hebben te reguleren* . . . (Middelburg: Johan Misson, February 21, 1665), Article XXX,13. See also Bruijn, "Dutch Privateering," 402. The rate was $f.20,000$ during the Second and Third Anglo-Dutch Wars, $f.25,000$ in 1702 at the beginning of the War of the Spanish Succession, and $f.30,000$ by 1705. Also see Verhees-van Meer, *De Zeeuwse Kaapvaart*, 21.
29. Oudendijk, *The Dutch Republic and Algiers*, 156, n. 36.
30. Bruijn, "Dutch Privateering,"402.
31. States-General, "Resolutie, ordre omtrent de Commissievaarders . . .," July 10, 1692, *Recueil van Alle de Placaten . . . Betreffende de Admiraliteiten . . .*, Vol. II, 224 vs.
32. Bruijn, "Dutch Privateering,"402.
33. See, e.g., Verz. Thysius: *Artyckel-Brief van de . . . West-Indische Compagnie* . . . (Amsterdam: Nic. van Ravesteyn, 1657) ; and Verz. Thysius: *Artyckel-Brief van de . . . Oost-Indische Compagnie* . . . (t'Amsterdam: R. en G. Wetstein, 1672).
34. van der Oest, "De Praktijk van de Nederlandse Kaapvaart," 21.
35. Verz. Thysius: *Instructie ende Articulen* . . . (February 21, 1665).

36. Verz. Thysius: *Instructie ende Articulen* . . . (February 21, 1665), Article XII, 5; Articles XIII–XV, 5–6; and Article XVI, 6.
37. Verz. Thysius: *Instructie ende Articulen* . . . (February 21, 1665), Article XIX, 7.
38. Verz. Thysius: *Instructie ende Articulen* . . . (February 21, 1665), Articles IV–VI, 2–3; and Article IX, 4.
39. Verz. Thysius: *Instructie ende Articulen* . . . (February 21, 1665), Article VII, 3.
40. Verz. Thysius: *Instructie ende Articulen* . . . (February 21, 1665), Article XVII, 6.
41. Verz. Thysius: *Instructie ende Articulen* . . . (February 21, 1665), Article XXI, 8.
42. Verz. Thysius: *Instructie ende Articulen* . . . (February 21, 1665), Article XX, 7; and Articles XXII–XXV, 8–9.
43. Verz. Thysius: *Instructie ende Articulen* . . . (February 21, 1665), Article I, 1.
44. Verz. Thysius: *Instructie ende Articulen* . . . (February 21, 1665), Article II, 2; and Article VIII, 4.
45. Verz. Thysius: *Instructie ende Articulen* . . . (February 21, 1665), Article III, 2; and Article XI, 4.
46. Verz. Thysius: *Instructie ende Articulen* . . . (February 21, 1665), Article XIV, 5; Article X, 4; and Article XXIX, 10.
47. Verz. Thysius: *Instructie ende Articulen* . . . (February 21, 1665), Article XXIX, 12.
48. Verz. Thysius: *Instructie ende Articulen* . . . (February 21, 1665), 14. Bookkeepers could take the oath in the captain's place, if the captain could not attend the ceremony. See Verhees-van meer, *De Zeeuwse Kaapvaart*, 34.
49. Verz. Thysius: *Instructie ende Articulen* . . . (February 21, 1665), Article IV, 2.
50. Verz. Thysius: *Instructie ende Articulen* . . . (February 21, 1665), Article II, 2; and Article XI, 4.
51. Verz. Thysius: *Instructie ende Articulen* . . . (February 21, 1665), Article III, 2.
52. Verz. Thysius: *Instructie ende Articulen* . . . (February 21, 1665), Articles XIII and XIV, 5.
53. For more about this safety harness, see Mike Dash, *Batavia's Graveyard* (New York: Crown, 2002), 91.
54. Verz. Thysius: *Instructie ende Articulen* . . . (February 21, 1665), Articles XV and XVII, 6.
55. Verz. Thysius: *Instructie ende Articulen* . . . (February 21, 1665), Article VII, 3.
56. Verz. Thysius: *Instructie ende Articulen* . . . (February 21, 1665), Articles VIII and IX, 4; Articles XXII and XXIII, 8; and Article XXXI, 13.
57. Verz. Thysius: *Instructie ende Articulen* . . . (February 21, 1665), Article XVI, 6.
58. Verz. Thysius: *Instructie ende Articulen* . . . (February 21, 1665), Article IV, 2 Articles V and VI, 3; Article XII, 5; and Article XXIV, 9.
59. Verz. Thysius: *Instructie ende Articulen* . . . (February 21, 1665), Article XIX, 7; and Article XXIX, 10.
60. For an example of a treaty that treats privateering (in this case, explicitly forbidding its practice between the two signatories, France and the United Provinces), see ARA, AA, Verz. Bisdom #123: "Tractaat Van Commercie, Navigatie en Marine, Gemaakt, geslooten en vastgesteld tot Nimmegen den 10 August 1678 . . .," *Extract-Resolutien van de Staten Generaal, de Staten van Holland en de Admiraliteit op de Maze, plakaten, reglementen, instructien, enz. betreffende de commissievaart* . . ., 1590–1784, Section II, 5–6.
61. Verz. Thysius: States-General, *Placaet. De Staten Generael . . . Doen te weten . . . dat wy oock noodigh achten dat de Commissie-Vaerders* . . . ('s Graven-Hage: J. Scheltus), January 8, 1691.

62. ARA, AA, Verz. Bisdom #123: States-General, Placaat, June 27, 1627, and Placaat, April 26, 1653, "Lyste op de Placaten en Orders Rakende Commissievaarders en Vreemde Kapers," 1627–1673, *Extract-Resolutien van de Staten Generaal, de Staten van Holland en de Admiraliteit op de Maze, plakaten, reglementen, instructien, enz. betreffende de commissievaart . . .*, 1590–1784. The Dutch were not alone in making such a prohibition. See, e.g., the translation of a similar proclamation from King Louis XIV of France: ARA, AA, Verz. Bisdom #123: "Pub. Adm. Maze," August 17, 1658, "Lyste op de Placaten en Orders Rakende Commissievaarders en Vreemde Kapers," 1627–1673, *Extract-Resolutien van de Staten Generaal, de Staten van Holland en de Admiraliteit op de Maze, plakaten, reglementen, instructien, enz. betreffende de commissievaart . . .*, 1590–1784.
63. ARA, AA, Verz. Bisdom #123: States-General, Placaat, January 29, 1658, "Lyste op de Placaten en Orders Rakende Commissievaarders en Vreemde Kapers," 1627–1673, *Extract-Resolutien van de Staten Generaal, de Staten van Holland en de Admiraliteit op de Maze, plakaten, reglementen, instructien, enz. betreffende de commissievaart . . .*, 1590–1784.
64. Oudendijk, *The Dutch Republic and Algiers*, 156.
65. See, e.g., ARA, AA, Verz. Sweers #2: Isaac Sweers, *Journaal, ghehouden door Sweers . . . op 's Lands schip De Maen . . .*, April 5, 1649–November 16, 1649, entries for May 12 and August 23. In this instance, Sweers reported that he had "visited" two Zeelands privateers carrying letters against Portugal. The Dutch *kapers* had captured two "pirates" from Salé, as well as six vessels by the Cape of Finisterre, and four frigates, each carrying 50 men. Additionally, he "visited" another privateer from Zeeland who had seized an English prize.
66. Bruijn, "Dutch Privateering," 406 and 410. Collectively, these representatives for the Admiralties were known as the *Commissarissen op den Prinsen* (the "Commissioners of Prizes"). The extent of these consuls' correspondence suggests that they took the responsibilities of their job—for which they received a 2% commission on all prize sales in their port—very seriously. And indeed, Admiralty of the Maas sentencing records corroborate this speculation, at least to some degree. At least one wayward captain—in this instance, a navy officer, Willem van Heden, who auctioned his captured booty in Gibraltar without the local consul's authorization—paid a price for such cavalier disregard for the rules: he had to forfeit all proceeds from the prize, a sum that was instead given entirely to the Admiralty's *Vendumeester* (Auctioneer). See ARA, AA, Verz. Bisdom #167: *Copie -Crimineele Vonnissen van de Admiraliteit op de Maas*, 1575–1710, November 16, 1678, fol. 215 vs.
67. Verhees-van Meer, *De Zeeuwse Kaapvaart*, 35.
68. van der Oest, "De Praktijk van de Nederlandse kaapvaart," 31.
69. See, for instance, ARA, WIC #745: *Korte inhoud van den notulen*, 1674–1764, entry for July 2, 1676, fol. 57.
70. For example, see ARA, AA, Verz. Bisdom #123: "Brief aan de Staten Generael van Adm. op de Maze," September 23, 1605, *Extract-Resolutien van de Staten Generaal, de Staten van Holland en de Admiraliteit op de Maze, plakaten, reglementen, instructien, enz. betreffende de commissievaart . . .*, 1590–1784.
71. For example, Verz. RLP: *Naerder Openbaringe, van Nederlants Engelschen Oorloge, Oorsake, Ende Tegenweer. Ontsteken over 'onEngelschen off Duyvelschen Handel en Misdandel der Engelsche Regeeringe . . .* (Leyden: Wilhelm Christiaans vander Boxc, 1653), 80–81.

72. Verz. Thysius: Gidion de Wildt and Hans Wargaren, *Copie. Uyt het Schip Sint Benita den 18 November 1657...* (Amsterdam: Otto Barentsz. Smient, 1657).
73. For instance, see ARA, AA, Verz. Bisdom #123: "Notulen over de VOC en WIC en de Admiraliteiten," Extract uijt het boek geintituleert Missiven en Bijlagen van Staaten Generael, entry for February 5, 1650, *Extract-Resolutien van de Staten Generaal, de Staten van Holland en de Admiraliteit op de Maze, plakaten, reglementen, instructien, enz. betreffende de commissievaart...*, 1590–1784. The general public, too, understood that privateers in the West Indies went after sugar. See Verz. RLP: *Amsterdams Tafel-Praetje Van Wat Goets en Wat Quats En Wat Noodichs* (Gouda: Iasper Cornelisz, 1649), 17.
74. ARA, AA #1806–#1808 (Admiraliteit van Amsterdam): *Rekeningen van den vendumeester wegens zijn ontvang van de prinsen, mulcten en confiscatien*, 1665–1667; and ARA, AA #1813–#1816 (Admiraliteit van Amsterdam): *Rekeningen van den vendumeester wegens zijn ontvang van de prinsen, mulcten en confiscatien*, 1672–1675.
75. ARA, AA, Verz. Van Der Heim #155: *Extracten uit de role van Proceduren voor den Raad ter Admiralteit op de Maze over Prinsen der Commissievaarders verovert...*, October 12, 1652–August 18, 1690, entries for the years 1652–1653; 1665–1667; 1672–1673.
76. Verhees-van Meer, *De Zeeuwse Kaapvaart*, Appendix VII, 208–215.
77. For more details on this process, see van der Oest, "De Praktijk van de Nederlandse Kaapvaart," 25–26.
78. van der Oest, "De Praktijk van de Nederlandse Kaapvaart," 26.
79. Bruijn, "Dutch Privateering," 402.
80. Baetens, "Organisatie...," 105.
81. These numbers come from the following sources: ARA, AA #1806, #1807, #1808, #1813, #1814, #1815, and #1816 (Admiraliteit van Amsterdam): *Rekeningen van den vendumeester wegens zijn ontvang van de prinsen, mulcten en confiscatien*, 1665–1667 and 1672–1675.
82. de Meij, "Oorlogsvaart," 307–334.
83. F. Binder, "Die Zeeländische Kaperfahrt, 1654–1662," *Mededelingen van het Koninklijk Zeeuwsch Genootschap der Wetenschappen* (1976), 67. Furthermore, the Admiralty of Zeeland's prize auctions alone during the Second and Third Anglo-Dutch Wars yielded over ƒ.9 million worth of prize booty, while the Admiralty of Amsterdam recorded approximately ƒ.3 million in profit. The Admiralty of Rotterdam made at least ƒ.316,000 during the Third War (and this figure represents the value of only 239 prizes and retaken ships). See Jaap R. Bruijn, "Kaapvaart in de tweede en derde Engelse Oorlog," *Bijdragen en Mededelingen betreffende de Geschiedenis der Nederlanden*, 90 (1975), 422; and Bruijn, "Dutch Privateering," 411. He also notes that the Admiralty of Zeeland received ƒ.172,000 in prize money during the period 1672–1674, but that this figure is difficult to interpret. See J.C. de Jonge, *Geschiedenis van het Nederlandsche Zeewezen*, Vol. II (Haarlem: Kruseman, 1858–1862), 477, n. 1.
84. Bruijn, "Dutch Privateering," 411.
85. At the beginning of the conflict, the Admiralty of Zeeland already had some 31 ships and 948 crewmen devoted to privateering, and by the end, there were at least 18 ships and 1,800 seamen involved in the trade. Verhees-van Meer, *De Zeeuwse Kaapvaart*, n. 36 and n. 38, 10.
86. Verhees-van Meer, *De Zeeuwse Kaapvaart*, 167.
87. van der Oest, "De Praktijk van de Nederlandse Kaapvaart," 26.

88. This is according to a late-eighteenth-century legal review of the administration and apportioning of prize plunder. See ARA, AA, Verz. Van Der Heim #155: *Memoria over de Buytgelden* (ca. 1770). For another governmental review of the various laws pertaining to booty division, see an essay produced by authorities at the Admiralty of the Maas, which recounts the legal history of prize money apportionment, beginning with the year 1597: ARA, AA, Verz. Van Der Heim #155: *Afspraak Van de Gecommitteerden uit de Respe. Collegien ter Admiralteit, wegens den Tiende van den Admiraal de Repartitien der buitgelden, de behandeling der Prinsen en Prinsen goederen, en wat dies meer is*, November 9, 1781. This opinion was seconded by a States-General resolution from 1653. See ARA, AA, Verz. van der Hoop #53: States-General, *Extract uit het Register der Resolutien van de Hoog Mo. Heeren Staaten Generaal de Vereenigde Nederlanden*, June 23, 1653.
89. AA, ARA, Verz. van der Hoop #53: *Extract uit het Register der Resolutien . . .*, June 23, 1653.
90. For records listing the amount of privateering booty appropriated to the Admiral-Generals/Stadholders by the Admiralty of the Maas during the period 1621–1631, see ARA, AA, Verz. XLVII #29 (Stukken betreffende zee- en admiraliteitszaken, als losse aanwinsten door het Algemeen Rijksarchief verworven voor het jaar 1888): *Copie-Rekeningen van het aan Prins Maurits en Prins Frederik Hendrik toekomend aandeel in de buiten, gemaakt door de kapiteins en commissievaarders onder de Admiraliteit op de Maze*, 1621–1631. For another interpretation of the profit distributions, see van der Oest, "De Praktijk van de Nederlandse Kaapvaart," 27–28.
91. ARA, AA, Verz. Bisdom #107: *Extract uijt het Register der Resolutien van H.H.M. of de geregtigheijd van den Admirall in de Prinsen bij particuliere verovert, welk volgens het placaat geheel aen de veroveraars zijn belooft*, February 18, 1639.
92. Bruijn, "Dutch Privateering," 402.
93. van der Oest, "De Praktijk van de Nederlandse Kappvaart," 27.
94. ARA, AA, Verz. Bisdom #123: "Brief aan de Staten Generael van Adm. op de Maze," September 23, 1605, *Extract-Resolutien van de Staten Generaal, de Staten van Holland en de Admiraliteit op de Maze, plakaten, reglementen, instructien, enz. betreffende de commissievaart . . .*, 1590–1784.
95. ARA, AA, Verz. Van Der Heim #155: *Memoria over de Buytgelden* (ca. 1770); and ARA, AA, Verz. Van Der Heim #155: *Afspraak Van de Gecommitteerden uit de Respe. Collegien ter Admiralteit, wegens den Tiende van den Admiraal de Repartitien der buitgelden, de behandeling der Prinsen en Prinsen goederen, en wat dies meer is*.
96. See, e.g., ARA, AA, Verz. Bisdom #34: *Alphabetische index op de extract-resolutien . . .*, Section on "Prinsen en Buiten"; ARA, AA, Verz. Bisdom #123: *Extract-Resolutien van de Staten Generaal, de Staten van Holland en de Admiraliteit op de Maze*, plakaten, reglementen, instructien, en3. *betreffende de commissievaart . . .*, 1590–1784; and ARA, AA, Verz. Evertsen #38: *Stukken raakende de buijtgelden der prinsen, tot Vlissingen, Middelburgh en Veere opgebragt . . .*, 1701.
97. ARA, AA, Verz. Bisdom #107: "Resolutien van H.H.M. houdende . . . een voet van verdeeling der Prinsen . . .," January 28, 1631, *Recueil van verscheijde oude stukken, rakende de directie van en over de equipagien ter zee, de tractementen der zeeofficieren, den articulbrief te water, en de vaart der neutralen, en de prinsen en buijten*. This resolution discusses myriad hypothetical situations in which a capture

might take place (e.g., if the prize is in an offensive or defensive position, etc.). Always, the States-General stresses, the Dutch fleet is obligated to support and defend one another.

98. The ultimate outcome of the case is unknown. For all the details discussed here, see Verz. Thysius: *Copye van seeckeren Brief, geschreven uyt Middelburch, van den eenen vriendt aen den anderen* . . . (Middelburgh: March 26, 1645), 1–3.

99. For more on VOC prize proceeds to the Admiralties in general, see ARA, VOC #11188: *Register Bavattende Memorie van de Bewindhebbers Betreffende het Deel van het Opbrengst van door de VOC Genomen Prijzen dat aan de Admiraliteitscolleges toekomt*, 1691. For more on the VOC's appropriations of prize proceeds to the Admiralty of Amsterdam from 1623 to 1707, see ARA, VOC #307: *Zakenindex op de resoluties van de kamer Amsterdam, 1602–1743*, fols. 400–401.

100. See, e.g., resolutions from the Zeeland Chamber's Archives: ARA, VOC #7417: *Trefwoordenreportorium op de Resoluties van de Heren XVII, 1602–1716*, fols. 136–149. For an example of Company documents detailing the apportionment of specific prizes, see ARA, VOC #13389: *Lijst Waarop de Verdeling Staat Aangegeven van . . . Veroverde Portuguese Goederen*, 1606.

101. ARA, AA, Verz. Bisdom #123: States-General, "Placcaet . . .," July 10, 1606, *Extract-Resolutien van de Staten Generaal, de Staten van Holland en de Admiraliteit op de Maze, plakaten, reglementen, instructien, enz. betreffende de commissievaart . . .*, 1590–1784; and ARA, VOC #543: Pieter Willemsz. Verhoeff, *Lijst van de . . . Buitgemaakte Goederen uit het Veroverde Schip Nosa Senhora del Para*, December 12, 1608.

102. ARA, AA, Verz. Bisdom #123: Notulen over de VOC en WIC en de Admiraliteiten, "Extract uit het Collegiaal boek van de Gecommitteerde Raden ter Admiraliteit resideerende tot Amstelredam," June 11, 1610 and June 12, 1610, *Extract-Resolutien van de Staten Generaal, de Staten van Holland en de Admiraliteit op de Maze, plakaten, reglementen, instructien, enz. betreffende de commissievaart . . .*, 1590–1784.

103. Verz. Thysius: *Ordonnantien ende Articulen . . . op het toerusten . . . van een West-Indische Compagnie* (1623), 1. The charter also cites these other reasons for the establishment of a monopolistic company dedicated to trade to and from the Americas: commerce and shipping lead to the general welfare of the United Provinces; a general company can more easily conform to the various treaties, alliances, and agreements forged with other states; and a general company can be the sole recipient of help and investment from the entire society, thereby making the Company stronger.

104. The States-General granted the Company the right to issue its own letters of marque in 1624. For an example of the WIC's issuing of *commissiebrieven*, in this instance against the French, see ARA, WIC #468: *Kopieboeken van brieven naar Amerika, 1684–1689*, letter dated January 5, 1689. For an example of some of the WIC's own rules concerning prizes, see Verz. Thysius: *Artyckel-Brief Van de Generale Geoctroyeerde West-Indische Compagnie in de Vereenighde Nederlanden* . . . ('t Amsterdam: Nicolaes van Ravesteyn, 1657), clauses XXVI–XXVIII, 15–17.

105. Verz. Thysius: *Ordannantien ende Articulen . . . op het toerusten . . . van eene West-Indische Compagnie* (1623), 13, Clause 43.

106. ARA, AA, Verz. Bisdom #123: "Extract uijt het boek geintituleert Missiven en Bijlagen van Staaten Generael," February 5, 1650, *Extract-Resolutien van de Staten Generaal, de Staten van Holland en de Admiraliteit op de Maze,*

plakaten, reglementen, instructien, enz. betreffende de commissievaart..., 1590–1784. This is clause #44 in the WIC's Charter.

107. See, e.g., sample prizes declared in Curaçao by the WIC from 1674 to 1690, in ARA, WIC #865: *Alphabetisch zakelijke registers op de notulen der vergadering van Tienen, Zeeland Kamer*, passim.
108. ARA, AA, Verz. Bisdom #123: "Extract uijt boek geintituleert Missiven en Bijlagen van Staaten Generael," February 5, 1650, *Extract-Resolutien van de Staten Generaal, de Staten van Holland en de Admiraliteit op de Maze, plakaten, reglementen, instructien, enz. betreffende de commissievaart...*, 1590–1784.
109. ARA, AA, Verz. Bisdom #123: "Voorslag van accommodatie tusschen de ... Admiraltiet ... in Zeeland, ende de ... Westindische Comp ..." (no date), Notulen over de VOC en WIC en de Admiraliteiten, *Extract-Resolutien van de Staten Generaal, de Staten van Holland en de Admiraliteit op de Maze, plakaten, reglementen, instructien, enz. betreffende de commissievaart...*, 1590–1784.
110. ARA, WIC #745: *Korte inhoud van den notulen..., Zeeland Kamer*, fols. 57–60. For another example of such a situation, this time occurring in 1711 and again concerning a French prize, see fol. 288.
111. ARA, AA, Verz. Bisdom #10: *Deductie gedaan maken, ende d'Ed. Mogen... Raden ter Admiraliteyt, resideerende binne Amsterdam...*, June 1, 1675.
112. ARA, AA, Verz. van der Hoop #1: *Aanteekeningen uit de resolutiën van de Staten van Holland betreffende de Admiraliteiten...*, 1575–1716, Section II: Particulariteijten ontrent Goede of Quade Prises, Resolution #95, July 9–August 2, 1631.
113. ARA, AA, Verz. van der Hoop #1: *Aanteekeningen uit de resolutiën van de Staten van Holland betreffende de Admiraliteiten...*, 1575–1716, Section II: Particulariteijten ontrent Goede of Quade Prises, Resolution #51, March 22, 1629.
114. States-General, "Placaat, de Scheepen van de Visscherye genoomen by de Vyanden, niet te moogen werden ingekogt als by de Eigenaars zelfs," February 28, 1678, *Recueil van Alle de Placaten... Betreffende de Admiraliteiten...*, Vol. I, 839.
115. Bruijn, "Dutch Privateering," 402.
116. The remainder of the sums went to various places, but primarily to cover storage and auction costs (*ongeld*). One must assume that the government, Admiralty, and Stadholder had already extracted the amount they were due.
117. The 1665 entry for privateers Oultman Eijldon and Pieter Jansz. de Vries indicates that they received 3.5%; note, however, that this is for two privateers, meaning that each one would actually enjoy approximately 1.25%.
118. See ARA, AA, Verz. Bisdom #107: States-General, *Extract uijt het Register der Resolutien van H.H.M of de geregtigheijd van den Admiral in de Prinsen bij particuliere verovert,...*, February 18, 1639.
119. Verz. Thysius: States-General, "Placcaet..." ('s-Gravenhage: J. Scheltus, October 10, 1673).
120. Verhees-van Meer, *De Zeeuwse Kaapvaart*, 54–55.
121. Verz. Thysius: States-General, *Prijzen uitgeloofd op het veroveren or vernielen van schepen...*, March 11, 1632.
122. Verz. Thysius: States-General, *Publicatie* ('s Gravenhage: Iac. Scheltus, 1672), April 14, 1672, Articles I–XIX. The premiums were as follows: for those who

captured the warship of the first French or English Admiral, the reward of *f.*50,000; for the capture of all other Admirals' ships, *f.*30,000; for the capture of any ship of the remaining officers, *f.*20,000; for all other warships with at least 40 guns, *f.*10,000; for ships with fewer than 40 guns, *f.*6,000; for the removal of the first Admiral's flag, *f.*5,000 or 2,000 rijksdaalders; for the flags of the other Admirals, *f.*2,500 or 1,000 rijksdaalders; for the flags of lesser officers, *f.*250–1,250; for those who supplied ships that came to destroy enemy vessels, one-third of the above sums; for those who destroyed an enemy warship that was poised to attack a Dutch warship, *f.*6,000; for those who rescued an endangered Dutch warship, a special premium to be determined by the States-General; for those who recaptured a Dutch warship seized by the enemy, half of the sums stipulated above; and for those who captured enemy ships anywhere in the world, outside of battle, half of the sums stated above.

123. Verz. Thysius: States-General, *Publicatie*, February 28, 1678. For other examples of States-General laws concerning privateer premiums, see the following mandates from the *Recueil van Alle de Placaten . . . Betreffende de Admiralteiten . . .*: "Placaat houdende praemie voor de Commissievaarders die eenige Vyandelyke Oorlogscheepen koomen te veroveren," May 31, 1697, Vol. II, 288; "Resolutie weegens het ontfangen van het extraordinaris Lasten Veilgeld ten behoeve van de zoogenaamde Praemievaarders," June 29, 1697, Vol. II, 287 vs.; "Placaat, praemie op het veroveren van Vyandelyke Scheepen," June 6, 1702, Vol. III, 192; "Resolutie, praemie voor Commissievaarders, en verhooginge van het Lasten Veilgeld," June 7, 1702, Vol. III, 215; "Renovatie-Placaat. Praemie voor die geene die eenige Vyandlyke Scheepen of Branders ruineeren," October 20, 1703, Vol. III, 292; "Amplicatie van het Placaat van den 6 June 1702, weegens de Praemie voor Commissievaarders," June 20, 1704, Vol. III, 298; and "Resolutie, Theodorus Ryswyk toegevoegt twee derde van de Praemie by Placaat aan de Commissievaarders toegelegt," June 19, 1706, Vol. III, 486. For a proclamation stipulating premiums during the early phase of the War of the Spanish Succession, see Verz. Thysius: States-General, *Placaet, Van de praemien voor de Commissie-vaerders deser Landen, dewelcke eenige Oorlogh-schepen van den Vyandt sullen komen te veroven*, June 6, 1702 ('s Gravenhage: P. Scheltus, 1702).
124. ARA, AA, Verz. van der Hoop #1: *Aanteekeningen uit de resolutien van de Staten van Holland betreffende de Admiraliteiten . . .*, 1575–1716, Resolution #254, September 30, 1627.
125. Verz. RLP: *Vervolg van Het Rotterdams Zee-Praatje Tusschen Drie Personen, een Koopman, een Borger en een Stierman . . .* (Middelburg: Gerrit Jansz. van Hoorn, 1653).
126. Verz. RLP: *Vervolg van Het Rotterdams Zee-Praatje . . .* (1653), 7.
127. Verz. RLP: *Amsterdams Tafel-Praetje Van Wat Goets en Wat Quats En Wat Noodichs* (Gouda: Iasper Cornelisz, 1649); Verz. RLP: *Amsterdams Vuur-Praetje, Van 't Een ende 'tander datter nu om gaet* (Amstelredam: Claes Pietersz, 1649), especially 22–23; and Verz. RLP: *Amsterdams Dam-Praetje, Van Wat Outs en Wat Nieuws En Wat Vreemts* (Amsterdam: Ian van Soest, 1649), 5.
128. Verz. RLP: *Amsterdams Dam-Praetje* (1649), 5.
129. Verz. RLP: *Goede Apparentie tot Spoedige opkomst, Der Vrye Nederlandens Magtige Zee-Vaart . . .* (1653).
130. Bruijn, "Dutch Privateering," 400 and 405.

131. J.S. Bromley, "The North Sea in Wartime (1688–1713)," *Bijdragen en Mededelingen betreffende de Geschiedenis der Nederlanden*, Vol. 92 (1977), 292.
132. Verhees-van Meer explains that during the War of the Spanish Succession, each privateering ship required a crew of 20–350 men. Bruijn argues that crew sizes during the Second and Third Anglo-Dutch Wars probably ranged from 20 to 100 men (with most ships needing 20–40 hands, and 50–100 souls working the bigger North Sea vessels). Clark, moreover, refers to a list of 31 Zeelands privateers during the Nine Years War who sailed with a complement of 948 men, thus producing an average of 30.58 (or 31) sailors per privateering vessel. Clark, "English and Dutch Privateers," 210–211 and 216. He also adds that the majority of English privateers at the time carried crews ranging from 10 to 40 men. A Spanish source affirms that each ship belonging to a fleet of Dutch privateers that prowled the Pacific coast in 1600 carried 12 guns and 26 men. See AGI: Patronata 268, N. 2, R. 4: *Corsario Holandás que Fue à Filipinas desde Perú*, 1601.
133. See Bruijn, "Dutch Privateering," 400 and 403–404. He cites the "*Commissieboeken*" of the Algemeen Rijksarchief (AA #1328 and #2429–2430) and the minutes of the Zeeland Admiralty (AA #2484–2499) as his main sources of information; G.N. Clark, "English and Dutch Privateers under William III," *Mariner's Mirror*, Vol. 7 (1921), 209; Bromley, "North Sea . . ."; and Verhees-van Meer, *De Zeeuwse Kaapvaart*, 29, 38, 47–48, and 163–164; for specific details about these commissions, see appendix IV, 179–200.
134. The source for this estimate is Clark, "English and Dutch Privateers," 210–211 and 216. This figure also coincides somewhat closely with the projections made by Bruijn, "Dutch Privateering," 404.
135. van der Oest, "De Praktijk van de Nederlandse Kaapvaart," 16.
136. Bruijn, "Dutch Privateering," 404.
137. Verhees-van Meer, *De Zeeuwse Kaapvaart*, 43–44, 47, and 164.
138. Verhees-van Meer, *De Zeeuwse Kaapvaart*, Appendix IV, 179–200.
139. Verhees-van Meer, *De Zeeuwse Kaapvaart*, 163–164.
140. Verhees-van Meer, *De Zeeuwse Kaapvaart*, 47–48 and 164.
141. Jonathan I. Israel, *The Dutch Republic: Its Rise, Greatness, and Fall 1477–1806* (Oxford: Oxford University Press, 1995), 623.
142. Bruijn, "Dutch Privateering," 403.
143. van der Oest, "De Praktijk van de Nederlandse Kaapvaart," 15–16.
144. van der Oest, "De Praktijk van de Nederlandse Kaapvaart," 14.
145. Verhees-van Meer, *De Zeeuwse Kaapvaart*, 45. For more on the issue of insuring privateers, especially during the early eighteenth century, see Verhees-van Meer, *De Zeeuwse Kaapvaart*, 33–34.
146. Verhees-van Meer, *De Zeeuwse Kaapvaart*, 44–45.
147. Bruijn, "Dutch Privateering," 404; and van der Oest, "De Praktijk van de Nederlandse Kaapvaart," 16.
148. Verz. RLP: *Naerder Openbaringe* . . . (1653), 40, 54–57, 69–70, and 77–87.
149. Verhees-van Meer, *De Zeeuwse Kaapvaart*, 44–45 and 164; van der Oest, "De Praktijk van de Nederlandse Kaapvaart," 18.
150. Bruijn, "Dutch Privateering," 404.
151. Bruijn, "Dutch Privateering," 404. He found these names in W. Voorbeijtel Cannenburg and J.P. Kruseman, *Scheepsnamen Vroeger en Nu* (Amsterdam, 1960).

152. Verhees-van Meer, *De Zeeuwse Kaapvaart*, Appendix IV, 179–200.
153. During the Fourth Anglo-Dutch War (1780–1784), e.g., many "Dutch" privateer captains were, in fact, French. See van der Oest, "De Praktijk van de Nederlandse Kaapvaart," 18–19.
154. van der Oest, 18–19; and Verhees-van Meer, *De Zeeuwse Kaapvaart*, 52. Verhees-van Meer cites the name of Jan Hurgronje, who served as a *kaper kapitein* during the War of the Spanish Succession, as a member of an elite family.
155. Verhees-van Meer, *De Zeeuwse Kaapvaart*, 51–53.
156. ARA, VOC #307, *Zakenindex op de resoluties van de kamer Amsterdam*, 1602–1743, October 22, 1714, fol. 472.
157. Such men included former captains Michiel Brijs, Anthonie Crijnsen de Vlaminck, Jacques Cool, and Anthonie Claesz. Stokvis. See Bruijn, "Dutch Privateering," 403. He cites the following records in the Admiralty Archives of the *Algemeen Rijksarchief*: AA #2429 (December 24, 1666; July 26, 1672; August 14, 1672; and September 28, 1672); and AA #2430 (October 10, 1673; December 8, 1673; January 15, 1674; and February 1676).
158. Verhees-van Meer, *De Zeeuwse Kaapvaart*, 16, 20, and 24.
159. Verhees-van Meer, *De Zeeuwse Kaapvaart*, 47–48.
160. Data from appendix III derives from Verz. RLP: *Naerder Openbaringe . . .* (1653), 40, 54–57, 69–70, and 77–87.
161. Verhees-van Meer, *De Zeeuwse Kaapvaart*, 48, 50–51 and 164. Unfortunately, due to lacunae in the archival documents one cannot know the composition of such privateering crews in great detail.
162. AGI: Patronata 268, N. 2, R. 3: *Declaracíon de Rodrigo Girardi, Capitande Filibote Flamenco* (1600).
163. Verhees-van Meer, *De Zeeuwse Kaapvaart*, 49–50; and van der Oest, "De Praktijk van de Nederlandse kaapvaart," 19.
164. C.R. Boxer, *The Dutch Seaborne Empire, 1600–1800* (London: Penguin Books, 1990), 91–93. Boxer, in turn, cites See J. Veirac and B. Hussem, *Verhandelingen over de besmettelijke rotkoorts op de uitgaande Oost-Indische schepen* (Middelburg, 1778) in J. Hullu, *Bijdragen tot de Taal-land en Volkenkunde van Nederlandsche Indië*, Vol. 67 (1913), 249–250.
165. van der Oest, "De Praktijk van de Nederlandse kaapvaart," 19 and 21; and Verhees-van Meer, *De Zeeuwse Kaapvaart*, 52 and 54–55. The *anker-*, *touw-*, and *zeilgeld* represented the money earned from the sale of a prize's best anchors, lines, and sails. Sometimes sailors also enjoyed *dekgeld* and *kajuitgeld* (money earned from the sale of the objects from a ship's deck and cabin, respectively), *plunderage* (the personal belongings of the prize ship's crewmembers, such as clothing and seachests), and other incidental bonuses.
166. Verhees-van Meer, *De Zeeuwse Kaapvaart*, 45.
167. D. de Waard, "De Zeeuwsch Expeditie naar de West onder Cornelis Evertsen den Jonge, 1672–1674," *Werken Linschoten Vereeniging*, 30 (1928), 58–59, cited in Bruijn, "Dutch Privateering," 406.
168. AGI, Patronata 268, N. 2, R. 4: *Corsario Holandás que Fue a Filipinas desde Perú* (1601), and AGI, Patronata 268, N. 2, R, *Declaracíon de Rodrigo Girarddo, Capitan de Filibote Flamenco* (1600), 3.
169. AGI, Patronata 267, N. 1, R. 59: *Los Rebeldes de los Paises Bajos contra la Armada Española* (1571).
170. For example, navy officer Isaac Sweers mentions in the log of his ship, *The Moon*, that they encountered two Zeelands privateers on May 12, 1649.

It appears that these two vessels were working together, and had captured two Barbary corsair ships, as well as six ships carrying assorted goods, and four frigates manned by 50 seamen. See ARA, AA, Verz. Sweers #2: Isaac Sweers, *Journaal, ghehouden door Sweers als adelborts op 's Lands schip De Maen, kruisende lange de kusten van Spanje en Portugal*, April 5, 1649–November 16, 1649; May 12, 1649, 42. A Spanish source comments that a fleet of privateerships that attacked the Pacific coast in 1600 consisted of five vessels; see AGI, Patronata 268, N. 2, R. 3: *Declaracíon de Rodrigo Girardo, Capitan de Filibote Flamenco* (1600). Verhees-van Meer observed in her research that Zeelands privateers sometimes traveled in small groups of two to five vessels; see Verhees-van Meer, *De Zeeuwse Kaapvaart*, 64.

171. Verz. RLP: *Amsterdams Vuur-Praetje, Van 't Een ende 'tander nu om gaet* (1649), 17.
172. For general information about shipboard conditions, see Boxer, *The Dutch Seaborne Empire*, Chapter 3.
173. Verhees-van Meer, *De Zeeuwse Kaapvaart*, 61–62.
174. Verhees-van Meer, *De Zeeuwse Kaapvaart*, 62–64.
175. ARA, AA, Verz. Sweers #2: *Journal, ghehouden door Sweers* . . .
176. In the fifteenth century, the cities of Zierikzee and Brouwershaven served as bases for *kapers* assaulting ships in nearby Flemish waters. See H.A.H. Boelmans Kranenburg, "Zierikzee als visscherijplaats," *Zeeuws Tijdschrift*, 20 (1970), 78, cited in Verhees-van Meer, *De Zeeuwse Kaapvaart*, 7.
177. Verhees-van Meer, *De Zeeuwse Kaapvaart*, 8.
178. Girardo himself was based in Amsterdam and Rotterdam. See AGI, Patronata 268, N. 2, R. 3: *Declaracíon de Rodrigo Girardo, Capitan de Filibote Flamenco* (1600).
179. Bruijn, "Dutch Privateering," 411. See also Baetens, "Organisatie . . .," 98–99 and 106–109.
180. Verz. RLP: *Amsterdams Vuur-Praetje, Van 't Een ende 'tander datter nu om gaet* (Amstelredam: Claes Pietersz, 1649), 16.
181. AGI, Indiferente 430, L. 42, F. 271v–272: *Real Cédula a Don Rafael Capri y Sanz, gobernador de Cartagena* . . ., November 20, 682.
182. Bruijn, "Dutch Privateering," 403; and Verhees-van Meer, *De Zeeuwse Kaapvaart*, 29.
183. Verhees-van Meer, *De Zeeuwse Kaapvaart*, 3; and G.N. Clark, "Neutral Commerce in the War of the Spanish Succession and the Treaty of Utrecht," *The British Yearbook of International Law* (1928), 74.
184. Verz. RLP: *Goede Apparentie tot Spoedige opkomst, Der Vrye Nederlandens Magtige Zee-Vaart* . . . (1653), 10.
185. Verz. RLP: *Goede Apparentie tot Spoedige opkomst, Der Vrye Nederlandens Magtige Zee-Vaart* . . . (1653), 9.
186. Verz. Thysius: *Buere-Praetje Tusschen een Borger en een Matroos* . . . (1665?), 2 and 4.
187. Verz. RLP: *Amsterdams Tafel-Praetje* . . . (1649), passim.
188. All bear similar titles, but represent three different—albeit similar—texts. See Verz. RLP: *Amsterdams Tafel-Praetje Van Wat Goets en Wat Quats En Wat Noodichs* (Gouda: Iasper Cornelisz, 1649); Verz. RLP: *Amsterdams Vuur-Praetje, Van 't Een ende 'tander datter nu om gaet* (Amstelredam: Claes Pietersz, 1649); and Verz. RLP: *Amsterdams Dam-Praetje, Van Wat Outs en Wat Nieuws En Wat Vreemts* (Amsterdam: Ian van Soest, 1649).

189. In fact, a number of firms in the Walcherse region—home of Vlissingen and Middelburg—had been devoted to this goal since 1621, when the Twelve Years' Truce with Spain came to an end. By 1636, the Zeelanders had captured and brought in 547 official prizes, the majority of which consisted of Portuguese ships traveling from Brazil. A number of the Zeelands privateering firms united in the "*Brasilse Directie*" (Brazilian Directorate) in Middelburg in 1646. Within two years, those privateers affiliated with the *Directie* had seized some 220 Portuguese prizes, as well as a number of vessels of various nationalities that were in Portuguese service. See Verhees-van Meer, *De Zeeuwse Kaapvaart*, 8–9.
190. ARA, AA, Verz. Bisdom #123: "Extract uijt boek geintituleert Missiven en Bijlagen van Staaten Generael," February 5, 1650, *Extract-Resolutien van de Staten Generaal, de Staten van Holland en de Admiraliteit op de Maze, plakaten, reglementen, instructien, enz., betreffende de commissievaart, het beheer van de buitgemoakte en gestande vijandelijke schepen en goedeven, de vaart der neutralen, enz.*, 1590–1784.
191. Verz. RLP: *Amsterdams Tafel-Praetje* . . . (1649).
192. Verz. RLP: *Amsterdams Dam-Praetje* . . . (1649), 5–7.
193. Verz. RLP: *Amsterdams Dam-Praetje* . . . (1641), 9, 5–7.
194. Verz. RLP: *Amsterdams Tafel-Praetje* . . . (1649), 14.
195. Verz. RLP: *Amsterdams Tafel-Praetje* . . . (1649), 18–19.
196. Verz. RLP: *Amsterdams Tafel-Praetje* . . . (1649), 22.
197. Verz. RLP: *Amsterdams Tafel-Praetje* . . . (1649), 14.
198. Verz. RLP: *Amsterdams Vuur-Praetje* . . . (1649), 23.
199. Verhees-van Meer, *De Zeeuwse Kaapvaart*, 9, n. 30.

2   A "Malicious Business": Piracy in the Dutch Republic

1. J.J. Baud, *Proeve eener Geschiedenis der Strafwetgeving tegen de Zeerooverij* (Utrecht: D. Post Uiterweer, 1854), 79–80.
2. Baud, *Proeve eener Geshiedenis*, 82.
3. States-General, "Placaet tegen de Zee-Roovers . . .," August 25, 1611, ed. C. Cau, *Groot Placaet-Boeck van de Staten-Generaal en van Holland en Zeeland*, Vol. I (The Hague/Amsterdam, 1658–1796), 968.
4. Article LXXV, "Vredestractaat met Spanje te Munster," January 30, 1648, *Groot Placaet-Boeck*, Vol. II, 79.
5. *Groot Placaet-Boeck*, Vol. II, 2850.
6. *Groot Placaet-Boeck*, Vol. II, 2910.
7. *Groot Placaet-Boeck*, Vol. II, 2868.
8. Verz. Thysius: Staten van Zeeland, Placaet vande . . . Staten van Zeeland, teghens den Vagabunden, Bedelaers, etc. . . . (Middelburgh: R. Schilders, 1596); Verz. RLP: Staten van Zeeland, Placaet vande . . . Staten van Zeeland, teghens den Vagabunden, Bedelaers, etc. . . ., July 19, 1607 (Middelburgh: R. Schilders, 1607). Other such infractions included begging, vagabondage, and thievery, as well as violent acts such as housebreaking, animal theft, and the burglary of mills and canals. For examples of how crimes such as thievery, burglary, vagabondage, rioting, and begging were prosecuted and punished during the very early years of the Republic, see ARA, Hof van Holland Archief Index op de Crimineele Sententien van het Hof van Holland, 1538–1572.

9. Verz. Thysius: *Placcaet vande Staten van Gelderlant . . . tegen alle Roovers ende Stroopers . . .* March 30, 1621.
10. See, e.g., *Groot Placaet-Boeck*, Vol. II, 65, 311, and 499; and Vol. III, 229.
11. For an example, see *Groot Placaet-Boeck*, Vol. IV, 211.
12. The States-General, for instance, made a practice of widespread distribution of their proclamations so that no citizen could plead ignorance of the contents. For reference to this custom of ubiquitous dissemination, see Verz. Thysius: States-General, *Placaet . . . (tegen 't varen naer West-Indie buiten de W. I. Comp.)*, June 14, 1632.
13. Verz. Thysius: *Ordinantie Ghemaeckt op 't Stuck van de Admiralieteit, ende Teghens de Zeeroouers*, November 13, 1583 ('t Antwerpen: Chr. Plantijn, 1583).
14. ARA, AA, Verz. Bisdom #107: *Aanschrijving van de Staten Generaal om in diligentie eenige scheepen van oorlog toe te rusten om te agterhalen de vrijbuiters uijt dese Landen . . .*, March 6, 1607.
15. Oldenbarnevelt's mandate notes that the neighboring states of France, England, and Germany had threatened reprisals if the Dutch government did not stop the guilty *vrijbuiters*. See the last sentence of ARA, AA, Verz. Bisdom #107: *Aanschrijving van de Staten Generaal om in diligentie eenige scheepen van oorlog toe te rusten om te agterhalen de vrijbuiters uijt dese Landen . . .*, March 6, 1607.
16. ARA, AA, Verz. Bisdom #123: "Excessen door Vrijbuijters &c. dezer Landen tegen Neutrale Vrienden gepleegt," Het Memoriale Admt. Maze, September 18, 1605, *Extract-Resolutien van de Staten Generaal, de Staten van Holland en de Admiraliteit op de Maze, plakaten, reglementen, instructien, enz. betreffende de commissievaart . . .*, 1590–1784.
17. ARA, AA, Verz. Bisdom #123: "Excessen door Vrijbuijters &c. dezer Landen tegen Neutrale Vrienden gepleegt," Het Memoriale Admt. Maze, October 8, 1605, *Extract-Resolutien van de Staten Generaal, de Staten van Holland en de Admiraliteit op de Maze, plakaten, reglementen, instructien, enz. betreffende de commissievaart . . .*, 1590–1784.
18. Verz. ZBP: *Placcaet van de Staten-Generaal . . . tegen de buitensporigheden der kaapvaarders*, July 10, 1606.
19. ARA, AA, Verz. Bisdom #123: "Excessen door Vrijbuijters &c. dezer Landen tegen Neutrale Vrienden gepleegt," Het Memoriale Admt. Maze, October 6, 1606, *Extract-Resolutien van de Staten Generaal, de Staten van Holland en de Admiraliteit op de Maze, plakaten, reglementen, instructien, enz. betreffende de commissievaart . . .*, 1590–1784.
20. ARA, AA, Verz. Bisdom #123: "Excessen door Vrijbuijters &c. dezer Landen tegen Neutrale Vrienden gepleegt," Het Memoriale Admt. Maze, March 6, 1607, *Extract-Resolutien van de Staten Generaal, de Staten van Holland en de Admiraliteit op de Maze, plakaten, reglementen, instructien, enz. betreffende de commissievaart . . .*, 1590–1784.
21. States-General, "Placaet tegen de Zee-Roovers," May 12, 1611, *Groot Placaet-Boeck*, Vol. I, 970.
22. Baud, *Proeve eener Geschiedenis*, 85. This phenomenon occurred in other states as well, e.g., England. See Verz. Thysius: *Proclamatie ofte Placcaet des Conings van Groot Britanien / tot wederroepinghe der Engelsche Natie die haer ter Zee zijn generende met Rooff . . .* (Delf: J. Andriesz., 1605).
23. C.R. Boxer, *The Dutch Seaborne Empire, 1600–1800* (New Yerk: Alfred A. Knopf, 1965; London: Penguin, 1990), 75.
24. Verz. Thysius: States-General, *Pardon aan de zeelieden . . .* August 25, 1651 ('s-GravenHage: Wed. en Erfg. van H. Jzn. v. Wouw, 1651).

25. States-General, "Publicatie, tegens de geene die met dubbele Commissie in Zee zyn . . .," January 29, 1658, in *Groot Placaet-Boeck*, Vol. II, 499.
26. Verz. Thysius: *Hollandtze Mercurius*, 16th edition (Haerlem: Pieter Casteleyn, 1666), 31.
27. Verz. Thysius: States-General, *Placcaet* . . ., October 10, 1673 ('s-Gravenhage: J. Scheltus, 1673).
28. Verz. Thysius: States-General, *Placcaet* . . ., October 10, 1673 ('s-Gravenhage: J. Scheltus, 1673).
29. Verz. Thysius: States-General, *Placcaet* . . ., December 23, 1673 ('s-Gravenhage: J. Scheltus, 1673).
30. Indeed, Jaap Bruijn's research reveals that privateer *reders*, too, could contribute to such problems. At times they were recalcitrant about following government policy, and even actively encouraged unlawful privateering. Some *reders*—especially those in Zeeland—illegally sponsored and outfitted privateering vessels during times when the States-General forbade the trade. Bruijn has found that this happened, e.g., in 1665 and again in 1673. See Jaap R. Bruijn, "Dutch Privateering during the Second and Third Anglo-Dutch Wars," ed. Commission Internationale d'Histoire Maritime, *Course et Piraterie* . . . (Paris: Institut de Recherche et d'Histoire des Textes/Editions du Centre National de la Recherche Scientifique, 1975), Vol. I, 406.
31. Verz. Thysius: Stadthouder Hendrick Casimyr, *Waerschouwinge Nopens de Zee-roveryen op de Friesse Kusten* (Leeuwarden: R.S. Arumsma, 1677).
32. States-General, "Placaat tegens het misbruiken van Commissien van Oorlog aan Particulieren verleent . . .," October 23, 1690, *Recueil van Alle de Placaten . . . Betreffende de Admiraliteiten* . . ., Vol. II ('s-Gravenhage: Isaac Scheltus, 1730–1780), 172–173 vs.
33. States-General, "Resolutie tot nakoominge der Tractaaten met Neutraalen ten reguarde van het opbrengen van Scheepen door Commissievaarders," January 4, 1692, *Recueil van Alle de Placaten . . . Betreffende de Admiralteiten* . . ., Vol. II, 218 vs; and States-General, "Resolutie, ordre omtrent de Commissievaarders en precautie tegens het opbrengen van Neutraale Scheepen," July 10, 1692, *Recueil van Alle de Placaten . . . Betreffende de Admiralteiten* . . ., Vol. II, 224 vs.
34. States-General, "Resolutie, ordres omtrent de Commissievaart en het opbrengen van Neutrale Scheepen," January 2, 1694, *Recueil van Alle de Placaten . . . Betreffende de Admiralteiten* . . ., Vol. II, 250.
35. It is important to note that this was not solely a Dutch phenomenon. Indeed, an English proclamation from 1605 laments that the same tendency held true within Albion's shores as well. Specifically, the proclamation which had been translated into Dutch concerned English seafaring men who had been legally employed during the recently ended Anglo-Spanish hostilities. Although formerly practitioners of "normal and admirable" occupations, these mariners now had taken up service as "Men of War" for various foreign governments. Cunningly, they used the trappings of this foreign service—*commissies van retorsie* and the like—as a facade to follow a more nefarious course, "making themselves . . . no better than pirates . . ." and robbing "our own subjects . . . and the subjects of other princes and neighbors . . ." Verz. Thysius: *Proclamatie Ofte Placcaet des Conings van Groot Britanien / tot wederroepinghe der Engelsche Natie die haer ter Zee zijn generende met Rooff* . . . (Delf: J. Andriesz., 1605).
36. ARA, Hof van Holland #5213.18: *Stukken inzake Cornelis Dielofs te Oegstgeest wegens zeeroverij*, 1610.

37. ARA, Hof van Holland #5220.29: *Informatie tegen Corn. Claesz. van Uitgeest, impretrant van pardon en gevangene op de voorpoort, zeerover*, 1615.
38. ARA, Hof van Holland Archief: *Chronologisch Register op de Criminele Papieren van het Hof van Holland uit de periode 1572 tot en met 1810*, 1572–1699; and ARA, Hof van Holland #5220.21: *Request etc. voor Jan Lievensz. Rijckewaert, zeerover, om gratie*, September 1615.
39. ARA, Hof van Holland Archief: *Chronologisch Register op de Criminele Papieren van het Hof van Holland uit de periode 1572 tot en met 1810*, 1572–1699; and ARA, Hof van Holland #5217.2: *Stukken betreffende het arresteren te Medemblik van eenschip dat tot zeeroverij gediend had*, June 18, 1613.
40. ARA, Hof van Holland #5346.23: *Mandament van purge voor H. Hogencamp, beschuldigd van zeeroverij, met een antal bewijsstukken*, 1687; and ARA, Hof van Holland #5345.9: *Informatie inzake Hendrick Hoogenkamp beschuldigd van zeeroverij*, 1687.
41. See the "Repertorium" in ARA, AA, Verz. Bisdom #167: *Copie-Crimineele vonnissen van de Admiraliteit op de Maas...*, 1575–1710.
42. ARA, AA, Verz. Bisdom #167: *Copie-Crimineele vonnissen van de Admiraliteit op de Maas...*, 1575–1710, fols. 286 vs–293 vs.
43. The court cited a States-General *Placaat* of December 1, 1640, as well as the 12th Article of the most recent declaration of war against France, and the 57th Article of Sissingh's *Articulbrief*.
44. ARA, AA, Verz. Bisdom #167: *Copie-Crimineele vonnissen van de Admiraliteit op de Maas...*, 1575–1710, fols. 2 vs–4.
45. J.C.A. de Meij, *De Watergeuzen en de Nederlanden 1568–1572* (Amsterdam: N.V. Noord-Hollandsche Uitgevers, 1972). Sea Beggar officers were nobles from both northern and southern provinces, but came primarily from Holland and Friesland (see 149–150). These two provinces also dominated the crews, which included men originating from througout the region (see 157).
46. de Meij, *De Watergevzen en de Nederlanden*, 166–168.
47. Boxer, *The Dutch Seaborne Empire*, 18.
48. R.B. Prud'homme van Reine, "Nederlandse Kaapvaart en Piraterij in Beeld," *Kapers op de Kust: Nederlandse Kaapvaart en Piraterij, 1500–1800* (Vlissingen: Uitgerverij ADZ, 1991), 35.
49. E.W. van der Oest, "De Praktijk van de Nederlandse Kaapvaart en Piraterij, 1500–1800," *Kapers op de Kust: Nederlandse Kaapvaart en Piraterij, 1500–1800* (Vlissingen: Uitgerverij ADZ, 1991), 12.
50. van der Oest, "De Praktijk van de Nederlandse Kaapvaart," 23.
51. Baud, *Proeve eener Geschiedenis*, 76–77. For examples of complaints about Sea Beggar "excesses" and William of Orange's feelings about the subject, see Lettre CCCXXXV, "Le Prince d'Orange au Comte Jean de Nassau; Inconduite de M. de de Dolhain: nouvesses diverses"; Lettre CCCXXXIX, "Le Prince d'Orange au Comte Jean de Nassau, Sur les excès des Gueux de mer et l'inconduite du Seigneur de Dolhain"; and Lettre CCCXLIII, "Le Cardinal De Châtillon au Prince d'Orange, Affaires de France; pirateries des Gueux de mer" in G. Groen van Prinsterer, *Archives ou Correspondance inédite de la maison d'Orange-Nassau*, Première Série, Vol. III, 1567–1572 (Leiden, 1836), 351–354, 363–365, and 373–377.
52. Olfert Dapper, *Historische Beschryving der Stadt Amsterdam* (Amsterdam: Jacob van Mevrs, 1663) 213–214.
53. van der Oest, "De Praktijk van de Nederlandse Kaapvaart," 23.

54. van der Oest, "De Praktijk van de Nederlandse Kaapvaart," 24.
55. ARA, AA, Verz. Bisdom #167: *Copie-Crimineele vonnissen van de Admiraliteit op de Maas...*, 1575–1710, fols. 104 vs–105 vs.
56. ARA, AA, Verz. Bisdom #167: *Copie-Crimineele vonnissen van de Admiraliteit op de Maas...*, 1575–1710, fols. 103–104 vs.
57. ARA, AA, Verz. Bisdom #167: *Copie-Crimineele vonnissen van de Admiraliteit op de Maas...*, 1575–1710, fols. 104 vs–105 vs, fols. 194 vs–197.
58. ARA, AA, Verz. Bisdom #167: *Copie-Crimineele vonnissen van de Admiraliteit op de Maas...*, 1575–1710, fols. 208 vs–209.
59. J.Th.H. Verhees-van Meer, *De Zeeuwse Kaapvaart tijdens de Spaanse Successieoorlog 1702–1713* (Middelburg: Werken Uitgegeven door het Koninklijk Zeeuwsch Genootschap der Wetenschappen, Deel 3, 1986), 50.
60. Verhees-van Meer, *De Zeeuwse Kaapvaart*, 50.
61. Rijke was especially fortunate—not only did he escape the death penalty, but he was released altogether. Verhees-van Meer, *De Zeeuwse Kaapvaart*, 50.
62. ARA, AA, Verz. Bisdom #167: *Copie-Crimineele vonnissen van de Admiraliteit op de Maas...*, 1575–1710, fols. 11 vs–12 vs.
63. Verhees-van Meer, *De Zeeuwse Kaapvaart*, 71.
64. Verhees-van Meer, *De Zeeuwse Kaapvaart*, 8–9.
65. Verz. RLP: *Amsterdams Vuur-Praetje, Van 't Een ende 'tanger nu om gaet* (Amstelredam: Claes Pietersz, 1649), 17.
66. Verz. RLP: *Amsterdams Vuur-Praetje* (1649), 16.
67. Verz. RLP: *Amsterdams Vuur-Praetje* (1649), 14.
68. Verz. RLP: *Amsterdams Vuur-Praetje* (1649), 21.
69. Verz. RLP: *Amsterdams Vuur-Praetje* (1649), 14.
70. Verz. RLP: *Amsterdams Vuur-Praetje* (1649), 22.
71. Verz. RLP: *Amsterdams Vuur-Praetje* (1649), 22.
72. ARA, AA, Verz. Bisdom #107: *Extract uijt het Register der Resolutiën van de Ho: Mo: Heeren Staaten Generaal... op de besetting van de Vlaamsche Kust*, April 16, 1627.
73. ARA, Hof van Holland Archief: *Index op de Criminele Sententien van het Hof van Holland*, 1623–1811; and ARA, Hof van Holland #5654–5657: *Registers van criminele sententies, Hof van Holland*, 1571–1674.
74. ARA, AA, Verz. Bisdom #167: *Copie-Crimineele vonnissen van de Admiraliteit op de Maas...*, 1575–1710, fols. 73 vs–74 vs.
75. ARA, AA, Verz. Bisdom #167: *Copie-Crimineele vonnissen van de Admiraliteit op de Maas...*, 1575–1710, fols. 33–33 vs.
76. ARA, AA, Verz. Bisdom #167: *Copie-Crimineele vonnissen van de Admiraliteit op de Maas...*, 1575–1710, fols. 27 vs–28.
77. ARA, AA, Verz. Bisdom #167: *Copie-Crimineele vonnissen van de Admiraliteit op de Maas...*, 1575–1710, fols. 21 vs–23 vs. The authorities altered Lenart Jorisz.'s sentence a bit after its pronouncement. After the serious supplications of the residents of Dordrecht, who indicated that Jorisz. had a house full of children, the judges promised Jorisz. that his body would be buried in the *Kerkhove* of the Hague, so as to shield his family from scandal.
78. ARA, AA, Verz. Bisdom #167: *Copie-Crimineele vonnissen van de Admiraliteit op de Maas...*, 1575–1710, fols. 34 vs–35.
79. ARA, AA, Verz. Bisdom #167: *Copie-Crimineele vonnissen van de Admiraliteit op de Maas...*, 1575–1710, fols. 45–45.

80. ARA, AA, Verz. Bisdom #167: *Copie-Crimineele vonnissen van de Admiraliteit op de Maas...*, 1575–1710, fols. 39 vs–40.
81. Also convicted that day was one Diedirik Verhoogt (a.k.a. *Jongbloed* or "Youngblood") of undisclosed origin. See ARA, AA, Verz. Bisdom #167: *Copie-Crimineele vonnissen van de Admiraliteit op de Maas...*, 1575–1710, fols. 45–45 vs.
82. ARA, AA, Verz. Bisdom #167: *Copie-Crimineele vonnissen van de Admiraliteit op de Maas...*, 1575–1710, fols. 45–46 vs.
83. ARA, AA, Verz. Bisdom #167: *Copie-Crimineele vonnissen van de Admiraliteit op de Maas...*, 1575–1710, fols. 31 vs–32.
84. ARA, AA, Verz. Bisdom #20: "Res. Holl," April 28, 1611, *Extract-Resolutien van de Staten-Generaal, de Staten van Holland, enz.*, 1581–1746.
85. ARA, Hof van Holland #5219.16: *Informaties nopens Maritgen Jacobs Laedigat en enige zeerovers...*, 1615. Because of Grote Piet's involvement in violence and mayhem committed in Oudskarspel, he was banned from Holland, Zeeland, Vriesland, and Utrecht for 18 years. See also ARA, Hof van Holland Archief: *Chronologisch Register op de Criminele Papieren van het Hof van Holland uit de periode 1572 tot en met 1810*, Band I, 1572–1699.
86. *Ordinaire Leydse Courant*, June 6, 1686, "Nederlanden" section.
87. K. Heeringa, *Bronnen tot de Geschiedenis van de Levanthandel 1560–1660*, Rijks Geschiedkundige Publicatie 9 and 10 ('s-Gravenhage: Martinus Nijhoff, 1910–1911); see Vol. II, 977. See also H. Dunlop, *Hollandsche Zeeroovers in de 17e Eeuw* (Zutphen: W.J. Thieme & Cie, 1938), 4. For a more general treatment of Dutchmen who became Barbary corsairs, see Arne Zuidhoek, *Zeerovers van de Goude Eeuw* (Bussum: De Boer Maritiem, 1977).
88. Nicolaes Wassenaer, *Historisch Verhael Aller Gedenkwaerdiger Geschiedenissen die Hier en Daer in Europa.... Voorgevallen Sijn.*, Vol. 13 (Amsterdam: Jan Jansz., 1627–1628), 30 vs. Wassenaer's words were also reiterated verbatim in the preface of Claes Compaen's biography, *'t Begin, Midden en Eynde Der Zee-Rooveryen van den Alderfamieusten Zee-Roover, CLAES G. COMPAEN...* (1659), iv.
89. Simon de Vries, *Historie van Barbaryen, en des zeys Zee-Roovers...*, trans. G.V. Broekhuizen (Amsterdam: Jan ten Hoorn, 1684) 65.
90. For seventeenth-century accounts of Simon de Danser the Elder (called "Dansker" or "Danseker" by the English), see Andrew Barker, *A True and Certaine Report of the Beginning, Proceedings, Overthrowes, and now present Estate of Captain WARD and DANSEKER, the two late famous Pirates...* (London: William Hall, 1609), 23–26; and William Lithgow, *The Rare Adventures and Painful Peregrinations of William Lithgow* (London, 1632; London: The Folio Society, 1974), 220–221. A Dutch edition of Lithgow's work appeared in 1632.
91. *'t Begin, Midden en Eynde Der Zee-Rooveryen van den Alderfamieusten Zee-Roover...*, 8–9.
92. Wassenaer, *Historisch*, Vol. 13, 31 vs.
93. ARA, Hof van Holland Archief: *Index op de Criminele Sententien van het Hof van Holland*, 1538–1572.
94. ARA, Hof van Holland Archief: *Index op de Criminele Sententien van het Hof van Holland*, 1538–1572.
95. ARA, Hof van Holland Archief: *Index op de Criminele Sententien van het Hof van Holland*, 1538–1572.

96. ARA, Hof van Holland Archief #5217.2: *Stukken betreffende het arresteren te Medemblik van eenschip dat tot zeeroverij gediend had*, June 18, 1613; and ARA, Hof van Holland Archief: *Chronologisch Register op de Criminele Papieren van het Hof van Holland . . .*, 1572–1699.
97. ARA, Hof van Holland Archief: *Chronologisch Register op de Criminele Papieren van het Hof van Holland . . .*, 1572–1699.
98. ARA, Hof van Holland Archief: *Chronologisch Register op de Criminele Papieren van het Hof van Holland . . .*, 1572–1699.
99. ARA, Hof van Holland Archief: *Chronologisch Register op de Criminele Papieren van het Hof van Holland . . .*, 1572–1699; and ARA, Hof van Holland # 5220.21: *Request etc. voor Jan Lievensz. Rijckewaert, zeerover, om gratie*, September 1615.
100. ARA, Hof van Holland #5220.29: *Informatie tegen Corn. Claesz. van Uitgeest, impetrant van pardon en gevangene op de voorpoort, zeerover*; and ARA, Hof van Holland Archief: *Chronologisch Register op de Criminele Papieren van het Hof van Holland . . .*, 1572–1699.
101. ARA, Hof van Holland Archief: *Chronologisch Register op de Criminele Papieren van het Hof van Holland . . .*, 1572–1699.
102. Verz. ZBP: *Sententie By mijn Ed. Heeren van den Gerechte der Stadt Dordrecht, gepronuncieert tegens Laurens Davidsz. . . . Ter saecke van de Zee-rooveryen ende pirateryen . . .* (Dordrecht: Mattheus van Nispen, 1663); ARA, VOC #307: *Zakenindex op de resoluties van de kamer Amsterdam*, 1602–1743; ARA, Hof van Holland Archief #5270A.2: *Stukken en informatie in zake Laurens Davids wegens zeeroverij in de Rode Zee en elders*, 1663; and ARA, Hof van Holland Archief: *Chronologisch Register op de Criminele Papieren van het Hof van Holland . . .*, 1572–1699.
103. ARA, Hof van Holland Archief #5346.23: *Mandament van purge voor Hendrick Hoogencamp, beschuldigd van zeeroverij met een aantal bewijsstuken*, January–March 1687; ARA, Hof van Holland Archief #5345.9: *Informatie inzake Hendrick Hoogenkamp beschuldigd van zeeroverij*, 1687; and ARA, Hof van Holland Archief: *Chronologisch Register op de Criminele Papieren van het Hof van Holland . . .*, 1572–1699.
104. ARA, Hof van Holland #5369.4: *Informatie inzake Gerrits Gysson Bloek van zeeroverij onder Scheveningen en dreigementen*, 1697; and ARA, Hof van Holland Archief: *Chronologisch Register op de Criminele Papieren van het Hof van Holland . . .*, 1572–1699
105. ARA, Hof van Holland Archief: *Index op de Criminele Sententien van het Hof van Holland*, 1538–1572.
106. ARA, AA, Verz. Bisdom #167: *Copie-Crimineele vonnissen van de Admiraliteit op de Maas . . .*, 1575–1710, fols. 6–7.
107. ARA, AA, Verz. Bisdom #167: *Copie-Crimineele vonnissen van de Admiraliteit op de Maas . . .*, 1575–1710, fols. 35–36.
108. ARA, AA, Verz. Bisdom #167: *Copie-Crimineele vonnissen van de Admiraliteit op de Maas . . .*, 1575–1710, fols. 86–88 vs.
109. ARA, VOC #307: *Zakenindex op de resoluties van de kamer Amsterdam*, 1602–1743, November 15, 1663, fol. 435. See entry under "Zeeroverij"; and for more on this topic, VOC #237.
110. Specifically, they attacked "Gonseratsee, moorse en andere shepen."
111. ARA, VOC #656: *Kopie-resoluties van President en Raden van de Kantoren in Bantam en Jakarta* (January 8, 1618) (January 22, 1618) (March 13, 1618) (May 19, 1618); and van der Chijs, *Realia*, I, 418.

112. Except for the data specifically footnoted to David Marley, the information in the following two paragraphs comes from these archival documents: ARA, WIC #24: *Algemeene alphabetisch register op de notulen . . . Vergadering van Tienen, 1674–1748*, heading of "Zeeroverijen" (March 11, 1683); ARA, WIC #337: *Notulen der Vergadering van Tienen, Kamer Amsterdam*, February 20, 1682; ARA, WIC #338: *Notulen der Vergadering van Tienen, Kamer Amsterdam*, March 11, 1683; ARA, WIC #339, *Notulen der Vergadering van Tienen, Kamer Amsterdam*, December 29, 1684; ARA, WIC #468: "Aenden Directeur van Curaçao, Jan van Erpecum," *Kopieboeken van brieven naar Amerika, 1684–1689*, August 16, 1684, fol. 16; August 31, 1684, fol. 17 vs; October 6, 1684, fol. 26 vs; and July 6, 1685, fols. 48–48 vs; and ARA, WIC # 833: *Notulen der Vergadering van Tienen, Kamer van Zeeland*, March 11, 1683, fols. 12–12 vs.

113. David F. Marley, *Pirates and Engineers: Dutch and Flemish Adventurers in New Spain (1607–1697)* (Windsor, Ontario: Netherlandic Press, 1992), 53.

114. AGI: Escribania, 25A–25C: *Comisiones Audencia de Santo Domingo*, 1684; AGI: Escribania, 297A: *Comisión por el Conde de Paredes . . .* (1683); and David F. Marley, *Pirates and Privateers of the Americas* (Santa Barbara, CA: ABC-Clio, 1994), 11–12 and 106–107. According to the first source, the Spanish considered Van Hoorn to be not only Dutch, but "Zeelands" (*zelandés*). For more on Van Hoorn's attack on Veracruz, see David F. Marley, *The Sack of Veracruz: The Great Pirate Raid of 1683* (Windsor, Ontario: Netherlandic Press, 1993); and Carlos Saiz Cidoncha, *Historia de la Piratería en América Española* (Madrid: Editorial San Martin, 1985), 313–318.

115. AGI: Escribania, 297A: *Comisión por el Conde de Paredes . . .* (1683); and Marley, *Pirates and Privateers of the Americas*, 106–107.

116. For more biographical details about these men, as well as fellow Dutchman Michel Andrieszoon, see Marley, *Pirates and Privateers of the Americas*; and Cidoncha, *Historia*, 313–332.

117. Alexander O. Exquemelin, *The Buccaneers of America*, trans. Alexis Brown (Mineola, NY: Dover, 2000), 80; and Alexander Olivier Exquemelin, *De Americaensche Zee-Roovers . . .* (Amsterdam: Jan ten Hoorn, 1678), 42–44.

118. Exquemelin, *Buccaneers of America*, 80; and Exquemelin, *De Americaensche Zee-Roovers . . .*, 42–44.

119. See, e.g., the sentence meted out by the States of Holland on May 27, 1581 against "pirates imprisoned in Enkhuizen." ARA, AA, Verz. Bisdom #20: "Res. Holl," May 27, 1581, *Extract-Resolutien van de Staten-Generaal, de Staten va Holland, enz., 1581–1746*.

3 Collective Identity, Nationalism, and the Golden Age Netherlands

1. *Ordinaire Leydse Courant*, November 26, 1686 (No. 104) (Leiden: Daniel van Gaesbeeck, 1686), "Neederlanden" section.
2. *Ordinaire Leydse Courant*, November 28, 1686 (No. 105), "Neederlenden" section.
3. *Ordinaire Leydse Courant*, November 30, 1686 (No. 106), "Neederlenden" section.
4. *Ordinaire Leydse Courant*, December 3, 1686 (No. 107), "Neederlenden" section.
5. *Ordinaire Leydse Courant*, December 3, 1686 (No. 107), "Neederlenden" section.
6. For example, *Oprechte Haerlemse Saturdaegse Courant*, November 30, 1686 (No. 48) (Haerlem: Abraham Casteleyn, 1686).

7. For example, this history of the city of Haarlem claims to discuss all the storms that have riddled the city in the past, in addition to other important happenings: Verz. Thysius: P. Sterlincx, *Beschrijvinghe (Een Corte waerachtighe), van alle Gheschiedenissen, Aenslaghen, Stormen, Schermutsingne, ende Schieten voor de vrome Stadt Haerlum in Hollandt gheschiet* (Delft, 1574).
8. For example, Wou's *Ships in a Tempest*; de Vlieger's *Shipwreck on a Rocky Coast*; Bellevois's *Ships in Distress on a Rocky Coast*; and Blankerhoff's *A Shipwreck*.
9. For example, The *Sea Storm*, attributed to Joost de Momper; the *Shipwreck on the Netherlands Coast*, attributed to Jan Bruegel the Younger; Theodore Galle's *Shipwreck in a Storm*; and Hendrick Cornelisz. Vroom's *Ships in a Tempest*.
10. See, e.g., Verz. Thysius: *Warachtighe beschrijvinghe van het groote Jammer droesheydt ende ellende datter nu ghebuert is op Zee* . . . (Rotterdam: Jan de Kramer, 1615), which describes a catastrophic storm in England and Ireland that sank ships, drowned animals and more than 200 people, and engulfed seven villages.
11. Verz. Thysius: *Deductie, Op het subject van de handelinge op de Straet, en de Navigatie in de Middellantsche Zee* (1687).
12. For example, for a representative text, see this pamphlet from 1616: Verz. Thysius: *Een waerachtighe beschryvinghe van het goot jammer, droesheydt ende ellende datter nu ghebeurt is op de Zee ende schade die daer oock gheschiet is in Tessel* . . . (Amsterdam: Gerrit van Breughel, 1616), 1–2.
13. Verz. Thysius: *Hollandtze Mercurius* (Haerlem: Pieter Casteleyn, 1666),158.
14. Verz. Thysius: *Duyns-Kerckens Naeckende Sterff-Dagh* . . . (ca. 1645), 7.
15. Ralph Davis, *The Rise of the Atlantic Economies* (London: Weidenfeld and Nicolson, 1973), 180.
16. C.R. Boxer, *The Dutch Seaborne Empire 1600–1800* (London: Penguin Books, 1990; London: Hutchinson, 1965; New York: Alfred A. Knopf, 1965), 29.
17. Richard W. Unger, Dutch Shipbuilding Before 1800: Ships and Guilds, *Aspects of Economic History: The Low Countries* (Assen: Van Gorcum, 1978), 11.
18. Boxer, *The Dutch Seaborne Empire*, 323.
19. Charles Henry Wilson, *Anglo-Dutch Commerce and Finance in the Eighteenth Century* (Cambridge: Cambridge University Press, 1941), 3, cited in Immanuel Wallerstein, *The Modern World System II*: Mercantilism and the Consolidation of the European World Economy, 1600–1750 (New York: Academic Press, 1980), 39. Charles M. Andrews traces this expression to a States-General proclamation on July 19, 1624. See his "Anglo-French Commercial Rivalry, 1700–1750: The Western Phase," *American Historical Review*, Vol. XX, Part I, 3 (April 1915), 541.
20. Meynert Semeyns, *Corte Beschryvinge over de Haring Vischerye in Hollandt*, cited in Wallerstein, *The Modern World System II*, 39.
21. Wallerstein, *The Modern World System II*, 38–39. Wallerstein explains that hegemony "may be defined as a situation wherein the products of a given core state are produced so efficiently that they are by and large competitive even in other core states, and therefore the given core state will be the primary beneficiary of a maximally free world market." In other words, "there is a . . . moment in time when a given core power can manifest *simultaneously* productive, commercial, and financial superiority *over all other core powers*. This momentary summit is what we call hegemony."
22. L. Goedde, *Tempest and Shipwreck in Dutch and Flemish Art: Convention, Rhetoric and Interpretation* (University Park: Pennsylvania State University Press, 1989), 9.
23. G. Keyes, *Cornelis Vroom: Marine and Landscape Artist* (Alphen aan de Rijn: Canaletto, 1985), 17.

24. Olfert Dapper, *Historische Beschryving der Stadt Amsterdam* (Amsterdam: Jacob van Meurs, 1663), 251.
25. Stanza from "Visscherslied" (1702), D.F. Scheurleer, *Van Varen en Van Vechten*, Vol. III ('s-Gravenhage: Martinus Nijhoff, 1914), 161–162. The lyrics in Dutch read: *De zee is ons vermaken / Daer vinden wy oock lust / Hoewel sy altijd hobbelt / En selden blijft in rust . . .*
26. Verz. Thysius: *Deductie, Op het subject van de handelinge op de Straet, en de Navigatie in de Middellantsche Zee* (1687).
27. Simon Schama, *The Embarassment of Riches: An Interpretation of Dutch Culture in the Golden Age* (Berkeley: University of California Press, 1988), 44–45.
28. Schama, *The Embarassment of Riches*, 43–44. For the Vierlingh quote, see Andries Vierlingh, *Tractaet van Diekgie*, eds. J. de Hullu and A.G. Verhoeven ('s-Gravenhage, 1920), 396.
29. For evidence of this cultural predilection, see the sailor's complaints about the fussy tastes and imperious manner of Admiral Obdam vis-à-vis the probity, valor, and integrity of Admiral Tromp in Verz. RLP: *Een Praatje Van Den Ouden en Nieuwen Admiraal . . .* (Amsterdam: Jacob Volkers Hoofdbreker, 1653), 4–5.
30. Benedict Anderson, *Imagined Communities: Reflections on the Origins and Spread of Nationalism*, 2nd edition (New York: Verso, 1991), 12. Anderson himself judged nationalism to be an eighteenth- and nineteenth-century phenomenon.
31. Anderson, *Imagined Communities*, 4.
32. Elaborating upon this description, Anderson posits that this "imagined community" is limited because "even the largest of them, encompassing perhaps a billion living human beings, has finite, if elastic boundaries, beyond which lie other nations. No nation imagines itself coterminous with mankind." The idea of this community as sovereign arose because the "legitimacy of the divinely-ordained, hierarchical dynastic realm"—the standard medieval model in Europe—faded away as history unfolded. See Anderson, *Imagined Communities*, 6–7.
33. Anderson, *Imagined Communities*, 12 and 37–46.
34. Ernest Renan, "Qu'est-ce qu'une nation?" *Oeuvres Complètes*, 1, 892, quoted in Anderson, *Imagined Communities*, 199.
35. Anderson, *Imagined Communities*, 201.
36. Lewis A. Coser, Introduction to Maurice Halbwachs, *On Collective Memory*, ed. and trans. Lewis A. Coser (Chicago: University of Chicago Press, 1992), 22.
37. Coser, *On Collective Memory*, 24.
38. Eric Hobsbawm, e.g., terms the "nation" (and its associated phenomena, nationalism, the nation-state, national symbols, and national histories) as "that comparatively recent historical innovation." He has pinpointed the "nation" and "nationalism" as developments arising in the late eighteenth and early nineteenth centuries. Likewise, Ernest Gellner, predicating his thoughts on the work of Max Weber, views it as a phenomenon occurring only after the establishment of the modern, industrial, bureaucratized state. See Eric Hobsbawm, "Introduction: Inventing Traditions," ed. Eric Hobsbawm and Terence Ranger, *The Invention of Tradition* (Cambridge: Cambridge University Press, 1983), 13; and Eric Hobsbawm, *Nations and Nationalism Since 1780: Programme, Myth, Reality* (Cambridge and New York: Cambridge University Press), passim. Hobsbawm does acknowledge the existence of a pre-nineteenth-century phenomonenon, "popular proto-nationalism," which he defines as expressions of preexisting feelings of collective belonging that are potentially congruent with modern nations. Such expressions might include patriotic feelings resulting from a shared language,

religion, symbols, or rituals, or from opposition to foreign control, or from the consciousness of belonging to an enduring political entity (*Nations and Nationalism*, 46–79). Also Ernst Gellner, *Nations and Nationalism* (Oxford: Basil Blackwell, 1983), 4–5. The literature on the creation of the modern nation-state and nationalism is vast. Representative examples include J.A. Armstrong's *Nations Before Nationalism* (Manchester, England: Manchester University Press, 1982); Miroslav Hroch's *Social Preconditions of National Revival in Europe*, trans. Ben Fowkes (Cambridge: Cambridge University Press, 1985); Anthony Smith's *The Ethnic Origins of Nations* (Oxford: Basil Blackwell, 1987); and P. Chatterjee's *Nationalist Thought and the Colonial World* (London: Zed Books for the United Nations University, 1986).

39. For works asserting the existence of national identity in the Dutch Republic, see Schama, *The Embarassment of Riches*; Benjamin Schmidt, *Innocence Abroad: The Dutch Imagination and the New World, 1570–1670* (Cambridge: Cambridge University Press, 2001); and Herbert H. Rowen and Craig E. Harline, "The Birth of the Dutch Nation," *Politics, Religion & Diplomacy in Early Modern Europe: Essays in Honor of DeLamar Jensen*, ed. Malcom R. Thorp and Arthur J. Slavin (Kirksville, MS: Sixteenth Century Journal Publishers, 1994).
40. For works asserting the existence of national identity in the Dutch Republic, see Schama, *The Embarassment of Riches*; Schmidt, *Innocence Abroad*; and Rowen and Harline, "The Birth of the Dutch Nation."
41. Anderson, *Imagined Communities*, 39–40 and 44.
42. Geoffrey Parker, *The Dutch Revolt*, 2nd edition (London: Peregrine Books, 1988), 270. Censorship occasionally did occur, however, as evidenced by criminal sentences meted out by the *Hof van Holland* for publishing taboo materials. See ARA, Hof van Holland Archief, *Registers van Criminele Sententies*, Inventory #5655 (the cases of Michiel van Staat, September 1, 1650; and Machteld Fynemans, February 23, 1652); Inventory #5656 (the case of Michiel Staal, April 23, 1652); and Inventory #5657 (the case of Margaretha Tromp, 1667; and Christiaan Moekwater, May 14, 1667). For more information on books prohibited in the United Provinces, see W.P.C. Knuttel, *Verboden Boeken in de Republiek der Vereenigde Nederlanden* ('s-Gravenhage, 1914).
43. Craig E. Harline, *Pamphlets, Printing, and Political Culture in the Early Dutch Republic* (Dordrecht: Martinus Nijhoff Publishers, 1987), 72.
44. Harline, *Pamphlets*, 3.
45. Harline, *Pamphlets*, 5 and 21.
46. For more information on these collections, see, e.g.: G. van Alphen, *Catalogus der Pamfletten van de Bibliiotheek der Rijksuniversiteit te Groningen (1542–1853)* (Groningen: J.B. Wolters, 1944); J. Broekema, *Catalogus van de Pamfletten, Tractaten, Enz. Aanwezig in de Provinciale Bibliotheek van Zeeland* (Middelburg: Auer, 1892); W.P.C. Knuttel, *Catalogus van de Pamfletten-Verzameling Berustendein de Koninklijke Bibliotheek* (Utrecht: HES Publishers, 1978; 's-Gravenhage, 1890–1920) and available in English in *Dutch Pamphlets, ca. 1486–1648: The Collection in the Royal Library, the Hague on Microfiche* (Zug: Inter Documentation Co., 1980) and *Dutch Pamphlets, 1649–1750: The Collection in the Royal Library, the Hague on Microfiche* (Zug: Inter Documentation Co., 1986); Louis D. Petit, *Bibliotheek van Nederlandsche Pamfletten. Verzamelingen van Joannes Thysius en de Bibliotheek der Rijks-Universiteit te Leiden* (Leiden: A.W. Sijthoff, 1925–1934); and J.F. van Someren,

Bibliotheek der Rijksuniversiteit Utrecht. Pamfletten Niet Voorkomende in Afzonderlijke Gedrukte Catalogi . . . (Utrecht: A. Oosthoek, 1915–1922).

47. F. Adama van Scheltama, *Nederlandsche Letterkunde: Populaire Prozaschrijvers der XVIIe en XVIIIe Eeuw* . . . (Amsterdam: Frederick Muller & Cie, 1893), reprinted in *Muller/Vries/Scheepers: Populaire Prozaschrijvers der XVIIe en XVIIIe Eeuw* . . ., ed. H.W. de Kooker (Utrecht: HES Publishers, 1981), 26.

48. J.Fzn.M. Buisman, *Populaire Prozaschrijvers 1600–1815: Romans, Novellen, Verhalen, Levensbeschrijvingen, Arcadias, Sprookjes. Alphabetische Naamlijst* (Amsterdam: Israel, 1960), 8.

49. Buisman, *Populaire Prozaschrijvers*, 5.

50. See, e.g., two works by Lambert van den Bos(ch): *Prael-Toneel Der Doorluchtige Mannen, Of Het Leven en Bedrijf der beroemder Vorsten, uytheemsche Veldt-Oversten en Vorstelijcke bedienaers deses Tijdts* . . . (Amsterdam: Jacob van Meurs en Compagnie, 1676); and *De Reysende Mercurius. Verhandelende De hedendaegsche en onlangs tegenwoordige staet en verrichtingen van Europa* . . . (Amsterdam: Jan Bouman, 1674).

51. For more information on elite literature in the Dutch Republic, see M.A. Schenkeveld, *Dutch Literature in the Age of Rembrandt: Themes and Ideas* (Amsterdam and Philadelphia: Benjamins, 1991). For information on Dutch reading habits in general, see Emma Dronckers, *Verzameling F.G. Waller: Nederlandsche en Vlaamsche Populair Boeken* ('s-Gravenhage: Martinus Nijhoff, 1936).

52. Parker, *The Dutch Revolt*, 269.

53. See, e.g., extant copies of the *Ordinaire Leydse Courant*. As efficient as these publishers attempted to be, various problems could interfere with their timely reporting of the news. For instance, in the March 30 edition, the publisher felt compelled to apologize for the tardiness of his correspondents' reports, which were late due to inclement weather. Moreover, on April 9, poor weather prevented ships from arriving, delaying the news "from the sea."

54. Parker, *The Dutch Revolt*, 269. The particular paper was the *'Courantier in 't Legher van Sijn Princelijke Excellentie.*

55. See, e.g., a pamphlet detailing a 1600 victory of the Dutch over the Spanish at Oostende, which emphasizes that "Dit is beminde Leser, by een ghestelt, uyt de Brieven end Schriftelicke Rapportten, die belanghende het beleyt ende de uytcomste deser Bataillie over ghefonden zijn": Verz. Thysius: *Waerachtich Verhael van den grooten Slach ende gheluckighe Victorie* . . . (Haerlem: G. Rooman, 1600), 3.

56. See, e.g., Verz. Thysius: *Hollandtze Mercurius . . . Het sesthiende Deel* (Haerlem: Pieter Casteleyn, 1666), passim. The first of this series of almanacs appeared in Haarlem in 1651. For more information on the series' history, see John Landwehr, *De Nederlander Uit en Thuis: Spiegel van het Dagelijkse Leven uit Bijzondere Zeventiende-Eeuwse Boeken* (Alphen aan den Rijn: A.W. Sijthoff, 1981), 96–97. Another title representative of this genre was the *Amsterdamze Mercurius*.

57. See, e.g., Verz. RLP: *Politicq Memoriael, Der hedendaeghsche Geschiedenissen ende Maximen van Staet* . . . (Amsterdam: C.v. G., 1663).

58. Harline, *Pamphlets*, 57.

59. Harline, *Pamphlets*, 60. For the year 1630, the rates for grooms and brides were 57% and 32% respectively; for the year 1660, the rates were 64% and 37%. For more information on this study, see Simon Hart, *Geschrift en Getal: een Keuze*

uit de Demografisch-, Economisch-en Social Historische Studien op Grond van Amsterdamse en Zaanse Archivalia, 1600–1800 (Dordrecht: Historische Vereniging Holland, 1976), 130–132 and 178–179.

60. Harline, *Pamphlets*, 60–62.
61. Harline, *Pamphlets*, 64–65 and 67–70.
62. ARA, AA, Verz. Bisdom #34: *Alphabetische index op de extract-resolutien, enz . . .*, Inventory #VI, fol. 355; Inventory #VI, fol. 356; and Inventory #VII, fol. 299 (February 22, 1680).
63. ARA, Hof van Holland Archief #5346.23: *Mandament van purge voor Hendrick Hoogencamp . . .* January–March 1687. The government authorities of Enkhuizen reported how they learned of the criminal Giel Tobias from the "*voorleden donderdagse Courant . . .*"
64. One such case was an invitation to participate in a new trade company. Demonstrating the role of the paper in disseminating information to the public, the advertisement stipulated that updates on the status of the company, as well as any new resolutions, would be periodically published in the "*Courant*" for public notice. See Verz. Thysius: *Propisitien van d'Ondernemers tot het Vast-Stellen van een Vrye Haven in West-Indien* (1679).
65. Verz. RLP: *Goede Apparentie tot Spoedige Opkomst, Der Vrye Nederlandens Magtige Zee-Vaart . . .* (1653), 4.
66. Anderson, *Imagined Communities*, 37–46.
67. Verz. Thysius: J. Liefs, *Den Lof vande Geoctr. Oost ende West-Indische Compagnye ende Lofrijcke Zee-vaert . . .* (Delf: J. Pz. Waelpots, 1630), 11.
68. Verz. Thysius: *Den Lof vande Geoctr. Oost ende West-Indische Compagnye ende Lofrijcke Zee-vaert . . .*, 12–13. For other similar examples, see Verz. ZBP: Adr. van Nierop, *Echo ofte Galm, dat is Weder-klickende Ghedicht van de teghenwoordighe Vrede-handelinghe . . .* (1608); Verz. RLP: *Reden Van dat die West-Indische Compagnie oft Handelinge . . . noodtsaeckellijck is . . .* (1636); and Verz. ZBP: *Levendich Discours Vant ghemeyne Lants welvaert, voor desen de Oost, ende nu oock de West-Indische generale Compaignie aenghevanghen, seer notabel om lesen. Door een Lief-Hebber des Vaterlandts . . .* (Amsterdam: Broer Jansz., 1622). The last source also can be found at the KB.
69. Verz. Thysius: *Den Lof vande Geoctr. Oost ende West-Indische Compagnye ende Lofrijcke Zee-vaert . . .*, 13.
70. Simon de Vries, *Historie van Barbaryen, En de zelfs Zee-Roovers . . . Tweede Deel . . .* (Amsterdam: Jan ten Hoorn, 1684), 6–7. Part I of this work was written by Pierre Dan and translated by G.V. Broekhuizen.
71. See, e.g., Verz. ZBP: *Anderde Discourse, By Forma van Missiven. Daer in kortelijck ende grondich verthoondt wort, de nootwendicheyt . . . [van de] West-Indiaensche Compagnie . . . te contribueren, ten eynde . . . beter success tot krenckinghe van de Castiliaensche Trafijcke ghewinne . . .* (1622); Verz. ZBP: *Missive. Daer in Kortelijck ende grondigh wert verthoont . . . dat door de Gheoctroyeerde West Indische Navigatie . . . grooter schade ende afbreuk voor den Coninck van Spangien zy te verwachten . . .* (Amsterdam: Broer Jansz., 1621); and Verz. ZBP: *Korte Onderrichtinghe ende vermaeninge aen alle liefhebbers des Vaderlandts, om liberalijcken te teeckenen inde West-Indische Compagnie . . .* (Leyden: Isaak Elzevier, 1622).
72. Verz. RLP: "Pambonen Vreimundima," *Den Hollantschen Apocalypsis . . .* (1626), 17.
73. Verz. Thysius: *Triumphe Van weghen de Geluckighe ende Over-Rijcke Victorie . . . vanden Heer Generael Pieter Pietersz. Heyn . . .* (1628), 64–65.

74. Verz. Thysius: *Den Lof vande Geoctr. Oost ende West-Indische Compagnye ende Lofrijcke Zee-vaert . . .*, 4 and 13.
75. M. Aleman, *Het Leven van Gusman d'Alfarache, 't Afbeeltsel van 't Menschelijk Leven: Onder de ghedaente van een Spaenschen Landtlooper, en Bedelaar . . .*, 2nd edition (Amsterdam: Baltus Boekholt, 1669). In the preface, the publisher pleads, "Ick bid u haet hem niet om dat hy een Spangiaert is . . ." Moreover, the printer adds that he has removed the main character's original Spanish clothing and dressed him in "een mager Hollands Kleedtje . . ." (see 5–6).
76. Landwehr, *De Nederlander uit en Thuis*, 18. For an early extant edition of this text, see Don Fray Bartholome de las Casas, *Spieghel der Spaenscher tyrannye in West-Indien . . .* (Amstelredam: Cornelis Claesz., 1607).
77. Willem Ysbrantsz Baudaert, *Morghen-wecker der vrye Nederlantsche provintien . . .* (Danswick: Crijn Vermeulen de Jonge, 1610). Another example of such a pamphlet is Verz. RLP: I.v.H., *Ondeckinghe Vanden Raed Achitophels . . .* (Ziericzee: Balthasar Doll, 1636).
78. For a sample of such works, see Schama, *The Embarassment of Riches*, 84–91.
79. See Verz. Thysius: *Waerachtigh verhael, van het Succes van de Vlote . . .* (1625). For an account of Spanish violence in Germany, see KB Pamfletten: *Eyghentlijck ende treffelijck bewijs . . . van alle . . . sacken oock grouwelycke daden ende onmenschelijcke beestighe shier noyt gheboorde tyrannie . . .* (Herman Allertsz., 1599). For another example of men whom the Spanish caught supplying intelligence to the Dutch, see AGI, Contratacion 167: *Autos Fiscales*, Número 7 (Contra Nicolás de Porta, Andrés Enríques y Felipe Juan), 1618–1619.
80. *Spieghel der Jeught, ofte: een kort verhael der voornaemste Tyrannie, en Barbarishce wreetheden . . .* (Amsterdam: de Wed. van Theunis Jacobsz., ca. 1650). Initially published in 1614, this chapbook was extremely popular and was reprinted nine times by 1631 and twenty-nine times before 1740. See, e.g., the 1615 edition: Willem Baudaert, *Spieghel der jeught, Ofte Corte Cronijcke der Nederlantsche geschiedenissen . . .* (Amsterdam: Herman Allertz. Coster, 1615). For more on this text, see de Kooker, *Muller/Vries/Scheepers*, 163.
81. Landwehr, *De Nederlander uit en Thuis*, 19.
82. See Dronckers, *Verzameling F.G. Waller*, cite #208. The original text was: Willem Baudaert, *Morghen-wecker der vrye Nederlantsche provintien . . .*, which was published a myriad of times. For a sample edition, see Verz. RLP: Willem Baudaert, *Morghen-wecker der vrye Nederlantsche provintien: Ofte Een cort verhael van de bloedighe vervolghinghen ende wreetheden door de Spaenjaerden ende haere Adherenten inde Nederlanden gheduerende dese veertich-jarighe Troublen ende Oorloghen begaen . . .* (Danswick: Crijn Vermeulen de Jonge, 1610).
83. Coster quoted in Landwehr, *De Nederlander uit en Thuis*, 18–19. Landwehr notes that Coster's schoolbook reappeared in yet another incarnation in 1672, after the close of the war with France, as *The New Youth's Mirror of French Tyranny, Being a Short Tale of the Origins and Proceedings of the War*.
84. Verz. Thysius: *Waerachtich Verhael van den grooten Slach ende gheluckighe Victorie . . .* (Haerlem: G. Rooman, 1600), 3; Verz. RLP: *Spaenschen Raedt. Om die Geunieerde Provincien . . . onder Spaensche Tyrannije to brengen . . .* ('s Gravenhage: Aert Meuris, 1626); and Baudaeart's *Spieghel der jeught, Ofte Corte Cronijcke der Nederlandsche geschiedenissen . . .* (Amsterdam: Herman Allertz. Coster, 1615).
85. For examples of use of the term "Fatherland" in popular literature, see *Spiegel der Jeught . . .* (1650); *Eyghentlijck ende treffelijck bewijs . . . van alle . . . grouwelycke*

daden ende onmenschelijcke beestighe shier noyt ghehoorde tyrannie ende schenderie welcke des Spaensche Coninghs krijghsvolck inde Nederlandtsche Westphaelsche Kreijs . . . teghen alle menschen volbracht hebben (Herman Allertsz., 1599); and Verz. Thysius: *Den Lof vande Geoctr. Oost ende West-Indische Compagnye ende Lofrijcke Zee-vaert . . . .* States-General documents also employed this terminology, specifically, the "United Fatherland." See, e.g., Verz. RLP: *Artickels-Brief ende Instructie roerende den Oorloghe ter Zee . . .* (April 27, 1629).

86. *Eyghentllijck ende treffelijck bewijs ende summaris waerachtich bericht . . .* (1599).
87. Verz. ZBP and Verz. KB Pamfletten: Adr. van Nierop, *Echo ofte Galm . . . Door Een Lief-hebber des Vaderlandschen Vryheyds* (1608).
88. See, e.g., Verz. ZBP: *Missive. Daer in Kortelijck ende grondigh wert verthoont . . . dat door de Gheoctroyeerde West Indische Navigatie . . . grooter schade ende afbreuk voor den Coninck van Spangien zy te verwachten. Geschreven aen een seker Vrient ende Liefhebber van de Welstant des Vader-landts . . .* (Amsterdam: Broer Jansz., 1621); and Verz. ZBP: *Korte Onderrichtinghe ende vermaeninge aen alle liefhebbers des Vaderlandts, om liberalijcken te teeckenen inde West-Indische Compagnie . . . Door een liefhebber des Vaderlandts inghestelt . . .* (Leyden: Isaak Elzevier, 1622).
89. Verz. RLP: *Ondeckinghe Vanden Raed Achitophels . . .* (Ziericzee: Balthasar Doll, 1636).
90. In Dutch, "goede Ingesetenen ende Patrotten onses lieve en diergekochte Vaderlants." See Verz. RLP: *Naerder Openbaringe, van Nederlants Engelschen Oorloge, Oorsake, Ende Tegenweer . . .* (Leyden: Wilhelm Christiaans vander Boxc, 1653), 14.
91. Schama, *The Embarassment of Riches*, 104–125.
92. The inscription was composed by the Netherlands' greatest Golden Age poet, Vondel. See Dapper, *Historiche*, 386.
93. Verz. RLP: *Naerder Openbaringe, van Nederlants Engelschen Oorloge . . .*, 14.
94. The Dutch noted this fact in reports sent back during the Dutch Revolt. See, e.g., Verz. Thysius: *Ample ende waerachtige beschrijvinghe waerinne verhaelt wort alle de circunstantien in wat manieren de ses groote Galleyen . . . zijn . . . overvallen . . .* (Delff: J. Cz. Vennecool, 1602), 3.
95. G.H.P. De Jonge claims that many of the misdeeds attributed to the Barbary corsairs are the product of a stubborn historical stereotype and are not based on fact. See his "Het Fabeltje van de Verschrikkelijke Barbarijse Zeerover," *Spiegel Historiael*, Vol. 24 (1989), 68–74.
96. For more on the damage to Dutch trade by the Barbary corsairs, see K. Heeringa, *Bronnen tot de Geschiedenis van den Levantschen Handel*, Rijks Geschiedkundige Publicatiën 9, 10, 34, and 95 ('s-Gravenhage: Martinus Nijhoff, 1910–1952), Part I, Vol. II, Chapters IV–VI; and R.E.J. Weber, *De Beveiliging van de Zee Tegen Europeesche en Barbarijsche Zeerovers, 1609–1621* (Amsterdam: Werken uitgeg. door de Commssie voor Zeegeschiedenis der Kon. Adad. van Wetensche. III, 1936).
97. Peter Earle, *Corsairs of Malta and Barbary* (London: Sidgwick and Jackson, 1970), 97–144; and Fernand Braudel, *The Mediteranean and the Mediteranean World in the Age of Philip II*, trans. Sian Reynolds (New York: W.W. Norton, 1973), 877–879.
98. de Vries, *Historie van Barbaryen*.
99. de Vries, *Historie van Barbaryen*, 47.
100. See, e.g., de Vries, *Historie van Barbaryen*, 54, 71, and 153–154.

101. de Vries, *Historie van Barbaryen*, 34. See also Verz. Thysius: *Seeckere tydinge van tgene aldereerst ghepasseert is . . . hoe 36. Turchsche Zee-roovers het Eylant Lanceroote hebben afgheloopen, geplondert, ende duysent mensche tot slaven ghemaecht . . .* (Amstelredam: Broer Jansz. op de Kolck, 1618).
102. Those who died were denied the decency of a proper burial, and their corpses were left to rot and be eaten by dogs. Verz. RLP: *Een Cort ende warachtich verhael vande ghedenckweerdige gheschiedenisse in Barbaryen . . .* ('s Gravenhage: Hill. Jacobsz., 1607).
103. See, e.g., Emanuel de Airanda, *Turckse Slavernie . . .* ('s-Gravenhage: Christoffel en Jasper Doll, 1666); and *De overzelzame Historie van de Markgravinne de Frene, door haar eigen man aan een Turkschen zeeroover verkoft . . .* (Rotterdam, 1702).
104. *De Ontschaakte Amsterdamsche Helena . . .* (Steenwyk: Hendrik Stuifzand, 1693).
105. *De Joodse Swerver Of De Historie Van Sekere Niet Onbekende Slaaf . . .* (Enkhuizen: C. Klenk, ca. 1750); and *Zonderlinge Levensloop Van Een Ongelukkig Reisgezel, Of Beschryving Van de door hem geledene Droevige Slaverny, Onder de Turken in Turkyen en Barbaryen . . .* (ca. 1750).
106. The list of cities and towns includes shops in Enkhuizen, Alkmaar, Purmerend, Hoorn, Harlingen, Arnhem, Vlissingen, Middelburg, Dort, Schiedam, Rotterdam, Utrecht, Amsterdam, Haarlem, Leiden, Delft, the Hague, Leeuwaarden, Zwol, and Zardam.
107. Verz. Thysius: *De Snelle Mercurius . . .* (T'Amstelredam: Otto Barentsz. Smiet, 1686), May 5 and July 11.
108. Verz. Thysius: *Hollandtze Mercurius . . .* (1666), 64–65, where the almanac explains that the Turks were persecuting the resident Christians in the Holy Land "more and more" in retaliation for French attacks on the Barbary corsairs.
109. Verz. RLP: *Amsterdamse Dingsdaegse Courant*, February 7, 1690, 1; and *Ordinaire Leydse Courant* (1686), passim.
110. *Ordinaire Leydse Courant*, August 22, 1686 (No. 63), "Nederlanden" section.
111. ARA, Archief Bisdom #151: *Register van Criminele Sententies van het Hof van Holland*, Case #74, October 19, 1599. Another source that reveals this fear is AVS #1912: *Een Waerachtigh Liedt van een Schip datmen in Tessel heeft gekregen daer 26. Knechtjens en 2. Meyskens op waren die sy meynden aenden Turck te leveren . . .* (1645). The verses here describe a purportedly true case in which Dutch Christian children had been kidnapped from all over the country and were en route to Turkey and North Africa when one youth jumped off to seek help.
112. de Vries, *Historie van Barbaryen*, 104.
113. ARA, AA, Verz. Schrijver #8: *Lyste of Rolle van all de Slaaven, soo van de Neederlandsche Natie . . . door de Algiersche Kaapers genoomen . . . 1690–1726*.
114. See, e.g., ARA, AA, Verz. Schrijver #8: *Bylage by missive van den Capitein Thomas Hees . . .: Lijste van de geloste Nederlandsche Slaven tot Algiers*, January 18, 1683. According to this document, numerous Dutch women had been captured and enslaved, and one family, the Borstels from Amsterdam, endured the same fate.
115. de Vries, *Historie van Barbaryen*, 162–168. The vast majority of the 178 slaves included here were Dutch; a scant few were of Scandinavian, English, and German descent. Many of the Dutch slaves originated from Amsterdam, and only eight of them were women. For an eighteenth-century roll, see Hendrik Cornelis Steenis, *Journaal Wegens De Rampspoedige Reys-Tocht, Van . . . Capiteyn Hendrik Cornelis Steenis . . .* (Amstelredam: Bernardus Mourik, ca. 1751–1791).

116. ARA, AA,Verz. Schrijver #8: *Lyste of Rolle van alle de Slaaven . . . 1690–1726.*
117. For more on this topic, see C.J. den Ridder, "Gedenk de gevangenen alsof gij mede gevangenen waart. De loskoop van Hollandse zeelieden uit Barbarijse gevangenschap (1600–1746)," *Tijdschrift voor Zeegeschiedenis,* Vol. V (1986), 3–22.
118. For a typical example of how Dutch slaves were discussed in political agreements with the North Africans, see Point #4 in the September 29, 1662 treaty between the United Provinces and Tunis in Verz. RLP: Heeren ter Admiraliteyt, *Deliberatien ende Resolutien Genomen op Verscheyde Poincten, Ende Berechtingen vande Heeren ter Admiraliteyt . . .* (1663).
119. For an example of this government enthusiasm, see Verz. Thysius: States-General, *Waerschouwinge. De Staten Generael,* December 29, 1677 ('s-Gravenhage: J. Scheltus, 1677).
120. E.W. van der Oest, "De Praktijk vande Nederlandse Kaapvaart en Piraterij 1500–1800," *Kapers op de Kust: Nederlandse Kaapvaart en Piraterij 1500–1800,* ed. Prud'homme van Reine and van der Oest (Vlissingen: Uitgeverij ADZ, 1991), 23. The records of at least one, the so-called *Slavenkas* ("Slaves Coffer"), established in 1735 in Zierikzee, Zeeland, are still extant. This particular institution was financed as a mutual insurance scheme; every Zierikzee ship that left the city's harbor contributed an amount to the *Slavenkas.* Then, whenever the need arose, funds were available for the release of Zierikzee sailors taken into North African captivity. See the collection "Commissarissen van de Slavenkas" in Zierikzee's municipal archive. For more information, see R.B. Prud'homme van Reine, "Nederlandse Kaapvaart en Piraterij in Beeld," *Kapers op de Kust: Nederlandse Kaapvaart en Piraterij, 1500–1800* (Vlissingen: Uitgeverij ADZ, 1991), 50–51.
121. van der Oest, "De Praktijk vande Nederlandse Kaapvaart," 23. The historian claims, "Pogingen om de ongelukkigen los te kopen werden door de overheid niet of nauwelijks ondernomen."
122. ARA, AA, Verz. Van Der Heim #481: States-General, *Extract-Resolutien van de Staten-Generaal, aanteekeningen, enz. betreffende de lossing van christenslaven te Algiers en het overbrengen derwaarts van de gebruikelijke jaarlijksche geschenken,* 1642–1757.
123. See ARA, AA, Verz. Schrijver #8: *Slaven, waar voor te Amsterdam collectien zyn geobtineerd . . . ,* ca. 1715. Entries reveal that wives, mothers, fathers, brothers, friends, ostensibly unrelated individuals, and even notaries sponsored the collection efforts in this case.
124. ARA, AA, Verz. Schrijver #8: *Bylage by missive van den Capitein Thomas Hees . . . Lijste van de geloste Nederlandsche Slaven tot Algiers,* January 18, 1683.
125. de Vries, *Historie van Barbaryen,* 162–168.
126. ARA, AA, Verz. Schrijver #8: *Lyste of Rolle van alle de Slaaven . . . 1690–1726.*
127. See, e.g., Verz. Thysius: States-General, *Waerschouwinge . . . ,* December 29, 1677.
128. Hendrik Cornelis Steenis, *Kort, Dog Naauwkeurig en Opregt Verhaal, Van alle de Behandelingen, Wreedhedens en Ongemakken, in hunne Slavernye . . . Met hunne Verlossing en te rugkomst in ons Vaderland* (Amsterdam: Wed. J. van Egmont, ca. 1726–1761). Note the title.
129. Verz. Thysius: States-General, *Placaet . . .* ('s-Gravenhage: J. Scheltus, September 9, 1679). The sickness is presented as, ". . . Salée met de Pestilentiale Sieckte van Godt den Heere Almachtig zijn besocht . . ."

130. ARA, AA, Verz. Sweers #2: Isaac Sweers, *Journaal, gehouden door Sweers... uitgezonden naar de kust van Barbarije... te zuiveren van de zeerovers*, March 10, 1650–May 20, 1651. Note "te zuiveren" in the title.
131. ARA, AA, Verz. Sweers #2: Isaac Sweers, *Journaal, gehouden door Sweers... op's Lands schip De Maen, kruisende langs de kusten... op de Turksche en andere zeerovers*, April 5, 1649–November 16, 1649, entry for May 27.
132. ARA, AA, Verz. Bisdom #42: *Extract uit de Resolutien van haar Hoog. Mo. van 1604, 1605, 1606*. See section under the heading of "Prinsen."
133. ARA, AA#1839 (College van het Admiraliteit te Amsterdam): *Rekening ven den vendumeester wegens zijn ontvang van de princen en veroverde Turcken en Mooren op de kust van Barbarije onder den vice-admiral De Ruijter*, 1661–1662. See entry for March 4, 1661; the last two figures do not indicate the date of sale.
134. For a reference to this practice, see de Vries, *Historie van Barbaryen*, Chapter VI. De Vries also notes that North African corsairs were held in Dutch jails (42).
135. See, e.g., *Ordinaire Leydse Courant* (1686), passim; and Verz. Thysius: *Courante uyt Italien ende Duytschlandt* (Amsterdam), No. 9, February 26, 1639, 2.
136. For example, Verz. RLP: *Ordinarise Middel-weeckse Courante* (Amsterdam), No. 33, August 12, 1653.
137. For example, *Ordinaire Leydse Courant*, No. 112, December 14, 1686. The paper notes, "Gisteren is den kloekmoedigen Zee-Held den Heer Admirael Tromp alhier gearriveert."
138. Verz. Thysius: *Hollandtze Mercurius...* (1666), 68.
139. See, e.g., a pamphlet that related the history of all "courageous" Dutch battles against the English from 1588 to 1665—Verz. Thysius: *Opweckingh en moedgevingh aen de Bataviers van't wydt Beroempt Nederlandt, om Couragieus te strijden tegen die van Engelandt, Verhandlende mede de prinsipaelste Victorien en Overwinningen ter Zee...* (Schoonhoven: Samuel Knudde, 1665).
140. For example, Verz. Thysius: *Copie van een Brief van den Heere Admirael Spilberghen...* (Delf: Andriessz., 1617); Verz. Thysius: *Pertinant Verhael van alle het gene in de Zeeslagt tusschen de Engelse, France, en Vereenighde nederlandsche Vlooten is vorrgevallen, op den 7 Junij 1672 en vervolgens* (Amsterdam: P. Arentsz, 1672); Verz. Thysius: *Verhaal Van de Zee-Battailje, Tusschen het Frans Konings-Schip... en het Schip De Faam, van Zeeland...* (Middelburg: S. Bruilois, 1689); Verz. Thysius: *Extract van een Brief, Geschreven uyt Parijs...* ('s-Gravenhage: Abraham de Hondt, November 10, 1702); and Verz. ZBP: Martinum Bruynvisch, *De Banieren des Heeren, Ofte... Ter gedachtenisse van die... Victorye,... over de machtige Spaensche Vlote...* (Ziericzee: Balthazar Doll, 1640; and Middleburgh: Hans vander Hellen, 1640).
141. See, e.g., Verz. RLP: *Rotterdams Zee-Praatjen; Tusschen Een Koopman, een Borger en een Stierman...* (Schiedam: de Rechte Liefhebbers van de Vrye Nederlandsche Republik, 1653), which discusses the virtues of Admirals de Ruyter and Tromp in battle, dubbing them "Sea Lions" for their courage (8 and 29); and Verz. RLP: *Een Praatje Van Den Ouden en Nieuwen Admiral...*), which lauds Maarten Tromp.
142. See, e.g., the letter from Admiral Cornelis Tromp, written "at the front" and giving an account of a battle against the English in 1665 in Verz. Thysius: *Hollandtze Mercurius* (1666), 72–74.
143. Lambert Van Den Bosch, *Leven en Daden van de Doorluchtige Zeehelden* (Amsterdam: Jan Claesz. ten Hoorn & Jan Bouman, 1676). For more on this volume, see Scheltama, *Nederlandsche Letterkunde*, 136, #778.

144. Jean Pierre Camus Belley, *De Groote Schouwplaets der jammerrlijcke bloed-en-moord geschiedenissen* . . ., trans. Simon de Vries (Utrecht: J. Ribbius, 1670), see dedication.
145. Belley, *De Groote Schouwplaets* . . ., 6.
146. Verz. RLP: *Een Praatje Van Den Ouden en Nieuwen Admiraal* . . ., title page, 4 and 22.
147. Verz. RLP: *Rotterdams Zee-Praatjen* . . ., 8 and 29.
148. Verz. Thysius: *Victori-liedt op en Scheep-strijt tusschen de Armade des Conings van Spagnien, ende de Schepen van Oorloge . . . Onder 't beleyt van . . . Jacob van Heemskerk, Gheschiet den 25sten April Anno 1607 . . . voor Gibralter* (1607), see title.
149. Scheurleer, *Van Varen en Van Vechten*, Vols. I–III.
150. Verz. Thysius: *Copye van Seeckenen Brief, geschreven uyt Mideelburch* . . . (Middelburgh, 1645).
151. Verz. RLP: *Vervolg van Het Rotterdams Zee-Praatje* . . . (Middelburg: Gerrit Jansz. van Hoorn, 1653), 3.
152. Gerard Brandt, *Het Leven en Bedryf van den Heere Michiel de Ruiter* (Amsterdam: Voor Wolfgang, Waasberge, Boom, Van Someren en Goethals, 1687). The third edition was printed in Amsterdam, The Hague, and Rotterdam in 1732.
153. Verz. RLP: *Vervolg van Het Rotterdams Zee-Praatje* . . . (1653), 3–4 notes that Zeelanders were upset and angry about the portrayal of their admiral, Jan Evertszoon, in an earlier pamphlet. Consequently, the States-General banned further publication of this incendiary work, and slapped fines on both the pamphlet's author and printer.
154. Cynthia Lawrence, "Hendrick de Keyser's Heemskerk Monument: The Origins of the Cult and Iconography of Dutch Naval Heroes," *Simiolus: Netherlands Quarterly for the History of Art*, Vol. 21, No. 4 (1992), 268.
155. Lawrence, "Dutch Naval Heroes," 272. See also Schama, *The Embarassment of Riches*, 246–247. This is not to say that the army did not receive some public adulation as well. Complimentary pamphlets appeared when the Dutch army won battles, and nationalistic language was used to report the victories. See, e.g., two pamphlets about the Dutch victory over the Spanish army at Oostende: Verz. Thysius: *Waerachtick Verhael van den grooten Slach* . . . (Dordrecht: Jac. Canin, 1600); and Verz. Thysius: *Waerachtich Verhael vanden grooten Slach, ende gheluckighe Victorie . . . tusschen Oosteynde ende Nieupoort* . . . (Haerlem: G. Rooman, 1600).
156. Lawrence, "Dutch Naval Heroes," 272. See also Schama, *The Embarassment of Riches*, 246.
157. Lawrence, "Dutch Naval Heroes," 272.
158. Lawrence, "Dutch Naval Heroes," 269.
159. Lawrence, "Dutch Naval Heroes," 269.
160. Verz. Thysius: *Victori-liedt op en Scheep-strijt tusschen de Armade des Conings van Spagnien, ende de Schepen van Oorloge . . . Onder 't beleyt van . . . Jacob van Heemskerk* . . . (1607), see verse 10.
161. Lawrence, "Dutch Naval Heroes," 277–278. She notes also that three later naval hereos Piet Heyn (d. 1629), Maerten Tromp (d. 1653), and Michiel de Ruyter (d. 1677) were similarly honored.
162. Lawrence, "Dutch Naval Heroes," 274 and 280. Lawrence adds that Heemskerk's grave in the Oude Kerk served as the site for a general shrine for the Admiralty of Amsterdam's famous slain officers.

163. For a description of the Heemskerk memorial, as well as an explication of its complicated iconography, see Lawrence, "Dutch Naval Heroes," 280–290.
164. Verz. RLP: *Een Praatje Van Den Ouden en Nieuwen Admiraal . . .* (1653), 3.
165. Verz. RLP: *Een Praatje Van Den Ouden en Nieuwen Admiraal . . .* (1653), 8.
166. "Aan den Deurlugtigen Zeehelt, Cornelis Tromp, Vice-Admiral van Hollandt" (1666), in Scheurleer, *Van Varen en Van Vechten*, Vol. II, 200. For other poems and songs about the admiral, see Scheurleer, *Van Varen en Van Vechten*, Vol. II, 197–201.
167. See, e.g., the widely circulated engraving, Verz. ZBP: *Zee-triomph vanden Manhaften E. Admirael Marten Harpensen Tromp mitsgaders den slagh ter zee tusschen hem en de Duynkerckers, Anno 1639* ('t Amsterdam: Cornelis Danckertsz, 1639).
168. Dapper, *Historische*, 251–252.
169. Prud'homme van Reine, "Nederlandse Kaapvaart," 53.
170. See, e.g., Verz. RLP: *Rouwklage, over de dood van Hollands grooten Admirael, de Heer Michaël de Ruyter* (Rotterdam: J. Oudaan, 1676); and Verz. ZBP: *Het klagende Vaderland, Over het afsterven Van . . . Michael de Ruiter, Ridder . . .* (1676). For many more pamphlets on this same subject, see Broekema, *Catalogus*, #1346–1354 and #1378.
171. See Scheurleer, *Van Varen en Van Vechten*, Vol. II, 497–539.
172. Verz. Thysius: *Hollandtze Mercurius* (1666), 68. It is interesting to note that one of the ships in the fleet was named the *Tromp*. Whether this title was intended to honor the admiral(s), or meant to invoke the "muzzle of a gun" (as the word *tromp* can be translated) is difficult to determine. However, one might guess the latter, since the ship was actually sailing under Admiral Cornelis Tromp's command, and such an extreme manifestation of admiral worship seems a bit excessive, the Republic's intense adulation of its naval heroes notwithstanding.
173. George S. Keyes, *Mirror of Empire: Dutch Marine Art of the Seventeenth Century* (Cambridge: Cambridge University Press), 146.
174. Verz. Thysius: *Hollandtze Mercurius* (1666), 92.
175. Lawrence, "Dutch Naval Heroes," 291.
176. Lawrence, "Dutch Naval Heroes," 272.
177. That is, that members of the nation are bound together by the awareness—the memory—of certain fundamental transformative events whose very divisive details they decided to transcend and "forget."
178. For an exhaustive compilation of these songs, see E.T. Kuiper, *Het Geuzenliedboek*, 2 vols. (Zutphen: W.J. Thieme & Cie, 1925).
179. See the photo of the title page of this 1581 edition in Kuiper, *Het Geuzenliedboek*, Vol. II, ii.
180. See, e.g., *Het Nieuwe Bossche Geuse Lied-Boek Anders genaemt Oranjens Triumph-Liedekens* (Dordrecht: Hendrik Walpot, 1728–1759). Dronckers notes that this edition originally appeared shortly after 1629. See Dronckers *Varzameling F.G. Waller*, #605.
181. See *Het Geuse Liedt-Boeck, Waer in begrepen is den Oorspronk ven de troublen der Nederlantsche Oorlogen en het gene daer op gevolght is . . .* (Dordrecht: Symon Onder de Linde, 1687). The book includes a woodcut portrait of a typical Beggar with the motto "Vive le Geus."
182. For example, see *Het Geuse Liedt-Boeck . . .*, whose extended title advertises that the work is *Van nieuws over-sien en met verscheyde Refereynen en Liedekens vermeerdert.*

183. Simon Schama calls the *Wilhelmus* "the first recognizable national anthem in European history." See Schama, *The Embarassment of Riches*, 103.
184. Verz. RLP: Jan van Hilten, *Waerachtich verhael vande victorieuse Zee-Strijt tusschen acht Portugysche Galeoenen ende vier Hollandsche met vier Enghelsche Schepen* . . . (Amsterdam:Weduwe van Jacob Jacobsz, 1626), 2.
185. Schama, *The Embarassment of Riches*, 93.
186. See, e.g., Verz. Thysius: *Ten Waer Saecke (Goede Vrunden) dat U Luyder Ooghen* . . . (Leiden: October 5, 1574).
187. J.J. Orlers, *Beschrijvinge der Stadt Leyden* (Leiden, 1641), 520–522.
188. Jacob Duym, *Belegering der Stad Leyden* (1606).
189. Reynerius Bontius, *Belegering en Ontsetting der Stad Leyden, Geschied in den Jare 1574* . . ., 2nd edition (Leyden: Iacob Tinnekens, 1646). Date of first printing unknown.
190. *Amsterdam Donderdaghse Courant*, September 20, 1685 (No. 38).
191. *Ordinaire Leydse Courant*, October 5, 1686 (No. 82), "Nederlanden" section.
192. Van Der Werff Park is named after the man who was the mayor of Leiden during the siege. This stalwart leader, rather than surrender to the reviled Spanish, offered his own body as food for his fellow citizens and encouraged them to hold out bravely. Fortunately, the Sea Beggars arrived before the townspeople had to resort to cannibalism.
193. For example, see Geeraert Brandt, *Historie der vermaerde zee- en koopstad, Enkhuizen* . . . (Enkhuisen: Egbert van den Hoof, 1666), 111–112, for a copy of a Sea Beggar commission given by William the Silent to Enkhuizen resident Pieter L. Buiskes.
194. These mock battles are still reenacted each year. See Schama, *The Embarassment of Riches*, 93.
195. Schama, *The Embarassment of Riches*, 93.
196. For example, "Victory-Liedeken: Van de Zeeslag in Duyns" (1639); "Roomsche-Vreucht, op de Spaensche-Winst Door den Hollantschen Tromp" (1639); and "Geuse-Bril, op Paepse Neusen" (1639); in Scheurleer, *Van Varen en Van Vechter*, Vol. I, 296–299, 305–307, and 308–309.
197. Verz. Thysius: *Waerachtigh verhael Van het success van de Vlote onder den Admirael Jaques L'Hermite* . . . *Hier is Een Spaensche Brief by-ghevoeght* . . . (1625), 12.
198. See the "Zeeusche Nachtegael" in Landwehr, *De Nederlander uit en Thuis*, 53–54.
199. Verz. Thysius: *Sommiere Loffelijcke beschrijvinge van* . . . *Zeelandt. Midtsgaders de Daden* . . . *der* . . . *Zeelanderen* (Amsterdam: J.Fz. Stam,1636), 1 and 6. For other chronicles of the province, see Johan Reygersbergen, *Chroniik van Zeeland, Eertijds Beschreven door d'Heer Johan Reygersbergen, Nu Verbetert ende Vermeerderdt door Marcus Zuerius Boxhorn* (Middelburg: Zacharius ende Michiel Roman, 1644); and M. Smallegange, *Nieuwe Cronyk van Zeeland* (Middelburg: Joannes Meertens, 1696).
200. Verz. Thysius: States of Zeeland, *Propositie van de* . . . *Staten van Zeelant, Aen de* . . . *Staten Generael, om ordre te stellen tegens de Portugaelsche Commissie vaerders* . . ., May 23, 1662 (Vlissingen: T. Tyssen, 1662).
201. J.Th.H. Verhees-van Meer, *De Zeeuwse Kaapvaart Tijdens de Spaanse Successieoorlog 1702–1713* (Middelburg: Werken Uitgegeven door het Koninklijk Zeeuwsch Genootschap der wetenschappen, Deel 3, 1986), passim.
202. ARA, AA, Verz. Bisdom #13: *Index op het Recueil 'T Admiraliteit*, Vol. I, fol. 29. Entry reads: "Klagten aan de Admiraliteit te Amsterdam over die aan Zeeland nopens het te regt stellen den Prinse. 14 October 1604."

203. Verz. RLP: *Rotterdams Zee-Praatjen* ... (1653), 21.
204. Verz. RLP: *Vervolg van Het Rotterdams Zee-Praatje* ... (1653), 3–4.
205. Verz. RLP: *Vervolg van Het Rotterdams Zee-Praatje* ... (1653), 4–5.
206. Verz. Thysius: *Copye Van seeckeren Brief, geschreven uyt Middelburch* ... (1645).
207. Verz. Thysius: *Copye Van seeckeren Brief, geschreven uyt Middelburch* ..., 1–6. I do not know how this matter was eventually resolved.
208. Verz. Thysius: H. van V, *Den Oprechten Hollandsen Bootgesel. Vertoond in een t'Zamenspraak tussen drie Persoonen ... Gehoord, gezien en te zamen gesteld. Tot onderrechtinge van de vrome en welmeende Patriotten* (Rotterdam: Jan Isaakse, 1666).
209. Verz. Thysius: *Den Oprechten Hollandsen Bootgesel* ..., 5.
210. Verz. Thysius: *Den Oprechten Hollandsen Bootgesel* ..., 5.
211. Simon Groeneveld, "Beeldvorming en realiteit. Geschiedschrijving en achtergronden van de Nederlandse Opstand tegen Filips II," in P.A.M. Geurts and A.E.M. Janssen, eds., *Geschiedschrijving in Nederland* ('s-Gravenhage: Nijhoff, 1981), 64. See also his "Natie en nationaal gevoel in de sestiende-eeuwse Nederlanden," in *Scrinium et Scriptura. Opstellen betreffende de Nederlandse geschiedenis aangeboden aan J.L. van der Gouw* (Groningen: Erven B. van der Kamp, 1980), 372–387.
212. Schama, *The Embarassment of Riches*, 57.
213. Verz. RLP: *Goede Apparentie tot Spoedige opkomst, Der Vrye Nederlandens Magtige Zee-Vaart* ... (1653), 8.
214. "Een Nieuw Lied over de Tegenwoordige Toerustinge van Oorlog," in Scheurleer, *Van Varen en Van Vechten*, Vol. II, 358–361.
215. Johan de Witt quoted in Herbert H. Rowen, *John de Witt: Grand Pensionary of Holland* (Princeton: Princeton University Press, 1978), 388–389.
216. Verz. Thysius: *Den Oprechten Hollandsen Bootgesel* ..., 1.
217. Verz. Thysius: *Den Oprechten Hollandsen Bootgesel* ..., 1.
218. Verz. Thysius: *Den Oprechten Hollandsen Bootgesel* ..., 3–5.
219. Verz. Thysius: *Den Oprechten Hollandsen Bootgesel* ..., 4.
220. Verz. Thysius: *Den Oprechten Hollandsen Bootgesel* ..., 5. It should be noted that he is criticizing Admiral Cornelis Tromp in this passage.
221. For more on this idea, see Rowen and Harline, "The Birth of the Dutch Nation."
222. Verz. RLP: *Goede Apparentie tot Spoedige opkomst, Der Vrye Nederlandens Magtige Zee-Vaart* ..., 8.
223. See, e.g., this poetic work—Verz. ZBP: *Sonnet op d'onsterskijcke Lof van onse Bataefsche Zee-Heldin* (Amsterdam: Cornelis Danckertsz, 1639); and this pamphlet—Verz. Thysius: *Opweckingh en moed-gevingh aen de Bataviers van 't wydt Beroempt Nederlandt* ... (Schoonhoven: Samuel Knudde, 1665).
224. Schama, *The Embarassment of Riches*, 76. As Schama points out, it is hardly surprising that seventeenth-century scholarship depicted the Batavians as "hardy, frugal, industrious, pious, brave, hospitable ... and addicted to cleanliness and liberty," for all were qualities that Golden Age Dutch culture revered (78).
225. Examples are almost too numerous to cite, but see, e.g., a pamphlet such as Verz. Thysius: *Den Lof vande Geoctr. Oost ende West-Indische Compagnye ende Lofrijcke Zee-vaert* ... (1630), a praise poem that lauds the maritime commerce of "dit Landt" (11); States-General edicts, such as Verz. Thysius: *Publikatie* ..., April 14, 1672 ('s-Gravenhage: Iac. Scheltus, 1672), which was intended for the "goede Ingesetenen ende Patriotten van den Lande" who are

"ten dienste van het lieve Vaderlant ge-encourageert..."; and Verz. RLP: *Artickels-Brief ende Instructie roerende den Oorloghe ter Zee* ... (April 27, 1629); a laudatory, patriotic pamphlet, Verz. Thysius: *Opweckingh en moed-gevingh aen de Bataviers van 't wydt Beroempt Nederlandt*... (Schoonhoven: Samuel Knudde, 1665); "Lyk-Klacht" (1676), in Scheurleer, *Van Varen en Van Vechten*, Vol. II, 509–510; and Simon de Vries's reference to his country as "Nederland" rather than "Nederlanden" in de Vries, *Historie van Barbaryen*, 64.

226. See, e.g., Gerard Brandt, *Chronyxken Der voornaemste Nederlantsche Gheschiedenissen, soo Kerckelijck asl Politijcq*..., 3rd edition (Amsterdam: Borrit Iansz. Smit, 1657); and Romyn de Hoogh, *Spiegel van Staat Des Vereenigde Nederlands*... (1706–1707).
227. See, e.g., *Realia*: GGR, VOC, October 31, 1643; and Dionisius van der Sterre, *Zeer aenmerkelijke reysen gedaan door Jan Erasmus Reying*... (Amsterdam: Jan ten Hoorn, 1691), 27.
228. H. van de Waal, *Drie Eeuwen Vanderlandsche Geschied-Uitbeelding, 1500–1800* ('s-Gravenhage, 1917), Vol. 1, 62, cited in Schama, *The Embarassment of Riches*, 71 and 72.
229. Dapper, *Historische*, 249–250.
230. *Amsterdamze Mercurius*, April 1689, 29.
231. Verz. RLP: M. van Bohemen, *Practijcke van den Spaenschen Aes-Sack op de Veroveringe, en Victorie van den Loffelicken, Voorsienighen, Manlijck-hertighen Heer Generael Pieter Pietersz. Heyn*... ('s-Gravenhage, 1629).

4 Piracy, the Dutch, and the Seventeenth-Century Seas

1. Andrew Barker, *A True and Certaine Report of the Beginning, Proceedings, Overthrowes, and now Present Estate of Captaine WARD and DANSEKER, the Two Late Famous Pirates*... (London: William Hall, 1609; New York and Amsterdam: Da Capo Press & Theatrum Orbis Terrarum Ltd., 1968), 13.
2. An incredibly popular text, *The Buccaneers of America* went through a number of reprintings and translations during the early modern period. From edition to edition and country to country, Exquemelin's name took on different forms and spellings. I will use a variant spelling only if the text lists it as such.
3. Alexander O. Exquemelin, *The Buccaneers of America*, trans. Alexis Brown (1684; Mineola, NY: Dover, 1969), 106–107.
4. Primary accounts such as those of Basil Ringrose, William Dampier, Edward Barlow, and Robert Drury have formed the bedrock of firsthand knowledge about piracy. The 1724 "bestseller" by Captain Charles Johnson (perhaps Daniel Defoe) *The General History of the Robberies and Murders of the Most Notorious Pyrates*—a compendium of contemporary data about piracy, including transcriptions of piracy trials and articles from London newspapers, as well as possible interviews of seamen and former pirates—represents one of the more important primary sources. See William Dampier, *A Collection of Voyages* (1729); Basil Lubbock, ed., *Barlow's Journal of His Life at Sea in King's Ships, East and West Indiamen and Other Merchantmen from 1659–1703* (London: Hurst & Blackett, 1934); and Charles Johnson, *A General History of the Robberies and Murders of the Most Notorious Pyrates* (London, 1724). For a modern edition of Dampier, see William Dampier, *A New Voyage Round the World* (New York: Dover, 1968). For a recent, annotated edition of Johnson's text, see Daniel Defoe, ed. Manuel Schonhorn, *A General History of the Pyrates* (Mineola, NY: Dover, 1999).

5. Notable, informative accounts include Raveneau de Lussan, *Journal du voyage fait à la Mer du Sud* (Paris, 1689); also see the English translation, Ravenau de Lussan, trans. M.E. Wilbur, *Journal of a Voyage into the South Seas* (Cleveland, OH: Arthur H. Clark, 1930); E. Ducéré, *Journal de bord d'un flibustier (1686–1693)* (Bayonne, 1894); Montauban, *Relation du Voyage Du Sieur Montauban, Capitaine des Flibustiers . . . en l'an 1625* (Amsterdam: de Lorme, 1698); Jean-Baptiste Lepers, *La tragique histoire des Flibustiers: Histoire de Saint-Domingue et de l'ile de la Tortue, repaiers des flibustiers, écrite vers 1715*, ed. Pierre-Bernard Berthelot (Paris: G. Crès, 1925); and Louis Adhemar Timothée Le Golif, *Memoirs of a Buccaneer . . .* (London: George Allen & Unwin, 1954). Gérard A. Jaeger's bibliography of French memoirs and studies is most helpful in identifying such relevant material. See Gérard A. Jaeger, *Les Aventuriers de la Mer: Biblographie Thematique (XVIe–XXe Siècle)* (Lausanne: Editions Le Front Litteraire, 1983), 73–79.
6. David Cordingly, *Under the Black Flag: The Romance and the Reality of Life Among the Pirates* (New York: Random House, 1995), xvi.
7. Marcus Rediker, *Between the Devil and the Deep Blue Sea: Merchant Seamen, Pirates and the Anglo-American Maritime World, 1700–1750* (Cambridge: Cambridge University Press), 254–255.
8. In the face of such difficulties, it is admirable that Marcus Rediker even attempts to provide estimates of the pirate population, although it must be remembered that he deals only with what he terms "Anglo-American" pirates. Citing both primary sources (such as contemporary estimates and "records which describe the activities of pirate ships and reports or projections of crew sizes") and other secondary literature, Rediker guesses that there were 1,800–2,400 Anglo-American pirates between 1716 and 1718; 1,500–2,000 between 1719 and 1722; and 1,000–1,500 between 1723 and 1726, before ultimately declining to 200. He adds that one extant eighteenth-century source written by pirates themselves calculates that their folk numbered approximately 2,400 men at that moment, or during the years of the early eighteenth century generally, a total of 4,500–5,500 individuals. At any rate, Rediker's calculations indicate that the pirate community he profiles was formidable in size and strength, and therefore represented a truly fearsome threat to merchant shipping. See Rediker, *Between the Devil and the Deep Blue Sea*, 256. In note 4 on this page, Rediker details his many sources and how he arrived at his estimates.
9. For a history of piracy in the Mediterranean, see Fontenay and Tenenti, "Course et Piraterie Méditerranéennes de las Fin du Moyen Age au Début du XIXème Siècle," *Course et Piraterie*, ed. Commission Internationale d'Histoire Maritime (Paris: Institut de Recherche et d'Histoire des Textes/Editions du Centre National de la Recherche Scientifique, 1975).
10. Carlos Saiz Cidoncha, *Historia de la Piratería en América Española* (Madrid: Editorial San Martin, 1985), 26–27.
11. See, e.g., the report in the *Ordinaire Leydse Courant*, August 29, 1686, "Nederlanden" section, which relates that the French had just sent four frigates to America, "to suppress the pirates there."
12. For more on beleaguered Spanish outposts and the crown's attempts to protect them, see the following documents: AGI, Panama 30, N. 68: *Cartas y Expedientes de Cabildos Seculares: Panamá*, 1616; AGI, Mexico 28, N. 28; Panama 95: *Entrada de Piratas en Portobelo, Darien y Mar del Sur*, 1679–1681; AGI, Panama 96: *Entrada de Piratas en Portobelo, Darien y Mar del Sur*, 1682–1687; AGI, Indiferente 2578: *Piratas en las Costas de Barlovento*,

1681–1684; AGI, Santo Domingo 856: *Invasión de Piratas en la Florida*, 1684–1702; AGI, Guatemala 42, N. 77: *Caratas de Cabildos Seculares*, March 18, 1671; AGI, Panama 81: *Empréstito de 1000,000 Pesos para Rescutar Portobelo*, 1678; and AGI, Panama 99: *Resguardo del Darién y Tierra Firme contra la Pirateria*, 1683–1694.
13. Jack Beeching, Introduction to Exquemelin, *Buccaneers of America*, 13.
14. Auguste Toussaint, "Rapport: La Course et la Piraterie dans l'Océan Indien," *Course et Piraterie...*, Vol. III ed. Commission Internationale d'Histoire Maritime (Paris: Institut de Recherche et d'Histoire des Textes/Editions de Centre National de la Recherche Scientifique, 1975), 101–102.
15. Toussaint, "Rapport," 101–102. For a historical overview of piracy in this region, see Toussaint's, "La Course et la Piraterie dans l'Océan Indien," *Course et Piraterie*, Vol. II, 703–743.
16. Rediker, *Between the Devil and the Deep Blue Sea*, 258 and 260.
17. See, for instance, a seventeenth-century pamphlet that describes the pirate crew which pursued the Dutch ship the *Aernem*: Verz. RLP: Johannes van Kerckhoven, *Wijtloopig breede en waerachtige Beschrijvinge Van de Ongeluckige Voyage van 't Schip AERNEM...* (Amsterdam: Jacobus vander Fuyck, 1664).
18. Robert C. Ritchie, *Captain Kidd and the War Against the Pirates* (Cambridge: Harvard University Press, 1986), 22. Also, for various examples, see Exquemelin, *Buccaneers of America*, passim.
19. Defoe, *A General History of the Pyrates*, 148–165.
20. Rediker, *Between the Devil and the Deep Blue Sea*, 260–261.
21. See, e.g., Cordingly, who writes of Exquemelin: "Careful comparison of his stories with the events described in Spanish documents of the period has shown that he gets most of the facts right but is often mistaken about place-names and dates. Some of his wilder stories appear to be secondhand accounts which he probably heard in taverns, but it is clear that he took part in a number of buccaneer expeditions... Exquemelin's book... has provided the basis for all serious histories of the buccaneers and, in spite of some inaccuracies, remains the standard work on the subject." Cordingly, *Under the Black Flag*, 40. For another balanced appraisal of Exquemelin, Cordingly further recommends Peter Earle, *The Sack of Panama* (New York: Viking Press, 1982), 265–266.
22. Exquemelin, *Buccaneers of America*, passim.
23. Exquemelin, *Buccaneers of America*, 151.
24. It is seems fitting that according to Exquemelin, L'Ollonais met his own horrible end, imprisoned by native American peoples, at the hands of whom he "was hacked to pieces and roasted limb by limb..." Exquemelin, *Buccaneers of America*, 104 and 117.
25. Cordingly, *Under the Black Flag*, 127, 129, 131–132.
26. See, e.g., ARA, VOC #7417: *Trefwoordenrepertorium op de Resoluties van de Heren XVII*, December 2, 1688, fol. 222; and ARA, VOC #345: *Zakenindex op de uitgaande missiven van de Heren XVII aan de kantoren in Indie*, April 21, 1690, fol. 573.
27. For example, ARA, VOC #680: *Kopie-Resolutie, GGR, Ingekomen Stukken uit Indie* (Heren Zeventien en Kamer Amsterdam): "Het roven op de Cust...," November 25, 1665; and *Realia*, Vol. I, 224: Generale Resolutie, GGR. By 1700, the Company decided to exempt the Papuaese people—at least those sailing along the coasts of Ceram—from such a label. See ARA, VOC #715: *Kopie-Resolutie, GGR, Ingekomen Stukken uit Indie* (Heren Zeventien en Kamer

Amsterdam): "De Papoese vaartuijgen op de Noordcust...," January 22, 1700; and *Realia*, Vol. I, 224: "Generale Resolutie," GGR.
28. *Ordinaire Leydse Courant*, October 3, 1686 (No. 81), "Spanjen" section.
29. J.J. Baud, *Proeve eener Geschiedenis der Strafwetgeving tegen de Zeerooverij* (Utrecht: D. Post Uiterweer, 1854), 100.
30. Verz. RLP: Johannes van Kerckhoven, *Wijtloopig breede en waerachtige Beschrijvinge Van de ongeluckige Voyage van 't Schip AERNEM*... (Amsterdam: Jacobus vander Fuyck, 1664); and Andries Stokram, *Korte Beschryvinge Van de Ongeluckige Weerom-reys van het Schip Aernhem*... (Amsterdam: Jacob Venckel, 1663).
31. ARA, VOC #4043 (Overgekomen brieven en papieren uit Kaap de Goede Hoop en Mauritius aan de Heren XVII en de Kamer Amsterdam): *Brief van Capitein Jan Coin*, February 13, 1700.
32. ARA, VOC #4043 (Overgekomen brieven en papieren uit Kaap de Goede Hoop en Mauritius aan de Heren XVII en de Kamer Amsterdam): April 8, 1699, fol. 280.
33. ARA, VOC#7417: *Trefwoordenrepertorium op de Resoluties van de Heren XVII*, December 2, 1688, fol. 222.
34. *Ordinaire Leydse Courant*, December 12, 1686 (No. 111), "Spanjen" section.
35. *Ordinaire Leydse Courant*, July 9, 1686 (No. 44), "Nederlanden" section.
36. *Ordinaire Leydse Courant*, November 12, 1686 (No. 98), "Nederlanden" section.
37. ARA, WIC #24: *Algemeene alphabetisch register op de notulen... Vergadering van Tienen*, section on "Zeeroverijen," June 6, 1682; October 11, 1682; November 11, 16, and 20, 1684; April 13, 1685; and November 28, 1686.
38. ARA, WIC #24: *Algemeene alphabetisch register op de notulen... Vergadering van Tienen*: Section on "Retorsie," November 10, 1706.
39. ARA, WIC #468: *Kopieboek van brieven naar Amerika*, November 17, 1684, fol. 38.
40. ARA, WIC #468: *Kopieboek van brieven naar Amerika*, December 13, 1686, fol. 106.
41. Verz. Thysius: *Placcaet ende Ordonnantie op de Verzeeckerheyt vande Scheepvaert tusschen Hollandt ende Zeelandt* (Delff: A. Hendricxz, 1589).
42. *Ordinaire Leydse Courant*, July 23, 1686 (No. 50), "Nederlanden" section.
43. See, e.g., "Tot den Zee-Man in 't Generael" (ca. 1655), and "Aan de Hollandsche Matrozen" (ca. 1658), in D.F. Scheurleer, *Van Varen en van Vechten*, Vol. II ('s-Gravenhage: Martinus Nijhoff, 1914), 2 and 60.
44. ARA, AA, Verz. Bisdom #123: *Lyste op de Placaten en Orders Rakende Commissievaarders en Vreemde Kapers*, 1627–1673.
45. For example, States-General, "Placaat tot weeringe van Vyandeliyke Kaapers," February 24, 1696, *Recueil van Alle de Placaten... betreffende de Admiraliteiten...*, Vol. II, 283; and "Placaat tegens Vyandelyke Kaapers binnen de Tonnen en Stroomen," May 28, 1702, *Recueil van Alle de Placaten... betreffende de Admiraliteiten...*, Vol. III, 178.
46. ARA, AA, Verz. Bisdom #123: Placaat, August 9, 1658, *Lyste op de Placaten en Orders Rakende Commissievaarders en Vreemde Kapers*, 1627–1673.
47. See, in *Recueil van Alle de Placaten... betreffende de Admiraliteiten...*, "Placaat tegens het rantçoeneeren van Scheepen," June 12, 1690, Vol. II, 165; and "Resolutie tot stricte observantie van de Placaten tegens het rantçoeren van genoomen Scheepen," June 28, 1692, Vol. II, 218 vs.
48. *Ordinaire Leydse Courant*, October 8, 1686 (No. 83), "Nederlanden, s'Gravenhage..." section.

49. See, e.g., Verz. Thysius: *Placcaet ende Ordonnantie op de Verzeeckerheyt vande Scheepvaert tusschen Hollandt ende Zeelandt* (Delff: A. Hendricxz, 1589); and *Ordinaire Leydse Courant*, October 8, 1586 (No. 83), "Nederlanden: s'Gravenhage . . ." section.
50. ARA, AA, Verz. Bisdom #107: *Advis van de Lieutenanten Admiraals van Holland en Zeeland en de Aanwesende Gecommt. uijt de Collegien ter Admirl. tegens het Placcat van de Koning van Spagne op de vrijbuijt . . .*, March 19, 1622.
51. R.A. Stradling, "The Spanish Dunkirkers, 1621–48: A Record of Plunder and Destruction," *Tijdschrift voor Geschiedenis*, Vol. XCIII (1980), 543. For more on this general Spanish strategy, see 541–544.
52. ARA, AA, Verz. Bisdom #107: *Advis van de Lieutenanten Admiraals van Holland en Zeeland en de Aanwesende Gecommt. uijt de Collegien ter Admirl. tegens het Placcat van de Koning van Spagne op de vrijbuijt . . .*, March 19, 1622.
53. Verz. ZBP: *Placaat van de Staten-Generaal dd. 4 Juli 1625, waarbij sommen worden uitgeloofd voor het veroveren of vernielen van Spaansche Schepen* ('s-Gravenhage: de Weduwe . . . van wijlen Hillebrandt Jacobssz van Wouw, 1625). See also *Groot Placaet-Boeck van de Staten-Generaal en van Holland en Zeeland* (The Hague/Amsterdam, 1658–1796), I, 975.
54. Verz. RLP: *Placcaet ende Ordonnantie opte Wapeninge ende Manninge vande Schepen, soo ter coopvaerdye als Visscherye uytte Vereen. Nederlanden over Zee varende . . .* ('s-Gravenhage: Wed. en Erfg. van H. Jzn. v. Wouw . . ., 1625).
55. Verz. RLP: *Amsterdams Tafel-Praetje Van Wat Goets en Wat Quats En Wat Noodichs* (Gouda: Iasper Cornelisz, 1649), 17.
56. *Ordinaire Leydse Courant*, June 4, 1686 (No. 29), "Nederlanden" section. The captain of the captured ship was listed as one Boudewijn Joannisse.
57. ARA, WIC #1180: *Brief van Lucas Schorck aan de Zeeland Kamer*, April 17, 1688.
58. Nicolaes Wassenaer, *Historisch Verhael aller gedenkwaerdiger geschiedenissen . . .*, Vol. 14 (Amsterdam: Jan Jansz., 1627–1628), 24.
59. Wassenaer, *Historisch*, 24–25.
60. Verz. Thysius: *Propositie van de Edele Mogende Heeren Staten van Zeelant Aen de Hoogh-Mogende Heren Staten Generael, om ordre te stellen tegens de Portugaelsche Commissie vaerders . . .*, May 23, 1662 (Vlissingen: T. Tyssen, 1662).
61. ARA, Verz. Radermacher #86: *Acte tegen het aandoen van de Zoute Eylanden*, 1683.
62. Stradling, "The Spanish Dunkirkers," 544.
63. Henri Malo's archival research in 1913 yielded the first significant figures when he reproduced an official seventeenth-century table that tallied prizes captured during the years 1627–1634. It was not until fairly recently, however, that any other scholar contributed further to this question. Using many of the same records that Malo consulted, the work of the Belgian scholar R. Baetens, as well as that of Spanish historian J. Alcalá-Zamora, has made new inroads, although since the two men's sums differ significantly, their assessments have created some confusion too. Therefore, R. Stradling's estimates, based upon an entirely different set of archival sources, represents something of a breakthrough. See Henri Malo, *Les Corsaires: les corsaires Dunkerquois et Jean Bart*, Vol. I (Paris, 1913), 333–334; R. Baetens, "The Organization and Effects of Flemish Privateering in the Seventeenth Century," *Acta Historiae Neerlandica*, Vol. IX (1976), 48–75; J. Alcalá-Zamorra y Queipo de Llano, *España, Flandes, y el Mar del Norte, 1618–1639* (Barcelona, 1975); and Stradling, "The Spanish Dunkirkers", 546. Stradling was especially thorough: his main sources are the *somaires des prises*

(monthly lists of prize captures), documents that were kept in the office of the chief clerk (*greffier*) of the Admiralty; they are now preserved in the *Archives du Royaume* in Brussels. He also consulted quarterly and annual registers that were sent to Madrid, as well as other Spanish records.

64. Stradling, "The Spanish Dunkirkers," 547, Table 1.
65. See Stradling, "The Spanish Dunkirkers," 555, Table 4.
66. Stradling, "The Spanish Dunkirkers," 553, Table 3. He estimates that the number ranges from 325 to 533 vessels.
67. R. Baetens, "Organisatie en resultaten van de Vlaamse Kaapvaart in de 17e eeuw," *Mededelingen van de Belgische Marine Academie*, Vol. 21 (1969/1970), 106.
68. Jaap Bruijn, "Dutch Privateering during the Second and Third Anglo-Dutch Wars," *Course et Piraterie* ... ed. Commission Internationale d'Histoire Maritime, Vol. I (Paris: Institut de Recherche et d'Historie des Textes/Editions du Centre National de la Recherche Scientifique, 1975), 401.
69. After Dunkirk became a part of France in 1645, the city was again used as a base from which to attack Dutch shipping. See, e.g., a letter from the WIC archives, which notes that a captured WIC ship, the *Pelican*, was brought by French privateers to Dunkirk: ARA, WIC #467 (Tweede Comp., Kamer van Amsterdam): April 1, 1677, fol. 29 vs. For a brief overview of Jean Bart's illustrious career, see R.B. Prud'homme van Reine, "Nederlandse Kaapvaart en Piraterij in Beeld," *Kapers op de Kust: Nederlandse Kaapvaart en Piraterij, 1500–1800*, ed. Prud'homme van Reine and van der Oest (Vlissingen: Uitgervij ADZ, 1991).
70. Stradling, "The Spanish Dunkirkers," 546.
71. Prud'homme van Reine, "Nedertandse Kaapvaart en Piraterij," 39.
72. Geeraert Brandt, *Historie der vermaerde zee- en koopstad, Enkhuizen* ... (Enkhuizen: Egbert van den Hoof: 1666), 187, 200, and 202–205.
73. Velius, *Hoorn*, 525; and Brandt, *Enkhuizen*, 275–276, both cited in Baud, *Proeve eener* ... , 81.
74. ARA, AA, Verz. Bisdom #167: *Copie-Crimineele Vonnissen van de Admiraliteit op de Maas*, 1575–1710, fols. 11 vs–12 vs.
75. ARA, AA #2840 (College ter Admiraliteit in Zeeland): *Quitantie van Kapitin Legier Pietersen aan de Admiraliteit voor het nemen van een Duinkerker schip*, July 5, 1592; and ARA, AA, Verz. Bisdom #42: *Extract uit de Resolutien van haar Hoog. Mo. van 1604, 1605, 1606*, section under "Prinsen." The Dunkirkers appear here frequently.
76. ARA, AA, Verz. Bisdom #167: *Copie-Crimineele Vonnissen van de Admiraliteit op de Maas*, fols. 27 vs–28. Six other crewmembers were given lighter sentences, "because of their youth and other reasons." See fols. 28–28 vs.
77. ARA, AA, Verz. Bisdom #167: *Copie-Crimineele Vonnissen van de Admiraliteit op de Maas*, fols. 47–47 vs.
78. ARA, AA, Verz. Bisdom #167: *Copie-Crimineele Vonnissen van de Admiraliteit op de Maas*, fols. 54–54 vs.
79. ARA, AA, Verz. Bisdom #167: *Copie-Crimineele Vonnissen van de Admiraliteit op de Maas*, fols. 60 vs–63.
80. ARA, AA, Verz. Bisdom #167: *Copie-Crimineele Vonnissen van de Admiraliteit op de Maas*, fols. 98 vs–99 vs.
81. ARA, AA, Verz. Bisdom #107: *Extract uit het Register der Resolutien van de Ho. Mo. Heeren Staten Generaal der Vereenigde Nederlanden, op de besetting van de Vlaamsche kust, en de veijliging van de Zee* ... , February 6, 1626, The document indicates that the warships were to be 150 *lasten* in size, and the yachts

50–60 *lasten*. There are many such resolutions in this particular collection of documents.
82. Prud'homme van Reine, "Nederlandse Kaapvaart en Piraterij," 41.
83. Prud'homme van Reine, "Nederlandse Kaapvaart en Piraterij," 40–41.
84. Verz. Thysius: States-General, *Placaat*, February 28, 1678.
85. De Bosch Kemper, *Armoede* (1860 edition), 103 quoted in C.R. Boxer, *The Dutch Seaborne Empire, 1600–1800* (London: Hutchinson, 1965; London: Penguin Books, 1990), 76.
86. Verz. Thysius: *Duyn-Kerckens Naeckende Sterff-Dagh* . . . (ca. 1645), 5.
87. Verz. Thysius: Dionysium Spranckhuysen, *Triumphe Van weghen de Geluckighe ende Over-Rijcke Victorie . . . vanden Heer Generael Pieter Pietersz. Heyn . . .* (Delf: Jan Andriesz. Kloeting, 1629), 71.
88. Verz. Thysius: *Apologie of verdedingh van Capiteyn Pieter de Russchuer . . .* (Amsterdam), August 1, 1639, 3.
89. For examples of this practice, see the proclamations authorizing exchanges in 1634 and 1636, coordinated on the Dutch side by the *Schout* (Sherriff) of Rosendaal in *Recueil van Alle de Placaten . . . betreffende de admiraliteiten . . .*, Vol. II, 385 (December 8, 1634); and Vol. II, 386 vs (June 10, 1636).
90. See, e.g., Verz. Thysius: States-General, *Placaat*, February 28, 1678.
91. Verz. Thysius: *Duyn-Kercken Naeckende Sterff-Dagh* . . ., 6.
92. Verz. Thysius: *Duyn-Kerckens Naeckende Sterff-Dagh* . . ., 1–2.
93. ARA, WIC #23: *Algemeene alphabetishe register op de notulen . . . Vergadering van Tienen*, 1674–1748. This document states that French piracies took place on November 11, 16, and 20, 1685; April 13, 1685; and October 16, 1688. See heading of "Frankrijk."
94. All of the aforementioned cases can be found in ARA, WIC #467: *Kopieboeken van brieven naar Amerika . . .*, 1675–1684, fols. 22 vs, 29 vs, 36 vs, and 76 vs.
95. ARA, WIC #468: *Kopieboeken van brieven naar Amerkia . . .*, 1684–1689, fols. 16, 17 vs, 18 vs, and 26 vs.
96. ARA, WIC #24: *Algemeene alphabetisch register op de notulen, H-Z, Vergadering van Tienen*, 1674–1748.
97. ARA, WIC #865: March 20, 1675, *Alphabetisch zakelijke registers op de notulen der vergadering van Tienen, Zeeland Kamer*, 1674–1690, fol. 108.
98. *Realia*, I, 418: Generale Resolutie, GGR, March 13, 1618 (ARA, VOC #656: *Kopie-resolutie van President en Raden van de Kantoren in Bantam en Jakatra*, GGR). See also *Realia*, I, 418: Generale Resolutie, GGR, May 19, 1618 (ARA, VOC #656: *Kopie-resolutie . . .*, GGR).
99. ARA, VOC #718: *Kopie-Resolutie . . .*, GGR, "Twee Franse kapers . . .," December 16, 1703; *Realia*: Generale Resolutie, GGR, I, 269.
100. *Realia*, II, 95: Generale Resolutie, GGR, October 16, 1703 (see ARA, VOC #718: Kopie Resolutie . . ., GGR); and *Realia*, I, 269 and II, 95: Generale Resolutie, GGR, December 16, 1703 (see also ARA, VOC #718: *Kopie Resolutie*, GGR).
101. ARA, AA, Verz. Sweers #4: Isaac Sweers, *Journaal, gehouden door Sweers, op s' Land schip Der Goes . . .*, February 22, 1657–December 20, 1657.
102. ARA, AA, Verz. Sweers #4: Isaac Sweers, *Journaal, gehouden door Sweers, op s' Land schip Der Goes . . .*, entries for May 23, 1657; June 26, 1657; and June 27, 1657. One should note that the ship's scribe Isaac Sweers points out

that the Dutch assumed that the two ships off of the coast of Pantalleria were French because the vessels flew red flags.
103. Verz. Thysius: *Hollantse Mercurius* (Haerlem: Pieter Casteleyn, 1651).
104. Baud, 86–87.
105. See the cases of "Thomas Smit" and "Jan Dael" in ARA, Hof van Holland Archief: *Index op de Criminele Sententien van het Hof van Holland, 1538–1572 en 1623–1811,* 1572.
106. See the case of "Claas Thomsz." in ARA, AA, Verz. Bisdom #167: *Copie-Crimineele vonnissen van de Admiraliteit op de Maas,* fols. 86–88 vs.
107. Ralph Davis, *The Rise of the English Shipping Industry in the Seventeenth and Eighteenth Centuries* (London: Macmillan, 1962), 48–54.
108. Violet Barber, "Privateers and Pirates of the West Indies," *American Historical Review,* Vol. 16 (1910–1911), 547–551.
109. Verz. Thysius: *Hollandtze Mercurius...,* 16th edition (Haerlem: Pieter Casteleyn, 1666), 15–16. VOC records indicate that English privateers had been successful in the First Anglo-Dutch War as well, capturing at least one Company ship, the *Dolfijn,* in 1654. See ARA, VOC #11517 (Zeeland Kamer): *Sententie van het Hoge Hof van de Admiraliteit in Engeland betreffende de confiscatie van het VOC-schip Dolfijn,* 1654.
110. Verz. Thysius: *Hollandtze Mercurius...* (1666), 27.
111. Verz. Thysius: *Hollandtze Mercurius...* (1666), 27.
112. Verz. Thysius: *Hollandtze Mercurius...* (1666), 3.
113. Verz. Thysius: *Hollandtze Mercurius...* (1666), 6–7.
114. Verz. Thysius: *Hollandtze Mercurius...* (1666), 18.
115. Verz. Thysius: *Hollandtze Mercurius...* (1666), 31.
116. See, e.g., the various examples found in Scheurleer, *Van Varen en Van Vechten,* Vol. II, 79–88; 162–165; and 193.
117. Verz. RLP: *Goede Apparentie tot Spoedige opkomst, Der Vrye Nederlandens Magtige Zee-Vaart...* (1653), 5–6.
118. Verz. Thysius: L.B., *Klaght en Kort Verhael, Over de Engelschen haer hooghmoedige begeerlijckheyt, ongeregelde Zee-rooversche proceduren...* (1672).
119. Verz. Thysius: *Buere-Praetje Tusschen een Borger en een Matroos, Aengaende De ghelegentheydt deses Tijdts* (ca. 1665).
120. Verz. RLP: *Vervolg van Het Rotterdams Zee-Praatje Tusschen Drie Personen, een Koopman, een Borger en een Stierman...* (Middelburg: Gerrit Jansz. van Hoorn, 1653), 9–10.
121. Specifically, the almanac reports, Scottish "privateers" (*Kaep-vaerders*) hid along the coast of Ireland and the island of Jersey, and had enjoyed some success. See Verz. Thysius: *Hollantse Mercurius...* (Haerlem: Pieter Casteleyn, 1651), entries for February 10, 1650, 10.
122. Verz. Thysius: L.B., *Klaght en Kort Verhael...* (1672).
123. See, e.g., ARA, VOC #345: *Zakenindex op de uitgaande missiven van de Heren XVII aan de kantoren in Indie,* 1614–1707, fols. 117, 296, 350, and 360.
124. See, e.g., this case concerning English pirates who preyed upon both the Dutch and the Portuguese in the East Indies. They were captured by the VOC only after they had amassed a handsome stash of valuable plunder: States-General, "Resolutie waar by de Oostindische Compagnie gelast werd elf Gevangenen van een Engelsche Roofschip ter judicature van de Admiraliteit van Amsterdam

over te leeveren," July 31, 1700, *Recueil van alle de Placaten . . . betreffende de admiraliteiten . . .*, Vol. II, 298 vs.

125. *Realia*, III, 386: "Eeen dood-vonnis tegens Engelsche zeeroovers geveld . . .," Generale Resolutie, GGR, April 27, 1702; see also ARA, VOC #717: *Kopie Resolutie . . .*, April 27, 1702.

126. Realia, III, 386: "Uijt Europa herwaarts terug gezonden twee Engelsche zeeroovers aan den Advocaat-Fiscaal te geeven met de stukken ten hunnen Lasten . . .," Generale Resolutie, GGR, November 4, 1701; see also ARA, VOC #716: *Kopie-Resolutie . . .*, GGR, November 4, 1701.

127. States-General, "Resolutie waar by de Oostindische Compagnie gelast werd elf Gevangenen van een Engelsche Roofschip . . .," July 31, 1700, *Recueil van alle de Placaten . . . betreffende de admiraliteiten . . .*, Vol. II, 298 vs.

128. *Realia*, I, 312: "Van twee Engelse Jagten Frederik Francois en Jan . . .," Generale Resolutie, GGR, November 15, 1657; see also ARA, VOC #677: Kopie-Resolutie, GGR, November 15, 1657.

129. *Realia*, III, 386: "Zeven Engelsche zeeroovers uijt de boeijen gelargeerd en tot nadere ordre voor soldaten naar de Oostersche Provintien gezonden . . .," Generale Resolutie, GGR, August 29, 1704; see also ARA, VOC #719: *Kopie-Resolutie*, GGR, August 29, 1704.

130. ARA, VOC #7417: *Zakenindex op de Resoluties de Heren XVII*, 1602–1736, December 2, 1688, fol. 222. This same reference can also be found in ARA, VOC# 221, fol. 590. For a fuller discussion of this issue, see ARA, VOC #7355 and ARA, VOC #110.

131. Barber, "Privateers and Pirates," 531.

132. ARA, WIC #865: *Alphabetisch zakelijke registers op de notulen der vergadering van Tienen, Zeeland Kamer*, 1674–1690, March 20, 1675, fol. 108.

133. *Realia*, III, 386: "Een befaamd zee-roover alhier, in de stad door den Engelschen capitein Jacob Wright ontmoet . . ." Generale Resolutie, GGR, December 8, 1702 (see also ARA, VOC #717: *Kopie-Resolutie . . .*, GGR, December 8, 1702); and *Realia*, III, 386: "Die rover . . . te doen examineeren . . .," Generale Resolutie, GGR, December 11, 1702 (see also ARA, VOC #717: *Kopie-Resolutie*, GGR, December 11, 1702).

134. *Realia*, I, 346: "Dien swerver naar deze Gewesten staande . . .," Generale Resolutie, GGR, December 19, 1704 (see also ARA, VOC #719: *Kopie-Resolutie*, GGR, December 19, 1704); and *Realia*, I, 346: "Bij ontmoeting van dezelve in eenige plaatsen onder de Koningen van Ternate en Tidor sorteerende . . .," Generale Resolutie, GGR, January 8, 1705 (see also ARA, VOC #720: *Kopie-Resolutie*, GGR, January 8, 1705).

135. *Realia*, I, 346: "Met een Schip op Batchian vervallen . . .," Generale Resolutie, GGR, July 27, 1706; see also ARA, VOC #722: Kopie-Resolutie, GGR, July 27, 1706.

136. *Realia*, I, 384: "Aan gem[e] Dampier werden twee Spaanse gevangenen overgelevert," and "De Acte van den Notaris werd produceert wegens 't examen van Dampier . . .," Generale Resolutie, GGR, August 2, 1706; see also ARA, VOC #722: *Kopie-Resolutie*, GGR , August 2, 1706, fols. 564–566.

137. *Realia*, I, 384: "Gedagte Dampier zal na dat zekere kist . . .," Generale Resolutie, GGR , August 3, 1706; ARA, VOC #722: *Kopie-Resolutie*, GGR, August 3, 1706, fols. 568–569.

138. *Realia*, I, 385: "Het volk van Dampier's schip . . ."; "Blijven persisteren bij de weigering . . ."; and "Dit volk gaat eijndelijk na boord," Generale Resolutien,

GGR, August 6, 10, and 12, 1706; see also ARA, VOC #722: *Kopie-Resolutie* . . ., GGR, August 6, 10, and 12, 1706, fols. 579 and 582–596.

139. *Realia*, I, 384–385: "De voorm^c twee Gecommitteerde Leden der Hoge Regeering dienen van berigt over de zaak van Dampier . . ." and "Alle de papieren tot de zaak van Dampier . . .," Generale Resolutien, GGR, August 5 and 27, 1706 (see also ARA, VOC #722: *Kopie-Resolutie*, GGR, August 5 and 27, fols. 572–573); *Realia*, I, 346: "D'attestation rakende zijne zaak zullen niet voor den Raad van Justitie werden overgegeven," Generale Resolutie, GGR, August 28, 1706 (see also ARA, VOC #722: *Kopie-Resolutie*, GGR, August 28, 1706); and *Realia*, I, 385: "De Attestatien rakende de zaak van Dampier . . .," and "Op een ingediend berigt van den Advocaat fiscaal werd de zaak van Dampier afgedaan . . .," Generale Resolutien, GGR, September 28 and October 5, 1706 (see also ARA, VOC #722: *Kopie-Resolutie*, GGR, September 28 and October 5, 1706).

140. See, e.g., Verz. Thysius: *Hollandtze Mercurius* . . . (1666), 47; Verz. Thysius: L. B., *Klaght en Kort Verhael* . . . (1672); and Verz. RLP: *Vervolg van Het Rotterdams Zee-Praatje Tusschen Drie Personen, een Koopman, een Borger en een Stierman: Noodig, In der haast gelesen te werden* (Middelburg: Gerrit Jansz. van Hoorn, 1653), 9–10.

141. J.K. Oudendijk, "The Dutch Republic and Algiers, 1662–1664," *Course et Piraterie: Etudes présentées à la Commission International d'Histoire Maritime* . . ., ed. Commission Internationale d'Histoire Maritime (Paris: Institute de Recherche et d'Histoire des Textes/Editions du Centre National de la Recherche Scientifique, 1975), 155.

142. See, e.g., the terminology used by the authorities of the Admirality of Amsterdam when they sent the warship *Ter Goes* out on an expedition to combat the Barbary corsairs: ARA, AA, Verz. Sweers #4: *Journaal, gehouden door Sweers op 's Land schip Der Goes bestemd naar de Middellandsche zee ter beteugeling van de zeeroovers*, February 22, 1657–December 20, 1657. Likewise, the instructions given to Captain Moy Lambert by the united Admiralities, ARA, AA, Verz. Bisdom #107: *Instructie voor den Capiteijn Moij Lambert Commandeur over de naervolgende veerthien Scheepen van Oorloge, gaande naar de Middelandsche Zee teegens de rovers*, May 2, 1618.

143. States-General, "Capitulatie van de Turkschen Keiser voor de Onderdaanen van deezen Staat . . . vernieuwt is," 1681, *Recueil van alle de Placaten . . . betreffende de admiraliteiten* . . . Vol. III, 317.

144. Oudendijk, 146. For more on the Capitulation itself, see J. Dumont, *Corps Universal Diplomatique du Droit des Gens*, Vol. V, Part II (Amsterdam, 1726–1731), 210. For more on early Dutch–Ottoman relations generally, see A.H. de Groot, *The Ottoman Empire and the Dutch Republic: A History of the Earliest Diplomatic Relations, 1610–1630* (Leiden, 1978).

145. Simon de Vries, *Historie van Barbaryen En de zelfs Zee-Roovers*, Vol. II (Amsterdam: Jan ten Hoorn, 1684), Chapter 2.

146. For more on the Barbary states' general position in international law, see J.M. Mössner, *The Barbary Powers in International Law* (The Hague: Grotian Society Papers, 1972).

147. Oudendijk, "The Dutch Republic and Algiers," 152–153.

148. Andrew Barker, *A Report of Captaine Ward and Dansekar, Pirates*. The English Experience: Its Record in Early Printed Books Published in Facsimile, Number 21

149. Barker, *Captaine Ward*, 22–23.
150. de Vries, *Historie van Barbaryen*, 28–29.
151. K. Heeringa, "Bronnen tot de geschiedenis van de Levanthandel 1560–1660," *Rijks Geschiedkundige Publicatien*, Nos. 9, 10, and 34 ('s-Gravenhage: Martinus Nijhoff, 1910–1966).
152. See, e.g., ARA, VOC# 7417: *Trefwoordenreportorium op de Resoluties van de Heren XVII*, 1602–1716, September 19, 1698, fol. 101, which notes the death of one Dirk Loveld in a battle against two Algerian "rover" ships. See also ARA, VOC #221, fol. 159 and ARA, VOC #358 for more details on this case.
153. de Vries, *Historie van Barbaryen*, 30 and 36–38.
154. de Vries, *Historie van Barbaryen*, 28–30, 90, and 97.
155. ARA, AA, Verz. Bisdom #167: *Copie-Crimineele Vonnissen van de Admiraliteit op de Maas*, December 23, 1614, fols. 89 vs–90.
156. Verz. Thysius: *Belijdenisse, Sententie, ende Namen der Zee-roovers, die soo tot Rotterdam als t'Amsterdam met der koorde gheexecuteert zijn . . . mede een verhael wat schade de Zee-roovers ghedaen hebben sints den Treves . . .* (Amsterdam: Broer Jansz, 1615).
157. Several men (David Paule, Richard Stein, and Francois Claving) were of unspecified background, and one of the North African corsairs was actually identified as a "Morisco," i.e., a Spaniard of Arab descent.
158. de Vries, *Historie van Barbaryen*, 29–30.
159. de Vries, *Historie van Barbaryen*, 97.
160. ARA, AA, Verz. Bisdom #167: *Copie-Crimineele Vonnissen van de Admiraliteit op de Maas*, December 23, 1614, fols. 89 vs–90.
161. Verz. Thysius: *Belijdenisse, Sententie, enn Namen der Zee-roovers . . .* (1615).
162. Verz. Thysius: *Belijdenisse, Sententie, enn Namen der Zee-roovers . . .* (1615); Verz. Thysius: *Bekentenisse van Hugo Clerck Capiteyn der Zee Roovers . . .* (1615); and ARA, AA, Verz. Bisdom #167: *Copie-Crimineele Vonnissen van de Admiraliteit op de Maas*, fols. 89 vs–90. Likewise, de Vries mentions that another gang of Barbary corsairs was hanged in Amsterdam in 1619. See de Vries, *Historie van Barbaryen*, 36.
163. de Vries, *Historie van Barbaryen*, 86.
164. *Ordinaire Leydse Courant*, August 29, 1686 (No. 66), "Nederlanden" section.
165. ARA, WIC #468: *Kopieboeken van Brieven naar Amerika*, 1684–1689, "Letter to Willem Kerckrinck, Director in Curacao," October 20, 1687, fol. 129.
166. ARA, VOC #7417: *Trefwoordenreportorium op de Resoluties van de Heren XVII*, 1602–1716, entry for April 5, 1692, fol. 190. This incident is covered in more detail in ARA, VOC #7356.
167. ARA, WIC #468: *Kopieboeken van brieven naar Amerika*, 1684–1689, "Letter to Willem Kerckrinck, Director in Curacao," October 20, 1687, fol. 129.
168. de Vries, *Historie van Barbaryen*, 86.
169. See, e.g., ARA, AA, Verz. Sweers #2: *Journaal, gehouden door Sweers . . . uitgezonden . . . te zuiveren van de zeerovers*, March 10, 1650–May 20, 1651 (N.B.: zuiveren means "to clean, to purify"); and ARA, AA, Verz. Sweers #2: *Journaal, ghehouden door Sweers . . . kruisende langs de kusten van Spanje en Portugal op de Turksche en andere zeerovers*, April 5, 1649–November 16, 1649.
170. Verz. Thysius: *Hollantse Mercurius . . .* (1651), July 1650, 38–39.

171. "Relaes uyt het Hollands Fregat, de Stad Harderwijk, voor Harwitz in het gesigt van een Turksen Roover ten Anker leggende," *Ordinaire Leydse Courant*, October 17, 1686 (No. 87), "Engelant" section.
172. ARA, AA, Verz. Bisdom #167: *Copie-Crimineele Vonnissen van de Admiraliteit op de Maas*, fols. 89 vs–90; and Verz. Thysius: *Bekentenisse van Hugo Clerck Capiteyn der Zee Roovers, die met zijn Complicen ende aenhang gejusticeert zijn tot Amsterdam, den 24 Jan. 1615* . . . (Amsterdam, 1615); and Verz. Thysius: *Belijdenisse, Sententie, ende namen der Zee-roovers, die soo tot Rotterdam als 't Amsterdam met der koorde gheexecuteert zijn enz* . . . *den 24 Jan* (Amsterdam: Broer Jansz., 1615).
173. Verz. Thysius: Belijdenisse, *Sententie, enn Namen der Zee-roovers* . . . (1615), 1.
174. *Ordinaire Leydse Courant*, June 20, 1686 (No. 36), "Nederlanden" section.
175. de Vries, *Historie van Barbaryen*, 57.
176. *Ordinaire Leydse Courant*, July 23, 1686 (No. 50), "Nederlanden" section.
177. This agreement also stipulated that any Christians found aboard Barbary ships in Dutch waters would be manumitted immediately. See Oudendijk, "The Dutch Republic and Algiers," 154.
178. ARA, AA, Verz. Bisdom #246: *Extract uit het Register der Resolutien van de Hoog Mogende Heeren Staaten generale* . . ., April 2–16, 1686, entries for April 2 and April 13.
179. Such agreements that were typically printed and circulated among the Dutch public. See, e.g., Verz. Thysius: *Historisch journael vanden Tocht op de Barbare Turcken; Door . . . M . . . A . . . de Ruyter . . . beneffens de twee Tractaten van vrede . . . respective vande Stadt Thunis: ende van Algiers* . . . (June 5, 1662); Verz. Thysius: *Exhibitum den 7 Juny 1679. Traitte de Paix & de Commerce, entre . . . Les Estats Generaux des Provinces Unies des Pays-Bas & . . . Alger . . . le 30 . . . Avril 1679* (1679); Verz. ZBP: *Nieuw opgerecht Tractaet Tusschen . . . de Heer Michiel Adriaen de Ruyter . . . Ende de Koninck, ende die vande Regeringe van Tunis* . . . (Amsterdam: Michielsen Verbiest, 1662); and Verz. ZBP: *Tractaat Van Vrundtschap en Verbintenisse, Geslooten den negenden Februarii 1651. tusschen de . . . Staaten Generaal . . . en . . . de Steeden van Salé in Barbarye* . . . ('s-Gravenhage: Weduwe . . . van wylen Hillebrandt Jacobsz. van Wouw, 1651). The history of relations between the Dutch Republic and the Barbary powers is recounted in Simon de Vries's *Historie van Barbaryen*; de Vries includes various treaties as well in his work.
180. Verz. Thysius: States-General, *Placaet Opte Groote Equipagie Monture Manninge ende Admiraelschappen derr Scheppen* . . . ('s-Gravenhage: Weduwe ende Erfgenamen van wylen Hillebrandt Jacobsz. van Wouw, 1655). For other examples, see in *Recueil van alle de Placaten . . . betreffende de admiraliteiten* . . . : "Placaat op de Manningen en Monture van Scheepen na de Straat van Gibraltar, Middelandsche Zee en Levanten," December 2, 1667, Vol. I, 693; and "Resolutie, observantie van de Reglementen voor de Scheepen na de Middelandsche Zee," July 25, 1687, Vol. II, 72.
181. Verz. Thysius: *Placaet Opte Groote Equipagie* . . . (1655), 2.
182. Verz. Thysius: *Placaet Opte Groote Equipagie* . . . (1655), 3–10. The proclamation stipulates that the money garnered from any fine would be divided as follows: one-fourth would go to the person who reported the crime; one-fourth would go to the officer who made the indictment; one-fourth would go to poor relief; and the last fourth would go to the general penalty fund;

see 9–10. For an earlier example of such a government proclamation, see Verz. Thysius: States-General, *Placaet Opte Grootte Equipagie, Monture, Manninge ende Admiraelschappen der Schepen varende door de Strate van Gibralter naer de Middellandtsche Zee ende op Levanten* ('s-Gravenhage: Weduwe, ende Erf. van wijlen Hillebrant Jacobsz van Wouw, 1652). Yet another pamphlet in the Thysius Collection (Petit #326), contains the same information.

183. ARA, AA, Verz. Bisdom #107: *Instructie voor den Capiteijn Moij Lambert Commandeur* . . . May 2, 1618. The trade companies also sent ships to combat the Barbary corsairs. See the reference to the VOC's fleet of 18 vessels destined to fight the "Turkish pirates" in Verz. Thysius: *Donderdaeghsche Mercurius* (Utrecht), February 17, 1661, 8.

184. See, e.g., the log for a 1649 trip: ARA, AA, Verz. Sweers #2: Isaac Sweers, *Journaal, ghehouden door Sweers . . . op 'l Lands schip De Maen, kruisende langs de kusten van Spanje en Portugal op de Turksche en andere zeeroovers*, April 5, 1649–November 16, 1649.

185. An example of the profits raised by such expeditions can be found in ARA, AA #1839 (College van het Admiraliteit te Amsterdam): *Rekening van den vendumeester wegens zijn ontvang van de princen en veroverde Turcken en Mooren op de kust van Barbarije onder den vice-admiral De Ruijter, 1661–1662*. Money produced from the sale of captured goods (and apprehended North Africans, who were sold as slaves) totaled $f.51,397$.

186. For more on this topic, see R.E.J. Weber, *De Beveiliging van de Zee Tegen Europeesche en Barbarijsche zeerovers, 1609–1621* (Amsterdam: Werken uitgeg. door de Commissie voor Zeegeschiedenis der Kon. Akad. van Wetensch. III, 1936).

187. Verz. Thysius: *Ordonnantie dienende tot versekeringe vande Schepen uyt dese Landen nae Oosten ende Noorweghen varende* . . . (Amstelredam: Cornelis Claesz, 1596), 1–2.

188. Verz. Thysius: *Ordonnantie dienende tot versekeringe vande Schepen* . . . (1596), 3.

189. Verz. Thysius: *Ordonnantie dienende tot versekeringe vande Schepen* . . . (1596), 4.

190. Verz. Thysius: *Ordonnantie dienende tot versekeringe vande Schepen* . . . (1596), 1–5.

191. Willem Ysbrantsz. Bontekoe, *Gedenckwaardige beschrijving, van de achtjarige en zeer avontuurlyke reise van Willem Ysbrandtsz. Bontekoe van Hoorn* (Amsterdam: B. Koene, 1625). Another edition was published in Hoorn by Jan Janzoon Deutel in 1646. For an English translation of this text, see trans. C.B. Bodde-Hodgkinson and Pieter Geyl, *Memorable Description of the East Indian voyage, 1618–25* (London: G. Routledge & Sons, 1929).

192. Another three editions were published during the nineteenth century, and three in the twentieth (the last appeared in 1930). See J. Fzn. Buisman, *Populaire Prozaschrijvers 1600–1815. Romans, Novellen, Verhalen, Levensbeschrijvingen, Arcadias, Sprookjes* (Amsterdam: Israel, 1960), 45–51.

193. Translations of non-Dutch travelers' accounts were popular as well. See, e.g., *De Zeltzame Wedervaringen van Louis Marot, Koninklyke Loots-Man Over de Galeyen van Vrankrijk* . . . (Utecht: Johannes Ribbius, 1675), a translation of an original French text.

194. *Wonderlicke Avontuer van twee Goelieven, de eene ghenaemt Sr. Waterbrandt ende de ander Joufvrouw Wintergroen* . . . (Leyden: Nickolaes Geelkerck, 1624). Dutch literary scholars consider this text a notable early attempt to create an original Dutch novel. See Buisman, 24, #76.

195. For an extensive bibliography of seventeenth-century Dutch travel literature, see P.A. Tiele, *Memoire Bibliographique sur les Journaux des Navigateurs Neerlandais Reimprimés dans les Collections Hollandaises du XVIIe Siècle*... (Amsterdam: Frederik Muller, 1867). Also very helpful are the bibliographies found in ed. H.W. de Kooker, *Muller/De Vries/Scheepers: Populaire Prozaschrijvers der XVIIe en XVIIIe Eeuw* (Utrecht: HES Publishers, 1981), 142–151; and 330–344.
196. For example, *Eerste Schip-Vaert Der Hollanders naer Oost-Indien, Met vier Schepen onder 't beleydt van Cornelis Houtman van Alckmaer*... (Amsterdam: Ioost Hartgers, 1650); Aernout van Overbeke's *Geestige en Vermaeckelicke Reys-Beschryvinge, Van den Heer Aernout van Overbeke, Naer Oost-Indien gevaren*... (Jan Joosten oop de Voor-Burgwal, 1671). This text was very popular, and consequently was reprinted in 1672, 1678, 1685, 1691, 1696, and 1699; E. Melton, *Zeldzaame en Gedenkw. zee- en landreizen door Egypten, West-Indien... Oost-Indien enz. 1660–77* (Amstedam: J. ten Hoorn, 1681); Jean Mocquet, *Reysen in Afrique Asien Oost- en West-Indien gedaen door Jan Mocquet*... (Dordrecht: Abraham Andriessz., 1656); and *Journael van de Voyagie Gedaen met twaelft Scheepen naer Oost-Indien... Waer in verhaelt wordt her veroveren der Portugeesche Forten op Amboyna en Tydoor*... (Amsterdam: Gillis Joosten Saeghman, ca. 1660–1670). Probably the most significant work was *The Beginning and Continuing Progress of the United Dutch East India Company*, a "biography" of the VOC originally published in 1646 which was a compendium of tales and data about the region. This fascinating work describes everything from the most famous journeys made by Dutchmen to the area's resources and topography; to the religion, politics, and culture of the indigenous peoples; to the trade practices of the both the Dutch and native inhabitants. Included as well were fine illustrations, maps, and tables.
197. Among the more famous texts are Jan Huygen van Linschoten, *Histoire de la navigation de Iean Hvgves de Linscot Hollandois et de son voyage*... (Amstelredam: Theodore Pierre, 1610); and Johannes de Laet, *Nieuwe wereldt ofte Beschrijvinghe van West-Indien* (Leyden, 1625). Linschoten's work was translated into English as *Iohn Hvighen van Linschoten. his Discours of Voyages into yet Easte & West Indies. Deuided into foure Bookes* (London: Iohn Wolfe, 1598); and is available in a modern rendition as *The Voyage of John Huygen van Lischoten to the East Indies*, ed. Arthur Coke Burnell (New York: Burt Franklin, 1970).
198. For examples of such reports, see any of the extant 1686 editions of the paper housed at the Universiteits Bibliotheek, Rijksuniversiteit Leiden (Leiden, The Netherlands).
199. *Ordinaire Leydse Courant*, October 12, 1686 (No. 85), "Nederlanden" section.
200. For example, Verz. RLP: *Amsterdamse Dingsdaegse Courant*, February 7, 1690, 2, "Vranckryck" section.
201. For example, Verz. RLP: *Amsterdamse Dingsdaegse Courant*, February 7, 1690, 2, "Nederlanden" section.
202. Verz. RLP: *Amsterdamse Dingsdaegse Courant*, February 7, 1690, 2, "Vranckryck" section.
203. *Ordinaire Leydse Courant*, August 28, 1686, "Nederlanden" section; *Ordinaire Leydse Courant*, September 12, 1686 (No. 72), "Nederlanden"

section; and *Ordinaire Leydse Courant*, September 21, 1686 (No. 76), "Nederlanden" section. For a case involving corruption and counterfeiting from the earlier part of the century, see the pamphlet Verz. RLP: *Cort ende waerachtich Verhael wt de Sententie . . . den 26 September . . . in 's Gravenhage ghepronuncheert . . . over . . . den Fiscael Berck, van der Mast, enz . . . Geweest zynde van de Admiraliteyt tot Rotterdam* (Rotterdam: H. Pietersz., 1626).

204. Verz. Thysius: *Hollandtze Mercurius . . .* (1666), 72–74, 77, 90–99, and 107.
205. Verz. Thysius: *Hollantse Mercurius . . .* (1651), 38–39; and Verz. Thysius: *De Snelle Mercurius* (Amstelredam: Otto Barentsz. Smient, 1686), 8.
206. See, for e.g., Verz. Thysius: *Spieghel Der grau-same ongherechticheyt ende vervloeckte giericheyt vande . . . Conincklicke Comp^e. van Oost-Indien . . .* (1638).
207. For example, Gysbert Bastiaensz., *Ongeluckige Voyagie, Van 'T Schip Batavia Nae Oost-Indien . . .* (Amsterdam: Joost Hartgers, 1648). This is a copy of a letter written by Gysbert Bastiaensz from Batavia, which in addition to a discussion of the nature of VOC navigation and commerce, describes a particular voyage to the East Indies during which several murders (and their consequent punishment) took place.
208. For example, Verz. Thysius: *Copie Van een Brief van den Heere Admirael Spilberghen: Inhoudende de Voyage by hem gedaen door de Strate Magelanica, tot inde Zuydt Zee . . .* (Delf: Andriessz., 1617); and KB Pamfletten, *Een warachtich Verhael, hoe . . . de Vlote van hare Majesteyt van Enghelandt verovert heeft . . . een van des Conincks van Spaengien rijcke Oost-Indien varende Schepen . . .* (Delft: Jacob Cornelissz Vennecool., 1602).
209. For example, Verz. ZBP: *(Lijst) Van alle des vyandts veroverde Chaloupen, Ponten, Pleyten ende Seuyen . . . Midtsgaders de Lijste van alle de Gevangenen* (1631).
210. See, e.g., the news reports on the "Zee-Schrick," an innovative, semisubmersible craft designed in 1653–1654: Verz. Thysius: Isaac Burghoorn, *Terror terroris, Werelts Wonder-schrick . . .* ('s-Gravenhage: Isaac Burghoorn, 1654); Verz. Thysius: *Wonderen en Mirakelen welcke doen sal het . . . Rotterdams Zee-Schrick . . .* (Rotterdam: Pieter Flipsen, 1653); and Verz. Thysius: *Het Malle Schip van Rotterdam* (1654).
211. For example, Gysbert Bastiaensz., *Ongeluckige Voyagie, Van 'T Schip Batavia Nae Oost-Indien . . .* (1648); and Verz. Thysius: *Sententien By de Gecommitteerde Raden Admiraliteyt . . . binnen Rotterdam . . .* (Rotterdam: Anth. de Haes, 1629), 1–4.
212. See, e.g., Verz. Thysius: *Sententien By de Gecommitteerde Raden Admiraliteyt . . . binnen Rotterdam . . .* (1629).
213. For example, a sailors' riot in the port of Medemblik. See *Donderderdaeghsche Mercurius* (Utrecht), February 17, 1661 (No. 14), 8.
214. For more information on this social phenomenon, especially during the eighteenth century, see P.J. Buijnsters, *Levens van Beruchte Personen: Over de Criminele Biografie in Nederland gedurende de 18e Eeuw* (Utrecht, 1980).
215. For example, Verz. Thysius: Staten van Hollandt, *Placaet By de Ed. Mo. Heeren Staten van Hollandt ende West-Vrieslant, geemaneert jegens de Dieven, Dieverijen, ende aenhouders van dien* ('s-Gravenhage: Weduwe, ende Erf. van wijlen Hillebrandt Iacobsz van Wouw, 1635); Verz. RLP: Staten van Utrecht, *Placaet Van de Heeren Staten van den Lande van Utrecht tegens den Vagabunden, Bedelaars, Dieven, etc.* (January 24, 1596); and Verz. ZBP: Regeerders der Stadt Utrecht, *Ordonnantie . . . op 't Stuck vanden Armen, tegens de Bedelarye, ende alle vremde Bedelaers . . .* (Utrecht: Salomon de Roy, 1619).

216. See, e.g., this early-seventeenth-century description of the Amsterdam *Tuchthuis*, the new penal institution that sought both to punish and reform its residents: *Historie Van de wonderlijcke Mirakelen . . . In een plaets ghenaempt het Tucht-huys . . .* (Amstelredam: Marten Gerbrantsz., 1612). By the late eighteenth century, the public could read not only about the misfortunes of the great, but about the character and punishments of the average crime-prone Dutchman as well: see *Naam-Lyst Van Alle Persoonen, Die Binnen Amsterdam, Sederd het Jaar 1693 tot 1774 in Cluys . . .* (Amersfoort: Maurits Langenwagen, 1774). For a modern, scholarly study of the *Tuchthuis*, see Thorsten Sellin's *Pioneering in Penology: The Amsterdam Houses of Correction in the Sixteenth and Seventeenth Centuries* (Philadephia: University of Pennsylvania Press, 1944).
217. See, e.g., Verz. RLP: *'t Proces en executie van den grootes Moorder Philip Beeckern* (Utrecht: Anthony Benedick, 1661).
218. For example, *Ordinaire Leydse Courant*, October 3, 1686 (No. 83), "Nederlanden" section; *Waerachtige Beschryvinghe van een jammerlicke nieuwe Tijdinghe van een deerlicke Moort . . .* (Middelborch: Adriaen Leenaertsz, 1618). Other examples of pamphlets about foreign crime include: *Cort verhael Van het grouwelick ende verradelijck vergiftighen van eenen Edelen Ridder, Sir Thomas Overberry ghenaemt . . .* (Amsterdam: Desiderius de la Tombe, 1616); and *Omstandig en waaragtig Verhaal, van veele gepleegde en nooit gehoorde diefstallen . . . En een groot getal huisbraaken . . . in Duitsland gepleegd* (Amsterdam, 1710); Verz. KB Pamfletten: *Een Waerachtighe . . . Geschiedenisse, van drie Studenten van Cloppenburch, die welcke twee Jonghe dochters eerst hebben vercracht ende . . . vermoort . . .* (Lambert Raesvelt, 1610); and Verz. KB Pamfletten: *Een warachtighe beschrijvinge van drie moordenaers . . .* (Rotterdam: Jan Ghelen, n.d.).
219. For example, Lambert van den Bos(ch), *Het toneel der ongevallen . . . mitsg. het spicilegium van vorstelycke treur-gevallen* (Dordrecht, 1683); Lambert van den Bos(ch), *Keur-Stof Deses Tydts, Behelsende de voornaemste Geschiedenissen of Rampsaligheden Der Grooten, Meest voorgavallen zedert het Jaer 1640* (Dordrecht: Geemen van Cappel, 1672); Johan Reynolds, *Tonneel Der Wereldtse Rampsaligheden, Vertoonende Godts Wraake . . .* (Amsterdam: Gerrit van Goedesbergh, 1667); Jean Pierre Camus Belley, *De Groote Schouwplaets der jammerrlijcke bloed-en-moord geschiedennissen*, trans. Simon de Vries (Utrecht: J. Ribbius, 1670); and I.H.G., *Het Treur-Tooneel Der Doorluchtige Mannen Onser Eeuwe . . .* (Amsterdam, 1650), 3 vols. A second edition was published in 1698; the author was presented as Lambert van den Bos(ch).
220. For example, *Histori oft Practycke der dieven* (Utrecht: Wed. van Esdras Snellaert); *Histori oft Practycke der dieven* (Utrecht: Wed. van Esdras Snellaert); Don Garcia, *Oudheit en Afkomst der Dieven* (Amsterdam: Timotheus ten Hoorn, 1687); F. de Calvi, *Legende ofte Historye Vande snoode practicquen, ende de behendige listicheden der Dieven* (Leyden: David Lopez de Haro, 1645); *Den Gepredestineerden Dief, Ofte, Een t'Samen-spreeckinge gehouden tusschen een Predicant der Calvinus-gesinde ende een Dief, die gesententieert was om te sterven* (Hamburgh: Barent Adriaensz., ca. 1641); A. de Castillo Solersano, *'t Leeven en bedrijf van den doorsleepen bedrieger, meester van bedrogh en fieltery* (Amsterdam: B. Boekholt, 1669). Another edition was published in 1670; Mateo Aleman, *Het Leven van Gusman d'Alfarache, 't Afbeeltsel van 't Menschelijk Leven . . .*, 2nd edition (Amsterdam: Baltus Boekholt, 1669);

Mateo Aleman, *Het Tweede Deel van 't Leven van Gusman d'Alfarache*... (Amsterdam: Baltus Boekholt, 1670); H.A.B., *Den politycken dief* (Amsterdam: Johannes Colum, 1650); Michel de Servantes Savedra (i.e., Miguel de Cervantes Savedra), *Monipodios Hol of 't Leven, Bedrijf, en oefning der Gauwdieven, haer onrust en schelmerijen* (Amsterdam: Evert Nieuwenhof, 1658); *Den Engelschen Schelm, afgebootst in 't leven van Mariton Latroon, een doorsleepen Guyt* (Amsterdam: Jan ten Hoorn, ca. 1678); *Den Jacobitsche Rover, ofte het fameuse leven en daden van Jacob Whitney*... ('s-Gravenhage, 1693); *'t Leven van den wereldberuchten kapitein der moordenaren Louis Dominique de Cartouche*... (Delft: H. Boitet, 1722); Monsieur Le Grand, *Cartouche of de Rovers. Blyspel*..., trans. G. Tysens (Amsterdam: Jacob van Egmont, 1722); *Cartouche, of de gestrafte Booswigt*... (Amsterdam: Joh. de Ruiter, 1731); W.B.M., *De wonderlijke en niet min zeltzame levensloop van den doorluchtige gauwdief Duval* (Amsterdam: Jac. Groot, 1732); and C. Lonius, *De mislukte list of de bedroge Landsdief, zijnde het verhaal eenes gevangen Grutter* (Westzaandam, 1737).

221. *'t Begin, Midden en Eynde der Zee-rooveryen van den alder-famieusten zee-roover, Claes G. Compaen, van Oostzanen in Kennemer-landt: vervattende sijn wonderlijcke vreemde en landts-schadelijcke drijf-tochten* (1659). Alexander Olivier Exquemelin, *De Americaensche Zee-Roovers. Behelsende eene pertinente en waerachtige Beschrijving van alle de voornaemste Roveryen en onmenscheliycke wreedheden die Englese en France Rovers tegens de Spanjaerden in America gepleeght hebben*... (Amsterdam: Jan ten Hoorn, 1678). William Lithgow, *The Rare Adventures and Painful Peregrinations of William Lithgow* (London, 1632). The first Dutch edition of this work was also published in 1632. For a modern edition, see the version edited by Gilbert Phelps (London: Folio Society, 1974). Lithgow's text was known well-enough in the Netherlands that the anonymous author of Claes Compaen's biography recommended it to his readers in 1659 (see *'t Begin, Midden en Eynde der Zee-rooveryen*, iv). Charles Johnson, *Historie der Englesche zee-roovers... behelseen verhaal van hunne zee-rooveryen, moorderyen, wreedheden, en mishandelingen*... (Amsterdam: Hermanus Uytwerf, 1725).

222. Verz. Thysius: "Auctentijck Verhael van 't gene gepasseert is in den Slach ter Zee voor Duynkercken den 18 Februarij, tusschen den Admirael Marten Harpersz Tromp ende den Spaenschen Admirael Michiel van Doorn," *Courante uyt Italien ende Duytschlandt* (Amsterdam), February 26, 1639 (No. 9), 2.

223. That is, "The Authentic Tale of What Happened in the Sea-Battle By Dunkirk on February 18, Between Admiral Marten Harpersz. Tromp and the Spanish Admiral Michiel van Doorn."

224. For example, *Ordinaire Leydse Courant*, July 23, 1686 (No. 50), see "Nederland" section for a report on a helmsman and ship's boy from Vlissingen who survived capture by pirates along the coast of West Africa.

225. For example, *Ordinaire Leydse Courant*, September 26, 1686 (No. 78), see "Neederlanden" [*sic*] section for a report on the pirate capture of three English vessels.

226. For example, *Ordiniare Leydse Courant*, June 8, 1686 (No. 31), see "Nederlanden" section for a report on the return of Captain Warewijk of the ship *Josias*, who came home from the "Spanish West Indies" with a load of cocoa, but he lamented, no news about pirates in the Carribbean.

227. Verz. Thysius: *De Snelle Mercurius* (Amsterdam: Otto Barentsz. Smient, 1686).

228. Verz. Thysius: *Hollandtze Mercurius*... (1666), 15–18. To combat these English privateers, the States-General ordered the Admiralties to ready 72 warships to fight the English. Also, the Admiralty of Amsterdam mandated that all English vessels, whether merchant or naval, were to be captured as prizes. Lastly, the VOC donated 25 "substantial, courageous ships of war" to serve the nation during the duration of the hostilities.
229. For example, *Een schoone historie van de Verduldige Helena van Constantinopel*... (Amsterdam: Weduw' van Theunis Jacobsz Loots-man, 1684). See Chapter 3, which details Helena's kidnapping by sadistic pirates who drown the rest of her party and prepare to rape her, before God intervenes and carries her to England.
230. Franciscus Heerman, *Guldene Annotatien van Franciscus Heerman*... 16th edition (1670). This very popular book of moral instruction illustrates the ignoble deeds and character of classical pirates on pages 101 and 221.
231. Dionisius van der Sterre, *Zeer aenmerkelijcke reysen gedaan door Jan Erasmus Reyning, meest in West-Indien en ook in veel andere deelen des Werelds* (Amsterdam: Jan ten Hoorn, 1691).
232. See, e.g., these two pamphlets recounting the nerve-racking misadventures of the beleaguered VOC ship, the *Aernem*: Andries Stokram, *Korte Beschryvinge Van de Ongeluckige Weer-om-reys van het Schip Aernhem*... (Amsterdam: Jacob Venckel, 1663); and Verz. RLP: Johannes van Kerckhoven, *Wijtloopig breede en waerachtige Beschrijvinge Van de ongeluckige Voyage van 't Schip AERNEM; Van Batavia vortrocken den 23 December 1661*... (Amsterdam: Jacobus vander Fuyck, 1664). Among other calamities, the *Aernem* encountered and was pursued by Red Sea pirates lurking around Mauritius.
233. For example, Verz. Thysius: *Vande Heerlijcke Victorie verkregen tegen de Zee-Roovers*... (Amsterdam, 1614); and Verz. Thysius: *Seeckere tydinge van tgene aldereerst ghepasseert is tusschen onse Hollandtsche Oorlochschepen... [en] 36. Turcksche Zee-roovers*... (Amstelredam: Broer Jansz. op de Kolck, 1618).
234. For example, Verz. Thysius: *De achtervolgende Dagh-Register Van het Parlement En Resolutien wegens Arlington, Benevens een aerdighe Rescontre Van een France Kaper, en een Engels Fregat, Welcke Kaper na eenigh tegenweer is genomen en tot Pleymuyen opgebracht* (Amsterdam: Wed. van J. Bruyning en Steven Swart, 1674).
235. See, e.g., Verz. Thysius: *Belijdenisse, Sententie, ende namen der Zee-roovers, die soo tot Rotterdam als 't Amsterdam met der koorde gheexecuteert zijn enz... den 24 Jan.* (Amsterdam: Broer Jansz., 1615); and Verz. Thysius: *Vande Heerlijcke Victorie verkregen tegen de Zee-Roovers*... (Amsterdam, 1614).
236. Verz. Thysius: *Bekentenisse van Hugo Clerck Capiteyn der Zee Roovers, die met zijn Complicen ende aenhang gejusticeert zijn tot Amsterdam, den 24 Jan. 1615* (Amsterdam, 1615).
237. Verz. Thysius: *Vande Heerlijcke Victorie verkregen tegen de Zee-Roovers*... (Amsterdam, 1614).
238. Verz. Thysius: *Vande Heerlijcke Victorie tegen de Zee-Roovers*..., 2. And such virtue was not enjoyed by the elite alone. Even rank-and-file Dutchmen were capable of such heroic action vis-à-vis dastardly pirates and privateers, and were praised for it. See, e.g., "Een Nieuw Lied van de Helddadige Visschers van Scheveninge..." (1704), in Scheurleer, *Van Varen en Van Vechten*, Vol. III, 172–176.

239. Verz. Thysius: *Vande Heerlijcke Victorie tegen de Zee-Roovers* . . ., back side of pamphlet.
240. van der Sterre, *Zeer aenmerkelijcke reysen gedaan door Jan Erasmus Reyning* . . . (1691).
241. van der Sterre, *Zeer aenmerkelijcke reysen gedaan door Jan Erasmus Reyning* . . . (1691), 2.
242. Exquemelin, *Buccaneers of America*, 40 and 41.
243. "Op de Zee-Rover Klaas Kompaan," ca. 1656, Scheurleer, *Van Varen en Van Vechten*, Vol. II, 6.
244. *'t Begin, Midden en Eynde der Zee-rooveryen* . . . (1659), Preface.
245. *'t Begin, Midden en Eynde der Zee-rooveryen* . . . (1659), ii.
246. *'t Begin, Midden en Eynde der Zee-rooveryen* . . . (1659), i.
247. *'t Begin, Midden en Eynde der Zee-rooveryen* . . . (1659), ii.
248. Verz. Thysius: *De Snelle Mercurius* (Amsterdam: Otto Barentswz. Smient, 1686), 5.
249. J. de Decker, "Verzoek van de Middellandsche Zee aan de Zeemagt van Holland" (1661), in Scheurleer, *Van Varen en Van Vechten*, Vol. II, 70.
250. de Vries, *Historie van Barbaryen*.
251. E. de Airanda, *Turckse Slavernie, Beschreven door Emanuel De Airanda, soo hy selfs die geleden heeft* . . . ('s-Gravenhage: Christoffel en Jasper Doll, 1666).
252. Albrecht Schiel, *Beschryvingh sijns levens in Barbaryen* (ca. 1670s). This source is cited in de Vries's *Historie van Barbaryen*, 151, and may no longer be extant.
253. *Aanhangsel, Behelzende de rampzalige en zeer gedenkwaardige Wedervaaringen van een Slaaf Die te Salé vier jaaren in de Slaaverny der Ongeloovigen versleeten heelft* (by ca. 1684). Included as a recommended selection at the end of de Vries's *Historie van Barbaryen*, and translated from the French by G.V. Broekhuizen, this source may no longer be extant.
254. *De overzelzame Historie van de Markgravinne de Frene, door haar eigen man aan een Turkschen zeeroover verkoft* . . . (Rotterdam, 1702). The frontispiece of this book swears that it is a true story, but one that is so exceptional and peculiar that it almost seems to be fictional. The Marquess' own introduction affirms that her tale is a bizarre but authentic one, and that few people in France were unfamiliar with it, for "It is so unusual that a woman of my station has a husband, who [would] sell her to a pirate."
255. de Vries, 54.
256. Barker, *A True and Certaine Report* . . . (1609), 16.
257. Barker, *A True and Certaine Report* . . . (1609), 15.
258. See, e.g., Verz. Thysius: *Historisch journael vanden Tocht op de Barbare Turcken Door . . . M . . . A . . . de Ruyter* . . . (June 5, 1662); and "Italien: Livorno den 16 Ianuary," *Amsterdamse Dingsdaese Courant*, February 7, 1690, 1.
259. For example, Wassenaer, *Historisch Verhael Aller Gedenkwaerdiger Geschiedenissen* . . ., Vol. 14.
260. For instance, see Verz. RLP: *Een Cort ende warachtich verhael vande ghedenckweerdige gheschiedenisse in Barbaryen, ende vanden grooten slagh ontrent Maroques* . . . ('s-Gravenhage: Hill. Jacobsz., 1607).
261. See, e.g., J. de Decker, "Op den zeeslag tusschen den Turk en Venetiaan in den jare 1656" (1656); J. van Vondel, "Op den Zeetriomf der Heerschappye van Venetië" (1656); and "Nederlaeg der Turken . . ." (1670); in Scheurleer, *Van Varen en van Vechten* Vol. II, 3–6 and 341–344.

262. *Seeckere tydinge van... hoe 36. Turcksche Zee-roovers het Eylant Lanceroote hebben... geplondert, ende duysent mensche tot slaven ghemaecht, ende hoe... Moy Lambert met syn... Oorlochschepen... erlicke Roovers becomen hebben, hun haer loon gegeven, ende arme Christen slaven een deel ontset...* (Amstelredam: Broer Jansz. op de Kolck, 1618). For an example of a characteristic newspaper article, see "Relaes uyt het Hollands Fregat, de Stad Harderwijk, voor Harwitz in her gesigt van een Turksen Roover ten Anker leggende," in *Ordinaire Leydse Courant*, October 17, 1686 (No. 87), "Engelant" section.

263. See the *Penningen* (1620) bearing this image in the permanent exhibition of the Nederlandse Scheepvaartmuseum, Amsterdam.

264. For example, Hendrik Cornelis Steenis, *Kort, Dog Naauwkeurig En Opregt Verhaal, Van alle de Behandelingen, Wreedhedens en Ongemakken, in hunne Slavernye onder de Mooren...* (Amsterdam: Wed. J. van Egmont, ca. 1726–1761); Hendrik Cornelis Steenis, *Journaal Wegens De Rampspoedige Reys-Tocht, Van de Ed: Gestrengen Heer Capiteyn Hendrik Cornelis Steenis... Gestrand op de Moorsche Kust in Afrika...* 3rd edition (Amsterdam: Bernardus Mourik, ca. 1751–1791); and *Zonderlinge Levensloop Van Een Ongelukkig Reisgezel, Of Beschryving Van de door hem geledene Droevige Slaverny, Onder de Turken in Turkyen en Barbaryen...* (ca. 1750).

265. See Marcus Rediker and Peter Linebaugh, *The Many-Headed Hydra: Sailors, Slaves, Commoners, and the Hidden History of the Revolutionary Atlantic* (Boston: Beacon Press, 2000).

266. For the text of the inscription on van Galen's elaborate tombstone, see Olfert Dapper, *Historische Beschryving der Stadt Amsterdam* (Amsterdam: Jacob van Meurs, 1663), 386.

267. To read many such tombstone inscriptions, see Scheurleer, *Van Varen en van Vechten*, passim.

5 Prizes and "Excesses": The Golden Age Pirate

1. For instance, see the numerous sentences meted out by the Hof van Holland for the crimes of begging and thievery in ARA, Archief Bisdom #151: *Register van Criminelse sententies van het Hof van Holland* (July 1, 1585–September 27, 1622).

2. ARA, AA, Verz. Bisdom #123: States-General, "Placcaet...," July 10, 1606, *Extract-Resolutien van de Staten Generaal, de Staten van Holland en de Admiraliteit op de Maze, plakaten, reglementen, instructien, enz. betreffende de commissievaart...*, 1590–1784.

3. See, e.g., William of Orange, Lettre CCCXXXV, "Le Prince d'Orange au Comte Jean de Nassau; Inconduite de M. de de Dolhain: nouvesses diverses"; Lettre CCCXXXIX, "Le Prince d'Orange au Comte Jean de Nassau, Sur les excès des Gueux de mer et l'inconduite du Seigneur de Dolhain"; and Lettre CCCXLIII, "Le Cardinal De Châtillon au Prince d'Orange, Affaires de France; pirateries des Gueux de mer," in G. Groen van Prinsterer, *Archives ou Correspondance inédite de la maison d'Orange-Nassau*, Première Série, Vol. III, 1567–1572 (Leiden, 1836), 351–354, 363–365, and 373–377; Verz. Thysius: *Ordinantie Ghemaeckt op 't Stuck van de Admiraliteit, ende Teghens de Zeerooeurs*, November 13, 1583 ('t Antwerpen: Chr. Plantijn, 1583); ARA, AA, Verz. Bisdom #123: "Excessen door Vrijbuijters &c. dezer Landen...," Het Memoriale Admt. Maze, September 18, 1605,

October 8, 1605, October 6, 1606, and March 6, 1607, *Extract-Resolutien van de Staten Generaal...*, 1590–1784; and ARA, AA, Verz. Bisdom #107: *Aaanschrijving van de Staten Generaal om in diligentie eenigh scheepen van oorlog toe te rusten om te agterhalen de vrijbuiters uijt dese Landen...*, March 6, 1607.

4. A. Th. van Deursen, *Resolutien der Staten-Generaal*, Nieuwe Reeks (The Hague, 1971), 257, n. 1, cited in C.G. Roelofsen, "Grotius and State Practice of His Day: Some Remarks on the Place of *De Jure Belli ac Pacis* within the Context of Seventeenth-Century 'Christendom' and the Role of Contemporary Precedents in Grotius' Works," *Grotiana*, 10 (1989), 24, n. 96.
5. van Deursen, *Resolutien*, 257, n. 1, cited in Roelofsen, "Grotius and State Practice of His Day," 24, n. 96.
6. Verz. Thysius: *Hollantse Mercurius, Brenghende In een kort Tractaet het remarcabelst in den Iaere 1650...* (Haerlem: Pieter Casteleyn, 1651), 91.
7. Simon de Vries, *Historie van Barbaryen... Tweede Deel...* (Amsterdam: Jan ten Hoorn, 1684), 65–66.
8. de Vries, *Historie van Barbaryen*, 74.
9. de Vries, *Historie van Barbaryen*, 78; and Nicolaes Wassenaer, *Historisch Verhael aller Gedenkwaerdiger Geschiedenissen...*, Vol. 13 (Amsterdam: Jan Jansz., 1627–1628), 30–31.
10. de Vries, *Historie van Barbaryen*, 65; and Wassenaer, *Historisch*, Vol. 13, 31.
11. de Vries, *Historie*, 65–66.
12. de Vries, *Historie*, 57–59 and 66.
13. de Vries, *Historie*, 64–65.
14. Wassenaer, *Historisch*, Vol. 13, 30–31.
15. *'t Begin, Midden en Eynde Der Zee-Rooveryen van den Alderfamieusten Zee-Roover, Claes G. Compaen...* (1659), 8–9 and 35. For more details on the career of the illustrious Jansz., see A. van der Moer, "Jan Jansz. van Haerlem, alias Murat Reys (15?–16?), *Marineblad* (January 1996), 18–21.
16. Dionisius van der Sterre, *Zeer aenmerkelijke reysen gedaan door Jan Erasmus Reyning...* (Amsterdam: Jan ten Hoorn, 1691).
17. van der Sterre, *Zeer aenmerkelijke...*, 3.
18. Verz. Thysius: States-General, *Placcaet...* (*Verbod om dienst te nemen op vreemde schepen...*), March 23, 1629 ('s-Gravenhage: Wed. en Erfg. van H. Jz. van Wouw, 1629); and Verz. Thysius: States-General, *Placaet...* (*tegen 't dienst nemen op vreemde schepen...*), March 19, 1640 ('s-Gravenhage: Wed. en Erfgen. van H. Jz. v. Wouw, 1640).
19. van der Sterre, *Zeer aenmerkelijke...*, 10.
20. van der Sterre, *Zeer aenmerkelijke*, 12. Other concurrent Dutch sources, such as the almanac *De Snelle Mercurius* called the Jamaican marauders "*Rovers*"—i.e., pirates—not *kapers*—i.e., privateers. And of course, even if Casten had been a privateer, Dutch law still would have proscribed Reyning's service aboard his ship. See Verz. Thysius: *De Snelle Mercurius...* (T'Amstelredam: Otto Barentsz. Smient, 1686), 14, "September" section.
21. Van der Sterre claimed that Reyning was given a privateering commission, but complained that Exquemelin had come to the opposite conclusion. See van der Sterre, *Zeer aenmerkelijke...*, 27.
22. Van der Sterre, *Zeer aenmerkelijke...*, 13 and 18.
23. Van der Sterre, *Zeer aenmerkelijke...*, 24–26. van der Sterre notes that Exquemelin also discussed this "Rokje," so one assumes that he is the same man as the aforementioned "Rok de Bresiliaan."

24. van der Sterre, *Zeer aenmerkelijke* . . ., 34.
25. van der Sterre, *Zeer aenmerkelijke* . . ., 49.
26. Alexander Olivier Exquemelin, *De Americaensche Zee-Roovers* . . ., (Amsterdam: Jan ten Hoorn, 1678), 200.
27. van der Sterre, *Zeer aenmerkelijke* . . ., 57.
28. van der Sterre, *Zeer aenmerkelijke* . . ., 67–69.
29. van der Sterre, *Zeer aenmerkelijke* . . ., 123.
30. van der Sterre, *Zeer aenmerkelijke* . . ., 124 and 134–135.
31. van der Sterre, *Zeer aenmerkelijke* . . ., 93–94.
32. van der Sterre, *Zeer aenmerkelijke* . . ., Preface.
33. van der Sterre, *Zeer aenmerkelijke* . . ., 42 and 62.
34. van der Sterre, *Zeer aenmerkelijke* . . ., 30–31.
35. Verz. Thysius: Collegien ter Admiraliteyt, Zeeland Kamer, *Instructie ende Articulen, Waer naer de Capiteynen, Officieren ende Bootsgesellen ter vryer Neeringhe uytvarende, op behoorlicke Commissie hun sullen hebben te reguleren* . . ., February 21, 1665 (Middelburgh: Johan Misson, 1665), Articles IV, V–VI, XII, XXIV, XIX, and XXXIX.
36. Jaap Bruijn, "Dutch Privateering During the Second and Third Anglo-Dutch Wars," *Course et Piraterie* . . ., ed. Commission Internationale d'Histoire Maritime, Vol. I (Paris: Institut de Recherche et d'Histoire des Textes/Editions du Centre National de la Recherche Scientifique, 1975), 410.
37. ARA, AA, Verz. Bisdom #167: *Copie-Crimineele vonnissen van de Admiraliteit op de Maas* . . . *1575–1710*, fols. 388–389 and 391–392 vs.
38. See, e.g., ARA, Hof van Holland #5655: *Registers van criminele sententies, Hof van Holland* for the case of Lysbeth Hendriks, whom on March 31, 1651 the Court decreed had "violated banishment, [and will be] banished again." For a general list of High Court of Holland sentences, see ARA, Hof van Holland Archief: *Index op de Criminele Sententien van het Hof van Holland, 1623–1811*.
39. ARA, AA, Verz. Bisdom #167: *Copie-Crimineele vonnissen van de Admiraliteit op de Maas* . . . *1575–1710*, fols. 388–392 vs.
40. ARA, AA, Verz. Bisdom #167: *Copie-Crimineele vonnissen van de Admiraliteit op de Maas* . . . *1575–1710*, fols. 210–211.
41. ARA, AA, Verz. Bisdom #167: *Copie-Crimineele vonnissen van de Admiraliteit op de Maas* . . . *1575–1710*, fols. 303–307 and 319 vs–327 vs.
42. ARA, AA, Verz. Bisdom #167: *Copie-Crimineele vonnissen van de Admiraliteit op de Maas* . . . *1575–1710*, fols. 303–307 and 319 vs–327 vs.
43. ARA, AA, Verz. Bisdom #167: *Copie-Crimineele vonnissen van de Admiraliteit op de Maas* . . . *1575–1710*, fols. 303–307 and 319 vs–327 vs.
44. ARA, AA, Verz. van der Heim #339 (re: Admiraliteit op de Maze: Rechtspraak):*Register der Voornaamste Crimineele Sententien van den Raad Ter Admiraliteit op de Maze van den Jare 1575 tot 1710*; and ARA, AA, Verz. Bisdom #167: *Copie-Crimineele vonnissen van de Admiraliteit op de Maas* . . . *1575–1710*, fol. 28 vs.
45. ARA, AA, Verz. van der Heim #339 (re: Admiraliteit op de Maze: Rechtspraak): *Register der Voornaamste Crimineele Sententien van den Raad Ter Admiraliteit op de Maze van den Jare 1575 tot 1710*; and ARA, AA, Verz. Bisdom #167: *Copie-Crimineele vonnissen van de Admiraliteit op de Maas* . . . *1575–1710*, fol. 28 vs.
46. Verz. Thysius: States-General, *Publikatie* . . ., April 14, 1672 ('s-Gravenhage: Iac. Scheltus, 1672), Clause XXI.

47. J.Th.H. Verhees-van Meer, *De Zeeuwse Kaapvaart Tijdens de Spaanse Successicoorlog 1703–1713*, Werken Vitgeven door het Koninklijk Zeeusch Genootschap der Wetenschappen, Vol. 3 (Middleburg: koninklijk Zeeusch Genootschap der Wetenschappen, 1986), 265, n. 43. She notes that Jacobsen was imprisoned and taken to Dunkirk, from where he could not obtain a passport to return to the Dutch Republic. In a bind, "he had to take up service on an enemy ship."
48. ARA, AA, Verz. Bisdom #167: *Copie-Crimineele vonnissen van de Admiraliteit op de Maas . . . 1575–1710*, fols. 273 vs–273. By comparison, when the same Admiralty court convicted Navy Lieutenant Adriaan van der Hoeven of "piracy" (*Roverijen*) in absentia in 1690, the judges sentenced him to eternal banishment from the United Provinces; should he ever return, they condemned him to hang at the Rotterdam gallows. See ARA, AA, Verz. Bisdom #167: *Copie-Crimineele vonnissen van de Admiraliteit op de Maas . . . 1575–1710*, fols. 250–251. The harshness of this punishment is echoed in other in absentia cases as well, e.g., ARA, AA, Verz. Bisdom #167: *Copie-Crimineele vonnissen van de Admiraliteit op de Maas . . . 1575–1710*, fols. 325 vs–327 vs, fols. 322 vs–324 vs; and fols. 319 vs–322.
49. ARA, AA, Verz. #167: *Copie-Crimineele vonnissen van de Admiraliteit op de Maas . . .*, 1575–1710, fols. 181–182.
50. ARA, AA, Verz. Bisdom #167: *Copie-Crimineele vonnissen van de Admiraliteit op de Maas . . . 1575–1710*, fols. 60–60 vs. For more on this gang, see fols. 57 vs–58.
51. ARA, AA, Verz. Bisdom #167: *Copie-Crimineele vonnissen van de Admiraliteit op de Maas . . . 1575–1710*, fols. 265 vs–266 vs.
52. ARA, AA, Verz. Bisdom #34: *Alphabetische index op de extract-resolutien . . .*, December 23, 1692, Rec. I, fol. 60, "Zeevaart" heading.
53. ARA, AA, Verz. Bisdom #123: "Extract uit de Resolutien van den Raedt ter Admiralit. op de Maeze," June 2, 1695, *Extract-Resolutien van de Staten Generaal, de Staten van Holland en de Admiraliteit op de Maze, plakaten, reglementen, instructien, enz. betreffende de commissievaart . . .*, 1590–1784.
54. ARA, AA, Verz. Bisdom #167: *Copie-Crimineele vonnissen van de Admiraliteit op de Maas . . . 1575–1710*, fols. 246–249.
55. ARA, AA, Verz. Bisdom #167: *Copie-Crimineele vonnissen van de Admiraliteit op de Maas . . . 1575–1710*, fols. 28–28 vs.
56. ARA, AA, Verz. Bisdom #167: *Copie-Crimineele vonnissen van de Admiraliteit op de Maas . . . 1575–1710*, fol. 332.
57. ARA, AA, Verz. Bisdom #167: *Copie-Crimineele vonnissen van de Admiraliteit op de Maas . . . 1575–1710*, fols. 84–85 vs.
58. The document also states that the *Kraantgen* patrolled the waters of "Capo Augustijn," "Cape Clancre (Clanche?)," and the island of "Bona Sista."
59. The sentence also notes that one fugitive still remained at large. ARA, AA, Verz. Bisdom #167: *Copie-Crimineele vonnissen van de Admiraliteit op de Maas . . . 1575–1710*, fols. 84–85 vs.
60. Verz. Thysius: *Bekentenisse van Hugo clerck capiteyn der zee Roovels . . .* (Amsterdam, 1615). Verz. Thysius: *Belijdenisse, Sententie, ende namen der Zeeroovers, die soo tot Rotterdam als 't Amsterdam met der koorde gheexecuteert zijn enz . . . den 24 Jan . . .* (Amsterdam: Broer Jansz., 1615); and ARA, AA, Verz. Bisdom #167: *Copie-Crimineele vonnissen van de Admiraliteit op de Maas . . . 1575–1710*, fols. 89 vs–90 vs.

61. ARA, AA, Verz. Bisdom #167: *Copie-Crimineele vonnissen van de Admiraliteit op de Maas . . . 1575–1710*, fols. 310–318. The record notes that the second sentence was declared at the Loo Palace.
62. ARA, AA, Verz. Bisdom #20: "Res. Holl: Versoek van Capitijn Simon Maartsz Stuijt . . .," April 28, 1611, *Extract Resolutien van de Staten Generaal, de Staten van Holland, enz.*
63. ARA, Hof van Holland #5220.29: *Informatie tegen Corn. Claesz. van Uitgeest, impetrant van pardon en gevangene op de voorpoort, zeerover*, 1615; ARA, Hof van Holland Archief: *Chronologisch Register op de Criminele Papieren van het Hof van Holland uit de periode 1572 tot en met 1810*; and ARA, Hof van Holland #5222.22: States-General, *Pardon voor Pieter Pack*, 1615.
64. ARA, Hof van Holland Archief: *Chronologisch Register op de Criminele Papieren van het Hof van Holland uit de periode 1572 tot en met 1810*; ARA, Hof van Holland #5220.21: *Request etc. voor Jan Lievensz. Rijckewaert, zeerover, om gratie*, September 1615; and ARA, Hof van Holland #5222.22: States-General, *Pardon voor Pieter Pack*, 1615.
65. Rijckewaert defended his behavior by claiming that his assaults were justified during time of war (i.e., the Dutch Revolt), since the ships he had targeted were en route to Spain. See ARA, Hof van Holland #5220.21: *Request etc. voor Jan Lievensz. Rijckewaert, zeerover, om gratie*, September 1615.
66. To wit, 24 came from England, 1 from Scotland, 1 from Ireland, 5 from France, 1 from Lübeck, 2 from Flanders, 1 from Italy, and 1 from Sweden.
67. ARA, AA, Verz. Bisdom #107: "Aanschrijving van H. H. M. om de Fregatten waer op de Banditen waren gelogeert, aftedanken," March 6, 1609, *Recueil van verscheijde oude stukken, rakende de directie van en over de equipagien ter zee, de tractementen der zeeofficieren, den articulbrief te water, en de vaart der neutralen, en de prinsen en buijten*, 1589–1698.
68. Verz. Thysius: *Pardon aan de zeelieden die bij de "Piraten" dienen of gediend hebben . . .*, August 25, 1651 ('s-Gravenhage: Wed. en Erfg. van H. Jzn. v. Wouw, 1651).
69. M.R.C. Fuhrmann-Plemp van Duiveland, Introduction to *Der Untergang der Batavia und andere Schiffsjournale* (Tubingen and Basel: Erdmann, 1976).
70. R.B. Prud'homme van Reine, "Nederlandse Kaapvaart en Piraterij in Beeld," *Kapers op de Kust: Nederlandse Kaapvaart en Piraterij 1500–1800*, ed. Prud'homme van Reine and van der Oest (Vlissingen: Uitgeverij ADZ, 1991), 48.
71. The schoolteacher notes in the Preface that he used the recollections of a Sardammer man named "Soeteboom," who had known Compaen personally, the chronicle of Nicolaes Wassenaer, and information from Compaen's Oostzaan neighbor, Ian Vechtersz. Smit.
72. *'t Begin, Midden en Eynde Der Zee-Rooveryen van den Alderfamieusten Zee-Roover/Claes G. Compaen, Van Oostzanen in Kennermer-landt . . .* (Gedruckt by een Liefhebber van all Nieuwigheden, 1659).
73. J.Fzn.M. Buisman, *Populaire Prozaschrijvers 1600–1815* (Amsterdam: Israel, 1960), 30–32, #112–129.
74. Isaac Commelin, *Begin ende Voortgangh van de Vereenighde Nederlantsche Geoctroyeerde Oost-Indische Compagnie . . .*, Vol. II (Amsterdam: J. Janssonius, 1646), account #20.
75. Nicolaes Wassenaer, *Historisch Verhael aller gedenkwaerdiger geschiedenissen . . .*, Vol. 13 (1627).

76. Lambert Van Den Bosch, *Leven en Daden van de Doorluchtige Zeehelden* (Amsterdam: Jan Claesz. ten Hoorn & Jan Bouman, 1676).
77. Johan van Twist, *Generale Beschrijvinghe van Indien . . . Hier is noch bygevoecht 't Iournael van d'Heer Admirael Wybrant Schram, met de Zee-Slagh tegen Claes Compaen . . .*, 2nd edition (Amsterdam: Hendrick Doncker, 1650).
78. Wybrant Schram, *Journael ende Verhael Vande Oost-Indische Reyse, gedaen by den Heer Admiral Wybrant Schram . . . Met een Beschryvinghe van de See-Slach/die hy gheslagen heeft met den vermaerden See-roover Claes Compaen* (Amsterdam: Hendrick Doncker, 1650).
79. *'t Begin, Midden en Eynde Der Zee-Rooveryen . . .*, ii.
80. de Vries, *Historie van Barbaryen*, 81–83.
81. Alexander O. Exquemelin, *The Buccaneers of America*, trans. Alexis Brown (New York: Dover, 2000; orig. edition Amsterdam, 1678), 80.
82. van der Sterre, *Zeer aenmer Kelijke . . .*, 24–26.
83. *'t Begin, Midden en Eynde Der Zee-Rooveryen . . .*, 3; and Wassenaer, 31 vs.
84. *'t Begin, Midden en Eynde Der Zee-Rooveryen . . .*, 3.
85. *'t Begin, Midden en Eynde Der Zee-Rooveryen . . .*, 7, which reveals that Compaen captured the cargo of an English pirate.
86. Wassenaer, *Historisch*, 31 vs.
87. *'t Begin, Midden en Eynde Der Zee-Rooveryen . . .*, 3.
88. Bartholomew Roberts is tradionally viewed as the most prolific of the deep-sea pirates in terms of number of documented captures. See Daniel Defoe, *A General History of the Pyrates*, ed. Manuel Schonhorn, 2nd edition (Mineola, NY: Dover, 1999; originally published London, 1724), 194–287.
89. These individuals included a governor in Ireland (one William Hol, with whose assistance Compaen sold at least ƒ.16,000 worth of captured Spanish goods), and the Moroccan King Muley Zidan [sic], who presented Compaen with a passport naming the pirate as his personal friend and proclaiming him "Master of the Sea." See *'t Begin, Midden en Eynde Der Zee-Rooveryen . . .*, 4 and 8–9; and Wassenaer, *Historisch*, 31 and 32 vs.
90. Coincidentally enough, his *handelaer*—i.e., the dealer who sold Compaen's stolen goods—in that North African city was none other than Dutch Barbary corsair Simon de Dansser the Younger. See *'t Begin, Midden en Eynde Der Zee-Rooveryen . . .*, 8–9; and Wassenaer, *Historisch*, 31 vs.
91. *'t Begin, Midden en Eynde Der Zee-Rooveryen . . .*, 10.
92. Wassenaer, *Historisch*, 32.
93. Wassenaer, *Historisch*, 33.
94. For example, see *'t Begin, Midden en Eynde Der Zee-Rooveryen . . .*, 6 on aggressive happenings in Ireland; and 36 for Compaen's kidnapping of the *Alcaide* in Salé, whom he ransomed for ƒ.50,000.
95. *'t Begin, Midden en Eynde Der Zee-Rooveryen . . .*, 4.
96. *'t Begin, Midden en Eynde Der Zee-Rooveryen . . .*, 36.
97. *'t Begin, Midden en Eynde Der Zee-Rooveryen . . .*, 14–16.
98. *'t Begin, Midden en Eynde Der Zee-Rooveryen . . .*, 34–35.
99. *'t Begin, Midden en Eynde Der Zee-Rooveryen . . .*, 19.
100. *'t Begin, Midden en Eynde Der Zee-Rooveryen . . .*, 19.
101. The report is contained in the following logbook: ARA, VOC #5050: Wijbrant Jansz. Schram, *Journaal gehouden op het Schip Hollandia tijdens de Reis van de Republiek naar Batavia onder Beval van Wijbrant Jansz. Schram*, 1626.

102. *'t Begin, Midden en Eynde Der Zee-Rooveryen* . . ., 19; and Wassenaer, *Historisch*, 33 vs.
103. *'t Begin, Midden en Eynde Der Zee-Rooveryen* . . ., 19.
104. *'t Begin, Midden en Eynde Der Zee-Rooveryen* . . ., 18.
105. Wassenaer, *Historisch*, 33 vs.
106. *'t Begin, Midden en Eynde Der Zee-Rooveryen* . . ., 20; Wassenaer, *Historisch*, 34. At this point, the accounts presented in these two works begins to differ. For instance, Compaen's biography claims that Schram opened fire, while Wassenaer's chronicle contends that Compaen released the first shot. Also, Wasseaner affirms that Compaen sent his letter only after the hostilities had broken out (see 34 vs).
107. *'t Begin, Midden en Eynde Der Zee-Rooveryen* . . ., 19.
108. *'t Begin, Midden en Eynde Der Zee-Rooveryen* . . ., 21; and Wassenaer, *Historisch*, 34 vs.
109. *'t Begin, Midden en Eynde Der Zee-Rooveryen* . . ., 21–23.
110. Wassenaer, *Historisch*, 36.
111. *'t Begin, Midden en Eynde Der Zee-Rooveryen* . . ., 18.
112. *'t Begin, Midden en Eynde Der Zee-Rooveryen* . . ., 37–39.
113. *'t Begin, Midden en Eynde Der Zee-Rooveryen* . . ., 39.
114. *'t Begin, Midden en Eynde Der Zee-Rooveryen* . . ., 40.
115. *'t Begin, Midden en Eynde Der Zee-Rooveryen* . . ., 40; and Wassenaer, *Historisch*, 33.
116. *'t Begin, Midden en Eynde Der Zee-Rooveryen* . . ., 40; and Wasseaner, *Historisch*, 33.
117. *'t Begin, Midden en Eynde Der Zee-Rooveryen* . . ., 39-40; and Wassenaer, *Historisch*, 33.
118. Wassenaer, *Historisch*, 33.
119. *'t Begin, Midden en Eynde Der Zee-Rooveryen* . . ., 40.
120. van der Sterre, *Zeer aenmerkelijke* . . ., 93.
121. van der Sterre, *Zeer aenmerkelijke* . . ., 96.
122. The Spanish, e.g., were not immune from the convenience of illicit commerce with pirates. See, e.g., AGI: Guatemala #359, *Comercio ilícito con piratas y comisos de esclavas negros*, 1703–1704; and AGI, Escribania #964: *Sentencias del Consejo*, 1696.
123. Verhees-van Meer, *De Zeeuwse Kaapvaart*, 9. For specific instances of WIC captures of prize vessels, as well as inventories of the booty and notes on proceeds from the auctions, see, e.g., Diederick Kortland, ed., *Inhoudslijsten van Overgekomen Brieven en Papieren uit Brazilie (1630–1654)* (Algemeen Rijksarchief, Eerste Afdeling, 1994); ARA, WIC #49: *Brieven en papieren uit Brazilië*, 1630–1632; ARA, WIC #51: *Brieven en papieren uit Brazilië*, 1636, documents #14–16; ARA, WIC #52, *Brieven en papieren uit Brazilië*, 1637, documents #37–38, 47, 50–52, 62, 67–68, 109, 113, and 114; WIC #53, *Brieven en papieren uit Brazilië*, 1638, documents #9, 11-14, 100–101, 184, and 189; and ARA, WIC #54, *Brieven en papieren uit Brazilië*, 1639, documents #6, 37, 150–151, and 154.
124. Jack Beeching, Introduction to John Esquemeling, *The Buccaneers of America* (London: The Folio Society, 1972), 8–9; and J.J. Baud, *Proeve eener Geschiedenis der Strafwetgeving tegen de Zeerooverij* (Utrecht: D. Post Uiterweer, 1854), 106.

125. ARA, WIC #617: "Interrogatorien van Pieter Doncker," February 8, 1683, *Secrete Brieven & Papieren van Curaçao, 1680–1689*, fol. 263.
126. ARA, WIC #617: "Interrogatorien van Juan Barofso Y Pozzo," February 22, 1683, *Secrete Brieven en Papieren van Curaçao, 1680–1689*, fols. 259–260.
127. ARA, WIC #617: "Interragatorien van Elisabeth Pieters, Weduwe de heer Joan Pedro van Collen, Manuel Epina, Benjamin Carvallo, en Ysaacque Omar Chena," February 11, 1683, *Secrete brieven en papieren van Curaçao, 1680–1689*, fol. 291.
128. ARA, WIC #617: "Brief van Nicolaes van Liebergen, Directeur over Curacao, van Balthazar Beck," February 10, 1682, *Secrete Brieven en Papieren van Curaçao, 1680–1689*, fol. 146.
129. ARA, WIC #617: "Interrogatorien van Gisberto Hippesack," February 10, 1683, *Secrete brieven en papieren van Curaçao, 1680–1689*, fol. 295. This individual's name is sometimes also spelled "Hoppesack."
130. ARA, WIC #617: "Attestatie van G. Hoppesack," February 25, 1683, *Secrete brieven en papieren van Curaçao, 1680–1689*, fol. 290.
131. ARA, WIC # 617: "Aanteckingen van Gisberto Hoppesack, Secretarias, aan de Raad van Curaçao," April 12, 1681, *Secrete Brieven en Papieren van Curaçao, 1680–1689*, fol. 47.
132. The source notes that English "*Capers*" who had captured a WIC ship transporting slaves were carrying French letters of commission. See ARA, WIC #467: "Brief aan Jan Doncker...," December 3, 1677, *Kopieboeken van brieven naar Amerika, met Register*, 1675–1684, fol. 41 vs.
133. ARA, WIC #617: *Aanteckingen van Gisberto Hoppesack, Secretarias, aan de Raad van Curaçao*, April 12, 1681, *Secrete Brieven en Papieren van Curaçao, 1680-1689*, fol. 47.
134. ARA, WIC #617: "Nicolaas van den Hoorn, Auditeur Extraordinaris... Contra Antheunis Klincke, Capitein often Schipper van... de Jonge Jacob," September 3, 1680, *Secrete Brieven en Papieren van Curaçao, 1680–1689*, fols. 53–54.
135. ARA, WIC #617: "Interrogatorien van David Abendana," February 22, 1683, *Secrete brieven en papieren van Curaçao, 1680–1689*, fol. 299.
136. ARA, WIC #617: "Artijckelen aen Nicolaas van Liebergen," March 2, 1683, *Secrete brieven en papieren van Curaçao, 1680–1689*, fol. 324. According to Company records, Grammont was a formidable sea robber, commanding 4 ships, 2 barks, and approximately 130 men. Spanish vessels were his customary target. See ARA, WIC #617: "Brieven naar de Bewinthebberen van de Camer Amsterdam, Gecommitteert tot de Secrete Saechen," April 14, 1681, *Secrete Brieven en Papieren van Curacao, 1680–1689*, fols. 15–22.
137. ARA, WIC #617: "Interrogatorien van Jan Elkis," February 27, 1683, *Secrete Brieven en Papieren van Curaçao, 1680–1689*, fols. 245–247; and ARA, WIC #617: "Interrogatorien van Gerritt Slocker," 1683, *Secrete Brieven en Papieren van Curaçao, 1680–1689*, fols. 249–250. The Spanish authorities also investigated the wheeling and dealing of Balthazar Beck. See AGI, Escribania 597A: *Comisiones Gobernacion de Cartagena*, 1684.
138. ARA, WIC #617: Article 13, "Pointen ende Articulen bij de Heeren Bewinthebberen vande WIC ter Vergaderinge Vande Thienen," ca. 1683, *Secrete brieven en papieren van Curaçao, 1680–1689*, fol. 349.
139. ARA, WIC #617: Article 1, "Artijckelen van beschuldinge ten laste van de geweesene Director Nicolaes van Liebergen," ca. 1683, *Secrete brieven en papieren van Curaçao, 1680–1689*, fol. 448.

140. ARA, WIC #468: "Brief aan Willem Kerckrink, Directeur van Curaçao," July 2, 1688, *Kopieboeken van brieven naar Amerika*, 1684–1689, fols. 155 vs–156.
141. For some instances of general VOC misconduct, see ARA, Hof van Holland #5213.8: *Stukken betreffende zekere misbruiken gepleegd bij de Oostindische Compagnie*, 1610.
142. ARA, AA, Verz. Bisdom #123: States-General, Placcaet, July 10, 1606, *Extract-Resolutien van de Staten Generaal, de Staten van Holland en de Admiraliteit op de Maze, plakaten, reglementen, instructien, enz. betreffende de commissievaart...*, 1590–1784.
143. ARA, VOC# 307: *Zakenindex op de resoluties van de kamer Amsterdam*, 1602–1743, fol. 472. For additional details on this case, see ARA, VOC #248.
144. C.G. Roelofsen, "The Sources of Mare Liberum: The Contested Origins of the Doctrine of the Freedom of the Seas," ed. W.P. Heere, *International Law and Its Sources; Liber Amicorum Maarten Bos* (Deventer, 1988), 103.
145. ARA, VOC #345: *Zakenindex op de uitgaande missiven van de Heren XVII aan de kantoren in Indie*, 1614–1707, June 27, 1699, fol. 117. For more information on this entry, see ARA, VOC #323.
146. Verz. ZBP: *Sententie By... den Gerechte der Stadt Dordrecht... gepronuncieert tegens Laurens Davidsz...* (Dordrecht: Matteus van Nispen, 1663); F.W. Stapel, "Hubert Hugo: Een Zeeroover in Dienst van de Oostindische Compagnie," *Bijdragen tot de Taal-, Land-, en Volkenkunde van Nederlandsch-Indië*, Vol. 86, Afl. III en IV (1930), 1; and J.J. Beyerman, "Een Zeeroover als Zee-Officier onder de Ruyter" (Den Haag, 1934), 1–2. An off-print of this hard-to-find piece is available in Amsterdam, at the Nederlandse Scheepvaart Museum, #N. i. I. K II 196.
147. Stapel, "Hubert Hugo," 2.
148. Beyerman, "Een Zeeroover...," 1–2.
149. Verz. ZBP: *Sententie... tegens Laurens Davidsz.* (1663), 1.
150. ARA, Hof van Holland #5270A.2: "Letter from Cezar Duc de Vandosme...," July 13, 1663, *Stukken en informatie in zake Laurens Davids wegens zeeroverij in de Rode Zee en elders*, 1663; ARA, Hof van Holland #5270A.2: "Noten," *Stukken en informatie in zake Laurens Davids wegens zeeroverij in de Rode Zee en elders*, 1663; and Verz. ZBP: Sententie... *tegens Laurens Davidsz.* (1663).
151. Verz. ZBP: *Sententie... tegens Laurens Davidsz.* (1663), 1–2.
152. Verz. ZBP: *Sententie... tegens Laurens Davidsz.* (1663), 2.
153. ARA, Hof van Holland #5270A.2: "Lettre de Cézar Duc de Vandosme...," July 13, 1663, *Stukken en informatie in zake Laurens Davids wegens zeeroverij in de Rode Zee en elders*, 1663.
154. Verz. ZBP: *Sententie... tegens Laurens Davidsz.* (1663), 2.
155. ARA, Hof van Holland #5270A.2: Examination of Laurens Davidsz., *Stukken en informatie in zake Laurens Davids wegens zeeroverij in de Rode Zee en elders*, 1663.
156. ARA, Hof van Holland #5270A.2: Examination of Laurens Davidsz., *Stukken en informatie in zake Laurens Davids wegens zeeroverij in de Rode Zee en elders*, 1663; Verz. ZBP: *Sententie... tegens Laurens Davidsz.* (1663), 2–3; and "John Dutton's Account of Hugo," MS in the Public Records Office, England (see *Calendar of State Papers, Domestic, 1663–1664*, 148), reprinted in R.B. Serjeant, *The Portuguese off the South Arabian Coast: Hadrami Chronicles: With Yemeni and European Accounts of Dutch Pirates off Mocha in the Seventeenth Century* (Oxford: Clarendon Press, 1963), 127.

157. "English Records at the India Office, 1661–4," in Serjeant, *Hadrami Chronicles*, 128.
158. *The Travels of Monsieur de Thevenot into the Levant* (London, 1687), iii, 21, reprinted in Serjeant, *Hadrami Chronicles*, 128; and "Manucci's Account of Hugo," *Storia do Mogor*, Indian Texts Series, trans. William Irvine (London, 1907), ii, 45–46, reprinted in Serjeant, *Hadrami Chronicles*, 129.
159. al-Mutahhar al-Djarmuzi, "History," 315, trans. and reprinted as "Al-Djarmuzi's History," in Serjeant, *Hadrami Chronicles*, 125–126.
160. "John Dutton's Account," MS, Public Records Office, cited in the *Calendar of State Papers, Domestic, 1663–4*, 148, reprinted in Serjeant, *Hadrami Chronicles*, 127.
161. ARA, Hof van Holland 5270A.2: Examination of Laurens Davidsz.; and *Sententie . . . tegens Laurens Davidsz.*, 1663, 4.
162. ARA, Hof van Holland # 5270A.2: Examination of Laurens Davidsz., *Stukken en informatie in zake Laurens Davids wegens zeeroverij in de Rode Zee en elders*, 1663.
163. ARA, Hof van Holland 5270A.2: *Stukken en informatie in zake Laurens Davids wegens zeeroverij in de Rode Zee en elders*, 1663.
164. ARA, Hof van Holland 5270A.2: *Stukken en informatie in zake Laurens Davids wegens zeeroverij in de Rode Zee en elders*, 1663.
165. ARA, Hof van Holland 5270A.2: *Stukken en informatie in zake Laurens Davids wegens zeeroverij in de Rode Zee en elders*.
166. See ARA, Hof van Holland# 5270A.2: *Chronologisch Register op de Criminele Papieren van het Hof van Holland uit de Periode 1572 tot en met 1810, 1602–1743*, Band I: 1572–1699.
167. ARA, Hof van Holland #5270A.2: *Stukken en informatie in zake Laurens Davids wegens zeeroverij in de Rode Zee en elders*, 1663.
168. ARA, VOC #307: *Zakenindex op de resoluties van de kamer Amsterdam*, fol. 435; VOC #237, May 31, 1663 and June 7, 1663; and Verz. ZBP: *Sententie . . . tegens Laurens Davidsz.* (1663), 4.
169. Verz. ZBP: *Sententie . . . tegens Laurens Davidsz.* (1663), 4–5.
170. Verz. ZBP: *Sententie . . . tegens Laurens Davidsz.* (1663), 5.
171. Beyerman, "Een Zeeroover . . .," 17.
172. Beyerman, "Een Zeeroover . . .," 18.
173. For more information on this matter, see ARA, VOC #307: *Zakenindex op de resoluties van de kamer Amsterdam*, fol. 435; ARA, VOC #237, June 30 and July 14, 1663; and Beyerman, "Een Zeeroover . . .," 13–16.
174. Beyerman, "Een Zeeroover . . .," 19, n. 1.
175. All information from this paragraph comes from Beyerman, "Een Zeeroover . . .," 18–20.
176. All information from this paragraph comes from Stapel, "Hubert Hugo," 621–635.

6 The Dutch Freebooter in the Golden Age

1. For instance, in one 1589 case tried by the Admiralty of the Maas in which the defendants were pardoned, the sentence explained that Prince Maurits had felt moved to pronounce such lenient judgments—despite the fact that many of the defendants hailed from the Southern Netherlands—because of the men's "youth," as well as for unnamed "other reasons." See ARA, AA, Verz. Bisdom #167: *Copie-Crimineele vonnissen van de Admiraliteit op de Maas . . . 1575–1710*, fols. 28–28 vs.

2. By using the phrase "symbolic meaning," I mean to utilize Clifford Geertz's semiotic definition of culture. To Geertz, culture is an amalgam of signs and symbols that hold import and meaning; the human being, then, is "an animal suspended in webs of significance he himself has spun..." See Clifford Geertz, *The Interpretation of Cultures* (New York: Basic Books, 1973), 5.
3. Verz. RLP: *Amsterdams Vuur-Praetje, Van 't Een ende 'tander nu om gaet* (Amstelredam: Claes Pietersz., 1649), 16–23.
4. J.Th.H. Verhees-van Meer, *De Zeeuwse Kaapvaart Tijdens de Spaanse Successieoorlog 1702–1713* (Middelburg: Werken Uitgegeven door het Koninklijk Zeeuwsch Genootschap der Wetenschappen, 1986), 29–31.
5. Verz. Thysius: States of Zeeland, *Propositie... Om ordre te stellen tegens de Portugaelsche Commissie vaerders...* (Vlissingen: T. Tyssen, 1662).
6. See, e.g., Verz. Thysius: States-General, *Alsoo mijn Heeren die Staten Generael... zijn gheresolveert hen ter zee te wapenen...*, May 20, 1599.
7. Verhees-van Meer, *De Zeeuwse Kaapvaart*, 9.
8. Jaap R. Bruijn, "Dutch Privateering during the Second and Third Anglo-Dutch Wars," ed. Commission Internationale d'Histoire Maritime, *Course et Piraterie...*, Vol. I (Paris: Institut de Recherche et d'Histoire des Textes/Editions du Centre National de la Recherche Scientfique, 1975), 405.
9. Verz. RLP: *Amsterdams Vuur-Praetje...* (1649), Preface and 16.
10. States-General, *Groot Placaet-Boeck van de Staten-Generaal en van Holland en Zeeland*, Vol. I (The Hague and Amsterdam: 1648–1796), 984.
11. Verz. Thysius: *Deductie, Op het subject van de handelinge op de Straet, en de Navigatie in de Middellantsche Zee* (1687), 1.
12. Verz. Thysius: *Memorie Door mijn Heer de Graaf van Avaux...*, November 28, 1681 ('s-Gravenhage, 1681).
13. Verz. Thysius: *Deductie, Op het subject van de handelinge op de Straet...* (1687).
14. Verz. Thysius: Dionysium Spranckhuysen, *Triumphe Van weghen de Geluckighe ende Over-Rijcke Victorie... vanden Heer Generael Pieter Pietersz. Heyn...* (Delf: Jan Andriesz. Kloeting, 1629), 53–54.
15. Verz. Thysius: J. Liefs, *Den Lof vande Geoctr. Oost ende West-Indische Compagnye ende Lofricke Zee-vaert van dese vrye vereenighde Nederlandse Provintien* (Delf: J. Pz. Waelpots, 1630), 1–2.
16. Verz. Thysius: J. Liefs, *Den Lof vande Geoctr. Oost ende West-Indische Compagnye...* (1630), 4.
17. Verz. Thysius: J. Liefs, *Den Lof vande Geoctr. Oost ende West-Indische Compagnye...* (1630), 5.
18. Verz. RLP: *Amsterdams Vuur-Praetje...* (1649), 23.
19. *Realia*, I, 310: "Eenige Goederen van de Portugeesen Verovert, door de Comp.aan die Natie te Laten Doen," Generale Resolutie, GGR, October 31, 1643; and ARA, VOC #718. For another occurrence of VOC patriotic giving, see *Realia*, I, 311: "Zal het Zandelhout... in een verovert Portugees schip prijs gemaakt...," Generale Resolutie, GGR, February 4, 1653. And for a reference to the WIC's donation of prize moneys to the state, as stipulated in the WIC's charter, see Verz. Thysius: *Ordonnantien ende Articulen... op het toerusten... van eene West-Indische Compagnie* (1623), 12–13, clause 42.
20. For the specific details about the States-General's defense arrangements, see Verz. Thysius: *Ordonnanatien ende Articulen... op het toerusten... van eene West-Indische Compagnie* (1623), 11–12, clauses 39–41.
21. See, e.g., the following sources, all in the AGI: Patronata 267, N. 1, R. 59: *Los Rebeldes de Los Paises Bajos contra la Armada Española*, 1571; Patronata 268,

N. 2, R. 3: *Declaración de Rodrigo Girardo, Capitan de Filibote Flamenco*, 1600; Patronata 268, N. 2, R. 4: *Corsario Holandés que Fue a Filipinas desde Perú*, 1600; Indiferente 428, L. 32, F: *Real Cédula a las Justicias de Indias* . . ., 1602, 53 vs–54 vs; Mexico 28, N. 28: *Cartas del Virrey Marques de Guadalcazar*, 1614; and Panama, 30, N. 68: *Cartas y Expedientes de Cabildos Seculares: Panamá*, 1616.

22. Verz. RLP: *Extraordinaire du XXII Novembre 1634. Contenant . . . a prise de la belle Isle de Curacao . . . par les Holandais sur les Espagnols . . .*, November 22, 1634 (Paris, 1634).

23. Verz. Thysius: *Waerachtigh verhael, van het success van de Vlote, onder den Admirael* Jacques L'Hermite . . . (1625), 2–9. The source calls Huygen "een seer couragieus / maer wreed Man . . ." (9). For information on other damaging Dutch raids in Peru, see the following documents at the AGI: Patronata 268, N. 2, R. 3: *Declaración de Rodrigo Girardo, Capitan de Filibote Flamenco*, 1600; Patronata 268, N. 2, R. 4: *Corsario Holandés que Fue a Filipinas desde Perú* (1600); and Mexico 28, N. 28: *Cartas del Virrey Marques de Guadalcazar*, 1614.

24. Verz. Thysius: *Goede nieuwe tijdinghe . . . afghesonden vanden Generael Iacob Wilckens uyt Brasilien* . . . (Amsterdam: Broer Jansz., 1624).

25. Verz. RLP: Joannem Baers, *Olinda, Ghelegen int Landt van Brasil, inde Capitania van Phernambuco . . . geluckelijck verovert* . . . (Amsterdam: Hendrick Laurentsz., 1630), title and appendix.

26. Verz. Thysius: *Ordonnantien ende Articulen . . . op het toerusten . . . van eene West-Indische Compagnie* (1623), 6, Clause 11.

27. E.W. van der Oest, "De Praktijk vande Nederlandse Kaapvaart en Piraterij 1500–1800," *Kapers op de Kust: Nederlandse Kaapvaart en Piraterij 1500–1800*, ed. Prud'homme van Reine and van der Oest (Vlissingen: Uitgeverij ADZ, 1991), 14.

28. Verhees-van Meer, 36.

29. van der Oest, "De Praktijk vande Nederlandse," 16.

30. Probably foremost among this group was Benjamin Raule(1634–1707), a merchant and a member of the Middelburg city council who sponsored at least 17 privateering vessels during the Second and Third Anglo-Dutch Wars. See Bruijn, "Dutch Privateering," 403–404. Other prominent investors included Jacob van Hoorn and Abraham van Pere, both from Vlissingen, and both of whom acted as bookkeepers. For more on Benjamin Raule, see R. Häpke, "Benjamin Raule und seine Handlungbücher," *Economish-Historish Jaarboek*, Vol. 9 (1923), 214–220; G. Gieraths, "Benjamin Raule, seine Leben und insbesondere seine volkswirtschaflichen Ansichten," *Economisch-Historisch Jaarboek*, Vol. 10 (1924), 219–302; and F. Jorberg, "Benjamin Raule," *Mededelingen Nederlandse Vereniging voor Zeegeschiedenis*, Vol. 10 (1965), 1–9.

31. Prud'homme van Reine, "Nederlandse Kaapvaart," 59–62. For a more complete list of successful bookkeepers during this era, see Verhees-van Meer, *De Zeeuwse Kaapvaart*, 146–157.

32. Verhees-van Meer, *De Zeeuwse Kaapvaart*, 36.

33. Verhees-van Meer, *De Zeeuwse Kaapvaart*, 36 and 163.

34. For more on this famous episode, see Simon Schama, *The Embarassment of Riches* (Berkeley: University of California Press, 1988), 350–366.

35. Verz. RLP: *Amsterdams Tafel-Praetje Van Wat Goets en Wat Quats En Wat Noodichs* (Gouda: Iasper Cornelisz., 1649), 19–20.

36. Verhees-van Meer, *De Zeeuwse Kaapvaart*, 37 and 163.
37. Jaap Bruijn makes this claim based upon his research on privateering during the Second and Third Anglo-Dutch Wars. See Bruijn, "Dutch Privateering," 411. For a comparison to the prize profits produced by Dutch naval men-of-war, see F. Snapper, *Oorlogsinvloeden op de overzeese handel van Holland 1551–1719* (Amsterdam, 1959), 301 and Appendix 13.
38. Bruijn, "Dutch Privateering," 411.
39. For a reference to this practice in a seventeenth-century newspaper, see Verz. Thysius: *Courante uyt Italien ende Duytschlandt, &tc.* (Amsterdam), February 26, 1639 (No. 9), 1. In this case, the Admiralty of Zeeland allowed a French privateer captain to sell his prize—a *fluit*-ship named *Salvater*, which had been en route from Riga—in Vlissingen.
40. Verhees-van Meer, *De Zeeuwse Kaapvaart*, 2, 79–91, and 165.
41. Stanhope to Hedges, The Hague, August 7, 1703, Public Records Office, State Papers, 84/224, f. 319, quoted in J.S. Bromley, "Some Zeeland Privateering Instructions: Jacob Sautyn to Captain Salomon Reynders 1707," *William III and Louis XIV*, ed. Ragnhild Hatton and J.S. Bromley (Liverpool, 1968), 162–163.
42. Verhees-van Meer, *De Zeeuwse Kaapvaart*, 2–3, 93–108, and 165–166.
43. Verhees-van Meer, *De Zeeuwse Kaapvaart*, 109–120 and 166.
44. Verhees-van Meer, *De Zeeuwse Kaapvaart*, 2.
45. Verhees-van Meer, *De Zeeuwse Kaapvaart*, 2–3.
46. Verhees-van Meer, *De Zeeuwse Kaapvaart*, 166–167.
47. Verhees-van Meer, 2 and 165–166.
48. The matter was deemed negotiable for those who came from no fixed address. See ARA, AA, Verz. van der Hoop #1: "Particulariteijten ontrent Goede of Quade Prises," September 30, 1627, Section II, *Aanteekeningen uit de resolutiën van de Staten van Holland betreffende de Admiraliteiten ... de prijzen, de uitrustingen van schepen, de commissievaart en strandvonderij*, 1575–1716, fol. 36.
49. C.G. Roelofsen, "Grotius and State Practice of His Day: Some Remarks on the Place of *De Jure Belli ac Pacis* within the Context of Seventeenth-Century 'Christendom' and the Role of Contemporary Precedents in Grotius' Works," *Grotiana*, 10 (1989), 16.
50. Roelofsen, "Grotius," 21.
51. Roelofsen, "Grotius," 22–23. Roelofsen cites the case of Amsterdam privateer Dierck Diercks, who was accused by the duke of Pomerania of unlawful attacks. Pressured by the fear that the duke might order reprisals against the Dutch as a consequence, the States-General gave the Pomeranians the option of trying the case in either the Admiralty Court—the traditional arbiter in such situations—or the High Court of Holland and Zeeland (the "Hof") and the Supreme Court of Holland and Zeeland (the "Hoge Raad"). While the Pomeranians chose the latter forum, they recieved no real justice: Diercks himself was presumably insolvent, and the owners of his ship could avail themselves of a Dutch legal rule that restricted the liability of shipowners. See Roelofsen, "Grotius," 23–25.
52. Verhees-van Meer, *De Zeeuwse Kaapvaart*, Appendix IV, 179–200.
53. See Chapter 3.
54. Verz. RLP: *Amsterdams Vuur-Praetje* ... (1649), 18.
55. Verhees-van Meer, *De Zeeuwse Kaapvaart*, 36–37.
56. For example, of the seamen who sailed for the *Middelburgse Commercie Compagnie* a merchant trading company that existed from 1732 to 1802 and was based in Zeeland's capital, only 40% hailed from the home province. Indeed, 20% of

the sailors originated from other regions in the Dutch Republic, and 35% were foreign-born. See Verhees-van Meer, *De Zeeuwse Kaapvaart*, 51.
57. See ARA, AA #1844, 1845, 1846, and 1847: *Rekeningen van den vendumeester wegens zijn uitgaaf van de prinsen, mulcten en confiscatien*, 1665–1667; and ARA, AA #1806, 1807, and 1808: *Rekeningen van den vendumeester wegens zijn ontvang van de prinsen, mulcten en confiscatien*, 1665–1667.
58. van der Oest, "De Praktijk vande Nederlandse Kaapvaart," 24.
59. Verz. Thysius: *Waerachtige goede Tijdinge Hoe de Vesting Blockzijl Stormenderhandt door de Hollandsche Kapers is ingenomen*, September 2, 1672 (Amsterdam, 1672).
60. See a 1572 letter from the city government of Zierikzee to that in Goes, quoted in Van de Spiegel, *Historie van de Satisfactie der Stadt Goes* (1777), 111–112, cited in J.J. Baud, *Proeve eener Geschiedenis der Strafwetgeving tegen de Zeeroverij* (Utrecht: D. Post Uiterweer, 1854), 76.
61. Geeraert Brandt, *Historie der vermaerde zee- en koopstad, Enkhuisen, vervaetende Haere Herkomste, en Voortgangh. Mitsgaders Verscheide gedenkwaerdige Geschiedenissen, aldaer voorgevallen* (Enkhuisen: Egbert van den Hoof, 1666), 116.
62. Brandt, *Historie der vermaerde zee- en koopstad, Enkhuisen . . .*, 123.
63. W. Martin, G.A.J. Tops et al., *Van Dale Groot Woordenboek Nederlands-Engels*, 2nd edition (Utrecht: Van Dale Lexicographie, 1991), 1523.
64. Verz. Thysius: *Placcaet byden welchen alle vrybuiters anderwaerf . . . ghecasseert zijn . . .* March 5, 1577 (Ghendt: Jan vanden Steene, 1577).
65. ARA, AA, Verz. Bisdom #123: States-General, "Excessen door Vrijbuijters &c. dezer Landen tegen Neutrale Vrienden gepleegt," 1605–1606, Notulen uit het Memoriael van het Admiraliteit op de Maze, *Extract-Resolutien van de Staten Generaal, de Staten van Holland en de Admiraliteit op de Maze, plakaten, reglementen, instructien, enz. betreffende de commissievaart . . .*, 1590–1784.
66. ARA, AA, Verz. Bisdom #167: *Copie-Crimineele vonnissen van de Admiraliteit op de Maas 1575—1710*, fols. 6–7; fols. 104 vs–105 vs; and fols. 194 vs–197.
67. ARA, AA, Verz. Bisdom #167: *Copie-Crimineele vonnissen van de Admiraliteit op de Maas 1575–1710*, fols. 47–47 vs.
68. "Lof-Dicht, ter Eeren des Vrye Vaerts" (ca. 1630), D.F. Scheurleer, *Van Varen en Van Vechten: Verzen van Tijdgenooten op Onze Zeehelden en Zeeslagen, Lof- en Schimpdichten, Matrozenliederen*, Vol. I ('s-Gravenhage: Martinus Nijhoff, 1914), 234–237.
69. "Aan de Hollantse, en Zeeuwse Vrybuyters" (1665), Scheurleer, *Van Varen en Van Vechten*, Vol. II, 178.
70. "Lof des Vrye Vaearts, ende Berisp Tegen het Misbrvck der Selver" (1629), in Scheurleer, *Van Varen en Van Vechten*, Vol. I, 224–234.
71. Nicolaes Wassenaer, *Historisch Verhael Aller Gedenkwaerdiger Geschiedenissen . . .*, Vol. 13 (Amsterdam: Jan Jansz., 1627–1628), 30 vs.
72. See also, e.g., Verz. RLP: *Naerder Openbaringe, van Nederlants Engelschen Oorloge . . .* (Leyden: Wilhelm Christiaans vander Boxc, 1653), passim.
73. ARA, AA, Verz. Bisdom #167: *Copie-Crimineele vonnissen van de Admiraliteit op de Maas . . . 1575–1710*, fols. 86–88 vs.
74. For more on the concept of "pollution" in culture, see Mary Douglas, *Purity and Danger: An Analysis of the Concepts of Pollution and Taboo* (London and New York: Routledge, 1995; orig. edition 1966).
75. Verz. RLP: *Amsterdams Vuur-Praetje . . .* (1649), 22.

76. Verz. RLP: *Amsterdams Vuur-Praetje* . . . (1649), 16–23.
77. Verz. Thysius: *Goede nieuwe tijdinghe ghecomen . . . vande Gheoctroyeerde West-Indische Compagnie* (Amsterdam: Broer Jansz., 1624).
78. Verz. RLP: *Practijcke van den Spaenschen Aes-Sack aengewesen Op de Veroveringe, en Victorie van den Loffelicken, Voorsienighen, Manlijck-hertighen Heer Generael Pieter Pietersz. Heyn* . . . ('s-Gravenhage, 1629).
79. Verz. Thysius: States-General, *Placcaet* . . ., October 10, 1673 ('s-Gravenhage: J. Scheltus, 1673).
80. Verz. Thysius: States-General, *Publikatie* . . ., April 14, 1672 ('s-Gravenhage: Iac. Scheltus, 1672).
81. De Ruyter was 29 years old when he served as a *commissievaart* captain. See the permanent exhibition at the Nederlandse Scheepvaartmuseum, Amsterdam.
82. Verz. Thysius: States-General, *Publikatie* . . ., April 14, 1672 ('s-Gravenhage: Iac. Scheltus, 1672), clauses II, VI, XIII, and XV.
83. Verhees-van Meer, *De Zeeuwse Kaapvaart*, 52.
84. Simon de Vries, *Historie van Barbaryen . . . Tweede Deel* . . . (Amsterdam: Jan ten Hoorn, 1684), 65–66 and 87.
85. For instance, see the regular stories about Willem Credo in the *Amsterdamsche Mercurren*, described in Prud'homme van Reine, "Nederlandse Kaapvaart en Piraterij," 56.
86. For example, see Verz. Thysius: *Hollandtze Mercurius*, 16th edition (Haerlem: Pieter Casteleyn, 1666), 56, 130, and 159.
87. For example, Verz. Thysius: *Copie Uyt het Schip Sint Benita den 18 November, 1657* (Amsterdam: Otto Barentsz. Smient, 1657).
88. Verz. RLP: *Goede Apparentie tot Spoedige opkomst, Der Vrye Nederlandens Magtige Zee-Vaart* . . . (1653), 13.
89. Verz. RLP: *Naerder Openbaringe, van Nederlants Engelschen Oorloge* . . . (Leyden: Wilhelm Christiaans vander Boxc, 1653).
90. Verz. RLP: *Naerder Openbaringe* . . . (1653), 40.
91. Verz. RLP: *Naerder Openbaringe* . . . (1653), passim. For specific examples of such terminology, see 54–57 and 78.
92. Verz. RLP: *Naerder Openbaringe* . . . (1653), 80–81.
93. Verz. RLP: *Naerder Openbaringe* . . . (1653), 78.
94. For the melody of this seventeenth-century song, see A. Valerius, *Neder-lantsche Gedenck-clanck* (Haarlem, 1626), 164; for the text, see J. Veldkamp and K. Boer, *Kun je nog zingen, zing dan mee!* (Groningen, 1972), 32; cited in Verhees-van Meer, *De Zeeuwse Kaapvaart*, Vol. III, 6.
95. "Aan de Hollantse, en Zeeuwse Vrybuyters" (1665), in Scheurleer, *Van Varen en Van Vechten*, Vol. II, 178.
96. "Lof der vrye vaerts, ende berisp tegen het misbrvvyck der selver" (1629), in Scheurleer, *Van Varen en Van Vechten*, Vol. I, 224–234.
97. "Lof-Dicht, ter eeren des vrye vaerts" (1629), in Scheurleer, *Van Varen en Van Vechten*, Vol. I, 243–237.
98. "Rouwklagt over de Dood van den Dapperen Zeekapiteyn Pieter Borrens . . ." (1711), in Scheurleer, *Van Varen en Van Vechten*, Vol. III, 198–199. Borrens inspired another poem as well; see 202–203.
99. "Op de Lyckstatie van Capiteyn Mathys Jacobsz. Pruis . . ."; J. van Schrieck, J.Cz., "Graf-Schrift," and W. van Focquenbroch, "Grafschrift van den manhaften Kapitein Pruyst . . ." in Scheurleer, *Van Varen en Van Vechten*, Vol. II, 179–181.

100. "*Pié-de-Palo*" in Spanish and "*Perna de Páu*" in Portuguese. W.J. van Balen, *Hollandsche Kapers op Amerikaansche Kusten* (Leiden: A.W. Sijthoff, 1942), 176.
101. "Bijschrift," in Scheurleer, *Van Varen en Van Vechten*, Vol. I, 318.
102. Verz. RLP: *Naerder Openbaringe* . . . (1653), 40.
103. Olfert Dapper, *Historische Beschryving der Stadt Amsterdam* (Amsterdam: Jacob van Meurs, 1663), 380.
104. S. Savrij, *De Slagh vant Hantie tegens Twee Duijnkerckers Aen* (1633), Atlas Van Stolk #1748.
105. L. Reael, "Graf-schrift van Kornelis Jansen, toegenaemt het Haantjen," in Scheurleer, *Van Varen en Van Vechten*, Vol. I, 271; and Jan Vos, "Grafschrift op den Manhaftigen Wataerhopman de Haan," in Scheurleer, *Van Varen en Van Vechten*, Vol. I, 271.
106. "Van de Zee-slag van 't Schip de Haan," in Scheurleer, *Van Varen en Van Vechten*, Vol. I, 265–268; and "See-gevecht van kapiteyn Cornelis Jansz. de Haen, tegens twee Duynkerckers," in Scheurleer, *Van Varen en Van Vechten*, Vol. I, 268–271. Instructions directed the public to sing the former piece to the tune of *Ontwaakt gy Batavieren koen* and the latter to the tune of *O Heyligh! zalig Betlehem*.
107. Dapper, *Historische*, 380.
108. Epitaph of Kornelis Jansz. quoted in Dapper, *Historische*, 380. "Decien" is probably a reference to Publius Decies Mus, a military tribune whom Livy profiled. In 340 B.C., Decies fought the Latins and perished, sacrificing himself for Rome. Subsequently, he was celebrated for his patriotic devotion. Decies's son and grandson, both of whom were also known as Decies, died in battle as well and were likewise admired for their matrydoms. See Simon Hornblower and Anthony Spawforth, eds., *Oxford Classical Dictionary*, 3rd edition (Oxford: Oxford University Press, 1996), 436.
109. C.R. Boxer, "Piet Heyn and the Silver-Fleet," *History Today*, Vol. 13 (June 1963), 398.
110. Boxer, "Piet Heyn," 402–404.
111. Boxer, "Piet Heyn," 405.
112. van Balen, *Hollandsche Kapers*, 129–130; and Boxer, *Piet Heyn*, 406. For a firsthand account of the contents of Heyn's booty, see Verz. Thysius: Piet Heyn, *Extract uyt den Brief van den E. Generael Pieter Pietersz: Heyn* . . . (1628).
113. For example, Verz. Thysius: *Rapport aen hare Ho. Mo. ende Sijn Excell., van den Capiteyn Salomon Willemsz., over 't veroveren vande Silver-Vlote . . . door 't beleyt van . . . Pt. Psz. Heyn* ('s-Gravenhage: Wed. en Erfg. van H. Jzn. v. Wouw, 1628); and Verz. Thysius: Piet Heyn, *Extract uyt den Brief van den E. Generael Pieter Pietersz: Heyn* . . . (1628).
114. For example, see the medals on permanent display at the Nederlandse Scheepvaart Museum (Amsterdam), one of which celebrates Heyn's 1628 capture of the Silver Fleet, and the other which commemorates his death at the hands of the Dunkirkers.
115. And that accordingly, all historians, orators, and poets should describe Heyn's "*voorsichtigheydt, onvertsaeghtheydt, wackerheydt, dapperheydt*, ende met een woort, uwe *Volmaecktheydt* in het behaelen ende voltrecken van een Victorie ter Zee." Verz. Thysius: Spranckhuysen, *Triumphe van weghen . . . Victorie . . .* (1628), 2–3.
116. Verz. Thysius: I. Liefs, *Lof-dicht over de wijt-vermaerde . . . victorie, by het veroveren vande schatriicke Silver-vloot des Konings van Spangien* . . . (1629).

117. Verz. Thysius: Spranckhuysen, Preface to *Triumphe van weghen ... de Victorie ...*, 2–3. The author also argues that Heyn's triumph is equal to many of the miraculous deeds depicted in the Old Testament.
118. Scheurleer's collection *Van Varen en Van Vechten* alone includes 22 different poems and songs. See Scheurleer, *Van Varen en Van Vechten*, Vol. I, 167–224.
119. See the following works in Scheurleer, *Van Varen en Van Vechten*, Vol. I: "Zee-Zangh, over de veroveringthe, van de Silvere Vlote ..." (177); "Spotlied" (184); "Protest ... 't Welck den Coninck van Spagnen is doende. ... Ter occasie van 't veroveren vande Silver-Vlote ..." (190); "Op het Ontset van Piet Heins Buit ..." (207); and "Clare ende naeckte Afbeeldinghe hoe het Schip Hollandia ..." (209).
120. See Scheurleer, *Van Varen en Van Vechten*, Vol. I: "Een nieuwe Liedeken, ter Eeren van ... Pieter Pietersz. Heyn ..." (171 and 173); "Triumph-Lied op de Scheeps-Victorie der West-Indische Compagnie" (180, 182–183); "Protest ... 't Vvelck den Coninck van Spagnen is doende ..." (188 and 193); "Op de Goude Krone ... onder 't beleyd van Pieter Heyn den Spanjaerden benomen ..." (197); "Op Piet Heyn" (198); "Welcomst aan den gemelten Generael ..." (199); "Op het ontset van Piet Heyns Buit ..." (207); "Clare ende naeckte Afbeeldinghe ..." (210); "LIICK-KLACHT" (222); and "Op het portret" (223).
121. "LIICK-KLACHT," Scheurleer, *Van Varen en Van Vechten*, Vol. I, 221.
122. Verz. Thysius: I. Liefs, *Lof-dicht over de wijt-vermaerde ... victorie*, 2.
123. D. Lommelin, "Lof-dicht, ter Eeren ende tot weerde Fame vanden ... Generael P. Pz. Heyn, ... inghekomen met de Silver-vlote ... hier in ons Vaderlandt ..." (1629), 1–2.
124. "LIICK-KLACHT," Scheurleer, *Van Varen en Van Vechten*, Vol. I, 221.
125. See, e.g., Spranckhuysen, passim. The poet specifically calls Heyn "a servant and instrument of God" on page 1.
126. See, e.g., "Een nieuwe Liedeken, ter Eeren van den Generael Pieter Pietersz. Heyn, over den grooten schadt die hy op de Zee bekomen heeft," in Scheurleer, *Van Varen en Van Vechten*, Vol. I, 167–174. The piece was to sung to the tune of the *Wilhelmus*.
127. Verz. RLP: *Practijcke van den Spaenschen Aes-Sack ...* (1629).
128. Verz. RLP: Johannes Hasselbekium, *Triumph-Dicht, over de gheluckighe Veroveringhe van de Spaensche Silver-Vlote ...* (Leeuwarden: Claude Fonteyne, 1629), 3. This pamphlet also refers to the "Oragnie-vlaggen" on page 22.
129. See, e.g., Verz. RLP: Dionysium Spranckhuysen, *Tranen, over den doodt van den grooten Admirael van Hollandt, loffelijcker, ende onsterffelijcker ghedachtenisse, Pieter Pietersz. Heyn ...* (Delf: A.T. Kloetingh, 1629).
130. Prud'homme van Reine, "Nederlandse Kaapvaart en Piraterij," 55.
131. Prud'homme van Reine, "Nederlandse Kaapvaart en Piraterij," 58.
132. Quote by Gerard Bacot, Credo's son-in-law, in Prud'homme van Reine, "Nederlandse Kaapvaart en Piraterij," 56.
133. Quote by Gerard Bacot, in Prud'homme van Reine, "Nederlandse Kaapvaart en Piraterij," 56.
134. Dionisius van der Sterre, *Zeer aenmerkelijcke reysen gedaan door Jan Erasmus Reyning, meest in West-Indien en ook in veel andere deelen des Werelds* (Amsterdam: Jan ten Hoorn, 1691), 40.
135. van der Sterre, *Zeer aenmerkelijcke ...*, 27. He reiterates this point on page 87.
136. van der Sterre, *Zeer aenmerkelijcke ...*, 64. van der Sterre makes the same point, with very similar language, on page 27 as well.

137. van der Sterre, *Zeer aenmerkelijcke* . . ., 85.
138. van der Sterre, *Zeer aenmerkelijcke* . . ., 83.
139. van der Sterre, *Zeer aenmerkelijcke* . . ., 71.
140. van der Sterre, *Zeer aenmerkelijcke* . . ., 71.
141. Prud'homme van Reine, "Nederlandse Kaapvaart en Piraterij," 56.
142. Prud'homme van Reine, "Nederlandse Kaapvaart en Piraterij," 55.
143. Prud'homme van Reine, "Nederlandse Kaapvaart en Piraterij," 57–58.
144. Prud'homme van Reine, "Nederlandse Kaapvaart en Piraterij," 55–57.
145. Prud'homme van Reine, "Nederlandse Kaapvaart en Piraterij," 55–57.
146. van der Oest, "De Praktijk vande Nederlandse Kaapvaart," 19; and Prud'homme van Reine, "Nederlandse Kaapvaart en Piraterij," 53.
147. W. Voorbeijtel Cannenburg and J.P. Kruseman, *Scheepsnamen Vroeger en Nu* (Amsterdam, 1960), cited in Bruijn, "Dutch Privateering," 404.
148. Verhees-van Meer, *De Zeeuwse Kaapvaart*, Appendix IV, 179–200.
149. Verz. Thysius: *Hollantse Mercurius* . . . (Haerlem: Pieter Casteleyn, 1651), 52.
150. Verz. Thysius: *Hollantse Mercurius* . . . (1651), 53.
151. ARA, AA, Verz. Bisdom #123: "Excessen door Vrijbuijters &c. dezer Landen tegen Neutrale Vrienden gepleegt," Het Memoriale Admt. Maze, September 18, 1605, *Extract-Resolutien van de Staten Generaal, de Staten van Holland en de Admiraliteit op de Maze, plakaten, reglementen, instructien, enz. betreffende de commissievaart* . . ., 1590–1784.
152. ARA, AA, Verz. Bisdom #167: *Copie-Crimineele vonnissen van de Admiraliteit op de Maas . . . 1575–1710*, fols. 194 vs–197.
153. Verhees-van Meer, *De Zeeuwse Kaapvaart*, 50.
154. ARA, AA, Verz. Bisdom #167: *Copie-Crimineele vonnissen van de Admiraliteit op de Maas . . . 1575–1710*, fols. 181–182.
155. Schama, *The Embarassment of Riches*, Chapter 7, 481–561.
156. ARA, AA, Verz. Bisdom #167: *Copie-Crimineele vonnissen van de Admiraliteit op de Maas . . . 1575–1710*, fols. 84–85 vs.
157. J.J. Beyerman, "Een Zeeroover als Zee-Officier onder de Ruyter" (Den Haag, 1934), 2–3. An offprint of this rare publication is available at the Nederlandse Scheepvaart Museum Library (Amsterdam), #N. i. I. K II 196.
158. Legal historian C.G. Roelofson affirms that in matters concerning hegemony over the East Indies trade, the VOC "showed an aggressiveness, which quickly earned the Dutch a reputation as 'pirates.' "
159. Verz. RLP: *Pambonem Vreimundima, Den Hollantschen Apocalypsis Vrijmoedelijck uytgheleet door Pambonem Vreimundima* . . . (1626).
160. Verz. Thysius #1916: *Rijpen Raed, ende Salige Resolute gheraemt door eenen Lief-hebber des Vaderlandts* ('s-Gravenhage, 1635), 4 and 6–8.
161. Verz. Thysius: *Spieghel der grau-same ongherechticheyt ende vervloeckte giericheyt, vande factie der Contremineurs, die nu veel Jaeren tot groot achterdeel der Conincklicke Comp^f. van Oost-indien, een schantloose Roovery bedreven hebben* . . . (1638), 1.
162. Verz. Thysius: *Spieghel der grau-same ongherechticheyt ende vervloeckte giericheyt* . . . (1638), 3.
163. Verz. Thysius: *Spieghel der grau-same ongherechticheyt ende vervloeckte giericheyt* . . . (1638), 3.
164. The Dutch authorities had to promulgate legislation specifically forbidding such acts. See, e.g., a States-General proclamation that admonished all Dutch seamen—including those who worked for the VOC, WIC, navy, and merchant

shipping—who had the right to capture enemy ships to refrain from attacking and plundering them: ARA. AA, Verz. Thysius: *Extract wt 't Register der Resolutien van de ... St. Generael ... (Ordre om) alle Engelsche Schepen ... nae vermoghen ... te vermeesteren ...*, July 18, 1652. See also a *placaat* issued by the Prince of Orange (as Admiral General) to the navy, promising to punish navy seamen who stole from or made off with their captured prizes: Verz. Thysius: *Placaet Van ... den Heere Prince van Orange ...*, 1673 ('s-Gravenhage: J. Scheltus, 1673). This last proclamation reiterated States-General edicts of September 3, 1665 and August 30, 1666.

165. The Spanish often referred to the Dutch as *Rebeldes*. See, e.g., AGI, Patronato 267, N. 1, R. 59: *Los Rebeldes de los Paises Bajos contra la Armada Española*, 1571; and AGI, Mexico 29, N. 91: *Cartas del Virrey Marques de Gelves*, Block 3 ("Copia del aviso de la compania que se hace en las ys. Las Rebeldes Para las yndias ..."), July 30, 1622. They also often made no distinction between pirates and the Dutch Navy and Dutch privateers, calling them "*corsarios*," "*piratas*," and other pirate-like names. See, e.g., AGI, Patronata 268, N. 2, R. 4: *Corsario Holandés que Fue a Filipinas desde Perú ...*, 1600; and AGI, Contratacion 368, N. 5: *Bienes de Difuntos: Domingo Bohorquez*, 1626.

Bibliography

Primary Sources

Archival Collections

I. Algemeen Rijksarchief (The Hague, the Netherlands)

General Collections
Archief Bisdom #151: *Register van criminele sententies van het Hof van Holland*, July 1, 1585–September 2, 1622.
Verzameling Radermacher #86: *Acte tegen het aandoen van de Zoute Eylanden*, 1683.

Admiraliteits Archieven (AA)
AA #742 (College ter Admiraliteit op de Maze): *Register van de opbrengst der van wege de Admiraliteit in het openbaar verkochte aangehaalde en veroverde goederen*, March 21, 1637–October 18, 1645.
AA #1328: *Commissieboeken.*
AA #1806–1808 (Admiraliteit van Amsterdam): *Rekeningen van den vendumeester wegens zijn ontvang van de prinsen, mulcten en confiscatien*, 1665–1667.
AA #1813–1816 (Admiraliteit van Amsterdam): *Rekeningen van den vendumeester wegens zijn ontvang van de prinsen, mulcten en confiscatien*, 1672–1675.
AA #1839 (College van het Admiraliteit te Amsterdam): *Rekening van den vendumeester wegens zijn ontvang van de princen en veroverde Turcken en Mooren op de kust van Barbarije onder den vice-admiral De Ruijter*, 1661–1662.
AA #1844–1846 (Admiraliteit van Amsterdam): *Rekeningen van den vendumeester wegens zijn uitgaaf van de prinsen, mulcten en confiscatien*, 1665–1667.
AA #2429–2430: *Commissieboeken.*
AA #2840 (College ter Admiraliteit in Zeeland): *Quitantie van kapitein Legier Pietersen aan de Admiraliteit voor het nemen van een Duinkerker schip*, July 5, 1592.

Special Collections, Admiralty Archives (Admiraliteits Archieven)
Verzameling Bisdom #8: "Betaling aan 't volk van 't gebleven Schip Wassenaar, Wede. en Ergenamen te doen," April 16, 1681, *Retroacta Wegens genomen & gebleven Schepen*, 1681–1781.
Verzameling Bisdom #8: "Retroacta nopens gebleven of genomen Scheepen van Oorlog Sedert 1681," 1681, *Retroacta Wegens genomen & gebleven Schepen*, 1681–1781.
Verzameling Bisdom #10: *Deductie gedaan . . . uyt den naam ende van wegen Jacques Thierry, Koopman tot Amsterdam Voorsz., Impetrant in cas van revisie ter eenre, op ende jegens den Heer en Mr. Hendrick Hooft de Jonge . . . gevoeght met Capitein Willem Jansz, gedient hebbende met commissie van Retorsie . . .*, June 1, 1675, fols. 45–84.

Verzameling Bisdom #13: *Index op het Recueil 't Admiraliteit*, no date.
Verzameling Bisdom #20: *Extract-Resolutien van de Staten-Generaal, de Staten van Holland, de Admiraliteiten op de Maze en te Amsterdam, aanteekeningen enz. betreffende admiraliteits-zaken*, 1581–1746.
Verzameling Bisdom #107: "Aanschrijving van de Staten Generaal om in diligentie eenige scheepen van oorlog toe te rusten om te agterhalen de vrijbuiters uijt dese Landen die Neutralen en Vriende beschadighen," March 6, 1607, *Recueil van verscheijde oude stukken, rakende de directie van en over de equipagien ter zee, de tractementen der zeeofficieren, den articulbrief te water, en de vaart der neutralen, en de prinsen en buijten*, 1589–1698, fol. 43.
Verzameling Bisdom #107: "Aanschrijving van H.H.M. om de Fregatten waer op de Banditen waren gelogeert, aftedanken," March 6, 1609, *Recueil van verscheijde oude stukken, rakende de directie van en over de equipagien ter zee, de tractementen der zeeofficieren, den articulbrief te water, en de vaart der neutralen, en de prinsen en buijten*, 1589–1698, fol. 47.
Verzameling Bisdom #107: "Advis van de Lieutenanten Admiraals van Holland en Zeeland en de Aanwesende Gecommt. uijt de Collegien ter Admirl. tegens het Placaat van de Koning van Spagne op de vrijbuijt, en hoe men Zekere Galeijen zoude beletten over te komen," March 19, 1622, *Recueil van verscheijde oude stukken, rakende de directie van en over de equipagien ter zee, de tractementen der zeeofficieren, den articulbrief te water, en de vaart der neutralen, en de prinsen en buijten*, 1589–1698, fol. 97.
Verzameling Bisdom #107: "Commissie van retorsie voor een Keulsche Schipper," September 2, 1672, *Recueil van verscheijde oude stukken, rakende de directie van en over de equipagien ter zee, de tractementen der zeeofficieren, den articulbrief te water, en de vaart der neutralen, en de prinsen en buijten*, 1589–1698, fol. 160.
Verzameling Bisdom #107: "Extract uijt het Register der Resolutien van de Ho: Mo: Heeren Generaal der Vereenigde Nederlanden op de besetting van de Vlaamsche Kust," April 16, 1627, *Recueil van verscheijde oude stukken, rakende de directie van en over de equipagien ter zee, de tractementen der zeeofficieren, den articulbrief te water, en de vaart der neutralen, en de prinsen en buijten*, 1589–1698, fol. 107.
Verzameling Bisdom #107: "Extract uijt het Register der Resolutien van H.H.M. of de geregtighejd van den Admiral in de Prinsen bij particuliere verovert, welk volgens het placaat geheel aen de veroveraars zijn belooft," February 18, 1639, *Recueil van verscheijde oude stukken, rakende de directie van en over de equipagien ter zee, de tractementen der zeeofficieren, den articulbrief te water, ende vaart der neutralen, en de prinsen en buijten*, 1589–1698, fol. 149.
Verzameling Bisdom #107: "Extract uit het Register der Resolutien van de Ho. Mo. Heeren Staten Generaal der Vereenigde Nederlanden, op de besetting van de Vlaamsche Kust, en de veijliging van de Zee voor het somer saijsoen," February 6, 1626, *Recueil van verscheijde oude stukken, rakende de directie van en over de equipagien ter zee, de tractementen der zeeofficieren, den articulbrief te water, en de vaart der neutralen, en de prinsen en buijten*, 1589–1698, fol. 105.
Verzameling Bisdom #107: "Instructie voor den Capiteijn Moij Lambert Commandeur over de naervolgende veerthien Scheepen van Oorloge, gaande naar de Middelandsche Zee teegens de roovers," May 2, 1618, *Recueil van verscheijde oude stukken, rakende de directie van en over de equipagien ter zee, de tractementen der zeeofficieren, den articulbrief te water, en de vaart der neutralen, en de prinsen en buijten*, 1589–1698, fol. 71.

Verzameling Bisdom #107: "Resolutien van H.H.M. houdende een ordre en reglement in het abordeeren, vervolgen en veroveren van den vijand, en een voet van verdeeling der Prinsen ten op sigte van de Vice Admiraels en de Capiteijnen," January 28, 1631, *Recueil van verscheijde oude stukken, rakende de directie van en over de equipagien ter zee, de tractementen der zeeofficieren, den articulbrief te water, en de vaart der neutralen, en de prinsen en buijten*, 1589–1698.

Verzameling Bisdom #123: "Brief aan de Staten Generael van de Admiraliteit op de Maze," September 23, 1605, *Extract-Resolutien van de Staten Generaal, de Staten van Holland en de Admiraliteit op de Maze, plakaten, reglementen, instructien, enz. betreffende de commissievaart, het beheer van de buitgemaakte en gestande vijandelijke schepen en goederen, de vaart der neutralen, enz.*, 1590–1784.

Verzameling Bisdom #123: "Extract uijt boek geintituleert Missiven en Bijlagen van Staaten Generael," February 5, 1650, *Extract-Resolutien van de Staten Generaal, de Staten van Holland en de Admiraliteit op de Maze, plakaten, reglementen, instructien, enz. betreffende de commissievaart, het beheer van de buitgemaakte en gestande vijandelijke schepen en goederen, de vaart der neutralen, enz.*, 1590–1784.

Verzameling Bisdom #123: "Brief van Marque/Brief van Commissie," 1672–1674, *Extract-Resolutien van de Staten Generaal, de Staten van Holland en de Admiraliteit op de Maze, plakaten, reglementen, instructien, enz. betreffende de commissievaart, het beheer van de buitgemaakte en gestande vijandelijke schepen en goederen, de vaart der neutralen, enz.*, 1590–1784.

Verzameling Bisdom #123: "Extract uijt de Resolutien van de Raedt ter Admiraliteit op de Maeze," June 2, 1695, *Extract-Resolutien van de Staten Generaal, de Staten van Holland en de Admiraliteit op de Maze, plakaten, reglementen, instructien, enz. betreffende de commissievaart, het beheer van de buitgemaakte en gestande vijandelijke schepen en goederen, de vaart der neutralen, enz.*, 1590–1784.

Verzameling Bisdom #123: "Lyste op de Placaten en Orders Rakende Commissievaarders en Vreemde Kapers," 1627–1673, *Extract-Resolutien van de Staten Generaal, de Staten van Holland en de Admiraliteit op de Maze, plakaten, reglementen, instructien, enz. betreffende de commissievaart, het beheer van de buitgemaakte en gestande vijandelijke schepen en goederen, de vaart der neutralen, enz.*, 1590–1784.

Verzameling Bisdom #123: "Notulen over de VOC en WIC en de Admiraliteiten, 1610 and 1650," *Extract-Resolutien van de Staten Generaal, de Staten van Holland en de Admiraliteit op de Maze, plakaten, reglementen, instructien, enz. betreffende de commissievaart, het beheer van de buitgemaakte en gestande vijandelijke schepen en goederen, de vaart der neutralen, enz.*, 1590–1784.

Verzameling Bisdom #123: "Notulen uit het Memoriael van het Admiraliteit op de Maze," 1605–1607, *Extract-Resolutien van de Staten Generaal, de Staten van Holland en de Admiraliteit op de Maze, plakaten, reglementen, instructien, enz. betreffende de commissievaart, het beheer van de buitgemaakte en gestande vijandelijke schepen en goederen, de vaart der neutralen, enz.*, 1590–1784.

Verzameling Bisdom #123: "Placaet, den Staten Generael," July 10, 1606, *Extract-Resolutien van de Staten Generaal, de Staten van Holland en de Admiraliteit op de Maze, plakaten, reglementen, instructien, enz. betreffende de commissievaart, het beheer van de buitgemaakte en gestande vijandelijke schepen en goederen, de vaart der neutralen, enz.*, 1590–1784.

Verzameling Bisdom #123: "Tractaat Van Commercie, Navigatie en Marine, Gemaakt, geslooten en vastgesteld tot Nimmegen den 10 Augusty 1678, tusschen . . . Vrankryk ter eenre, en de . . . vereenigde Nederrlanden, ter andere zyde," August 10, 1678, *Extract-Resolutien van de Staten Generaal, de Staten van Holland en de Admiraliteit op de Maze, plakaten, reglementen, instructien, enz. betreffende de commissievaart, het beheer van de buitgemaakte en gestande vijandelijke schepen en goederen, de vaart der neutralen, enz.*, 1590–1784.

Verzameling Bisdom #123: "Uit het Memoriael Admiraliteit op de Maze," April 13, 1599, *Extract-Resolutien van de Staten Generaal, de Staten van Holland en de Admiraliteit op de Maze, plakaten, reglementen, instructien, enz. betreffende de commissievaart, het beheer van de buitgemaakte en gestande vijandelijke schepen en goederen, de vaart der neutralen, enz.*, 1590–1784.

Verzameling Bisdom #167: *Copie-Crimineele vonnissen van de Admiraliteit op de Maas. Met repertorium, 1575–1710.*

Verzameling Bisdom #246: *Extract uit het Register der Resolutien van de Hoog Mogende Heeren Staaten generale der vereenigde Nederlanden*, April 2–16, 1686.

Verzameling Bisdom #34: *Alphabetische index op de Extract-Resolutien, enz. vermeld onder de nummers 18–33*, no date.

Verzameling Bisdom #42: *Extract uit de Resolutien van haar Hoog. Mo. van 1604, 1605, 1606*, February 23, 1605, March 8, 1605, and March 17, 1605.

Verzameling De Jonge #2–3: Alkamade, K. and van der Schelling, P. *Proceduren vande HH: Staten Generaal tegens de Raaden en Officieren vande Admiraliteit opde Maas, wegens hunne begane excessen*, 1625.

Verzameling Evertsen #7: Ruijter, Michael de. *Orders van De Ruijter voor den schout-bij-nacht Cornelis Evertsen oop den kruistocht tegen de Barbarijsche zeeroovers*, September 8, 1661–November 10, 1661.

Verzameling Evertsen #38: *Stukken raakende de buijtgelden der prinsen, tot Vlissingen, Middelburgh en Veere opgebragt, waarvan de luitenant-admiraal cornelis Evertsens erven compteerden* (sic) *het aandeel . . .*, 1701.

Verzameling Schrijver #8: Hees, Capitein Thomas. *Missive vanCapitein Thomas Hees [aan de Staten Generaal] en Bylage by missive van den Capitein Thomas Hees . . .: Lijste van de geloste Nederlandsche Slaven tot Algiers*, January 18, 1683.

Verzameling Schrijver #8: *Lyste of Rolle van alle de Slaaven, soo van de Neederlandsche Natie, of die met Scheepen in den Staat der vereenigde Nederlanden t'huis hoorende t'seedert het jaar 1690 tot 1712, en van het jaar 1715 tot 1726 incluis, door de Algiersche Kaapers genoomen, ent tot Algiers opgebragt zyn*, 1690–1726.

Verzameling Schrijver #8: *Slaven, waar voor te Amsterdam collectien zyn geobtineerd . . .*, ca. 1715.

Verzameling Sweers #2: Sweers, Isaac. *Journaal, gehouden door Sweers als secretaris op het sinaldeel van Van Galen, uitgezonden naar de kust van Barbarije om de haven van Salee te bezetten en de Spaansche kust te zuiveren van de zeerovers*, March 10, 1650–May 20, 1651.

Verzameling Sweers #2: Sweers, Isaac. *Journaal, ghehouden door Sweers als adelborst op 's Lands schip De Maen, kruisende langs de kusten van Spanje en Portugal op de Turksche en andere zeeroovers*, April 5, 1649–November 16, 1649.

Verzameling Sweers #4: Sweers, Isaac. *Journaal, gehouden door Sweers op 's Land schip Der Goes bestemd naar de Middellandsche zee ter beteugeling van de zeeroovers*, February 22, 1657–December 20, 1657.

Verzameling Van der Heim #155: *Afspraak Van de Gecommitteerden uit de Respe. Collegien ter Admiraliteit, wegens den Tiende van den Admiraal de Repartitien der buitgelden, de behandeling der Prinsen en Prinsen goederen, en wat dies meer is*, November 9, 1781.

Verzameling Van der Heim #155: *Extracten uit de rol van Proceduren voor den Raad ter Admiraliteit op de Maze over Prinsen der Commissievaarders verovert daar tegens is ageert of door den Hr. Advt. Fiscaal, of door de rheders, omtyds de Jusce. als gevoegde.* October 2, 1652–August 18, 1690.

Verzameling Van der Heim #155: *Memoria over de Buitgelden.* ca. 1770.

Verzameling Van der Heim #339 (re: Admiraliteit op de Maze: Rechtspraak): *Register der Voornaamste Crimineele Sententien van den Raad Ter Admiraliteit op de Maze van den Jare 1575 tot 1710.*

Verzameling Van der Heim #481: Staten Generaal. *Extract-Resolutien van de Staten-Generaal, aanteekeningen, enz. betreffende de lossing van christenslaven te Algiers en het overbrengen derwaarts van de gebruikelijke jaarlijksche geschenken,* 1642–1757.

Verzameling Van der Hoop #1: *Aanteekeningen uit de resolutien van de Staten van Holland betreffende de Admiraliteiten, het college van Superintendentie . . . de prijzen, de uitrustingen van schepen, de commissievaart en strandvonderij,* 1575–1716.

Verzameling Van der Hoop #53: Staten Generaal. *Extract uit het Register der Resolutien van de Hoog Mog. Heeren Staaten Generael der Vereenigde Nederlanden . . . ,* June 23, 1653.

Verzameling XLVII #29 (Stukken betreffende zee- en admiraliteitszaken, als losse aanwinsten door het Algemeen Rijksarchief verworven voor het jaar 1888): *Copie-Rekeningen van het aan Prins Maurits en Prins Frederik Hendrik toekomend aandeel in de buiten, gemaakt door de kapiteins en commissievaarders onder de Admiraliteit op de Maze,* 1621–1631.

Hof van Holland Archief

Hof van Holland #5213.18: *Stukken inzake Cornelis Dielofs te Oegstgeest wegens zeeroverij,* 1610.

Hof van Holland #5217.2: *Stukken betreffende het arresteren te Medemblik van eenschip dat tot zeeroverij gediend had,* June 18, 1613.

Hof van Holland #5217.2: "Brief van Volckert Cornelisz., Schout, aan 't Hof van Holland," August 6, 1613, *Stukken betreffende het arresteren te Medemblik van eenschip dat tot zeeroverij gediend had,* 1613.

Hof van Holland #5219.16: *Informaties nopens Maritgen Jacobs Laedigat en enige zeerovers over oproer en gewelddadigheden gepleegd te Oudkarspel,* 1615.

Hof van Holland #5220.21: *Request etc. voor Jan Lievensz. Rijckewaert, zeerover, om gratie,* September 1615.

Hof van Holland #5220.29: *Informatie tegen Corn. Claesz. van Uitgeest, impetrant van pardon en gevangene op de voorpoort, zeerover,* 1615.

Hof van Holland #5222.22: Staten Generael, *Pardon voor Pieter Pack,* 1615.

Hof van Holland #5270A.2: *Stukken en informatie in zake Laurens Davids wegens zeeroverij in de Rode Zee en elders,* 1663.

Hof van Holland #5345.9: *Informatie inzake Hendrick Hoogenkamp beschuldigd van zeeroverij,* 1687.

Hof van Holland #5346.23: *Mandament van purge voor Hendrick Hoogencamp, beschuldigd van zeeroverij met een aantal bewijsstuken,* January–March 1687.

Hof van Holland #5369.4: *Informatie inzake Gerrits Gysson Bloek van zeeroverij onder Scheveningen en dreigementen,* 1697.

Hof van Holland #5654–5657: *Registers van criminele sententies, Hof van Holland,* 1571–1674.

Hof van Holland Archief (Reading Room): *Index op de Criminele Sententien van het Hof van Holland, 1538–1572; 1623–1811.*

Hof van Holland Archief (Reading Room): *Chronologisch Register op de Criminele Papieren van het Hof van Holland uit de periode 1572 tot en met 1810*, Band I: 1572–1699.

Hoge Krijgsraad en Zeekrijsraden Archieven
Hoge Krijgsraad en Zeekrijgsraden #249–252: *Registers van resolutien, sententien, . . . advysen . . . en andere stukken van verschillende krygsraden*, 1607–1629.
Hoge Krijgsraad en Zeekrijgsraden #262: *Criminele Sententie (1682–1709)*, 1682–1709.
Hoge Krijgsraad en Zeekrijgsraden #352: *Register van crimineele sententie van den Hoogen Krijgsraad der Vereenighde Nederlanden (16 Nov. 1672–21 April 1674)*, November 16, 1672–April 2, 1674.

Verenigde Oostindische Compagnie (VOC) Archieven
VOC #221: *Zakenindex op de Resoluties van de Heren XVII*, 1602–1736.
VOC #307: *Zakenindex op de resoluties van de kamer Amsterdam*, 1602–1743.
VOC #345: *Zakenindex op de uitgaande missiven van de Heren XVII aan de kantoren in Indie*, 1614–1707.
VOC #439: *Notariële akte van de Staten-Generaal . . . waarbij op de vloot van veertien schepen voor criminele zaken de brede raad wordt ingesteld*, May 13, 1602.
VOC #513: *Aantekeningen betreffende de mutaties in de bemanning van het schip Gelderland*, April 26–June 29, 1610.
VOC #522: *Verslagen van verhoren, afgenomen door de scheepsraad van het schip Kleine Zon over op dit schip door bemanningsleden gepleegde muiterij*, May 15–22, 1608.
VOC #543: Verhoeff, Pieter Willemsz. *Lijst van de door Verhoeff Buitgemaakte Goederen uit het Veroverde Schip Nossa Senhora del Pare*, December 12, 1608.
VOC #582: *Vonnissen, geveld door de scheepsraad van het schip Zwarte Leeuw, met lijst van de gestrafte personen en de door hen ondergane straffen*, February 25, 1610–July 6, 1614.
VOC #656: "Den Franschen Admiraal van twee andere Fransche schepen de St. Michiel en de Sant Malo genaamd Dekker were in arrest genomen als apparent een Nederlander zijnde . . .," January 8, 1618, *Kopie-Resolutie van Gouveurner-Generaal en Raden, Ingekomen Stukken uit Indie, Heren Zeventien en Kamer Amsterdam.*
VOC #656: "Dezen arrestant ontvlugt door behulp der Engelsen en salveerd zig in 't huijs van den pangerang . . .," January 22, 1618, *Kopie-resolutie van president en raden van de kantoren in Bantam en Jakatra.*
VOC #656: "De bovenstaande Fransche schepen, heben onder een prince vlag Gonssouratse en andere Moorse scheepen als Zeerovers vermeesterd . . .," March 13, 1618, *Kopie-resolutie van President en Raden van de Kantoren in Bantam en Jakatra.*
VOC #656: "Werd nadere annotitie gehouden wegens de zee roverijen door die schepen in de Indische Zee, onder een prince vlagge gepleegd . . .," May 19, 1618, *Kopie-resolutie van president en raden van de kantoren in Bantam & Jakatra.*
VOC #676: "Zal het Zandelhout van Iodia Soliman Brapinto en Jan de Britto in een verovert Portugees schip prijs gemaakt, aan den evengeme goed doen, wijl zij lieden de pennigen daartoe voor den Oorlog uijtgezet hadden . . .," February 14, 1653, *Kopie-Resolutie van Gouverneur-Generaal en Raden, Ingekomen Stukken uit Indie, Heren Zeventien en Kamer Amsterdam.*

VOC #677: "Van twee Engelse Jagten Frederik Francois en Jan . . .," November 15, 1657, *Kopie-Resolutie van Gouverneur-Generaal en Raden, Ingekomen Stukken uit Indien, Heren Zeventien en Kamer Amsterdam.*
VOC #680: "Het roven op de Cust, door de Papoese Inwoonders tegen te gaan . . .," November 25, 1665, *Kopie-Resolutie van Gouverneur-Generaal en Raden, Ingekomen Stukken uit Indie, Heren Zeventien en Kamer Amsterdam.*
VOC #710: "Op Timor over geene Europianen to vellen, maar de misdoende herwarts te senden . . .," February 2, 1695, *Kopie Resolutie van Gouverneur-Generaal en Raden, Ingekomen Stukken uit Indien, Heren Zeventien en Kamer Amsterdam.*
VOC #715: "De papoese vaartuijgen op de Noordcust van Ceram moeten niet als zeeroovers geconsidereert worden . . .," January 22, 1700, *Kopie-Resolutie van Gouverneur-Generaal en Raden, Ingekomen Stukken uit Indie, Heren Zeventien en Kamer Amsterdam.*
VOC #716: "Uijt Europa herwaarts terug gezonden twee Engelsche zeeroovers aan den Advocaat-Fiscaal te geeven met de stukken ten hunnen Lasten . . .," November 4, 1701, *Kopie-Resolutie van Gouveurner Generaal en Raden, Ingekomen Stukken uit Indie, Heren Zeventien en Amsterdam Kamer.*
VOC #717: "Eeen dood-vonnis tegens Engelsche zeeroovers geveld, in zijn geheel en ongeexecuteerd te laten, tot nadere dispositie en finale ordre der Heeren Meesters . . .," April 27, 1702, *Kopie-Resolutie van Gouveurneur-Generaal en Raden, Ingekomen Stukken uit Indie, Heren Zeventien en Amsterdam Kamer.*
VOC #717: "Zekere Isaac Coleman, met de zeeroovers gevaren hebbende, en tot de ketting gecondemneert, daarvan te pardonneeren, en met de eerste scheepen voor de kost naar 't Vaderland to zenden . . .," May 5, 1702, *Kopie-Resolutie, van Gouveurneur-Generaal en Raden, Ingekomen stukken uit Indie, Heren Zeventien en Amsterdam Kamer.*
VOC #717: "Die rover, ingevolge het besluijt in verzekering genomen en zijn Chialoup verzegeld, te doen examineeren door den Advocaat-Fiscaal . . .," December 11, 1702, *Kopie-Resolutie van Gouveurneur-Generaal en Raden, Ingekomen stukken uit Indien, Heren Zeventien en Amsterdam Kamer.*
VOC #718: "Twee Franse kapers van St. Malo zig in de straat Drioens onthoudende, werd de nodige voorsiening daartegens gedaan tot beveijliging onzer schepen door 't equipeeren van oorlogschepen . . .," October 18, 1703, *Kopie-Resolutie van Gouverneur-Generaal en Raden, Ingekomen Stukken uit Indie, Heren Zeventien en Kamer Amsterdam.*
VOC #718: "Twee Franse kapers in de rivier van Canton sijnde gezien, word ordre gesteld om dezelve in de straat Zunda of die van Malacca te laten waarnemen . . .," December 16, 1703, *Kopie-Resolutie van Gouveurneur-Generaal en Raden, Ingekomen Stukken uit Indie, Heren Zeventien en Kamer Amsterdam.*
VOC #719: "Zeven Engelsche zeeroovers uijt de boeijen gelargeerd en tot nadere ordre voor soldaten naar de Oostersche Provintien gezonden . . .," August 29, 1704, *Kopie-Resolutie van Gouverneur-Generaal en Raden, Ingekomen Stukken uit Indie, Heren Zeventien en Kamer Amsterdam.*
VOC #835–839: *Repertorium op de realia (onderwerpen) in de resoluties van gouverneur-general en raden. Met inhoudsopgaven,* 1632–1784.
VOC #4043 ("Overgekomen brieven en papieren uit Kaap de Goede Hoop en Mauritius aan de Heren XVII en de Kamer Amsterdam"): *Brief van Capitein Jan Coin,* February 13, 1700, fols. 821–822.
VOC #5050: Schram, Wijbrant Jansz. *Journaal gehouden op het schip Hollandia tijdens de reis van de Republiek naar Batavia onder beval van Wijbrant Jansz. Schram,* 1626.
VOC #7322: *Betreffende een door de Duinkerkers gevangenomen VOC–schipper,* 1633.

VOC #7417: *Trefwoordenrepertorium op de Resoluties van de Heren XVII*, 1602–1716.
VOC #7423: *Trefwoordenreportorium op de resoluties van de Heren XVII*, 1602–1716.
VOC #11129: *Stukken betreffende de klachten van de Portugezen over de verovering van het schip St. Antonio, komend uit Brazilie, door VOC-schepen*, 1613–1614.
VOC #11188: *Register Bavattende Memorie van de Bewindhebbers Betreffende het Deel van de Opbrengst van door de VOC Genomen Prijzen dat aan de Admiraliteitscolleges toekomt*, 1691.
VOC #11517: *Sententie van het Hoge Hof van de Admiraliteit in Engeland betreffende de confiscatie van het VOC-schip Dolfijn*, 1654.
VOC #13389: *Lijst Waarop de Verdeling Staat Aangegeven van door de Schepen Vlissingen en Dordrecht Veroverde Portuguese Goederen*, 1606.

West Indische Compagnie (WIC) Archieven

WIC #23: *Algemeene alphabetisch register op de notulen, A-G, Vergadering van Tienen*, 1674–1748.
WIC #24 *Algemeene alphabetisch register op de notulen, H-Z, Vergadering van Tienen*, 1674–1748.
WIC #49: *Brieven en papieren uit Brazilië*, 1630–1632.
WIC #51: *Brieven en papieren uit Brazilië*, 1636.
WIC #52: *Brieven en papieren uit Brazilië*, 1637.
WIC #53: *Brieven en papieren uit Brazilië*, 1638.
WIC #54: *Brieven en papieren uit Brazilië*, 1639.
WIC #137: *Plakaat, Kust van Guinea*, June 23, 1692.
WIC #337: *Notulen der Vergadering van Tienen, Kamer Amsterdam*, February 20, 1682.
WIC #338: *Notulen der Vergadering van Thienen, Kamer van Amsterdam*, March 11, 1683.
WIC #339: *Notulen der Vergadering van Tienen, Kamer Amsterdam*, December 29, 1684.
WIC #467: *Kopieboeken van brieven naar Amerika, met Register*, 1675–1684.
WIC #468: *Kopieboeken van brieven naar Amerika*, 1684–1689.
WIC #617: "Nicolaas van den Hoorn, Auditeur Extraordinaris . . . Contra Antheunis Klincke, Capitein ofte Schipper van . . . de Jonge Jacob," September 3, 1680, *Secrete Brieven en Papieren van Curaçao, 1680–89*, fols. 53–54.
WIC #617: "Resolutie, Raad van Curaçao," November 28, 1680, *Secrete Brieven en Papieren van Curaçao, 1680–89*, fols. 29–30.
WIC #617: "Aanteckingen van Gisberto Hoppesack, Secretarias, aan de Raad van Curaçao," April 12, 1681, *Secrete Brieven en Papieren van Curaçao, 1680–89*, fol. 47.
WIC #617: "Brieven naar de Bewinthebberen van de Camer Amsterdam, Gecommitteert tot de Secrete Saechen," April 14, 1681, *Secrete Brieven en Papieren van Curaçao, 1680–89*, fols. 15–22.
WIC #617: "Brief aan Nicolaes van Liebergen, Directeur over Curaçao, van Balthazar Beck," February 10, 1682, *Secrete Brieven en Papieren van Curaçao, 1680–89*, fol. 146.
WIC #617: "Artijckelen van beschuldinge ten laste van de geweesene Directeur Nicolaes van Liebergen," *Secrete Brieven en Papieren van Curaçao, 1680–89*. ca. 1683. fol. 448.

WIC #617: "Poincten ende Articulen bij de Heeren Bewinthebberen vande WIC ter Vergaderinge Vande Thienen," ca. 1683, *Secrete Brieven en Papieren van Curaçao, 1680–89*, fol. 349.

WIC #617: "Interrogatorien van Gerrit Slocker," 1683, *Secrete Brieven en Papieren van Curaçao, 1680–89*, fols. 249–250.

WIC #617: "Interrogatorien van Pieter Doncker," February 8, 1683, *Secrete Brieven en Papieren van Curaçao, 1680–89*, fol. 263.

WIC #617: "Interrogatorien van Gisberto Hippesack," February 10, 1683, *Secrete Brieven en Papieren van Curaçao, 1680–89*, fol. 295.

WIC #617: "Interrogatorien van Elisabeth Pieters, Weduwe de Heer Joan Pedro van Collen, Manuel Epina, Bejamin Carrello, en Ysaacque Omar Chena," February 11, 1683, *Secrete Brieven en Papieren van Curaçao, 1680–89*, fol. 291.

WIC #617: "Interrogatorien van David Abendana," February 22, 1683, *Secrete Brieven en Papieren van Curaçao, 1680–89*, fol. 299.

WIC #617: "Interrogatorien van Juan Barofso Y Pozzo," February 22, 1683, *Secrete Brieven en Papieren van Curaçao, 1680–89*, fols. 259–260.

WIC #617: "Attestatie van G. Hoppesack," February 25, 1683, *Secrete Brieven en Papieren van Curaçao, 1680–89*, fol. 290.

WIC #617: "Interrogatorien van Jan Elkis," February 27, 1683, *Secrete Brieven en Papieren van Curaçao, 1680–89*, fols. 245–247.

WIC #617: "Artijckelen aen Nicolaas van Liebergen," March 2, 1683, *Secrete Brieven en Papieren van Curaçao, 1680–89*, fol. 324.

WIC #617: "Papieren over Willem de Penijn, Vrij Coopman," 1687, *Secrete Brieven en Papieren van Curaçao, 1680–89*, fol. 542vs.

WIC #617: "Memorial, Anno 1688," 1688, *Secrete Brieven en Papieren van Curaçao, 1680–89*, fol. 50b.

WIC #617: "Brief aan de Kamer Amsterdam," July 19, 1688, *Secrete Brieven en Papieren van Curaçao, 1680–89*, fol. 143.

WIC #745: *Korte inhoud van den notulen, met alfabetisch register*, 1674–1764.

WIC #833: *Notulen der Vergadering van Tienen, Kamer van Zeeland.*

WIC #865: *Alphabetisch zakelijke registers op de notulen der vergadering van Tienen, Zeeland Kamer*, 1674–1690.

WIC #1180: "Brief van Lucas Schorck aan de Zeeland Kamer," April 17, 1688, *Brieven & Papieren van St. Eustatius*.

WIC #1180: "St. Eustatius: Debent en Credunt Rekening," 1688, *Brieven en Papieren van St. Eustatius*.

II. Archivo General de Indias (Seville, Spain)

Contratacion 167: *Autos Fiscales*, Número 7 (Contra Nicolás de Porta, Andrés Enríques y Felipe Juan), 1618–1619.

Contratacion 368, N. 5: *Bienes de Difuntos: Domingo Bohorquez*, 1626.

Escribania 25A–25C: *Comisiones Audencia de Santo Domingo*, 1684.

Escribania 297A: *Comisión por el Conde de Paredes . . .*, 1683.

Escribania 597A: *Comisiones Gobernacion de Cartagena*, 1684.

Escribania 964: *Sentencias del Consejo*, 1696.

Guatemala 42, N. 77: *Caratas de Cabildos Seculares*, March 18, 1671.

Guatemala 359: *Comercio ilícito con piratas y comisos de esclavas negros*, 1703–1704.

Indiferente 2578: *Piratas en las Costas de Barlovento*, 1681–1684.

Indiferente 428, L. 32, F: *Real Cédula a las Justicias de Indias . . .*, 1602.

Indiferente 430, L. 42, F. 271v–272: *Real Cédula a Don Rafael Capri y Sanz, gobernador de Cartagena* . . ., November 20, 1682.
Mexico 28, N. 28: *Cartas del Virrey Marques de Guadalcazar*, 1614.
Mexico 29, N. 91: *Cartas del Virrey Marques de Gelves*, 1622.
Panama 30, N. 68: *Cartas y Expedientes de Cabildos Seculares: Panamá*, 1616.
Panama 81: *Empréstito de 1000, 000 Pesos para Rescutar Portobelo*, 1678.
Panama 95: *Entrada de Piratas en Portobelo, Darien y Mar del Sur*, 1679–1681.
Panama 96: *Entrada de Piratas en Portobelo, Darien y Mar del Sur*, 1682–1687.
Panama 99: *Resguardo del Darién y Tierra Firme contra la Pirateria*, 1683–1694.
Patronata 267, N. 1, R. 59: *Los Rebeldes de Los Paises Bajos contra la Armada Española*, 1571.
Patronata 268, N. 2, R. 3: *Declaracíon de Rodrigo Girardo, Capitan de Filibote Flamenco*, 1600.
Patronata 268, N. 2, R. 4: *Corsario Holandás que Fue à Filipinas desde Perú*, 1601.
Santo Domingo 856: *Invasión de Piratas en la Florida*, 1684–1702.

III. Atlas van Stolk (Rotterdam, the Netherlands)

Atlas van Stolk #407: *De Spaensche Tiranye Gheschiet in Neder-lant, Waer in te sien is, De Onmenschelijcke ende wreede handelingen der Spaeniaerden* . . . . t'Amsterdam, Jacob Pietersz. Wachter, 1567–1597, plate #8.
Atlas van Stolk #484: *Herstelde Hongers-Dwangh, of Haerlems langh en strenghe Belegeringhe*. Haerlem: Kornelus Theunisz. Kas, 1660.
Atlas van Stolk #1659: *Veroevering van de Silver-vloot inde Bay Matanca*. t'Amsterdam: Claes Iansz. Visscher, 1628.
Atlas van Stolk #1748: S. Savrij, *De Slagh vant Hantie tegens Twee Duijnkerckers Aen*, 1633.
Atlas van Stolk #1760: *Victorie Liedt over het innemen vaneen Duynkercker met 136. coppen ende 13 stucken groot 100 last verder hoe de Manhaftighe Capiteynen Jan van Galen ende den Goyer met zijn Haentjen bracht tot Amsterdam den 13 October 1634*, 1634.
Atlas van Stolk #1912: *Een Waerachtigh Liedt van een Schip datmen in Tessel heeft gekregen daer 26. Knechtjens en 2. Meyskens op waren die sy meynden aenden Turck te leveren* . . ., 1645.
Atlas van Stolk #2229: C. van Dalen (?), *Eer en lof zij Tromp*.

Pamphlet collections

*I. Verzameling Thysius, University of Leiden
(Leiden, the Netherlands)*

Ample ende waerachtige beschrijvinghe . . . in wat manieren de ses groote Galleyen (ghesonden wt Spaengien na de Nederlanden) zijn vergaen, overvallen, ende ghestrant . . . Alles beschreven opt Schip van Capiteyn Gerrit Evertsz . . . den 7 Oct. 1602. Delff: J. Cz. Vennecool, 1602.
Apologie of verdedingh van Capiteyn Pieter de Russchuer. Van wegen de Sententie over hem gepronunciert by de . . . Staten van Holland op den 23 Febr. Anno 1638 jegenw. sittende in 't Tuchthuys te Amsterdam . . ., August 1, 1639. Amsterdam, 1639.
Artyckel-brief van de Generale Nederlandsche Geoctroyeerde West-Indische Compagnie. 's Graven-hage: Jac. Scheltus, 1675.
Bekentenisse van Hugo Clerck Capiteyn der Zee Roovers, die met zijn Complicen ende aenhang gejusticeert zijn tot Amsterdam, den 24 Jan. 1615. Met een antwoort Liet tusschen den Capiteyn ende de gasten . . . . Amsterdam, 1615.

Belijdenisse, Sententie, ende namen der Zee-roovers, die soo tot Rotterdam als 't Amsterdam met der koorde gheexecuteert zijn enz . . . den 24 Jan . . . . Amsterdam: Broer Jansz, 1615.

Buere-Praetje tusschen een Borger en een Matroos, Aengaende De ghelegentheydt deses Tijdts. . . . ca. 1665.

Casimyr, Hendrick (Stadthouder). *Waerschouwinge Nopens de Zee-roverijen op de Friesse Kusten . . .* June 9, 1677. Leeuwarden: R.S. Arumsma, 1677.

Collegien ter Admiraliteyt, Zeeland Kamer. *Instructie ende Articulen, waer naer de Capiteynen, Officieren ende Bootsgesellen ter Vryer Neeringe, uytvarende op behoorlicke Commissie, hun sullen hebben te reguleren . . . .* February 21, 1665. Middelburgh: Johan Misson, 1665.

Copie. Uyt het schip Sint Benita den 18 November 1657. [Aan de Raden ter Admiraliteit binnen Amsterdam, verslag van schipper Hans Wargaren omtrent het prijs maken van eenige vijandelijke koopvaardijschepen]. Amsterdam. Otto Barentsz. Smient, 1657.

Copie. Ongeteekende missiven naar de Staten Generael uit Alicante. January 11, 1683.

Copye van seeckeren Brief, geschr. uyt Middelburch (26 Maart) . . . Waer in verhaelt wort 't ghene gepasseert is in 't nemen vanden Duynkercker, geschiet op den 1 en 2 Martij . . . 1645, 1645.

Cort verhael van sulx alsser ghepasseert is, soo binnen als buyten Oostende, 't zedert den 7den Jan. 1602 (tot het einde dier maand) . . . Mitgaders de namen van de Hoofden . . . . Dordrecht: Jac. Canin, 1602.

Courante uyt Italien ende Duytschlandt. February 26, 1639. Amsterdam: voor J. v. Hilten by J. Fz. Stam, 1639.

De achtervolgende Dagh-Register Van het Parlement En Resolutien wegens Arlington, Benevens een aerdighe Rescontre Van een France Kaper, en een Engels Fregat, Welcke Kaper na eenigh tegenweer is genomen en tot Pleymuyen opgebracht. Amsterdam: Wed. van J. Bruyning en Steven Swart, 1674.

De Snelle Mercurius. Op nieu mede brengende, al het gene in 't Jaar Sestien hondert vijfentagtig, In al de vier Gedeelten des Werelts is voorgevallen . . . . Amstelredam: Otto Barentsz. Smient, 1686.

Deductie, Op het subject van de handelinge op de Straet, en de Navigatie in de Middellantsche Zee, 1687.

Donderdaeghsche Mercurius. No. XIV (February 17, 1661). Utrecht: Anthony Benedicti, 1661.

Donderdaechsche Mercurius . . . Nieuwen Stijl. July 2, 1665. Utrecht: Anthony Benedicti, 1665.

Duyn-Kerckens Naeckende Sterff-Dagh: Verhandelt in bondighe Redenen, aen de Gheun. Nederl. Provincien . . . . ca. 1645.

Een waerachtige beschryvinghe van het groot jammer . . . datter nu ghebeurt is op de Zee, ende schade die daer oock gheschiet is in het Tessel . . . den 20 Jan . . . . Amsterdam: Gerrit van Breughel, 1616.

Exhibitum den 7 Juny 1679. Traitte de Paix & de Commerce, entre . . . Les Estats Generaux des Provinces Unies des Pays-Bas & . . . Ismael Basscha, Hadgi Mahomed Day Baba Hassan, Gouverneur, Aga . . . de la Ville et du Royaume d'Alger . . . Confirme, signe & scelle en presence de Dieu, le 30 . . . . Avril 1679. 1679.

Extract van een Brief, Geschreven uyt Parijs, den 10 November, 1702 . . . 's Gravenhage: Abraham de Hondt, November 10, 1702.

Goede nieuwe tijdinghe ghecomen met het Iacht de Vos ghenaemt, afghesonden vanden Generael Jacob Wilcken uyt Bresilien, aen . . . Bewint-Hebbers vande . . . . West-Indische Compagnie . . . . Amsterdam: Broer Jansz., 1624.

Graaf van Avaux. *Memorie Door mijn Heer de Graaf van Avaux . . . Ambassadeur van zijn Allerchristelijckste Majesteit, gepresenteert aan de . . . Staten Generaal der Vereenigde Nederlanden.* November 28, 1681. 's-Gravenhage, 1681.

H. van V. *Den Oprechten Hollandsen Bootgesel. Vertoond in een t'Zamenspraak tussen drie Persoonen, Een van Delf, Een van Amsterdam, En eenen Bootsgesel Geweest zijnde in de laaatste Zeeslag. Gehoord, gezien en te zamen gesteld, Tot onderrechtinge van de vrome en welmeende Patriotten.* Rotterdam: Jan Isaakse, 1666.

Het Malle Schip van Rotterdam, 1654.

Heyn, Pieter Pietersz. *Extract uyt den Brief van den E. Generaal Pieter Pietersz Heyn aen de Geotr. West-Indische Comp., gheschreven in 't Schip Amsterdam, ghedateert den 26 Sept. 1628 140 mylen bywesten 't Eylandt Bermuda.* 1628.

Hollandtze Mercurius, Behelzende de gedenckweerdichste voorvallen in't Jaer 1665 binnen Christenryck . . . . 16th ed. Haerlem: Pieter Casteleyn, 1666.

Hollantse Mercurius, brenghende in een kort Tractaet het remarcabelst in den Iaere 1650 voor ghevallen in Christenryck . . . . Haerlem: Pieter Casteleyn, 1651.

L.B. *Klaght en Kort Verhael, Over de Engelschen haer hooghmoedige begeerlijckheyt, ongeregelde Zee-rooversche proceduren . . . ,* 1672.

Liefs, I. *Lof-dicht over de wijt-vermaerde . . . victorie, by het veroveren vande schatriicke Silver-vloot des Konings van Spangien . . . Geschiet Ao. 1628,* 1629.

———. *Sommiere Loffelijcke beschrijvinge van . . . Zeelandt. Midtsgaders de Daden . . . der . . . Zeelanderen. By een vergadert ende in Rhijm ghestelt . . . .* Amsterdam: J. Fz. Stam, 1636.

Liefs, J. *Den Lof vande Geoctr. Oost ende West-Indische Compagnye ende Lofrijcke Zee-vaert van dese vrye vereenighde Nederlandse Provintien.* Delf: J. Pz. Waelpots, 1630.

Lommelin, D. *Lof-dicht, ter Eeren ende tot weerde Fame vanden . . . Generael P. Pz. Heyn . . . inghekomen met de Silver-vlote . . . hier in ons Vaderlandt den 10 January 1629,* 1629.

Magistraet van 's Graven-Hage. *Keure ende Ordonnantie byde Magistraet van 's Graven-Hage gedaen maecken, op 't stuck vande Vagabonden ende Bedelaers . . . .* April 2, 1640. 's-Gravenhage: Wed. en Erfgen. an H. Jz. van Wouw, 1640.

Opweckingh en moed-gevingh aen de Bataviers van't wydt Beroempt Nedelandt, om Couragieus te strijden tegen die van Engelandt, Verhandlende mede de prinsipaelste Victorien en Overwinningen ter Zee . . . Schoonhoven: Samuel Knudde, 1665.

Ordinantie Ghemaeckt op t' Stuck van de Admiraliteit, ende Teghens de Zeeroouers (13 Nov. 1582). 't Antwerpen: Chr. Plantijn, 1583.

Ordonnatie, dienende tot versekeringe vande Schepen uyt dese Landen nae Oosten ende Noorweghen varende . . . . Amstelredam: Cornelis Claesz, 1596.

Ordonnantien ende Articulen . . . op het toerusten . . . van eene West-Indische Compagnie. 1623.

Pertinant Verhael van alle het gene in de Zeeslagt tusschen de Engelse, France, en Vereenighde nederlandsche Vlooten is vorrgevallen, op den 7 Junij 1672 en vervolgens. Amsterdam: P. Arentsz, 1672.

Placaat opde Commercien van de Coopluyden adventuriers van de Engelsche Natie. March 22, 1599. 's Gravenhage: Aelbr. Heyndricksz., 1599.

Placcaet byden welcken alle vrybuiters anderwaerf . . . ghecasseert zijn . . . . March 5, 1577. Ghendt: Jan vanden Steene, 1577.

Placcaaet Ende Ordonnantie beroerende die Boodtsghesellen die haer metten Stierluyden veryhuyren/ hoe lange sy varen moeten/ ende hoe sy betaelt sullen worden. 's Graven-Haghe: Hillebrant Iacobssz, 1619.

Prince van Orange, Wilhem Hendrick. *Placcaet, Van Syne Hoogheyt den Heere Prince van Orange, Op het verbranden ende in den grondt booren van veroverde Schepen* . . . . April 24, 1673. 's Graven-hage: J. Scheltus, 1673.

Proclamatie ofte Placaat des Conings van Groot Britanien, tot wederroepinghe der Engelsche Natie die haer ter Zee zijn generende met Rooff enz. March 1, 1605. Delf: J. Andriesz., 1605.

Proeve, over eenen Rypen-Raet, ende Zalige resolutie, onlangs uytgheghelen door een Lief-hebber des Vaderlandts . . . Ghetrouwelijck ingestelt by . . . I.G.B.S.G.M. Ter Tholen: Christoffel Speeckaert, 1636.

Propositien Van d'Ondernemers tot het vast-stellen van een vrije Haven in West-Indien. 1679.

Rapport aen hare Ho. Mo. ende Sijn Excell., van den Capiteyn Salomon Willemsz., over 't veroveren vande Silver-Vlote . . . door 't beleyt van . . . Pt. Psz. Heyn . . . . 's Gravenhage: Wed. en Erfg. van H. Jzn. v. Wouw, 1628.

Rijpen Raedt, ende Salige Resolutie gheraemt door eenen Lief-hebber des Vaderlandts, ende voor-ghehouden onse vereenighde Nederlanden . . . . 's Graven-Haghe: 1635.

Seeckere tydinge van 'tgene aldereest ghepasseert is tusschen onse Hollandtsche Oorlochschepen naer Venitien/ende de Spaensche. Maer insonderheyt hoe 36. Turcksche Zee-roovers het Eylant Lancerotte hebben afgheloopen/geplondert / ende duysent menschen tot slaven ghemaeckt . . . . Amstelredam: Broer Jansz. op de Kolck, 1618.

Sententien over Capiteyn Reynhart Tijtfort. Vlissinghen: Maerten Abraham van der Nolck, 1621.

Sententien By de Gecommitteerde Raden Admiraliteyt . . . binnen Rotterdam . . . (Rotterdam: Anth. de Haes, 1629).

Sententien . . . over eenige persoonen, gedient hebbende de . . . O.I. Comp. Rotterdam: Anth. de Haes, 1629.

Spieghel der grau-same ongherechticheyt ende vervloeckte giericheyt, vande factie der Contremineurs, die nu veel Jaeren, tot groot achter-deel der Conincklicke Compagnie van Oost-Indien, een schantloose Roovery bedreven hebben ende noch doen, 1638.

Spilberghen, Admirael. *Copie van een Brief van den Heere Admirael Spil-berghen: Inhoudende de Voyage by hem gedaen door de Strate magelanica, tot inde Zuydt Zee, al waer hem bejeghent is de Vlote van Don Rodrigo de Mendosa daer hy Mannelijcken tegen gevochten, ende de victorije behouden heeft.* Delf: Andriessz., 1617.

Spranckhuysen, Dionysium. *Triumphe van weghen de . . . Victorie, welcke de Heere onse God op den 8 Sept . . . . 1628 verleent heeft aen de Vlote . . . onder het beleydt van Pieter Pietersz. Heijn, teghen de Silver-vlote.* Delf: Jan Andriesz. Kloeting, 1628.

Staten Generael. *Placcaet ende Ordonnantie op de Verzeeckerheyt vande Scheepvaert tusschen Hollandt ende Zeelandt.* Delff: A. Hendricxz, 1589.

———. *Alsoo mijn Heeren die Staten Generael . . . . zijn gheresolveert hen ter zee te wapenen tot affweeringe van het ghewelt der Spaignaerden* . . . . May 20, 1599.

———. *Placcaet. Die Staten Generael der Vereenighde Nederlanden [verbieden alle moetwillicheden tegens de Commisen der recherche op de stroomen vant Vlye ende Texel . . .].* April 13, 1620. 's Graven-Haghe: Hillebrant Iacobssz., 1620.

———. *Placcaet ende Ordonnantie vande . . . St. Gen . . . . tegens Wechloopers die hun in dienst vande Oost- ofte West Indische Compagnien begeren hebbende, verloopen* . . . . May 30, 1625. 's Gravenhage: Wed. en Erfgen. van H. Jzn. v. Wouw, 1625.

———. *Placcaet. De Staten Generael . . . (Verbod om dienst te nemen op vreemde schepen . . .*). March 23, 1629. 's Gravenhage: Wed. en Erfg. van H.Jz. van Wouw, 1629.

Staten Generael. *De Staten Generael enz. (Prijzen uitgeloofd op het veroveren of vernielen van schepen, in d. 11 Maart 1632)* . . . . 1632a.

———. *Placaet. De St. Gen. (tegen 't varen naer West-Indie buiten de W.I. Comp., 14 Juni 1632)*, 1632b.

———. *Placaet. De St. Generael (tegen 't dienst nemen op vreemde schepen . . .*). March 19, 1640. 's Gravenhage: Wed. en Erfgen. van H. Jz. v. Wouw, 1640.

———. *Placaet Van mijn Heeren de Staten Generael der Vereenighde Nederlanden. Inhoudende verbodt, van niet te moghen varen opte Havenen van Grevelingen, Duynkercke, Nieupoort, Sluys ende andere, buyten 's Duyns van Vlaenderen gelegen* . . . . 's Graven-Hage: Wed. ende Erf. van wijlen Hillebrandt Iacobssz van Wouw, 1641.

———. *Pardon aan de zeelieden die bij de "Piraten" dienen of gediend hebben* . . . . August 25, 1651. 's Graven-Hage: Wed. en Erfg. van H. Jzn. v. Wouw, 1651.

———. *Extract wt 't Register der Resolutien van de . . . St. Generael . . . (Ordre om) alle Engelsche Schepen . . . nae vermoghen . . . te vermeesteren* . . . . July 18, 1652.

———. *Placaet Opte Grootte Equipagie, Monture, Manninge ende Admiraelschappen der Schepen varende door de Strate van Gibralter naer de Middelandtsche Zee ende op Levanten.* 's Graven-Hage: Weduwe, ende Erfgenamen van wijlen Hillebrant Jacobsz van Wouw, 1652.

———. *Placaet Opte Groote Equipagie Monture Manninge ende Admiraelschappen derr Scheppen varende door de Strate van Gibralter naer de Middelandtsche Zee ende op Levanten.* May 17, 1655. 's Graven-Hage: Weduwe ende Erfgenamen van wylen Hillebrandt Jacobsz. van Wouw, 1655.

———. *Publikatie. De Staten Generael der Vereenigde Nederlanden* . . . . April 14, 1672. 's Gravenhage: Iac. Scheltus, 1672.

———. *Placcaet. De Staten Generael der Vereenighde Nederlanden* . . . . October 10, 1673. 's-Gravenhage: J. Scheltus, 1673a.

———. *Placcaet. De Staten Generael der Vereenighde Nederlanden . . . den Hage* . . . . December 23, 1673. 's Gravenhage: J. Scheltus, 1673b.

———. *Waerschouwinge. De Staten Generael* . . . . December 29, 1677. 's Graven-Hage: J. Scheltus, 1677.

———. *Publicatie. De Staten Generael* . . . . February 28, 1678.

———. *Placaet. De Staten Generael der Vereenighde Nederlanden* . . . . September 9, 1679. 's Graven-Hage: J. Scheltus, 1679.

———. *Traitte de Paix & de Commerce entre les . . . Estats Generaux des Provinces Unies des Pays-Bas, et le . . . Prince d'Orange d'une part; et . . . Ismael Basscha Hadji Mahometh Day, Baba Hassan, Gouverneur . . . de la Ville & du Royaume d'Alger d'autre part* . . . . May 1, 1680.

———. *Nader Placaet, Tegens Brantstichtingen, Dootslagen, Moorderyen, Dieveryen, Vechteryen, en het dragen van onbehoorlyck Geweer, Tegens Vagabonden . . . ende andere delicten en ongeregeltheden, soo over de Steden, als ten platten Lande, onder het ressort van desen Staet* . . . . April 28, 1691. 's Graven-Hage: J. Scheltus, 1691.

———. *Placaet. De Staten Generael . . . Doen te weten . . . dat wy oock noodigh achten dat de Commissie-Vaerders, tegenwoordigh noch in Zee zynde, ten spoedighsten wederom herwaerts komen* . . . . January 8, 1691. 's Graven-Hage: J. Scheltus, 1691.

———. *Placaet, Van de praemien voor de Commissie-vaerders deser Landen, dewelcke eenige Oorlogh-schepen van den Vyandt sullen komen te veroven,* June 6, 1702. 's Gravenhage: P. Scheltus, 1702.

Staten van Gelderlant. *Placcaet vande Staten van Gelderlant . . . tegen alle Roovers ende Stroopers, die van wegen den vijant int selve lant souden mogen comen* . . . . March 30, 1621.

Staten van Holland. *Ordonnantie op 't Stuck vande Justitie Binnen den Steden, ende ten platten Lande van Hollandt*, 1635.
Staten van Hollandt. *Placaet By de Ed. Mo. Heeren Staten van Hollandt ende West-Vrieslant, geemaneert jegens de Dieven, Dieverijen, ende aenhouders van dien.* 's Graven-Haghe: Weduwe, ende Erf. van wijlen Hillebrandt Iacobszvan Wouw, 1635.
Staten van Zeelandt. *Placcaet vande . . . Staten van Zeelandt, teghens den Vagabunden, Bedelaers, Dieven Lantloopers, enz . . . .* Middelburgh: R. Schilders, 1596.
Staten van Zeelant. *Propositie van de . . . Staten van Zeelant, Aen de . . . Staten Generael, om ordre te stellen tegens de Portugaelsche Commissie vaerders, dewelcke dagelijcx noch de goede Inwoonders berooven, ende bestealen, tot een volcomen suppressie der selvige, en voorts tenderende om mede nieuwe Commissien aen de Nederlandtsche Inwoonders uyt te deelen tegens de Portugesen.* May 23, 1662. Vlissingen: T. Tyssen, 1662.
Sterlincx, P. *Beschrijvinghe (Een Corte waerachtighe), van alle Gheschiedenissen, Aenslaghen, Stormen, Schermutsinge, ende Schieten voor de vrome Stadt Haerlum in Hollandt gheschiet.* Delft, 1574.
Ten Waer Saecke (Goede Vrunden) dat U Luyder Ooghen enz . . . . October 5, 1574. Leyden, 1574.
Terror terroris, Werelts Wonder-schrick. Seldsame . . . vondt, mitsgaders . . . Beschryvinge van seecker . . . onverwinnelyck Vaer-tuygh, ghenaemt den Oorlogs-Blixem ter Zee . . . Opgericht ende gebouwt binnen Rotterdam . . . . 's Graven-hage: Isaac Burghoorn, 1654.
Vande Heerlijcke Victorie verkregen tegen de Zee-Roovers, hoe Capitein Jacob Jansson van Edam, Moy Lambert, ende noch twee ander Oorlochschepen eenen welghemonteerden Zee-Roover onder Yrlandt hebben doen stranden . . . 't Amsterdam, 1614.
Verhaal Van de Zee-Battailje, Tusschen het Frans Konings-Schip . . . en het Schip De Faam, van Zeeland . . . Middelburg: S. Bruilois, 1689.
Verhael van het Gevecht vande Vloot van . . . Blaeck tegens de Spaense West-Indische Vloot . . . in Canarien . . ., 1657.
Victori-liedt op en Scheep-strijt tusschen de Armade des Conings van Spagnien, ende de Schepen van Oorloge . . . Onder 't beleyt van . . . Jacob van Heemskerk . . . voor Gibralter, 1607.
Waerachtich Verhael vanden grooten Slach, ende gheluckighe Victorie . . . tusschen Oosteynde ende Nieupoort, op den 2den Julij Anno 1600 . . . . Haerlem: G. Rooman, 1600.
Waerachtige goede Tijdinge Hoe de Vesting Blockzijl Stormerdenhandt door de Hollandsche Kapers is ingenomen . . . . September 2, 1672. Amsterdam, 1672.
Waerachtigh verhael, van het success van de Vlote, onder den Admirael Jacques L'Hermite, in de Zuyt-zee, op de Custen van Peru, en de Stadt Lima in Indien, 1625.
Warachtighe beschrijvinghe van het groote Jammer . . . datter nu ghebeurt is op Zee, alwaer veel schepen zijn vergaen . . . . Rotterdam: Jan de Kramer, 1615.
West-Indische Compagnie. *Artyckel-brief van de . . . West-Indische Compagnie . . . voor de Officieren, Boots-ghesellen, soldaten ende andere die hun in ders. Dienst sullen begeven . . . ghearrest. in . . . Julio 1657.* Amsterdam: Nic. van Ravesteyn, 1657.
Wonderen en Mirakelen welcke doen sal het . . . Rotterdams Zee-Schrick, sijnde een gemaeckt Instrument . . . Geinventeert door den . . . Mathesios le Sieur DE LISSON . . . . Rotterdam: Pieter Flipsen, 1653.

II. Verzameling Pamfletten, Rijksuniversiteit Leiden
(Leiden, the Netherlands)

Amsterdams Dam-Praetje, Van Wat Outs en Wat Nieuws. En Wat vreemts. Amsterdam: Ian van Soest, 1649.

Amsterdams Tafel-Praetje Van Wat Goets en Wat Quats En Wat Noodichs. Gouda: Iasper Cornelisz, 1649.

Amsterdams Vuur-Praetje, Van 't Een ende 'tander datter nu om gaet. Amstelredam: Claes Pietersz, 1649.

Baers, Joannem. *Olinda, Ghelegen int Landt van Brasil, inde Capitania van Phernambuco, met Mannelijcke dapperheyt ende groote couragie inghenomen, ende geluckelijck verovert op den 16 Februari Ao. 1630 . . . .* Amsterdam: Hendrick Laurentsz, 1630.

Cort ende waerachtich Verhael wt de Sententie . . . den 26 September . . . in 's Gravenhage ghepronuncheert . . . over . . . den Fiscael Berck, Van der Mast, enz . . . . Geweest zynde van de Admiraliteyt tot Rotterdam. Rotterdam: H. Pietersz., 1626.

Een Cort ende warachtich verhael vande ghedenckweerdige gheschiedenisse in Barbaryen, ende vanden grooten slagh ontrent Maroques, Gheschiet 25 Apr. 1607 . . . . 's Graven-haghe: Hill. Jacobsz., 1607.

Een Praatje Van Den Ouden en Nieuwen Admiraal. Zynde Een noodige verantwoordinge van den Overtreffelijken Zeeheld, Marten Harpertzoon Tromp, Tegen verscheyden valsche beschuldigingen. Door een Oprecht Hollands Zeeman. Amsterdam: Jacob Volkers Hoofdbreker, 1653.

Extraordinaire du XXII Novembre 1634. Contenant . . . La prise de la belle Isle de Curacao . . . par les Holandais sur let Espagnols . . . . November 22, 1634. Paris, 1634.

Generale Sententie door den Heer Gouverneur Generael . . . ende den Breeden Raed der seven Schepen, Nieuw Amsterdam, Fredrick Hendrick, enz . . . . uyt-gesproocken ende ghe-executeert jegensClaes Garbrantsen van Schiebroeck . . . . enz . . . op het schip Nieuw Amsterdam, ten Ancker leggende inde Tafelbay vande Caep de bona Esperance den 29 Maert Anno 1636. Amsterdam: Gerrit Jansz., 1636.

Goede Apparentie tot Spoedige opkomst, Der Vrye Nederlandens Magtige Zee-Vaart; en vorige Negotie: En daar tegens, de Spoedige ondergang der tegenwoordighe Engelsche Regeeringh Haar Zee-Vaart en Nogotie, 1653.

Hasselbekium, Johannes. *Triumph-Dicht, over de gheluckighe Veroveringhe van de Spaensche Silver-Vlote, geschiet den 8 Sept. 1628. Item, Over de rasse Veroveringhe van de Bahia de Todos os Sanctos. Den 10 Maij, Anno 1624. Beyde door cracht van Schrick of Vreese, die hier Poetischer wijse, als een Personagie werdt aff-ghebeeldet, op de Mate ende wijse van 't Grieckschc Hexameter. [Mitsgaders een] Eer-Dicht, Op de vrome Scharmutsinge Van den manhaften Zee-Capiteyn Gerrit van Swol Tegens twee Duyn-Kerckers. Geschiet nae by der Schellinge, Anno 1627 in October. Nae de Maete van 't Sapphicum.* Leeuwarden: Claude Fonteyne, 1629.

Heeren ter Admiraliteyt. *Deliberatien ende Resolutien Genomen op Verscheyde Poincten, Ende Berechtingen vande Heeren ter Admiraliteyt, joncxst inden Haegh versamelt,* 1663.

I.v.H. *Ondeckinghe van den Raed Achitophels uyt-ghegheven onder den on saligen ende vermomden Tytel van Rijpen Raed ende salighe Resolutie, etc . . . Door den Vaderland Recht-lief-hebbenden Patriott I. v. H.* Ziericzee: Balthasar Doll, 1636.

Naerder Openbaringe, van Nederlants Engelschen Oorloge, Oorsake, Ende Tegenweer. Ontsteken over 'onEngelschen off Duyvelschen Handel en Misdandel der Engelsche Regeeringe, tegens haren Staet. Mitsgaders Enige herde Scheeps-ontmoetingen, en Bloedige Voorvallen ter Zee . . . . Leyden: Wilhelm Christiaans vander Boxc, 1653.

Oost-Indisch-praetjen, Voorgevallen in Batavia, Tusschen vier Nederlanders, Den eenen een Koopman, d'ander een Krijghs-Officier, den derden een Stuyrman, en den vierden of den laeste een Kranke-besoeker, 1663.

Ordanarise Middel-weeckse Courante. No. 33 (August 12, 1653). Amsterdam: Jacques Bourse (?), 1653.

Politicq Memoriael, Der hedendaeghsche Geschiedenissen ende Maximen van Staet. Verhalende 't gepasseerde in de Maenden October, November ende December, Anno 1662. Het derde deel. Amsterdam: C.v.G., 1663.

Practijcke van den Spaenschen Aes-Sack aengewesen Op de Veroveringe, en Victorie van den Loffelicken, Voorsienighen, Manlijck-hertighen Heer Generael Pieter Pietersz. Heyn. 's Gravenhage, 1629.

"Quesnelium Ium. Middele, Petrum." *Den Strick Vanden Openbare Lasteraer, oft Wederlegginghe vanden Hollandtschen Apocalypsis*. Delf: Felix van Sambix, 1626.

Reden Van dat die West-Indische Compagnie oft Handelinge, niet alleen profijtelijck, maer oock noodtsaeckellijck is, tot behoudenisse van onsen Staet, 1636.

Rotterdams Zee-Praatjen; Tusschen Een Koopman, een Borger en een Stierman. Aangaande de handelingen ter Zee: Ende De laatste Slag tusschen den Heer Admirael Tromp, Ende de Engelsche. Schiedam, 1653.

Rouwklage, over de dood van Hollands grooten Admirael, de Heer Michaël de Ruyter. Rotterdam: J. Oudaan, 1676.

Spaenschen Raedt. Om die Geunieerde Provincien, te Water ende te Lande te benauwen, van alle Neeringen ende welvaren te beroovan, om soo voorts de selvige weder onder de Spaensche Tyrannije te brengen. Tot waerschouwinge aen deser zij de uytgegeven. s' Graven-haghe: Aert Meuris, 1626.

Spranckhuysen, Dionysium. *Tranen, over den doodt vn den grooten Admirael van Hollandt, loffelijcker, ende onsterffelijcker ghedachtenisse, Pieter Pietersz. Heyn. Mitsgaders syn Testament Aen de Generale Gheoctroyeerde West-Indische Compagnie. Ofte Onbedriegh'lijcke LEYD-STERRE, Tot geluckige Voyagie van der selver Scheeps-Vloten*. Delf: A.T. Kloeting, 1629.

Staten Generael. *Sententien, ofte vonnissen ghewesen binnen utrecht teghens verscheyden persoonen* . . . . 1612.

———. *Placcaet ende Ordonnantie opte Wapeninge ende Manninge vande Schepen, soo ter coopvaerdye als Vissherye uytte Vereen. Nederlanden over Zee varende* . . . . 's Gravenhage: Wed. en Erfg. van H. Jzn. v. Wouw, 1625.

———. *Artickels-Brief Ende Instructie, roerende den Oorloghe ter Zee, waer naer allen ende eenen yegelijck, 't zy Admirael, Vice-Admirael, Capiteynen, Lieutenanten, Edelluyden, Schippers, Officiers, Soldaten ende ghemeense Matrosen ter Zee dienende, hen te reguleren hebben, op de straffen, penen, boeten, ende Correctien daer inne begrepen*. April 27, 1629.

Staten van Utrecht. *Placaet Van de Heeren Staten van den Lande van Utrecht tegens den Vagabunden, Bedelaars, Dieven, etc*. January 24, 1596.

Staten van Zeelant. *Placaet vande . . . Staten van Zeelant, teghens den Vagabunden, Bedelaers* . . . . July 19, 1607. Middelburgh: R. Schilders, 1607.

't Proces en executie van den grootes Moorder Philip Beeckern. Utrecht: Anthony Benedick, 1661.

van Hilten, Jan. *Waerachtich verhael van de victorieuse Zee-strijt tusschen acht Portugysch galeonen ende vier Hollantsche met vier Engelsche schepen omtrent Ormus ende de Persische Kust voorgevallen*. Amsterdam: de Weduwe van Jacob Jacobsz, 1626.

van Kerckhoven, Johannes. *Wijtloopig breede en waerachtige Beschrijvinge Van de ongeluckige Voyage van 't Schip AERNEM* . . . . Amsterdam: Jacobus vander Fuyck, 1664.

Vervolg van Het Rotterdams Zee-Praatje Tusschen Drie Personen, een Koopman, een Borger en een Stierman: Noodig, In der haast gelesen te werden. Middelburg: Gerrit Jansz. van Hoorn, 1653.

"Vreimundima, Pambonem." *Den Hollantschen Apocalypsis*...., 1626.

Waerachtich verhael, Belanghende de aenkomste tot Constantinoplen, van den Ambassadeur der Edele Moghende Heeren Staten Generael de Vereenighde Nederlanden.... Jacob Harmantz Verblack, 1612.

III. Verzameling Zeeuwse Biblitheek

Anderde Discours. By Forma van Messieve. Daer in kortelijck ende grondich verthoondt wort, de nootwendicheyt des Oost ende West Indische Navigatie, oock met goede fondamentale redenen bewesen dat door geen ander middel, eenen vasten versekerden vrede en is te verwachten of te verhopen..., 1622.

Bruynvisch, Martinum. *De Banieren des Heeren, Ofte Victory-vlagge, Op-ghesteken Ter gedachteisse van die.... Victorye.... over de machtige Spaensche Vlote, den 21. ende eenighe volghende daghen van October Anno 1639. Onder het beleydt Van.... Maerten Harperssen Tromp....* Ziericzee; Middelburch: Balthazar Doll, 1640; en Hans vander Hellen, 1640.

Discours Van Franciscus Campanella, Hoe de Nederlanden onder des Conings van Hispaengien ghehoorsaemheyt weder te brenghen zijn. Dienende tot opmerckinge aller getrouwe Voester-Heeren onses Lieven Vaderlandts, 1618.

Het klagende Vaderland, Over het afsterven Van... Michael de Ruiter, Ridder.... 1676.

Korte Onderrichtinghe ende vermaeninge aen alle liefhebbers des Vaderlandts, om liberalijcken te teeckenen inde West-Indisce Compagnie:.... Leyden: Isaak Elzevier, 1622.

Levendich Discours Vant ghemeyne Lants welvaart, voor desen de Oost, ende nu oock de West-Indische generale Compaignie aenghevanghen, seer notabel om lesen. Amsterdam: Broer Jansz., 1622.

(Lijst) Van alle des vyandts veroverde Chaloupen, Ponten, Pleyten ende Seuyen, met spedificatie van alle de Metale Stucken, Steen-Stucken als anders. Verovert by d'Heer Vice-Admirael Marinus Hollaer op den XIIJ Septemb. 1631. Midtsgaders de Lijste van alle de Gevangenen, 1631.

Missive. Daer in Kortelilјck ende grondigh wert verthoont, hoe veel de Vereenighde Nederlanden gelegen is aen de Oost ende West-Indische Navigatie.... Amsterdam: Broer Jansz., 1621.

Nieuw opgerecht Tractaet Tusschen den Nederlantschen Admirael de Heer Michiel Adriaen de Ruyter Ter eender. Ende de Koninck, ende die vande Regeringe van Tunis ter andere, op den Tweeden September 1662. Amsterdam: Michielsen Verbiest, 1662.

Regeerders der Stadt Utrecht. *Ordonnantie Vande Regeerders der Stadt Utrecht op 't Stuck vanden Armen, tegens de Bedelarye, ende alle vremde Bedelaers, ende den genen die d'selve in hare huysen innemen, logeren ofte Cameren verhuyren, mitsgaders d'ordre tusschen die schamele Ambachts-kinderen ende hare Meysters.* Utrecht: Salomon de Roy, 1619.

Sententie By mijn Ed. *Heeren van den Gerechte der Stadt Dordrecht, op den xxvj. September, 1663,gepronuncieert tegens Laurens Davidsz.... Ter saecke van de Zee-rooveryen ende pirateryen... in't... Roode Meer gepleegt.* Dordrecht: Mattheus van Nispen, 1663.

Sonnet op d'onsterskijcke Lof van onse Bataefsche Zee-Heldin. Amsterdam: Cornelis Danckertsz, 1639.

Staten Generaal. *Placcaet van de Staten-Generaal . . . tegen de buitensporigheden der kaapvaarders.* July 10, 1606.

———. *Placaat van de Staten-Generaal . . . waarbij sommen worden uitgeloofd voor het veroveren of vernielen van Spaansche Schepen.* July 4, 1625. 's Graven-haghe: de Weduwe, ende erfghenamen van wijlen Hillebrandt Jacobsz. van Wouw, 1625.

Tractaat Van Vrundtschap en Verbintenisse, Beslooten den negenden Februarii 1651. tusschen de . . . Staaten Generaal . . . . en de Heeren Gouverneurs en Superieuren van de Steeden van Sale in Barbarye . . . . 's Gravenhage: Weduwe . . . van wylen Hillebrandt Jacobsz. van Wouw, 1651.

van Nierop, Adr. *Echo ofte Galm, dat is Weder-klickende Ghedicht van de teghenwoordighe Vrede-handelinghe,* 1608.

Zee-triomph vanden Manhaften E. Admirael Marten Harpensen Tromp mitsgaders den slagh ter zee tusschen hem en de Duynkerckers, Anno 1639. 't Amsterdam: Cornelis Danckertsz, 1639.

IV. Verzameling Koninklijke Bibliotheek

Een Waerachtighe . . . Geschiedenisse, van drie Studenten van Cloppenburch, die welcke twee Jonghe dochters eerst hebben vercracht ende daer nae iver jonghe Dochters . . . vermoort . . . waer over zy eyndelicken gevangen ende daer na gerabraeckt zijn geworden. Lambert Raesvelt, 1610.

Een warachtich Verhael, hoe . . . de Vlote van hare Majesteyt van Enghelandt verovert heeft een Caracque, wesende een van des Conincks van Spaengien rijcke Oost-Indien varende Schepen . . . . Delft: Jacob Cornelissz Vennecool., 1601.

Een warachtighe beschrijvinge van drie moordenaers, de welcke binnen zeven Jaer in Danswijck ende buyten Danswijck, wel XXXIX. persoonen vermoort hebben: Ende zijn gejustificeert den 21 Junij 1609 . . . . Rotterdam: Jan Ghelen, no date.

Warachtighe Verclaringhe, in wat manieren de dry Ambassadeurs des Conincx van Barbaryen by hare Ma. van Enghelandt zijn ghecomen, ende audientie hebben verkreghen . . . . 1600.

Other Primary Sources (i.e., Books, Almanacs, Newspapers, Plastic Arts)

Aanhangsel, Behelzende de rampzalige en zeer gedenkwaardige Wedervaaringen van een Slaaf Die te Salé vier jaaren in de Slaaverny der Ongeloovigen versleeten heelft. ca. 1684.

Aleman, Mateo. *Het Leven van Gusman d'Alfarache, 't Afbeeltsel van 't Menschelijk Leven: Onder de ghedaente van een Spaenschen Landtlooper, en Bedelaar. Waer in de allergheslepenste Fielterijen en de Schelmstucken der Wereldt vermaeckelijck, yder ten nut, werden ontdekt.* 2nd ed. Amsterdam: Baltus Boekholt, 1669.

———. *Het Tweede Deel van 't Leven van Gusman d'Alfarache. 't Afbeeltsel van 't Menschelyk Leven: Onder de gedaente van een Spaenschen Gaudief. Waer in de allergeslepenste Fielteryen en Schelmstucken der Wereldt vermaeckelijck yeder -een ten nut, werden ontdeckt.* 2nd ed. Amsterdam: Baltus Boekholt, 1670.

Amsterdam Donderdaghse Courant. No. 38 (September 20, 1685). Amsterdam: Adriaen Van Gaesbeeck, 1685.

Amsterdamse Dingsdaegse Courant. February 7, 1690. Amsterdam: Casparus Commelin, 1690.

Amsterdamze Mercurius: Behelzende de Voornaamste in Europa, Voorgevallen in April 1689. Amsterdam: Johannes Landsmeer, April 1689.

Barker, Andrew. *A Report of Captaine Ward and Danseker, Pirates.* The English Experience: Its Record in Early Printed Books Published in Facsimile, Number 21. London: William Hall, 1609. Reprint, New York & Amsterdam: Da Capo Press & Theatrum Orbis Terrarum Ltd., 1968.

Bastiaensz, Gysbert. *Ongeluckige Voyagie, Van 'T Schip Batavia Nae Oost-Indien*.... Amsterdam: Joost Hartgers, 1648.

Baudaert, Willem. *Morghen-wecker der vrye Nederlantsche provintien: Ofte Een cort verhael van de bloedighe vervolghinghen ende wreetheden door de Spaenjaerden ende haere Adherenten inde Nederlanden ghedurende dese veertich-jarighe Troublen ende Oorloghen begaen aen vele Steden ende ettelijcke duysent particuliere Persoonen*.... Danswick: Crijn Vermeulen de Jonge, 1610.

———. *Spieghel der jeught, Ofte Corte Cronijcke der Nederlantsche geschiedenissen. In de welcke naecktelijck verhaelt en voor ooghen ghestelt worden de voornaemste Tyrannien ende onmenschelijcke wreedtheden die door het beleydt der Coningen van Hispaengien, onder hare Stadt-houders, hier in Nederlandt bedreven zijn aen menich duysent menschen*.... 2nd ed. Amsterdam: Herman Allertz. Coster, 1615.

Belley, Jean Pierre Camus. *De groote schouwplaets der jammerlijcke bloed- en moord-geschiedenissen, vervatt. onder 75 opschriften ontrent 200 voorbeelden der ellendige uytwerckselen van haet, toorn, yversught, ontrouw, bedrogh, Hooghmoed, Wanhoof en allerley ongeregelde Menschlijke Herts-toghten.* Utrecht: J. Ribbius, 1670.

Bodde-Hodgkinson, C.B. and Pieter Geyl, Trans. *Memorable description of the East Indian voyage, 1618–25.* London: G. Routledge & Sons, 1929.

Bontekoe, Willem Ysbrantsz. *Gedenckwaardige beschrijving, van de achtjarige en zeer avontuurlyke reise van Willem Ysbrandtsz. Bontekoe van Hoorn.* Amsterdam: B. Koene, 1625.

———. *Gedenckwaardige beschrijving, van de achtjarige en zeer avontuurlyke reise van Willem Ysbrandtsz. Bontekoe van Hoorn.* Hoorn: Jan Janzoon Deutel, 1646.

Bontius, Reynier. *Belegering en Ontsetting der Stad Leyden, Geschied in den Jare 1574. beginnende den 27. May, en eyndigende den derden Octobris.* Leyden: Iacob Tinnekens, 1646.

Brandt, Geeraert. *Historie der vermaerde zee- en koopstad, Enkhuisen, vervaetende Haere Herkomste, en Voortgangh. Mitsgaders Verscheide gedenkwaerdige Geschiedenissen, aldaer voorgevallen.* Enkhuisen: Egbert van den Hoof, 1666.

Brandt, Gerard. *Chronyxken Der voornaemste Nederlantsche Gheschiedenissen, soo Kerckelijck als Politijcq, tzedert den Jare 1600.* 3rd ed. Amsterdam: Borrit Iansz. Smit, 1657.

Cartouche, of de gestrafte Booswigt. Amsteldam: Joh. de Ruiter, 1731.

Commelin, Isaac. *Begin ende Voortgangh Van De Vereenighde Nederlantsche Geoctroyeerde Oost-Indische Compagnie*.... Amsterdam: J. Janssonius (Jan Jansz.), 1646.

Cort verhael Van het grouwelick ende verradelijck vergiftighen van eenen Edelen Ridder, Sir Thomas Overberry ghenaemt: In 's werck ghestelt door den Grave van Sommerset, met syn Huysvrou ende hare Complicen: waer in haren grouwelijcken handel verhaelt wordt, midtsgaders hare ghevanckenisse, examinatie, sententie, ende executie. Amsterdam: Desiderius de la Tombe, 1616.

Dampier, William. *A Collection of Voyages*, 4 vols. 1729.

———. *A New Voyage Round the World.* 1697. Reprint, NY: Dover, 1968.

Dan, Pieter and Simon de Vries. *Historie van Barbaryen, en des zelfs Zee-Roovers....* Trans. G.v. Broekhuizen. Amsterdam: Jan ten Hoorn, 1684.

Dapper, Olfert. *Historische Beschryving der Stadt Amsterdam.* Amsterdam: Jacob van Meurs, 1663.

de Airanda, E. *Turckse Slavernie, Beschreven door Emanuel De Airanda, soo hy selfs die geleden heeft: Mitsgaders Versheyde particuliere en vermaeckelijcke Verhalingen van veelderhande dinghen die geschiet zyn terwijl hy in Slavernie is gheweest....* 's Gravenhage: Christoffel en Jasper Doll, 1666.

De Berugte Land- en Zee-heldin, Of De Wonderbare Levensgevallen van Anna Blound, Anders Robert Stafford.... Amsterdam: Steven van Esveldt, 1756.

de Calvi, F. *Legende ofte Historye Vande snoode practijcquen, ende de behendige listicheden der Dieven.... achter is noch by gevoecht Gielers Vocabulaer Hael Tael.* Leyden: David Lopez de Haro, 1645.

———. *Historien ofte Practyke der Dieven, in dewelcke begrepen zijn seer jammerlycke Feyten, subtyle Dieveryen, en bedriegelijcke stratagemens van Gaudieven en Kleyers....* Utrecht: Willem van Paddenburg, 1688.

de Castillo Solersano, A. *'t Leeven en bedrijf van den doorsleepen bedrieger, meester van bedrogh en fieltery.* Amsterdam: B. Boekholt, 1669.

De Groote Nieuwe Hollandsche Boots-Gezel, Ofte Bataviers Helden-Stuk. Zijnde een groot deel vermeerderd en dat met de Vermaakelijkste Melody en Min-gezangen. Amsterdam: Joannes Kannewet, 1763.

de Hooghe, Romyn. *Spiegel van Staat Des Vereenigde Nederlands. Waar in De Macht en 't Vry Bestier, Van yder der Zeven Verbonde Provincien en haar byzondere Steeden, Zo in Rechten als Regeeringen werd ontvouwd. Aanwyzende Aan, de In, en Uytheemschen, alle de Hooge en Lage Recht-banken, Collegien en Ampten, dewelke in de zelve, tot dienst van den Staat, en het Recht, zijn ingesteld....* Amsterdam: Jan ten Hoorn, 1706–1707.

De Joodse Swerver Of De Historie Van Sekere Niet Onbekende Slaaf; Vervattende de aller Aanmerklykse Gevallen, doe ooit Imand ontmoet zyn, of in enige Historien voorkomen; gedurende zyn vier Jarige Slaverny te Sale.... Enkhuizen: C. Klenk, ca. 1750.

de Laet, Johannes. *Nieuwe wereldt ofte Beschrijvinghe van West-Indien.* Leyden, 1625.

de Lussan, Ravenau. *Journal du voyage fait à la Mer du Sud.* Paris, 1689.

———. *Journal of a Voyage into the South Seas.* Trans. M.E. Wilbur. Cleveland, Ohio: Arthur H. Clark, 1930.

De Ontschaakte Amsterdamsche Helena. Behelzende de wonderlyke Voorvallen, so van Liefde als van Geval, die een voorname Juffer van Amsterdam in verscheiden gewesten des Waerelts, en van gelyken in Turkse Slaverny, sedert weinige jaren herwaarts, overgekomen zyn. Steenwyk: Hendrik Stuifzand, 1693.

De overzelzame Historie van de Markgravinne de Frene, door haar eigen man aan een Turkschen zeeroover verkoft, en weder te regt gebragt, met alle de voor vallen voor en na dien stand overgekomen. Rotterdam, 1702.

de Servantes Savedra, Michel. *Monipodios Hol of 't Leven, Bedrijf, en oefning der Gauwdieven, haer onrust en schelmerijen. Als mede 't Bedrieghlick Houwelick, en Philosophische t' Samenspraeck, van twee Gasthuis-houders. Waer in van verscheyden Ampten en Staten seer kluchtif ghehandelt werdt.* Amsteldam: Evert Nieuwenhof, 1658.

De Silesische Robinson.... Doormengt met veele byzonderheden, zo van zeldzame als verbazende ongevallen, en wonderlyke ontmoetingen. Amsterdam: Steven van Esveldt, 1755.

de Vries, Simon. *Historie van Barbaryen, en des zelfs Zee-Roovers . . . . Tweede Deel, Bevattende de Handelingen en Geschiedenissen tusschen den Staat der Vereenigde Nederlanden, en die van de Zee-Roovers in Barbaryen, van 't Jaer 1590. tot op 't jaar 1684. met ondermenging van verscheidene Aanmerkelijkheden . . . .* Trans. G. v. Brockhuizen. Amsterdam: Jan ten Hoorn, 1684.

De Wispeltuurige Turkin, Of de Onkuische Hattiga; Behelzende Een verhaal van het ongestadig en wonderlijk leeven, 't geen een overschoone Turkin in Turkyen, Malta, en Venetien, sedert weinige Jaarin herwaarts gevoerd heeft . . . . Amsterdam: Timotheus ten Hoorn, 1680.

De wonderlijcke Reyse Van Ian Mandevyl Naer het H. Landt, ghedaen in 't Jaer 1322. Beschrijvende niet alleen sijne Reyse, maer oock de heele geleghentheyt van 't Landt der Beloften, Aegypten, Arabien, Persen, Ethiopien ende Indien, met vele vremde gewoonten onder de menschen aldaer bevonden oft ghehoort . . . . 2nd ed. Antwerpen: Jacobus de Bodt, 1677.

De wonderlijke en niet min zeltzame levensloop van den doorluchtige gauwdief Duval. Amsterdam: Jac. Groot, 1732.

De Zeltzame Wedervaringen van Louis Marot, Koninklyke Loots-Man Over de Galeyen van Vrankrijk. Bestaande in een geestigh Verhaal van wonderlijkke voorvallen ende onbedenkkelijke uitkomsten. Utrecht: Johannes Ribbius, 1675.

Den Engelschen Schelm, afgebootst in 't leven van Mariton Latroon, een doorsleepen Guyt. Amsterdam: Jan ten Hoorn, ca. 1678.

Den Gepredestineerden Dief, Ofte, Een t'Samen-spreeckinge gehouden tusschen een Predicant der Calvinus-gesinde ende een Dief, die gesententieert was om te sterven. Hamburgh: Barent Adriaensz., ca. 1641.

Den Jacobitsche Rover, ofte het fameuse leven en daden van Jacob Whitney, capiteyn v.e. bende rovers op de groote wegen in Engelant . . . op den 11. Feb. 1693 tot London geexecut. en gehangen. 's Grav., 1693.

Drury, R. *Madagascar, or Robert Drury's Journal during Fifteen Years of Captivity in that Island.* London, 1729.

Ducéré, E. *Journal de bord d'un flibustier (1686–1693).* Bayonne, 1894.

Dumont, J. *Corps Universal Diplomatique du Droit des Gens.* 8 vols. Amsterdam, 1726–1731.

Duym, Jacob. *Belegering der Stad Leyden,* 1606.

Een schoone historie van de Verduldige Helena van Constantinopel, eens Konings Dochter, die 27 jaren achter Lande doolde, in grooter armoede, broodt biddende: seer pleysant ome te lese, en met schoone figuren versiert. Amsterdam: Weduw' van Theunis Jacobsz Loots-man, 1684.

Eerste Schip-Vaert Der Hollanders naer Oost-Indien, Met vier Schepen onder 't beleydt van Cornelis Houtman van Alckmaer, uyt Texel t'zeyl gegaen, Anno 1595 . . . . Amsterdam: Ioost Hartgers, 1650.

Esquemeling, John. *The Buccaneers of America: A true account of the most remarkable assaults committed of late year upon the coasts of the West Indies by the Buccaneers of Jamaica and Tortuga (both English and French).* Dover Classics of Travel, Exploration, True Adventure, 1684. Reprint, New York: Dover, 1967.

Exquemelin, Alexander O. *The Buccaneers of America.* Trans. Alexis Brown. Mineola, New York: Dover, 2000.

Exquemelin, Alexander Olivier. *De Americaensche Zee-Roovers. Behelsende eene pertinente en waerachtige Beschrijving van alle de voornaemste Roveryen en onmenscheliycke wreend heden die Englese en France Rovers tegens de Spanjaerden in America gepleeght hebben . . . .* 't Amsterdam: Jan ten Hoorn, 1678.

Eyghentlijck ende treffelijck bewijs ende summaris waerachtich bericht van alle ende jeghelicke saken oock grouwelycke daden ende onmenschelijcke beestighe shier noyt gehoorde tyrannie ende schenderie welcke des Spaensche Coninghs krijghsvolck inde Nederlandtsche Westphaelsche Kreijs Oock op des Rijcks grondt ende bodem in desen (als nu noch durende) inval sonder onderscheyt teghen alle menschen volbracht hebben.... Herman Allertsz., 1599.

Garcia, Don. *Oudheit en Afkomst der Dieven. Haer onderscheid, eigenschappen en listigheden, geestig en vermakelijk in 't Spaens beschreven door Don Garcia.* Amsterdam: Timotheus ten Hoorn, 1687.

H.A.B. *Den politycken dief.* Amsterdam: Johannes Colum, 1650.

Heerman, Franciscus. *Guldene Annotien van Franciscus Heerman: Vertoonende de Heerlickste Deughden, Daden, Leeringen ende Sententien, van de alderdoorluchtighste ende vermaertste Mannen der Werelt.* 11th ed. Dordrecht: Jacob Braat, 1654.

———. *Guldene Annotatien van Franciscus Heerman*.... 16th ed., 1670.

Het Geuse Liedt-Boeck, Waer in begrepen is den Oorspronk van de troublen der Nederlantsche Oorlogen en het gene daer op gevolght is. Mitsgaders het weede en derde. Deel: zijnde met veele schoone Figueren verciert. Van nieuws over-sien en met verscheyde Refereynen en Liedekens vermeerdert. Dordrecht: Symon Onder de Linde, 1687.

Het Nieuwe Bossche Geuse Lied-Boek Anders genaemt Oranjens Triumph-Liedekens. Beplant met alle Victory-Gezangen tot Lof van zijn Doorlugtige Hoogheyt Fredrik Hendrik Van Nassouw. De laatsten Druk met veel schone Figuren verciert. Dordrecht: Hendrik Walpot, ca. 1728–1759.

Het wonderlijk Leeven; en de Dappere Oorlogs-daaden, van de Kloekmoedige Land-en Zee-Heldin. Waarachtige Geschiedenis. Amsterdam: Weduwe van Gysbert de Groot, 1694.

Histori oft Pracktycke der dieven. Utrecht: Wed. van Esdras Snellaert.

Historie van de drie laatste Turckse Keysers, ca. 1690.

Historie Van de wonderlijcke Mirakelen die in menichte ghebeurt zijn ende noch dagelijcx ghebeuren binnen de vermaerde Coopstadt Aemstelredam: ... Amstelredam: Marten Gerbrantsz., 1612.

Historie Van den Grooten Visier Cara Mustapha Inhoudende Sijn Opvoeding, sijn Liefde-oeffening in het Sarrail, sijn verscheide Bedieningen, het ware onderwerp dat hem het beleg van Weenen heeft doen ondernemen, en de bysonderheden van sijn Dood. Leyden: Joannes Prins, 1684.

Historisch journael vanden Tocht op de Barbare Turcken; Door... M.... A.... de Ruyter.... Naer sijn eygen brieven aende Staten Generael, beneffins de twee Tractaten van vrede, gesloten met de regeringe, respective vande Stadt Thunis: ende van Algiers... voor Ambrosius Turckschaep. June 5, 1662.

Johnson, Ch. *Historie der Englesche zee-roovers, beginn. met de geschiedenisse van Capiteyn Avery en zyne makkers, 1692, behels. een verhaal van hunne zee-rooveryen, moorderyen... enz. By gev. het leeven van Mary Read en Anne Bonney, twee zee-roovende vrouwen.* Amsterdam, 1725.

Johnson, Charles. *A General History of the Robberies and Murders of the Most Notorious Pyrates, from Their First Rise and Settlement in the Island of Providence in 1717 to the Present Time.* London, 1724.

———*A General History of the Pyrates.* Ed. Manuel Schonhorn. Reprint, London: Dent, 1972.

Journael van de Voyagie Gedaen met twaelft Scheepen naer Oost-Indien, Onder 't beleydt van den Heer Admirael Steven van der Hagen, Waer in verhaelt wordt het veroveren der Portugeesche Forten op Amboyna en Tydoor . . . . Amsterdam: Gillis Joosten Saeghman, ca. 1660–1670.

Kalbergen, D. *Muliassus, de Turk. Treurspel. Gerijmt.* Amsterdam: D.C. Houthaeck, 1645.

Kemp, A. *Droeff-eyndick-spel van de moort van Sultan Osman, Keyser van Turckyen, 20 Mey 1622.* Amsterdam: D.C. Houthaeck, 1639.

Las Casas, Fray Bartholome de. *Spieghel der Spaenscher tyrannye in West-Indien. Waar inne verhaelt wordt de moordadighe schandelijcke ende grouwelijcke feyten die de selve Spaenjaerden ghebruyckt hebben inde selve Landen* . . . . Amstelredam: Cornelis Claesz., 1607.

Le Golif, Louis Adhemar Timothée. *Memoirs of a Buccaneer.*

Lepers, Jean-Baptiste. *La tragique historire des Flibustiers: Histoire de Saint-Domingue et de l'ile de la Tortue, repaiers des flibustiers, écrite vers 1715.* Ed. Pierre-Bernard Berthelot. Paris: G. Crès, 1925.

Levensgevallen en euveldaden van versch. befaamde Englesche zee-, struik- en straatrovers, moordenaars, huisbrekers en andere fielten . . . waar- in vele . . . gebeurtenissen, zelfs hier te lande voorgevallen . . . . Amsterdam, 1752.

Lithgow, William. *The Rare Adventures and Painful Peregrinations of William Lithgow.* London, 1632. Reprint, London: The Folio Society, 1974.

Lonius, C. *De mislukte list of de bedroge Landsdief, zijnde het verhaal eenes gevangen Grutter. Versierd met veele merkwaardige Historien, schrandere uitvindingen en listige bedriegerijen, gesteld in V. Zamenspraken.* Westzaandam, 1737.

Lubbock, Basil, ed. *Barlow's Journal of His Life at Sea in King's Ships, East and West Indiamen and Other Merchantmen from 1659–1703.* 2 vols. London: Hurst & Blackett, 1934.

Marana, G.P. *Alle de Brieven en Gedenkschriften van eenen Turkschen Spion in de hoven van Europe: Waar in men ziet de ontdekkingen, door hem gedaan in alle de Hoven, die hy bezocht heeft, met eene aanmerkelyke Redenering over haare krachten, regeerkunde, en godsdienst, beginnende met het Jaar 1637, en eindigende met dat van 1682.* Amsterdam: Philip Verbeck; Nicolaas ten Hoorn, 1710–1720.

Melton, E. *Zeldzaame en Gedenkw. zee- en landreizen door Egypten, West-Indien . . . Oost-Indien enz. 1660–77.* Amstedam: J. ten Hoorn, 1681.

Mocquet, Jean. *Reysen In Afrique Asien Oost- en West-Indien gedaen door Jan Mocquet, Bewaerder van 't Cabinet der ongemeene Aerdigheden van de Koninck van Vranckrijck in de Tuillerie binnen Paris.* Dordrecht: Abraham Andriessz., 1656.

Montauban. *Relation du Voyage Du Sieur Montauban, Capitaine des Flibustiers . . . en l'an 1625.* Amsterdam: de Lorme, 1698.

Naam-Lyst Van Alle Persoonen, Die Binnen Amsterdam, Sederd het Jaar 1693 tot 1774 in Cluys. Door Scherpregters Handen zyn ter Dood gebragt; Met eene korte aanwyzinge van hunne Afkomst, en Misdaden om welcke zy gevonnist zyn, en op wat wys, zy hunne Executie desweegens ontfangen hebben Merkelyk vermeerdert en verbeeterd. Amersfoort: Maurits Langenwagen, 1774.

Omstandig en waaragtig Verhaal, van veele gepleegde en nooit gehoorde diefstallen: als voornamentlyk aan de zeer beruchte goude tafel . . . in 't Hooge Autaar van St. Michiels Kerke to Lunenburg . . . En een groot getal huisbraaken . . . in Duitsland gepleegd. Amsterdam, 1710.

Oprechte Haerlemse Saturdaegse Courant. No. 48 (November 30, 1686). Haerlem: Abraham Castelyen, 1686.

Ordinaire Leydse Courant. Nos. 8, 29, 30–31, 36, 44, 50, 63, 66, 72, 76, 78, 81–83, 85, 87–88, 98, 104–107, 111–112 (all from 1968). Leiden: Daniel van Gaesbeeck, 1686.

Orlers, J.J. *Beschrijvinge der Stadt Leyden*. Leiden, 1641.
Penningen (1620) of Moy Lambert, Permanent Collection, Nederlandse Scheepvaart Museum, Amsterdam, the Netherlands.
Rapport gedaen ... by den Capiteyn Salomon Willemssz.,over 't veroveren vande Silver-Vlote enz. (16 November).'s Gravenhage: Wed. en Erfg. van H. Jzn. van Wouw, 1628.
Recueil van Alle de Placaten, Ordonnaties, Resolutien, Instructies, Lijsten en Waarschuwingen Betreffende de Admiraliteiten, Convooyen, Licenten en Verdere Zee-Saaken (van 1597–1771). 12 vols. 's-Gravenhage: Isaac Scheltus, 1730–1780.
Reygersbergen, Johan. *Chroniik van Zeeland, Eertijds Beschreven door d'Heer Johan Reygersbergen, Nu Verbetert ende Vermeerderdt door Marcus Zuerius Boxhorn*. Middelburch: Zacharius ende Michiel Roman, 1644.
Reynolds, Johan. *Tonneel Der Wereldtse Rampsaligheden, Vertoonende Godts Wraake, Over de roepende en verfoeyelijke zonde der moedtwillige en voor-bedachte Moordery. Welkers wonderlijke ontdekkingen en gestrenge straffe beschreven worden in XXX. bezondere jammerlijke Historien: vervattende veel droevige en gekenkwaardige Geschiedenissen: Historische, Zedelijke en Goddelijke lessen*. Amsterdam: Gerrit van Goedesbergh, 1667.
Saadi, "Perssiaansche Roosengaard." *Den Perssiaanschen Boogaard. Beplant met zeer uitgeleesen spruiten der historien, en bezaait met zeltzame voorvallen, leerzame- en aardige geschiedenissen etc ....* Amsterdam: J. ten Hoorn, 1688.
Saadi, Schich. *Perssiaansche Roosengaard Beplant met vermaaklijke historien, ... en leerrijke sin-spreuken. Voor omtr. 400 jaaren in 't Perssiaans beschreeven, doch onlangs ... in 't Hoogd. overgeset ... d. A. Olearium, die daar by gevoegd heeft de aartige fabelen v. Lokman ....* Amsterdam: T. Houthaak voor J. Rieuwertsz. en H. Hendricksz., 1654.
Schiel, Albrecht. *Beschryvingh sijns levens in Barbaryen*. ca. 1670s.
Schram, Wybrant. *Journael ende Verhael Vande Oost-Indische Reyse, gedaen by den Heer Admiral Wybrant Schram. Uytgaven met een Vloot van 9 Schepen, den 3 May 1626. Met een Beschryvinghe van de See-Slach/die hy gheslagen heeft met den vermaerden See-roover CLAES COMPAEN*. Amsterdam: Hendrick Doncker, 1650.
Serwouters, J. *Den Grooten Tamerlam, met de doodt van Bayaset de I, Turks keizer*. 2nd ed. 1661.
Smallegange, M. *Nieuwe Cronyk van Zeeland*. Middelburg: Joannes Meertens, 1696.
Spiegel der Jeught, ofte: een kort verhael der voornaemstre Tyrannie, en Barbarische wreetheden, welcke de Spangiaerden hier in Nederlandt bedreen hebben .... 19th ed. Amsterdam: de Wed. van Theunis Jacobsz., ca. 1650.
Steenis, Hendrik Cornelis. *Journaal Wegens De Rampspoedige Reys-Tocht, Van de Ed: Gestrengen Heer Capiteyn Hendrik Cornelis Steenis, In Dienst van het Edel Moogende Collegie ter Admiraliteit, Resideerende te Amsterldam. Met het Oorlogschip genaamt Het Huys In 'T Bosch, Gestrand op de Moorsche Kust in Afrika, Tusschen Ceuta en Kaap Porkes, op Maandag Middag den 20 December 1751. Als meede en Korte Beschriyvinge van de Steeden Tetuan en Fez, de Handeling met den Keizer Van Marokko, de Vreedemaaking met Haar Hoog Moogende, en de Elende en Behandelinge van het Scheeps Volk; Nevens een Lyst der Genoomene Scheepen door de Saleesche en Tetuansche Roovers, zedert 't Jaar 1732, en de Naamen der geloste Hollandsche Gevangenen*. 3rd ed. Amsteldam: Bernardus Mourik, ca. 1751–1791.
———. *Kort, Dog Naauwkeurig En Opregt Verhaal, Van alle de Behandelingen, Wreedhedens en Ongemakken, in hunne Slavernye onder de Mooren, geleeden door de Equipage van 's Lands Schip Het Huys In 'T Bos, Gecommandeerd door de Ed. Gestrenge Heer Capt. Hendrik Cornelis Steenis En ongelukkig Gestrand aan de*

Moorsze Kust, Met hunne Verlossing en te rugkomst in ons Vaderland. Amsterdam: Wed. J. van Egmont, ca. 1726–1761.

Stokram, Andries. *Korte Beschryvinge Van de Ongeluckige Weer-om-reys van het Schip Aernhem, Nevens noch zes andere Schepen, onder 't gebiedt van den Heer Arnout de Vlaming van Outshoorn, van Batavia na het Vaderlandt afgevaren, op den 23. December 1661*. . . . Amsterdam: Jacob Venckel, 1663.

't Begin, Midden en Eynde der Zee-rooveryen van den alder-famieusten zee-roover, Claes G. Compaen, van Oostzanen in Kennemer-landt: vervattende sijn wonderlijcke vreemde en landts-schadelijcke drijf-tochten. 1659.

't Leven van den wereldberuchten kapitein der moordenaren Louis Dominique de Cartouche, behelz. een verhael van deszelfs . . . gauwdieveryen, gevangenemming, uitbreking u.h. gevankenis en executie. Delft: H. Boitet, 1722.

Tysens, G. *Cartouche of de Rovers. Blyspel. Vehandelende zyn voornaamste Schelmeryen, gevolgd naar 't Franse van Monsieur Le Grand*. Amsterdam: Jacob van Egmont, 1722.

Valerius. A. *Neder-lantsche Gedenck-clanck*. Haarlem, 1626.

van Aitzema, L. *Saken van Staet en Oorlogh* . . . . 7 vols. 's Gravenhage: Johan Veely, Johan Tongerloo, & Jasper Doll, 1669–1672.

van den Bos(ch), L. *Het toneel der ongevallen . . . mitsg. het spicilegium van vorstelycke treur-gevallen*. Dordrecht, 1683.

van den Bos(ch), Lambert. *De Reysende Mercurius. Verhandelende De hedendaegsche en onlangs tegenwoordige staet en verrichtingen van Europa; afbeeldinge der Volckeren; Staets-handelingen; bysondere voorvallen, en afbeeldinge der Zeden, &c*. . . . Amsterdam: Jan Bouman, 1674.

———. *Keur-Stof Deses Tydts, Behelsende de voornaemste Geschiedenissen of Rampsaligheden Der Grooten, Meest voorgavallen zedert het Jaer 1640. Vertoonende Het laetste Tooneel der Doorluchtige Mannen*. Dordrecht: Geemen van Cappel, 1672.

———. *Leven en Daden van de Doorluchtige Zeehelden*. Amsterdam: Jan Claesz. ten Hoorn & Jan Bouman, 1676.

———. *Het Treur-Tooneel Der Doorluchtige Mannen Onser Eeuwe*. Amstedam: Jan ten Hoorn, 1698.

———. *Prael-Toneel Der Doorluchtige Mannen, Of Het Leven en Bedrijf der beroemder Vorsten, uytheemsche Veldt-Oversten en Vorstelijcke bedienaers deses Tijdts* . . . .Amsterdam: Jacob van Meurs en Compagnie, 1676. van der Capellen, Robert Jaspar. *Gedenkschriften van Jonkheer A. van der Capellen*. Utrecht, 1777.

van der Sterre, Dionisius. *Zeer aenmerkelijcke reysen gedaan door Jan Erasmus Reyning, meest in West-Indien en ook in veel andere deelen des Werelds*. Amsterdam: Jan ten Hoorn, 1691.

van Linschoten, Jan Huygen. *Iohn Hvighen van Linschoten. his Discours of Voyages into yet Easte & West Indies. Deuided into foure Bookes*. London: Iohn Wolfe, 1598.

———. *Histoire de la navigation de Iean Hvgves de Linscot Hollandois et de son voyage* . . . Amstelredam: Theodore Pierre, 1610.

———. *The Voyage of John Huygen van Lischoten to the East Indies*. Ed. Arthur Coke Burnell. Reprint, New York: Burt Franklin, 1970.

van Overbeke, Aernout. *Geestige en Vermaeckelicke Reys-Beschryvinge, Van den Heer Aernout van Overbeke, Naer Oost-Indien gevaren, ten dienste van de E E. Heeren Bewinthebberen van de Oost-Indische Compagnie, Voor Raet van Justitie, in den Jare 1668*. Jan Joosten oop de Voor-Burgwal, 1671.

van Twist, Johan. *Generale Beschrijvinghe van Indien*. . . . *Hier is noch bygevoecht 't Iournael van d'Heer Admirael Wybrant Schram, met de Zee-Slagh tegen Claes Compaen* . . . . 2nd ed. Amsterdam: Hendrick Doncker, 1650.

van Yk, Cornelis. *De Nederlandsche Scheeps-bouw-konst Open Gestel*. Amsterdam: Jan ten Hoorn, 1697.

Vierlingh, Andries. *Tractaet van Diekgie*. Ed. J. de Hullu and A.G. Verhoeven. Reprint, 's Gravenhage, 1920.

Waerachtige Beschryvinghe van een jammerlicke nieuwe Tijdinghe van een deerlicke Moort die gheschiet is in West-Engelant by de Stadt Excester, in een Dorp Littelen ghenaemt . . . Al waer dry Moordenaers gejustificeert zijn, dewelcke eenen Huysman in syn eyghen huys hebben vermoort ende den hals afgesneden, ende thuys in brant ghesteken, meynende hunne misdaedt hier door verborghen te sijn. Middelborch: Adriaen Leenaertsz, 1618.

Wassenaer, Nicolaes. *Historisch Verhael Aller Gedenkwaerdiger Geschiedenissen die Hier en Daer in Europa, als in Duytschlant, Vranckrijck, Enghelant, enz. en Nederlant . . . Voorgevallen Sijn*. Vols. 13 and 14. Amsterdam: Jan Jansz., 1627–1628.

Wonderlicke Avontuer van twee Goelieven, de eene ghenaemt Sr. Waterbrandt ende de ander Joufvrouw Wintergroen . . . . Leyden: Nickolaes Geelkerck, 1624.

Zonderlinge Levensloop Van Een Ongelukkig Reisgezel, Of Beschryving Van de door hem geledene Droevige Slaverny, Onder de Turken in Turkyen en Barbaryen . . . . ca. 1750.

Published Compendia of Primary Sources

Cau, C, ed. *Groot Placaet-Boeck van de Staten-Generaal en van Holland en Zeeland*. 9 vols. The Hague, Amsterdam, 1658–1796.

Coolhaas, W. Ph. *Generale Missiven van Gouverneurs-Generaal en Raden aan Heren XVII der Verenigde Oost-Indische Compagnie 1610–1672*. Rijks Geschiedkundige Publikatiën. Vol. 104. Den Haag: Nijhoff, 1960.

Fuhrmann-Plemp van Duiveland, M.R.C. *Der Untergang der Batavia und andere Schiffsjournale*. Tubingen and Basel: Erdmann, 1976.

General Index over de Elf Deelen van het Recueil der Placaaten, Ordonnantien, Resolutien, en Reglementen, betreffende de Convoyen, en verdere Zeezaaken. Na ordre der respectieve jaaren en datums gesteld, beginnende met den jaare 1492 tot den jaare 1771 inclusive. Tweede deel: Volgens de Letters van het Alphabeth. 's Gravenhage: Isaac Scheltus, 1773–1775.

Heeringa, K. *Bronnen tot de Geschiedenis van de Levanthandel 1560–1660*. Rijks Geschiedkundige Publicatiën. Vols. 9, 10, 34, and 95. 's-Gravenhage: Martinus Nijhoff, 1910–1952.

Japikse, N. and H.H.P. Rijperda. *Resolutien der Staten-Generaal van 1576 tot 1609*. Rijks Geschiedkundige Publikatiën. Vols. 26, 33, 41, 43, 47, 51, 55, 57, 62, 71, 85, 92, 101, and 131. 's-Gravenhage: Nijhoff, 1915–1970.

Kuiper, E.T. *Het Geuzenliedboek*. 2 vols. Zutphen: W.J. Thieme & Cie, 1925.

Scheurleer, D.G. *Van Varen en Van Vechten: Verzen van Tijdgenooten op Onze Zeehelden en Zeeslagen, Lof- en Schimpdichten, Matrozenliederen*. 3 vols. 's-Gravenhage: Martinus Nijhoff, 1914.

Schiltkamp, J.A and J.Th. de Smidt. *West Indisch Plakaatboek: Suriname: Plakaten, Ordonnantien en Andere Wetten, Uitgevaardigd in Suriname 1667–1816*. Werken der Vereeniging tot Uitgaaf der Bronnen van het Oud-Vaderlandsche Recht. Amsterdam: S. Emmering, 1973.

———. *West Indisch Plakaatboek: Publikaties en Andere Wetten Alsmede de Oudste Resoluties Betrekking Hebbende op Curacao, Aruba, Bonaire*. Werken der Stichting tot Uitgaaf der Bronnen van het Oud-Vaderlandse Recht. Amsterdam: S. Emmering, 1978.

Schiltkamp, J.A and J.Th. de Smidt. *West Indisch Plakaatboek: Publikaties en Andere Wetten Betrekking Hebbende op St. Maarten, St. Eustatius, Saba: 1648/1681–1816.* Werken der Stichting tot Uitgaaf der Bronnen van het Oud-Vaderlandse Recht. Amsterdam: S. Emmering, 1979.

Serjeant, R.B. *The Portuguese Off the South Arabian Coast: Hadrami Chronicles; With Yemeni and European Accounts of Dutch Pirates off Mocha in the Seventeenth Century.* Oxford: The Clarendon Press, 1963.

van der Chijs, J.A. *Realia. Register op de Generale Resolutien van het Kasteel Batavia, 1632–1805.* Uitgegeven door het Bataviaasch Genootschap voor Kunsten & Wetenschappen. 3 vols. Batavia & 's Gravenhage: W. Bruining; & Mart. Nijhoff, 1882–1886.

———. *Nederlandsch-Indisch Plakaatboek 1602–1811.* 17 vols. Het Bataviaansch Genootschap van Kunsten en Wetenschappen met Medewerking van de Nederlandsch-Indische Regering. Batavia: Landsdrukkerij, 1885–1900. 's Hage: Nijhoff, 1885–1900.

van Prinsterer, G. Groen. *Archives ou Correspondance inédite de la maison d'Orange-Nassau.* Première Série. Vol. III (1567–1572). Leiden, 1836.

Reference Works

Adema van Scheltama, F. *Nederlandsche Letterkunde: Populaire Prozaschrijvers der XVIIe en XVIIIe Eeuw. Romans en Verhalen. Spectatoriale Geschriften. Vertalingen der Klassieken. Anecdoten. Hekelschriften. Facetiae. "Hoffsche Welleventheyt." "Fatsoenlicke Zend-Brief-Schrijver." Geschriften over Vrouwen. Beruchte Personen. Demonologie. Strichtelijke Lectuur. Volksboeken: Ridderromans, Sprookjes, Natuurkunde, Geschiedenis, Reizen en schipbreuken. Met een aanhang oper opvoeding en onderwijs.* Amsterdam: Frederick Muller & Cie, 1893.

———. *Nederlandsche Letterkunde: Populaire Prozaschrijvers der XVIIe en XVIIIe Eeuw....* Amsterdam: Frederick Muller & Cie, 1893, reprinted in *Muller/Vries/Scheepers: Populaire Prozaschrijvers der XVIIe en XVIIEe Eeuw. Foromechanische Herdruk...* Ed. H.W. de Kooker. Utrecht: HES Publishers, 1981.

Afd. Centrale Catalogi Koninklijke Bibliotheek. *Centrale catalogus van dag-, nieuws- en weekbladen van algemene inhoud in Nederland verschenen (CCD).* 's-Gravenhage: Stichting Bibliographia Neerlandica, 1985.

Algemeen Rijksarchief, Eerste Afdeling. *Inventarissen van Instellingen in Suriname tot 1828.*

Bos-Rops, J.A.M.Y. et al. *De Archieven in het Algemeen Rijksarchief.* Overzichten van de Archieven en Verzamelingen in de Openbare Archiefbewaarplaatsen in Nederland. Alphen aan den Rijn: Samsom, 1982.

Broekema, J. *Catalogus van de Pamfletten, Tractaten, enz. Aanwezig in de Provinciale Bibliotheek van Zeeland.* Vol. I (1568–1795). Middelburg: Auer, 1892.

Buisman, J.Fzn. M. *Populaire Prozaschrijvers 1600–1815. Romans, Novellen, Verhalen, Levensbeschrijvingen, Arcadias, Sprookjes. Alphabetische Naamlijst.* Amsterdam: Israel, 1960.

Carter, A.C. "The Dutch Notarial Archives." *The Bulletin of the Institute of Historical Research*, Vol. 26 (1953): 86–91.

Catalogus eener Verzameling van Pamfletten, Tractaten en Andere Stukken, Zoowel met Betrekking tot de Geschiedenis Elders Voorgevallen; Allen in Nederland

Uitgegeven van het Eind der Zestiende Tot he Midden der Achtiende Eeuw. 2 vols. Goes: F. Kleeuwens & Zoon, no date.

Coolhaas, W.P. *A Critical Survey of Studies on Dutch Colonial History.* Koninklijk Instituut voor Taal-, Land- en Volkenkunde, Bibliographical Series #4. The Hague: Martinus Nijhoff, 1980.

de Hullu, J. *De Archieven der Admiraliteitscolleges.* 's-Gravenhage: Algemeene Landsdrukkerij, 1924.

de Kooker, H.W. *Muller/De Vries/Scheepers: Populaire Prozaschrijvers der XVIIe en XVIIIe Eeuw. Fotomechanische Herdruk van de Magazijncatalogi van de Firma's Frederick Muller & Cie (1893) en R.W.P. de Vries (1907) en de Veilingcatalogi van de Collectie J.F.M. Scheepers (1947 en 1949).* Utrecht: HES Publishers, 1981.

de Vries, R.W.P. *Nederlandsche Letterkunde. Populaire Prozaschrijvers der XVIIe en XVIII Eeuw. Romans en Verhalen. Anecdoten en Raadsels. Leven van Beroemde en Beruchte Personen. Vertalingen van Grieksche en Latijnsche Klassieken. Stichtelijke en Zedekundige Werken. Spectatoriale Geschriften. Geneeskundige en Wiskundige Werken. Brievenboeken. Keukenboeken. Goochelboeken en Spelen.* Amsterdam: R.W.P de Vries, 1907.

Dronckers, Emma. *Verzameling F.G. Waller: Nederlandsche en Vlaamsche Populaire Boeken.* 's-Gravenhage: Martinus Nijhoff, 1936.

Formsma, R.W.J. and F.C.J. Ketelaar. *Gids voor de Nederlandse Archieven.* Bussum: de Haan (Unieboek), 1975.

Gieles, J.L.M and A.P.J. Plak. *Bibliographie van het Nederlandstalig Narratief-Fictioneel Proza/Bibliography of Prose Fiction Written in or Translated into Dutch, 1670–1700.* Bibliotheca Bibliographica Neerlandica, Vol. XXIV. Nieuwkoop: De Graaf Publishers, 1988.

Hornblower, Simon and Anthony Spawforth, eds. *Oxford Classical Dictionary.* 3rd ed. Oxford: Oxford University Press, 1996.

Knuttel, W.P.C. *Catalogus van de Pamfletten-Verzameling Berustenden de Koninklijke Bibliotheek.* 9 vols. Utrecht: HES Publishers, 1978.

Kortland, Diederick, ed. *Inhoudslijsten van Overgekomen Brieven en Papieren uit Brazilie (1630–1654).* 's Gravenhage: Algemeen Rijksarchief, Eerste Afdeling, 1994.

Landwehr, John. *VOC: A Bibliography of Publications Relating to the Dutch East India Company, 1602–1800.* Utrecht: HES Publishers, 1991.

Martin, W.G.A.J. Tops et al. *Van Dale Groot Woordenboek Nederlands-Engels.* 2nd ed. Utrecht: Van Dale Lexicographie, 1991.

Metselaars, H.J.A.H.G. *Particuliere Archieven in Nederland. Overzichten van de Archieven en Verzamelingen in de Openbare Archiefbewaarplaatsen in Nederland.* Houten/Zaventem: Bohn Stafleu van Loghum, 1992.

Muller, Frederick. *De Nederlandsche Geschiedenis in Platen. Beredeneerde Beschrijving van Nederlandsche Historieplaten, Zinneprenten en Historische Kaarten.* Amsterdam: Frederick Muller, 1863–1870.

Pennings, Joyce. *Inventaris van het Archief Bisdom.* Den Haag: Algemeen Rijksarchief (Eerste Afdeling), 1986.

Petit, Louis D. *Bibliotheek van Nederlandsche Pamfletten. Verzamelingen van Joannes Thysius en de Bibliotheek der Rijks-Universiteit te Leiden.* 3 vols. 's-Gravenhage: M. Nijhoff, 1882–1884. Leiden: A.W. Sijthoff, 1925–1934.

Raben, M.A.P. and H. Spikerman. *De archieven van de Verenigde Oostindische Compagnie: The Archives of the Dutch East India Company.* Algemeen Rijksarchief, Eerste Afdeling, 's-Gravenhage: Sdu Uitgeverij Koninginnegracht, 1992.

Ruys, H.J.A. *Bibliotheek van Nederlandsche en Andere Pamfletten. Verzameling van de Bibliotheek van Joannes Thysius te Leiden. Supplement.* Leiden: A.W. Sijthoff, 1934.

Scheepers, J.F.M. *Catalogus van een Zeer Belangrijke Verzameling Fraaie en Zeldzame Boeken der 16e–18e Eeuw. Zijnde het Eerste Gedeelte der Bibliotheek van wijlen J.F.M. Scheepers te Rotterdam. Nederlandsche Dichters en Prozaschrijvers. Rederijkersboeken. Tooneelspelen. Emblemataboeken. Liedboeken. Oude Reisbeschrijvinge.* Utrecht: J.L. Beijers' Antiquariatt, 1947.

Schultz, G.W. *Catalogus van Belangrijke Verzameling Zeldzame en Merkwaardige Boeken der 17e–19e Eeuw: het Tweede Gedeelte der Bibliotheek van wijlen J.F.M. Scheepers te Rotterdam: Nederlandsche Literatuur, Volksboeken, Vertalingen uit de Oude en Moderne Talen, Curiosa, Reizen, Etc.* Utrecht: J.L. Beijer's Antiquariaat, 1949.

The Holy Bible. New Revised Standard Version. Nashville: Thomas Nelson Publishers, 1989.

Tiele, P.A. *Memoire Bibliographique sur les Journaux des Navigateurs Neerlandais Reimprimes dans les Collections Hollandaises du XVIIe Siecle, et sur les Anciennes Editions Hollandaises des Journaux de Navigateurs Etrangers; La Plupart en la Possession de Frederik Muller à Amsterdam.* Amsterdam: Frederik Muller, 1867.

van Alphen, G. *Catalogus der Pamfletten van de Bibliiotheek der Rijksuniversiteit te Groningen (1542–1853).* Groningen: J.B. Wolters, 1944.

van Dijk, J.J.C., R.L. Koops, and H. Uil. *De Archieven in Zeeland.* Overzichten van de Archieven en Verzamelingen in de Openbare Archiefbewaarplaatsen in Nederland. Alphen aan den Rijn: Samsom Uitgeverij, 1979.

van Hoek Ostede, J.H. de et al. *De Archieven in Amsterdam.* Overzichten van de Archieven en Verzamelingen in de Openbare Archiefbewaarplaatsen in Nederland. Alphen aan den Rijn: Samsom Uitgeverij, 1981.

van Rijn, G. and C. van Ommeren. *Atlas van Stolk. Katalogus der historie-, spot- en zinneprenten betrekkelijk de geschiedenis van Nederland, verzameld door A. van Stolk Cz.* 10 vols. Amsterdam: Frederick Muller & Co., 1895–1933.

van Someren, J.F. *Bibliotheek der Rijksuniversiteit Utrecht. Pamfletten Niet Voorkomende in Afzonderlijke Gedrukte Catalogi . . . .* Utrecht: A. Oosthoek, 1915–1922.

van Sterkenburg, P.G.J. *Een glossarium van Zeventiende-Eeuws Nederlands.* Groningen: Wolters-Noordhoff, 1977.

Secondary Sources

Acda, G.M.W. *Voor en Achter de Mast: Het Leen van de Zeeman in de 17de and 18de Eeuw.* Bussum: De Boer Maritiem, 1976.

Alcalá-Zamorra y Queipo de Llano, J. *España, Flandes, y el Mar del Norte, 1618–39.* Barcelona, 1975.

Anderson, Benedict. *Imagined Communities: Reflections on the Origin and Spread of Nationalism.* New York and London: Verso, 1991.

Andrews, Charles M. "Anglo-French Commercial Rivalry, 1700–1750: The Western Phase." *American Historical Review,* Vol. XX, Part I (April 1915).

Armstrong, J.A. *Nations Before Nationalism.* Chapel Hill: University of North Carolina Press, 1982.

Baetens, R. "Organisatie en resultaten van de Vlaamse Kaapvaart in de 17e eeuw." *Mededelingen van de Belgische Marine Academie* 21 (1969/1970).

———. "The Organization and Effects of Flemish Privateering in the Seventeenth Century." *Acta Historiae Neerlandica*, IX (1976): 48–75.
Barber, Violet. "Privateers and Pirates of the West Indies." *American Historical Review*, Vol. 16 (1910–1911): 547–551.
Barlow, Edward. *Barlow's Journal of His Life at Sea in King's Ships, East and West Indiamen and Other Merchantmen from 1659–1703.* Ed. Basil Lubbock. London: Hurst & Blackett, 1934.
Baud, J.J. *Proeve eener Geschiedenis der Strafwetgeving tegen de Zeerooverij.* Utrecht: D. Post Uiterweer, 1854.
Beeching, Jack. *The Buccaneers of American.* Introd. John Equemeling. London: The Folio Society, 1972.
Beyerman, J.J. "Een Zeeroover als Zee-Officier onder de Ruyter." Den Haag, 1934. Offprint available at the Nederlandse Scheepvaart Museum, #N. i. I. K II 196.
Binder, F. "Die Zeeländische Kaperfahrt, 1654–1662," *Mededelingen van het Koninklijk Zeeuwsch Genootschap der Wetenschappen*, 1976: 40–92.
Boxer, C.R. "The Dutch East-Indiamen: their sailors, their navigators, and life on board, 1602–1795." *Mariner's Mirror*, Vol. 49 (May 1963): 81–104.
———. "Piet Heyn and the Silver-Fleet." *History Today*, Vol. 13 (June 1963): 398.
———. *The Dutch Seaborne Empire, 1600–1800.* New York: Alfred A. Knopf, 1965. Reprint, London: Penguin Books, 1990.
Braudel, Fernand. Trans. Sian Reynolds. *The Mediterranean and the Mediterranean World in the Age of Philip II.* New York: W.W. Norton, 1973.
———. *The Structures of Everyday Life: The Limits of the Possible.* Civilization & Capitalism, 15th–18th Century. Vol. I. New York: Harper & Row, 1981.
Breuilly, John. *Nationalism and the State.* Manchester, England: Manchester University Press, 1982.
Bromley, J.S. "Some Zeeland Privateering Instructions: Jacob Sautyn to Captain Salomon Reynders 1707." *William III and Louis XIV.* Ed. Ragnhild Hatton and J.S. Bromley. Liverpool, 1968.
———. "The Importance of Dunkirk (1688–1713) Reconsidered." *Course et Piraterie: Etudes presentees a la Commission Internationale d'Histoire Maritime a l'occasion de son XVe colloque international pendant le XIVe Congres International des Sciences historieques.* Vol. I. Ed. Commission Internationale d'Histoire Maritime. Paris: Institute de Recherche et d'Histoire des Textes/Editions du Centre National de la Recherche Scientifique, 1975: 231–270.
———. "The North Sea in Wartime (1688–1713)." *Bijdragen en Mededelingen betreffende de Geschiedenis der Nederlanden*, Vol. 92 (1977): 270–299.
Bruijn, Jaap R. "Dutch Privateering during the Second and Third Anglo-Dutch Wars." *Course et Piraterie: Etudes presentees a la Commission Internationale d'Histoire Maritime a l'occasion de son XVe colloque international pendant le XIVe Congres International des Sciences historieques.* Vol. I. Ed. Commission Internationale d'Histoire Maritime. Paris: Institut de Recherche et d'Histoire des Textes/Editions du Centre National de la Recherche Scientifique, 1975a: 397–415.
———. "Kaapvaart in de tweede en derde Engelse Oorlog." *Bijdragen en Mededelingen betreffende de Geschiedenis der Nederlanden* 90 (1975b): 408–429.
———. *The Dutch Navy of the Seventeenth and Eighteenth Centuries.* Columbia: University of South Carolina Press, 1993.
Bruijn, J.R., F.S. Gaastra, and I. Schöffer. *Dutch-Asiatic Shipping in the 17th and 18th Centuries.* Vol. I. The Hague: Martinus Nijhoff, 1987.

Buijnsters, P.J. *Levens van Beruchte Personen: Over de Criminele Biografie in Nederland gedurende de 18e Eeuw.* Utrecht: HES, 1980.

Burg, B.R. *Sodomy and the Pirate Tradition: English Sea Rovers in the Seventeenth-Century Caribeean.* New York: New York University Press, 1984.

Carter, Alice. "The Dutch Privateering Arm in Mid-and-Late Eighteenth Century." *Course et Piraterie: Etudes presentees a la Commission Internationale d'Histoire Maritime a l'occasion de son XVe colloque international pendant le XIVe Congres International des Sciences historieques.* Vol. I. Ed. Commission Internationale d'Histoire Maritime. Paris: Institut de Recherche et d'Histoire des Textes/Editions du Centre National de la Recherche Scientifique, 1975: 441–452.

Chatterjee, P. *Nationalist Thought and the Colonial World: A Derivative Discourse?* London: Zed Books for the United Nations University, 1986.

Cidoncha, Carlos Saiz. *Historia de la Piratería en América Española.* Madrid: Editorial San Martin, 1985.

Cipolla, Carlo M. *Guns, Sails and Empires: Technological Innovation and the Early Phases of European Expansion, 1400–1700.* Manhattan, KS: Sunflower University Press, 1985.

Clark, G.N. "English and Dutch Privateers under William III." *Mariner's Mirror*, Vol. 7 (1921): 162–167 and 209–217.

———. "Neutral Commerce in the War of the Spanish Succession and the Treaty of Utrecht." *The British Yearbook of International Law* (1928): 69–83.

Commission Internationale d'Histoire Maritime, ed. *Course et Piraterie: Etudes presentees a la Commission Internationale d'Histoire Maritime a l'occasion de son XVe colloque international pendant le XIVe Congres International des Sciences historieques.* 3 vols. Paris: Institute de Recherche et d'Histoire des Textes Editions du Centre National de la Recherche Scientifique, 1975.

Cordingly, David. *Under the Black Flag: The Romance and the Reality of Life Among the Pirates.* New York: Random House, 1995.

Coser, Lewis A. *On Collective Memory.* Introd. Maurice Halbwachs. Ed. and Trans. Lewis A. Coser. Chicago: University of Chicago Press, 1992.

Darnton, Robert. "History and Anthropology." *The Kiss of Lamourette: Reflections in Cultural History.* New York: W.W. Norton, 1990: 329–353.

Davies, D.W. *A Primer of Dutch Seventeenth-Century Overseas Trade.* The Hague: M. Nijhoff, 1961.

Davis, Natalie Zemon. *Society and Culture in Early Modern France.* Stanford, CA: Stanford University Press, 1965.

Davis, Ralph. *The Rise of the English Shipping Industry in the Seventeenth and Eighteenth Centuries.* London: Macmillan, 1962.

———. *The Rise of the Atlantic Economies.* World Economic History. London: Weidenfeld and Nicolson, 1973.

de Groot, A.H. *The Ottoman Empire and the Dutch Republic: A History of the Earliest Diplomatic Relations, 1610–1630.* Leiden: Nederlands Historisch-Archaeologisch Instituut Leiden, 1978.

de Jonge, G.H.P. "Het Fabeltje van de Verschrikkelijke Barbarijse Zeerover." *Spiegel Historiael: Maandblad voor Geschiedenis en Archeologie*, Vol. 24 (1989): 68–74.

de Jonge, J.C. *Geschiedenis van het Nederlandsche Zeewezen.* 6 vols. Haarlem: Kruseman, 1858–1862.

de Meij, J.C.A. *De Watergeuzen en de Nederlanden 1568–1572.* Amsterdam: N.V. Noord-Hollandsche Uitgevers, 1972.

———. "Oorlogsvaart, Kaapvaart en Zeeroof." Ed. G. Asaert, Ph. M. Bosscher, J.R. Bruijn, and W. J. van Hoboken. *Maritieme Geschiedenis der Nederlanden.* Vol. I. Bussum, 1976–1978: 307–337.

de Wilde, P.A. "Some Remarks on Dutch Privateering in the Indian Ocean till the Fall of Java in 1811." Ed. Commission Internationale d'Histoire Maritime. *Course et Piraterie: Etudes presentees a la Commission Internationale d'Histoire Maritime a l'occasion de son XVe colloque international pendant le XIVe Congres International des Sciences historieques.* Vol. II. Paris: Institut de Recherche et d'Histoire des Textes/Editions du Centre National de la Recherche Scientifique, 1975: 802–817.

den Ridder, C.J. "Gedenk de gevangenen alsof gij mede gevangenen waart. De loskoop van Hollandse zeelieden uit Barbarijse gevangenschap (1600–1746)." *Tijdschrift voor Zeegeschiedenis*, Vol. V (1986): 3–22.

Douglas, Mary. *Purity and Danger: An Analysis of the Concepts of Pollution and Taboo.* London/New York: Routledge, 1995; orig. ed. 1966.

Dunlop, H. *Hollandsche Zeeroovers in de 17e Eeuw.* Zutphen: W.J. Thieme & Cie, 1938.

Ducéré, E. *Journal de bord d'un flibustier (1686–1693) d'après un manuscrit de la Bibliotheque Nationale.* Bayonne: Impr. A. Lamaignere, 1894.

Earle, Peter. *Corsairs of Malta and Barbary.* London: Sidgwick and Jackson, 1970.

———. *The Sack of Panama: Sir Henry Morgan's Adventures on the Spanish Main.* New York: Viking Press, 1982.

Emmer, Pieter C. "The History of the Dutch Slave Trade, A Bibliographical Survey." *The Journal of Economic History*, Vol. 32 (1972): 728–747.

Fontenay, M. and A. Tenenti. "Course et Piraterie Méditerranéennes de las Fin du Moyen Age au Début du XIXème Siècle." Ed. Commission Internationale d'Histoire Maritime. *Course et Piraterie: Etudes presentees a la Commission Internationale d'Histoire Maritime a l'occasion de son XVe colloque international pendant le XIVe Congres International des Sciences historieques.* Paris: Institut de Recherche et d'Histoire des Textes/Editions du Centre National de la Recherche Scientifique, 1975: 78–136.

Friedman, Ellen G. *Spanish Captives in North Africa in the Early Modern Age.* Madison: University of Wisconsin Press, 1983.

Geertz, Clifford. "Thick Description: Toward an Interpretive Theory of Culture." *The Interpretation of Cultures.* New York: Basic Books, 1973: 3–32.

Gellner, Ernst. *Nations and Nationalism.* Oxford: Basil Blackwell, 1983.

Gieraths, G. "Benjamin Raule, seine Leben und insbesondere seine volkswirtschaflichen Ansichten." *Economisch-Historisch Jaarboek*, Vol. 10 (1924): 219–302.

Goedde, Lawrence. *Tempest and Shipwreck in Dutch and Flemish Art: Convention, Rhetoric and Interpretation.* University Park: Pennsylvania State University Press, 1989.

Gosse, Philip. *The Pirates' Who's Who.* London: Dulau, 1924.

———. *The History of the Pirates.* London: Longmans Green, 1932.

Groeneveld, Simon. "Natie en nationaal gevoel in de sestiende-eeuwse Nederlanden." *Scrinium et Scriptura. Opstellen betreffende de Nederlandse geschiedenis aangeboden aan J.L. van der Gouw.* Groningen, 1980: 372–387.

———. "Beeldvorming en realiteit. Geschiedschrijving en achtergronden van de Nederlandse Opstand tegen Filips II." Ed. P.A.M. Geurts and A.E.M. Janssen. *Geschiedschrijving in Nederland: Studies Over de Historiografie van de Nieuwe Tijd.*'s Gravenhage, Nijhoff, 1981.

Halbwachs, Maurice. *The Collective Memory*. New York: Harper-Colophon Books, 1950.

———. *On Collective Memory*. Ed. and Trans. Lewis A. Coser. Chicago: University of Chicago Press, 1992.

Häpke, R. "Benjamin Raule und seine Handlungbücher." *Economish-Historish Jaarboek*, Vol. 9 (1923): 214–220.

Harline, Craig E. *Pamphlets, Printing and Political Culture in the Early Republic*. Archives Internationales d'Histoire des Idées (International Archives of the History of Ideas). Dordrecht: Nijhoff, 1987.

Hart, Simon. *Geschrift en Getal: een Keuze uit de Demografisch-, Economisch- en Social Historische Studien op Grond van Amsterdamse en Zaanse Archivalia, 1600–1800*. Dordrecht: Historische Vereniging Holland, 1976.

Hobsbawm, Eric. *Nations and Nationalism since 1780: Programme, Myth, Reality*. Cambridge and New York: Cambridge University Press.

Hobsbawm, Eric and Terence Ranger, eds. *The Invention of Tradition*. Cambridge: Cambridge University Press, 1983.

Hofdijk, W.J. *De Triomf der Piraten: Eene Feestgave bij Neerlands derde Jubil'e* (Amsterdam: Funke, 1872).

Hroch, Miroslav. *Social Preconditions of National Revival in Europe: A Comparative Analysis of the Social Composition of Patriotic Groups Among the Smaller European Nations*. Trans. Ben Fowkes. Cambridge: Cambridge University Press, 1985.

Israel, Jonathan I. *Dutch Primacy in World Trade, 1585–1740*. Oxford: Clarendon Press, 1989.

———. *The Dutch Republic: Its Rise, Greatness, and Fall, 1477–1806*. Oxford History of Early Modern Europe. Oxford: Clarendon Press, 1995.

Jaeger, Gérard A. *Les Aventuriers de la Mer: Bibliographie Thematique (XVIe-XXe Siècle)*. Lausanne: Editions Le Front Litteraire, 1983.

———. *Pirates, Flibustiers et Corsairs: Histoire & Légendes d'Une Société d'Exception*. Avignon: Aubanel, 1987.

Jorberg, F. "Benjamin Raule." *Mededelingen Nederlandse Vereniging voor Zeegeschiedenis*, Vol. 10 (1965): 1–9.

Kemp, Peter K. and Christopher Lloyd. *The Brethren of the Coast: The British and French Buccaneers in the South Seas*. London: Heinemann, 1960.

Keyes, George S. *Cornelis Vroom: Marine and Landscape Artist*. Alphen aan de Rijn: Canaletto, 1985.

———. *Mirror of Empire: Dutch Marine Art of the Seventeenth Century*. Cambridge: Cambridge University Press, 1990.

Knuttel, W.P.C. *Verboden Boeken in de Republiek der Vereenigde Nederlanden*. 's Gravenhage, 1914.

Kohn, Hans. *German History: Some New German Views*. Ed. and Trans. Herbert H. Rowen. London: Allen & Unwin, 1954.

Kranenburg, H.A.H. Boelmans. "Zierikzee als visscherijplaats." *Zeeuws Tijdschrift*, Vol. 20 (1970): 77–85.

Landwehr, John. *De Nederlander uit en Thuis: Spiegel van het dagelijkse leven uit bijzondere zeventiende-eeuwze boeken*. Alphen aan den Rijn: A.W. Sijthoff, 1981.

Lawrence, Cynthia. "Hendrick de Keyser's Heemskerk Monument: The Origins of the Cult and Iconography of Dutch Naval Heroes." *Simiolus: Netherlands Quarterly for the History of Art.*, Vol. 21, No. 4 (1992): 265–295.

Le Golif, Louis Adhemar Timothée. *Memoirs of a Buccaneer: Being a Wondrous and Unrepentant Account of the Prodigious Adventures and Amours of King Louis*

XIV's Loyal Servant, Louis Adhemar Timothée Le Golif. . . . London: George Allen & Unwin, 1954.

Lepers, Jean-Baptiste (ed.) and Berthelot, Pierre-Bernard. *La tragique historire des Flibustiers: Histoire de Saint-Domingue et de l'ile de la Tortue, repaires des flibustiers, écrite vers 1715.* Collection littéraire des roman d'adventures. Paris: G. Crès, 1925.

Linebaugh, Peter and Rediker, Marcus. *The Many-Headed Hydra: Sailors, Slaves, Commoners, and the Hidden History of the Revolutionary Atlantic.* Boston: Beacon Press, 2000.

Malo, Henri. *Les Corsaires: les corsaires Dunkerquois et Jean Bart.* Paris, 1913.

Marley, David F. *Pirates and Engineers: Dutch and Flemish Adventurers in New Spain (1607–1697).* Windsor, Ontario: Netherlandic Press, 1992.

———. *The Sack of Veracruz: The Great Pirate Raid of 1683.* Windsor, Ontario: Netherlandic Press, 1993.

———. *Pirates and Privateers of the Americas.* (Santa Barbara, CA: ABC-Clio, 1994).

Meinecke, Friedrich. *Weltbürgertum und Nationalstaat: Studien zur Genesis des deutschen Nationalstaates.* 7th ed. Munich: Oldenbourge, 1928.

Mollat, Michel. "De la Piraterie Sauvage a la Course Réglementée (XIVe–XVe Siecle)." *Course et Piraterie: Etudes presentees a la Commission Internationale d'Histoire Maritime a l'occasion de son XVe colloque international pendant le XIVe Congres International des Sciences historieques.* Vol. I. Ed. Commission Internationale d'Histoire Maritime. Paris: Institut de Recherche et d'Histoire des Textes/Centre National de la Recherche Scientifique, 1975: 162–184.

Mollema, J.C. *Geschiedenis van Nederland ter Zee.* 4 vols. Amsterdam: Vitg. mij. "Joost van Vondel," 1939–1942.

Mössner, J.M. *The Barbary Powers in International Law.* The Hague: Grotian Society Papers, 1972.

Osborne, Lawrence. "A Pirate's Progress: How the Maritime Rogue Became a Multicultural Hero." *Lingua Franca: The Review of Academic Life.* Vol. 8, No. 2 (March 1998): 35–42.

Oudendijk, J.K. "The Dutch Republic and Algiers, 1662–1664." *Course et Piraterie: Etudes presentees a la Commission Internationale d'Histoire Maritime a l'occasion de son XVe colloque international pendant le XIVe Congres International des Sciences historieques.* Vol. I. Ed. Commission Internationale d'Histoire Maritime. Paris: Institut de Recherche et d'Histoire des Textes/Editions du Centre Nationalde la Recherche Scientifique, 1975: 146–160.

Parker, Geoffrey. *The Dutch Revolt.* 2nd ed. London: Peregrine Books, 1988.

Prud'homme van Reine, R.B. "Nederlandse Kaapvaart en Piraterij in Beeld." *Kapers op de Kust: Nederlandse Kaapvaart en Piraterij, 1500–1800.* Vlissingen: Uitgeverij ADZ, 1991.

Prud'homme van Reine, R.B. and E.W. van der Oest, eds. *Kapers op de Kust: Nederlandse Kaapvaart en Piraterij, 1500–1800.* Vlissingen: Uitgeverij ADZ, 1991.

Rankin, Hugh F. *The Golden Age of Piracy.* Williamsburg in American Series. New York: Holt, Rhinehart & Winston: 1969.

Rediker, Marcus. *Between the Devil and the Deep Blue Sea: Merchant Seamen, Pirates and the Anglo-American Maritime World, 1700–1750.* Cambridge: Cambridge University Press, 1987.

Ritchie, Robert C. *Captain Kidd and the War Against the Pirates.* Cambridge: Harvard University Press, 1986.

Roelofsen, C.G. "Grotius and State Practice of His Day: Some Remarks on the Place of *De Jure Belli ac Pacis* within the Context of Seventeenth-Century 'Christendom' and the Role of Contemporary Precedents in Grotius' Works." *Grotiana*, Vol. 10 (1989): 3–46.

———. "The Sources of Mare Liberum; The Contested Origins of the Doctrine of the Freedom of the Seas." *Practice & Doctrine in Particular Regard to the Law of Naval Warfare in the Low Countries from Circa 1450 until the Early 17th Century*. Studies in the History of International Law. University of Utrecht: Proefschrift (dissertation), 1991: 41–71.

Rowen, Herbert H. *John de Witt: Grand Pensionary of Holland*. Princeton: Princeton University Press, 1978.

——— and Craig E. Harline. "The Birth of the Dutch Nation." *Politics, Religion & Diplomacy in Early Modern Europe: Essays in Honor of DeLamar Jensen*. Ed. Malcolm R. Thorp, and Arthur J. Slavin. Kirksville, Missouri: Sixteenth Century Journal Publishers, 1994.

Schama, Simon. *The Embarassment of Riches*. Berkeley: University of California Press, 1988.

Schenkeveld, M.A. *Dutch Literature in the Age of Rembrandt: Themes and Ideas*. Amsterdam & Philadelphia: Benjamins, 1991.

Schmidt, Benjamin. *Innocence Abroad: The Dutch Imagination and the New World, 1570–1670*. Cambridge: Cambridge University Press, 2001.

Sellin, Thorsten. *Pioneering in Penology: The Amsterdam Houses of Correction in the Sixteenth and Seventeenth Centuries*. Philadelphia: University of Pennsylvania Press, 1944. London: Humphrey Mould, 1944. Oxford: Oxford University Press, 1944.

Senior, Clive M. "The Confederation of Deep-Sea Pirates: English Pirates in the Atlantic 1603–25." *Course et Piraterie: Etudes presentees a la Commission Internationale d'Histoire Maritime a l'occasion de son XVe colloque international pendant le XIVe Congres International des Sciences historieques*. Vol. I. Ed. Commission Internationale d'Historie Maritime. Paris: Institut de Recherche et d'Histoire des Textes/Editions du Centre National de la Recherche Scientifique, 1975: 331–359.

———. *A Nation of Pirates: English Piracy in Its Heyday*. New York: Crane, Russak, 1976.

Smith, Anthony. *The Ethnic Origins of Nations*. Oxford: Basil Blackwell, 1987.

Snapper, F. *Oorlogsinvloeden op de overzeese handel van Holland 1551–1719*. Amsterdam: Proefschrift (dissertation), 1959.

Spooner, F.C. "The European Economy 1609–1650." *The Decline of Spain and the Thirty Years War 1609–48/59*. The New Cambridge Modern History IV. Ed. J.P. Cooper. Cambridge: Cambridge University Press, 1970: 98–103.

Staatkundige Historie van Holland, Behelzende eene Staatkundige bespiegeling van de voornaamste Gevallen der Nederlandsche Geschiedenissen, volgens het Natuur, Staats, aller Volkeren en het beschreven Recht; de geaardheid der Zaaken en de gezonde Reden, om gezond over het voorledene te redeneeren, en tot een Richtsnoer voor het toekomende te dienen. 82 vols. Amsterdam: Bernardus Mourik, 1756–1802.

Stanley, Jo, ed. *Bold in Her Breeches: Women Pirates Across the Ages*. San Francisco, CA: Pandora, 1995.

Stapel, F.W. *Geschiedenis van Nederlandsch-Indie*. Nederlandsche Historische Bibliotheek. Vol. 16. Amsterdam: Meulenhoff, 1930a.

———. "Hubert Hugo: Een Zeeroover in Dienst van de Oostindische Compagnie." *Bijdragen tot de Taal-, Land-, en Volkenkunde van Nederlandsch-Indië*, Vol. 86, Afl. III en IV (1930a): 615–635. Offprint available at Nederlandse Scheepvaart Museum, #Ni. I. K II 259.

Stradling, R.A. "The Spanish Dunkirkers, 1621–48: A Record of Plunder and Destruction." *Tijdschrift voor Geschiedenis*, Vol. XCIII (1980): 541–558.

Theunissen, H. "Barbaren en ongelovigen: Turcica in de Nederlanden 1500–1800." Ed. H. Theunissen et al. *Topkapie en Turkomanie. Turks-Nederlandse onmoetingen sinds 1600*. Amsterdam: De Bataafsche Leeuw, 1989: 37–53.

Toussaint, Auguste. "La Course et la Piraterie dans l'Océan Indien." *Course et Piraterie: Etudes presentees a la Commission Internationale d'Histoire Maritime a l'occasion de son XVe colloque international pendant le XIVe Congres International des Sciences historieques*. Vol. II. Ed. Commission Internationale d'Histoire Maritime. Paris: Institut de Recherche et d'Histoire des Textes/Editions du Centre National de la Recherche Scientifique, 1975a: 703–743.

———. "Rapport: La Course et la Piraterie dans l'Océan Indien." *Course et Piraterie: Etudes presentees a la Commission Internationale d'Histoire Maritime a l'occasion de son XVe colloque international pendant le XIVe Congres International des Sciences historieques*. Vol. III. Ed. Commission Internationale d'Histoire Maritime. Paris: Institut de Recherche et d'Histoire des Textes/Editions du Centre National de la Recherche Scientifique, 1975b: 101–102.

Turner, Victor. *The Ritual Process: Structure and Anti-structure* (Chicago: Aldine, 1969).

Unger, Richard W. *Dutch Shipbuilding Before 1800: Ships and Guilds*. Aspects of Economic History: The Low Countries. Assen: Van Gorcum, 1978.

van Balen, W.J. *Hollandsche Kapers op Amerikaansche Kusten*. Leiden: A.W. Sijthoff, 1942.

van der Moer, A. "Jan Jansz. van Haerlem, alias Murat Reys (15?–16?)." *Marineblad*, Januari 1996: 18–21.

van der Oest, E.W. "De Praktijk van de Nederlandse Kaapvaart en Piraterij 1500–1800." Ed. R.B. Prudhomme van Reine and E.W. van der Oest. *Kapers op de Kust: Nederlandse Kaapvaart en Piraterij 1500–1800*. Vlissingen: Uitgeverij ADZ, 1991: 11–31.

van Deursen, A.Th. and H. de Schepper. *Willem van Oranje: Een Strijd voor Vrijheid en Verdraagzaamheid*. Weesp: Fibula-Van Dishoeck, 1984. Tielt: Lannoo, 1984.

van Eeghen, P. and J.Ph. van der Kellen. *Het Werk van Jan en Casper Luyken*. Amsterdam: Frederick Muller & Co., 1905.

van Royen, P.C. *Zeevarenden op de Koopvaardijvloot Omstreeks 1700*. Amsterdam: De Bataafsche Leeuw, 1987.

van Werkeke, H. "The Low Countries." *The Cambridge Economic History of Europe*. Vol. III. Cambridge: Cambridge University Press, 1963: 340–361.

Verhees-van Meer, J.Th.H. *De Zeeuwse Kaapvaart Tijdens de Spaanse Successieoorlog 1702–1713*. Werken Uitgegeven door het Koninklijk Zeeusch Genootschap der Wetenschappen. Vol. 3. Middelburg: Koninklijk Zeeusch Genootschap der Wetenschappen, 1986.

Vrijman, L.C. *Zeer Aenmerkelijcke Reysen Gedaan door Jan Erasmus Reyning*. Amsterdam: Van Kampen, 1937.

Wallerstein, Immanuel. *The Modern World System I: Capitalist Agriculture and the Origins of the European World-Economy in the Sixteenth Century*. Studies in Social Discontinuity. Orlando, FL: Academic Press, 1974.

Wallerstein, Immanuel. *The Modern World-System II: Mercantilism and the Consolidation of the European World-Economy, 1600–1750.* New York: Academic Press, 1980.

Weber, R.E.J. *De Beveiliging van de Zee Tegen Europeesche en Barbarijsche Zeerovers, 1609–1621.* Amsterdam: Werken uitgegeven door de Commssie voor Zeegeschiedenis der Kon. Adad. van Wetensche. III, 1936.

Williams, Neville. *Captains Outrageous: Seven Centuries of Piracy.* London: Barrie and Rockliff, 1961.

———. *The Sea Dogs: Privateers, Plunder and Piracy in the Elizabethan Age.* London: Weidenfeld and Nicolson, 1975.

Wright, Leigh R. "Piracy in the Southeast Asian Archipelago." *Course et Piraterie: Etudes presentees a la Commission Internationale d'Histoire Maritime a l'occasion de son XVe colloque international pendant le XIVe Congres International des Sciences historieques.* Vol. II. Ed. Commission Internationale d'Histoire Maritime. Paris: Institut de Recherche et d'Histoire des Textes/Centre National de la Recherche Scientifique, 1975: 881–915.

Zuidhoek, Arne. *Zeeroovers van de Gouden Eeuw.* Bussum: De Boer Maritiem, 1977.

Index

Aartszoon, Geert 55
Abrahamszoon, Claas 150, 151
Admiralty of Amsterdam 15, 19, 21, 42, 50, 94, 115, 126, 157, 167, 242n83
Admiralty of the Maas 6, 15, 16, 18, 19, 26, 34, 43, 47, 48, 49, 51, 54, 55, 57, 58, 60, 63, 76, 89, 110, 121, 122, 126, 142, 144, 149, 150, 151, 152, 153, 154, 155, 156, 157, 158, 159, 170, 174, 178, 192, 213, 241n66, 243n88, 243n90, 300n1
Admiralty of Zeeland 12, 19, 20, 25, 32, 90, 93, 94, 112, 123, 179, 185, 186, 189, 194, 205, 239n28, 242n83, 242n85, 309n33
Adriaanszoon, Daniel 59
Algiers 56, 57, 80, 81, 83, 84, 121, 123, 124, 134, 143, 180, 229, 231
Amsterdam 11, 15, 16, 19, 23, 25, 26, 28, 29, 32, 38, 42, 46, 50, 51, 59, 67, 68, 69, 70, 71, 74, 75, 76, 80, 83, 84, 87, 88, 91, 95, 98, 101, 107, 113, 120, 121, 127, 128, 129, 130, 142, 144, 145, 152, 153, 156, 157, 158, 170, 171, 172, 173, 174, 189, 197, 199, 205, 206, 207, 208, 220, 221, 222, 223, 224, 225, 229, 230, 231, 233, 149n178, 265n106, 265n114, 265n115, 287n216, 303n51
Anderson, Benedict 72, 73, 74, 259n30, 259n32
Andrieszoon, Michiel 61, 257n116
Anglo-Dutch Wars, *also see* First, Second and Third Anglo-Dutch Wars 9, 17, 18, 23, 26, 27, 28, 31, 115, 148, 184, 206, 242n83, 247n132, 302n30
Antwerp 50, 51, 53, 54, 55, 74

Africa 2, 20, 25, 79, 80, 104, 105, 107, 108, 117, 119, 121, 125, 144, 164, 165, 179, 181, 203, 234, 265n111, 288n224
Arianszoon, Sander 158
article brief, article brieven 12, 13, 14, 29, 48, 148

bandit(s) 52, 103, 104, 106, 146
banditry 36, 43, 127, 136, 151, 209
Bank, Adriaan 149, 150
Barbary Corsair(s) 2, 56, 57, 79, 80, 84, 98, 103, 104, 105, 116, 119, 120, 121, 122, 123, 124, 128, 134, 137, 142, 143, 144, 146, 157, 160, 163, 180, 195, 203, 209, 249n170, 255n87, 264n95, 264n96, 265n108, 281n142, 282n162, 284n183, 296n90
Bart, Jean 110, 154, 277n69
Batavia 97, 118, 126, 158, 159, 165, 175, 286n207
Batavian(s) 79, 97, 98, 99, 181, 195, 197, 198, 200, 220, 221, 222, 224, 225, 271n224
Baudaert, Willem 78, 263n80
Billeker, Jacob 58
Blackbeard 115
Bloek, Gerrits Gyssen 58
boekhouder(s), bookkeeper 11, 12, 15, 27, 28, 29, 183
Bonny, Anne 105
bookkeeper, see *boekhouder*
Borrens, Pieter 197
Bouwerszoon, Willem 47
Brant, Maximus 156
Brazil 19, 20, 23, 32, 62, 108, 157, 179, 183, 199, 225, 250n189
Bremen 186

Bresiliaan, Rock de 62, 145, 163, 292n23
Brits, Adriaan Jansen den 44, 45, 46
buccaneer(s) 61, 62, 101, 104, 105, 106, 107, 116, 118, 131, 132, 144, 145, 146, 163, 166, 167, 168, 202, 274n21

Campeche 61
Cape Verde Islands 107, 109, 157
Capitulation of the Sultan 119, 120, 281n144
Captain Kidd, *see* Kidd, William
Caribbean 15, 20, 61, 62, 101, 104, 105, 107, 109, 115, 144, 145, 146, 166, 167, 168, 169, 171, 197, 202
Cattendyk, Volchert Janszoon 58
Cavendish, Sir Thomas 105
Charles II (King of England) 39, 117
Chevalier de Grammont (aka Monsieur de Grammont) 61, 168, 298n136
Claaszoon, Cornelis 153
Claaszoon, Jan 60, 192
Claeszoon, Cornelis 42
Clerk, Hugo 128, 129, 158
Cleuter, Captain 130
Colaert, Jacques 112
collective memory 4, 73, 74, 79, 89, 93, 99, 175, 200
commissie van retorsie 10
commission 1, 10, 11, 13, 14, 15, 18, 20, 24, 25, 27, 28, 29, 31, 32, 33, 38, 42, 45, 47, 48, 49, 51, 52, 55, 56, 61, 116, 118, 144, 145, 146, 152, 153, 154, 155, 156, 157, 168, 170, 171, 179, 185, 186, 202, 241n66, 270n193, 292n21, 298n132
Compaen, Claes 1, 2, 3, 6, 9, 57, 127, 128, 131, 132, 134, 144, 161, 162, 163, 164, 165, 166, 192, 255n88, 288n221, 295n71, 296n85, 296n89, 296n90, 296n94, 297n106
Cordingly, David 106, 274n21
Cornelisdogter, Maritge 156
Corneliszoon, Adriaan 53, 54
Coster, Herman 78, 263n83
Courtszoon, Laurens 111
Crap, Hendrick van der 158, 159
Credo, Willem 201, 202, 205, 305n85
Cruidaan, Hendrik Franszoon 50, 51

Cruidman, Hendrikk 156
Curaçao 107, 114, 122, 146, 167, 168, 169, 202, 205, 245n107

Dampier, William 118, 119, 272n4
Danser, Simon de (the Elder and the Younger) 57, 255n90
Davidszoon, Laurens (aka Laurens Davids) 58, 170, 171, 172, 173, 174, 208
Dekker, Hans (Jan?) 61
Delft 54, 58, 95, 155, 189, 199, 265n106
den Briel 44, 60, 77, 191
Devil of Dordrecht 53
Dielofs, Cornelis 41
Dongen, Willem Hendrikszoon van 54, 55
Dordrecht 10, 11, 18, 26, 50, 53, 54, 97, 113, 170, 171, 172, 173, 174, 189, 208, 254n77
d'Oudenaarde, Pieter 59, 192
Drake, Sir Francis 4, 104
Dreitz, J.C. 37
Dunkirk 1, 9, 17, 18, 21, 23, 31, 52, 53, 59, 60, 104, 109, 110, 111, 112, 113, 114, 127, 137, 144, 149, 151, 152, 154, 179, 192, 193, 197, 198, 222, 277n69, 288n223, 294n47
Durkheim, Emile 74
Dutch East India Company (aka VOC) xi, xvii, 19, 24, 25, 60, 106, 115, 116, 126, 148, 158, 161, 162, 165, 169, 170, 171, 174, 175, 180, 181, 184, 186, 198, 208, 109, 244n99, 279n109, 279n124, 285n196, 286n207, 289n228, 289n232, 299n141, 308n158, 308n164
Dutch Navy xiii, 4, 5, 6, 12, 17, 18, 22, 24, 30, 39, 48, 52, 55, 85, 86, 87, 88, 89, 93, 99, 111, 112, 124, 126, 128, 129, 130, 136, 154, 155, 158, 174, 182, 185, 194, 195, 198, 203, 209, 241n66, 294n48, 308n64, 309n164, 309n165
Dutch Revolt xvii, 4, 31, 46, 74, 89, 90, 108, 120, 264n94, 295n65
Dutch West India Company (aka WIC) xvii, 10, 17, 19, 20, 21, 25, 27, 28, 32, 33, 60, 61, 62, 76, 77, 106, 107,

108, 109, 114, 115, 118, 122, 152, 166, 167, 168, 169, 179, 180, 181, 182, 183, 184, 193, 197, 198, 199, 202, 203, 208, 209, 244n104, 245n106, 245n107, 277n69, 297n123, 298n132, 301n19, 308n164

East India Company, *see* Dutch East India Company
Eighty Years War   xvii, 35, 42, 45, 78, 108, 109
England   4, 21, 28, 31, 35, 37, 39, 43, 46, 48, 76, 88, 98, 103, 104, 106, 111, 117, 118, 119, 120, 121, 122, 148, 202, 220, 221, 222, 223, 224, 225, 226, 227, 228, 233, 234, 251n15, 251n22, 258n10, 289n229, 295n66
English Channel   18, 29, 47, 56, 116, 122, 123
Enkhuizen   28, 41, 42, 52, 67, 76, 84, 93, 110, 113, 158, 191, 222, 224, 225, 226, 233, 257n119, 262n63, 265n106, 270n193
Evertsen, Johan   112
Exquemelin, Alexander   62, 101, 102, 105, 106, 127, 128, 131, 132, 133, 145, 202, 272n2, 274n21, 274n24, 292n21, 292n23
extortion   xiii, 43, 45, 46, 47, 49, 55, 142, 153, 181, 208

Feringhis   105
First Anglo-Dutch War   xvii, 17, 18, 22, 23, 26, 31, 38, 79, 116, 117, 195, 219, 279n109
Florisse, Heijndrik   148, 149
France   xvii, 10, 17, 21, 35, 37, 41, 42, 48, 50, 96, 109, 121, 122, 170, 171, 174, 186, 187, 190, 202, 208, 220, 224, 228, 233, 234, 236n2, 240n60, 241n62, 251n15, 253n43, 263n83, 277n69, 290n254, 295n66
Friesland   9, 27, 40, 206, 253n45

Gabrielszoon, Jacob   59, 192
Galen, Jan van   79, 88, 137, 291n266
Gan, Claas van   111
Geertz, Clifford   5, 236n18, 301n2

Gelder, Dirk de   152
Gellner, Ernest   259n38
Gerrits, Cornelis   194, 201
Gerrits, Egbert   53
Gijsbregtszoon, Cornelis, *see* Gysbregtszoon, Cornellis
Gijsbregtszoon, Wouter   156
Graaf, Laurens de (aka Lorencillo)   61, 62
Grammont, Chevalier de, *see* Chevalier de Grammont
Groenevelt, Quartermaster   150, 151
Grote Piet   9, 56, 58, 255n85
Gysbregtszoon, Cornellis (aka Cornelis Gijsbregtszoon)   50, 51, 156

Haas, Jan de   48, 49, 207
Haentje (aka Kornelis Jansz.)   197
Hague, the   42, 54, 56, 91, 166, 254n77, 265n106
Halbwachs, Maurice   73, 74
Halfkraagh, Captain   149
Hamburg   42, 43, 48, 155, 156, 157, 186, 220, 222, 223, 226
Hamers, Pieter   194, 201
Havre de Grâce   170, 171, 174
Heemskerk, Jacob van   86, 87, 197, 268n162, 269n163
Hermite, Jan   182
Heyn, Piet   xvii, 197, 198, 199, 200, 201, 268n161, 306n112, 306n114, 306n115, 307n117, 307n125
High Court of Holland (aka *Hof van Holland*)   xiii, 6, 34, 41, 52, 56, 57, 58, 61, 63, 91, 160, 169, 170, 171, 172, 174, 237n3, 260n42, 291n1, 293n38
Hispaniola   61, 109, 145, 167
Hobsbawm, Eric   259n38
Hoen, 't (the Chicken)   46
Hoeven, Cornelis van der   154, 155
Hof van Holland, *see* High Court of Holland
Hofdijk, W.J.   4
Hoogencamp, Hendrick   42, 43
hooliganism   53, 55, 59, 110
Hoorn   11, 19, 28, 44, 93, 113, 160, 223, 225, 229, 265n106
Hoorn, Nicolaes van   61, 62, 257n114

Hugo, Hubert 170, 171, 172, 173, 174, 175, 208
Huygen, Jan 182, 302n23

imagined community 73, 74, 76, 98, 190, 210, 259n32
Ireland 28, 37, 41, 107, 121, 233, 258n10, 279n121, 295n66, 296n89, 296n94

Jacobsen, Hendrik 152, 294n47
Jacobsen, Jan 44, 45, 46
Jacobszoon, Jan 47
Jamaica 62, 127, 145, 292n20
Janssen, Adriaan 54
Janssen, Jacob 52, 53, 130
Janssen, Jan 151, 152
Jansz., Kornelis, *see* Haentje
Janszoon, Geraart 55
Janszoon, Gullis 55
Janszoon, Hendrik 158
Janszoon, Herman 44
Janszoon, Jan 142, 143, 144, 146, 180
Janszoon, Jan/Cornelis 58
Janszoon, Joris 158
Janszoon, Laurens Adriaan 55
Janszoon, Steven 48
Janszoon, Willem 55
Jeliszoon, Marten 47
Jol, Cornelis 197
Joppen, Leendert 44, 45, 46
Joriszoon, Jan 59
Joriszoon, Lenart 53, 54

kaperbrief xiii, 10, 146
keelhaul 13, 40, 47, 64
Kennedy, Daniel 118
Kidd, William 105
Knole, Jan Corneliszoon 152, 153, 207
Knollendam, Jan Theuniszoon 58

L'Olonnais, François (aka François Lolonois) 101, 102, 103
Lagge Bagge 55
Lambert, Moy 110, 111, 122, 124, 128, 130, 136, 197, 281n142
Lange Bagger 54
Las Casas, Bartholome 77, 78

Lawrence, Cynthia x, 86, 87, 268n162
Leiden 45, 55, 58, 67, 88, 90, 91, 93, 107, 191, 265n106, 270n192, 285n198
letter of commission, *see* commission
letter of marque 115, 116, 118, 119, 120, 170, 178, 182, 213, 236n2, 244n104
letter of reprisal 107
liminal, liminality 5, 6, 167, 178, 192, 193, 210, 235n16
Linden, Barent vander 58
Lolonois, François, *see* L'Olonnais, François
Lorencillo, *see* Graaf, Laurens de
Lübeck 186, 220, 222, 295n66

Maartenszoon, Floris 150
Maasluis 112
Mamora 56, 121, 160
Marnix, Philip de 44
Medemblik 21, 42, 286n213
Mediterranean 17, 25, 30, 42, 56, 85, 104, 112, 115, 121, 122, 123, 136, 160, 180, 196, 198, 224
Middelburg 11, 26, 31, 95, 184, 189, 201, 205, 206, 221, 230, 250n189, 265n106, 302n30
Montbars of Languedoc 106
Moos, Gysbrecht 58
Morgan, Sir Henry 104, 145, 202
Mulato, Jan Merida 58, 59

Nassau, Philips van 55
nation, nationalism 72, 73, 74, 76, 83, 88, 97, 98, 99, 130, 175, 188, 189, 190, 202, 203, 205, 206, 259n30, 259n32, 259n38, 269n177
navy, *see* Dutch Navy
Nine Years War xvii, 17, 21, 22, 26, 27, 247n132
Nobel, Ysbrand Willemzoon 52, 58
North Africa 2, 79, 80, 119, 121, 144, 203, 234, 265n111
North Sea 18, 29, 53, 68, 107, 110, 113, 155, 247n132

Oldenbarnevelt 251n15
Ottoman Empire 56, 119, 120, 281n144

Index

Pack, Cornelis and Peter 58, 160
Panama 31, 128, 145, 202
Pegelin, Ali, *see* Pisselingh, Ali
Pellecoren, Captain 130
Peru 78, 107, 182, 199, 302n23
Philip III (king of Spain) 187
Philip IV (king of Spain) 108
Philepszoon, Arij 151, 152
Pieterszoon, Goris 58, 59
Pisselingh, Ali (aka Pegelin, Ali) 57, 163
Portugal 1, 23, 32, 33, 35, 121, 122, 179, 187, 188, 209, 225, 241n65
Pot, Barent van der 158
praatje xiv, 23, 30, 31, 32, 76, 88, 95, 97, 116, 184, 193, 195
premium(s) 21, 22, 23, 27, 29, 108, 112, 124, 125, 149, 179, 186, 194, 245n122, 246n123
Prince of Orange 10, 11, 16, 45, 54, 99, 166, 202, 206, 207, 309n164
Pruis, Mathys Jacobszoon 197

Quirynk, Jan 58

Read, Mary 105
Red Sea 61, 106, 122, 170, 171, 172, 174, 289n232
Rediker, Marcus 103, 105, 273n8
Renan, Ernest 73
Reynders, Salomon 205
Reyning, Jan Erasmus 128, 131, 144, 145, 146, 147, 163, 166, 167, 169, 202, 203, 292n20
Rijckewaert, Jan Lievenszoon 42, 160, 295n65
Rijke, Albert 50, 207, 254n61
Rijp, J.C. 37
Ringelszoon, Captain 18, 19, 95
Rochussen, Isaac 205
Rock de Bresiliaan, *see* Bresiliaan, Rock de
Roose, Willem Jacobszoon 42, 58
Rotterdam 6, 11, 16, 25, 26, 28, 37, 38, 43, 44, 49, 51, 52, 53, 55, 56, 59, 60, 61, 62, 64, 88, 89, 94, 95, 97, 107, 110, 111, 113, 114, 128, 144, 148, 152, 153, 154, 155, 156, 157, 158, 159, 189, 198, 199, 206, 221, 222, 223, 224, 229, 233, 242n83, 249n178, 265n106, 294n48
Rundere, Laurens de 55, 56
Ruth, Johan 58, 160
Ruyter, Michiel de 85, 86, 88, 89, 94, 194, 267n141, 268n161

Salé 56, 57, 84, 121, 122, 123, 134, 143, 144, 164, 166, 233, 234, 241n65, 296n94
Samuelszoon, Engel 150, 151
Schama, Simon ix, 72, 79, 96
Schram, Wybrant 163, 165, 297n106
Scotland 58, 59, 121, 150, 187, 221, 233, 234, 295n66
Sea Beggars 4, 5, 44, 45, 46, 89, 90, 91, 92, 93, 181, 190, 191, 192, 193, 194, 270n192
Sea Dogs 4
Second Anglo-Dutch War xvii, 17, 18, 21, 23, 24, 26, 28, 31, 32, 88, 97, 116, 148, 174, 179, 206, 242n83, 247n132, 302n30
Segelare, Jan de 111
Sierra Leone 89, 165
Silver Fleet xvii, 182, 198, 199, 200, 306n114.
Simonszoon, Jan 59, 192
Sissingh, François 43, 44
slave, slavery 4, 15, 27, 28, 62, 77, 78, 79, 80, 81, 82, 83, 84, 85, 88, 99, 105, 106, 117, 119, 120, 130, 134, 135, 136, 143, 146, 180, 193, 196, 202, 203, 206, 229, 265n114, 265n115, 266n118, 266n120
Sluis, Jan 150, 151
Spain xvii, 1, 9, 17, 22, 26, 35, 37, 38, 42, 45, 57, 59, 70, 72, 74, 76, 77, 78, 85, 89, 97, 98, 99, 108, 109, 120, 122, 143, 144, 146, 157, 179, 182, 187, 188, 190, 192, 198, 200, 209, 238n18, 250n189, 295n64
Spienink, Jan 53, 110
Stadholder xiv, 9, 10, 11, 17, 40, 44, 46, 89, 93, 98, 118, 152, 153, 243n90, 245n116
States of Holland 11, 21, 56, 91, 107, 124, 160, 174, 187, 238n18, 257n119

States of Zeeland   19, 33, 94, 109, 179, 185, 186, 187, 189, 238n18
States-General   xiv, 1, 10, 11, 12, 13, 14, 16, 17, 18, 19, 20, 21, 22, 23, 24, 32, 33, 35, 36, 38, 39, 40, 41, 42, 48, 51, 52, 60, 61, 63, 84, 86, 87, 93, 94, 99, 107, 108, 109, 110, 111, 112, 114, 116, 121, 122, 123, 124, 142, 144, 149, 152, 153, 157, 160, 161, 165, 166, 169, 172, 179, 181, 183, 185, 186, 187, 188, 192, 193, 194, 207, 238n14, 238n15, 238n16, 238n18, 243n88, 244n97, 244n104, 246n122, 251n12, 252n30, 258n19, 264n85, 268n153, 271n225, 289n228, 301n20, 303n51, 308n164
Steenwers, Pieter   151, 152
Stogwoning, Jop Ariense   153, 154
Stuijt, Simon Maartsszoon   56, 160
Surinam   107, 144

Thijs, Bartell   47
Third Anglo-Dutch War   xvii, 24, 26, 27, 31, 115, 117, 148, 205, 206, 242n83, 247n132, 302n30
Thoeniss, Jan   58
Thomasszoon, Ellert   122, 128
Thomaszoon, Claas   60, 192
Thomaszoon, Claaszoon   59, 192
trade company, trade companies   xiii, 12, 19, 38, 41, 51, 60, 76, 99, 106, 107, 120, 126, 166, 181, 183, 209, 262n64, 284n183
Treaty of Münster   xvii, 35, 108
Tripoli   56, 121
Tromp, Cornelis   86, 95, 267n142, 269n172, 271n220
Tromp, Maarten   18, 19, 86, 88, 94, 95, 112, 197, 199, 259n29, 267n141, 268n161
Tulip Mania   184
Tunis   56, 114, 120, 121, 123, 124, 136, 266n118
Turk, Jan   50
Turner, Ephraim   20, 21
Turner, Victor   235n16
Twelve Years Truce   xvii, 38, 42, 108, 109, 120, 157, 250n189

Uitsingam, Joris   59, 60, 192
Union of Utrecht   xvii, 93, 94
Utrecht   33, 50, 96, 255n85, 265n106

Veenboer   56
Veere   9, 123, 143, 189, 196, 223, 224, 236n3, 237n4
Vera Cruz   61
Verbrugge, Willem Teunisse   150, 151
Vierlingh, Andries   72, 87
Vlissingen   2, 11, 20, 26, 28, 31, 37, 44, 57, 59, 60, 88, 93, 112, 123, 144, 158, 184, 189, 196, 205, 206, 220, 221, 223, 224, 225, 226, 228, 230, 231, 233, 237n4, 250n189, 265n106, 288n224, 302n30, 303n39
VOC, *see* Dutch East India Company
Vonk, Reinier Claaszoon   49
vrijbuiter, vrijbuiterij   xiv, 3, 91, 192, 193

War Against Piracy   103
Waterman, Quinijn den   153
Weber, Max   259n38
Wegh, Cornelis Claaszoon   61
West India Company, *see* Dutch West India Company
West Indies   9, 17, 20, 25, 31, 125, 126, 144, 157, 169, 224, 242n73, 288n226
WIC, *see* Dutch West India Company
Wilckens, Jacob   183
Wilhelmus   90, 130, 200, 270n183, 307n126
Willemszoon, Hendrik   156, 157, 208
Willemszoon, Huig   48
William of Orange (aka William the Silent)   9, 10, 17, 27, 44, 46, 50, 87, 89, 90, 118, 253n51, 270n193, 291n3
William the Silent, *see* William of Orange
Witt, Johan de   96
Wittebak, Heindrik   59, 60

yardarm (thrown from)   13, 14, 49, 64, 149, 151

Zuijlen, Jan   158, 159